Environmental Justice

Environmental Justice

Law, Policy & Regulation

FOURTH EDITION

Clifford Villa
PROFESSOR OF LAW, UNIVERSITY OF NEW MEXICO

Nadia B. Ahmad
PROFESSOR OF LAW, BARRY UNIVERSITY

Rebecca Bratspies
OLIVER HOUCK PROFESSOR OF ENVIRONMENTAL LAW, TULANE LAW SCHOOL

Patrice Simms
VICE PRESIDENT OF LITIGATION FOR HEALTHY COMMUNITIES, EARTHJUSTICE
VISITING PROFESSOR, HARVARD LAW SCHOOL
CO-FOUNDER AND STRATEGIC ADVISOR, COUNTERSTREAM MEDIA

Carlton Waterhouse
ENVIRONMENTAL AND CLIMATE JUSTICE CENTER, FOUNDING DIRECTOR
PROFESSOR OF LAW, HOWARD UNIVERSITY SCHOOL OF LAW

Clifford Rechtschaffen
CO-FOUNDER, GOLDEN GATE UNIVERSITY ENVIRONMENTAL LAW AND JUSTICE CLINIC

Eileen Gauna
PROFESSOR EMERITA, UNIVERSITY OF NEW MEXICO

Catherine O'Neill
ENVIRONMENTAL SCHOLAR AND ADJUNCT PROFESSOR OF LAW,
LEWIS & CLARK LAW SCHOOL
PRINCIPAL, O'NEILL CONSULTING

Roger Lin
FORMER CLINICAL SUPERVISING ATTORNEY, UNIVERSITY OF CALIFORNIA, BERKELEY

CAROLINA ACADEMIC PRESS
Durham, North Carolina

Library of Congress Cataloging-in-Publication Data

Names: Villa, Clifford author | Ahmad, Nadia Batool author | Bratspies, Rebecca M., 1965- author | Simms, Patrice author | Waterhouse, Carlton author | Rechtschaffen, Clifford, 1957- author | Gauna, Eileen P., 1953- author | O'Neill, Catherine A. author | Lin, Roger author
Title: Environmental justice : law, policy & regulation / Clifford Villa, Nadia Ahmad, Rebecca Bratspies, Patrice Simms, Carlton Waterhouse, Clifford Rechtschaffen, Eileen Gauna, Catherine O'Neill, Roger Lin.
Description: Fourth edition. | Durham : Carolina Academic Press, 2026. | Includes bibliographical references and index.
Identifiers: LCCN 2025049197 | ISBN 9781531033538 paperback | ISBN 9781531033545 ebook
Subjects: LCSH: Environmental law—United States | Environmental justice—United States | LCGFT: Casebooks (Law)
Classification: LCC KF3817 .R385 2026
LC record available at https://lccn.loc.gov/2025049197

Carolina Academic Press
700 Kent Street
Durham, North Carolina 27701
Telephone (919) 489-7486
www.cap-press.com
Printed in the United States of America

For all dedicated public servants, present and past, who remain committed to protecting human health and the environment for all people.

C.V.

For all those who fight for breath, land, water, and dignity, may justice rise like the tide.

N.A.

For the young people in New York City (and everywhere)
who are speaking out and stepping up
for a just transition.

R.B.

For the children, families, and communities on the front lines of toxic exposures around the country and around the world.
Your fight is our fight!

P.S.

For the countless unrecognized and routinely unnamed people of all ages, races, tribes, clans, religions, and nationalities devoting their time and talents to fight to protect their homes, neighborhoods, communities, villages, and environment by standing up for environmental and climate justice.

C.W.

Summary of Contents

Contents

Preface and Thanks

Environmental justice is one of the most significant developments in environmental law since modern environmental legislation emerged in the 1970s. Drawing upon principles from environmental law, civil rights legislation, and broader movements for social and economic justice, the environmental justice movement originally focused attention on the disparate environmental harms experienced by low-income communities and communities of color. At the same time, the critical methodologies of environmental justice have drawn attention to other groups who may similarly experience disparate impacts from environmental degradation, including women, children, older adults, immigrants, LGBTQIA+ individuals, and persons with disabilities. While the scope of environmental justice may thus have broadened over time, original concerns remain no less relevant today, particularly as stark examples of racism continue to rise and our national commitment to social welfare continues to erode. Consider the drinking water crises in Flint, Michigan, and Jackson, Mississippi, for example, or construction and operation of the Dakota Access Pipeline over the massive opposition and protest of Indigenous peoples.

This book will provide readers with a comprehensive introduction to environmental justice. Oriented towards legal issues and law students, the book also draws from other disciplines including sociology, geography, and economics. As such, in addition to law school, the book may be used in undergraduate or graduate courses. The sixteen chapters of this book provide readings for a single semester of study in environmental justice, or supplemental materials for studies in environmental law, civil rights, and related subjects. To improve readability for a broader audience, we have generally omitted footnotes and legal citations from excerpted materials.

At the same time, this book is intended as a reference guide for practitioners, government officials, and community activists. For lawyers, as promised in the subtitle of the book, we provide a selection of laws and regulations that may help address specific problems in a given context. For government officials, we provide selections of law and policy to assist their important work in protecting the public health and welfare. For EJ activists and advocates, we provide examples of how environmental justice concerns have been addressed in circumstances that may be different or perhaps similar to their own.

EJ activists remind, "We speak for ourselves." Accordingly, this book reflects legal scholarship but also listening and learning from community members and advocates across the United States: from Maui to Puerto Rico; the Arctic to Miami; northern Minnesota to New Orleans; Los Angeles to Memphis; the Navajo Nation in the Southwest to the Onondaga Nation of Upstate New York; Selma to Atlanta; Seattle, Denver, Chicago, Detroit, and Cleveland; Washington, D.C., Chester, PA; Newark and New York City; and innumerable cities, towns, and rural spaces in between. Many of the communities we have visited and people we have met appear in images included in this fourth edition—a reminder that environmental justice is about real people and places.

This book is about understanding the real challenges of environmental justice across the country, but also about how to begin addressing these challenges. Thus, Chapter 3 introduces the concepts of risk assessment and risk management, to encourage and empower community advocates to participate in these vital processes for characterizing threats to public health. Chapter 5 provides background on how regulatory agencies make rules for protecting public health and how communities may engage in promoting or defending such rules. Chapter 6 explains how community protection may be enhanced through permits for industrial facilities, and how these permits may be influenced or challenged by community advocates.

Where proper regulations or permits fail to prevent disparate environmental impacts, this edition of the book provides an expanded examination of legal tools available to address cases of environmental injustice. Thus, Chapter 4 provides a broad review of constitutional law, civil rights legislation, and implementing regulations, with applications illustrated through cases including the drinking water contamination in Flint, Michigan. Chapter 7 provides an overview of enforcement authorities available to government agencies under such federal laws as the Clean Air Act and the Clean Water Act. Chapter 8 provides a deep examination of legal authorities for cleaning up contaminated sites, focusing on the federal Superfund program. Chapter 9 considers unique questions of environmental justice for Indian tribes and Indigenous people. Chapter 10 considers federal and state initiatives to promote environmental justice, concluding with a note on private governance. Chapter 11 examines environmental review under authorities such as the National Environmental Policy Act, and also addresses information disclosure under authorities such as FOIA and the Emergency Planning and Community Right-to-Know Act. Chapter 12 reviews opportunities for legal action by community advocates, including citizen suits under environmental statutes as well as claims under common law. Chapter 13 reflects a new addition to this fourth edition, recognizing environmental justice as a global movement and providing an introduction to some norms and principles of international environmental law.

The last three chapters of the book consider special challenges for environmental justice in contexts including climate change, disaster response, and food systems. As we will see, each of these contexts may affect all people on the planet, but the disparate effects on certain groups of people are important to comprehend and address. Readers interested in deeper explorations of these and many other related subjects will benefit from pathfinders included throughout the book.

Finally, the authors of this fourth edition would like to express their gratitude to the many people who contributed to this book in different ways. First and foremost, we would like to thank the prior authors of this book, Clifford Rechtschaffen, Eileen

Gauna, Catherine O'Neill, and Roger Lin, whose earlier work truly advanced the study and practice of environmental justice, and who entrusted us with carrying forward this endeavor. We would also like to thank all those who reviewed draft chapters of this edition or otherwise inspired our thinking in this book, including Tony Arnold, Vicki Arroyo, Warigia Bowman, Sara Bronin, Robert Bullard, Robin Craig, Dan Farber, Lisa Grow Sun, Stacey Sublett Halliday, Jacquie Hand, Marianne Engelman Lado, Charles Lee, Seema Kakade, Alice Kaswan, Gregg Macey, Jimmy May, Matt Tejada, Vernice Miller-Travis, Michelle Nowlin, Catherine O'Neill, Jessica Owley and the Environmental Law Collaborative, Uma Outka, Quentin Pair, Mike Pappas and participants in his online workshop, Cliff Rechtschaffen, J.B. Ruhl, Rob Verchick, and Elizabeth Kronk Warner. We are particularly grateful for all those who gave of their time for interviews and community tours, including Frank and Cindy Aragon of Mora County, New Mexico; Jennifer Ganata and colleagues from Communities for a Better Environment; Richard Moore and Sofia Martinez of Los Jardines Institute; Mychal Johnson of South Bronx Unite; Mabel Franklin of the Navajo Nation; residents of the Red Water Pond Road Community; Dr. Johnnye Lewis, Chris Shuey, and other experts and advocates for tribal health; Father Phil Schmitter; Rep. Justin Pearson; Brandy Toft, Lenny Fineday, and all the welcoming members of the Leech Lake Band of Ojibwe; Paula Garcia of the New Mexico Acequia Association; Paulina López and the Duwamish River Community Coalition; Charlie Powell, Jilisa Milton, and other good folks of the Greater Birmingham Alliance to Stop Pollution (GASP); and Wasté Win Young, the dearly missed LaDonna Brave Bull Allard, and all the amazing women, Water Protectors, and indominable spirits of the Standing Rock Sioux Tribe.

For research support, **Cliff Villa** thanks Dean Camille Carey of the University of New Mexico School of Law. For research assistance, thanks go to Profs. Jennifer Laws and Ernesto Longa, UNM law librarians. For all-hours tech support: thank you, Morgan Roberts! For the opportunity to work with the best of the best in public service, Cliff thanks Michael Regan, Janet McCabe, Barry Breen, and all other current and former colleagues at EPA, to include Theresa Segovia, Charles Lee, Lilian Dorka, and Stacey Lobatos, all fonts of wisdom and good sense on environmental justice. For endless inspiration, Cliff thanks the EJ book team (4th ed.): Nadia Ahmad, Rebecca Bratspies, Patrice Simms, and Carlton Waterhouse. Deep gratitude as well for thoughtful conversations, observations, and insights from EJ seminar students of 2020 (pivoting gracefully from classroom to Zoom), 2022 (little did we know I would soon be decamping for D.C. to put theory into practice), and 2023 at Columbia Law School (making every Thursday commute from D.C. to N.Y.C. worthwhile). And, of course, endless love and appreciation to family including Angie, Mom, Christina and Curtis, and Oli and Julian (the best readers, writers, and travel partners a proud dad could ever have).

Rebecca Bratspies thanks the many community activists whose work is documented in these pages. In particular, gratitude goes to Peggy Shepard and the late (very missed) Cecil Corbin-Mark at WEACT, Gloria Boyce-Charles at the Eastern Queens Alliance, and Evie Hantzopoulos of the Queens Botanical Garden for inspiring an entire generation of young New Yorkers to speak up and step forward for environmental justice, and to former New York City Councilmember Costa Constantinides for the vision and leadership that crafted Renewable Rikers, the Climate Mobilization Act, and so much more. Rebecca thanks her husband Allen and son Sam for their endless support and encouragement, her colleagues Andrea McArdle, Laura Mott, and Sarah Lamdan for their generosity in sharing their insights and expertise, and the entire New York City Environmental Justice Advisory Board for the hard work that made EJNYC a reality. Working with co-authors Cliff Villa, Nadia Ahmad, Carlton Waterhouse, and Patrice Simms challenged and inspired Rebecca and pushed her thinking in new directions.

Nadia Ahmad extends her heartfelt gratitude for the institutional support she has received throughout this journey. She thanks Dean Leticia Diaz of Barry University School of Law, along with Michael Allen, Pablo Ortiz, John Murray, Jill Farrell, Jeff Larson, Margaret Stewart, Helia Hull, Dan O'Gorman, Stephen Leacock, Glen-Peter Ahlers, Wes Henricksen, and Sam Kan for their encouragement and guidance. She is deeply appreciative of her co-authors Cliff Villa, Rebecca Bratspies, Carlton Waterhouse, and Patrice Simms, whose collaboration enriched this work. Special thanks go to Dan Esty, Gerald Torres, Zhe Zhu, Luke Sanford, Indy Burke, and Peter Raymond for their invaluable insight and support. She is also grateful to Barry Law librarians Jason Murray and Diana Botluck, and to Melissa Bryan for her dedicated research assistance. With love and admiration, she acknowledges her partner, Akmal, whose affirmation and boundless love sustain her. She is endlessly inspired by her children, Senan, Hanan, and Jihan, whose unyielding energy carries her through hurricanes and high tides. Finally, she offers deep appreciation to her parents and siblings as well as her extended family for their enduring support.

Patrice Simms thanks his many mentors in the environmental justice space, especially Leslie Fields, Vernice Miller-Travis, Quentin Pair, Ben Wilson and Charles Lee, all of whom are not just valued colleagues but also dear friends. He is also deeply grateful for blessings of knowledge, wisdom, and inspiration that have come from working with incredible environmental justice leaders, advocates, thinkers, and champions like Dr. Beverly Wright, Dr. Robert Bullard, Peggy Shepard, the amazing Tricia Cortez, the unstoppable Ms. Sharon Lavigne, Catherine Flowers, Jacqui Patterson, the late Cecil Corbin-Mark, Lisa Garcia, Abré Conner, Amy Laura Cahn, Marianne Engelman Lado, Daria Neal, Mark Magaña, Al Huang, Michel Gelobter, and Mustafa Santiago Ali, among others. He especially recognizes the many incredible young leaders who hold the future in their hands, like Alexia Leclercq, Wawa Gatheru, Mary Black, and the ferocious Asia Simms. Patrice also deeply appreciates his friends and colleagues at Earthjustice who are committed to centering communities and justice in their work, including Angela Johnson-Meszaros and Rachel Rintelmann (and the entire Community Partnership Program), Jeremy Orr, Gussie Lord, Debbie Chizewer, Adrienne Bloch, Adrian Martinez, Marvin Brown, Raul Garcia, and so many others, and of course the incomparable Abbie Dillen. A special thanks to Shilpi Chhotray and the whole Counterstream crew helping people on the front lines of environmental justice tell their stories. And of course, this wonderful group of co-authors. *It really does take a village!*

Carlton Waterhouse thanks Vivian Malone Jones, Luke Cole, Jerry Balter, Connie Tucker, Damu Smith, Bunyan Bryant, Sister Joanne Chiaverini, Janice O'Neal, Willie Faye Bush, Margaret Williams, Hazel M. Johnson, State Senator Jean Breaux, Delegate Walter Fauntleroy, Congresswoman Julia Carson, and Congressman Donald McEachin. These environmental justice champions have gone before us, but their lives continue to speak loudly inspiring him to continue their fight for a clean environment for all. He also thanks his wife and family for their support, his co-authors for their hard work and great insights, and all the fellow travelers listed above by his co-authors who have also touched his life.

All authors of this edition extend our gratitude to Ryland Bowman and the fabulous team at Carolina Academic Press, who have supported this project through the years and made every edition possible. We also, of course, thank all readers of this book. Your support and feedback are always welcome as we continue the pursuit of environmental justice together.

Foreword

by Vernice Miller-Travis

When the first edition of this textbook was published and I received my copy, I cradled it to my chest and held it close, thinking that now there's an entire textbook that articulates environmental justice legal theory and practice. One of my personal sheroes, Eileen Gauna, Emeritus Professor of Law at the University of New Mexico School of Law, was also one of the editors.

For me, *Environmental Justice: Law, Policy & Regulation* signified that we in the environmental justice movement no longer needed to engage in endless debate about the existence of environmental injustice. Or provide Pythagorean Theorem-like proofs of the ways that congressionally established statutory and regulatory authorities, and even long-standing civil rights protections, did not anticipate or speak to the environmental threats and cumulative impacts and harms that too many low-income, Indigenous peoples, and communities of color were facing without the benefit of avenues for redress.

The period of time since publication of the third edition in 2020 and this updated fourth edition has been nothing short of momentous in terms of advancing climate, energy, and environmental justice.

During the Biden-Harris Administration, we saw:

- Unprecedented access to federal decision-making tables for environmental justice advocates and their allies, especially those representing community-based organizations.
- A whole-of-government, coordinated approach to advancing climate, energy, and environmental justice policy and practice.
- Almost every federal agency establishing or elevating their environmental justice and related external civil rights offices.
- Historic new federal offices stood up, most notably the Office of Environmental Justice and External Civil Rights at the U.S. EPA, the Office of Environmental Justice at the U.S. Department of Justice, the Office of Energy Justice and Equity at the U.S. Department of Energy, and the White House Office of Environmental Justice within the Council on Environmental Quality. All four of these historic federal offices were unfortunately disbanded by the current administration within weeks of their assumption of office.
- Several new presidential Executive Orders signed into existence, reinvigorating enforcement of environmental and civil rights laws, regulations. and statutes to enhance equal environmental protection for all communities.
- Congressionally appropriated federal financial assistance distributed to states, tribes, and local governments to modernize drinking water systems, clean up contaminated lands, expand clean energy, enhance flood mitigation, upgrade sewer and stormwater management, and improve transportation infrastructure, with a mandate to focus at least 40 percent of the benefits of those investments in underserved communities.
- More than $3 billion in federal grants to advance climate, environmental, and energy justice awarded through highly competitive and rigorous national selection processes by the U.S. EPA, DOE, DOT, HHS, HUD, and USDA.

Recently, the pendulum has swung in the opposite direction and the federal government is not inclined at this moment to continue to address this set of complex issues.

However, state, tribal, and local governments have been and continue to seek ways to use their statutory and regulatory authorities to strengthen enforcement and equal protection from environmental harms visited upon their residents.

Some states like California, Illinois, Massachusetts, Minnesota, New Jersey, New Mexico, New York, Rhode Island, Vermont, and Washington are passing new laws and promulgating regulations to provide more tools to advance environmental and climate justice policies and practices. North Carolina issued an Executive Order on Environmental Justice and Clean Energy; Maryland has appointed its first Assistant

Secretary for Environmental Justice at its Department of the Environment. The Bay Area Air District released a new strategic plan and Call to Action to focus on aggressively advancing environmental justice outcomes across the one hundred and four jurisdictions where it enforces clean air regulations. The Navajo Nation is aggressively pursuing a solar energy program to provide access to clean energy to its members.

Perhaps most importantly, due to the relentless advocacy of local environmental and climate justice groups and their allies in national environmental, public health, scientific, civil rights and legal advocacy organizations, tremendous progress is still being made, even in the face of strong resistance.

Students who believe environmental justice is a core value and organizing principle are joining the ranks every day. They are graduating from high school, college, and graduate schools every semester. They are bringing their skills, passion, technology, and values to help deepen the bench. This book will be an invaluable asset to them as they seek to learn more and grow in their knowledge of environmental justice

The fourth edition of *Environmental Justice: Law, Policy & Regulation* is an important tool in helping us learn and understand the depths of the environmental challenges and threats to life, liberty, and the pursuit of happiness to which we all are entitled but do not all enjoy equally. The ability to breathe clean air, drink clean water, have access to clean energy and sanitary sewage and stormwater systems, and the right to not be poisoned in our schools or workplaces is not too much to ask. It is the very least that we as a modern society can provide for all communities within the United States and its Territories.

So read this book until it's dog-eared, highlight the most salient parts, keep it nearby for quick reference, and donate a copy to a community or student group near you.

Lastly, if you think the light of environmental justice has been dimmed, fear not—remember it is always darkest just before dawn.

Onward,

Vernice Miller-Travis
June 20, 2025

Acknowledgments

The authors gratefully acknowledge the permissions granted to reproduce in this book images and excerpts of the following works:

Mallery Quetawki, *Merciless Laws of Nature* (2025), front cover.

Associated Press/Greg Gibson, Figure 1-1.

Robert R. Kuehn, *A Taxonomy of Environmental Justice*, 30 Envtl. L. Rep. 10,681 (2000).

Richard Lazarus, *Pursuing "Environmental Justice": The Distributional Effects of Environmental Protection*, 87 Northwestern U. L. Rev. 787 (1993).

Yale Rabin, *Expulsive Zoning: The Inequitable Legacy of Euclid*, *in* Zoning and the American Dream 101 (Charles M. Haar & Jerold S. Kayden eds., 1989).

Sarah Schindler, *Architectural Exclusion: Discrimination and Segregation through Physical Design of the Built Environment*, 124 Yale L.J. 1934 (2015).

Robin Saha & Paul Mohai, *Explaining Racial and Socioeconomic Disparities in the Location of Locally Unwanted Land Uses: A Conceptual Framework*, presented at the 1997 Annual Meeting of the Rural Sociological Society (Toronto, Aug. 1997).

Carmen G. Gonzalez, *An Environmental Justice Critique of Comparative Advantage: Indigenous Peoples, Trade Policy, and the Mexican Neoliberal Economic Reforms*, 32 U. Pa. J. Int'l L. 723 (2011).

Shirley Trout, Figure 2-2.

Brie D. Sherwin, *The Upside Down: A New Reality for Science at the EPA and Its Impacts on Environmental Justice*, 27 N.Y.U. Envt'l. L.J. 57 (2019).

Vicki Been, *Locally Undesirable Land Uses in Minority Neighborhoods: Disproportionate Siting or Market Dynamics?*, 103 Yale L.J. 1383 (1994).

Manuel Pastor, Jr., Jim Sadd & John Hipp, *Which Came First? Toxic Facilities, Minority Move-In, and Environmental Justice*, 23 J. Urban Aff. 1 (2001).

Shelly Taylor Page & Patricia A. Broussard, *Environmental Racism in America: Minority Communities As Dumping Grounds for Environmental Waste*, 49 S. Ill. U. L.J. 199 (2025).

Staff Sgt. Connie Jones/U.S. Army National Guard, Figure 3-1.

Carnegie Commission on Science, Technology, and Government, Risk and the Environment: Improving Regulatory Decision Making (1993).

Robert R. Kuehn, *The Environmental Justice Implications of Quantitative Risk Assessment*, 1996 U. Illinois L. Rev. 103 (1996).

Cary Coglianese & Gary E. Marchant, *Shifting Sands: The Limits of Science in Setting Risk Standards*, 152 U. Pa. L. Rev. 1255 (2004).

Philip J. Landrigan, Virginia A. Rauh, & Maida P. Galvez, *Environmental Justice and the Health of Children*, 77 Mount Sinai J. Med. 178 (2010).

Marianne Engelman Lado, *No More Excuses: Building a New Vision of Civil Rights Enforcement in the Context of Environmental Justice*, 22 U. Pa. L. & Soc. Change 281 (2019).

Daniel Farber, *Inequality and Regulation Revisited*, 4 Am. J. Law & Equality 347 (2024).

Richard J. Lazarus & Stephanie Tai, *Integrating Environmental Justice nto EPA Permitting Authority*, 26 Ecology L.Q. 617 (2000).

Sara A. Colangelo, *Forging Complete Justice: Equitable Relief in Environmental Enforcement*, 46 Harvard Envtl. L. Rev. 315 (2022).

Patrice L. Simms, *Leveraging Supplemental Environmental Projects Toward an Integrated Strategy for Empowering Environmental Justice Communities*, 47 Envtl. L. Rep. News & Analysis 10,511 (2017).

Elizabeth Kronk Warner, *Environmental Justice: A Necessary Lens to Effectively View Environmental Threats to Indigenous Survival*, 26 Transnat'l L. & Contemp. Probs. 343 (2017).

Elizabeth Kronk Warner, *Sovereignty over Box Checking: Effective Tribal Consultation Leading to Consent*, 38 J. Land Use & Envtl. L. 131 (2023).

Rebecca Tsosie, *Tribal Environmental Policy in an Era of Self-Determination: The Role of Ethics, Economics, and Traditional Ecological Knowledge*, 21 Vermont L. Rev. 225 (1996).

Jeanette Wolfley, *Tribal Environmental Programs: Providing Meaningful Involvement and Fair Treatment*, 29 J. Envtl. L. & Litig. 389 (2014).

Lisa Murkowski, *Alaska's Contaminated Lands Are an Environmental Injustice*, 62 ABA Judges' Journal 17 (2023).

Michael Gerrard & Edward McTiernan, *New York Adopts Nation's Strongest Environmental Justice Law*, New York Law Journal, May 10, 2023.

Vien Truong, *Addressing Poverty and Pollution: California's SB 535 Greenhouse Gas Reduction Fund*, 49 Harvard Civil Rights-Civil Liberties L. Rev. 493 (2014).

Seema Kakade, *A Contractual Relationship with Environmental Justice*, 73 American U. L. Rev. 343 (2023).

Sarah Lamdan & Rebecca Bratspies, T*aking a Page from the FDA's Prescription Medicine Information Rules: Reimagining Environmental Information for Climate Change*, 40 U. Ark. Little Rock L. Rev. 573 (2018).

Francis Calpotura, *Why the Law?*, Third Force (May/June 1994).

Luke W. Cole, *Empowerment as the Key to Environmental Protection: The Need for Environmental Poverty Law*, 19 Ecology L.Q. 619 (1992).

Joshua Weichman, Figure 12-2.

Helen Kang, *Pursuing Environmental Justice: Obstacles and Opportunities—Lessons from the Field*, 31 Wash. U. J. L. & Pol'y 121 (2009).

Richard T. Drury, *Moving a Mountain: The Struggle for Environmental Justice in Southeast Los Angeles*, 38 Envtl. L. Rep. News & Analysis 10,338 (2008).

Roselynn Loaiza, Figure 12-3.

Sumudu Atapattu, *The Right to a Healthy Life or the Right to Die Polluted?: The Emergence of a Human Right to a Healthy Environment Under International Law*, 16 Tulane Envtl. L.J. 65 (2002).

Russell A. Miller, *Pandemic as Transboundary Harm: Lessons from the Trail Smelter Arbitration*, 55 N.Y.U. J. Int'l L. & Pol. (2023).

Giovanni Chiarini, *Ecocide in War and Peace: From the Air Pollution Consequences of the War in Ukraine to Japan's Disposal of Fukushima Water into the Ocean*, 56 Case W. Res. J. Int'l L. 242 (2024).

Carlton Waterhouse, *Climate Redress Revisited: Loss and Damage, Compensation and Reparations*, 101 Iowa L. Rev. 2201 (2025).

Subhankar Banerjee, Figure 14-1, from Arctic Voices: Resistance at the Tipping Point (Seven Stories Press, pbk, 2013). Used by permission.

Scripps Institute of Oceanography at UC San Diego, Figure 14-2.

Solmari Perez Oliveras, Figure 14-3.

Maxine Burkett, *Rehabilitation: A Proposal for a Climate Compensation Mechanism for Small Island States*, 13 Santa Clara J. Int'l L. 81 (2015).

Maria A. Tigre, *Climate Change and Indigenous Groups: The Rise of Indigenous Voices in Climate Litigation*, 9 E-Publica 214 (2022).

Alice Kaswan & Catalina Gonzalez, *Environmental Justice in State Climate Planning: Learning from California* (Center for Progressive Reform, 2024).

Rebecca Bratspies, *Climate Justice Begins at Home*, 37 New York Int'l. Rev. 13 (2024).

Maytal Gilboa, Yotam Kaplan & Roee Sarel, *Climate Change as Unjust Enrichment*, 112 Georgetown L.J. 1039 (2024).

Georgetown Climate Center, Opportunities for Equitable Adaptation in Cities (2017).

Simon Romero, *"Burning Down a Way of Life": Wildfire Rips Through a Hispanic Bastion*, N.Y. Times, May 5, 2022. All rights reserved. Used by permission.

Robert R.M. Verchick, *Disaster Justice: The Geography of Human Capability*, 23 Duke Envtl. L. & Pol'y Forum 23 (2012).

Zacary E. Wilson-Fetrow, *Meaningless Involvement: How Traditional Modes of Involvement Exclude Transgender People from Environmental Justice*, 48 Ecology L.Q. 843 (2021).

Sidney Shapiro, *Preface: An Ounce of Prevention*, *in* From Surviving to Thriving: Equity in Disaster Planning and Recovery (Center for Progressive Reform, 2018).

Danielle Arigoni, Climate Resilience for an Aging Nation (2023).

Tony Anderson, University of New Mexico School of Law, Figure 15-4.

Smita Narula, *Beyond Reform: Food Sovereignty and the Future of Global Food Systems*, 31 Ind. J. Glob. Legal Studs. 141 (2024).

Deborah N. Archer & Tamara C. Belinfanti, *We Built It and They Did Not Come: Using New Governance Theory in the Fight for Food Justice in Low-Income Communities of Color*, 15 Seattle J. Soc. Justice 307 (2016).

Intergovernmental Panel on Climate Change, Special Report: Climate Change and Land (2019).

Rebecca M. Bratspies, *Hunger and Equity in an Era of Genetic Engineering*, 7 U.C. Irvine L. Rev. 195 (2017).

Danielle M. Purifoy, *Food Policy Councils: Integrating Food Justice and Environmental Justice*, 24 Duke Envtl. L. & Pol'y Forum 375 (2014).

Shirley Trout, Figure 16-3.

Rebecca L. Goldberg, *No Such Thing as a Free Lunch: Paternalism, Poverty, and Food Justice*, 24 Stanford L. & Pol'y Rev. 35 (2013).

Andrea Freeman, *The Unbearable Whiteness of Milk: Food Oppression and the USDA*, 3 U.C. Irvine L. Rev. 1251 (2013).

Environmental Justice

Chapter 1

An Introduction to Environmental Justice

A. Environmental Injustice

Environmental justice, as a field of study and practice, exists because environmental *injustice* exists all around us. Within the bounds of the United States, consider the following:

On the **Navajo Nation**, sprawling across Arizona, New Mexico, and Utah, the legacy of uranium mining during the Cold War has left Diné communities today facing risks of lung cancer and other diseases from soil contamination 800 times above the action levels established by the U.S. Environmental Protection Agency (EPA).

In the **Dallas, Texas**, metro area, the unincorporated community of Sandbranch, settled by freed Blacks after the Civil War, to this day lacks running water or sewage treatment, with residents depending upon bottled water deliveries to replace contaminated wells.

In Reserve, Louisiana, within the heart of **"Cancer Alley"** between New Orleans and Baton Rouge, surrounded by stacks of the petrochemical industry, cancer rates are fifty times above the national average, the poverty rate is almost double the national average, and the Black population is more than four times the national average.

In **Central Appalachia**, including rural communities of Kentucky and West Virginia, generations of coal mining and other extractive industries have left local residents suffering health impacts such as black lung disease plus widespread ecological devastation.

In **Duplin County, North Carolina**, near the town of Warsaw, where Blacks and Latinos account for more than three-quarters of the population, residents often cannot hang laundry to dry outside or keep windows open on summer days because of the massive waste from industrial hog farms blowing in the air and fouling local waters.

In **Puerto Rico**, residents of this U.S. territory continue to live with regular blackouts and other consequences of poverty, colonization, and failed governance, exacerbated by climate disasters including Hurricane Maria in 2017.

In **New York City**, residents of Manhattan's Upper East Side enjoy an average lifespan ten years longer than residents of neighborhoods just across the Bronx River—a disparity reflecting many factors including differences in income, proximity to freeways, and attendant air pollution.

In **Flint, Michigan**, with a population 57 percent Black and 42 percent below the poverty line in 2015, state and local officials precipitated the "Flint Water Crisis" by failing to properly treat a new source for city water and exposing some 8,657 young people to dangerous levels of lead, risking permanent neurological impairments.

In **Cahokia Heights, Illinois**, with a Black population more than 70 percent, residents in this community across the Mississippi River from **St. Louis** regularly experience floodwaters and raw sewage in their streets and homes, the result of persistent failures by local utilities to maintain water infrastructure.

In **North Dakota**, members of the Standing Rock Sioux Tribe live with constant threats to their water and lifeways posed by the risk of crude oil escaping from the Dakota Access Pipeline, which was constructed without consent from the Tribe, and whose protest in 2016 drew supporters from more than 300 tribal nations.

In **Alaska**, residents of Arctic villages witness the alarming impacts of a rapidly warming environment, including accelerated coastal erosion on the order of 23 feet per year in locations along the Beaufort Sea.

In **Seattle, Washington** and many other urban areas, fisherfolk from Vietnamese, Filipino, Latino, and Indigenous communities catch native fish from polluted waterways and take the fish home to feed their families.

In the **Central Valley** of California, as in many other agricultural areas, immigrant farmworkers face constant health threats from pesticide exposure, air pollution, inadequate housing, and—increasingly—extreme heat.

In the ***colonias*** along the U.S.-Mexico border from Southern California to Texas, low-income Latino families continue to live without municipal water, sanitation, electricity, and many other public services that other communities take as given.

In **Wichita, Kansas**, North End neighborhoods where the Black population comprises 62 percent and the Latino population comprises 16 percent, toxic air pollutants rank in the 98th percentile nationally and risk of exposure to lead-based paint ranks in the 97th percentile nationally.

Look around your community, wherever you live, learn, work, play, or pray, and you will likely find more examples of environmental injustice. If this concerns you, there are things you can do about it, actions grounded in law and policy to promote environmental justice. That is the subject of this book.

B. "The Arc of the Moral Universe"

2022 was a good year for environmental justice. In September, Michael Regan, President Biden's EPA Administrator, signed an order creating a new EPA Office of Environmental Justice and External Civil Rights, placing this new office on par with other major program offices at EPA Headquarters. The new EJ office would coordinate with new EJ offices in each of the ten EPA Regions and would administer more than $3 billion in grant funding provided by the Inflation Reduction Act of 2022.

Figure 1-1. Rev. Benjamin Chavis raises his fist joining fellow protesters at the Warren County PCB landfill near Afton, North Carolina. Sept. 16, 1982. Photo: AP/Greg Gibson. Used by permission.

Significantly, Administrator Regan signed the order in Warren County, North Carolina, surrounded by EJ luminaries including Dr. Benjamin Chavis. Forty years prior, in September 1982, Dr. Chavis led a protest against a toxic waste dump in Warren County, which had the highest percentage of Blacks in the state and was also one of the poorest counties in the state. The 1982 protest attracted support from a broad coalition of national civil rights leaders, elected officials, environmental activists, and labor leaders. Dr. Chavis, who had worked alongside Dr. Martin Luther King, Jr., in the 1960s, could see what was happening in Warren County. Toxic waste spread out across 14 counties in North Carolina was being hauled and dumped in Warren County for reasons that Dr. Chavis termed "environmental racism." The Warren County protests would not stop that dumping but did help inspire the enduring movement we know today as environmental justice. EILEEN MCGURTY, TRANSFORMING ENVIRONMENTALISM: WARREN COUNTY, PCBS, AND THE ORIGINS OF ENVIRONMENTAL JUSTICE (2007).

After Warren County in 1982, communities of color alarmed conventional environmental organizations, regulators, and industry leaders with further allegations of environmental racism. These charges reflected long-standing frustration on the part of such communities, and their view that people of color systematically receive disproportionately greater environmental risk while white communities systematically receive better environmental protection. Across the country, communities of color began to challenge the siting of hazardous waste facilities, landfills, industrial activities, and other risk-producing land practices within their community. The roots of the environmental justice movement lie in diverse political projects, including the Civil Rights Movement of the 1960s, the environmental movement of the 1970s, organizing efforts for worker health and safety, and movements supporting tribal sovereignty and Indigenous lifeways. *See generally* Luke Cole & Sheila Foster, From the Ground Up: Environmental Racism and the Rise of the Environmental Justice Movement (2001).

"Environmental justice" soon came to mean more than skewed distributional consequences of environmental burdens to communities of color. Becoming multi-issue and multi-racial in scope, the movement began to address disparities borne by the poor as well as by people of color, acknowledging the substantial overlap between the two demographic categories. Concerns about regulatory processes surfaced as well. Often, the communities most impacted by environmentally risky activities had been excluded from important decision-making proceedings, sometimes intentionally so and sometimes because of a lack of resources, specialized knowledge, and other structural impediments.

Largely in response to these early concerns, several investigations and studies were undertaken which lent support to charges of environmental injustice. In 1987, for example, a national study by the United Church of Christ found a positive correlation between racial minorities and proximity to commercial hazardous waste facilities and uncontrolled waste sites. United Church of Christ, Commission for Racial Justice, Toxic Wastes and Race in the United States (1987). Significantly, the study found that race was a more statistically significant variable than income. Early activism also included an extraordinary gathering of grassroots activists at the First National People of Color Environmental Leadership Summit in Washington, D.C., in October 1991, where delegates adopted the Principles of Environmental Justice, reprinted below.

In response to public pressure, the EPA under President George Bush conducted an investigation and issued a report which among other things recognized that "race and income ... appear to be correlated with" the distribution of "some types of pollutants...." U.S. EPA, Environmental Equity: Reducing Risk for All Communities 2 (June 1992). In 1993, under President Bill Clinton, the EPA convened a National Environmental Justice Advisory Council (NEJAC), charged with making recommendations to the EPA concerning a broad range of environmental justice matters. In 1994, President Clinton signed Executive Order 12898, requiring all federal agencies to make environmental justice part of their mission. While not carrying force of law, Executive Order 12898 established norms that courts cited repeatedly for aid in statutory interpretation. *See* Clifford J. Villa, *No "Box To Be Checked": Environmental Justice in Modern Legal Practice*, 30 N.Y.U. Envtl. L.J. 157, 180–88 (2022) (summarizing cases).

After progress on environmental justice during the Clinton administration, the Bush-Cheney administration took an approach to environmental justice that de-emphasized focus on minority and low-income populations. During this time, EJ advocates shifted their attention to state and local governments to remedy environmental disparities. Reinvigorated efforts to address environmental justice returned to the federal government with the Obama administration—and went underground again with the first Trump administration, which attempted to eliminate funding for environmental justice programs and staff. *See* Uma Outka & Elizabeth Kronk Warner, *Reversing Course on Environmental Justice Under the Trump Administration*, 54 Wake Forest L. Rev. 393 (2019).

President Joe Biden made environmental justice a top priority for the entire federal government. On the day of his inauguration on January 20, 2021, President Biden signed Executive Order 13990, which declared "the Federal Government ... must advance environmental justice." One week later, Executive Order 14008, among other things, created a White House Environmental Justice Advisory Council (WHEJAC) and established the Justice40 initiative, whereby certain federal investments would work "toward a goal that 40 percent of the overall benefits flow to disadvantaged communities." In April 2023, President Biden signed Executive Order 14096, *Revitalizing Our Nation's Commitment to Environmental Justice for All*, which among other things established an updated definition of "environmental justice" applicable to all federal entities. *See generally*, Clifford J. Villa, *A New Day for Environmental Justice at the U.S. EPA*, 54 U. Memphis L. Rev. 867 (2024).

January 20, 2025, marked a radical reversal for environmental justice across the federal government as Donald Trump began a second term as president. On that day, President Trump signed Executive Order 14151, which among other things directed each federal agency to "terminate ... all DEI, DEIA, and 'environmental justice' offices and positions...." On the same day, Trump's Executive Order 14148 rescinded a long list of Biden orders addressing environmental justice, including Executive Orders 13990, 14008 (effectively abolishing the WHEJAC and Justice40 initiative), and 14096 (effectively repealing a new definition of "environmental justice" applicable to the entire federal government). The next day, Executive Order 14173 rescinded Executive Order 12898, President Clinton's original order on environmental justice that had remained in place for over 30 years. In the days and weeks that followed, President Trump's EPA Administrator announced mass firings of EJ staff and abolishment of EJ offices in EPA Headquarters and all EPA regional offices. *See* U.S. EPA, *EPA Terminates Biden's Environmental Justice, DEI Arms of Agency*, March 12, 2025.

In many ways, the Trump backlash against environmental justice in 2025 recalls the backlash against civil rights some 60 years before. In the face of progress including *Brown v. Board of Education* in 1954 and the Civil Rights Act of 1964, Alabama state troopers in March 1965 brutally attacked a group of peaceful protesters who were attempting to march from Selma to Montgomery in order to bring attention to racial violence and the denial of voting rights in the state. On the third try, the marchers, led by Dr. Martin Luther King, succeeded in crossing the Edmund Pettus Bridge in Selma and completing the march to Montgomery. In the shadow of the state capitol, Dr. King famously observed that "the arc of the moral universe is long, but it bends toward justice." But even as a man of faith, Dr. King knew that the "arc" would not bend on its own; it would bend only because advocates were prepared to act, to march, to face resistance even from their own government. Whether the arc will bend toward *environmental* justice may likewise depend on the continued actions of EJ advocates

Figure 1-2. Edmund Pettus Bridge, Selma, Alabama. Photo: Cliff Villa, 2025.

today. This book may provide some tools and starting points for action grounded in legal theory and authorities.

As federal support for environmental justice continues to diminish in this current administration, states, tribes, cities, and nongovernmental organizations may play increasingly important roles. In recent years, many states, including California, Colorado, Illinois, Maryland, Massachusetts, Minnesota, New Jersey, New York, and Washington, have passed legislation requiring consideration of environmental justice. For a useful online compendium of state authorities and policies for promoting environmental justice, drop "Environmental Justice State by State" into your Internet browser.

Ultimately, environmental justice remains a grassroots movement, with community organizations and members empowered to advocate for themselves using a variety of political and legal tools. Chapter 4 explores the possibility of pursuing environmental justice through constitutional law and civil rights legislation. Chapters 5 and 6 focus on the federal regulatory process, identifying how government regulators and community activists may work cooperatively to establish new environmental regulations and permits. Chapter 7 examines environmental enforcement by government agencies, allowing limited, but potentially significant, opportunities for public engagement. Chapter 8 provides an overview of legal authorities and resources for addressing contaminated sites, including Superfund cleanup and Brownfields grants. Chapter 9 considers some of the unique EJ concerns for Indian tribes and Indigenous people. Chapter 10 focuses on federal and state initiatives to promote environmental justice, with a concluding note on private governance. Additional authorities available to community advocates, including citizen suit provisions of environmental statutes, are evaluated in Chapter 11 (Information Disclosure and Environmental Review) and Chapter 12 (Citizen Enforcement and Common Law Remedies). Chapter 13 provides an introduction to EJ in international law. Finally, Chapters 14, 15, and 16 explore emerging dimensions of environmental justice in climate justice, disaster justice, and food justice, respectively.

Overall, the thrust of this book is twofold: first, to examine the complexities presented by environmental inequity; and second, to explore the potential that exists within the current legal system to move environmental regulation forward in a responsible manner toward a more just society and sustainable environment. Solutions to many cases of environmental injustice are out there: our project in this book is to help readers find those solutions through the best tools of law and policy.

Pathfinder on Environmental Justice Generally

Scholarship on environmental justice is rich and varied. Among the numerous books addressing themes on environmental justice are Catherine Coleman Flowers, Holy Ground: On Activism, Environmental Justice, and Finding Hope (2025); Barry E. Hill, Environmental Justice: Legal Theory and Practice (5th ed. 2022); Dina Gilio-Whitaker, As Long as the Grass Grows: The Indigenous Fight for Environmental Justice, from Colonization to Standing Rock (2020); Jill Lindsey Harrison, From the Inside Out: The Fight for Environmental Justice within Government Agencies (2019); Katrina Smith Korfmacher, Bridging Silos: Collaborating for Environmental Health and Justice in Urban Communities (2019); Harriet A. Washington, A Terrible Thing to Waste: Environmental Racism and Its Assault on the American Mind (2019); The Routledge Handbook of Environmental Justice (Ryan Holifeld, Jayajit Chakraborty & Gordon Walker eds. 2018); Carmen G. Gonzalez et al., Energy Justice: US and International Perspectives (2018); Dorceta Taylor, Toxic Communities: Environmental Racism, Industrial Pollution, and Residential Mobility (2014); Robert Bullard & Beverly Wright, The Wrong Complexion for Protection (2012); The Law of Environmental Justice: Theories and Procedures to Address Disproportionate Risks (Michael B. Gerrard & Sheila R. Foster eds., 2d ed. 2008); Craig Anthony Arnold, Fair and Healthy Land Use: Environmental Justice and Planning (2007); Luke Cole & Sheila Foster, From the Ground Up: Environmental Racism and the Rise of the Environmental Justice Movement (2001); Bunyan Bryant, Environmental Justice: Issues, Policies and Solutions (1995); Confronting Environmental Racism: Voices from the Grassroots (Robert D. Bullard ed., 1993); Unequal Protection: Environmental Justice and Communities of Color (Robert D. Bullard ed., 1994); Race and the Incidence of Environmental Hazards: A Time for Discourse (Paul Mohai & Bunyan Bryant eds., 1992); and the classic work by Robert D. Bullard, Dumping in Dixie: Race, Class, and Environmental Quality (1990).

Among the wealth of scholarly articles on environmental justice are Danielle Stokes, *From Redlining to Greenlining*, 71 UCLA L. Rev. 628 (2024); Sara A. Colangelo, *Bridging Silos: Environmental and Reproductive Justice in the Climate Crisis*, 112 Cal. L. Rev. 1255 (2024); Michele Okoh, *Forgotten Waters*, 111 Georgetown L.J. 723 (2023); Seema Kakade, *A Contractual Relationship with Environmental Justice*, 73 American U. L. Rev. 343 (2023); Richard L. Revesz, *Air Pollution and Environmental Justice*, 49 Ecology L.Q. 187 (2022); Nadia B. Ahmad, *The Cliodynamics of Mass Incarceration, Climate Change, and "Chains on Our Feet,"* 49 Fordham Urban L.J. 371 (2022); Clifford J. Villa, *Don't Blame the Flint River*, 52 Envtl. L. 341 (2022); Rebecca Bratspies, *Underburdened Communities*, 110 Cal. L. Rev. 101 (2022); Warigia M. Bowman, *Dikos Nitsaa'igii-19 ("The Big Cough"): Coal, COVID-19, and the Navajo Nation*, 73 Hastings L.J. 975 (2022); Britney R. Wilson, *Making Me Ill: Environmental Racism and Justice as Disability*, 170 U. Penn. L. Rev. 1721 (2022); Charles Lee, *Another Game Changer in the Making? Lessons from States Advancing Environmental Justice Through Mapping and Cumulative Impact Strategies*, 51 Envtl. L. Rep. 10676 (2021); Zacary E. Wilson-Fetrow, *Meaningless Involvement: How Traditional Modes of Involvement Exclude Transgender People from Environmental Justice*, 48 Ecology L.Q. 843 (2021); Clifford J. Villa, *Remaking Environmental Justice*, 66 Loyola L. Rev. 469 (2020); Sarah Krakoff, *Environmental Justice and the Possibilities for Environmental Law*, 49 Envtl. L. 229 (2019); Oliver A. Houck, *Shintech: Environmental Justice at Ground Zero*, 31 Geo. Int'l. Envtl. L. Rev. 455 (2019); Spencer Banzhaf, Lala Ma & Christopher Timmins, *Environmental Justice: The Economics of Race, Place, and Pollution*, 33 J. Econ. Perspectives 185 (2019); Brigham Daniels, Michalyn Steele & Lisa Grow Sun, *Just Environmentalism*, 37 Yale L. & Pol'y Rev. 1 (2018); Jedediah Purdy, *The Long Environmental Justice Movement*, 44 Ecology L.Q. 809 (2018); Benjamin F. Wilson, *It's Not "Just" Zoning: Environmental Justice and Land Use*, 49 Urb. Law. 717 (2017); Rachael E. Salcido, *Reviving the Environmental Justice Agenda*, 91 Chi.-Kent L. Rev. 115 (2016); Carmen G. Gonzalez, *Environmental Justice, Human Rights, and the Global South*, 13 Santa Clara J. Int'l. L. 151 (2015); Gregg Macey, *Boundary Work in Environmental Law*, 53 Houston L. Rev. 103 (2015); Paul Mohai & Robin Saha, *Which Came First, People or Pollution? Assessing the Disparate Siting and Post-Siting Demographic Change Hypotheses of Environmental Injustice*, 10 Envtl. Res. Letters, no. 11 (Nov. 18, 2015); Tonya Lewis & Jessica Owley, *Symbolic Politics for Disempowered Communities: State Environmental Justice Policies*, 29 BYU J. Pub. L. 183 (2014); Alice Kaswan, *Environmental Justice and Environmental Law*, 24 Fordham Envtl. L. Rev. 149 (2013); Patrice Lumumba Simms, *On Diversity and Public Policymaking: An Environmental Justice Perspective*, 13 Sustainable Dev. L. & Pol'y 14 (2012–2013); Uma Outka, *Environmental Justice Issues in Sustainable Development: Environmental Justice in the Renewable Energy Transition*, 19 J. Envtl. & Sustainability L. 60 (2012); Jonathan C. Augustine, *Environmental Justice and Eschatology in Revelation*, 58 Loy. L. Rev. 325 (2012); Carlton Waterhouse, *Abandon All Hope Ye That Enter? Equal Protection, Title VI, and the Divine Comedy of Environmental Justice*, 20 Fordham Envtl. L. Rev. 51 (2009); Clifford Rechtschaffen, *Advancing Environmental Justice Norms*, 37 U.C. Davis L. Rev. 95 (2003); Robert D. Bullard et al., *Toxic Wastes and Race at Twenty: Why Race Still Matters After All of These Years*, 38 Envtl. L. 371 (2008);

Catherine O'Neill, *Mercury, Risk, and Justice*, 34 Envtl. L. Rep. 11070 (2004); Tseming Yang, *Melding Civil Rights and Environmentalism: Finding Environmental Justice's Place in Environmental Regulation*, 26 Harv. Envtl. L. Rev. 1 (2002); Carita Shanklin, *Pathfinder: Environmental Justice*, 24 Ecology L.Q. 333 (1997); Denis Binder, *Index of Environmental Justice Cases*, 27 Urb. Law. 163 (1995), *Environmental Justice Index II*, 3 Chapman L. Rev. 309 (2000), and *Environmental Justice Index III*, 35 Envtl. L. Rep. 10,606 (2005); Eileen Gauna, *An Essay on Environmental Justice: The Past, the Present, and Back to the Future*, 42 Nat. Resources J. 701 (2002) and *Farmworkers as an Environmental Justice Issue: Similarities and Differences*, 25 Environs Envtl. L. & Pol'y J. 67 (2002); Craig Anthony Arnold, *Planning Milagros: Environmental Justice and Land Use Regulation*, 76 Denver U. L. Rev. 1 (1998); Robert R. M. Verchick, *In a Greener Voice: Feminist Theory and Environmental Justice*, 19 Harv. Women's L.J. 23, 73–74 (1996); Richard J. Lazarus, *"Environmental Racism! That's What It Is."*, 2000 U. Ill. L. Rev. 255; *Pursuing "Environmental Justice": The Distributional Effects of Environmental Protection*, 87 Nw. U. L. Rev. 787 (1993); Robert W. Collin, *Environmental Equity: A Law and Planning Approach to Environmental Racism*, 11 Va. Envtl. L.J. 495 (1992); Gerald Torres, *Race, Class, and Environmental Regulation, Introduction: Understanding Environmental Racism*, 63 U. Colo. L. Rev. 839 (1992); and Luke W. Cole, *Empowerment as the Key to Environmental Protection: The Need for Environmental Poverty Law*, 19 Ecology L.Q. 619 (1992).

In addition to these and many other important works of legal scholarship, environmental justice advocates may find useful materials through myriad other sources, including multidisciplinary journals such as the bimonthly, peer-reviewed Environmental Justice, and websites maintained by academic institutions, nonprofit organizations, and government agencies. Among useful websites for environmental justice materials, see those for the Deep South Center for Environmental Justice (www.dscej.org) and the NAACP Environmental & Climate Justice Program (www.naacp.org/issues/environmental-justice). For readers of all levels interested in environmental justice concerns, see also the series of EJ comic books by Professor Rebecca Bratspies, available at the following link: https://www.rebeccabratspies.com/environmental-justice-chronicles. The authors of this book also maintain a website for updates on the world of environmental justice: www.environmentaljusticebook.org.

C. The Meaning of "Environmental Justice"

A fundamental question for this book and for related study and practice is the meaning of "environmental justice," which has evolved over time and remains open to diverse perspectives. In the following excerpt from an influential article, Professor Robert Kuehn attempts to elucidate the meaning of environmental justice through proposed definitions as well as four concepts of justice: distributive, procedural, corrective, and social justice.

Robert R. Kuehn, *A Taxonomy of Environmental Justice*

30 Envtl. L. Rep. 10,681 (2000)

Efforts to understand environmental justice are [] complicated by the term's international, national, and local scope; by its broad definition of the environment—where one lives, works, plays, and goes to school; and by its broad range of concerns—such as public health, natural resource conservation, and worker safety in both urban and rural environs. Disputes at the international level include allegations that governments and multinational corporations are exploiting indigenous peoples and the impoverished conditions of developing nations. At the national level, although an overwhelming number of studies show differences by race and income in exposures to environmental hazards, debate continues about the strength of that evidence and the appropriate political and legal response to such disparities. At the local level, many people of color and lower income communities believe that they have not been treated fairly regarding the distribution of the environmental benefits and burdens....

Shifting Perspectives and Uses of Terms

The U.S. Environmental Protection Agency (EPA) initially used the term "environmental equity," defined as the equitable distribution of environmental risks across population groups, to refer to the environmental justice phenomenon. Because this term implies the redistribution of risk across racial and economic groups rather than risk reduction and avoidance, it is no longer used by EPA, though it is still used by some states.

In some instances, the phrase "environmental racism," defined as "any policy, practice or directive that differentially affects or disadvantages (whether intended or unintended) individuals, groups, or communities based on race or color," is used to explain the differential treatment of populations on environmental issues. Commentators disagree over the proper usage of this term, particularly over whether an action having an unequal distributive outcome across racial groups would in itself be a sufficient basis to label an action environmental racism or whether the action must be the result of intentional racial animus. Today, many environmental justice advocates and scholars avoid the term "environmental racism," though the phrase continues to be employed and is useful in identifying the institutional causes of some environmental injustices. This shift is attributable to a desire to focus on solutions rather than mere identification of problems, as well as a desire to encompass class concerns and not to be limited by issues of intentional conduct....

In 1994, President Clinton issued Executive Order No. 12898 ... and adopted the phrase "environmental justice" to refer to "disproportionately high and adverse human health or environmental effects ... on minority populations and low-income populations." The Executive Order's use of the term "environmental justice" is significant in at least three respects. First, the Executive Order focuses not only on the disproportionate burdens addressed by the term environmental equity, but also on issues of enforcement of environmental laws and opportunities for public participation. Second, the Executive Order identifies not just minorities but also low-income populations as the groups who have been subject to, and entitled to relief from, unfair or unequal treatment. Finally, the Executive Order, and in particular the accompanying memorandum, refers to environmental justice as a goal or aspiration to be achieved, rather than as a problem or cause....

Going beyond the issues of disproportionate exposures and participation in the development and enforcement of laws and policies, EPA further elaborated that environmental justice:

> is based on the premise that: 1) it is a basic right of all Americans to live and work in "safe, healthful, productive, and aesthetically and culturally pleasing surroundings;" 2) it is not only an environmental issue but a public health issue; 3) it is forward-looking and goal-oriented; and 4) it is also inclusive since it is based on the concept of fundamental fairness, which includes the concept of economic prejudices as well as racial prejudices.

Professor Bunyan Bryant defines environmental justice as referring "to those cultural norms and values, rules, regulations, behaviors, policies, and decisions to support sustainable communities, where people can interact with confidence that their environment is safe, nurturing, and protective." Some critics of environmental justice contend that these definitions of environmental justice by government agencies and environmental justice advocates are so broad and aspirational as not to state clearly the ends of environmental justice.

An alternative approach to defining environmental justice that does state its desired ends, albeit very ambitious ones, was developed by environmental justice leaders during the 1991 First People of Color Environmental Leadership Summit. Its "Principles of Environmental Justice" sets forth a 17-point paradigm [excerpted below]....

Dr. Robert Bullard has distilled the principles of environmental justice into a framework of five basic characteristics: (1) protect all persons from environmental degradation; (2) adopt a public health prevention of harm approach; (3) place the burden of proof on those who seek to pollute; (4) obviate the requirement to prove intent to discriminate; and (5) redress existing inequities by targeting action and resources. In his view, environmental justice seeks to make environmental protection more democratic and asks the fundamental ethical and political questions of "who gets what, why and how much."

Students and lawyers are often left without an understanding of unifying themes or common political, legal, or economic approaches to addressing allegations of injustice. The classification method set forth in this [a]rticle seeks to overcome this shortcoming and to advance the understanding of environmental justice by disassembling the term into the four traditional notions of "justice" that are implicated by allegations of environmental injustice....

Environmental Justice as Distributive Justice

... Distributive justice has been defined as "the right to equal treatment, that is, to the same distribution of goods and opportunities as anyone else has or is given." Aristotle is often credited with the first articulation of the concept and explained it as involving "the distribution of honour, wealth, and the other divisible assets of the community, which may be allotted among its members." The focus of this aspect of justice is on fairly distributed outcomes, rather than on the process for arriving at such outcomes.

In an environmental context, distributive justice involves the equitable distribution of the burdens resulting from environmentally threatening activities or of the environmental benefits of government and private-sector programs. More specifically, in an environmental justice context, distributive justice most commonly involves addressing the disproportionate public health and environmental risks borne by people of color and lower incomes....

Distributive justice in an environmental justice context does not mean redistributing pollution or risk. Instead, environmental justice advocates argue that it means equal protection for all and the elimination of environmental hazards and the need to place hazardous activities in any community. In other words, distributive justice is achieved through a lowering of risks, not a shifting or equalizing of existing risks.

With such a strong focus on the inequitable distribution by race and income of environmental hazards, an often overlooked aspect of distributive justice is that it also involves the distribution of the benefits of environmental programs and policies, such as parks and beaches, public transportation, safe drinking water, and sewerage and drainage....

Some of the best known local environmental justice disputes have involved dramatic evidence of distributive inequities.

In *Chester Residents Concerned for Quality Living v. Seif* [132 F.2d 925 (3rd Cir. 1997), *vacated*, 524 U.S. 974 (1998)], residents of Chester, Pennsylvania, alleged that the state's issuance of a permit for a new waste facility would create an unlawful disparate impact on African-American residents. As evidence, they noted that Chester, with a population of 42,000, 65% of which are African-American, had become the designated dumping grounds for the rest of Delaware County, with a population of 502,000, 91% of which are white. Though one-twelfth the size of the county, Chester already has five permitted waste facilities, while the rest of Delaware County has only two. All of Delaware County's municipal waste and sewage is processed in Chester, although only 7.5% of the county's population resides in the town. Most dramatically, the permitted capacity for the waste facilities in the much smaller city of Chester [is] 1,500 times greater than the permitted capacity for the remaining facilities in Delaware County (2.1 million tons vs. 1,400 tons), and the capacity per person for the waste facilities in the 65% African-American Chester area is almost 18,000 times greater than the capacity per person for the facilities in 91% white Delaware County.

Figure 1-3. Delaware County, Pennsylvania. Photo: Cliff Villa, 2024.

The dispute over a proposal by Shintech to build a new polyvinyl chloride (PVC) plant in the lower income, 84% African-American community of Convent, Louisiana, also raised substantial distributive justice concerns. An analysis of toxic air emissions from the 10 existing petrochemical plants in the Convent area revealed that residents were already exposed to 251,179 pounds of toxic air pollution per square mile per year, and Shintech proposed to emit an additional three million pounds of air pollution per year, over 600,000 pounds of which would be toxic. This existing cumulative impact on the 84% African-American Convent-area residents is 67 times greater than the toxic air pollution burden for the rest of St. James Parish (the third most polluted parish in the state and 43.5% African American), 93 times greater than the average toxic air pollution exposure per square mile for the heavily polluted Louisiana Mississippi River industrial corridor (36.8% African American), 129 times greater than Louisiana's average exposure per square mile (the second most polluted state in the nation and 30.8% African American), and 658 times higher than the average toxic air pollution exposure per square mile in the United States (12% African American). EPA's disparate impact analysis, using its "relative emissions burden ratio" method, found that, were Shintech permitted to operate, African Americans in St. James Parish would experience a 71% to 242% greater toxic air pollution burden than non-African Americans in the parish....

Environmental Justice as Procedural Justice

Claims of procedural injustice also are common in environmental justice disputes, and it is not [unusual] for people of color and low-income communities to complain about both the distributive and procedural aspects of an environmental policy or decision. Indeed, in many situations, a community's judgment about whether or not an outcome was distributively just will be significantly determined by the perceived fairness of the procedures leading to the outcome.

Procedural justice has been defined as "the right to treatment as an equal. That is the right, not to an equal distribution of some good or opportunity, but to equal concern and respect in the political decision about how these goods and opportunities are to be distributed." Aristotle referred to this as a status in which individuals have an "equal share in ruling and being ruled." It involves justice as a function of the manner in which a decision is made, and it requires a focus on the fairness of the decision-making process, rather than on its outcome....

The Executive Order on environmental justice has a strong focus on procedural justice, directing agencies to ensure greater public participation and access to information for minority and low-income populations. The Principles of Environmental Justice demand that public policy be based on mutual respect and justice for all peoples and free from bias or discrimination, affirm the fundamental right to self-determination, and insist on the right to participate as equal partners at every level of decision-making.

Environmental justice complaints raise both *ex ante* and *ex post* considerations of procedural fairness. Looking at the process in advance of its use (*ex ante*), they question whether the decision-making and public participation procedures are fair to all concerned or whether they favor one side over the other. Also, looking back (*ex post*), the complaints question whether the completed decision-making process did, in fact, treat all with equal concern and respect.

One way to judge procedural justice *ex ante* is to determine if those to be affected by the decision agree in advance on the process for making the decision. Thus, procedural justice requires looking not just to participation in a process but to whether the process is designed in a way to lead to a fair outcome. In this respect, environmental decision-making processes have been roundly criticized by commentators who have examined issues of environmental justice and public participation. One common observation is that the predominant expertise-oriented, interest-group model of environmental decision-making favors those with resources and political power over people of color and low-income communities. Even the [civic] republican process, which outwardly seeks to advance community interests over private interests, may obscure the true private interests at issue and the continuing disparities in resources, power, and influence. In general, to achieve procedural justice, observers advocate developing more deliberative models of decision-making, providing disadvantaged groups with greater legal and technical resources, and ensuring equal access to decision-makers and the decision-making process....

A common procedural justice complaint at the national level is that people of color and lower income communities [have] little influence on the decision-making processes of legislatures and environmental agencies.... Even where citizens are able to participate, environmental decision-makers are skeptical of the validity of citizen information and are biased in favor of the scientific data submitted by regulated industries.

Underrepresentation on the technical or scientific boards and commissions that make environmental decisions and recommendations is also a problem, particularly since the actions of these boards often reflect politics and personal values....

Another procedural justice aspect is the manner in which the government collects and analyzes data on environmental exposures and public health. In one case, EPA and the National Institutes of Health announced a $15 million, 10-year epidemiological study on the health of farmers and farmworkers that would omit Hispanics from the study, even though farmworkers are largely Hispanic. The justification for the omission? The difficulty of tracking the highly mobile Hispanic population....

In addition to the procedural justice issues arising from the manner in which the state handled the permitting process, the Shintech case illustrates the *ex ante* obstacles that people of color and lower income communities confront. Under the state permitting process, the permit applicant has an automatic right, if requested, to an adjudicatory hearing, yet local residents have no such right....

The county's handling of a permit to build a hazardous waste incinerator near the Hispanic community of Kettleman City, California, illustrates the procedural barriers often encountered by ethnic communities. Despite the repeated, strong interest expressed by [Spanish]-speaking residents to participate in the permitting process, environmental impact documents, meeting notices, and public hearing testimony were never provided in Spanish. The court in *El Pueblo Para el Aire y Agua Limpio v. County of Kings* [22 Envtl. L. Rep. 20, 357 (Cal. Super. Ct. 1991)] held that the meaningful involvement of local residents was effectively precluded by the failure to provide Spanish translations and set aside the local permit. When similar translation concerns were raised by Vietnamese-speaking residents regarding efforts to reopen the Marine Shale hazardous waste incinerator in Amelia, Louisiana, the state responded that it would take care of the inability of the Vietnamese community to participate in the public hearing process *after* the permit was issued....

While environmental justice requires, at a minimum, a procedurally just process, the emphasis on disparate effects, rather than discriminatory intent, in the Executive Order, Principles of Environmental Justice, and Title VI's implementing regulations indicates that a fair process alone will not negate claims of distributive injustice....

Environmental Justice as Corrective Justice

The third aspect of justice encompassed by the term environmental justice is "corrective justice," a notion of justice that is sometimes referred to by other names and may be subsumed within claims for distributive or procedural justice....

"Corrective justice" involves fairness in the way punishments for lawbreaking are assigned and damages inflicted on individuals and communities are addressed.... Corrective justice involves not only the just administration of punishment to those who break the law, but also a duty to repair the losses for which one is responsible....

Therefore, as reflected in claims made in the environmental justice context, corrective justice encompasses many aspects of wrongdoing and injury and includes the concepts of "retributive justice," "compensatory justice," "restorative justice," and "commutative justice." I adopt the term corrective justice here because environmental justice seeks more than just retribution or punishment of those who violate legal rules of conduct. Corrective justice is also preferred over the phrase compensatory justice because the latter term may imply that, provided compensation is paid, an otherwise unjust action is acceptable. It is also important to note that although some concepts of corrective justice view fault or wrongful gain as a necessary condition for liability, environmental justice principles impose responsibility for damages regardless of fault (e.g., the polluter-pays principle). Corrective justice, therefore, is not used in the narrow Aristotelian rectificatory sense but instead in a broader, applied sense that violators be caught and punished and not reap benefits for disregarding legal standards and that injuries caused by the acts of another, whether a violation of law or not, be remedied....

The theme of corrective justice ... figures prominently in the efforts of indigenous people to achieve environmental justice. Native Americans have long complained that the federal government and mining and oil companies have failed to take responsibility for and address contamination caused by their nuclear testing and resource development activities on Indian lands. In addition, hundreds of open dumps, many originally operated by the Indian Health Service, currently exist in Indian country and are in need of cleanup. The recent, expanded ability of tribes to obtain authority to implement federal environmental laws presents tribal governments with the opportunity to promote corrective justice by directly enforcing compliance with environmental statutes on tribal lands, rather than having to rely on federal agencies, yet finding the financial and technical resources to carry out that authority remains a problem.

Local efforts to achieve corrective justice are illustrated by community efforts to address contamination from lead smelters in West Dallas—"the classic example of government inaction and callous disregard for the law." [Quoting Robert Bullard—eds.] As early as 1972, Dallas officials were aware of significantly elevated lead levels in the blood of children living in a minority neighborhood near a lead smelter that had repeatedly violated the law. EPA's own study in 1981 confirmed the high lead concentrations in children living near the smelters. In spite of repeated complaints by local residents, government officials took no action; EPA even rejected a voluntary cleanup plan, preferring still further tests of local children and suggesting that spreading dirt and planting grass would be sufficient.... Finally, after 50 years of operation without necessary local permits and 20 years after government officials became aware of the public health problems caused by the illegally operated smelter, authorities closed the facility and started a comprehensive cleanup program....

Environmental Justice as Social Justice

The fourth and final aspect of justice implicated by the term environmental justice is "social justice," a far-reaching, and some say nebulous, goal of the environmental justice movement...

Social justice is "that branch of the virtue of justice that moves us to use our best efforts to bring about a more just ordering of society—one in which people's needs are more fully met." "The demands of social justice are ... first, that the members of every class have enough resources and enough power to live as befits human beings, and second, that the privileged classes, whoever they are, be accountable to the wider society for the way they use their advantages."

Environmental justice has been described as a "marriage of the movement for social justice with environmentalism" integrating environmental concerns into a broader agenda that emphasizes social, racial, and economic justice. Dr. Bullard refers to this aspect of environmental justice as "social equity: ... an assessment of the role of sociological factors (race, ethnicity, class, culture, lifestyles, political power, and so forth) in environmental decision-making."

Professor Sheila Foster has argued that a narrow focus on issues of distributive justice neglects the search for social structures and agents that are causing the environmental problems. A social justice perspective presents environmental justice as part of larger problems of racial, social, and economic justice and helps illustrate the influence of politics, race, and class on an area's quality of life. This broader social perspective contrasts with traditional environmentalism and its narrower focus on wilderness preservation and the technological aspects of environmental regulation.

Environmental justice's focus on social justice reflects reality. As one community organizer explained, oppressed people do not have compartmentalized problems—they do not separate the hazardous waste incinerator from the fact that their schools are underfunded, that they have no daycare, no sidewalks or streetlights, or no jobs. The reason disadvantaged communities do not separate these problems is that their quality of life as a whole is suffering and the political, economic, and racial causes are likely interrelated....

[C]riticism of environmental justice as too myopic and a diversion of scarce resources away from other more important social and public health problems is not well-founded. Most often, environmental justice efforts do not wastefully divert a community's attention but instead bring residents together to focus on a broad array of social justice problems.... [G]overnment officials and firms seeking community acceptance for environmentally risky projects must as a practical, if not also moral, matter consider whether social justice is served by their projects. For if the environmental and other social burdens of a proposed project are imposed on the local community while the economic and other benefits flow elsewhere, "community opposition will be fierce and the chances for success lessened."

Notes and Questions

1. Scholarly conceptions of "environmental justice." Notice the distinct conceptions of "environmental justice" offered by Professors Kuehn, Bullard, and Bryant. Professor Bryant (University of Michigan Emeritus before his passing in 2024) conceived of "environmental justice" as "those cultural norms and values, rules, regulations, behaviors, policies, and decisions to support sustainable communities, where people can interact with confidence that their environment is safe, nurturing, and protective."

What about this conception most resonates with you? What do you believe "confidence" means in this context? Is confidence always a good thing?

Professor Bullard's vision of "environmental justice" includes such elements as "protect all persons from environmental degradation" and "obviate the requirement to prove intent to discriminate." If we really could "protect all persons from environmental degradation," would we still need any other "principles" for environmental justice? The "requirement to prove intent to discriminate" derives from an invention of the U.S. Supreme Court. *See, e.g., Washington v. Davis*, 426 U.S. 229 (1976). May this case law be reversed by public protest or popular vote? If not, how do you imagine EJ advocates might "obviate" this requirement, as Bullard suggests?

Professor Kuehn's conception of environmental justice deserves particular consideration. As noted in the excerpt, Kuehn approaches environmental justice through the four dimensions of distributive, procedural, corrective, and social justice. These four dimensions of "justice" provide one theoretical framework that students and practitioners of environmental justice may find useful today. As such, this book will continue to employ Kuehn's "justice" framework in the chapters that follow. In fact, consider these four dimensions of justice in the context of the federal definitions of "environmental justice" discussed immediately below. How are these four dimensions of justice reflected in these definitions? Are any dimensions of justice missing or underserved by these definitions?

2. Federal definitions of "environmental justice." Environmental justice has never been defined by any federal legislation or federal rulemaking. Environmental justice has been defined, however, by many expressions of federal policy, including Executive Orders and agency statements. As Kuehn notes, President Clinton's Executive Order 12898 from 1994 framed environmental justice as a program for addressing "disproportionately high and adverse human health or environmental effects ... on minority populations and low-income populations." § 1-103. This program would also "apply equally to Native American programs." § 6-606.

From the limited applicability to minority, low-income, and Native American populations, federal conceptions of environmental justice evolved and expanded, led by the U.S. EPA. EPA definitions of environmental justice fluctuated over time, but during the Bush-Cheney administration produced a definition that remains the most common conception of the environmental justice in use in the United States today. That definition appears in the box below:

> **Environmental Justice (EJ)** is the **fair treatment** and **meaningful involvement** of **all people** regardless of race, color, national origin, or income with respect to the development, implementation, and enforcement of environmental law, regulations, and policies.

From this definition, note three major elements: (1) "fair treatment" and (2) "meaningful involvement" of (3) "all people." Fair treatment and meaningful involvement will be considered in more depth below. For now, consider the significance of "all people." Broadening substantially beyond the original focus on minority and low-income populations, "all people" initially drew intense criticism from EJ advocates. *See* Clifford J. Villa, *Remaking Environmental Justice*, 66 Loyola L. Rev. 469, 496–500 (2020). What disadvantages do you see with this boundless scope? Do you see any advantages? Does "all people" open environmental justice to concerns for children? women? older adults? undocumented residents? members of LGBTQ communities? What about rural residents who oppose environmental regulation? White wealthy political donors? Does "all people" insulate environmental justice from conservative attacks on affirmative action?

After remaining in place for more than two decades, the EPA definition of environmental justice began to draw more attention from EJ scholars and advocates in light of developments including accelerating climate disasters, the COVID-19 pandemic, and the murder of George Floyd (and many other Black and Brown people) by police. With input from the White House Environmental Justice Advisory Council, President Biden in April 2023 issued Executive Order 14096, which for the first time established a definition of environmental justice that applied across the federal government. How does this Biden definition (presented in the box below) compare to the definition maintained previously by EPA? What common elements do you see? Why do you imagine "fair" treatment was replaced with "just" treatment? What additional concerns or aspirations do you see introduced in the Biden definition?

> **"Environmental justice"** means the **just treatment** and **meaningful involvement** of **all people** regardless of income, race, color, national origin, Tribal affiliation, or disability, in agency decision-making and other Federal activities that affect human health and the environment so that people:
>
> > are fully protected from disproportionate and adverse human health and environmental effects (including risks) and hazards, including those related to climate change, the cumulative impacts of environmental and other burdens, and the legacy of racism or other structural or systemic barriers; and have equitable access to a healthy, sustainable, and resilient environment in which to live, play, work, learn, grow, worship, and engage in cultural and subsistence practices.

The Biden definition reflected significant advancement in thinking about environmental justice. It was officially short-lived, however, as Executive Order 14096 was repealed immediately by President Trump in January 2025 and the definition was removed from the EPA website. Even so, the Biden definition may continue to inform understanding of environmental justice and inspire actions toward its achievement. For example, considerations of "cumulative impacts" and "cultural and subsistence practices" may help community advocates, agency staff, and the private sector make better decisions in the future than they did in the past when setting standards, ensuring compliance, and cleaning up contaminated sites, as we will discuss in later chapters of this book.

Three elements of the Biden definition and the prior EPA definition of environmental justice—commonly framed as "fair treatment" and "meaningful involvement" for "all people"—also remain established in the law and policy of many states and other jurisdictions. (See discussion in Chapter 10.) Accordingly, we will continue to refer to these three elements throughout this book. It is important to recognize, however, that individual states, tribes, local governments, and community organizations may adopt different conceptions and definitions of "environmental justice" for their own purposes. Good EJ advocates should be sure to check for alternate conceptions and definitions applicable in their local area.

3. Fair treatment. In the EPA definition of environmental justice noted above, what is the meaning of "fair treatment"? The EPA itself supplied a definition:

> **Fair treatment** means no group of people should bear a disproportionate share of the negative environmental consequences resulting from industrial, governmental and commercial operations or policies.

Consider the implications of this definition. How does it compare, for example, with the EJ principle that we should "protect all persons from environmental degradation"? Under the EPA's definition of fair treatment, may some people still be harmed by environmental degradation? If so, must all people be harmed equally?

Should fair treatment apply only to "negative environmental consequences"? What about positive environmental amenities? Should all people also have fair access to city parks, wilderness areas, swimming holes, and fishing ponds? How does the Biden definition respond to this question?

Definitions aside, anyone who had siblings growing up already knows (or thinks they know) what is *fair* and (especially) what is *not* fair. To paraphrase Supreme Court Justice Potter Stewart from a different context, with unfair treatment, "we know it when we see it." *Cf.*, *Jacobellis v. Ohio*, 378 U.S. 184 (1964), Stewart, J., concurring. But do we always know? Consider what fairness demands in the following scenarios:

- Homes in a diverse neighborhood range in property values from $40,000 to $1 million. Asbestos contamination from an old Navy base makes the entire neighborhood uninhabitable, dropping all property values to zero. Notwithstanding the zero value of each property, the Navy offers each property owner a buy-out of $50,000.

- A home in a poor, largely Latino neighborhood becomes severely contaminated with mercury brought into the home by two teenage boys who live there. The home is worth $50,000 and the EPA estimates the cleanup will cost $500,000.
- Sediments contaminated with polychlorinated biphenyls (PCBs) in an urban waterway make resident fish unsafe to eat. Cleanup of the waterway is estimated to cost $300 million and take 20 years. Instead of undertaking this massive clean-up, the government simply issues an order banning consumption of fish from the waterway. After the order goes into effect, the only groups who continue to eat fish from the waterway are homeless people and Asian-Pacific Islander families.
- High levels of asthma and other respiratory ailments are attributed to the cumulative emission of toxic air pollutants from six industrial facilities that surround a residential neighborhood. Each facility remains in compliance individually with its permit requirements under the Clean Air Act.
- Emissions of sulfur dioxide from an old coal-fired power plant owned and operated by a public utility violate federal standards under the Clean Air Act. To bring the old plant into compliance, the public utility would have to spend $50 million. The public utility cannot afford this upgrade and instead shuts down the plant, putting 220 plant employees out of work on an Indian reservation struggling to emerge from poverty.

Does "fairness" then not always seem intuitive? As used in the EPA definition of environmental justice, does fairness include protection of equity in million-dollar homes? Does fairness allow (or require?) spending ten times more to clean up a home than the home is worth on the market? Does fairness allow a blanket ban on fishing, regardless of the disproportionate impacts of the ban on certain groups? Does fairness support facility operators who comply with their permits individually yet contribute collectively to harm in neighboring communities? Does fairness require each facility operator to meet national standards, regardless of impacts on the local economy?

In the early years of attention to environmental justice, much of the concern involved the siting of industrial facilities in low-income and minority communities, as with the toxic waste site in Warren County. Much early scholarship on environmental justice thus addressed fairness in the context of siting such **Locally Undesirable Land Uses (LULUs)**. In one such article, Professor Vicki Been proposed several different models of fairness that could be summarized as follows: (1) even apportionment of LULUs among all neighborhoods; (2) compensation of communities hosting LULUs by other communities; (3) progressive siting—wealthier neighborhoods receive more LULUs; (4) cost internalization—those who benefit from LULUs bear the cost; (5) the siting process involves no intentional discrimination; (6) the siting process shows "equal concern and respect" for all neighborhoods; and (7) all communities receive an equal number of vetoes that can be used to exclude a LULU. Vicki Been, *What's Fairness Got to Do with It? Environmental Justice and the Siting of Locally Undesirable Land Uses*, 78 Cornell L. Rev. 1001 (1993).

What model of "fairness" would you favor for the siting of LULUs? Can you see any challenges for administering one or more of these models? For example, if we agreed to adopt "even apportionment" of LULUs among all neighborhoods, who would do this apportioning? The city? The state? What if different neighborhoods had different concerns based on local demographics, such as high populations of children or older adults? Moreover, how do we even know what a "LULU" is? Is an old coal-fired power plant necessarily "locally undesirable" if it is also a major employer in the area? As we will see in Chapter 9 (Environmental Justice for Indian Tribes and Indigenous People), even waste disposal sites—a classic LULU from many perspectives—may not be a LULU for some communities eager for economic development.

Fairness in the definition of environmental justice clearly remains subject to some level of subjectivity and differing perspectives. Nonetheless, it remains an important substantive dimension of environmental justice, placing some boundaries on the outcome of process to be explored in the following note.

4. Meaningful involvement. The second major element of environmental justice according to the EPA's historic definition is **meaningful involvement** in the development, implementation, and enforcement of environmental law and policy. As with fair treatment, the EPA provided a definition of "meaningful involvement" in this context:

> **Meaningful involvement** means:
>
> - People have an opportunity to participate in decisions about activities that may affect their environment and/or health;
> - The public's contribution can influence the regulatory agency's decision;
> - Community concerns will be considered in the decision-making process; and
> - Decision makers will seek out and facilitate the involvement of those potentially affected.

Meaningful involvement in this context may be usefully juxtaposed with older organizational notions of "public relations" or "public involvement." Even more recently, the Biden EPA embraced the idea of "meaningful *engagement*." *See, e.g.*, U.S. EPA, *Achieving Health and Environmental Protection Through EPA's Meaningful Engagement Policy* ("*Meaningful Engagement Policy*") (August 2024).

How do these terms differ? While "public relations" or "public involvement" may allow opportunities for public comment on proposed actions, *meaningful* involvement or meaningful *engagement* seeks to ensure that such comments may "influence" the final agency decision. As described in EPA's *Meaningful Engagement Policy* (2024), meaningful engagement seeks "to ensure that the public has timely, accessible, and accurate information about EPA programs."

To ensure that information is accessible, agency programs may need to ensure accommodations for community members with Limited-English Proficiency. Executive Order 13166, signed by President Clinton in 2000, required *Improving Access to Services for Persons with Limited English Proficiency.* This order was repealed by President Trump's Executive Order 14224, issued in March 2025, purporting to make English the official language of the United States. Even so, according to the U.S. Census Bureau, more than one-fifth of U.S. households may speak a language other than English at home—most commonly, Spanish, followed by Chinese, Vietnamese, and Tagalog. *See* U.S. Census Bureau, https://www.census.gov/newsroom/press-releases/2023/language-at-home-acs-5-year.html. In communities across the United States, many other languages may be spoken at home, including Russian, French, Arabic, and Navajo in the Southwest.

In addition to language, meaningful involvement may require accommodating differences in culture, education, or income. One EPA program, known as *Beyond Translation*, sought to use local theater to help educate largely Latino and Asian workers about the dangers of pesticide exposure. (For more information, drop "EPA Beyond Translation" into your Internet browser.) Other forms of communication including comic books and Indigenous art have also helped to bridge gaps across cultures and communities.

In many cases, meaningful involvement may require travel. While many meetings may be facilitated now via video conferencing, not everyone has access to this technology and some exchanges remain best in person. Travel may be required for agency staff or project proponents to learn more about community concerns. For example, to learn more about concerns with uranium contamination on the Navajo Nation, staff and leadership from EPA Headquarters and Regional offices held a series of listening sessions in different chapters of the Navajo Nation between 2022–2024. Travel may also be required for community members and advocates to engage directly in meetings and work sessions with agency staff. In some cases, compensation may be appropriate for a community member's time and travel expenses. For federal authority to provide such compensation, see EPA's *Meaningful Engagement Policy* at Table 2: EPA Compensation Types for Public Participation.

Note that meaningful involvement is intended to apply to all phases of the regulatory process, explicitly including the "development, implementation, and enforcement" of environmental laws, regulations, and policies. Meaningful involvement in "development" may include public engagement on draft regulations. Meaningful involvement in "implementation" may include public engagement on draft permits, such as the permits under the Clean Air Act for the six industrial facilities surrounding the neighborhood in the hypothetical above. But what does meaningful involvement in "enforcement" include? You may have heard that the U.S. Department of Justice does not comment on active investigations and litigation, but that does not mean there is no role for community engagement in enforcement. For ideas on what meaningful involvement may include in the enforcement context, *see* Chapter 7 (Government Enforcement).

5. Corrective justice. Recall the four dimensions of environmental justice articulated by Professor Kuehn: distributive justice, procedural justice, corrective justice, and social justice. As Kuehn describes the scope of corrective justice, to what extent does it appear to be encompassed within the historic EPA definition of environmental justice? Environmental justice, as defined by the EPA, can help correct current problems, such as permit violations or contaminated sites. But can it also reach elements of compensatory justice, such as compensation for the fish that cannot be eaten safely from a contaminated waterway? For exploration of this question, *see* Chapter 8 (Contaminated Sites).

6. Social justice. What is the relationship of environmental justice to social justice? As defined historically by the EPA? As envisioned by Kuehn? How would you draw the Venn diagram to explain this relationship? How does social justice figure into the conception of environmental justice expressed by grassroots environmental justice activists in the 17 Principles of Environmental Justice discussed in the next section?

Regardless of taxonomy and how one defines "environmental justice," environmental inequities certainly derive from many sources. These sources of inequitable protection surely include racism and other forms of invidious discrimination, but may also include deficiencies in the apparatus of environmental policymaking. For an investigation of these structural defects, see the following excerpt from the classic article by Harvard Law Professor Richard Lazarus:

Richard J. Lazarus,
Pursuing "Environmental Justice": The Distributional Effects of Environmental Protection

87 NORTHWESTERN U. L. REV. 787 (1993)

... There exist ... factors more endemic to environmental law itself that may exacerbate distributional inequities likely present in the context of any public welfare law. These factors suggest more than the disturbing, yet somewhat irresistible thesis, that the distributional dimension of environmental protection policy likely suffers from the same inequities that persist generally in society. They suggest the far more troubling, and even less appealing, proposition that the problems of distributional inequity may in fact be more pervasive in the environmental protection arena than they are in other areas of traditional concern to civil rights organizations, such as education, employment, and housing.

Indeed, it is the absence of that minority involvement so prevalent in the more classic areas of civil rights concern that may render the distributional problem worse for environmental protection. Minority interests have traditionally had little voice in the various points of influence that strike the distributional balances necessary to get environmental protection laws enacted, regulations promulgated, and enforcement actions initiated. The interest groups historically active in the environmental protection area include a variety of mainstream environmental organizations representing a spectrum of interests (conservation, recreation, hunting, wildlife protection, ... human health), as well as a variety of commercial and industrial concerns. Until very recently, if at all, the implications for racial minorities of environmental protection laws have not been a focal point of concern for any of these organizations.

Much of environmental protection lawmaking has also been highly centralized, with the geographic focus in Washington, D.C. The enactment of environmental statutes within that geo-political setting has required the expenditure of considerable political resources. As evidenced by the thirteen years required to amend the Clean Air Act, it is no easy task to obtain the attention of the numerous congressional committees, and to form the coalitions between competing interest groups, so necessary to secure a bill's passage.

Environmental legislation has ultimately been produced through intense and lengthy horse-trading among interest groups, a process necessary to secure a particular environmental law's passage. This process has often depended upon the forging of alliances between diverse interests both within the environmental public interest community and within government bureaucracy. Often, these unions have included so-called "unholy alliances" between environmentalists and commercial and industrial interests, where the latter have perceived an economic advantage to be gained (or disadvantage to be minimized) by their supporting an environmental protection law that allocates the benefits and burdens of environmental protection in a particular fashion....

It is not surprising, therefore, that those environmental laws enacted by Congress typically address some, but hardly all, environmental pollution problems. And, even with regard to those problems that are explicitly addressed, there are usually discrepancies and gaps within the statutory scheme. Which problems are confronted, and where the discrepancies and gaps occur, is quite naturally an expression of the priorities of those participants who wield the greatest influence and resources in the political process.

For this reason, much environmental legislation may not have focused on those pollution problems that are of greatest concern to many minority communities. For instance, air pollution control efforts typically have focused on general ambient air quality concerns for an entire metropolitan region rather than on toxic hot spots in any one particular area. Accordingly, while there has been much progress made in improving air quality as measured by a handful of national ambient air quality standards, there has been relatively less progress achieved over the last twenty years in the reduction of those toxic air emissions which tend to be of greater concern to persons, disproportionately minorities, who live in the immediate geographic vicinity of the toxic polluting source.... Likewise, and at the behest of mainstream environmental groups, substantial resources have also been directed to improving air and water quality in nonurban areas. Programs for the prevention of significant deteriorations in air quality, the reduction of "acid rain," and the protection of visibility in national parks and wilderness areas, all require significant financial expenditures. Substantial resources have similarly been expended on improving the quality of water resources that are not as readily accessible to many minorities because of their historical exclusion. Without meaning to suggest that these programs lack merit on their own terms (for the simple reason that they possess great merit), their return in terms of overall public health may be less than pollution control programs directed at improving the environmental quality of urban America's poorer neighborhoods, including many minority communities....

[R]acial minorities have had little influence on either the lawmaking or priority-setting processes at any of the legislative, regulatory, or local enforcement levels. They have not been well represented among the interest groups lobbying and litigating before governmental authorities on environmental protection issues. Nor have they been well represented, especially at the national level, within those governmental organizations actively involved in the relevant environmental processes. Their voices have not been heard in the mainstream environmental public interest organizations that participate in the policymaking debates and that, in the absence of governmental enforcement, are behind citizen suits filling the void. Traditional civil rights organizations have historically had little interest in, and have infrequently become involved with, environmental issues. At the same time, mainstream environmental organizations have historically included few minorities in policymaking positions. In 1990, this fact prompted several members of various civil rights organizations and minority groups to send a widely publicized letter to the national environmental public interest organizations charging them with being isolated from minority communities....

Notes and Questions

1. Progress? In the three-plus decades since publication of this article by Prof. Lazarus, the structural defects he identified remain largely in place. The U.S. Congress still has passed no federal statute dedicated to addressing concerns for environmental justice. Federal rulemaking to implement the aging collection of federal environmental laws (e.g., the Clean Air Act, Clean Water Act) remains mostly a matter of top-down administrative process. And today, almost every federal rule that is proposed to address real environmental concerns becomes the immediate subject of nationwide litigation or reversal by the next administration. *See, e.g., National Ass'n of Manufacturers v. Dept. of Defense*, 138 S.Ct. 617 (2018) (allowing challenges to rule defining Clean Water Act jurisdiction to be brought in U.S. district courts across the country).

2. Hope? Notwithstanding the lack of progress on defects within policymaking structures in the United States, some advancements must be noted. For example, through formation of the National Environmental Justice Advisory Council (NEJAC) in 1993 and the NEJAC's diligent work to investigate matters of environmental injustice across the country, grassroots activists developed direct channels for communications with EPA officials in Washington, D.C. EJ activists also established working relations not just with mainstream environmental organizations but also with supportive civil rights organizations. The American Civil Liberties Union (ACLU), for example, was an early advocate for safe drinking water when the lead contamination came to light in

Flint, Michigan. The ACLU has also taken the lead in litigation challenging construction of the proposed border wall along the U.S.-Mexico border, in support of interests from both environmental and immigrant rights groups. At the same time, the NAACP has become a recognized leader in developing tools and advocacy materials to address concerns for environmental and climate justice. *See* Chapter 14 (Climate Justice).

D. "We Speak for Ourselves"

Environmental justice advocates have long observed that environmental laws have not prevented disproportionate environmental harms from occurring. The reasons for this are many and examined throughout this book. One fundamental concern, noted by Professor Lazarus, is that environmental regulation often focuses on improving overall ambient environmental conditions but may not consider the distributional consequences of where pollution is occurring. Therefore, the relationship between EJ activists, on the one hand, and conventional environmental organizations, industry, and government agencies, on the other, has been marked by suspicion and hobbled to some degree by a legal framework that was not designed to consider the unique concerns of individual communities. The wariness felt by community leaders toward environmental regulators and mainstream environmental organizations reflected in a 1990 letter sent by EJ activists to leaders of the ten largest environmental organizations (the "Group of Ten" letter, reprinted below). In addition, many activists were concerned that business interests, academics, and others were misinterpreting their positions. Thus, in 1991, environmental justice activists gathered in an historic summit and developed a set of principles to guide their efforts and clearly state their positions. (These "Principles" are also reprinted below.) Through these writings and many other communications delivered consistently over time, community leaders have delivered and reinforced the powerful message that "We speak for ourselves."

"Group of Ten" Letter

March 16, 1990

Dear [Environmental Organization Representative]:

We are writing this letter in the belief that through dialogue and mutual strategizing we can create a global environmental movement that protects us all.

We are artists, writers, academics, students, activists, representatives of churches, unions, and community organizations writing you to express our concerns about the role of your organization and other national environmental groups in communities of people of color in the Southwest.

For centuries, people of color in our region have been subjected to racist and genocidal practices including the theft of lands and water, the murder of innocent people, and degradation of our environment. Mining companies extract minerals leaving economically depressed communities and poisoned soil and water. The U.S. military takes lands for weapons production, testing and storage, contaminating surrounding communities and placing minority workers in the most highly radioactive and toxic worksites. Industrial and municipal dumps are intentionally placed in communities of color, disrupting our cultural lifestyle and threatening our communities' futures. Workers in the fields are dying and babies are born disfigured as a result of pesticide spraying.

Although environmental organizations calling themselves the "Group of Ten" often claim to represent our interests, in observing your activities it has become clear to us that your organizations play an equal role in the disruption of our communities. There is a clear lack of accountability by the Group of Ten environmental organizations towards Third World communities in the Southwest, in the United States as a whole, and internationally.

Your organizations continue to support and promote policies which emphasize the clean-up and preservation of the environment on the backs of working people in general and people of color in particular. In the name of eliminating environmental hazards at any cost, across the country industrial and other economic activities which employ us are being shut down, curtailed or prevented while our survival needs and cultures are ignored. We suffer from the end results of these actions, but are never full participants in the decision-making which leads to them.

[Selected examples from the letter follow. Eds.]:

Organizations such as the National Wildlife Federation have been involved in exchanges where Third World countries will sign over lands (debt-for-nature swaps) to conservation groups in exchange for creditors agreeing to erase a portion of that country's debt.... This not only raises the specter of conservation groups now being "creditors" to Third World countries, but legitimizes the debt itself through the further expropriation of Third World resources....

The lack of people of color in decision-making positions in your organizations such as executive staff and board positions is also reflective of your histories of racist and exclusionary practices. Racism is a root cause of your inaction around addressing environmental problems in our communities.

Group of Ten organizations are being supported by corporations such as ARCO, British Petroleum, Chemical Bank, GTE, General Electric, Dupont, Dow Chemical, Exxon, IBM, Coca Cola, and Waste Management, Incorporated. Several of these companies are known polluters whose disregard for the safety and well-being of workers has resulted in the deaths of many people of color. It is impossible for you to represent us in issues of our own survival when you are accountable to these interests....

We again call upon you to cease operations in communities of color within 60 days, until you have hired leaders from those communities to the extent that they make up between 35–40 percent of your entire staff. We are asking that Third World leaders be hired at all levels of your operations....

Sincerely,

/s/ 117 signatures of organizations and individuals.

Figure 1-4. Environmental justice pioneers Dr. Sofia Martinez and Richard Moore. Among other credits, Mr. Moore signed the 1990 "Group of Ten" letter and served as chair of the National Environmental Justice Advisory Council and co-chair of the White House Environmental Justice Advisory Council. Albuquerque, New Mexico. Photo: Cliff Villa, 2019.

PRINCIPLES OF ENVIRONMENTAL JUSTICE

Proceedings, The First National People of Color Environmental Leadership Summit

October 24–27, 1991

WE THE PEOPLE OF COLOR, gathered together at this multinational *People of Color Environmental Leadership Summit*, to begin to build a national and international movement of all peoples of color to fight the destruction and taking of our lands and communities, do hereby re-establish our spiritual interdependence to the sacredness of our Mother Earth; to respect and celebrate each of our cultures, languages and beliefs about the natural world and our roles in healing ourselves; to ensure environmental justice; to promote economic alternatives which would contribute to the development of environmentally safe livelihoods; and, to secure our political, economic and cultural liberation that has been denied for over 500 years of colonization and oppression, resulting in the poisoning of our communities and land and the genocide of our peoples, do affirm and adopt these Principles of Environmental Justice:

1. Environmental justice affirms the sacredness of Mother Earth, ecological unity and the interdependence of all species, and the right to be free from ecological destruction.

2. Environmental justice demands that public policy be based on mutual respect and justice for all peoples, free from any form of discrimination or bias.

3. Environmental justice mandates the right to ethical, balanced and responsible uses of land and renewable resources in the interest of a sustainable planet for humans and other living things.

4. Environmental justice calls for universal protection from nuclear testing, extraction, production and disposal of toxic/hazardous wastes and poisons and nuclear testing that threaten the fundamental right to clean air, land, water, and food.

5. Environmental justice affirms the fundamental right to political, economic, cultural and environmental self-determination of all peoples.

6. Environmental justice demands the cessation of the production of all toxins, hazardous wastes, and radioactive materials, and that all past and current producers be held strictly accountable to the people for detoxification and the containment at the point of production.

7. Environmental justice demands the right to participate as equal partners at every level of decision-making including needs assessment, planning, implementation, enforcement and evaluation.

8. Environmental justice affirms the right of all workers to a safe and healthy work environment, without being forced to choose between an unsafe livelihood and unemployment. It also affirms the right of those who work at home to be free from environmental hazards.

9. Environmental justice protects the right of victims of environmental injustice to receive full compensation and reparations for damages as well as quality health care.

10. Environmental justice considers governmental acts of environmental injustice a violation of international law, the Universal Declaration of Human Rights, and the United Nations Convention on Genocide.

11. Environmental justice must recognize a special legal and natural relationship of Native Peoples to the U.S. government through treaties, agreements, compacts, and covenants affirming sovereignty and self-determination.

12. Environmental justice affirms the need for urban and rural ecological policies to clean up and rebuild our cities and rural areas in balance with nature, honoring the cultural integrity of all our communities, and providing fair access for all to the full range of resources.

13. Environmental justice calls for the strict enforcement of principles of informed consent, and a halt to the testing of experimental reproductive and medical procedures and vaccinations on people of color.

14. Environmental justice opposes the destructive operations of multinational corporations.

15. Environmental justice opposes military occupation, repression and exploitation of lands, peoples and cultures, and other life forms.

16. Environmental justice calls for the education of present and future generations which emphasizes social and environmental issues, based on our experience and an appreciation of our diverse cultural perspectives.

17. Environmental justice requires that we, as individuals, make personal and consumer choices to consume as little of Mother Earth's resources and to produce as little waste as possible; and make the conscious decision to challenge and reprioritize our lifestyles to insure the health of the natural world for present and future generations.

Adopted today, October 24, 1991, in Washington, D.C.

Notes and Questions

1. "Bottom-up" or "top-down"? What are the implications of a grassroots or "bottom-up" perspective for addressing environmental problems in fora dominated by formal professionalization? As you consider the various strategies—legal and technical—available to reduce environmental disparities, consider which of them are better equipped to work with and utilize a grassroots perspective. Many EJ advocates resist top-down government approaches, noting that the decisions of scientists, lawyers, policymakers, and judges are often paternalistic and disempowering. Is there an inherent tension between the movement's participatory goals of having greater voice and power, and the movement's substantive goals of eliminating risk of environmental harm altogether? Is it possible greater participation would not lead to the policy changes that EJ advocates desire?

2. Values. How do the Principles of Environmental Justice presented above compare to the elements of "fair treatment" and "meaningful involvement" in the EPA definition of environmental justice? How do these principles compare to Professor Kuehn's four dimensions of environmental justice? In your Venn diagram of environmental justice in relation to social justice, where do you place the principle of freedom from "military occupation"? Are these "Principles of Environmental Justice" only concerned with protecting human health? Or could they embrace broader values to include concern for non-human animals, culture, and sovereignty? Consider the following observation:

> For some racialized communities, [] environmental justice is not only, or even primarily, about immediate health concerns or burden distribution. Rather, for them, and particularly for some indigenous peoples, environmental justice is mainly about cultural and economic self-determination and belief systems that connect their history, spirituality, and livelihood to the natural environment....

Eric K. Yamamoto & Jen-L W. Lyman, *Racializing Environmental Justice*, 72 U. Colo. L. Rev. 311 (2001). In Chapter 9, we will explore values including cultural preservation and self-determination in the context of Indigenous communities. However, it is important to recognize that such values may also be cherished in different ways by other communities and may even be placed above more conventional environmental values such as a reduced risk of asthma attacks.

3. The Principles of Environmental Justice. What do you imagine the drafters hoped to accomplish with the 17 Principles of Environmental Justice? Are the principles directed at one government agency or one level of government? Are the principles framed more as objectives to be achieved or aspirations to be pursued? Are the demands all realistic? If it seems unrealistic to demand the "cessation of the production of all toxins," which might include the components of every penny and car battery, then what do you imagine the drafters of these principles did expect? Can these demands be reconciled with existing societal and legal norms, or do they call for radical social and legal reform? Are there middle grounds where progress toward environmental justice may be realized?

4. The "Group of Ten" letter. The writing of EJ activists is often hard-hitting. EJ activists have challenged dominant paradigms in all sectors including government, academia, and the broader environmental movement that began with events such as passage of the Wilderness Act in 1964 and the first Earth Day in 1970. While the "Group of Ten" letter in 1990 must have come as some shock to leaders of those mainstream environmental organizations, the letter also succeeded in drawing attention to failure of the broader environmental movement to address concerns such as worker protection, tribal sovereignty, economic development, and leadership within the organizations themselves. Since that time, many of these organizations have made important strides toward addressing these concerns. For example, the Sierra Club Legal Defense Fund (now Earthjustice) currently pursues a wide range of EJ matters, to include litigation against the Dakota Access Pipeline on behalf of the Standing Rock Sioux Tribe. The National Audubon Society and local chapters now offer a variety of programs to support diverse communities, including programs to provide naturalist training for at-risk youth. *See* https://www.audubon.org/magazine/november-december-2015/birds-offer-way-outside-troubled-kids. Newer environmental organizations, such as the Center for Biological Diversity—formerly dedicated to the preservation of animal species—now do work to protect human health, including through campaigns to address toxic exposures to lead, mercury, uranium, and pesticides. *See* https://www.biologicaldiversity.org/programs/environmental_health/. Regional environmental organizations such as the Southern Environmental Law Center have dedicated substantial efforts to pursuing environmental justice, such as the successful opposition to the Byhalia Pipeline through the Boxtown neighborhood of Memphis, Tennessee. *See* https://www.selc.org/news/byhalia-pipeline-basics/. Likewise, the Western Environmental Law Center, with origins in protecting the Northern Spotted Owl, has helped litigate extensively on behalf of tribal members and children who may be impacted disproportionately by climate change. *See* https://westernlaw.org/safeguarding-climate/. While major environmental organizations must continue to seek ways to support the concerns of diverse communities, 30 years after the Group of Ten letter, it is clear that much progress has been made toward that end.

E. Conclusion

In this chapter, we have only briefly sketched the history of the environmental justice movement, including the efforts of multiple and diverse groups to articulate a common critique of mainstream environmental approaches. However, the EJ movement is neither monolithic nor static. Instead, with the passage of time, the movement has evolved and expanded, identified newly pressing issues, enlisted new tools of law and policy, and, at times, refined earlier approaches, theories, and definitions.

Over time, EJ advocates have crafted inclusive, multi-racial, and multicultural coalitions, and scholars have attempted to articulate coherent theoretical frameworks for the common claims of this movement. But it is nonetheless important to recognize that each campaign for environmental justice is rooted in its locale and unique culture and history. We may use the term "environmental justice communities" or "environmental justice groups" in this book as a shorthand reference to all of the various groups that are affected by any particular issue. In doing so, we mean to embrace the inclusive posture of the EJ movement itself and to recognize common institutional and structural forces that generate environmental injustice. But, at the same time, we also recognize that each group's circumstances are, in fact, unique and that each group's claims for justice can only be understood properly in context.

Finally, for analytical coherence, we will generally apply throughout the book the EPA's historic definition of environmental justice, to require the "fair treatment" and "meaningful involvement" of "all people" in the administration of environmental programs. We do so, of course, recognizing the many diverse conceptions of environmental justice and the continuing responsibility of environmental justice advocates to listen and respect the distinct concerns of the communities and people they serve.

Chapter 2

Theories of Causation

Figure 2-1. Powerlines in San Juan, Puerto Rico, leaning over streets after Hurricane Maria. Photo: Cliff Villa, 2018.

A. Introduction

This chapter considers the *who* and *how* behind systemic environmental injustice. In the United States, many factors have led to environmental injustice. Explanatory theories are numerous and varied, drawing from economics, political science, urban planning, history, sociology, critical race studies, and other disciplines. This chapter outlines some of the major theories that have been advanced to explain the prevalence of environmental inequities. Many current disparities grew from past land-use practices, derived from centuries of land grabbing and exploitation of poor and vulnerable communities of color. More neutral market forces may have led to undesired outcomes both during the initial siting of polluting and risk-generating facilities and as the result of post-siting market dynamics. Alternative theories center on sociopolitical factors, such as a community's social capital, and how those factors interact within the structure of our environmental laws. Yet another explanation examines the forms of racial discrimination currently at play.

The origins of environmental injustice emerged long before the poor, rural, and predominantly Black community of Warren County, North Carolina, protested the siting of a hazardous waste facility in 1982. Indeed, the historical foundations of environmental injustice in the United States are deeply intertwined with the nation's colonial history, the displacement of Indigenous peoples, the institution of slavery, and the subsequent patterns of segregation and discriminatory land-use policies that persisted well into the 20th century and continue to shape our communities today.

Environmental justice scholarship has evolved significantly over the past four decades, moving from early descriptive studies documenting disparate environmental burdens to sophisticated analyses of the complex, multilayered causes of these disparities. In 2025, with mounting evidence of climate change disproportionately affecting vulnerable communities and infrastructure investments that often reinforce existing inequities, understanding the causal mechanisms behind environmental injustice has never been more critical. This evolving understanding has led to increasingly nuanced policy approaches that recognize the need to address not just the symptoms but also the root causes of environmental inequity.

While early environmental justice research often focused on documenting correlations between race, class, and environmental burdens, contemporary scholarship emphasizes the importance of understanding causation. Did polluting facilities deliberately target communities of color? Did vulnerable communities move to areas where land was less expensive due to existing environmental risks? How have historical patterns of segregation, discriminatory lending practices, and exclusionary zoning shaped the geography of environmental risk? Or are multiple causal mechanisms operating simultaneously, creating feedback loops that entrench and exacerbate environmental disparities over time?

This chapter does not aim to settle the debate by pinpointing a single causal explanation; rather, it presents various theoretical frameworks through which we might better understand the complex origins of environmental injustice. From the structural violence of colonialism to the bureaucratic indifference of regulatory agencies, from the "rational" decisions of market actors to the unconscious biases that influence decision-making at every level, environmental injustice arises from the complex interplay of numerous factors operating across different scales and timeframes.

Recent developments have further complicated our understanding of environmental justice causation. The COVID-19 pandemic revealed how environmental factors like air pollution significantly increased vulnerability to respiratory diseases in communities of color. Climate change has introduced new dimensions of environmental injustice, with historically marginalized communities often experiencing the earliest and most severe impacts of rising temperatures, extreme weather events, and resource scarcity. Digital technologies, while offering new tools for community organizing and environmental monitoring, have also introduced new forms of exclusion based on the digital divide. The theories presented in this chapter should be understood not as competing explanations but as complementary perspectives, each illuminating different aspects of a complex social phenomenon. A comprehensive understanding of environmental injustice requires integrating insights from multiple disciplines and considering how various causal mechanisms interact across different scales from individual decision-making to institutional structures to global economic systems.

By analyzing these causal theories, we gain a deeper academic understanding of environmental injustice and more effective tools for addressing it. Different causal explanations suggest different intervention points and policy solutions. If environmental injustice stems primarily from market failures, then economic instruments may offer the most promising remedies. If institutional racism plays a central role, then civil rights enforcement and structural reforms may be necessary. If multiple causes interact in complex ways, then multifaceted, holistic approaches will be required.

B. Land-Use Practices

In part, the current distribution of environmental hazards is the result of land-use and zoning practices that started centuries ago. Restrictive racial covenants, exclusionary zoning practices like density and use restrictions, urban renewal policies that displaced thousands of residents, and other land-use mechanisms all contributed to residential segregation and the prevalence of unwanted land uses in low-income communities and communities of color. In the following excerpt, the late Professor Yale Rabin described one such long-standing zoning practice.

Yale Rabin, *Expulsive Zoning: The Inequitable Legacy of Euclid*

ZONING AND THE AMERICAN DREAM 101
(Charles M. Haar & Jerold S. Kayden eds., 1989)

... What follows sets forth the hypothesis that zoning, in addition to its well-recognized use as an exclusionary mechanism, also has been frequently employed in ways that have undermined the character, quality, and stability of black residential areas; that zoning not only has been used to erect barriers to escape from the concentrated confinement of the inner city, it has been used to permit—even promote—the intrusion into black neighborhoods of disruptive incompatible uses that have diminished the quality and undermined the stability of those neighborhoods. For reasons explained later, I refer to this practice as *expulsive zoning*....

[T]here is evidence to suggest that expulsive zoning practices have been relatively commonplace in black residential areas. The record, while admittedly fragmentary, indicates that in the years following the [Supreme] Court's rejection of racial zoning in 1917 and continuing through the thirties, and perhaps much later, a number of cities—mainly, but not exclusively, in the South—zoned some low-income residential areas occupied mainly, but not exclusively, by blacks for industrial or commercial use. These practices were sometimes carried out even in neighborhoods of single-family detached houses, thus undermining the quality of the very types of neighborhood housing which zoning ostensibly was intended to protect. To the extent that these practices were effective—that is, to the extent that residential uses were replaced by industrial or commercial uses, residents were displaced. Therefore, the term *expulsive zoning*. Because it appears that such areas were mainly black, and because whites who may have been similarly displaced were not subject to racially determined limitations in seeking alternative housing, the adverse impacts of expulsive zoning on blacks were far more severe and included, in addition to accelerated blight, increases in overcrowding and racial segregation....

[T]hese expulsive zoning practices are entirely consistent with the more general findings of my studies: that the land-use-related policies and practices of government at all levels, but particularly the decisions and initiatives of local government, have been and continue to be instrumental influences on both the creation and perpetuation of racial segregation. Expulsive zoning, as one of these practices, does not occur as an isolated or independent action, but as one element in a web-like pattern of interacting public practices that serve to reproduce and reinforce the disadvantages of blacks. Urban renewal, public housing site selection, school segregation, highway route selection, and code enforcement are a few of the other frequently encountered cords in the web....

Summary and Conclusions

The adverse impacts evident in these ... cases of expulsive zoning vary widely. They include environmentally blighting nuisances, displacement, and life threatening hazards.... [T]he evidence to date does appear to support three significant generalizations. First, illustrated most vividly by the case of Detroit, the magnitude and severity of adverse impacts are not necessarily proportional to the scale of intrusion or the extent of displacement. A single intrusive use can sometimes have disastrous effects. Second, the blighting and disruptive effects of expulsive zoning grow, rather than diminish, with the passage of time. Finally, expulsive zoning is not merely an historical remnant of a racially unenlightened past, but a current practice that continues to threaten, degrade, and destabilize black and other minority neighborhoods....

* * *

Post-Hurricane Maria Displacement in Puerto Rico: A Case Study in Environmental Injustice

(2017–2025)

Hurricane Maria devastated Puerto Rico in September 2017, causing catastrophic destruction that revealed profound environmental justice concerns. The federal government's response exposed significant disparities in disaster assistance and recovery support compared to similar disasters on the mainland United States. The consequences of Hurricane Maria were immediate and severe. Approximately 2,975 excess deaths occurred in the six months following the hurricane, many attributable to lack of electricity, medical care, and clean water. Research demonstrates that over 30 percent of Puerto Rican households reported problems accessing medical care after the hurricane, including the inability to get medications, closed medical facilities, and not being able to call 911 services.

Federal oversight agencies documented significant challenges in Puerto Rico's recovery process. In 2017, Hurricanes Irma and Maria caused extensive damage throughout Puerto Rico, destroying roads and buildings and cutting power and communication lines. Puerto Rico estimates that $132 billion will be needed to repair and reconstruct its infrastructure and services.

Puerto Rico's recovery has faced ongoing infrastructure challenges. As of June 2023, FEMA has awarded $23.4 billion in Public Assistance funds for Puerto Rico to recover from the 2017 hurricanes and 2019 and 2020 earthquakes. Of that, it has spent $1.8 billion and a lot of work remains, but increased costs may lead to funding shortfalls for projects. The rebuilding process has proceeded unevenly, with some communities experiencing faster recovery than others. More than six years after hurricanes Irma and Maria, Puerto Rico's recovery is ongoing. This prolonged recovery timeline has had differential impacts on communities across the island, with environmental justice implications for vulnerable populations. The delayed federal response altered Puerto Rico's demographic landscape, forcing out those with the fewest resources while enabling land acquisition by external investors. These patterns reflect broader environmental justice concerns about how disaster response can exacerbate rather than alleviate existing inequities. *See* Nishant Kishore et al., *Mortality in Puerto Rico after Hurricane Maria*, 379 New Eng. J. Med. 162, 162–70 (2018); U.S. Gov't Accountability Off., GAO-19-256, *Puerto Rico Hurricanes: Status of FEMA Funding, Oversight, and Recovery Challenges* 1 (2019); Carlos E. Rodriguez-Díaz & Charlotte Lewellen-Williams, *Race and Racism as Structural Determinants for Emergency and Recovery Response in the Aftermath of Hurricanes Irma and Maria in Puerto Rico*, 4 Health Equity 232 (2020); U.S. Gov't Accountability Off., GAO-24-105557, *Puerto Rico Disasters: Progress Made, but the Recovery Continues to Face Challenges* 1 (2023).

Notes and Questions

1. Causal chains. When environmental harms result from the intersection of natural events and government policy decisions, complex causation issues arise. Consider a community of color located in a floodplain that experiences severe flooding during a hurricane. If residents argue that discriminatory zoning policies historically confined them to flood-prone areas, and that inadequate federal flood response exacerbated their vulnerability, how should courts analyze causation? Should the hurricane be treated as a superseding intervening cause that breaks the causal chain to government liability? Compare this to other contexts where natural events interact with alleged discrimination, such as communities of color disproportionately affected by heat waves due to lack of tree cover, or tribal lands experiencing severe drought impacts due to historical water rights allocations. What role should foreseeability play when government actors make policy decisions in areas known to be environmentally vulnerable?

2. Multiple causes. Environmental justice plaintiffs often face the challenge of establishing causation when their harms result from multiple, interconnected government decisions over decades rather than discrete discriminatory acts. Consider a community experiencing disproportionate pollution burden due to the cumulative effect of industrial permitting decisions, zoning policies, transportation planning, and enforcement patterns spanning multiple agencies and decades. Must plaintiffs prove that each individual decision was motivated by discriminatory intent, or can they establish causation by demonstrating that the cumulative effect of facially neutral policies systematically disadvantaged communities of color? How might this analysis differ in various contexts, such as environmental enforcement patterns that result in more lenient oversight of facilities in minority communities, or infrastructure investment decisions that systematically under-invest in environmental improvements for communities of color? What evidentiary standards should courts apply when evaluating claims of "environmental racism" as a causal force?

3. Temporal concerns. Environmental justice cases often involve significant temporal gaps between alleged discriminatory government action and current environmental harms. Consider a Superfund site where historical industrial activities contaminated soil and groundwater, but cleanup has been delayed for decades, allegedly due to the site's location in a low-income community of color. If residents develop health problems or property values decline, how should courts analyze the causal relationship between decades-old contamination, intervening cleanup decisions, and current harms? Should legal causation doctrine account for the persistent effects of historical environmental decisions, or does the passage of time break the causal connection? Compare this to other temporal causation scenarios in environmental justice, such as communities seeking to link current health disparities to historical pollution exposure, or residents arguing that past discriminatory housing policies caused their current vulnerability to climate change impacts. How should causation analysis differ when the alleged harm is ongoing environmental exposure versus discrete past events with continuing consequences?

* * *

Professor Sarah Schindler considers the impact of the built environment and how what she describes as "architectural exclusion" also leads to segregation with broader environmental justice impacts.

Sarah Schindler, *Architectural Exclusion: Discrimination and Segregation through Physical Design of the Built Environment*

124 YALE L.J. 1934 (2015)

The idea that architecture regulates is found at the core of much urban planning and geography scholarship, though that body of literature does not always describe architecture as "regulation." At the most general level, it is not controversial among planning and geography scholars to assert that the built environment often is constructed in a way that furthers political goals. Moreover, these scholars generally agree that architectural decisions will favor some groups and disfavor others. Many would also agree that architecture can be, and is, used to exclude. As one planning scholar acknowledged, "[r]ace is a ubiquitous reality that must be acknowledged ... if [planners] do not want simply to be the facilitators of social exclusion and economic isolation."

Despite this deep theoretical understanding of the powerful role that architecture plays in crafting experience, practicing planners sometimes fail to afford sufficient weight to the concept of exclusion by design....

The metaphorical use of architecture implies an underlying recognition—foundational to planners and architects—that physical design regulates and that the built environment controls human behavior. Legal scholars use architecture as an analogue in their work with the understanding that "small and apparently insignificant [architectural] details can have major impacts on people's behavior...."

Although legal scholars do not often write directly about architecture as regulation, some—especially law and geography scholars and critical race theorists—have confronted concepts like architecture, the built environment, municipal infrastructure, space, and place in the context of class and race. As one commentator has noted:

> It is hard to understate the central significance of geographical themes—space, place, and mobility—to the social and political history of race relations and antiblack racism in the United States.... [S]egregation, integration, and separation are spatial processes; ... ghettos and exclusionary suburbs are spatial entities; ... access, exclusion, confinement ... are spatial experiences....

Legal academics have also proposed the idea that spaces themselves have racial meanings. For example, Elise C. Boddie argues that places have racial identities based on their history of or reputation for exclusion, and that courts should consider this racial meaning for purposes of racial discrimination claims. She further suggests that the racial meaning of a place can allow those in charge, such as police officers, to determine who belongs in that place and who does not. Similarly, Stephen Clowney has addressed the way in which landscapes, parks, and statues create a narrative that often marginalizes African Americans. Despite this recognition from scholars, Boddie points out that "law overlooks the racial identifiability of spaces," and Clowney notes that "landscape is one of the most overlooked instruments of modern race-making...."

However, architectural exclusion is different in that it is concerned with the placement and location of infrastructure that physically separates and inhibits access, not just disparities in treatment based on geographic location.

Although regulation through architecture is just as powerful as law, it is less identifiable and less visible to courts, legislators, and potential plaintiffs. While this observation suggests that decision makers should be even more diligent in analyzing the impact of architecture, research demonstrates that they often fail to take it seriously. To be clear, officials may understand that an architectural decision could have an exclusionary effect—they might even intend that result—but they generally do not see their decisions as a form of regulation that should be analyzed and patrolled in the same way that a law with the same effect would be. Exclusion through architecture should be subject to scrutiny that is equal to that afforded to other methods of exclusion by law.

* * *

One of the most vexing questions in federal environmental law concerns the reach of the federal Clean Water Act, defined by the meaning of "waters of the United States" (WOTUS). In *Solid Waste Agency of Northern Cook County v. United States Army Corps of Engineers*, 531 U.S. 159 (2001) ("SWANCC"), the U.S. Supreme Court began defining limits on WOTUS, finding that "nonnavigable, isolated, intrastate waters" are not subject to Clean Water Act jurisdiction. Five years later, in *Rapanos v. United States*, 547 U.S. 715 (2006), a fractured Supreme Court (4–1–4) established two tests for CWA jurisdiction: (1) a "Scalia test" requiring "relatively permanent bodies of water"; and (2) a "Kennedy test" potentially extending WOTUS to additional waters (e.g., wetlands or ephemeral streams) where there is "significant nexus" to other traditionally navigable waters. Regulations to clarify WOTUS were promulgated by both the Obama and first Trump administrations—and both rules were challenged and struck down in district courts. After swinging farther to the right, the U.S. Supreme Court issued yet another opinion on WOTUS, excerpted below.

Sackett v. Environmental Protection Agency

598 U.S. 651 (2023)

Justice Alito delivered the opinion of the Court.

... The phrase "the waters of the United States" delineates the geographic scope of the Clean Water Act. In these cases, we consider whether that category of "waters" includes wetlands that do not abut a "water of the United States." We conclude that it does not....

The statutory phrase at issue—"the waters of the United States"—had an established meaning in 1972, when Congress enacted the Act. At that time, "the waters of the United States" were understood to include only relatively permanent, standing, or flowing bodies of water found in streams, oceans, rivers, lakes, and bodies of similar nature.

The text and structure of the Clean Water Act—in particular, the distinction it draws between "navigable waters" and "point sources"—confirms this understanding. The Act contemplates a system of point-source regulation for pollutants discharged into navigable waters. A "point source" is defined as "any discernible, confined and discrete conveyance, including but not limited to any pipe, ditch, channel, tunnel, conduit, well, discrete fissure, container, rolling stock, concentrated animal feeding operation, or vessel or other floating craft, from which pollutants are or may be discharged." 33 U.S.C. §1362(14). Many of the items in this list "ditch[es]," "channel[s]," and so forth—would typically constitute what ordinary speakers would identify as "waters" if the statutory term were given an expansive interpretation. The fact that the Act treats "ditches" and "channels" as distinct from "navigable waters" indicates that the latter term does not include structures that allow for the conveyance of water....

Construing the phrase "the waters of the United States" to include wetlands that lack a continuous surface connection to relatively permanent bodies of water also contradicts the ordinary meaning of that phrase. Simply put, a wetland is not a "water" in any ordinary sense of that term. Tellingly, the Act's definitional section draws a basic contrast between "waters" and "wetlands." It defines "wetlands" not as "waters" but as "areas ... inundated or saturated by surface or ground water." §1362(7) (emphasis added). In ordinary parlance, "wetlands" are different from "waters" precisely because they are areas characterized by the presence of water, not waters themselves....

We therefore hold that the CWA extends to only those wetlands with a continuous surface connection to bodies that are "waters of the United States" in their own right, so that they are "indistinguishable" from those waters. The EPA cannot regulate all wetlands simply because they are "adjacent" to a covered water....

The "significant nexus" test adopted by the Ninth Circuit and supported by the Government has no basis in the statutory text and contradicts fundamental principles reflected in the Act's text, structure, and history. It misconstrues the Act by giving the EPA and the Corps sweeping authority to regulate private property across much of the Nation. And it disregards this Court's reasoning in Riverside Bayview, SWANCC, and Rapanos.

In light of the foregoing, we reverse the judgment of the Ninth Circuit and remand the case for further proceedings consistent with this opinion.

It is so ordered.

* * *

The Supreme Court's 2023 decision in *Sackett v. EPA* offers an instructive case study for examining causative mechanisms of environmental injustice. By replacing the "significant nexus" test with a "continuous surface connection" requirement for Clean

Water Act jurisdiction, the Court fundamentally altered federal protection for approximately half of the nation's wetlands. The measurable consequences of this judicial action across different communities provide a rare opportunity to evaluate competing theories of causation in environmental justice. *Sackett's* impact illuminates how past land-use decisions create present vulnerabilities. Census tracts with majority-minority populations experienced substantially greater losses of federally protected wetlands than predominantly white areas—not by coincidence, but through the accumulated effects of discriminatory zoning and housing policies that relegated certain communities to environmentally marginal lands.

This pattern substantiates the spatial determinism theory advanced by Rabin and others who argue that contemporary environmental inequities stem directly from historical practices such as "expulsive zoning" and redlining. Communities forced into flood-prone areas and near non-navigable waters decades ago now face disproportionate harm from the Court's narrowed interpretation of protected waters. The *Sackett* majority also ignores the impact of its decision on relatively arid areas of the United States, including poor Latino and Indigenous communities of the Southwest. In the State of New Mexico, for example, some 90 percent of waters are ephemeral, with water bodies such as the Rio Puerco dry much of the year, but fed seasonally by spring snowmelt and summer monsoons, and giving life to communities such as the Pueblo of Laguna. *Sackett* thus reveals how seemingly neutral judicial decisions interact with historically embedded spatial inequities to produce racially disparate outcomes.

Post-*Sackett* development patterns demonstrate the market-based causation theory proposed by Been and other scholars. Following the ruling, newly unregulated wetlands could experience rapid increases in development activity. This development pattern reflects rational economic behavior: firms naturally gravitate toward locations with reduced regulatory oversight, lower land costs, and minimal organized opposition. The *Sackett* decision effectively reduced the transaction costs associated with developing previously protected areas, creating economic incentives that predictably led to environmental degradation in vulnerable communities. This observed pattern supports the thesis that market dynamics—independent of discriminatory intent—can systematically produce disparate environmental outcomes when regulatory protections are removed. The varied regulation of state waters by individual states before and after *Sackett* show how social capital theory explains environmental justice outcomes. The State of California has long regulated state waters, for example, while the State of Alaska, which has more isolated waters than any other state, has chosen not to regulate these waters. In response to *Sackett*, the State of New Mexico passed legislation in the spring 2025 legislative session to establish state authority over waters left unprotected by the *Sackett* decision. *Sackett* demonstrates how communities with greater civic capacity can successfully advocate for environmental protections even as federal safeguards recede. Conversely, communities lacking political influence and advocacy infrastructure remain vulnerable to environmental degradation despite facing disproportionate risks—precisely as predicted by social capital theories of environmental injustice.

At the most fundamental level, *Sackett* exposes how the architecture of environmental law itself generates disparate outcomes. The Clean Water Act's jurisdiction derives from Commerce Clause authority rather than public health protection or equitable principles. This statutory foundation creates an inherent disconnect between the law's scope and the lived experiences of environmental justice communities. The Court's textualist approach in *Sackett* accentuated these structural limitations, revealing what environmental justice scholars have long argued: environmental statutes primarily manage pollution within acceptable limits rather than prevent environmental harms altogether. The resulting system predictably distributes environmental benefits and burdens unequally, with marginalized communities bearing disproportionate risks. The *Sackett* decision's observed impacts demonstrate how multiple causative mechanisms operate simultaneously. Historical land-use patterns established the preconditions for vulnerability; market forces rapidly exploited regulatory changes; social capital disparities determined communities' adaptive capacity; and structural features of environmental law created the framework within which these dynamics unfolded.

Notes and Questions

1. **Hurricane Maria and theories of causation.** The Puerto Rico case study reveals multiple theories of causation working simultaneously to produce environmental injustice outcomes. Which causal mechanism do you find most compelling in explaining the post-disaster inequities: historical land-use practices, market forces, lack of social capital, or racial/colonial discrimination? How might an understanding of these causative factors inform more equitable disaster recovery policies? The population displacement, or "climate gentrification," introduced in this case study represents an emerging form of environmental injustice. How does this phenomenon differ from traditional gentrification? What legal or policy interventions might prevent climate disasters from becoming opportunities for wealth transfer and displacement?

2. **The built environment.** Professor Schindler draws attention to exclusionary practices embedded within architecture to show their adverse impacts on communities and local residents. How do controls and expectations of the built environment heighten disparities that lead to environmental injustice?

3. **Gentrification.** Another potential threat to neighborhood stability in many urban areas is **gentrification** or **displacement**, a phenomenon that grew substantially throughout the 1990s. In response to skyrocketing housing costs, the high market demand for land, the growth in information technology-based companies, and other factors, urban neighborhoods, including low-income communities or communities of color that had long received little development attention, became much more attractive to investors. While increased economic development can bring important benefits to these areas, it also can make neighborhoods unaffordable and displace longtime residents. San Francisco's Mission District, for example, long an enclave for working class and recent immigrant Latino families, was targeted for development by many investors. This had the result of "squeezing out longtime tenants, small mom-and-pop stores, non-profits,

artists and working class people of all colors." As noted by one environmental justice organization, such displacement is particularly devastating in San Francisco, where rental vacancies are scarce and 40 percent of renters pay more than a third of their incomes for housing. Antonio Diaz, People Organizing to Demand Environmental & Economic Rights (PODER), RACE & SPACE: DOT-COLONIZATION, DISLOCATION AND RESISTANCE EN LA MISÍON DE SAN FRANCISCO (2001).

4. Exclusionary and inclusionary zoning. Zoning has evolved to be a local government function, with profound impacts in the aggregate. Some of the most common zoning provisions, such as bans on multi-family housing and mandates for minimum lot sizes, have the effect of limiting housing supplies. Many studies have exposed the impacts of these types of zoning limitations—dubbed "exclusionary zoning"—on the supply and affordability of housing, and on the demographic composition of communities. Large-lot, single-family zoning correlates with wealthier, whiter, better-educated households—and thus with residential segregation. *See, e.g.*, Yonah Freemark, Lydia Lo & Sara Bronin, Research Report, *Bringing Zoning into Focus: A Fine-Grained Analysis of Zoning's Relationships to Housing Affordability, Income Distributions, and Segregation in Connecticut* (June 2023). Given the well-known impacts of local zoning, would federal or state preemption be justified?

Some localities have tried to address exclusionary zoning with practices known as "inclusionary zoning," namely requirements that a developer reserve either funding or a certain percentage of proposed housing units for people of modest incomes or certain low-paying occupations (such as teachers or artists). Such provisions aim to ensure that affordable housing is created. However, one zoning expert, Professor Sara Bronin, notes that such provisions may backfire. She points out that "existing research suggests that inclusionary zoning actually increases overall prices, because developers recoup the costs of building their units by charging more for market-rate units." SARA C. BRONIN, KEY TO THE CITY: HOW ZONING SHAPES OUR WORLD 79–87 (2024). Perhaps unintuitively, Bronin argues that in many of the nine hundred or so jurisdictions where inclusionary zoning has been implemented, such provisions thwart the production of all types of housing (including affordable housing). She argues instead that zoning for more housing by right would expand supply for all people, whether such housing units are designated as affordable or not. She argues that bringing in "residents of a different race, ethnicity, or economic status [] can be healthy for a place that has suffered as a result of long-entrenched racial segregation." *Id.* at 80. Is this consistent with the goals of environmental justice? What are your thoughts?

C. The Market

Many critics who challenge the salience of race and/or ethnicity in explaining environmental disparities argue that market forces best account for these differences. This section considers the debates surrounding two types of "market force" explanations—one focusing on market forces in the site-selection process, the other examining market-driven changes that occur after siting decisions are made.

1. Market Forces in Site Selection

Robin Saha & Paul Mohai, *Explaining Racial and Socioeconomic Disparities in the Location of Locally Unwanted Land Uses: A Conceptual Framework*

(Conference paper presented at the Annual Meeting of the Rural Sociological Society, Toronto, Canada, August 1997)

The economic explanation of disproportionate siting relies on classic economic theory and focuses on industry's site selection rationale, reducing it down to strictly economic criteria.... In calculating the feasibility of a particular location, a company evaluates the transaction costs associated with the siting process and anticipated operating costs which affect the competitiveness and profitability of the service that can be offered at a particular location.... The transaction costs are associated with site selection, design, permitting, and construction. These costs can be quite high, especially if public opposition results in long delays, court costs, large financial compensation packages, or other exactions....

It has been argued that disproportionate conditions arise coincidentally out of private site selection decisions concerning the transaction costs of acquiring land for proposed facilities. The sole purported basis of these decisions is to minimize property value costs. Disproportionate siting is said to occur because cost-efficient industrial areas with low property values are also likely to be near areas with low residential property values. These areas, in turn, typically suffer from depressed economic conditions relative to other areas. Thus, the reasonable presumption that areas with low property values coincide with areas with high proportions of persons of low socioeconomic status (SES) is used to explain disproportionate siting with respect to SES. In addition, the interaction between low SES and race has been used to explain racial siting disparities.

Another aspect of the economic explanation holds that the calculation of transaction costs stemming from potential public opposition may result in disproportionate siting....

A rejected proposal is a costly matter for a sponsoring firm. Numerous activities are involved with putting forward a siting proposal such as securing finances and guarantees, conducting site assessments (e.g., geotechnical testing), developing business plans, negotiating and letting design contracts, and filing permit applications. These efforts represent "sunk costs" and are largely unrecoverable, since these investments of time, personnel, and money do not simply transfer to another proposal but must be carried out anew if a different location must be selected....

[I]t has been suggested that industry considers the potential costs of public opposition and selects a location where the probability of incurring such costs is minimized.... One way of avoiding the high costs of siting delays or defeats is to select communities where the likelihood of public opposition is reduced.... Evidence exists to support the claim that middle-income, affluent, and better educated communities are better equipped to wage effective opposition campaigns....

[A]s part of their transaction and operating costs firms are likely to consider the compensation costs that might be demanded in order for a community to accept a proposal.... Studies on class differences in the value placed on environmental quality suggest that communities with relatively well-educated and affluent residents are willing to pay more to preserve environmental amenities than communities with less educated and low-income residents. Even though these findings may reflect differences in ability to pay, they suggest that communities of lower SES would accept relatively smaller compensation packages in order to accept new facilities (disamenities).... More importantly, it appears that anticipated class differences in levels of acceptable compensation could be a factor firms consider, which, in turn, may contribute to disproportionate siting....

* * *

The excerpt from Saha & Mohai illuminates how economic decision-making can systematically produce environmental inequities even without explicit discriminatory intent. Their analysis represents one of several key theoretical frameworks for understanding the causal mechanisms behind environmental injustice, focusing specifically on market dynamics as a driving force. According to this economic explanation, companies make siting decisions based primarily on two cost considerations. First, they seek locations with low property values to minimize acquisition costs. Second, they attempt to reduce transaction costs associated with community opposition, including expenses from regulatory proceedings, litigation, and potential compensation demands. Both considerations tend to steer locally unwanted land uses (LULUs) toward socioeconomically disadvantaged communities. This market-based theory offers several key insights. The search for low property values naturally directs hazardous facilities toward areas already experiencing economic depression. Since communities of color are disproportionately represented in low-income areas due to historical patterns of segregation and disinvestment, a seemingly race-neutral criterion (low cost) produces racially disparate outcomes. Similarly, the desire to avoid costly opposition leads companies to target communities with less political power and fewer resources to mount effective resistance campaigns.

The market forces framework remains highly relevant in contemporary environmental justice contexts. Recent studies of renewable energy development demonstrate how these same economic calculations shape the transition to clean energy. Large solar installations and wind farms disproportionately locate in rural, lower-income communities where land costs are minimal and political opposition is less organized. While these facilities don't produce traditional pollution, they create their own environmental impacts, habitat disruption, viewshed changes, and land use conflicts that follow familiar distributional patterns.

The rapid growth of e-commerce and logistics has created a modern corollary in warehouse siting decisions. In 2024, researchers from George Washington University published a study finding that e-commerce fulfillment centers such as those maintained by Amazon are disproportionately located near communities of color, resulting in disproportionate impacts of air pollution on surrounding communities. Gaige Hunter Kerr et al., *Air Pollution Impacts from Warehousing in the United States Uncovered with Satellite Data*, 15 NATURE COMMUNICATIONS 6006 (2024). (See also related discussion in Chapter 11.) Climate adaptation infrastructure follows similar patterns. In coastal communities facing sea-level rise, public investment in protective infrastructure increasingly flows to higher-property-value areas that promise better returns on investment, while managed retreat programs target lower-value properties often concentrated in historically marginalized communities, a market-driven approach that reinforces existing disparities.

The environmental justice implications of carbon offset markets also reflect Saha & Mohai's analysis. Companies seeking the lowest-cost carbon offsets often invest in projects far from the communities experiencing their emissions, creating a spatial disconnect between environmental costs and benefits that follows predictable socioeconomic patterns. Understanding these market dynamics has informed recent policy innovations. Some states, including Colorado, Minnesota, New Jersey, New York, and Washington, and cities, including Albuquerque and Newark, now require cumulative impact analyses before permitting certain new facilities, directly addressing the market tendency to concentrate environmental burdens in already-impacted communities. Environmental justice screening tools used by federal agencies attempt to identify communities where market forces have created disproportionate environmental burdens, targeting resources to counterbalance these forces. The market forces theory underscores a fundamental tension in environmental justice: the conflict between individual market transactions that may appear rational and neutral, and the cumulative patterns of inequity that emerge from these transactions. Addressing this tension requires interventions that acknowledge both the economic logic driving siting decisions and the broader social context that makes some communities systematically more vulnerable to environmental burdens than others.

Professor Carmen Gonzalez further explores how historical segregation and racism have impacted international investment and neoliberal trade formulations through U.S.-Mexico relations.

Carmen G. Gonzalez, *An Environmental Justice Critique of Comparative Advantage: Indigenous Peoples, Trade Policy, and the Mexican Neoliberal Economic Reforms*

32 U. Penn. J. Int'l. L. 723 (2011)

The theory of comparative advantage plays a central role in legitimating both the ideology of free trade and the economic policy recommendations of the World Trade Organization ("WTO"), the World Bank, and the International Monetary Fund ("IMF"). Developed by David Ricardo, the theory of comparative advantage posits that each country should specialize in the goods that it produces relatively more efficiently and should import the goods that it produces relatively less efficiently. For example, countries with abundant natural resources and scarce capital should specialize in agricultural exports and should import manufactured goods. Furthermore, subsidies and tariffs are inefficient because they distort comparative advantage and encourage countries to produce goods in which they do not have a comparative advantage and which might be produced more cheaply elsewhere. In order to elucidate the relevance of the theory of comparative advantage to contemporary debates over trade policy, it is useful to summarize the ongoing controversy over international trade in agricultural products. Global agricultural trade is currently distorted by high levels of protectionism in industrialized countries. The lavish agricultural subsidies provided by the United States and the European Union to domestic farmers encourage overproduction and depress world market prices for agricultural commodities. Many agricultural commodities are being sold in world markets at below the cost of production, thereby undermining the livelihoods of poor farmers in Asia, Africa, and Latin America....

The poverty and desperation produced by the collapse of Mexican corn prices caused many subsistence farmers to migrate to northern Mexico or to the United States in order to earn the cash necessary to support their families. Indeed, from 1990 to 2000, the highest levels of out-migration in Mexico occurred in the regions with the highest levels of cultural diversity and corn agro-biodiversity. This exodus of able-bodied male workers is fracturing families, leaving fields unplanted, and forcing women and children to work the land and to seek off-farm employment in order to supplement the family's income. Unfortunately, many of these rural migrants have been unable to find employment in Mexico's urban areas because trade liberalization under NAFTA failed to create sufficient manufacturing jobs to keep pace with the rural exodus. At least 500,000 Mexican workers migrate to the United States every year, many of them from Mexico's impoverished rural areas. Indeed, approximately two-thirds of the estimated twelve million undocumented workers in the United States came after 1995 and many are regarded as casualties of NAFTA. Recognizing the relationship between U.S. agricultural trade policy and immigration, a *New York Times* editorial acknowledged that "ending subsidies for agribusiness would be far more effective than beefing up the border patrol."

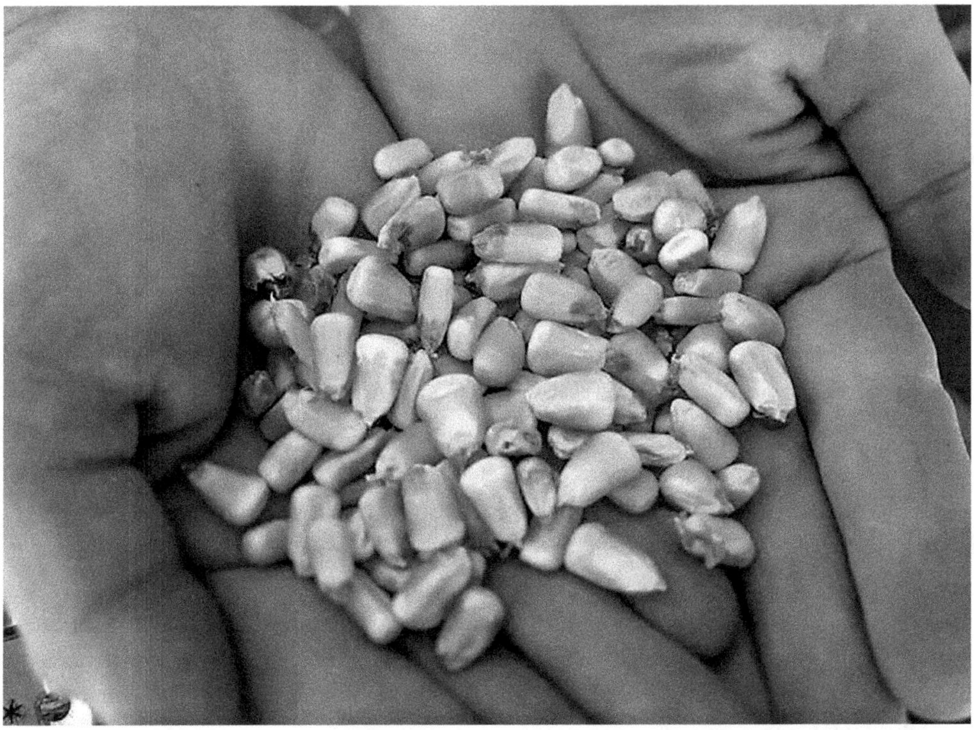

Figure 2-2. Nobel Prize winner and famed Mexican poet Octavio Paz once observed, "the invention of corn by Mexicans is only comparable to the invention of fire by man." Photo: Shirley Trout.

Migration also has important cultural, environmental, and economic consequences in Mexico and poses risks to global food security. Mexico's impoverished, indigenous peasants are the custodians of Mexico's genetically diverse varieties of corn. This genetic diversity protects farmers from catastrophic crop loss in the event of environmental disturbances and is also vital to global food security. The out-migration of farmers with traditional knowledge or experience may disrupt the transfer of this knowledge to future generations, leading to the replacement of traditional corn varieties with other crops or with commercial high-yield corn varieties, or, alternatively, to the abandonment of farming altogether. In short, the migration of Mexican farmers threatens Mexico's genetic diversity as well as the survival of Mexico's indigenous population.

Notes and Questions

1. **Market forces.** Saha & Mohai articulate how economic decision-making processes related to property values and anticipated community opposition can systematically produce environmental inequities. What specific market mechanisms do they identify, and how might these seemingly "race-neutral" economic calculations nevertheless produce racially disparate outcomes? Consider whether recognizing the role of market forces diminishes or reinforces the case for regulatory intervention in EJ contexts.

2. Even "green" infrastructure? The Soha & Mohai excerpt identifies several contemporary examples where market forces continue to shape the distribution of environmental burdens and benefits, including renewable energy development, e-commerce warehouses, and climate adaptation infrastructure. Analyze how these modern applications demonstrate continuity or evolution in market-driven environmental inequities. Does the transition to "green" infrastructure challenge or reinforce existing patterns of inequality?

3. Thinking globally. Professor Gonzalez's analysis of U.S.-Mexico agricultural trade extends market forces theory to an international context. How does her critique of comparative advantage theory complement or challenge the domestic market forces explanation offered by Saha & Mohai? Consider whether environmental justice requires fundamentally rethinking dominant economic paradigms rather than merely correcting for market failures.

4. Market efficiency vs. environmental equity. The conflict between individual market transactions that appear neutral, and the cumulative patterns of inequity that emerge from these transactions, represents a fundamental tension in environmental justice. Evaluate this tension by considering circumstances where market efficiency and environmental equity might align versus circumstances where they necessarily conflict. What implications does this tension have for policy approaches to environmental justice?

2. Market Forces vs. Science

Professor Brie Sherwin considers how data management and the interpretation of scientific results have strong guiding principles. She examines the rubric for environmental justice through the use of scientific studies and how this rubric can be manipulated through attacks on science.

Brie D. Sherwin, *The Upside Down: A New Reality for Science at the EPA and Its Impact on Environmental Justice*

27 N.Y.U. Envtl. L.J. 57 (2019)

The concept of environmental justice can best be measured by scientific studies of the effects of pollution on vulnerable populations. Science sheds light on disproportionate environmental risks in a way that is measurable and that provides public assurance that the process is honest, truthful, and reliable. Politicians, however, are increasingly questioning the integrity of the scientists who are involved in assessing risk; working to sow doubt in the minds of political constituents and the public.

But, there is a fundamental difference in how scientists and politicians work. Scientists aim to discover the truth. Indeed, many believe that science "is the pinnacle of human achievement not because of its actual successes but in virtue of the fact that its practice, both in attaining truth and in lapsing into error, is thoroughly informed by reason." These virtuous thoughts are the very ideals that scientists should, and for the most part do, ascribe to without fault. However, when scientists become involved in the administrative rulemaking process, science becomes politicized to a certain extent.

With the Trump administration's efforts to remove objective oversight of the scientific process, it is likely that the public's trust in science will continue to erode. The slow demise of public's trust in science has occurred over the past fifteen years, most notably with the Bush Administration's intervention in the scientific processes underlying environmental policy and rulemaking and its subsequent distortion or suppression of scientific findings. This included withholding comments from scientists at the U.S. Fish and Wildlife Service on the destructive impacts of proposed regulatory changes, stacking scientific advisory committees with unqualified members who had industry ties, altering websites, and suppressing agency reports. Most notably, in 2003, the White House infamously edited a discussion of climate change in EPA's *Draft Report on the Environment*. At that time, EPA's scientists complained that the altered draft "no longer accurately represented scientific consensus on climate change," which ultimately led the Agency to eliminate the discussion in its entirety from the report.

The distortion of scientific findings extends beyond policy to legislation also meant to protect environmental and human health. In 2005, Congress exempted hydraulic fracturing (fracking) from EPA oversight under the 1974 Safe Drinking Water Act based on a controversial 2002 draft EPA study which found that fracking posed a low risk to drinking water supplies. Many of these fracking sites are located in rural areas, where much of the population lives below the poverty level, triggering environmental justice concerns.

We have also seen profound impacts on environmental justice, particularly as it relates to safe drinking water, with industry insiders replacing scientists on scientific advisory boards. In the early 1990s, while high levels of lead in drinking water was a rising concern, the George H.W. Bush Administration replaced three national experts in lead poisoning on the Advisory Committee on Childhood Lead Poisoning Prevention with several individuals who had ties to the lead industry. In fact, one of the appointees was a leading industry consultant, who had previously testified that a lead level that was seven times higher than the current Center for Disease Control (CDC) recommendations was safe for children's brains. Over the following decade, little changed in the regulations that were meant to protect children from lead in drinking water. Arguably, it was that lack of urgency in revising the Lead and Copper Rule to better reflect the most recent scientific evidence of risk, along with the economic crisis and agency apathy, that culminated in the environmental justice crisis in Flint, Michigan, in 2015.

[Under the first Trump administration,] the apathy has been replaced with an outward rejection of EPA scientists who are meant to advocate for children. Dr. Ruth Etzel, a leading pediatrician and epidemiologist in the field of children's health for over thirty years, was put on administrative leave on September 25, 2018. John Konkis, an EPA spokesman, refused to provide a reason for her leave. Her office, the Department of Children's Health Protection, is, by design, meant to inform the Agency "on the specific health and environmental-protection needs of children," who often require more protective standards than adults. In addition to placing Dr. Etzel on leave, EPA also stalled a year-long project, headed by Etzel's former office, to develop an interagency effort to reduce children's lead exposure.

And, it was not long after President Trump took office that scientific data and reports quietly disappeared within EPA. Mere moments after President Trump's inauguration, the official website of the White House deleted almost all mention of climate change, save one: the new President's vow to eliminate climate change policies created by the Obama Administration. But, although the policy changes were alarming, scientists were even more concerned about the disappearance of climate change data gathered and stored by administrative agencies for years, which is considered some of the most complete and solid data in the world. Since his election, a minimum of fifty academic scientists have taken to preserving and monitoring data stored on government websites like those of EPA, NASA, and National Oceanic and Atmospheric Administration (NOAA).

* * *

The relationship between science, politics, and environmental justice presents one of the most complex challenges in addressing environmental inequities. Professor Sherwin's 2019 analysis of how scientific integrity affects environmental justice outcomes highlighted a critical but often overlooked causal mechanism in environmental inequality—the manipulation of scientific evidence that forms the foundation for environmental regulation and enforcement. The second Trump administration, after taking office in January 2025, rapidly accelerated these concerning patterns, creating new obstacles for environmental justice communities.

Environmental justice relies fundamentally on scientific evidence to establish causal relationships between environmental exposures and harmful outcomes in vulnerable communities. When political actors undermine scientific processes through various mechanisms—replacing qualified experts with industry representatives, suppressing scientific findings, eliminating data access, or creating artificial uncertainty—they effectively obscure the causal chains that otherwise might trigger regulatory action to protect overburdened communities. This disruption of scientific processes represents a distinct causal pathway for environmental injustice that operates alongside historical land use patterns, market forces, and sociopolitical factors. While these other causal mechanisms create the conditions for disproportionate exposures, scientific manipulation ensures these disparities remain unaddressed by preventing the establishment of causation supporting regulatory intervention.

The Trump administration's 2025 dismantling of the EPA's Office of Environmental Justice and External Civil Rights and regional EJ divisions represents an attack on institutional structures designed to identify and address environmental injustice across the country. The Trump administration's dismantling of the EPA Office of Research and Development represents an attack on science itself, impeding advancement and application of new knowledge and technology across all areas of environmental protection. For a thorough analysis of the Trump EPA's efforts to eliminate its Office of Research and Development (by the former head of that office under the Biden administration), see the blog maintained by Dr. Christopher Frey, *EPA's Proposal to Eliminate Its Office of Research and Development Will Affect You*, available at https://frey.wordpress.ncsu.edu/2025/03/18/what-are-the-benefits-of-taking-the-science-out-of-a-science-based-agency-epa-tldr-none/.

The political interference with scientific processes operates through several distinct mechanisms, each with implications for how we understand environmental justice causation. The Trump administration's reconstitution of the EPA's Science Advisory Board with new membership requirements mandating "balanced representation from regulated industries" has effectively shifted which evidence receives consideration and how uncertainties are resolved. Eight of the eleven new appointees announced in April 2025 have direct ties to industries regulated by the EPA, including representatives from petrochemical, mining, and agricultural sectors, a clear example of industry capture of scientific advisory processes.

On a broader level, President Trump's executive order, *Restoring Gold Standard Science*, May 23, 2025, may restrict scientific inquiry and advancement across the entire federal government. The "Gold Standard" order from the second Trump administration reintroduces many of the substantive flaws of the "Secret Science Rule" from first Trump administration, which was struck down quickly in federal court. *Envt'l. Defense Fund v. U.S. EPA*, 515 F. Supp. 3d 1135 (D. Mont. 2021). Trump's 2025 "Gold Standard" order provoked a strong response from House Democrats, who wrote:

> One of the most concerning elements of the order is the requirement that agencies publicly release all "data, analyses, and conclusions" underpinning major policies. While transparency is a fundamental scientific value, this language closely mirrors the flawed [Secret Science Rule] from your first term, a rule that sought to exclude essential studies from [EPA] policymaking unless raw data, including sensitive medical information, was made public. Such an approach does not enhance scientific integrity; it undermines it, while also weakening public health protections.

Letter from Paul D. Tonko, Member of Congress, et al., to The Honorable Donald J. Trump, June 26, 2025.

By setting impossible standards for scientific evidence, the "Gold Standard" order along with other actions to diminish scientific integrity creates a structural barrier to establishing causation for environmental harms affecting vulnerable communities.

The administration's proposed suspension of the PFAS National Primary Drinking Water Regulation finalized in 2023, which had established legally enforceable limits for six per- and polyfluoroalkyl substances in drinking water systems, demonstrates how regulatory rollbacks could disproportionately impact EJ communities. Officials have announced a "reassessment of economic impacts" despite these chemicals' prevalence in disadvantaged communities and substantial evidence linking them to adverse health effects.

Proposed revisions to the Lead and Copper Rule Improvements that extend compliance timelines and reduce requirements for lead service line inventories could particularly affect older urban communities where lead contamination remains a significant concern. This weakening of protections, justified through claims of economic burden, perpetuates the same pattern of regulatory neglect that contributed to crises like Flint, Michigan.

Perhaps most troubling from a causation perspective is the potential shelving of the cumulative risk assessment framework developed during the Biden administration, which specifically addressed how multiple chemical and non-chemical stressors affect vulnerable communities. Trump officials cited "methodological concerns" and "implementation costs," effectively attempting to block scientific recognition of the complex, multiple exposures that define environmental justice communities' experiences. The administration has also significantly altered public access to environmental data. The EPA's Environmental Justice Screening and Mapping Tool (EJSCREEN) had been removed from the EPA website, but has been preserved by institutions including Harvard University and may still be found at https://screening-tools.com/epa-ejscreen.

These recent developments illustrate how attacks on scientific integrity represent a sophisticated form of institutional discrimination that perpetuates environmental inequities without requiring explicit discriminatory intent. By controlling which causal relationships receive scientific recognition and regulatory response, political actors can effectively maintain environmental disparities while claiming commitment to objective, science-based decision-making.

Understanding these dynamics adds an important dimension to theories of environmental injustice causation. While historical theories focus on how discriminatory zoning, market forces, and political power disparities create vulnerability to environmental hazards, Sherwin's analysis and recent developments reveal how scientific manipulation maintains these disparities by preventing effective regulatory responses.

Effective environmental justice strategies must address not only the distribution of environmental hazards and benefits but also the institutional processes through which scientific evidence is evaluated and translated into regulatory action. This step requires scientific capacity building within environmental justice communities to enable independent verification of government and industry claims about environmental risks, particularly important in the current political climate where official data sources have become unreliable.

Data democratization through community-based participatory research and improved public access to environmental monitoring data creates alternative knowledge sources when official channels are compromised. The suspension of environmental monitoring programs in "low-priority areas" announced in 2025, which effectively reduces data collection in many rural and lower-income communities, could make these alternative data collection efforts even more critical. By recognizing scientific integrity as a critical causal factor in environmental justice outcomes, we gain a more complete understanding of how environmental inequities persist despite decades of advocacy and increased awareness. Addressing these root causes requires not only distributional and procedural justice but also what some scholars have termed "epistemic justice," fair and equitable processes for producing and evaluating the knowledge that informs environmental decision-making.

Notes and Questions

1. **Undermining science.** Professor Sherwin argues that politicians are questioning the findings of the scientists who are involved in assessing environmental risks. What are the environmental risks that are overlooked in this situation?

2. **Doubt.** How does creating doubt in the mind of political constituents and the public impact environmental compliance and enforcement?

3. Post-Siting Changes

One of the earlier arguments in environmental justice scholarship was that the prevalence of LULUs in low-income communities and communities of color resulted from market-driven changes that occurred in neighborhoods after an unwanted land use was located there. This thesis, called the "market dynamics" or "minority move-in" theory, was prominently developed by Professor Vicki Been, who also discusses why it is important to know which came first, the community or the unwanted land use.

Vicki Been, *Locally Undesirable Land Uses in Minority Neighborhoods: Disproportionate Siting or Market Dynamics?*

103 Yale L.J. 1383 (1994)

The environmental justice movement contends that people of color and the poor are exposed to greater environmental risks than are whites and wealthier individuals.... [R]esearch does not, however, establish that [communities hosting LULUs] were disproportionately minority or poor at the time the sites were selected. Most of the studies compare the *current* socioeconomic characteristics of communities that host various LULUs to those of communities that do not host such LULUs. This approach leaves open the possibility that the sites for LULUs were chosen fairly, but that subsequent events produced the current disproportion in the distribution of LULUs. In other words, the research fails to prove environmental justice advocates' claim that the disproportionate burden poor and minority communities now bear in hosting LULUs is the result of racism and classism in the *siting process* itself.

In addition, the research fails to explore an alternative or additional explanation for the proven correlation between the current demographics of communities and the likelihood that they host LULUs. Regardless of whether the LULUs originally were sited fairly, it could well be that neighborhoods surrounding LULUs became poorer and became home to a greater percentage of people of color over the years following the sitings. Such factors as poverty, housing discrimination, and the location of jobs, transportation, and other public services may have led the poor and racial minorities to "come to the nuisance"—to move to neighborhoods that host LULUs—because those neighborhoods offered the cheapest available housing....

Market Dynamics and the Distribution of LULUs

The residential housing market in the United States is extremely dynamic. Every year, approximately 17% to 20% of U.S. households move to a new home. Some of those people stay within the same neighborhood, but many move to different neighborhoods in the same city, or to different cities. Some people decide to move, at least in part, because they are dissatisfied with the quality of their current neighborhoods. Once a household decides to move, its choice of a new neighborhood usually depends somewhat on the cost of housing and the characteristics of the neighborhood. Those two factors are interrelated because the quality of the neighborhood affects the price of housing.

The siting of a LULU can influence the characteristics of the surrounding neighborhood in two ways. First, an undesirable land use may cause those who can afford to move to become dissatisfied and leave the neighborhood. Second, by making the neighborhood less desirable, the LULU may decrease the value of the neighborhood's property, making the housing more available to lower income households and less attractive to higher income households. The end result of both influences is likely to be that the neighborhood becomes poorer than it was before the siting of the LULU.

The neighborhood also is likely to become home to more people of color. Racial discrimination in the sale and rental of housing relegates people of color (especially African-Americans) to the least desirable neighborhoods, regardless of their income level. Moreover, once a neighborhood becomes a community of color, racial discrimination in the promulgation and enforcement of zoning and environmental protection laws, the provision of municipal services, and the lending practices of banks may cause neighborhood quality to decline further. That additional decline, in turn, will induce those who can leave the neighborhood—the least poor and those least subject to discrimination—to do so.

The dynamics of the housing market therefore are likely to cause the poor and people of color to move to or remain in the neighborhoods in which LULUs are located, regardless of the demographics of the communities when the LULUs were first sited....

If the siting process is primarily responsible for the correlation between the location of LULUs and the demographics of host neighborhoods, the process may be unjust under current constitutional doctrine, at least as to people of color....

On the other hand, if the disproportionate distribution of LULUs results from market forces which drive the poor, regardless of their race, to live in neighborhoods that offer cheaper housing because they host LULUs, then the fairness of the distribution becomes a question about the fairness of our market economy. Some might argue that the disproportionate burden is part and parcel of a free market economy that is, overall, fairer than alternative schemes, and that the costs of regulating the market to reduce the disproportionate burden outweigh the benefits of doing so. Others might argue that those moving to a host neighborhood are compensated through the market for the disproportionate burden they bear by lower housing costs, and therefore that the situation is just. Similarly, some might contend that while the poor suffer lower quality neighborhoods, they also suffer lower quality food, housing, and medical care, and that the systemic problem of poverty is better addressed through income redistribution programs than through changes in siting processes.

Even if decisionmakers were to agree that it is unfair to allow post-siting market dynamics to create disproportionate environmental risk for the poor or minorities, the remedy for that injustice would have to be much more fundamental than the remedy for unjust siting *decisions*. Indeed, if market forces are the primary cause of the correlation between the presence of LULUs and the current socioeconomic characteristics of a neighborhood, even a siting process radically revised to ensure that LULUs are distributed equally among all neighborhoods may have only a short-term effect. The areas surrounding LULUs distributed equitably will become less desirable neighborhoods, and thus may soon be left to people of color or the poor, recreating the pattern of inequitable siting....

The Evidence of Disproportionate Siting

Several recent studies have attempted to assess whether locally undesirable land uses are disproportionately located in neighborhoods that are populated by more people of color or are more poor than is normal.... [One frequently cited study,] which is often credited for first giving the issue of environmental justice visibility, was conducted by the United States General Accounting Office (GAO).... [The GAO found that in three of the four communities where hazardous waste landfills were sited in eight southeastern states, the population was disproportionately African American and poor. Eds.] Another frequently cited local study was conducted by sociologist Robert Bullard and formed important parts of his books, *Invisible Houston* and *Dumping in Dixie*. Professor Bullard found that although African-Americans made up only 28 percent of the Houston population in 1980, six of Houston's eight incinerators and mini-incinerators and fifteen of seventeen landfills were located in predominantly African-American neighborhoods.

[Professor Been then re-analyzed the GAO study and the Bullard study, looking at demographic characteristics of the host communities at the time of siting decisions and tracing subsequent changes in the demographics of these communities. She found mixed support for her thesis: of the four communities reviewed by the GAO, all were disproportionately Black at the siting, and in each case the percentage of Blacks decreased after siting decisions were made. For ten communities studied by Professor Bullard, she found 50 percent were sited in predominantly Black communities, and that the percentage of Blacks in all neighborhoods surrounding the landfills subsequently increased (as did the percentage of the population with incomes below the poverty level in all but two host neighborhoods). Eds.]

Notes and Questions

1. **Climate havens.** Recent studies document "reverse environmental migration" where climate havens attract higher-income residents while climate-vulnerable areas become more concentrated with low-income residents and communities of color who lack mobility options. How should environmental justice scholars analyze this phenomenon as evidence of market dynamics working as Been predicted, or as a new form of environmental inequality that transcends the original chicken-or-egg framework?

2. **"Climate redlining."** The emergence of "climate redlining," where insurance companies and lenders use climate risk data to restrict services in certain neighborhoods, often overlaps with historically redlined areas. Does this pattern represent a continuation of discriminatory market practices or does it suggest that contemporary environmental injustice operates through mechanisms distinct from traditional market dynamics?

3. **The rise of AI.** Consider the role of algorithmic decision-making in contemporary housing markets, where AI-driven property valuations, lending algorithms, and climate risk assessments may systematically undervalue properties in communities of color while directing green investments elsewhere. How do these technological intermediaries affect the market dynamics theory's assumptions about rational market actors and price signals driving demographic change?

Some scholars seeking to explain disproportionate siting point to a complicated set of sociopolitical and legal factors. Their theories are examined in the following section.

D. Politics and Social Capital

As described above, companies may choose to site noxious facilities in low-income communities or communities of color because this represents the path of least political resistance. In one recent case, an energy company concluded the "path of least resistance" for a new oil pipeline in Memphis, Tennessee, would be through the predominantly Black and history community known as Boxtown. In a significant victory for environmental justice, community members, led by Justin Pearson, organized and successfully resisted the proposal. *See*, Southern Environmental Law Center, *How the Byhalia Pipeline Would Have Impacted Memphis* (Mar. 10, 2021).

Minority and poor residents often have less political power than wealthier communities for a variety of reasons: lack of access to elected officials, lack of awareness of the appropriate officials to contact in order to express concerns about environmental conditions, and under-representation in local government. They are "likely to lack the know-how, the administrative, legal, and scientific expertise to participate effectively in administrative process of siting decisions." Saha & Mohai, *supra*, at 9, 11–13. Explana-

Figure 2-3. Justin Pearson, Memphis, Tennessee. After defeating the proposed Byhalia Pipeline through the Boxtown community, Pearson was elected to the Tennessee State Legislature, later removed for exercising First Amendment rights, and subsequently restored to his role in the legislature. Photo: Cliff Villa, 2021.

tions that center upon these sociopolitical factors essentially posit that environmental burdens are shifted to groups that lack social capital.

Social capital can be defined as resources embedded in a social structure that are accessed and/or mobilized in purposive actions. By this definition, the notion of social capital contains three ingredients: resources embedded in a social structure; accessibility to these social resources by individuals; and use or mobilization of them by individuals engaged in purposive action. Thus conceived, social capital contains both structural (accessibility) and action-oriented (mobilization or use) elements....

[S]ocial capital captures the extent to which individuals have differential accessibility to collective resources....

> [I]t is incumbent on a theory of social capital to delineate the patterns and determinants of the two ingredients of social capital or *the inequality of social capital* as accessible social resources and mobilized social resources....

Nan Lin et al., *The Position Generator: Measurement Techniques for Investigations of Social Capital, in* SOCIAL CAPITAL: THEORY AND RESEARCH 57, 58–59 (Nan Lin et al., eds. 2001).

With this in mind, consider that researchers found that ethnic demographic shifts, a previously overlooked variable in the empirical data on disparities, significantly correlated with the siting of commercial hazardous waste facilities (called treatment, storage, and disposal facilities, or "TSDFs," under federal hazardous waste law). The excerpt below, describing this study, attempts to identify and measure the lack of social capital that explains some environmental disparities.

Manuel Pastor, Jr., Jim Sadd & John Hipp, *Which Came First? Toxic Facilities, Minority Move-In, and Environmental Justice*

23 J. URBAN AFFAIRS 1 (2001)

... Many have assumed that contemporary inequity is the result of discriminatory siting practices. The general argument is that low levels of political power in minority communities may induce polluters to locate hazards in these areas. Such a political argument is often implicitly based on notions of social capital and community efficacy: Where residents have more ability to organize and affect policy, perhaps because of their income or racial status in a stratified society, they will be more able to resist the placement of a hazardous facility. Of course, social capital may in fact be affected by other factors, such as the level of education of residents or the ability to bridge differences between minority groups, a topic we explore below....

[W]e focus on the effects of a new dimension of ethnic change. Previous work has stressed the percentage of minorities. But while a 40% increase in Latinos that is matched by a corresponding 40% decrease in African Americans may leave the percentage of minorities unchanged, the neighborhood will in fact be transformed. Such ethnic transitions may weaken the usual social bonds constituted by race and make an area more susceptible to siting. We investigate this "social capital" effect [] finding that it does indeed have an effect on the likelihood of receiving a TSDF....

Black to Brown shifts have been especially prevalent in South Los Angeles, an area laden with hazardous or toxic facilities and air pollution.... Such shifting neighborhood patterns can cause tensions between minority groups, weakening neighborhood social capital and increasing the area's vulnerability to siting locally undesirable land uses.... We label this measure of dynamics within a census tract "ethnic churning." ...

To see whether a change in the ethnic composition of an area—even if it remains minority—weakens social capital and makes areas more vulnerable to disproportionate siting, we re-estimated the model by using ethnic churning during the 1970s and 1980s and TSDF siting over the same period.... [The researchers then found that the churning variable is highly significant at predicting TSDF siting at the one-mile level; they also found that, controlling for other factors, minorities attract TSDFs, but TSDFs do not generally attract minorities. Eds.]

This study offers a lesson consistent with the experience of many environmental justice advocates: Demographics reflecting political weakness—including a higher presence of minorities, a lower presence of home owners, or a significant degree of ethnic churning—seem to be the real attractors of TSDFs. A special challenge is posed by the fact that areas undergoing transition and unable to lay claim to pre-existing racially based social capital may be especially vulnerable. If this is so, then the current strategy of most of the environmental justice movement—building social capital across ethnic lines by an explicit commitment to a people of color movement—may be an effective way to combat the environmental degradation often found in urban minority communities.

E. Racial Discrimination

Another, and perhaps most obvious, set of explanations for disproportionate environmental burdens and benefits involves racial discrimination. In the recent past, given prevailing societal opprobrium, many people may have thought of racial discrimination as unlikely to occur in the open. But there is no denying that racial discrimination remains firmly entrenched in American culture, as demonstrated in 2020 with the police murder of George Floyd in Minneapolis and with the killing of so many other Black and Brown men, women, and children across the country. As we will see in Chapter 4, constitutional law concerns itself mostly with *intentional* discrimination: e.g., targeting individuals and communities of color based on pure racial bigotry. A softer, but related, view of intentional discrimination posits that communities of color are targeted for unwanted land uses and other environmental burdens by those who believe communities of color will be more willing to trade off environmental risks for possible economic benefits, less likely to organize effective opposition than white communities, or less worthy of environmental concern. For example, while deliberating whether or not to provide financial assistance to Flint, Michigan (57 percent Black, 42 percent below federal poverty line) in the middle of the Flint Water Crisis, one agency staff member commented, "I'm not so sure Flint is the community we want to go out on a limb for." *See* Clifford J. Villa, *Don't Blame the Flint River*, 52 Envtl. L. 341, 367 (2022).

A broader view of discrimination encompasses actions that are not grounded in intentional, conscious prejudice, but that, because of the structure or workings of social and political institutions, have discriminatory effects. For example, an all-white zoning board may render decisions with discriminatory effects because of unconscious racial prejudices, or because minority citizens, who do not live in the same neighborhoods and are not part of the same social networks as the board members, have less access to them, or because the white board members do not live in the area impacted by a proposed LULU, or because the decision-makers are less interested in the fate of minority residents for political reasons. In some respects, all of the above authors' insights point to specific mechanisms by which this form of "structural" or "institutional" racism works. In the following article, Professors Shelly Page and Patricia Broussard examine environmental racism and its definitions.

Shelly Taylor Page & Patricia A. Broussard, *Environmental Racism in America: Minority Communities As Dumping Grounds for Environmental Waste*

49 S. Ill. U. L.J. 199 (2025)

Inequity based on race is a significant issue in many parts of the world, particularly concerning access to necessary resources and services. The United States has taken steps to rectify this inequity by passing legislation to increase access to these essential resources and services; however, continuing egregious instances of environmental racism, such as the Flint, Michigan Water Crisis, illustrate the disparities in our society. Environmental racism refers to the disproportionate exposure of minority communities, primarily Black and low-income Americans, to pollution, toxic waste, and other environmental hazards. These communities often live in areas with fewer regulations and weaker protections, such as near factories, landfills, or industrial sites. Such conditions lead to higher rates of health issues like asthma, cancer, and other illnesses due to constant exposure to poor air quality, contaminated water, or unsafe living conditions. For example, Black and low-income communities are more likely to live near highways or areas where industrial waste is dumped.

Institutional racism fuels this issue by shaping policies, zoning laws, and economic opportunities in ways that grossly disadvantage these communities. Historically, redlining and segregation forced Black families into specific neighborhoods, many of which were in undesirable or hazardous areas. Even today, zoning laws and real estate practices often push poor Black Americans into areas that lack resources or environmental protections.

Both environmental and institutional racism fosters an environment where marginalized communities have limited access to safe, clean, and healthy living conditions, resulting in poorer health outcomes. Policies that prioritize the interests of wealthier, white neighborhoods while neglecting or exploiting the environment of poor and Black communities perpetuate this cycle of harm.

This Article explores environmental racism policies and how they manifest in the lives of those most impacted by their effects. This research also explores the proposed legislation that can be implemented to lessen the impact of environmental racism. By analyzing relevant laws and other public policies that have contributed to Superfund sites and disasters, such as Flint, Michigan, we can better understand how systemic failures, government oversight, corporate accountability, and environmental regulation disproportionately harm marginalized communities. Specifically, these policies have a particularly harmful impact on Black and low-income populations, perpetuating environmental injustice and institutional racism. This analysis reveals the urgent need for reforms prioritizing environmental health equity and stronger protections for vulnerable populations....

Throughout history and research, scholars have used the terms "environmental racism," "environmental inequality," and "environmental injustice" interchangeably to describe the different situations in which environmental discrimination has occurred. These terms often correlate with severe health implications for the members of the communities affected....

Before the U.S. House Committee of the Judiciary and a subcommittee on Civil Rights, Dr. [Benjamin] Chavis Jr. defined "environmental racism" as "racial discrimination in environmental [policymaking] and the unequal enforcement of environmental laws and regulations. It is the deliberate targeting of people of color communities for toxic waste facilities and the official sanctioning of a life threatening presence of poisons and pollutants in people of color communities." More simply put, it is the idea that those who are looking to build and operate waste facilities, factories that pollute, and harmful alternative ideas are intentionally targeting Communities of Color and are perpetuating health problems on a national scale. These activities make members in these marginalized communities sicker and unhealthier and lead to untimely, premature deaths.

... Dr. Robert D. Bullard ... defined "environmental racism" as "any policy, practice, or directive that differently affects or disadvantages (whether intentional or unintentional) individuals, groups or communities based on race or colour." The critical difference between Dr. Bullard's definition and that of ... Dr. Benjamin Chavis Jr., is that Bullard's does not require intent, whereas Chavis's does. Despite this difference, both definitions highlight the systemic forces that perpetuate the degradation and demise of Communities of Color and individuals inhabiting low-income environments....

Across America, a clear pattern exists in which specific populations face disproportionate exposure to pollution and risk due to systemic barriers preventing access to equitable resources. Rather than indicating a lack of action to combat the issue, it highlights the need for further eradication efforts. In that vein, several cases and legislation are pending or have already taken effect aimed at correcting issues surrounding environmental racism.

Notes and Questions

1. Intentional vs. unintentional. Consider the definition by Dr. Chavis requiring "deliberate targeting" versus Dr. Bullard's definition that includes "unintentional" effects. How do these definitional differences reflect competing theories of causation in environmental justice cases? If a plaintiff seeks to prove that a waste facility's location in a predominantly Black community violates civil rights laws, what are the advantages and challenges of proving intentional discrimination as the cause versus proving that facially neutral policies caused a disparate racial impact? Consider how different causation standards would affect the type and burden of evidence required.

2. Passage of time. The excerpt explains that "historically, redlining and segregation forced Black families into specific neighborhoods, many of which were in undesirable or hazardous areas," and that current environmental harms continue to affect these same communities. What causation challenges arise when environmental justice plaintiffs argue that historical discriminatory practices are the legal cause of contemporary environmental harms? How should courts analyze the causal chain between decades-old redlining policies and current pollution exposure? Should legal causation doctrine account for the persistent effects of historical discrimination, or does the passage of time break the causal connection?

3. Systemic forces. The excerpt describes how "institutional racism fuels this issue by shaping policies, zoning laws, and economic opportunities" and refers to "systemic barriers" and "systemic forces" that perpetuate environmental injustice. How should environmental justice doctrine address causation when alleged harm results from multiple, interconnected institutional practices rather than discrete discriminatory acts? When a community's disproportionate pollution burden stems from the cumulative effect of zoning decisions, permit approvals, enforcement patterns, and infrastructure investments over decades, what legal and practical challenges arise in establishing causation? Should environmental justice law recognize theories of "systemic causation" that differ from traditional tort causation principles?

Chapter 3

Risk and Health

Figure 3-1. A soldier with 66th Troop Command, Mississippi Army National Guard, puts water in the backseat of a car at the Smith-Wills Stadium in Jackson, Mississippi, Sept. 1, 2022. Nearly 600 Mississippi National Guardsmen were set up across seven sites throughout Jackson for residents to collect bottled water and non-potable water from water trucks to help relieve some effects of the Jackson water crisis. Photo: Staff Sgt. Connie Jones, U.S. Army National Guard.

A. Introduction

Environmental health risks permeate our daily lives. Everyone faces some degree of risk when they go outside, cross a street, or drive a car. These risks range from life-threatening events like car accidents to quality-of-life concerns such as developing asthma. Some health risks occur naturally; approximately one in five Americans will develop skin cancer in their lifetime. Others stem from environmental exposures, such as the increased skin cancer risk from stratospheric ozone depletion that allows greater ultraviolet radiation to reach Earth's surface. Health risks can be categorized as "acute" (resulting from short-term exposures with immediate adverse impacts) or "chronic" (developing after years of exposure).

Environmental justice focuses on the disproportionate health risks that certain communities experience based on who they are or where they live. These disparities affect various ethnic, racial, and socioeconomic groups and encompass impacts to physical, psychological, social, cultural, and spiritual health. Importantly, these harms often constitute affronts not just to individuals but to entire communities. As environmental justice advocates emphasize, these health disparities result from multiple contributing "stressors" that interact in complex ways. Consider mercury exposure through contaminated fish: to fully understand the health impacts, one must account for individual susceptibility and exposure circumstances (timing, duration, quantity), potential interactions with other chemical stressors like PCBs, and compounding social and economic factors such as inadequate healthcare access and nutritional deficiencies caused by poverty.

Jackson, Mississippi, represents just one of many American communities teetering on the brink of environmental health disaster. In 2022, Jackson's predominantly Black residents endured weeks without safe water after decades of infrastructure neglect culminated in a treatment plant failure. Similar conditions exist in numerous communities nationwide: Martin County, Kentucky, where residents receive cloudy, occasionally brown water; Lowndes County, Alabama, where failing septic systems create raw sewage backups; and Uniontown, Alabama, where coal ash disposal threatens groundwater. In each location, historical disinvestment in low-income communities and communities of color has created persistent, multifaceted environmental health risks.

These communities exemplify how the interaction of multiple stressors (failing infrastructure, limited political power, economic disinvestment, and environmental contamination) create conditions where basic needs for clean water, air, and soil remain unmet. This chapter examines the cascade of failures that led to ongoing environmental health tragedies, illuminates patterns that continue to threaten similar communities nationwide, and offers insights to help prepare advocates to engage in risk assessment and risk management discussions that affect the communities they serve.

The ongoing water crisis in Jackson, Mississippi shows how environmental health hazards disproportionately burden communities of color and low-income populations. With over 80 percent of residents identifying as Black and approximately 25 percent living below the poverty line, Jackson represents a clear case of environmental injustice where historical disinvestment has culminated in a public health emergency affecting nearly every aspect of community wellbeing.

Jackson's water system crisis reached national attention in August 2022 when flooding overwhelmed the already fragile O.B. Curtis Water Treatment Plant, leaving approximately 150,000 residents without reliable access to safe drinking water for weeks. However, this acute emergency merely exposed decades of systemic neglect. The Environmental Protection Agency (EPA) had been warning Jackson about its deteriorating water infrastructure since the 1970s, with a 2020 emergency order stating the system posed "an imminent and substantial endangerment" to residents. Between 2020 and 2022 alone, Jackson issued approximately 300 boil water notices, reflecting the chronic instability of the system. The city's water infrastructure includes approximately 1,500 miles of water mains, some over 100 years old, with an average of 55 breaks per 100 miles of line annually, far exceeding the "safe" rate of 15 breaks or less. Mayor Chokwe Antar Lumumba has estimated the cost of fully repairing the system at $2 billion, a staggering figure for a city with limited resources and a shrinking tax base.

Health Impacts: A Multidimensional Crisis

The health consequences of Jackson's water crisis extend far beyond immediate sanitation concerns. Lead contamination poses the most serious threat, particularly to vulnerable populations. In 2016, the Mississippi State Department of Health notified Jackson of elevated lead levels, yet the city continued accumulating violations for non-compliance with lead and copper regulations.

According to leading health researchers, "Low-level lead poisoning is a risk factor for preterm birth and for cognitive deficits and attention deficit-hyperactivity disorder (ADHD) ... in children. In adults, low-level lead poisoning is a risk factor for chronic kidney failure, hypertension, and cardiovascular disease." Bruce Lanphear, Ana Navas-Acien, & David C. Bellinger, *Lead Poisoning*, 391 New England J. Med. 1621–31 (2024). Some Jackson parents have linked long-term lead exposure to rare skin disorders and behavioral and neurologic conditions in their children.

These impacts compound Mississippi's existing public health challenges. The state has the lowest life expectancy in the U.S. and ranks worst for diabetes, hypertension, stroke, and infant mortality rates. Families divert limited resources to purchase bottled water, with some spending hundreds monthly. Healthcare costs from contamination-related conditions create additional financial strain on an economically vulnerable population.

Environmental Justice and Legal Responses

The crisis has sparked multiple legal actions reflecting environmental justice and civil rights intersections. In September 2022, the NAACP filed a Title VI complaint with the EPA against Mississippi, alleging discrimination in infrastructure funding allocation and prioritizing predominantly white communities over Jackson. By 2023, over 1,000 children had filed lawsuits against the City of Jackson and the Mississippi State Department of Health for lead poisoning. U.S. District Court Judge Carlton Reeves allowed these cases to proceed, describing the allegations against the state health department as "straight-up negligence." *J. W. v. City of Jackson, Mississippi*, 663 F. Supp. 3d 624 (2023). The federal Department of Justice also filed complaints in November 2022 for Safe Drinking Water Act violations, resulting in the appointment of an interim third-party manager. In March 2024, a federal court granted the Mississippi Poor People's Campaign intervention status in EPA proceedings, giving residents formal voice in decisions shaping their water system's future, an important step toward environmental justice community inclusion.

The crisis stems from historical racial segregation and white flight. Following 1970s–80s school integration, Jackson lost over 20 percent of its population in 40 years, dramatically reducing the tax base while leaving aging infrastructure requiring increasing maintenance. Political tensions between the Democratic city government and Republican state legislature have complicated solutions. When Jackson requested $47 million for sewer repairs, it received only $3 million. These patterns reflect nationwide environmental justice trends seen in Flint, Michigan; Martin County, Kentucky; and Lowndes County, Alabama, communities facing similar crises from historical disinvestment. Climate change will likely worsen these infrastructure vulnerabilities without comprehensive policy solutions. For further background on the roots of the Jackson water crisis, see Emily Brennan, *Environmental (In)Justice: Evaluating the Factors That Led to the Jackson Water Crisis & Proposing a Solution for Environmental Justice in Mississippi*, 41 Miss. Col. L. Rev. 244 (2023).

Congress approved $600 million in December 2022 for Jackson's water system—$150 million for technical assistance and $450 million for capital projects. The Biden EPA actively oversaw reforms, with Administrator Michael Regan making multiple city visits. Community organizations like the Mississippi Rapid Response Coalition distributed bottled water, installed filters, and advocated for systemic changes. Despite these efforts, challenges persist. Many residents distrust tap water despite safety assurances. Years of unsafe water created lasting community trauma. While emergency responses addressed immediate needs, long-term sustainability remains uncertain without continued investment and political support.

The Jackson water crisis exemplifies decades of environmental injustice and underinvestment in communities of color. As infrastructure ages and climate change intensifies, similar crises threaten vulnerable communities nationwide. Solutions require substantial infrastructure investment, meaningful community participation, legal accountability for environmental discrimination, and acknowledgment of historical inequities that created these disparities.

Catherine Coleman Flowers, environmental justice activist and founder of the Center for Rural Enterprise and Environmental Justice, observed:

> Today, Jackson is the embodiment of neglect, of collapsing infrastructure, of environmental justice at its most extreme. Families have been left without sufficient water pressure to flush toilets. Students must attend school virtually because of failing water and sanitation infrastructure. Cancer patients have been asked to leave hospitals because the water conditions are unsafe. These are the circumstances in a capital city—unheard of in the rest of America.

Catherine Coleman Flowers, *The "Blackest City in America" Is the Embodiment of Environmental Injustice*, Time Magazine, Jan. 28, 2025.

When health and environmental agencies evaluate and respond to the harms of environmental contamination, they frequently consider the problem in terms of risk to human health, understood in the narrow, individual, physiological sense of the term. Agencies for the most part proceed chemical by chemical and consider whether human contact with that chemical is expected to result in an increased likelihood of various human health "endpoints" such as neurological damage or cancer. Agencies make this determination by means of risk assessment, an analytical tool that often is intended to produce a quantitative prediction of health impacts for given levels of environmental contamination. For example, risk assessment may attempt to quantify the probability of IQ deficits in children associated with a certain level of exposure to lead in drinking water.

Quantitative risk assessment enjoyed ascendancy during the 1980s, when it was increasingly employed by health, environmental, and safety agencies to set human health-based standards. Although the use of risk assessment in the regulatory context has been criticized from numerous quarters, risk assessment continues to improve along with advances in physical and social sciences. In view of risk assessment's prominent role in environmental decision-making, it is important to understand the fundamentals of risk assessment as well as the paradigms within which it operates.

Section B of this chapter begins by outlining fundamental elements of quantitative risk assessment. Section C canvasses some of the early criticisms of risk assessment and risk management that have been raised from an environmental justice and other perspectives. Section D assesses recent policy shifts promoting approaches to risk assessment more attuned to concerns for environmental justice. Section E takes a brief look at risk concerns specific to children's health. Section F examines historic concerns and recent advances promoting consideration of cumulative impacts in risk assessment and risk management. Section G concludes the chapter with a look at integrating scientific evidence into action for the benefit of overburdened communities.

Generally, risk regulation is thought to involve a separation between risk assessment, which is the measurement of risk according to objective, scientific principles, and risk management, which involves subjective, value-laden policy judgments on how to address risks deemed "unacceptable." As will become apparent, however, a strict separation between risk assessment and risk management may not always be possible (or advisable) in practice.

The seminal discussion of the risk assessment process in the regulatory context is the National Research Council, RISK ASSESSMENT IN THE FEDERAL GOVERNMENT: MANAGING THE PROCESS (1983) (known as the "Red Book"). Three later reports of similar national significance are National Research Council, ISSUES IN RISK ASSESSMENT (1993); National Research Council, SCIENCE AND JUDGMENT IN RISK ASSESSMENT (1994); and National Research Council, SCIENCE AND DECISIONS: ADVANCING RISK ASSESSMENT (2009).

In addition to the materials discussed in this chapter, other pieces that examine risk assessment and environmental justice include Sheila R. Foster, VULNERABILITY JUSTICE: A NEW FRAMEWORK FOR ENVIRONMENTAL POLICY (2023); David Konisky & Sanya Carley, *Justice and Environmental Hazards: A Review of Evidence and Emerging Issues in the United States*, 13 ANN. REV. ENV'T & RESOURCES 1 (2023); Devesh Lal,

Racializing Risk: Identifying Why Environmental Justice Matters in the Clean Water State Revolving Fund Program, 56 Stan. L. Rev. 823 (2024); Patrick C. Breysse et al., *National Institutes of Health/Environmental Protection Agency Centers of Excellence on Environmental Health Disparities Research: Advances in Understanding Environmental Health Disparities*, 134 Am. J. Pub. Health 34 (2023); Martha E. Wadsworth & Alexandra F. Werntz, *Toxic Economic Inequality: Addressing the Mental Health Impacts of Environmental and Economic Injustice*, 93 Am. Psychologist 267 (2023); Kyle Whyte, *Indigenous Climate Change Studies: Indigenizing Futures, Decolonizing the Anthropocene*, 55 Eng. Lang. Notes 153 (2022); Brie D. Sherwin, *Pride and Prejudice and Administrative Zombies: How Economic Woes, Outdated Environmental Regulations, and State Exceptionalism Failed Flint, Michigan*, 88 U. Colo. L. Rev. 653 (2017); Catherine O'Neill, *Exposed: Asking the Wrong Question in Risk Regulation*, 48 Ariz. St. L.J. 704 (2016); Vincent R. Johnson, *Nanotechnology, Environmental Risks, and Regulatory Options*, 121 Penn. St. L. Rev. 471 (2016); Mike Ewall, *Legal Tools for Environmental Equity vs. Environmental Justice*, 13 Sustainable Dev. L. & Pol'y 4 (2013); Catherine A. O'Neill, *Environmental Justice in the Tribal Context: A Madness to EPA's Method*, 38 Envtl. L. 495 (2008); Carl F. Cranor, *Risk Assessment, Susceptible Subpopulations, and Environmental Justice*, *in* The Law of Environmental Justice: Theories and Procedures to Address Disproportionate Risks 341 (Michael B. Gerrard & Sheila R. Foster eds., 2d ed. 2008).

B. Fundamentals of Quantitative Risk Assessment

Although "risk" is not inherently or necessarily a quantitative concept, formalized assessments of the harm that can be expected to result from exposure to toxic contamination start from the assumption that risk can be estimated and expressed in numerical terms. Today, the dominant paradigm for considering risk from environmental hazards entails a quantitative description of the likelihood and severity of adverse effects. Of course, contamination may adversely affect both human and non-human components of ecosystems, and agencies may need to consider both sorts of effects. However, the assessment methods that have evolved for each are somewhat different, with assessments of the impacts on humans often termed "human health risk assessments" and assessments of the broader environmental impacts termed "ecological risk assessments." Throughout this chapter, we will be concerned primarily with efforts in the former category.

The basic quantitative risk assessment method is outlined in the following excerpt.

Carnegie Commission on Science, Technology, and Government, *Risk and the Environment: Improving Regulatory Decision Making*

(1993)

Risk assessment is a composite of established disciplines, including toxicology, biostatistics, epidemiology, economics, and demography. The goals of risk assessment are to characterize the nature of the adverse effects and to produce quantitative estimates of one or both of the following fundamental quantities: (1) the *probability* that an individual (a hypothetical or identified person) will suffer disease or death as a result of a specified exposure to a pollutant or pollutants; and (2) the *consequences* of such an exposure to an entire population (i.e., the number of cases of disease or death).

Risk assessment can either be generic (e.g., an estimate of the number of excess annual cancers caused by all 189 hazardous air pollutants identified in the 1990 Clean Air Act Amendments) or site- and/or chemical-specific (e.g., the probability that a specified child will suffer neurological impairment as a result of exposure to lead in his household drinking water).

The regulatory process is generally thought to encompass two elements, risk assessment and risk management. The distinction between the two components is important, though controversial. Risk assessment is usually conceived as the "objective" part of the process, and risk management the subjective part. In risk assessment the analyst decides how big the problem is, while in risk management political decision makers decide what to do about the problem. The "conventional wisdom" (which some believe needs rethinking) stresses that risk management must not influence the processes and assumptions made in risk assessment, so the two functions must be kept conceptually and administratively separate.

Numerical estimates derived from risk assessment serve as inputs to several very different kinds of decisions, including (1) "acceptable risk" determinations (wherein action is taken if the risk exceeds some "bright line," which can be zero); (2) "cost-benefit" determinations, where the risks reduced by a proposed action are translated into benefits (e.g., lives saved, life-years extended), expressed in dollar amounts, and compared to the estimated costs of implementing the action and some rule of thumb regarding how much cost it is wise to incur to achieve a given level of benefit (e.g., $10 million to save one additional life); and (3) "cost-effectiveness" determinations, where the action that maximizes the amount of risk reduction (not necessarily expressed in dollar terms) per unit cost is favored.

Since at least 1983 (with the publication of the National Research Council's "Red Book"), the dominant paradigm for risk assessment has been a sequential, four-step process:

- *Hazard Identification*: in which a qualitative determination is made of what kinds of adverse health or ecological effects a substance can cause. Typically, agencies have focused on cancer as the effect that drives further analysis and regulation. So, for example, a typical hazard identification for vinyl chloride released from industrial facilities would involve the collection and critical analysis of short-term test-tube assays (for mutagenicity, etc.), of long-term animal assays (typically, two-year rodent carcinogenicity tests), and of human epidemiologic data—either cohort studies (in which populations exposed to vinyl chloride are followed to assess whether their rates of any disease were significantly greater than those of unexposed or less-exposed populations) or case-control studies (which focus on victims of a particular disease to see whether they were significantly more likely to have been exposed to vinyl chloride than similar but disease-free individuals).

- *Exposure assessment*: in which a determination is made of the amounts of a substance to which a hypothetical person (usually the "maximally exposed individual") and/or the total population are exposed. To return to the vinyl chloride example, this part of risk assessment would bring to bear techniques of emissions characterization (how much vinyl chloride leaves the plant in a given time?), fate-and-transport analysis (how is the chemical dispersed in the atmosphere and transformed into other compounds?), uptake analysis (how much air do people breathe, both outdoors and indoors?), and demographic analysis (how many hours per day do people spend in various locations near the plant, and how long do they reside in one locale before moving away?).
- *Dose-response assessment*: in which an estimate is made of the probability or extent of injury at the exposure levels determined above, by quantifying the "potency" of the chemical in question. For vinyl chloride again, scientists would determine its carcinogenic potency by fitting the bioassay data (number of tumors produced at different exposure levels) to a mathematical model (usually one that is linear at low doses), and then transforming the resultant potency estimate for rodents into a human potency estimate through the use of a "scaling factor" (usually, a ratio of the body surface areas of the two species). Additionally, human epidemiologic data could be used to validate or supplant the animal-based potency estimate.
- *Risk characterization*: in which the results of the above steps are integrated to describe the nature of the adverse effects and the strength of the evidence and to present one or more "risk numbers." For example, EPA might say, "This vinyl chloride plant is estimated to produce up to 3 excess cases of liver cancer every 70 years among the 100,000 people living within 1 mile of the facility" or "the maximally exposed individual faces an excess lifetime liver cancer risk of 5.4 x 10-4."

Risk assessment is essentially a tool for extrapolating from scientific data to a risk number. The tool is made up of a host of assumptions, which are an admixture of science and policy. Sometimes either science or policy predominates, but it is often difficult to get a broad consensus that this is so. . . .

Notes and Questions

1. "Excess" cancers. In the preceding excerpt, note the references to "excess" cancers, a measure of the number of cancer cases that may be attributed directly to some exposure to an environmental toxin. Estimations of excess cancers recognize that people get cancer whether or not they are exposed to environmental toxins. Based on recent estimates, more than one third of all Americans will be diagnosed with cancer at some point in their lives. *See* National Cancer Institute, Cancer Statistics, available at www.cancer.gov. Given that more than three thousand in ten thousand people would be expected to be diagnosed with cancer anyway, should we still care that one additional person in that same group of ten thousand might get cancer from environmental exposure? What is your best argument for why we should still care about this one person?

2. Non-cancer risks. Often lost in the debate about risk calculations and "excess cancers" is the fact that many devastating health impacts from pollution have nothing to do with cancer. Poor air quality from smog and particulate matter may trigger asthma attacks in children and adults, a leading cause of emergency room visits and lost days of school and work. Accordingly, advocates for environmental justice should always consider the complete range of contaminants of concern in a particular community and the potential effects of each contaminant. For a comprehensive listing of toxic substances and associated health effects, *see* the website of the federal Agency for Toxic Substances and Disease Registry (ATSDR): www.atsdr.cdc.gov.

3. Risk perceptions. Psychologists and other researchers have long observed that the risks perceived by the public often vary dramatically from the risks calculated by experts. Explanations for the disparity between public and expert perceptions of risk often center around the concept of "dread risks." Drawing on the influential research of psychologist Paul Slovic, dread risks may be explained in large part using two variables:

> The first variable represents the extent to which a risk is dreaded—that is, "catastrophic, hard to prevent, fatal, inequitable, threatening to future generations, not easily reduced, increasing, involuntary, and [personally] threatening." The second variable relates to the familiarity of a risk—that is, its "observability, knowledge, immediacy of consequences, and familiarity." Examples of the high-dread, low-familiarity risks are nuclear power, nuclear waste disposal, uranium mining, liquefied natural gas, pollution associated with burning coal, DNA technology, and satellite crashes. Examples of low-dread, high-familiarity risks are bicycles, shock from electric appliances, recreational boating, chainsaws, and trampolines. As one might expect, the higher a risk is on the dread and unfamiliarity scales, the more people tend to want strict regulation in hopes of reducing the risk.
>
> Certainly not everyone perceives even high-dread risks in the same way. Cultural cognition theory (CCT) hypothesizes that individuals perceive risks in ways that reflect and reinforce their cultural worldviews—whether they are individualists, egalitarians, hierarchs, or fatalists. Take geographic variations

> in risk perception. France, for example, is far more accepting of nuclear power than the United States. French people, however, are more likely to hold hierarchical worldviews than individualistic Americans. Thus, they are both more accepting of the risks associated with nuclear power, and more comfortable with the ability of elite experts to manage those risks.

Emily Hammond, *Public Participation in Risk Regulation: The Flaws of Formality*, 2016 UTAH L. REV. 169, 174–175 (2016).

One conclusion flowing from these observations is that "merely educating the public will not lead to enlightened public opinions about risk. Instead, people are more likely to further entrench their views when confronted with new information that is inconsistent with their cultural predispositions." *Id.* at 175.

If education of the public will simply "further entrench" people in their own established views, how then should regulators seek meaningful public involvement in risk regulation? Should regulators such as the EPA still seek to address serious health risks such as indoor radon even if these risks are not widely recognized by the public? Is it wrong for the EPA to continue investing substantial resources on cleaning up hazardous waste sites even if these sites are not the highest health risks according to risk experts? What are the arguments on either side of this question?

In considering the disparity between the public and expert perceptions of risk, it must be observed that risk assessment is never perfect and always continues to develop.

C. Early Critiques of Quantitative Risk Assessment and Risk Management

Many of the early criticisms of quantitative risk assessment reflected concerns for environmental justice. The risk assessment process has been criticized historically for instating a highly technical process reserved to a cadre of "experts," one that ignores the expertise and lived experience of those most affected. The risk process, driven by technical experts, may diminish opportunities for public participation. Among other things, risk assessors may miss significant risks to community members based upon misunderstandings of lifeways, the totality of environmental exposures in a community, and other factors that may be unknown to outsiders. Professor Robert Kuehn discussed some of these points in one of the first critiques of risk assessment from the perspective of environmental justice.

Robert R. Kuehn, *The Environmental Justice Implications of Quantitative Risk Assessment*

1996 U. ILLINOIS L. REV. 103 (1996)

Methodological Limitations of Quantitative Risk Assessment and Their Impact on Environmental Justice

Quantitative risk assessment has problems addressing the aggregation of risks, which include multiple exposure, cumulative exposures, and existing exposures. Multiple exposures occur when a person is exposed to a combination of two or more different chemicals or pollutants, while cumulative exposures result when an individual is exposed to one or more chemicals or pollutants from different media or over time. Existing or "background" exposures or risks are those exposures that a person presently experiences, before the addition of any new exposures or risks. Risk assessments generally address the risks posed by one chemical or one source, and a regulatory decision of what is an "acceptable" risk customarily focuses on the risk posed by that single chemical or source. The total risk that a person faces, however, is an aggregate of these many, many risks, each of which individually may be deemed acceptable but in the aggregate may be quite substantial. If a person already has a significant level of existing or background exposure or risk, then the addition of even a small exposure or risk may have a greater effect on that person than on another person who is not already above or near some threshold of safety.... Because minorities and low-income communities face greater exposures to environmental contaminants, it is reasonable to conclude that the failure of risk assessment to account for multiple and cumulative exposures impacts these subpopulations more adversely than other population groups...

Synergistic effects among pollutants that mix also pose a methodological problem for quantitative risk assessment.... The phenomenon of synergism may be widespread among pollutants. Approximately 5% of chemicals exhibit effects that are more or less than additive. Although this percentage may seem relatively small, because there are so many chemicals, synergistic possibilities are huge. For example, if there were 12,000 chemicals in commerce today, and 2.5% reacted synergistically, almost 1.8 million pairs of chemicals would act synergistically.

Despite the propensity for chemicals to react synergistically and increase in toxicity, risk assessments rarely take synergism into account....

A 70 kg, White Male Complex

... There is a high degree of variability in the response of humans to different levels of pollution. Age, lifestyle, genetic background, sex, ethnicity, and race may all play an important role in enhancing the susceptibility of persons to environmentally related disease. Studies have shown human variability of more than 1,000-fold in drug metabolism and between 3 and 150-fold in the carcinogenic metabolism of various chemicals....

[R]isk assessment most accurately portrays the risks of a particular subgroup—the healthy, seventy-kilogram, white male. Risk assessments use a seventy-kilogram male with the general biology of a Caucasian, as a so-called reference man, in developing dose-response predictions and assume that this reference man is an appropriate surrogate for minorities, as well as women and children. In addition, the dose-response models used to extrapolate from high-dose animal studies to lower-dose human exposures are based on the assumption that the exposed population is of uniform susceptibility. The result of relying on this reference man is a risk assessment characterization that fits far less than half the nation's population, because the majority are women, children, the elderly, sick, or people of color....

* * *

Over 20 years ago, law professors Cary Coglianese and Gary Marchant theorized "four basic approaches" that agencies such as the EPA might adopt for greater consistency in risk management decisions. As you read the following article, consider the apparent virtues as well as the political and physical limitations to each theoretical approach.

Cary Coglianese & Gary E. Marchant, *Shifting Sands: The Limits of Science in Risk Standards*

152 U. Penn. L. Rev. 1255 (2004)

Regulatory decisions, such as the selection of air quality standards, involve enormous stakes in terms of both health consequences and economic burdens. How can EPA provide a more coherent justification for these significant decisions than it offered in its most recent NAAQS revisions? A regulatory agency such as EPA has four basic approaches available that it can use to provide a consistent justification for making risk management decisions such as setting ambient standards: (1) eliminate all risks (or all nonnaturally occurring risks); (2) avoid unacceptable risks; (3) avoid unacceptable costs (sometimes described as the feasibility approach); and (4) balance costs and benefits. Although these approaches are not all equally sound strategies—nor are they all currently permissible under the Supreme Court's interpretation of the Clean Air Act—they do illustrate the range of possible ways to provide a consistent explanation for risk management decision making.

Eliminate All Risks

The first approach is conceptually straightforward: eliminate all risks. This principle could be consistently applied if EPA set its standards at levels at which it believed there would be absolutely no health risks. The Agency also could take a consistent risk management approach if it chose to minimize risk by setting standards at background levels, thereby opting to eliminate all risks except those that are naturally occurring (a zero additive risk approach)....

Avoid Unacceptable Risks

A second approach would be for the Agency to establish a level of acceptable risk for its air quality standards. Rather than minimizing all risks, the Agency would only reduce risks to a consistent and tolerable level. As with the minimize risk principle, the acceptable risk approach focuses exclusively on the benefits to be reaped from a risk standard. It does not try to maximize those benefits, but simply to deliver a desirable level of health benefits.

The acceptable risk approach has been used in other regulatory contexts. For example, in setting standards for hazardous air pollutants, EPA has presumptively defined "acceptable risk" to mean a maximum individual mortality risk of no greater than one in ten thousand. The Agency has similarly set acceptable risk targets in other contexts, including the regulation of water quality, hazardous wastes, and pesticides. The Occupational Safety and Health Administration (OSHA) follows a similar approach, using a benchmark mortality risk of one in one thousand as the level of "significant risk" on which it bases its occupational health standards....

Avoid Unacceptable Costs

A third approach to consistent risk management is the mirror image of the acceptable risk approach. Instead of focusing exclusively on benefits, the cost of a regulation should be the key factor. In other words, EPA could set its standards as low as possible while keeping the costs of compliance below an acceptable level.

This approach typically has been couched in terms of feasibility—what can be achieved without high costs or severe economic disruptions. Saying that a standard is feasible implies that its costs are acceptable....

When regulatory agencies justify their risk management decisions based only on either costs or benefits, they can achieve consistent, principled decision making simply by using the same level of acceptable costs or risks across different rulemakings. Nevertheless, all the approaches we have discussed so far truncate the range of risk management criteria and may therefore lead regulatory agencies, in some cases, to make decisions that make little sense, even though they are consistent. Under the acceptable risk approach, however, agencies can affirm standards that impose significant costs without proportional health protection gains. Under the acceptable cost approach, agencies can reject opportunities to achieve significant net social benefits simply because costs are high.

Balance Costs and Benefits

With precisely these kinds of perverse outcomes in mind, a fourth approach for risk management would take both benefits and costs into consideration and seek to achieve a consistent balance of the two. By considering both costs and benefits, regulators could set risk management standards to maximize net benefits. Several environmental statutes other than the Clean Air Act actually require agencies to balance benefits and costs when they are setting risk standards. Indeed, absent statutory prohibitions to the contrary (such as now in the Clean Air Act), regulatory agencies are directed by

Executive Order No. 12,866 to assess both costs and benefits of significant proposed regulations and to "propose or adopt a [new] regulation only upon a reasoned determination that the benefits of the intended regulation justify its costs."

Of course, in practice, there will be important issues regarding measurement, valuation, and discount rates that must be treated consistently. But this is true for any other approach to risk management decision making, and regulators have developed guidelines for approaching these operational issues in consistent ways. When conducted responsibly, cost-benefit analysis can prove quite valuable in explaining regulatory agencies' decision making. It offers a consistent and systematic approach to risk management.

Notes and Questions

1. **Transparency.** Professor Kuehn accurately predicted that "some form of risk assessment is not just here to stay, but ... is likely to increase in use." Professor Kuehn accordingly advanced numerous suggestions for reforming the risk assessment process. For example, he proposed that distributional information (the demographic characteristics of the populations at risk) and information on multiple and cumulative exposures be included in all risk assessments. Another suggestion was to provide for meaningful public participation at all stages of the risk assessment process, including its design, data collection, and analysis. He also recommended that risk assessors should inform the public about the pervasive uncertainties underlying the risk assessment process, suggesting that "[w]hen these unknown factors and assumptions are revealed, the public may see the lack of confidence in the estimates and may well question the reliability and relevance of risk assessment in resolving questions about environmental exposures." *Id.* at 150–153, 158–166. The latter suggestion was essentially a call for greater transparency in the risk assessment enterprise.

2. **Susceptibility.** Among the issues that Professor Kuehn raised were those stemming from variability in *susceptibility*. As he explained, two people may be exposed to the same amount of a contaminant in the environment, for the same period of time, yet have markedly different responses. These differences in susceptibility may stem from a variety of factors, including sex, lifestage, and genetic predisposition.

3. **Exposure.** Variability in *exposure* is important to understand from the perspective of environmental justice. A group or subpopulation may be more vulnerable to a given level of environmental contamination because its members' circumstances and lifeways leave them more exposed to the contaminants than members of the general population. These people might, for example, live nearer to the fence-line of industrial facilities that emit multiple toxic air pollutants; they might live in older, deteriorated housing that harbors lead dust; they might depend to a greater extent on fish that has become contaminated with PCBs and other pollutants.

How should variability in exposure be taken into account in assessing risk? What if agencies were simply to assess the risk to the maximally exposed individual and then establish regulatory protections accordingly? Are there drawbacks to this protective response to variability in exposure?

4. Exaggerated risks? While environmental justice advocates often fear that quantitative risk assessment will underestimate health risks in certain communities, risk assessment has also come under substantial criticism from those who believe that, as currently practiced by environmental agencies, risk assessment leads to overestimates of risk and, consequently, an overinvestment by society in regulations requiring risk reduction. While supportive of risk assessment as a theoretical matter, they contend nonetheless that risk assessment methods ought to be refined in several ways. Two influential sources espousing this view are Cass R. Sunstein, Risk and Reason: Safety, Law, and the Environment (2002); and Stephen Breyer, Breaking the Vicious Circle: Toward Effective Risk Regulation (1993).

Critics have argued that environmental agencies inappropriately respond to both uncertainty and variability when they undertake a risk assessment, producing high-end estimates of risk. They cite the fact that EPA currently uses conservative responses to each instance of uncertainty, choosing, for example, an assumption about the mechanism of carcinogenesis that yields a much higher estimate of a chemical's potency than would competing assumptions. Additionally, they claim that EPA selects protective responses to each instance of variability, focusing on the highly exposed individuals represented by the 90th or 95th percentile of the distribution for the total population. While each of these assumptions might be plausible in isolation, they argue, taken together, they produce an effect of "cascading conservatism" such that the resulting estimate of risk is likely to be unrealistically high and to reflect no one's actual circumstances of exposure. For critical assessment of the "cascading conservatism" argument from an environmental justice perspective, see Catherine A. O'Neill, *Exposed: Asking the Wrong Question in Risk Regulation*, 48 Ariz. St. L.J. 703 (2016).

D. Transformations in Risk Assessment: Policy Shifts and Structural Changes

EPA and broader federal approaches to risk assessment have undergone substantial changes since the foundational frameworks of the 1980s and 1990s. While the "Red Book" (1983) established the foundational four-step risk assessment process, recent developments have significantly altered how agencies approach environmental and public health risks through both evolutionary improvements and structural reorganizations. The progression of risk assessment continued through the 2000s and 2010s with the National Research Council's Science and Decisions: Advancing Risk Assessment (the "Silver Book") in 2009, which emphasized better linkage between scientific analysis and decision-making contexts. This framework called for greater consideration of cumulative exposures, enhanced stakeholder involvement, and more explicit discussion of uncertainties in risk communication. By 2015, EPA's risk assessment approach expanded further with the *Framework for Human Health Risk*

Assessment to Inform Decision Making, which incorporated principles of problem formulation, planning and scoping, and risk management options into a more integrated framework.

The COVID-19 pandemic catalyzed additional changes in risk assessment methodologies. In 2021, federal agencies began integrating lessons from pandemic response into environmental health risk frameworks, including faster data synthesis methods, greater emphasis on risk communication, and explicit consideration of health disparities and environmental justice concerns. In 2024, consistent with 2016 amendments to the Toxic Substances Control Act, EPA published final regulations updating procedures for evaluating risk from individual chemicals, adding "overburdened communities" to the list of "potentially exposed or susceptible subpopulation," which already included infants, children, pregnant women, workers, and the elderly. *Procedures for Chemical Risk Evaluation Under the Toxic Substances Control Act (TSCA)*, 89 Fed. Reg. 37028 (May 3, 2024). The Biden administration also issued executive orders on artificial intelligence that included provisions for using AI to improve risk assessment methods, particularly for evaluating chemical mixtures and cumulative impacts. However, these executive orders were subsequently revoked by the Trump administration upon taking office in January 2025.

The Trump administration's return to power in January 2025 initiated significant policy changes across federal risk assessment and risk management programs with EPA Administrator Lee Zeldin announcing a comprehensive agenda of deregulation, as further explored in Chapter 5 (Environmental Regulations). As part of broader government "efficiency" initiatives, the Trump EPA announced organizational restructuring in 2025, including plans to reduce staffing levels and reorganize its Office of Research and Development (ORD). The restructuring purportedly involves redistributing scientific functions across EPA offices and consolidating certain programs. Administrator Zeldin stated that the reorganization aims to ensure the agency can fulfill its statutory obligations while operating more efficiently.

Parallel changes may occur at the Department of Health and Human Services (HHS) under Robert F. Kennedy Jr. Secretary Kennedy announced a substantial reorganization aimed at streamlining the department's structure and improving coordination across its various agencies. The restructuring includes consolidating administrative functions and centralizing certain policy oversight responsibilities that were previously distributed across individual agencies. Kennedy's approach to health risk assessment emphasizes what he terms a "precautionary framework" that focuses on prevention and early intervention. This approach purportedly reflects concerns about chronic disease rates in America and seeks to address what the administration views as systemic issues in the nation's health outcomes. The HHS has undertaken reviews of various assessment guidelines and advisory processes as part of this broader health policy initiative. The Trump administration has also made personnel changes to various advisory committees, including the CDC's Advisory Committee on Immunization Practices, appointing new members.

The COVID-19 pandemic provided important lessons about surveillance systems, risk communication, and emergency response that continue to inform federal risk assessment and risk management approaches. Various aspects of pandemic response, including vulnerability mapping and community-based monitoring, have been incorporated into ongoing environmental health risk assessment frameworks, though funding priorities and program emphasis have shifted under the second Trump administration. These organizational and policy changes represent a significant shift in federal risk assessment infrastructure. The current administration emphasizes regulatory efficiency, cost reduction, and streamlined decision-making processes as key priorities. Supporters argue these changes will reduce bureaucratic inefficiency and regulatory burden while maintaining essential public health protections.

The implications of these changes extend to state and local governments, regulated industries, and various stakeholder groups who interact with federal risk assessment processes. The long-term effects of current policy shifts on risk assessment methodology, scientific advisory processes, and public health outcomes continue to develop as implementation proceeds. The ultimate impact of current reforms on risk assessment practice, regulatory effectiveness, and public health outcomes will likely be evaluated over time as new organizational structures and policy approaches are fully implemented and assessed. *See also* U.S. Dep't. of Health & Human Servs., Office of Minority Health, *Minority Health Social Vulnerability Index,* https://minorityhealth.hhs.gov/minority-health-svi; UNC Superfund Research Program, *NC ENVIROSCAN: Environmental Justice Screening Tool,* https://enviroscan.org.

Notes and Questions

1. Political influence vs. scientific integrity. Secretary Kennedy's appointment at HHS represents a significant departure from traditional approaches to protecting public health. Kennedy has advocated replacing what he calls "regulatory capture" with a more precautionary, community-centered approach. How should environmental justice advocates navigate the potential benefits of increased precaution against the risks of decreased scientific rigor? Consider Kennedy's proposal to reexamine the safety of fluoride in drinking water, which could affect low-income communities that rely on public water systems. What strategic approaches might best balance community protection with evidence-based decision-making when regulatory standards are being reconsidered under this new approach? How might advocacy strategies need to shift when interacting with agencies that may be more responsive to anecdotal evidence of harm than traditional epidemiological studies?

2. Evidentiary standards and health protection. The standard of evidence required to justify regulatory action dramatically affects environmental justice outcomes. Historically, agencies have often required extensive proof of harm before taking protective action, with vulnerable communities bearing the burden of this delay. Kennedy's HHS could lower thresholds for action when potential harm disproportionately affects marginalized communities. What ethical frameworks should guide decisions about appropriate evidentiary standards when scientific uncertainty exists? How might standards of proof vary appropriately depending on factors like exposure vulnerability, hazard severity, and reversibility of potential harms? What institutional safeguards could prevent arbitrary application of different standards based on political considerations? Compare outcomes in cases where the precautionary principle was applied (e.g., European chemical regulation under REACH) versus those requiring more substantial proof of harm before action (e.g., U.S. regulation of PFAS chemicals). What practical guidelines could help agencies determine when sufficient evidence exists to take protective action, particularly for communities already facing multiple environmental stressors?

3. Pandemic lessons for environmental justice. The COVID-19 pandemic demonstrated how environmental and social factors create disproportionate vulnerability to health threats. In Chicago, for example, neighborhoods with higher levels of PM2.5 air pollution experienced significantly higher COVID-19 mortality rates, with the association strongest in low-income, predominantly Black communities. Similar, disproportionate impacts of COVID-19 were also identified in Louisiana, Indian reservations, and many other parts of the country where residents already faced struggles for clean air, clean water, and access to health care. *See* Clifford J. Villa, *Remaking Environmental Justice*, 66 Loyola L. Rev. 469, 473 (2020).

What specific methodological innovations from pandemic response (e.g., real-time data collection, vulnerability indices, community-based monitoring) should be permanently integrated into environmental justice work? What institutional changes would be needed to maintain these approaches beyond the pandemic recovery period? Consider how pandemic-era innovations in telemedicine and digital access might also transform how environmental health information is collected and disseminated in underserved communities.

4. Community participation in risk assessment. Despite decades of acknowledgment that community expertise is valuable, risk assessment remains largely dominated by technical experts using complex models often inaccessible to affected communities. In situations like the Jackson, Mississippi, water crisis, community members identified water quality concerns years before official recognition, yet lacked mechanisms to translate their observations into regulatory action. What specific structural changes to the risk assessment process would create space for meaningful community participation without simply adding token "community input" sessions?

How might traditional ecological knowledge and community expertise be incorporated alongside technical analysis when evaluating risks in Indigenous communities? What models of community-based participatory research have successfully balanced scientific rigor with genuine power-sharing in the risk assessment process? Identify examples where community knowledge has successfully influenced risk characterization and compare these with instances where community input was solicited but evidently ignored.

Figure 3-2. Wild rice, or *manoomin*, on the Reservation of the Leech Lake Band of Ojibwe in northern Minnesota. Wetlands on the Reservation that are the native home of *manoomin* may be at risk of contamination from a nearby Superfund site, threatening a significant source of the Tribe's food, income, and cultural identity. Across the Upper Midwest, *manoomin* may also be in decline from factors including climate change and habitat modification, impacting many tribal communities. For background, see Madeline Nyblade, *First We Must Consider Manoomin/Psiŋ: Impacts of Climate and Land Cover Change on Wild Rice* (Dissertation: U. Minn.) (2023). Photo: U.S. EPA, 2024.

5. Indigenous health assessment. Tribal members and researchers have developed alternatives to traditional risk assessment. One approach embraces identification of Indigenous Health Indicators to comprehend the unique values of individual tribes and tribal members. In the Swinomish Indian Tribal Community of Washington State, for example, "'health' is shaped by the many interrelated relationships between humans, non-human beings, nature, local natural resources, and the spiritual realm (i.e., social and cultural values). Moreover, health is thought of on familial and community scales, rather than an individual scale." Jamie Donatuto et al., *The "Value" of Values-Driven Data in Identifying Indigenous Health and Climate Change Priorities*, 158 Climatic Change 161 (2020).

E. Risks to Children

Risk assessment practices are increasingly recognizing the disproportionate risks faced by children. Children are especially vulnerable to environmental hazards because their systems are still developing, because they eat proportionately more food, drink more fluids, and breathe more air than adults, and because their behavior patterns, such as playing close to the ground and hand-to-mouth activity, increase their exposure to hazards. In 1995, EPA adopted a policy requiring that the environmental health risks of children be evaluated in risk assessments. EPA also pledged that it would set new regulatory standards at levels protective enough to address the potentially heightened risks faced by children and that it would re-evaluate a number of existing regulations to see if they met this standard. In 1997, President Clinton issued an executive order requiring that each agency make it a high priority to identify and assess environmental health and safety risks that may disproportionately affect children, and ensure that its actions address these disproportionate risks. *Protection of Children from Environmental Health Risks and Safety Risks*, Exec. Order No. 13,045, 62 Fed. Reg. 19,885 (April 23, 1997). The 1996 Food Quality Protection Act also explicitly requires EPA to address the special risks to infants and children when setting pesticide tolerances, the levels of chemical pesticide residues permissible on foods. If EPA does not have complete or reliable data to assess risks to children or infants, it can require an additional tenfold safety factor. 21 U.S.C. § 346a(b)(2)(C).

In 2008, EPA published a handbook setting forth the different factors that describe children's circumstances of exposure. U.S. EPA, CHILD-SPECIFIC EXPOSURE FACTORS HANDBOOK (2008). While EPA had previously provided some guidance as to how risk assessors ought to account for children's unique circumstances, this was the first time in which EPA issued comprehensive guidance exclusively devoted to children. The following excerpt from a medical journal shows the risk of environmental injustice to children and the link to toxic environmental exposures.

Philip J. Landrigan, Virginia A. Rauh & Maida P. Galvez, *Environmental Justice and the Health of Children*

77 MOUNT SINAI J. MEDICINE 178 (2010)

Evidence has been building for 100 years that toxic exposures in the environment can cause and aggravate disease in children. This body of evidence has become especially compelling in the past 2 decades:

- Rates of asthma are increased in children exposed to second-hand cigarette smoke.
- Rates of asthma are increased in children exposed to particulate air pollution.
- Risk of sudden infant death syndrome is increased in babies exposed to particulate air pollution.

- Neurodevelopmental impairment with a reduced intelligence quotient (IQ), shortening of attention span, and disruption of behavior is increased in children exposed to lead.
- Neurodevelopmental impairment with a reduction of IQ is increased in children exposed to polychlorinated biphenyls.
- Neurodevelopmental impairment with a reduction of IQ and shortening of attention span is increased in children exposed prenatally to methyl mercury.
- Lower birth weight, smaller head circumference at birth, and subsequent developmental delays are increased in children exposed prenatally to the organophosphate pesticide chlorpyrifos.
- Neurodevelopmental impairment with a reduction of IQ and disruption of behavior is increased in children exposed prenatally to ethyl alcohol; this is called fetal alcohol syndrome.
- There is an increased risk of preterm birth associated with prenatal exposure to tobacco smoke...

Disease of environmental origin is preventable. Disease caused by environmental degradation and environmental injustice is the result of human activity and is therefore preventable through modification or cessation of the activity that damages or pollutes the environment. To begin to address environmental injustice and its consequences for human health, we need solid evidence-based research on the long-term human health effects of exposure to a range of physical, chemical, and social exposures beginning before conception and continuing throughout childhood into adulthood....

In addition, we need to recognize that inequalities in exposures arise at both the community and individual levels, so efforts to redress these disparities cannot be limited to behavioral interventions. Broad societal efforts and a reordering of priorities are needed to redress social and structural conditions that result in unacceptably high levels of toxic exposure for whole populations. Protection of the vulnerable must become a moral and ethical beacon that guides decision making at all levels of government and business. An example of such enlightened decision making is to be found in the Food Quality Protection Act of 1996. This is [a] major federal pesticide law in the United States, and it is the only federal environmental statute that makes explicit provision for the protection of children's health in the setting of pesticide standards. As a result of environmental injustice, too many American children live their lives burdened by biological and social conditions that severely limit their potential for success. The effects on children are the cruelest consequences of environmental injustice.

Beyond childhood, the disproportionate exposure in early life of children in poor communities to environmental hazards sets the stage for a lifetime of suboptimal health and diminished achievement and thus helps to perpetuate the intergenerational cycle of disenfranchisement and poverty.

Notes and Questions

1. "Cycle of disenfranchisement." In the excerpt above, the authors posit that early childhood exposures to toxic substances may help "perpetuate the intergenerational cycle of disenfranchisement and poverty." How would you understand this "cycle" to work? Using childhood exposure to lead as an example, how do the neurological impacts on children perpetuate poverty in poor, urban communities?

2. Moving targets. Dr. Philip Landrigan is one of the leading advocates for children's health, following landmark studies he conducted in the early 1970s demonstrating the effects of lead smelter emissions on children's health. The standard test for children exposed to lead involves drawing a blood sample and analyzing it for lead, with results reported in micrograms (one millionth of a gram) per deciliter (μg/dL) of blood. In 1971, the threshold for childhood lead poisoning in the United States was defined as 40 μg/dL. By 1991, due in part to the work of Dr. Landrigan, the U.S. threshold had fallen to 10 μg/dL. By the early 2000s, scientists knew there was no safe level of lead in children, with amounts even between 0 and 5 μg/dL showing significant impacts in cognitive development as measured by decrements in IQ. Bruce P. Lanphear et al., *Low-Level Environmental Lead Exposure and Children's Intellectual Function: An International Pooled Analysis*, 113 Envtl. Health Persp. 894 (2005). Given that the early definitions of childhood lead poisoning (with industry influence) proved very wrong, how should environmental justice advocates today approach supposed "safe" levels of exposure for any toxic substances? What should be the respective roles of science and policy so that a community will feel confident that their health is being protected?

F. Cumulative Impacts

Environmental justice advocates have long argued that risk assessment, as historically practiced, grossly understated the risks actually faced by those in tribes, communities of color, and low-income communities. This was so, in part, because risk assessors typically focused on a single chemical or source in isolation (for example, "a risk assessment for dioxin," or "an assessment of risk from TCE in groundwater" at a particular contaminated site). But, as affected communities have pointed out, people are rarely exposed to only one chemical contaminant; rather, they are often exposed to multiple chemicals present in their environment (e.g., TCE and PCBs in contaminated soils) or chemicals present in multiple media (e.g., lead in drinking water and lead in the paint of older housing stock). While this historic failure to account for cumulative exposures has been a shortcoming of risk assessment generally, its import is amplified for communities with EJ concerns, who are often among the most exposed to mixtures of chemical contaminants in their environments. Indeed, thoughtful consideration of cumulative impacts in environmental decision-making has been described as the "Holy Grail" of environmental justice. Charles Lee, Guest Editor, *Special Issue: Cumulative Impacts and Government Decision-Making*, 18 Envtl. Justice, No. 8 (2025).

The need to consider cumulative impacts in risk assessment has long been understood and acknowledged. In 2004, for example, the National Environmental Justice Advisory Council (NEJAC) specifically advised the EPA to embrace consideration of cumulative impacts across the entire Agency. In its report to the EPA, the NEJAC concluded:

> The issue of cumulative risks/impacts is a unifying one, because it is a vehicle through which the impressive array of tools now available to ensure pollution prevention and risk reduction can be brought together and applied in new, innovative, and more effective ways. Exciting new approaches, partnerships, and models will surely emerge....

NEJAC, Ensuring Risk Reduction in Communities with Multiple Stressors: Environmental Justice and Cumulative Risks/Impacts (Dec. 2004).

Unfortunately, the "new approaches" to addressing cumulative impacts did not come quickly to the EPA. EPA did, in 2003, issue one early report embracing consideration of cumulative impacts in theory. U.S. EPA, Framework for Cumulative Risk Assessment (2003). However, while many communities continued to struggle with "multiple stressors," two decades went by until EPA appeared to move significantly toward incorporating consideration of cumulative impacts in its practices of risk assessment and risk management. As one recent example, in January 2024, EPA released a policy document identifying new screening levels for lead contamination in residential soils. Starting with screening levels of 400 parts per million (ppm) established in 1994, EPA in 2024 lowered the new screening level for lead generally to 200 ppm. However, for areas where "an additional source of lead is identified (e.g., lead water service lines, lead-based paint...)," EPA lowered the screening level even further to 100 ppm to account for the cumulative impacts of other sources of lead in the area. U.S. EPA Office of Land and Emergency Management, Updated Residential Soil Lead Guidance for CERCLA Sites and RCRA Corrective Action Facilities, Jan. 17, 2024.

In 2024, EPA issued a new guidance document which encouraged EPA staff to take cumulative impacts into consideration across all EPA programs. *See* U.S. EPA, Interim Framework for Advancing Consideration of Cumulative Impacts (2024). "Whenever possible," the guidance provided, "decisions informed by cumulative impacts work should aim to advance environmental justice goals to reduce existing impacts in overburdened and other communities with environmental justice concerns...." The framework also provided many examples of where cumulative impacts were already being taken into consideration in EPA programs and policies, including the 2024 screening levels for lead in residential soils, plus environmental rulemaking, permitting, and other actions under the Clean Air Act, Clean Water Act, and other environmental statutes.

Specifically concerning risk assessment, in January 2025, EPA issued new guidance to assist risk assessors with the significant technical questions that have long challenged quantitative risk assessment involving multiple chemicals and multiple media. *See* U.S.

EPA, GUIDELINES FOR CUMULATIVE RISK ASSESSMENT PLANNING AND PROBLEM FORMULATION (2025). Additional technical advances are emerging through integration of statistical modeling, Monte Carlo simulations, and "exposome" approaches that consider the totality of environmental exposures. For a brief introduction to exposome analysis, see Andrew M. Geller, *Cumulative Impacts: Scientific Drivers and Approaches from Exposomatics and Sustainability*, 18 ENVTL. JUSTICE ___ (May 28, 2025). For a broad and timely review of existing tools and methodologies for cumulative impact assessments (CIA) in different contexts, with recommendations for continued development, see NATIONAL ACADEMIES OF SCIENCE, ENGINEERING, AND MEDICINE, STATE OF THE SCIENCE AND THE FUTURE OF CUMULATIVE IMPACT ASSESSMENT (2025).

Beyond federal programs, consideration of cumulative impacts shows promise at state and local levels. New Jersey's environmental justice law requires cumulative impact statements for major permits, with authority to deny projects causing disproportionate impacts. Chicago has developed "the most robust and inclusive cumulative impact assessment in existence," featuring community co-design and compensation for participants. Minnesota expanded its cumulative impact law in 2023 to cover the Twin Cities metro area. These models demonstrate how cumulative risk assessment can move from theory to practice, though widespread implementation requires overcoming significant institutional, legal, and technical barriers while ensuring meaningful community engagement and equitable outcomes. *See generally*, City of Chicago, *Chicago Cumulative Impact Assessment 2023 Summary Report* (2023); Elena Reale et al., *Human Biomonitoring and Toxicokinetics as Key Building Blocks for Next Generation Risk Assessment*, 184 ENVT. INT'L 108474 (2024); En-Hsuan Lu et al., *Advancing Probabilistic Risk Assessment by Integrating Human Biomonitoring, New Approach Methods, and Bayesian Modeling: A Case Study with the Mycotoxin Deoxynivalenol*, 45 RISK ANALYSIS 457 (2025); NEJAC, REDUCING CUMULATIVE AND DISPROPORTIONATE IMPACTS AND BURDENS IN ENVIRONMENTAL JUSTICE COMMUNITIES (2024).

Beyond chemical exposures, the actual health consequences for any community member can only be understood by accounting for the complete suite of contributing stressors that affect human health, sometimes identified as **social determinants of health**. Thus, the same amount of a contaminant present in the environment can result in widely differing health consequences for members of two different communities or subpopulations, depending on the extent to which these other non-chemical (e.g., physical, social, cultural) stressors are also present. Communities with environmental justice concerns are often historically overburdened with contamination and disadvantaged in services (e.g., education, health care) that would permit members to withstand or recover from environmental insults. Failure to account for multiple stressors in assessments of risk, therefore, is likely again to lead to especially large underestimates of risk in these communities. *See* Michael Marmot, *Social Determinants of Health Inequalities*, 365 LANCET 1099 (2005); Michael Marmot & Jessica J. Allen, *Social Determinants of Health Equity*, 104 AM. J. PUB. HEALTH S517 (2014);

Paula A. Braveman et al., *The Social Determinants of Health: It's Time to Consider the Causes of the Causes,* 129 Pub. Health Rep. 19 (2014).

Notes and Questions

1. **In 2023, New Jersey** enacted the nation's first statewide environmental justice law requiring cumulative impact analysis for major industrial permits. *See* discussion in Chapter 6 (Environmental Permits). Under the law, permit applicants must prepare environmental justice impact statements and engage with local communities, and the state can deny, limit, or condition permits if they would cause disproportionate impacts. However, the law only applies to eight specific facility types (incinerators, large sewage treatment plants, etc.) and excludes many other pollution sources. Camden, New Jersey, which already hosts numerous industrial facilities, is now facing permit applications for additional waste and manufacturing operations. How should state regulators apply New Jersey's cumulative impact law in practice? Address (a) what constitutes "disproportionate impacts" when a community like Camden already bears significant pollution burdens, (b) how state agencies should weigh the cumulative effects of existing facilities against new permit applications, (c) whether the law's limitation to certain facility types creates gaps that undermine effective cumulative impact assessment, and (d) what role community input should play when residents oppose new facilities but local officials support them for economic development. Consider how the law's requirement that applicants "avoid and minimize stressors" might apply when a community is already overburdened.

2. **The Port of Long Beach** and surrounding communities in Los Angeles County face air pollution from multiple sources: diesel trucks, cargo ships, rail yards, oil refineries, and highways. Local residents have higher rates of asthma and other respiratory diseases. California's CalEnviroScreen tool (discussed further in Chapter 10) ranks these communities among the most environmentally burdened in the state, yet individual permit decisions continue to be made facility-by-facility without comprehensive cumulative impact analysis. How should local and state authorities in California address the cumulative environmental health impacts in port communities? In developing your response, consider: (a) what legal authority California Air Quality Management Districts have to deny or condition permits based on cumulative impacts rather than just individual facility emissions, (b) how local land use planning and zoning decisions might be used to address cumulative impacts, and (c) how economic concerns about port operations and trucking jobs should be balanced against community health impacts. Consider how truck routes, warehouse siting, or port expansion might be designed differently if cumulative impacts were a primary consideration rather than just individual project impacts.

G. Integrating Scientific Evidence into Advocacy and Policy

From the early days of the movement, including Dr. Bullard's analysis of waste disposal sites in Houston (discussed in Chapter 4), advocates for environmental justice have employed scientific methods and evidence to support their arguments. Environmental justice advocacy has evolved significantly over the past decades, increasingly incorporating rigorous scientific evidence to document disparities, establish causation, and drive policy change. The integration of methodologically sound research into environmental justice work has transformed what was once primarily a social movement into a powerful framework for addressing systemic environmental health inequities through evidence-based interventions. Environmental justice work has matured through the strategic use of scientific evidence across multiple disciplines. A 2023 article in the Journal of Exposure Science & Environmental Epidemiology illustrates this shift, proposing that environmental justice principles "should be the standard and not an afterthought or trend dismissed by those who believe that science should not be politicized." Yolanda O. Van Horne et al., *An Applied Environmental Justice Framework for Exposure Science*, 33 J. Exposure Sci. & Envt. Epidemiology 1, 1–11 (2023). This evolution represents a deliberate integration of community concerns with scientific methodologies, employing approaches that include geospatial analysis, biomonitoring, epidemiological studies, risk assessment models, and community-based participatory research.

The integration of scientific evidence has been particularly influential in addressing water contamination disparities. A nationwide study in Environmental Health employed sophisticated statistical methods to analyze data from nearly 40,000 community water systems, conclusively demonstrating that Latino communities face disproportionately high nitrate exposure, with 5.6 million Americans served by water systems exceeding health-based thresholds. Laurel A. Schaider et al., *Environmental Justice and Drinking Water Quality: Are There Socioeconomic Disparities in Nitrate Levels in U.S. Drinking Water?*, 19 Envtl. Health 3 (2019).

This scientific documentation of disparities has directly informed policy responses and legal remedies. In California's San Joaquin Valley, researchers developed the "Drinking Water Disparities Framework" that traced mechanisms through which socioeconomic factors constrain access to safe water, guiding the state's implementation of the Human Right to Water Act and establishing a $1.4 billion fund specifically targeting disadvantaged communities. *See* Camille Pannu, *Bridging the Safe Drinking Water Gap for California's Rural Poor*, 24 Hastings Envtl. L.J. 253 (2018); Carolina Balazs et al., *The Drinking Water Disparities Framework: On the Origins and Persistence of Inequities in Exposure*, 104 Am. J. Pub. Health 603, 603–611 (2014). Environmental scientists at UC Berkeley created a publicly accessible Drinking Water Tool providing community-specific water quality data, enabling residents and advocates to document contamination patterns, which, when presented to state officials, led to emergency water provisions for communities with persistent violations. Clare Pace et al., *Water Contaminants Identified, Addressed in Marginalized Communities,* ENVT. FACTOR (Oct. 2023), https://factor.niehs.nih.gov/2023/10/community-impact/drinking-water-contaminants-solutions. A 2023 study in WATER POLICY demonstrated that water systems serving predominantly low-income and minority communities experienced significantly higher violation rates for contaminants like arsenic; these findings were subsequently cited in successful litigation requiring state agencies to provide technical assistance to struggling water systems. Yusuke Kuwayama et al., *Disparities in Drinking Water Quality: Evidence from California,* 25 WATER POL'Y 69 (2023).

Scientific evidence has also strengthened environmental justice approaches to climate change impacts. The EPA's 2024 report on "Climate Change and the Health of Socially Vulnerable People" synthesized data showing how heat-related mortality, air pollution, and extreme weather events disproportionately affect low-income communities and communities of color. U.S. EPA, CLIMATE CHANGE AND THE HEALTH OF SOCIALLY VULNERABLE PEOPLE (2024), https://www.epa.gov/climateimpacts/climate-change-and-health-socially-vulnerable-people. These findings have directly influenced adaptation strategies, including targeted tree-planting initiatives in historically redlined neighborhoods, mandatory heat protection standards for outdoor workers in several states, and Harvard Medical School's implementation of a Climate Change, Environment, and Health curriculum responding to research on differential climate health impacts by creating "one of the first [programs] aimed at supporting future physicians' practical training to respond to the impact of climate change on patient health." Sandor Szabo et al., *A Review of the Increasing Global Impact of Climate Change on Human Health and Approaches to Medical Preparedness,* 25 MED. SCI. MONITOR e947411 (2024). The Health Affairs journal has further documented how climate change creates and exacerbates health inequities through differential exposure, sensitivity, and adaptive capacity across populations. Kristie L. Ebi et al., *Health Risks Due to Climate Change: Inequity in Causes and Consequences,* 40 HEALTH AFF. 1816 (2021).

The integration of scientific methods with community advocacy has proven particularly effective in addressing industrial pollution. A 2024 study in HEALTH & PLACE employed EPA risk screening methodology to document how over two billion pounds of industrial chemicals released into U.S. waterways created disproportionate health risks in minority communities. Haley E. Olig et al., *Racial and Ethnic Disparities in Health Risk from Industrial Surface Water Pollution in the United States,* 2011–2021, 89 HEALTH & PLACE 101710 (2024). Communities have leveraged such scientific evidence to secure tangible outcomes, as in North Carolina, where researchers detected PFAS "in 99 percent of blood samples from the neighboring community" near industrial facilities discharging into the Cape Fear River, supporting successful legal claims against chemical manufacturers and securing funding for alternative water supplies. The Superfund Research Program has documented disparities in drinking water contaminant exposure and supported community-engaged research that "ensures that a community's concerns around water are translated into actionable research that can be leveraged in the policy arena." Kenda Freeman, *Water Contaminants Identified, Addressed in Marginalized Communities*, Nat'l Inst. Env't. Health Sci. (Oct. 2023), https://factor.niehs.nih.gov/2023/10/community-impact/drinking-water-contaminants-solutions.

Practice Exercise

Part I: Risk Assessment Case Study Analysis

Scenario: The community of Riverdale (population 15,000) sits downriver from a 30-year-old chemical manufacturing facility. The community is 70 percent Black and Latino with median income 30 percent below state average. Recent testing revealed PFAS levels of 45 ppt in municipal water—above EPA's 2024 Maximum Contaminant Level standard (4 ppt) but below a standard (20 ppt) proposed by a new administration. Preliminary health assessments show elevated rates of thyroid conditions, certain cancers, and developmental delays compared to regional communities.

Questions:

1. Identify the health risks present (acute vs. chronic) and which populations might be most vulnerable. Explain your reasoning.
2. How might socioeconomic factors influence both PFAS exposure and the community's ability to respond to contamination?
3. As a public health official, what risk communication strategies would you employ with residents?

Part II: Scientific Evidence in Environmental Justice Cases

Select one case from: Flint water crisis, Cancer Alley (Louisiana), Central Valley farmworker pesticide exposure, Jackson water system failure, or Houston's Manchester Neighborhood air quality. Research and analyze:

1. **Data Collection:** How was health risk data gathered and by whom? What challenges existed in establishing causation between exposures and health outcomes?
2. **Evidence Presentation:** How was scientific evidence presented to decision-makers, and did different standards of proof apply compared to affluent communities?
3. **Outcomes:** What role did scientific evidence play in the case's resolution?

Part III: Risk Perception and Environmental Justice

1. How might risk perception differ between scientists, officials, and affected community members? What psychological, social, and cultural factors influence these differences?
2. How might the concept of "acceptable risk" vary depending on who determines it versus who bears it? What ethical principles should guide environmental risk distribution decisions?

3. How might your own background and social position influence your perception of environmental health risks?

* * *

The incorporation of scientific evidence into environmental justice work continues to evolve, with researchers increasingly adopting a "racism as a public health issue" framework that examines how "systemic racism is a fundamental cause of disproportionate exposures and associated health effects." Symma Finn et al., *Racism as a Public Health Issue in Environmental Health Disparities and Environmental Justice: Working Toward Solutions*, 23 Envtl. Health 8 (2024). This integration of rigorous science with environmental justice principles represents a powerful approach to addressing environmental health disparities. By documenting disparities through objective data, establishing causal mechanisms, and evaluating the effectiveness of interventions, environmental justice advocates can more effectively secure policy changes, legal remedies, and community-based solutions that address the fundamental inequities in environmental health. The Centers for Disease Control and Prevention has further supported this approach through its Environmental Justice Index, providing key insights on environmental justice indicators across the United States. CDC Environmental Justice Index, 2024 Update (2024), https://www.atsdr.cdc.gov/place-health/php/eji/environmental-justice-index-2024-update.html. As demonstrated across these recent studies, the marriage of scientific evidence with environmental justice advocacy has transformed how we understand, document, and address environmental health disparities, creating more effective pathways toward equitable risk assessment and risk management for all communities.

Chapter 4

Constitutional Law and Civil Rights Claims

A. Introduction

With inspiration from the Civil Rights Movement, it seems natural that environmental justice advocates would seek remedies from legal authorities such as the U.S. Constitution and the Civil Rights Act of 1964. Such authorities, however, have rarely succeeded in delivering judicial victories to plaintiffs seeking environmental justice (EJ). So far, there is nothing like a *Brown v. Board of Education* for environmental justice plaintiffs. Although the EPA has, on rare occasion, found a prima facie case of discrimination under Title VI of the Civil Rights Act, the agency has never denied or withdrawn financial assistance to a funding recipient because of a finding of discrimination under Civil Rights Act Title VI. The reasons the EPA has been so "spectacularly unsuccessful" with enforcing Title VI are varied and examined thoroughly in Marianne Engelman Lado, *No More Excuses: Building a New Vision of Civil Rights Enforcement in the Context of Environmental Justice*, 22 U. PENN. J. L. & SOC. CHANGE 281 (2019). Nevertheless, the U.S. Constitution, including the Equal Protection Clause of the Fourteenth Amendment, and civil rights legislation, including § 1983 and Title VI of the Civil Rights Act, have long been regarded as important authorities for seeking to advance the cause of environmental justice, providing bases for legal action as well as leverage for negotiation. The Biden administration took affirmative steps to enforce Title VI, with mixed success. Unfortunately, the Trump administration in 2025 directed EPA not to accept any new civil rights complaints and not to issue any findings of discrimination in the dozens of pending complaints. Despite this executive action, the agency still has a statutory and regulatory duty to enforce the Civil Rights Act.

This chapter reviews efforts by impacted communities to use constitutional and civil rights remedies to address environmental harms. Part B addresses whether EJ advocates should consider constitutional or civil rights claims at all, given many other alternatives, including citizen suits under the various environmental statutes (*see* Chapter 12). Part C examines claims under the Equal Protection Clause of the U.S. Constitution. Part D focuses on the Civil Rights Act Title VI, including Louisiana's aggressive effort to shut down Title VI disparate impact claims in the state. Part E takes a quick look at § 1983, through the lens of a case responding directly to the drinking water contamination in Flint, Michigan.

Pathfinder on Constitutional and Civil Rights Claims for Environmental Justice

In addition to the articles discussed in this chapter, the following is a selected group of materials that discuss constitutional rights or civil rights legislation in the environmental justice context: Deborah Sivas, *The Future of Environmental Justice Claims Under Title VI: Can the "Sleeping Giant" Finally Be Awakened?*, 20 Stanford J. Civil Rts. & Civil Liberties 105 (2025); Rebecca Bratspies, *Underburdened Communities*, 110 Cal. L. Rev. 1933 (2022); Mehmet K. Konar-Steenburg, *Root and Branch: The Thirteenth Amendment and Environmental Justice*, 19 Nevada L.J. 509 (2018); David A. Dana & Deborah Tuerkheimer, *After Flint: Environmental Justice as Equal Protection*, 111 Nw. U. L. Rev. 879 (2017); Elizabeth Ann Kronk, *Application of Title VI in Indian Country: The Key Is Tribal Sovereignty*, 6 Fla. A&M U. L. Rev. 215 (2011); Carlton Waterhouse, *Abandon All Hope Ye That Enter? Equal Protection, Title VI, and the Divine Comedy of Environmental Justice*, 20 Fordham Envtl. L. Rev. 51 (2009); Philip Weinberg, *Equal Protection*, and Bradford C. Mank, *Title VI*, *in* The Law of Environmental Justice: Theories and Procedures to Address Disproportionate Risks (Michael B. Gerrard & Sheila R. Foster eds., 2d ed. 2008). *See also* U.S. Comm. on Civil Rights, Environmental Justice: Examining the Environmental Protection Agency's Compliance and Enforcement of Title VI and Executive Order 12898 (Sept. 2016).

B. Constitutional Law and Civil Rights Claims for Environmental Injustice

Students and practitioners of environmental law understand that the United States (like most countries now) has a robust set of environmental statutes protecting the air we breathe and the water we drink. With these laws and implementing regulations that fill linear feet of shelf space, one might naturally wonder why environmental justice advocates would consider bringing claims under constitutional provisions or civil rights litigation, given the extraordinary hurdles some of these alternatives may present. Don't environmental laws guarantee clean air and clean water? For one compelling response to this question, consider the following excerpt:

Marianne Engelman Lado, *No More Excuses: Building a New Vision of Civil Rights Enforcement in the Context of Environmental Justice*

22 U. Penn. J. Law & Social Change 281 (2019)

The argument that civil rights enforcement is not necessary or, worse, is a distraction of needed resources, relies on a belief that if fully implemented and enforced, environmental laws are sufficiently protective. Most broadly, though, environmental

Figure 4-1. Hog farm and waste lagoon, eastern North Carolina. Photo: Cliff Villa, 2019.

laws have failed to eliminate the adverse and disparate impacts on communities of color that Title VI and its implementing regulations seek to forbid.

... [S]ignificant gaps in environmental protection create the space for exacerbating racial inequalities in the distribution of environmental benefits and burdens, especially when layered on top of geographic patterns of racial segregation created by racially explicit federal, state, and local government policies.... [E]nvironmental statutes, regulations, and standards are the outcome of political and administrative processes, which take into account statutory goals and an array of competing interests and criteria....

To examine the adequacy of environmental statutes in addressing racial disparities in exposure to sources of environmental pollution, it is worth returning to the complaint filed by groups in North Carolina against [the North Carolina Department of Environmental Quality (DEQ)] claiming that its decision to allow more than 2,100 hog facilities to operate on North Carolina's coastal plain has an unjustified disparate impact on the basis of race. Surely the alphabet soup of federal environmental laws, including the Clean Water Act (CWA), Resource Conservation and Recovery Act (RCRA), the National Environmental Policy Act (NEPA), the Endangered Species Act (ESA), the Clean Air Act (CAA), the Comprehensive Environmental Response, Compensation and Liability Act (CERCLA, otherwise known as the Superfund law), or the Emergency Planning and Community Right to Know Act (EPCRA), should provide ample protection, particularly when combined with state nuisance laws.... For years before filing their complaint, residents of the region complained to DEQ that the high concentration of swine facilities generated staggering quantities of feces and urine, which are stored in open-air cesspools, called lagoons, and sprayed on fields with high volume spreaders. Residents can live within three miles of upwards of ten facilities and, thus, ten such cesspools for facilities with 2,000 pigs or more.

Residents attest that the stench can be unbearable, and numerous studies over time have documented the adverse impacts of the industry on air and water. The Clean Water Act prohibits discharge of a pollutant from a point source—explicitly including confined animal feeding operations such as the swine facilities in eastern North Carolina—into waters of the United States, and residents and clean water advocates have, in fact, investigated and brought litigation to enforce the law. Yet enforcement actions face significant hurdles. Initially, although neighbors may be impacted by odors and the flow of waste from sprayfields to ditches and waterways, they lack access onto the property of nearby facilities to identify potential discharges. Even when advocates monitor pollutants such as fecal coliform and find high levels downstream from facilities, they must overcome a number of legal barriers to bringing claims under the Clean Water Act. To prove a discharge, for example, they must show that pollutants are entering jurisdictional "waters of the United States" and that the discharge will not be considered "agricultural stormwater" and thus allowed under the Clean Water Act.

These barriers to Clean Water Act enforcement fail to capture the full scale of the gap between the promise of environmental protection and the reality. In theory, [CERCLA] and EPCRA would require facility owners and operators to report releases from swine operations over certain threshold levels. However, a 2008 rule finalized in the closing hours of the Bush administration largely exempted confined animal feeding operations from the rule. Moreover, animal operations are all but exempted from coverage under the Clean Air Act....

Notes and Questions

1. Environmental compliance vs. environmental protection. In the above excerpt, the author (a long-time legal advocate for environmental justice and a senior official in the Biden administration) notes many of the means by which environmental law may fail to protect human health. Failures may stem from a lack of political will among agency leadership, and also from the design of environmental laws and regulations themselves. The design of the National Ambient Air Quality Standards (NAAQS) under the Clean Air Act is one classic example. Under the NAAQS, compliance with air quality standards is measured by Air Quality Control Regions or subregions, which may encompass multiple municipalities within the same county, or even multiple counties, masking localized impacts of air pollution. The Air Quality Control Region of the "South Coast Air Basin," encompassing the Los Angeles metro area, says nothing about the air quality that children breathe on a school playground in East L.A. Similarly, the NAAQS attainment status of eastern North Carolina may tell you nothing about the air quality in Warsaw, North Carolina, and a family home surrounded by 20,000 pigs on ten "industrial hog operations," with acrid odor and particulate matter wafting in the wind. Conflating environmental compliance with environmental protection is a common mistake—one made by EPA itself in the *Select Steel* decision, discussed later in this chapter.

2. Environmental compliance vs. civil rights compliance. As environmental compliance does not ensure environmental protection, nor does it ensure compliance with civil rights law. In 2024, the federal government issued an extraordinary statement to confirm that understanding. The statement, issued by federal agencies including DOJ, EPA, and HUD, "reminds recipients [of federal funding] that civil rights obligations are separate and distinct from recipients' other obligations, including obligations to comply with federal, state, territorial and local environmental laws." Press Release, *Five Federal Departments Join Justice Department in Reaffirming Shared Commitment to Uphold Civil Rights Laws and Advance Environmental Justice*, May 6, 2024. What's one circumstance you can imagine where full compliance with environmental requirements could still lead to civil rights violations? Hold that circumstance in mind as you read through this chapter and consider potential solutions.

3. Filling regulatory gaps. Students and scholars familiar with legislative or administrative processes may see many obvious needs for new laws or regulations to provide genuine protection for human health. Efforts to fill gaps in existing regulatory schemes have proven increasingly difficult, however, at least on a federal level. Even where there is widespread agreement on the need for regulation, such as the need to clarify the meaning of "waters of the United States" under the Clean Water Act (see discussion in Chapter 2), there is now likely to be years of litigation challenging any new federal rule, complemented by continuing proposals to withdraw or amend the rule as new administrations come and go. On a state, tribal, or municipal level, efforts to fill regulatory gaps may fare better, and will be explored later in this book. *See* Chapter 5 (Environmental Regulations) and Chapter 10 (Public and Private Initiatives). What is it about federal legislation and rulemaking now that makes progress toward protecting human health so difficult? What advantages do older authorities such as the U.S. Constitution or the Civil Rights Act bring to the problem of gaps in environmental regulation?

C. Equal Protection Claims

To address concerns for the disparate treatment of racial minorities and the inequitable distribution of environmental burdens, perhaps the most obvious authority for EJ advocates to consider is the Equal Protection Clause of the Fourteenth Amendment to the U.S. Constitution. The Equal Protection Clause provides that "[n]o State shall ... deny to any person within its jurisdiction the equal protection of the laws." By its plain terms, without limitation, the Equal Protection Clause should guarantee the equal protection of the environmental laws. Under this authority, some of the earliest legal challenges to the siting of undesirable land uses in communities of color alleged violations of the Equal Protection Clause. The challenges largely failed, however, for lack of evidence of discriminatory intent. While there is no textual requirement to prove discriminatory intent under the Equal Protection Clause, a majority of the U.S. Supreme

Court invented such a requirement in *Washington v. Davis*, 426 U.S. 229 (1976). Stating that the "central purpose of the Equal Protection Clause is the prevention of official conduct discriminating on the basis of race," the Court held that a plaintiff must prove that a defendant acted with discriminatory intent. The Court allowed that such intent may be inferred and provided additional guidance the following year in the case of *Village of Arlington Heights v. Metropolitan Housing Development Corp.*, 429 U.S. 252 (1977). In *Arlington Heights*, the Court identified five factors as potentially indicative of intentional discrimination: (1) disparate impact; (2) a "clear pattern, unexplainable on grounds other than race"; (3) historical background to the decision; (4) departures from normal sequence or substance; and (5) "contemporary statements" during legislative or administrative proceedings. The Court made clear that these five factors were not "exhaustive," but nevertheless, as indicated in cases below, courts have continued to apply the five-factor *Arlington Heights* test to determine whether facially neutral government action may actually be discriminatory.

In early cases in the mid-1980s, courts inferred discriminatory intent and found violations of the Equal Protection Clause based on the disparate provision of municipal services. In one notable case, a federal district court reviewing allegations against the City of Apopka, north of Orlando, Florida, "found intentional discrimination in the provision of street paving, the water distribution system, and storm drainage facilities in violation of the fourteenth amendment." Specifically, as the Eleventh Circuit affirmed on appeal:

> The district court found that 42% of the street footage in the black community was unpaved as compared to 9% in the white community and that 33% of the black community residences fronted on such unpaved streets while only 7% of the residences in the white community did so. As regards storm drainage, the court found that while 60% of the residential streets in the white community had curbs and gutters, no streets in the black community had curbs and gutters....

Dowdell v. City of Apopka, 698 F.2d 1181 (11th Cir. 1983).

Plaintiffs have had less success using the Equal Protection Clause in the facility siting context. The following decision involves one of the most famous cases in environmental justice, where field research led by Dr. Robert Bullard indicated disparate siting of waste facilities in minority neighborhoods of Houston, Texas. Plaintiffs filed suit seeking to invalidate a decision by the Texas Department of Health (TDH) to grant a permit to a company to operate a solid waste landfill in the East Houston-Dyersdale Road area in Harris County, Texas. They sought a preliminary injunction to restrain the project from going forward. The court ruled as indicated below.

Bean v. Southwestern Waste Management Corporation

482 F. Supp. 673 (S.D. Texas 1979), *aff'd* 780 F.2d 1038 (5th Cir. 1986)

McDonald, District Judge:

... The burden on [plaintiffs] is to prove discriminatory purpose. That is, the plaintiffs must show not just that the decision to grant the permit is objectionable or even wrong, but that it is attributable to an intent to discriminate on the basis of race. Statistical proof can rise to the level that it, alone, proves discriminatory intent, as in *Yick Wo v. Hopkins*, 118 U.S. 356 (1886), and *Gomillion v. Lightfoot*, 364 U.S. 339 (1960), or, this Court would conclude, even in situations less extreme than in those two cases, but the data shown here does not rise to that level. Similarly, statistical proof can be sufficiently supplemented by the types of proof outlined in *Arlington Heights* to establish purposeful discrimination, but the supplemental proof offered here is not sufficient to do that.

Two different theories of liability have been advanced in this case. The first is that TDH's approval of the permit was part of a pattern or practice by it of discriminating in the placement of solid waste sites. In order to test that theory, one must focus on the sites which TDH has approved and determine the minority population of the areas in which the sites were located on the day that the sites opened. The available statistical data, both city-wide and in the target area, fails to establish a pattern or practice of discrimination by TDH. City-wide, data was produced for the seventeen (17) sites operating with TDH permits as of July 1, 1978. That data shows that 58.8% of the sites granted permits by TDH were located in census tracts with 25% or less minority population at the time of their opening and that 82.4% of the sites granted permits by TDH were located in census tracts with 50% or less minority population at the time of their opening. In the target area, an area which roughly conforms to the North Forest Independent School District and the newly created City Council District B and is 70% minority in population, two (2) sites were approved by TDH. One, the McCarty Road site, was in a census tract with less than 10% minority population at the time of its opening. The other, the site being challenged here, is in a census tract with close to 60% minority population.... Of all the solid waste sites opened in the target area, 46.2 to 50% were located in census tracts with less than 25% minority population at the time they opened. It may be that more particularized data would show that even those sites approved in predominantly Anglo census tracts were actually located in minority neighborhoods, but the data available here does not show that. In addition, there was no supplemental evidence, such as that suggested by *Arlington Heights*, *supra*, which established a pattern or practice of discrimination on the part of TDH.

The plaintiffs' second theory of liability is that TDH's approval of the permit, in the context of the historical placement of solid waste sites and the events surrounding the application, constituted discrimination. Three sets of data were offered to support this theory. Each set, at first blush, looks compelling. On further analysis, however, each set breaks down. Each fails to approach the standard established by *Yick Wo*, *supra*, and *Gomillion*, *supra*, and, even when considered with supplementary proof, *Arlington Heights*, *supra*, fails to establish a likelihood of success in proving discriminatory intent.

The first set of data focuses on the two (2) solid waste sites to be used by the City of Houston. Both of these sites are located in the target area. This proves discrimination, the plaintiffs argue, because "the target area has the dubious distinction of containing 100% of the type I municipal landfills that Houston utilizes or will utilize, although it contains only 6.9% of the entire population of Houston." There are two problems with this argument. First, there are only two sites involved here. That is not a statistically significant number. Second, an examination of the census tracts in the target area in which the sites are located reveals that the East Houston-Dyersdale Road proposed site is in a tract with a 58.4% minority population, but that the McCarty Road site is in a tract with only an 18.4% minority population. Thus, the evidence shows that, of the two sites to be used by the City of Houston, one is in a primarily Anglo census tract and one is in a primarily minority census tract. No inference of discrimination can be made from this data.

The second set of data focuses on the total number of solid waste sites located in the target area. The statistical disparity which the plaintiffs point to is that the target area contains 15% of Houston's solid waste sites, but only 6.9% of its population. Since the target area has a 70% minority population, the plaintiffs argue, this statistical disparity must be attributable to race discrimination. To begin with, in the absence of the data on population by race, the statistical disparity is not all that shocking. One would expect solid waste sites to be placed near each other and away from concentrated population areas. Even considering the 70% minority population of the target area, when one looks at where in the target area these particular sites are located, the inference of racial discrimination dissolves. Half of the solid waste sites in the target area are in census tracts with more than 70% Anglo population. Without some proof that the sites affect an area much larger than the census tract in which they are in, it is very hard to conclude that the placing of a site in the target area evidences purposeful racial discrimination.

The third set of data offered by the plaintiffs focuses on the city as a whole. This data is the most compelling on its surface. It shows that only 17.1% of the city's solid waste sites are located in the southwest quadrant, where 53.3% of the Anglos live. Only 15.3% of the sites are located in the northwest quadrant, where 20.1% of the Anglos live. Thus, only 32.4% of the sites are located in the western half of the city, where 73.4% of the Anglos live. Furthermore, the plaintiffs argue, 67.6% of the sites are located in the eastern half of the city, where 61.6% of the minority population lives. This, according to the plaintiffs, shows racial discrimination.

The problem is that, once again, these statistics break down under closer scrutiny. To begin with, ... a large number of [] sites are located around Houston's ship channel, which is in the eastern half of the city. But those sites, the Assistant Attorney General argues persuasively, are located in the eastern half of the city because that is where Houston's industry is, not because that is where Houston's minority population is. Furthermore, closer examination of the data shows that the city's solid waste sites are not so disparately located as they first appear. If we focus on census tracts, rather than on halves or quadrants of the city, we can see with more particularity where the solid waste sites are located. Houston's population is 39.3% minority and 60.7% Anglo. The plaintiffs argue, and this Court finds persuasive, a definition of "minority census tracts" as those with more than 39.3% minority population and Anglo census tracts as those with more than 60.7% Anglo population.

Using those definitions, Houston consists of 42.5% minority tracts and 57.5% Anglo tracts. Again using those definitions, 42.3% of the solid waste sites in the City of Houston are located in minority tracts and 57.7% are located in Anglo tracts. In addition, if we look at tracts with one or more sites per tract, to account for the fact that some tracts contain more than one solid waste site, 42.2% are minority tracts and 57.8% are Anglo tracts. The difference between the racial composition of census tracts in general and the racial composition of census tracts with solid waste sites is, according to the statistics available to the Court, at best, only 0.3%. That is simply not a statistically significant difference. More surprisingly, from the plaintiffs' point of view, to the extent that it is viewed as significant, it tends to indicate that minority census tracts have a tiny bit smaller percentage of solid waste sites than one would proportionately expect....

Arlington Heights, supra, suggested various types of non-statistical proof which can be used to establish purposeful discrimination. The supplementary non-statistical evidence provided by the plaintiffs in the present case raises a number of questions as to why this permit was granted. To begin with, a site proposed for the almost identical location was denied a permit in 1971 by the County Commissioners, who were then responsible for the issuance of such permits. One wonders what happened since that time. The plaintiffs argue that Smiley High School has changed from an Anglo school to one whose student body is predominantly minority. Furthermore, the site is being placed within 1,700 feet of Smiley High School, a predominantly black school with no air conditioning, and only somewhat farther from a residential neighborhood. Land-use considerations alone would seem to militate against granting this permit. Such evidence seemingly did not dissuade TDH.

If this Court were TDH, it might very well have denied this permit. It simply does not make sense to put a solid waste site so close to a high school, particularly one with no air conditioning. Nor does it make sense to put the land[fill] site so close to a residential neighborhood. But I am not TDH and for all I know, TDH may regularly approve of solid waste sites located near schools and residential areas, as illogical as that may seem.

It is not my responsibility to decide whether to grant this site a permit. It is my responsibility to decide whether to grant the plaintiffs a preliminary injunction. From the evidence before me, I can say that the plaintiffs have established that the decision to grant the permit was both unfortunate and insensitive. I cannot say that the plaintiffs have established a substantial likelihood of proving that the decision to grant the permit was motivated by purposeful racial discrimination in violation of 42 U.S.C. § 1983....

Permanent Relief

The failure of the plaintiffs to obtain a preliminary injunction does not, of course, mean that they are foreclosed from obtaining permanent relief. Because of the time pressures involved, extensive pre-trial discovery was impossible in this case. Assuming the case goes forward, discovery could lead to much more solid and persuasive evidence for either side. Ideally, it would resolve a number of the questions which the Court considers unanswered.

Where, for instance, are the solid waste sites located in each census tract? The plaintiffs produced evidence that in census tract 434, a predominantly Anglo tract, the site was located next to a black community named Riceville. If that was true of most sites in predominantly Anglo census tracts, the outcome of this case would be quite different.

How large an area does a solid waste site affect? If it affects an area a great deal smaller than that of a census tract, it becomes particularly important to know where in each census tract the site is located. If it affects an area larger than that of a census tract, then a target area analysis becomes much more persuasive.

How are solid waste site locations selected? It may be that private contractors consider a number of alternative locations and then select one in consultation with city or county officials. If that is so, it has tremendous implications for the search for discriminatory intent. It may be that a relatively limited number of areas can adequately serve as a Type I solid waste site. If that is so, the placement of sites in those areas becomes a lot less suspicious, even if large numbers of minorities live there.... At this point, the Court still does not know how, why, and by whom the East Houston-Dyersdale Road location was selected.

What factors entered into TDH's decision to grant the permit? The proximity of the site to Smiley High School and a residential neighborhood and the lack of air conditioning facilities at the former were emphasized to the Court. It is still unknown how much, if any, consideration TDH gave to these factors. The racial composition of the neighborhood and the racial distribution of solid waste sites in Houston were primary concerns of the plaintiffs. It remains unclear to what degree TDH was informed of these concerns....

[P]laintiffs' Motion for a Preliminary Injunction ... [is] DENIED.

Notes and Questions

1. ***Arlington Heights* factors.** Consider the evidence analyzed by the *Bean* court in denying the preliminary injunction. Which of the *Arlington Heights* factors does this evidence relate to? Consider also the additional evidence that the court suggests might have been persuasive to it, including where the solid waste sites were located within each census tract, how large an area a solid waste site affects, how solid waste sites are selected, and what factors entered into the Texas Department of Health's decision to grant the permit. How do each of the requested pieces of evidence relate to the *Arlington Heights* factors?

2. Measuring discriminatory impact. How do you think discriminatory impact should be measured? This threshold question, which arises in many legal contexts including claims brought under the Fair Housing Act and Title VI of the Civil Rights Act, raises a host of difficult methodological questions. How do you define a community for purposes of determining whether it has suffered disparate impacts? Is "community" defined by political boundaries? Should it be defined by city blocks, neighborhoods, zip codes, census tracts, city quadrants, county lines? Or by a geographic radius extending from the unwanted land use? Should it vary depending on type of facility? As *Bean* demonstrates, the units chosen can have a significant impact on the outcome of a given case. For useful guidance and methodology for establishing disparate impacts, *see* the U.S. DOJ Title VI Legal Manual, available online at https://www.epa.gov/sites/default/files/2021-01/documents/titlevi_legal_manual_rev._ed_1.pdf.

3. Sympathies and statistics. Owing perhaps to the large amount of data collected and presented by plaintiffs, the hearing on the motion for preliminary injunction in this case took an extraordinary eleven days. In the decision, Judge McDonald clearly expressed sympathy with the plaintiffs' concerns, yet he seemed persuaded by statistics that appeared to negate a clear finding of discriminatory intent in this case. What kind of statistics would Judge McDonald find convincing? In his opinion, McDonald pointed to two cases where discriminatory intent was found: *Yick Wo v. Hopkins* (1886) and *Gomillion v. Lightfoot* (1960). In *Yick Wo v. Hopkins*, as some students may recall, the City of San Francisco established an ordinance requiring a permit to operate a laundry in a wooden building. Of 310 laundries in wooden buildings, 240 had Chinese operators—all of whom were denied city permits. At the same time, all but one non-Chinese laundry received city permits. In *Gomillion v. Lightfoot*, the city of Tuskegee, Alabama, redrew its city boundaries from a square to "an uncouth 28-sided figure" in order to disenfranchise "all save four or five of [the city's] 400 Negro voters." Writing for the Court, Justice Frankfurter observed that if the allegations were proven true, this would be "tantamount ... to a mathematical demonstration" of discriminatory intent. Is this the level of proof that Judge McDonald would have required in *Bean*? If you had eleven days to present the same case today, what statistical evidence would you like the court to consider?

4. *Bean* and the Bullards. Like Warren County, the *Bean* case was another epic moment in the development of environmental justice as a field of study and practice. Vigorously litigated by Linda McKeever Bullard, *Bean* plaintiffs included Margaret Bean and other residents of Houston's Northwood Manor neighborhood in one of the first cases to reach a courtroom in a challenge alleging racial discrimination in environmental siting. To support their allegations, plaintiffs relied on data collection and statistical analysis by Mrs. Bullard's husband, sociologist Dr. Robert Bullard, who served as an expert witness on the case. Although the litigation was obviously not decided as plaintiffs hoped, it did signal a new era where advocates for environmental justice would be prepared to turn from protests in the streets to challenges in the courtroom, drawing resources from statistical methods and litigation tactics. For further background on the *Bean* case and its place in EJ history, *see* Robert D. Bullard, DUMPING IN DIXIE: RACE, CLASS, AND ENVIRONMENTAL QUALITY 40–45 (1990).

5. Smiley High School. So, whatever happened to Smiley High School, where the lack of air conditioning required open windows in classrooms 1,700 feet away from the waste disposal site? As might be expected over the course of nearly 40 years, the school has seen changes resulting from social shifts as well as major incidents including Hurricane Ike in 2008. The school is known today as the North Forest High School. In 2018, North Forest students moved across the street to a new, $59.5 million campus funded by the state. The student population remains highly diverse, with approximately 51 percent of students Black and 46 percent Latino. 98 percent of students were classified as "economically disadvantaged" and, in 2023, only 18.5 percent were classified as "college ready" at graduation, half the district-wide level. Texas Education Agency, 2023–24 School Report Card, North Forest High School. As in so many neighborhoods across the country, the struggle for social justice in the community of the former Smiley High School clearly continues.

6. Discrimination contexts. Are courts (such as in *City of Apopka*) more willing to infer discriminatory intent on the part of government actors and find an equal protection violation when the issue is the inequitable provision of services, rather than when it is the inequitable siting of locally undesirable land uses? For example, in a case alleging racial discrimination in providing municipal services to single-family homeowners and residents of an area of town that was 98.5 percent minority and 46 percent low-income, the court applied the *Arlington Heights* factors and denied summary judgment to the city, finding that a genuine issue of material fact of discrimination existed despite an absence of direct evidence of discriminatory intent. *See Miller v. City of Dallas*, 2002 WL 230834 (N.D. Tex.). Consider the consequences that might follow from a successful equal protection claim under, respectively, the municipal services and the siting dispute cases.

7. Equal protection: dead end—or alive and kicking? Are equal protection challenges a dead end for environmental justice plaintiffs? While equal protection victories remain elusive, legal advocates continue to assert equal protection claims to address cases of environmental injustice. In 2023, for example, Louisiana community and religious groups sued St. James Parish alleging that the Parish violated their constitutional rights and intentionally discriminated against them by steering hazardous industrial development into Black neighborhoods. The plaintiffs, which included environmental justice advocates Rise St. James, alleged violations of 42 U.S.C. § 1983 as well as the Thirteenth and Fourteenth Amendments, and the Louisiana Constitution. They alleged that through intentionally discriminatory zoning and land use decisions, St. James Parish deprived them of their right to equal protection under the law. They further alleged that the exposure to hazardous pollutants they suffered from Defendants' land use decisions deprived them of the substantive due process right to bodily integrity. Judge Carl Bieber of the Eastern District of Louisiana dismissed the case as time barred and for lack of standing. *Inclusive Louisiana v. St. James Parish*, 702 F.

Supp. 3d 478 (E.D. La. 2023). The Fifth Circuit reversed, finding that plaintiffs had standing to bring the action, that the claims were not time barred, and that the claims survived a 12(b)(6) motion to dismiss for failure to state a claim. 134 F.4th 297 (5th Cir. 2025). While plaintiffs will still have to prove intentional discrimination to prevail in this litigation, the case potentially breathes new life into intentional environmental discrimination claims.

Also in 2023, the Supreme Court found affirmative action in college admissions to be a violation of equal protection rights. *Students for Fair Admission v. Harvard*, 600 U.S. 181 (2023). Professor Dan Farber wrote about the possible impacts of this Supreme Court decision on environmental justice claims.

Daniel Farber, *Inequality and Regulation Revisited*

4 Am. J. Law & Equality 347 (2024)

In June 2023, a bitterly divided Roberts Court ended the practice of affirmative action in higher education in *Students for Fair Admissions, Inc. v. President & Fellows of Harvard College* ("SFFA"). Writing for the six conservatives, Chief Justice Roberts emphasized that the "core purpose" of the Equal Protection Clause is to end all race discrimination imposed by government and that "[e]liminating race discrimination means eliminating all of it." Any exception to the Constitution's demand for equal protection," he wrote, "must survive a daunting two-step examination known in our cases as 'strict scrutiny,'" which Roberts thought neither admissions program came close to satisfying. In the Court's view, "[b]oth programs lack sufficiently focused and measurable objectives warranting the use of race, unavoidably employ race in a negative manner, involve racial stereotyping, and lack meaningful end points."

The SFFA decision clearly raises the threat level for some agency efforts at environmental justice. Still, the resemblance between affirmative action and the use of race in designing regulations to reduce racial inequality may be overstated. Affirmative-action programs make race a factor in each individual's admission decision. In contrast, a pollution regulation designed to reduce environmental harms to minority communities would be facially color blind. This poses a key constitutional question: are regulations targeting racial disparities in exposure to environmental and health risks subject to strict scrutiny?

A recent Fourth Circuit decision, *Coalition for TJ v. Fairfax County School Board*, highlighted judicial divisions about how to assess race-neutral means of pursuing racial equity. In a challenge brought by Asian students, the court upheld a race-neutral admission scheme designed to increase racial diversity at a public magnet school. The court emphasized that the admission scheme did not reduce the Asian students' admission rate below that of other groups and the motivation was not to decrease the Asian share of the student body. An analysis along similar lines would allow race-neutral regulations designed to improve health in minority communities so long as the regulation did not leave white people with poorer health outcomes than others and was not motivated by a desire to limit health benefits to white communities. But the panel was divided, highlighting the unsettled nature of the issue. The Supreme Court declined to hear the case, though with two Justices dissenting....

* * *

While *SFFA* upended the law of affirmative action, it was grounded in the Equal Protection Clause of the Fourteenth Amendment. For more progressive uses of the Equal Protection Clause, *see, e.g.*, *Washington v. Trump*, 847 F.3d 1151 (9th Cir. 2017) (considering *Arlington Heights* factors in denying government's motion to lift TRO against presidential order restricting foreign travel where evidence indicated president intended to establish a "Muslim ban"); *Veasey v. Abbott*, 830 F.3d 216 (5th Cir. 2016) (considering *Arlington Heights* factors in finding evidence "that the cloak of ballot integrity could be hiding a more invidious purpose" behind 2011 Texas voter ID requirement); *Arce v. Douglas*, 793 F.3d 968 (9th Cir. 2015) (applying *Arlington Heights* factors to reverse a finding of summary judgment against students who challenged elimination of the Mexican American Studies program in Tucson public schools).

It is worth noting that the International Convention on the Elimination of All Forms of Racial Discrimination defines racial discrimination to include any conduct that has the purpose *or effect* of denying racialized populations equal treatment. The United States is a party to this treaty and has garnered repeated international criticism for its failure to implement the Convention's prohibition on actions that cause disparate racialized impact. Committee on the Elimination of Racial Discrimination, *Concluding observations on the combined tenth to twelfth reports of the United States of America*, CERD/C/USA/CO.10-12 (Sept. 21, 2022).

8. Substantive due process? While arguments for environmental justice under the U.S. Constitution are most often framed under the Equal Protection Clause, could arguments also be framed effectively as requirements of Due Process? Under the Fifth Amendment (applicable to the federal government) and the Fourteenth Amendment (applicable to the states), no person shall be deprived "of life, liberty, or property, without due process of law...." As interpreted by the U.S. Supreme Court in a long line of cases, the Due Process Clause guarantees substantive as well as procedural rights. *See, e.g.*, *Meyer v. Nebraska*, 262 U.S. 390 (1923) (right of language teacher to engage in "the calling of modern language teachers"); *Pierce v. Society of Sisters*, 268 U.S. 510 (1925) (right of parents to send children to parochial schools); *Griswold v. Connecticut*, 381 US. 479 (1965) (right of married couples to use contraceptives).

In 2022, the Supreme Court upended 50 years of settled law to conclude that substantive due process did not support a right to an elective abortion. *Dobbs v. Jackson Women's Health Organization*, 597 U.S. 215 (2022). In so holding, the Court overturned holdings of *Roe v. Wade*, 410 U.S. 113 (1973) and *Planned Parenthood v. Casey*, 505 U.S. 833 (1992). In the context of climate justice, the only federal court decision so far to find a substantive due process right was in *Juliana v. United States*, 217 F.Supp.3d 1224 (D. Or. 2016), which was overturned on redressability grounds, 947 F.3d 1158 (9th Cir. 2020).

9. State constitutions. Where arguments under the U.S. Constitution appear unlikely to succeed, environmental justice advocates may also consider pursuing similar claims under state constitutions. Art. I §19 of the New York Constitution explicitly guarantees "everyone" the right to clean air, clean water, and a healthful environment. The Montana and Pennsylvania constitutions similarly guarantee environmental rights to everyone, and pair this guarantee with a state duty to protect and promote the rights. PA. CONST. art. I, § 27; MONT. CONST. art. IX, § 1. Article XI §§ 1, 9 of the Hawaii constitution creates a state duty to protect environmental rights. As Supreme Court Justice William Brennan once observed, "State constitutions, too, are a font of individual liberties, their protections often extending beyond those required by the Supreme Court's interpretation of federal law." William J. Brennan, Jr., *State Constitutions and the Protection of Individual Rights*, 90 HARV. L. REV. 489, 491 (1977). State courts have found fundamental rights under state constitutions where the U.S. Supreme Court under the U.S. Constitution has not. *Compare Serrano v. Priest*, 557 P.2d 929, 952 (Cal. 1976) (fundamental right to public education under California constitution), with *San Antonio Independent School District v. Rodriguez*, 411 U.S. 1 (1973) (no fundamental right to public education under U.S. Constitution). Moreover, even for rights recognized by both the U.S. and state constitutions, many state courts have established more protective standards for those rights. For example, equal protection clauses in some state constitutions have been interpreted to prohibit disparate impacts, not only actions that are intentionally discriminatory. For one excellent comparative analysis, *see* Robert J. Klee, *What's Good for School Finance Should Be Good for Environmental Justice: Addressing Disparate Environmental Impacts Using State Courts and Constitutions*, 30 COLUM. J. ENVTL. L. 135 (2005).

10. The Michigan Supreme Court grappled with substantive due process rights under the Michigan Constitution in the wake of the Flint water crisis.

Mays v. Governor of Michigan

506 Mich. 157 (2020)

This putative class action involves a series of events commonly referred to as the "Flint water crisis." Plaintiffs, who are water users and property owners in the city of Flint, sued former Governor Rick Snyder, the state of Michigan, the Michigan Department of Environmental Quality (MDEQ), and the Michigan Department of Health and Human Services (DHHS) (collectively, the state defendants). Plaintiffs also sued former city of Flint emergency managers Darnell Earley and Jerry Ambrose....

[W]e affirm the Court of Appeals and conclude that plaintiffs have alleged facts that, if proved, support a claim for a constitutional violation by defendants. Plaintiffs allege that defendants' decision to switch the city of Flint's water source to the Flint River, which defendants knew was contaminated, resulted in a nonconsensual entry of toxic water into plaintiffs' bodies. Plaintiffs contend that defendants neglected to upgrade Flint's water-treatment system before switching to the Flint River despite knowing and being warned that the system was inadequate. After receiving information that suggested the Flint River was contaminated with bacteria, toxic levels of lead, and other contaminants, defendants allegedly concealed scientific data and made misleading statements about the safety of the Flint River water.

There is obviously no legitimate governmental objective in poisoning citizens. Plaintiffs' allegations, if true, are so egregious and outrageous that they shock the contemporary conscience and support a finding of defendants' deliberate indifference to plaintiffs' health and safety. *See* Villanueva, 779 F.3d at 513; Mettler Walloon, L.L.C., 281 Mich. App. at 198, 761 N.W.2d 293; McClendon, 305 F.3d at 326. Plaintiffs' allegations make out more than a negligent decision to switch water sources. They allege that "Defendants had time for deliberation in their decisions to expose Flint residents to toxic water, and their decision to do so was made with deliberate indifference to the known serious medical risks." Their allegations paint a picture of a public health crisis of the government's own making, intentionally concealed by state actors despite their knowledge that Flint residents were being harmed so long as the untreated water continued to flow through their pipes. We find it difficult to characterize the actions that defendants allegedly took as anything short of shocking to the conscience. "When such extended opportunities to do better are teamed with protracted failure even to care, indifference is truly shocking." Sacramento Co. v. Lewis, 523 U.S. 833, 853 (1998)....

Plaintiffs allege that the city of Flint's choice to provide Flint residents with the Flint River water was approved and implemented by the state defendants, arguing that both sets of defendants were decision-makers in the adoption of a plan that, once effectuated, resulted in violations of their substantive due-process rights. Defendants then purportedly made decisions to conceal the consequences of the water-source switch and misled the public about the safety of the Flint River water. Plaintiffs allege that defendants' aforementioned actions exposed them to unnecessary harm for months after the switch was made. Plaintiffs' allegations, if proved, support a conclusion that defendants considered an array of options and made a deliberate choice to effectuate the Flint River switch despite knowing the potential harms of doing so.

... [W]e conclude that plaintiffs pleaded a recognizable due-process claim under Michigan's Constitution for a violation of their right to bodily integrity....

* * *

Note that *Mays v. Governor* relies upon constitutional precedent in both federal and state courts. Does this decision of the Michigan Supreme Court in 2020 survive the 2022 upheaval in substantive due process jurisprudence wrought by the U.S. Supreme Court in *Dobbs*? If the viability of constitutional rights generally appears to be diminishing as possible authority for addressing environmental injustice, may EJ advocates fare better with claims under civil rights legislation? Consider that question you read the following section.

D. Enforcement of Civil Rights Act, Title VI

1. Introduction

Because of lack of success of equal protection claims and the apparent reticence of environmental agencies—at local, state, and federal levels—to condition or deny permits on environmental justice grounds, in the 1990s activists and community residents turned to Title VI of the Civil Rights Act of 1964, a non-environmental statute, as a potential redress for environmental disparities. Title VI has two major provisions:

> **Sec. 601 (42 U.S.C. § 2000d).** No person in the United States shall, on the ground of race, color, or national origin, be excluded from participation in, be denied the benefits of, or be subjected to discrimination under any program or activity receiving Federal financial assistance.
>
> **Sec. 602 (42 U.S.C. § 2000d-1).** Each Federal department and agency which is empowered to extend Federal financial assistance to any program or activity, by way of a grant, loan, or contract ... is authorized and directed to effectuate the provisions of [§ 601] ... by issuing rules, regulations, or orders of general applicability which shall be consistent with achievement of the objectives of the [Civil Rights Act of 1964]....

Like the equal protection cases discussed above, section 601 has been interpreted by the Supreme Court to require proof of discriminatory intent to be actionable. The challenge for impacted communities, then, is that the bar is very high to go to court because of the extraordinary difficulty in proving that a state environmental agency specifically intended to discriminate on the basis of race in issuing a permit or taking other actions while administering federal environmental programs (for which it receives funding).

However, pursuant to Section 602, federal agencies issued regulations precluding recipients of federal funds from engaging in activities that have a discriminatory "effect," i.e., regulations that prohibit disparate impacts in addition to prohibiting intentional discrimination.

According to DOJ, 26 federal agencies have Title VI regulations with some version of a disparate impact standard. These regulations are intended to ensure that programs accepting federal money are administered in a fashion that, in the words of President Kennedy, does not "encourage, entrench, subsidize or result in racial discrimination." Special Message to Congress on Civil Rights and Job Opportunities (June 19, 1963).

To that end, and consistent with Title VI regulations of many other federal agencies, EPA's Title VI regulations specifically provide that "[a] recipient shall not use criteria or methods of administering its program or activity which have the effect of subjecting individuals to discrimination because of their race, color, national origin, or sex...." 40 C.F.R. § 7.35(b). Moreover, "A recipient shall not choose a site or location of a facility that has the purpose or effect of excluding individuals from, denying them the benefits of, or subjecting them to discrimination...." *Id.* § 7.35(c).

Title VI administrative complaints submitted to the EPA typically allege that federally funded actions of state and local environmental agencies have resulted in disparate impacts on the basis of race or national origin. Most commonly, these Title VI allegations assert that state permitting of industrial facilities causes or exacerbates disparate impacts in communities of color. Historically, EPA's response to these complaints was underwhelming, leading to a backlog of cases and suits for unreasonable delay. *See infra* discussion of cases including *Californians for Renewable Energy (CARE) v. U.S. EPA*, 2018 WL 11434811 (N.D. Cal. 2018).

Even for timely, well-pled complaints, the agency was not very responsive. Part of the problem was the agency's lack of infrastructure for addressing these complaints. EPA issued multiple draft guidance documents that attempted to lay out the investigative and adjudicative practices for enforcing disparate impact regulations. The backlog was finally resolved before the Biden administration, which focused on transparency and resolution of pending and new cases. For EPA's online docket of administrative complaints and related documents, including informal resolution agreements, see the following link: https://www.epa.gov/external-civil-rights/external-civil-rights-docket.

As noted in Chapter 1, upon returning to office in 2025, President Trump repealed a slew of executive orders issued by his predecessors, to include even President Johnson's 60-year-old Executive Order 11246 (1965) promoting equal employment opportunities in federal employment and nondiscrimination in federal contracting.

In March 2025, Trump issued Executive Order 14281, which purported to eliminate disparate impacts analysis from federal law. Declaring that disparate impact analysis created "a near insurmountable presumption [that] unlawful discrimination exists where there are any differences in outcomes in certain circumstances among different races, sexes, or similar groups," EO 14281 purported to withdraw presidential approval for Title VI regulations and to "deprioritize" enforcement of any statute or regulation that included disparate impact liability.

As an alternative to filing a Title VI administrative complaint, community advocates in different contexts filed civil lawsuits to enforce the "disparate impact" regulations promulgated under Title VI, Sec. 602. With a civil complaint in U.S. District Court, the community advocate could potentially bypass an agency's administrative process and directly ask a federal judge for the appropriate relief. *See, e.g., South Camden Citizens in Action v. New Jersey Dept. of Envtl. Protection*, 145 F. Supp. 2d 445 (D.N.J. 2001) (State's "failure to consider the totality of the circumstances surrounding the operation" of a proposed cement plant in a community 91 percent persons of color violates EPA's Title VI regulations), *reversed* 274 F.3d 771 (3rd Cir. 2001). However, the Supreme Court in *Alexander v. Sandoval*, 532 U.S. 275 (2001), ruled that there was no private right of action to enforce the Title VI regulations. According to the 5–4 majority opinion of Justice Scalia, plaintiffs could only bring civil claims under Sec. 601 of Title VI, which—like equal protection claims under the Fourteenth Amendment—required findings of intentional discrimination. One consequence of this ruling was renewed focus on administrative proceedings to enforce Title VI regulations.

In the following sections, we first discuss the Title VI administrative process generally and then examine two Title VI complaints filed on behalf of residents in Flint, Michigan, and a very recent third complaint. We then will turn to reforms and modern practice in Title VI enforcement, describing some recent Title VI settlements EPA reached on behalf of environmental justice communities using disparate impact analysis. The chapter then describes the recent backlash against Title VI enforcement in the environmental context, specifically Louisiana's suit challenging the constitutionality of Title VI disparate impact assessments, and a multi-state petition requesting rulemaking to repeal the rules that define racialized disparate impacts as violations of Title VI. Finally, the chapter ends with the limited role that Section 1983 plays as a tool for vindicating environmental justice claims, again in the context of Flint. As you read this section, consider whether this legal avenue for pursuing environmental justice has continued potential.

2. Title VI Administrative Complaints

Administrative complaints alleging violations of the EPA's Title VI regulations are the primary mechanism by which the public can report discrimination by recipients of EPA financial assistance. A Title VI complaint must be filed with the designated office of EPA Headquarters in Washington, D.C. EPA regulations at 40 C.F.R. §7.120, together with the EPA's *Case Resolution Manual* (2017), set forth the general process for Title VI complaints, to begin with a complaint letter and supporting information to the EPA, review by EPA for completeness and timely filing within 180 days of the last act of alleged discrimination, and a letter from EPA stating whether or not the complaint is accepted for investigation. Theoretically, an EPA finding of discrimination could ultimately result in an EPA decision to "terminate or refuse to award" financial assistance to a recipient of EPA funding. But this has never happened. What does often happen now, consistent with Title VI law and regulations, is settlement negotiations resulting in an informal resolution agreement including some form of injunctive relief. Very few Title VI complaints in EPA's history have ever reached a formal administrative decision. The first one that did arose from concerns for air pollution from a proposed steel mill on the northern edge of Flint, Michigan. Flint residents filed a Title VI complaint to challenge an air permit for the Select Steel facility issued by the Michigan Department of Environmental Quality (MDEQ). As the excerpt below suggests, resolution of this complaint provided no relief or encouragement to advocates for environmental justice.

The *Select Steel* Administrative Decision (1998)

Letter from Ann E. Goode, Director, EPA Office of Civil Rights, to Father Phil Schmitter and Sister Joanne Chiaverini et al.

Alleged Discriminatory Effect Resulting from Air Quality Impacts

As outlined in EPA's *Interim Guidance*, EPA follows five basic steps in its analysis of allegations of discriminatory effects from a permit decision. "The first step is to identify the population affected by the permit that triggered the complaint." ... If there is no adverse effect from the permitted activity, there can be no finding of a discriminatory effect which would violate Title VI and EPA's implementing regulations. In order to address the allegation that MDEQ's issuance of a PSD [Prevention of Significant Deterioration] permit for the proposed Select Steel facility would result in a discriminatory effect, EPA first considered the potential adverse effect from the permitted facility using a number of analytical tools consistent with EPA's *Interim Guidance*....

To evaluate the impact of VOCs, EPA examined the permit application submitted by Select Steel and a variety of analyses conducted by MDEQ.... In examining VOCs as ozone precursors, EPA studied the additional contribution of VOCs from the proposed Select Steel facility and has determined those emissions will not affect the area's compliance with the national ambient air quality standards (NAAQS) [under the Clean Air Act] for ozone.

The NAAQS for ozone is a health-based standard which has been set at a level that is presumptively sufficient to protect public health and allows for an adequate margin of safety for the population within the area; therefore, there is no affected population which suffers "adverse" impacts within the meaning of Title VI resulting from the incremental VOC emissions from the proposed Select Steel facility....

Similarly, to evaluate potential lead emissions from the facility, EPA studied the additional contribution of airborne lead emissions from the proposed Select Steel facility and has determined those emissions will not affect the area's compliance with the NAAQS for lead. As with ozone, there is a NAAQS for lead that has been set at a level presumptively sufficient to protect public health and allows for an adequate margin of safety for the population within the attainment area. Therefore, there would be no affected population which suffers "adverse" impacts within the meaning of Title VI resulting from the incremental lead emissions from the proposed Select Steel facility....

In this case, MDEQ also appropriately considered information concerning the effect of the proposed facility's lead emissions on blood lead levels in children in response to community concerns. EPA reviewed this information along with other available data on the incidence and likelihood of elevated blood lead levels in Genesee County, particularly in the vicinity of the site of the proposed facility. EPA considered this additional information in response to the Complainants' concerns that the existing incidence of elevated blood lead levels in children in the vicinity of the proposed facility were already high. Overall, EPA found no clear evidence of a prevalence of pre-existing lead levels of concern in the area most likely to be affected by emissions from the proposed facility....

To assess the allegations of discrimination concerning public process, EPA evaluated the information from interviews with Complainants and MDEQ, and from documents gathered from the parties. The first allegation was that the permit was "hastily sped through" by MDEQ to avoid permitting requirements (*i.e.*, conduct a risk assessment; provide opportunity for public comment on risk assessment; provide meaningful opportunity for all affected parties to participate in the permit process) imposed by a

State trial court that are under appeal. The five months between receipt of the complete permit application and permit approval is actually slower than the average time of one and a half months for the past twenty-six PSD permits approved by MDEQ. EPA's review found that the public participation process for the permit was not compromised by the pace of the permitting process. MDEQ satisfied EPA's regulatory requirements concerning the issuance of PSD permits....

The Complainants alleged that the manner of publication of the notice of the permit hearing also contributed to the alleged discriminatory process. The Complainants allege that publication in newspapers was insufficient to inform the predominantly minority community because few community members have access to newspapers—something the Complainants allege was brought to MDEQ's attention during the permitting process for another facility in Genesee Township. EPA's regulations for PSD permitting require that notice of a public hearing must be published in a weekly or daily newspaper within the affected area. In this case, MDEQ went beyond the requirements of the regulation and published notices about the hearing in three local newspapers.

Complainants also state that MDEQ's failure to provide individual notice of the hearing to more members of the community also contributed to the alleged discriminatory process. In addition to newspaper notice, EPA's regulations require that notice be mailed to certain interested community members. MDEQ mailed hearing notification letters a month in advance to Fr. Schmitter, Sr. Chiaverini, and nine other individuals in the community who had expressed interest in the Select Steel permit—an action which is consistent with the requirements of EPA's regulations. The mailing list that MDEQ developed was adequate to inform the community about the public hearing, in part, because the Complainants took it upon themselves to contact other members of the community.

The Complainants also alleged that the location of the public hearing (Mount Morris High School) made it difficult for minority members of the community to attend. Complainants felt that the hearing should have been held at Carpenter Road Elementary School. Both schools are approximately two miles from the proposed Select Steel site; however, the elementary school is located in a predominantly minority area, while the high school is in a predominantly white area. MDEQ explored other possible locations and chose the high school, among other reasons, because of its ability to accommodate the expected number of citizens and its close proximity to the proposed site. The high school also is accessible by the general public via Genesee County public transportation.

For all of these reasons, EPA finds that the public participation process for the Select Steel facility was not discriminatory or in violation of Title VI or EPA's implementing regulations....

Notes and Questions

1. Wrongly decided. The EPA's decision in *Select Steel* is widely recognized as badly reasoned and wrongly decided on many levels. As just one clear example of error, while the *Select Steel* opinion assumed that the affected area met national air quality standards for ozone, in fact, it did not. EPA's Office of Civil Rights (OCR) noted that the county hosting the facility had been formally designated nonattainment for ozone in 1978, but that it had demonstrated compliance with the one-hour standard based upon three years of air quality data prior to 1998. Thus, reasoned OCR, "[i]n practical terms, this means that the old classification of 'nonattainment' has been superseded by a determination that Genesee County was meeting the old ozone standard." *See* Investigative Report at 14 (a report that accompanied the decision). In other words, OCR did not feel bound by the legal designation of the area. This error was critical because the crux of the EPA's decision was that since the area in question was not violating a health-based standard, then by definition the impact (even assuming a disparity exists) could not be "adverse." The late environmental attorney Luke Cole criticized this approach and argued that, despite OCR's contentions, as a legal *and* a factual matter Genesee County was not in attainment in 1998, the time of the permit proceeding in the *Select Steel* Title VI investigation:

> When the MDEQ made the decision to grant the permit to Select Steel on May 27, 1998, the area was not in attainment for the "old" one-hour ozone standard. In fact, less than two weeks earlier, on May 15, 1998, Flint hit a one-hour ozone level of 130 parts per billion (ppb)—a full 60 percent above EPA's health-based NAAQS of 80 ppb. On July 22, 1998—after Michigan issued the permit and after the Title VI complaint had been filed—EPA revoked the one-hour NAAQS for the Flint area, and the area was then covered by the eight-hour ozone NAAQS. On both of these dates—May 27, 1998, for the permit decision and June 9, 1998, for the filing of the complaint—Flint was not in attainment with either the one-hour ozone standard or the eight-hour ozone standard.... Thus, the central underpinning of EPA's decision and theory of no adverse impact—that Flint was in attainment for ozone—is demonstrably false.

Luke W. Cole, *"Wrong on the Facts, Wrong on the Law": Civil Rights Advocates Excoriate EPA's Most Recent Title VI Misstep*, 29 ENVTL. L. REP. 10,775, 10,777–78 (1999).

2. Wrong—and *wronger*. Imagine that the Flint region had, in fact, been in compliance with all air standards for ozone when the Select Steel permit had been issued. Would that then have ensured the protection of the community's health? As noted earlier in this chapter, "attainment" of NAAQS under the Clean Air Act is measured in broad geographies designated as Air Quality Control Regions. Thus, the air quality of Genesee County, at issue in *Select Steel*, may have no relation to the air quality actually experienced by people living in the Flint neighborhood across the street or downwind of the Select Steel facility. Air quality in this neighborhood could potentially exceed the NAAQS by orders of magnitude, while the county as a whole remained in attainment. Moreover, even if the local air quality in this neighborhood remained in compliance with the NAAQS, there was no assurance that EPA set the NAAQS at a safe level. In fact, in the years since the *Select Steel* decision, EPA repeatedly recognized that the standards for ozone in place in 1998 were *not* protective of human health. EPA

Figure 4-2. Father Phil Schmitter. Flint, Michigan. Photo: Cliff Villa, 2020.

tightened standards for ozone in 2008 and again in 2015, which public health experts believe may still not be protective. *See*, *Murray Energy v. EPA*, 936 F.3d 597 (D.C. Cir. 2019) (generally upholding 2015 NAAQS for ozone against challenges by both industry and environmentalists).

Compounding all the errors concerning ozone was the fact that there were many other pollutants of concern in this case, raising the potential for cumulative impacts. In addition to ozone and dioxin, air emissions from the Select Steel facility were anticipated to include lead, which by 1998 was already a problem in Flint soils due to sources including lead-based paint. Lead air emissions from the Select Steel facility would only add to the lead contamination in the community. While the EPA appeared to consider existing data on elevated blood-lead levels in the community, the EPA appeared to dismiss the concern that more lead contamination in the community would lead to more children with lead poisoning.

3. Procedural justice. While the *Select Steel* decision may serve as an exemplar of distributive injustice, it may also teach lessons on procedural injustice. Consider the community complaints about notice by publication in local newspapers. If poor people in the Flint community were unable to afford newspapers, would publication in *more newspapers* do anything to relieve concerns about lack of notice? Direct mailings may help address this concern, but how many people actually received the direct mailing in this case? How are the mailing lists compiled and maintained? Are there people that direct mailings might never reach? May the EPA rely on the voluntary efforts of a Catholic priest and nun in order to provide actual notice to community members? What more might you have suggested in this case to genuinely serve the interests of procedural justice?

4. Epilogue. Perhaps due to the community protest against the Select Steel air permit, the proposed steel mill was never built in Flint. Fr. Phil Schmitter, for his part, remained a staunch advocate for the local community. The Title VI complaint for Select Steel was not, in fact, the first that Fr. Schmitter filed. In 1992, six years before his Select Steel complaint, Fr. Schmitter filed another Title VI complaint with the EPA, this one alleging that the Michigan Department of Natural Resources engaged in disparate treatment in its decision to approve a proposed facility to burn wood waste for energy, a facility to become known as the Genesee Power Station. The EPA, typically for that time, failed to respond to this complaint in a timely manner. A quarter century later, on the last day of the Obama administration, the EPA finally issued a written decision in this matter, as excerpted below.

EPA Letter to Father Phil Schmitter

U.S. ENVIRONMENTAL PROTECTION AGENCY
EXTERNAL CIVIL RIGHT [sic] COMPLIANCE OFFICE
EPA File No. 01R-R5 (Jan. 19, 2017)

Dear Father Schmitter:

This letter is to advise you that the US Environmental Protection Agency's (EPA) External Civil Rights Compliance Office (ECRCO) has completed its investigation of the above-referenced Complaint (Genesee Complaint) and is resolving and closing this case as of the date of this letter. The Genesee Complaint was dated December 15, 1992, and filed by you on behalf of the St. Francis Prayer Center (Complainants). The Genesee Complaint was filed under Title VI of the Civil Rights Act of 1964, as amended, 42 U.S.C. §§ 2000d et seq., (Title VI) and EPA's nondiscrimination regulations found at 40 C.F.R. Part 7.

EPA's investigation focused on allegations of discrimination by the Michigan Department of Natural Resources (MDNR) (later becoming the Michigan Department of Environmental Quality (MDEQ)) and the Michigan Air Pollution Control

Commission (MAPCC) based on race related to granting of a permit to the Genesee Power Station (GPS) in Flint, Michigan, under the Clean Air Act (CAA). The MAPCC and MDNR were recipients of EPA financial assistance at the time of the alleged discriminatory acts. The MDEQ has received, and continues to receive, federal grants from EPA to run the Michigan Air Pollution Control Program, which carries out the functions formerly delegated to the MAPCC and the MDNR. The CAA permit function currently resides in the Air Quality Division of the MDEQ....

Summary of Findings

Title VI provides that "[n]o person in the United States shall, on the ground of race, color, or national origin, be excluded from participation in, be denied the benefits of, or be subjected to discrimination under any program or activity receiving Federal financial assistance." 42 U.S.C. § 2000d. As implemented by EPA's regulation, these prohibitions include intentional discrimination as well as practices that have a discriminatory effect on the bases of race, color, or national origin. *See* 40 C.F.R. §§ 7.35(a), 7.35(b).

... EPA finds that the preponderance of evidence supports a finding of discriminatory treatment of African Americans by MDEQ in the public participation process for the GPS permit considered and issued from 1992 to 1994. In addition, EPA has concerns that MDEQ's current policies are insufficient to address the potential for discrimination given the deficiencies in MDEQ's public participation program and procedures.

With respect to the allegations of adverse disparate health effects raised in the original complaint, EPA conducted four analyses to assess risk of health effects and did not find sufficient evidence to establish adversity/harm with respect to health effects. Therefore, there is insufficient evidence to support a prima facie case of adverse disparate impact....

Requests to speak either in advance of or out of order at hearings

According to MAPCC Commissioners, the MAPCC regularly accommodated elected representatives at MAPCC meetings based upon their schedules. Commissioners stated that they would allow elected representatives to offer their comments on a particular permit before the scheduled hearing if their schedules dictated that they be elsewhere when that permit hearing was to take place. The MAPCC also accommodated other attendees with scheduling conflicts. One MAPCC Commissioner stated that the MAPCC was "in the business of listening to the public," and that it "typically went out of [its] way to try to listen to people who had taken the time to appear before the Commission."

During the December 1, 1992, meeting in Lansing, the MAPCC considered three permits in addition to five other agenda items. In addition to GPS, there were permit hearings scheduled related to two proposed facilities in Marquette County: one in Sands Township and one in Skandia. The GPS permit hearing was the 7th item on the agenda. The MAPCC began its meeting around 9:00 am. At 9:30 a.m. the MAPCC started the first scheduled public hearing for the Marquette County Solid Waste

Management Authority. By 11:45 a.m. only 3 people had commented on this permit application. The Chairman of the MAPCC indicated that the MAPCC would break for lunch, but that before it did so, Dr. Robert Soderstrom would speak on the GPS permit application because he had a scheduling conflict and had to leave. Dr. Robert Soderstrom, from the Genesee Medical Society, who is White, then spoke.

State Representative Floyd Clack and Ms. Janice O'Neal, both of whom are African American, each asked to address the MAPCC in advance of the GPS hearing because of scheduling conflicts created by the delay of the hearing. Neither request was granted. Ms. O'Neal provided her oral comments at the GPS hearing later that evening after traveling 120 miles to Flint and back. Ms. Bogardus, who is White, interrupted the MAPCC as they deliberated about whether to postpone the GPS hearing. She did not ask permission to speak in advance of the GPS hearing. She interrupted the Commissioners and was allowed to proceed with her remarks.

The MAPCC deviated from what was described as its standard operating procedures for handling requests to speak in advance of the public comment period resulting in African Americans' requests being denied while requests by Whites to speak in advance were granted....

The GPS hearing began at about 6:40 p.m. with public comment commencing at about 8:40 p.m. Community members interested in providing comments to the MAPCC were given their opportunity more than 11 hours after they had arrived from Flint and the MAPCC meeting had begun. The length of time before the GPS hearing began was irregular for the MAPCC, as most MAPCC meetings had concluded or were wrapping up in the early evening. At no other hearing held in 1992 were community members required to wait 9 hours before their hearing started and 11 hours before they were allowed to provide comment. The GPS public hearing lasted almost 6 hours....

The MAPCC had the discretion to postpone the December 1992 hearing and/or extend the comment period. The decision to continue the hearing into the night and to issue the permit without allowing time for those at the hearing to review and prepare comments on new permit conditions, new analyses, and other information resulted in the commenters from the predominantly African American community being treated less favorably than people at other permit hearings for facilities in predominantly non-African American communities....

Armed and uniformed officers at hearing

October 20, 1994, MDEQ held a hearing at the Carpenter Road School, in a predominantly African American neighborhood bordering the GPS facility in Flint, to receive public comment on the proposed Wood Waste Plan. This was the last hearing before GPS would begin normal operation. This was the second GPS public hearing held outside of Lansing and the first to take place in the predominantly African American neighborhood. Two uniformed and armed MDEQ Conservation Officers attended the hearing at the request of the MDEQ. The first two GPS public hearings had been held in Lansing without armed uniformed officers present at the doors of the hearing.

The Law Enforcement Division, for whom the conservation officers work, did not have any written policy on the use of armed and uniformed officers at hearings. In response to the question of why the armed and uniformed officers were present at the Carpenter Road hearing, Michigan state agencies gave a variety of answers. The Law Enforcement Division stated that upon request, conservation officers were typically assigned to state government real estate sales (strong box security) and other public meetings where it was anticipated that personnel safety may be a concern due to the controversial nature of an issue.

Both of the officers at the Carpenter Road hearing stated they had been assigned to guard hearings before, but according to both the officers and other MDEQ staff, having guards at MDEQ meetings was not a frequent occurrence and only occurred when the MDEQ anticipated popular disapproval of MDEQ actions.

There was no strong box to guard at the GPS hearing. There is no persuasive evidence in the record that personnel safety may have been a concern due to the controversial nature of an issue. The state office for whom the conservation officers worked had no record of a request for the presence of armed uniformed officers that might contain an explanation for their presence. Neither of the two Conservation Officers who were present at that GPS hearing recalled being briefed regarding the reason that their presence was required.

In 1999, MDEQ stated that no complaints had been filed regarding the presence of conservation officers at public hearings or meetings since 1994. MDEQ stated that it has held public hearings and meetings in the local affected communities without incident, and that many of these meetings were conducted in inner-city communities. MDEQ's recent response describes a number of reasons, including some not mentioned in 1999, why armed and uniformed officers might be present at hearings and indicates that depending on the circumstances, there are several different types of officers that might be present.

At the time, the use of armed and uniformed officers was uncommon and appears to have only happened at the hearing held in the African American community. In evaluating the use of armed and uniformed officers in this situation, EPA considered the intimidation factor through threat of police force as historically used against African Americans when attempting to exercise their rights.

Without any credible explanation, MDEQ deviated from its stated policy at the time by placing the armed and uniformed guards at the GPS hearing in Flint. MDEQ has not provided a copy of any current policies that apply to the use of armed and uniformed officers at hearings or the criteria used to evaluate whether and when certain types of officers should be used (e.g., plain clothes, armed and uniformed police, conservation officers).

Close of hearing during testimony

MDEQ adjourned the October 20, 1994, hearing during the testimony of an African American speaker and before everyone had been given a chance to testify.

The decision to adjourn the hearing surprised MDEQ staff. MDEQ staff stated that, before its adjournment, the October 20, 1994, hearing was not atypically controversial or heated, nor was the audience disorderly. MDEQ staff members stated that the audience at Carpenter Road Elementary was no more emotional than audiences at other hearings that had not been adjourned. One MDEQ employee stated that she had never seen any hearing adjourned before all of the commenters were allowed to speak.

In addition, another witness who attended most of the air permit hearings held in Michigan from 1990 to 1996 stated that he had never seen the MDEQ adjourn a hearing as it did at the October 20, 1994, GPS hearing. The witness stated that commenters at other hearings had made comments similar to Ms. O'Neal's, but the MDEQ had never adjourned a hearing because of it.

The evidence shows that Ms. O'Neal, an African American, was treated less favorably than all other commenters at any MDEQ hearing in anyone's memory. In addition, the witnesses say that to their knowledge the first time, and for some who attended many hearings afterward, the only time a hearing was closed before all commenters could speak was when it was held in the African American community in Flint....

The totality of the circumstances described above supported by a preponderance of the evidence in EPA's record would lead a reasonable person to conclude that race discrimination was more likely than not the reason why African Americans were treated less favorably than non-African Americans during the 1992–1994 public participation for the GPS permit.

[After finding likely race discrimination in the MDEQ permit procedures, the EPA letter proceeds to evaluate the likely health impacts from GPS air emissions. Finding no direct or indirect health effects above EPA's action levels (one in ten thousand excess chance of cancer), the EPA letter concluded that there was insufficient evidence of health impacts (thus insufficient evidence to support a finding of health impacts) on the African-American community of Flint. The EPA accordingly closed this Title VI complaint against MDEQ. Eds.]

Notes and Questions

1. Race discrimination. As recounted in the above excerpt, what exactly did the state do to support the EPA's finding that "African Americans were treated less favorably than non-African Americans" in the GPS permit process? If you were legal counsel for the state in 1992–1994, how might you have advised your agency clients to avoid any appearance of discrimination in each of the three contexts discussed in the excerpt?

2. Finally getting it right? What is the effect of an agency responding to a Title VI complaint 25 years after it has been filed? Is this a mockery of the administrative process? Or is the letter from the EPA in 2017 vindication of Fr. Schmitter and the Black community that the EPA found had been so mistreated by MDEQ in the GPS permit process? Could any good come from this?

While failing to find actual health impacts from the Genessee Power Station facility, the EPA letter found convincing evidence of procedural injustice in the GPS permit process and across MDEQ operations more broadly. After reviewing "30 years of [MDEQ] history," the letter stated that "EPA is deeply concerned that MDEQ will not fulfill its responsibility to implement a fully functioning and meaningful non-discrimination program as required under EPA regulations." EPA letter at 28. To address these "deep[] concerns," the EPA letter provided MDEQ with a number of specific recommendations for improving its public procedures, to include (1) updating and prominently displaying MDEQ's notice of non-discrimination; (2) updating MDEQ's grievance procedures; (3) providing explicit assurances against retaliation for invoking grievance procedures; (4) ensuring appropriate training for MDEQ personnel; (5) developing and updating appropriate public participation plans; (6) taking greater measures to involve Limited English Proficiency communities; and (7) ensuring MDEQ facilities are physically accessible for persons with disabilities.

While closing the Title VI complaint for the Genesee Power Station permit, the EPA letter further noted the existence of another Title VI complaint continuing against MDEQ where the EPA has "additional and serious concerns." This ongoing complaint arises from MDEQ's "administration of the Safe Drinking Water Act ... during the Flint drinking water crisis...."

3. Coda. In 2021, Flint-area advocates, including the St. Francis Prayer Center and working with Earthjustice, filed yet another Title VI administrative complaint with the EPA, alleging racialized disparate environmental impacts by Michigan's environmental agency—now known as the Michigan Department of Environment, Great Lakes, and Energy (EGLE). Specifically, the complaint alleged that EGLE discriminated against Black and Latino residents by issuing permits for the Ajax hot asphalt facility in Genessee Township. Although Genesee Township is nearly 90 percent white, and its board of trustees is all white, the nearly 3000 people living within one mile of the Ajax facility are overwhelmingly Black and Latino.

The complaint alleged that the siting of this asphalt facility was part of a pattern and practice of permitting toxic industry in or directly proximate to Flint, and that these actions had the intent and/or effect of discriminating on the basis of race, color, or national origin in violation of Title VI. The Ajax facility emits air toxics, including lead, sulfur, particulates, and other pollutants, adding to the pollution load in an already overburdened community still reeling from the lead-contaminated water crisis. The Ajax complaint, filed in 2021, was officially resolved in 2023 through entry of an Informal Resolution Agreement between EPA and EGLE. Among other things, the agreement provided for enhanced public engagement, installation of a fence-line air monitor, and other commitments by EGLE. Despite these commitments, the agreement left community advocates "outraged," as it failed to provide any substantive bar to permitting or operation of the asphalt facility. *See* Kayla Ruble, *EPA, Mich. Officials Resolve Genessee Co. Asphalt Plant Complaint, But Activists Aren't Happy*, Detroit News, Aug. 12, 2023.

Has the passage of time morphed Title VI into a procedural rather than a distributive justice requirement? In communities like Flint, has Title VI disrupted or solidified environmental injustice?

3. Title VI Citizen Litigation

The 25-year saga of the Genesee Power Station Title VI complaint was an extraordinary case on many levels. However, it represents just one of the hundreds of Title VI complaints that have been filed with the U.S. EPA over that same period of time. Historically, nearly all of the Title VI complaints filed with the EPA received delayed responses, if they received any response at all. This record of poor performance did not go unnoticed, including by federal courts and the EPA itself, both of which contributed to reforms of the Title VI program.

Even as EPA began making changes to its Title VI program during the Obama administration, the Agency's record of delay and inaction on Title VI complaints attracted the attention of federal courts. In a case brought seeking to compel EPA to respond to long-overdue Title VI complaints, the Ninth Circuit observed that "the EPA failed to process a single complaint from 2006 or 2007 in accordance with its regulatory deadlines." *Rosemere Neighborhood Ass'n v. U.S. EPA*, 581 F.3d 1169, 1175 (9th Cir. 2009). Other federal courts demonstrated similar concern for the EPA's failure to comply with Title VI regulatory deadlines. *See, e.g.*, *Padres Hacia Una Vida Mejor v. McCarthy*, 614 F.App'x 895, 897 (9th Cir. 2015) (describing as "simply deplorable" the EPA's 17-year delay in responding to a Title VI complaint filed in 1994 alleging discrimination against Latinos in the siting and operation of toxic waste disposal sites in Kettleman City); *see also*, *Californians for Renewable Energy (CARE) v. U.S. EPA*, 2018 WL 11434811 (N.D. Cal. 2018) (finding that over more than a decade EPA failed to respond to five different Title VI complaints alleging discriminatory siting of hazardous facilities in New Mexico, Michigan, Texas, Alabama and California.)

Granting plaintiffs' summary judgment motion, the *Californians for Renewable Energy* court issued the following judgment:

> 4. The EPA shall timely process any pending and future Title VI complaints submitted by Plaintiffs and accepted for investigation by EPA as follows: for any pending investigation into a Title VI complaint submitted by any Plaintiff, EPA must issue preliminary findings and any recommendations for voluntary compliance, or otherwise resolve the complaint, within 180 days of the date of entry of this judgment; for any Title VI complaint submitted by any Plaintiff and accepted by EPA after the date of entry of this judgment, EPA must issue preliminary findings and any recommendations for voluntary compliance, or otherwise resolve the complaint, within 180 days of acceptance. The requirements of this paragraph shall continue for a period of five years from the date judgment is entered.

5. The Court shall retain jurisdiction to enforce this judgment . . . as to those complaints subject to Paragraph 4 above.

IT IS SO ORDERED.

Does the outcome of cases like *Californians for Renewable Energy v. EPA* mean that the EPA must always be sued to compel compliance with Title VI regulations? Or might cases like that encourage the EPA to comply with Title VI requirements before it gets sued? For more on Title VI litigation and *Californians for Renewable Energy v. EPA* (by the attorney who served as counsel for the plaintiffs), *see* Engelman Lado, *No More Excuses*, *supra*, at 296.

Of course, victory in court does not necessarily mean progress on the ground. Did the lawsuit in *Californians for Renewable Energy* achieve any real benefit for community members concerned with environmental justice? For at least some of the individual plaintiffs, it does appear to have made a difference. As the court acknowledged in its opinion, the filing of the lawsuit seemed to encourage the EPA to provide some resolution to each of the five Title VI cases that had languished over a decade. The Michigan case was the one involving the Genesee Power Station, filed by Fr. Schmitter in 1992 and resolved by EPA letter of January 19, 2017 (reprinted in part above). On the same day, the EPA also resolved the New Mexico case, filed on behalf of the Citizens for Alternatives to Radioactive Dumping (CARD), by entering an Informal Resolution Agreement with the New Mexico Environment Department. Previously, the EPA had already closed the California case for "insufficient evidence of current non-compliance with Title VI" or the Title VI regulations. Within three months of resolving the Michigan and New Mexico cases, the EPA closed the Alabama case for "insufficient evidence" and closed the Texas case by entering into an Informal Resolution Agreement with Texas DEQ. *Californians for Renewable Energy* at 4.

While the California and Alabama Title VI complaints were dismissed, the continuing jurisdiction of the court for five years potentially gave the plaintiffs in these cases significant leverage in negotiations with local regulators, given the plaintiffs' continuing ability to file future Title VI complaints and seek enforcement of regulatory deadlines. The Genesee Power Station case in Flint, Michigan, resulted in a finding, by the preponderance of the evidence, that the state engaged in race discrimination—a finding any state would seek to avoid—plus specific recommendations from the EPA for improving the state's public involvement processes. For the New Mexico and Texas cases, through the Informal Resolution Agreements, the plaintiffs received specific commitments from state regulators to improve their environmental and community involvement practices. The New Mexico Environment Department, for example, developed a new public involvement policy and took affirmative measures to ensure that key regulatory documents would be translated for Spanish-speaking communities. (One of the book authors served as co-counsel to ensure compliance with the New Mexico agreement.)

Title VI complaints against the State of North Carolina alleging failure to address disproportionate impacts from industrial hog farms have had a mixed track record.

These concentrated animal feed operations (CAFOs) proliferated in the eastern part of the state, including Duplin County. The impacted communities were overwhelmingly communities of color. A complaint, filed in 2014 on behalf of the North Carolina Environmental Justice Network, community-based Rural Empowerment Association for Community Help (REACH), and Waterkeeper Alliance resulted four years later in a Settlement Agreement with the North Carolina Department of Environmental Quality. Under the Settlement Agreement, the DEQ agreed to specific concessions that include the following:

- Submission of the Swine Waste Management System General Permit to a public stakeholder process, including use of an independent facilitator;
- Conduct of local air monitoring and water monitoring, carried out in partnership with the complainant community organizations; and
- Development and implementation of policies to enhance public involvement and language access.

4. Title VI Administrative Complaints after 2020

The enhanced public engagement procedures required by the 2018 Settlement Agreement for Duplin County failed to relieve the substantial burdens that industrial hog farms posed to local residents. In 2021, the Southern Environmental Law Center filed another Title VI complaint on behalf of the NAACP alleging that North Carolina discriminated against residents of Duplin and Sampson counties by issuing permits allowing four hog farms to use cesspits and sprayfields, and to convert hog waste to energy without adequately protecting the hundreds of Black and Latino families living in close proximity to these operations. This complaint was never resolved. In 2023, Vermont Law School's Environmental Justice Clinic filed a Title VI complaint making similar allegations about the discriminatory impact of North Carolina DEQ's failure to adequately regulate industrial poultry farms in Duplin and Sampson counties.

The Biden administration changed course from the first Trump administration and made addressing discriminatory environmental and health impacts through enforcement of Title VI a top priority. The U.S. Department of Justice established an Office of Environmental Justice and developed a Comprehensive Environmental Justice Enforcement Strategy. EPA launched the Office of Environmental Justice and External Civil Rights (OEJECR), which provided training for EPA staff and education and technical assistance to recipients of EPA funding in order to promote Title VI compliance. OEJECR worked to bring communities into the Title VI complaint resolution process and also conducted its first affirmative compliance review, resulting in an agreement with the Colorado Department of Public Health and Environment. *See* EPA Press Release, *EPA and CDPHE Partner to Strengthen Civil Rights in Colorado*, Jan. 17, 2025. These actions produced some high-profile wins for environmental justice communities.

In November 2021, the DOJ announced a Title VI investigation against the Alabama Department of Public Health and Lowndes County Health Department in response to a 2018 Title VI complaint filed by environmental justice leader Catherine Coleman Flowers. The complaint alleged that both the Alabama Department of Public Health and the Lowndes County Health Department violated Title VI and discriminated against Black residents by failing to provide basic sanitation, failing to investigate a hookworm outbreak tied to inadequate sewage disposal, and threatening Lowndes County residents with criminal prosecution for sanitation conditions they had no power to prevent. For background on the extreme circumstances of environmental injustice in Lowndes County, Alabama, see CATHERINE COLEMAN FLOWERS, WASTE: ONE WOMAN'S FIGHT AGAINST AMERICA'S DIRTY SECRET (2020).

An 18-month DOJ investigation found that as many as 80 percent of Black and low-income residents of Lowndes County lacked basic sanitation and raised concerns that this situation was due to state agency actions and inactions in violation of Title VI. This investigation resulted in a 2023 informal settlement in which the Alabama Department of Public Health agreed, *inter alia,* to develop a long-term public health and infrastructure plan to improve access to adequate sanitation, to work with CDC to address public health risks associated with raw sewage exposure, and to stop arresting residents for being unable to afford a new septic system. However, in March 2025, the Trump DOJ abruptly terminated the Lowndes County agreement as part of what the administration described as an effort "to eradicate illegal DEI preferences and environmental justice across the government and in the private sector."

In 2022, DOJ opened a Title VI investigation into the City of Houston's solid waste management operations and enforcement practices. The investigation responded to a Title VI complaint brought on behalf of residents in Northeast Houston's Trinity/Houston Gardens Super Neighborhood 48 by Lone Star Legal Aid. The complaint alleged that the City ignored frequent complaints about illegal dumping in this predominantly Black and Latino neighborhood. The complaint alleged that these failures amounted to a denial of equal access to City services that disproportionately burdened the health and safety of Black and Latino Houstonians and devalued their real property in violation of Title VI. In 2023, DOJ announced an informal settlement of this Title VI complaint built around the City's *One Clean Houston Plan.* This plan prioritized combatting illegal dumping and rapid cleanup in areas severely impacted by illegal dumping. The City also agreed to create a neighborhood equity dashboard to analyze the City's responsiveness to complaints by neighborhood, and to improve community outreach.

Also in 2022, with the assistance of Earthjustice and Tulane's environmental law clinic, multiple Louisiana environmental justice groups filed two Title VI complaints with EPA alleging racial discrimination in air pollution permitting decisions by the Louisiana Department of Environmental Quality and the Louisiana Department of Health. The complaints involved state approvals for the Denka Performance Elastomer facility in St. John the Baptist Parish (see Chapter 5, Figure 5-3), and for the proposed Formosa Plastics facility ("Formosa") in St. James Parish. These permitting decisions would significantly increase air pollution in "Cancer Alley," an 85-mile stretch of land known for its concentration of industrial and petrochemical facilities in predominantly Black communities.

After preliminary investigation, EPA seemed ready to issue a finding of discrimination under Title VI. The agency issued a Letter of Concern detailing "significant evidence" indicating that Louisiana's regulatory actions or inactions over many years resulted in disparate adverse impacts on Black residents of St. John the Baptist Parish, St. James Parish, and the Industrial Corridor. The EPA Letter specifically identified substantially elevated cancer rates experienced by Black residents as a disparate impact and questioned whether the state methods for administering its air pollution control program had the intent or effect of subjecting persons to discrimination on the basis of race. A draft agreement negotiated between EPA and LDEQ contained major reforms that would have transformed Louisiana's air permitting program. Among other changes, the agreement would have required the LDEQ to use cumulative impacts assessments and to analyze whether pollution would disproportionately affect people of color when making permit decisions.

In response, then-state attorney general, now Governor Jeff Landry sued EPA and DOJ in federal court requesting an injunction to prevent the agencies from enforcing disparate impact regulations or requiring cumulative impacts analysis. The complaint alleged that EPA's Title VI disparate impact regulations exceeded the agency's authority under the Civil Rights Act, violated the Administrative Procedure Act, and implicated the major questions doctrine. Accusing EPA of being "fixated on race," Louisiana asserted that any move to remedy the environmental injustices suffered by Black Louisianians compelled the state to intentionally discriminate against white residents. The state disclaimed any obligation to avoid racially discriminatory effects in its environmental permitting. Against the backdrop of a recent call from experts on the United Nations Human Rights Council to end "environmental racism" in Cancer Alley, the complaint was an aggressive challenge to the very concept of environmental justice. Rather than fight, and in light of actions that EPA was taking to strengthen regulations applicable to emissions at the plant (see case study at conclusion of Chapter 5), EPA responded by closing its Title VI investigations.

In August 2024, Judge James D. Cain, Jr. of the Western District of Louisiana permanently enjoined EPA and DOJ from enforcing any Title VI disparate impact regulations against any entity in the state of Louisiana. Judge Cain found that such requirements went beyond Title VI's mandate and violated the Louisiana Constitution's ban on discrimination by requiring the decisionmaker to consider race. *State of LA v. EPA*, No. 2:23-cv-00692 (W.D. La. Jan. 23, 2024). Even before Judge Cain had issued a final injunction, Florida Attorney General Ashley Moody filed a petition for rulemaking on behalf of 23 states requesting EPA rescind the disparate impact provisions of its Title VI regulations. The petition falsely claimed that EPA's Title VI regulations "compel the imposition of quotas." Extrapolating from *Students for Fair Admissions v. Harvard College*, 600 U.S. 181 (2023), the petition argues that "any recipient choosing an alternative course of action to avoid a racial disparity would be taking action on the basis of race," contrary to the Equal Protection Clause.

The *Louisiana v. EPA* decision drew into question the EPA's authority to *require* disparate impact and/or a cumulative impacts analysis for projects with federal involvement. Trump's election to a second term ensured that this question will be at the center of American political discourse. Early in his second administration, Trump issued Executive Order 14281 purporting to eliminate federal enforcement of disparate impacts liability.

Notes and Questions

1. Appeal? If you represented the EPA in *Louisiana v. EPA* and believed Judge Cain's decision was wrong on the law or the facts, or both, would you appeal? Why or why not?

2. Title VI and other agencies. Advocates for environmental justice should consider every available pathway for relief, and that may include looking beyond EPA. Other federal agencies such as Housing and Urban Development (HUD), Health and Human Services (HHS), and the Department of Transportation (DOT) all receive Title VI complaints that may raise community concerns for environmental injustice. For example, in 2000, WE ACT for Environmental Justice, with support from legal counsel including Luke Cole, filed a Title VI complaint with DOT alleging the New York City Metropolitan Transportation Authority (MTA) had violated Title VI by siting six of its eight bus depots in Harlem and Washington Heights, thereby exposing community members to disproportionate levels of diesel exhaust. *See* Press Release, *WE ACT Files Title VI Complaint Against MTA*, Nov. 15, 2000. The complaint led to changes in MTA practices, including covered depots to reduce diesel exhaust emissions to ambient air. More recently, in 2022, HUD issued a finding of noncompliance with Title VI to the City of Chicago for facilitating the relocation of a metal recycling facility owned by General Iron from the majority white neighborhood of Lincoln Park to a predominantly Black and Hispanic neighborhood. *See* HUD, Letter of Findings of Noncompliance with Title VI and Section 109 *Southeast Environmental Task Force, et al. v. City of Chicago,* Case No. 05-20-0419-5/8/9 (July 19, 2022). In 2023, HUD and the City of Chicago entered a settlement agreement that required the City to complete a comprehensive study of environmental burdens, health conditions, and social stressors across Chicago and use that study to advance reforms in land use, permitting, and environmental enforcement policies. Voluntary Compliance Agreement Between [HUD] and The City of Chicago, May 12, 2023.

3. What now? Executive Order 14281 purported to make sweeping changes to federal civil rights law. Can the president do that unilaterally? Disparate impact theory is codified in federal law and supported by prior court decisions. Until the Supreme Court makes a ruling on this issue or Congress amends federal law, disparate impact should remain a viable theory under the federal civil rights laws. However, under the current state of Title VI law and policy, would you advise a client to pursue a Title VI complaint if the facts appeared to support a disparate impacts claim?

E. Environmental Justice through § 1983

With origins reaching back to the Civil Rights Act of 1871, the federal law known today as § 1983 provides as follows:

> Every person who, under color of any statute, ordinance, regulation, custom, or usage, of any State or Territory or the District of Columbia, subjects ... any citizen of the United States ... to the deprivation of any rights, privileges, or immunities secured by the Constitution and laws, shall be liable to the party injured in an action at law....

42 U.S.C. § 1983 (2019). As indicated, § 1983 establishes a private right of action against state employees for deprivation of rights established under the U.S. Constitution and other federal law. § 1983 is today a major authority for pursuing civil rights claims in every public arena, including education, voting rights, and criminal justice. While a thorough review of § 1983 theory and practice remains beyond the scope of this book, this concluding section of the chapter demonstrates that civil rights claims under § 1983 may also address concerns for environmental justice in certain contexts. Returning to drinking water poisoning in Flint, Michigan, discussed earlier in this chapter with the state court decision in *Mays v. Governor*, consider the following decision in federal court deciding a case brought by Flint residents under § 1983.

Boler v. Earley

865 F.3d 391 (6th Cir. 2017), *cert. denied*,
138 S.Ct. 1294 (2018)

JANE B. STRANCH, Circuit Judge

These [] cases arise from the water contamination crisis in Flint, Michigan. Plaintiffs, residents of Flint affected by the contaminated city water, bring suit against various state and local officials and entities, alleging violation of their constitutional rights, pursuant to 42 U.S.C. § 1983, along with other claims. In *Boler*, the district court determined that the § 1983 claims were preempted by the Safe Drinking Water Act (SDWA) and dismissed the case for lack of subject matter jurisdiction. Relying on its preemption analysis in *Boler*, the court dismissed the *Mays* case. The cases have been consolidated on appeal. For the reasons explained below, we REVERSE the judgment of the district court and REMAND for further proceedings.

I. BACKGROUND

A. Factual Background

In March 2011, the Michigan state Legislature passed the Local Government and School District Fiscal Accountability Act ("Act 4"), which authorized the governor to appoint an emergency manager for certain local governments....

In November 2013, Governor Snyder appointed Darnell Earley as Emergency Manager for the City of Flint. In January 2015, Earley was replaced by Gerald Ambrose.

Between 1967 and 2014, the City of Flint sourced its water from Lake Huron via the Detroit Water and Sewerage Department (DWSD). On March 29, 2013, ... the City of Flint decided to join a water supplier, the Karegnondi Water Authority (KWA), that was to be established. Sourcing water for Flint had been under review. In 2011, Flint had commissioned a study ("2011 Report" or "Report") to evaluate the cost of treating water from the Flint River for municipal use as an alternative to either purchasing from the future KWA or continuing its existing contract with DWSD. The Report determined that water from the Flint River would need to be treated to meet current water safety regulations. It also concluded that the cost of treating water from the Flint River to provide safe municipal use would be greater than the proposed KWA contract, but less than continuing the contract with DWSD. The officials thus decided to go with the cheapest long-term option—the KWA.

Shortly after the decision to switch to the KWA was made, DWSD notified Flint that its current contract would terminate in approximately one year, in April 2014. Because the KWA would take several years to construct, officials were tasked with choosing an interim water source: the Flint River or DWSD. Officials chose the Flint River....

In April 2014, Flint's emergency manager changed the source of the city's water from DWSD to the Flint River. The plaintiffs assert that at this time, the City knew "that the Flint River could not be a source of safe municipal water unless it underwent significant treatment, including the addition of anti-corrosive agents and treatment for microbial contaminants," as explained by the 2011 Report. The Report itself states that its comparison to other alternatives "assumed that the Flint [water treatment plant] w[ould] treat water from the river to provide a finished water of similar quality to other alternatives being considered." There is no evidence that the City upgraded the treatment plants or provided for additional safety measures prior to switching water supply sources on April 25, 2014. The Defendants contend that they operated in accordance with the SDWA's Lead and Copper Rule, which requires a two-step process that begins with "initial monitoring" over two separate six-month periods to determine if treatment is required. The first six-month period did not begin until June 2014.

Following the switch to the Flint River, residents immediately began to complain that the drinking water "smelled rotten, looked foul, and tasted terrible." Larger problems with the water supply soon became apparent. Testing conducted in August and September 2014 detected coliform and *E. coli* bacteria in the water supply. In October 2014, the water was linked to Legionnaire's disease. General Motors discontinued its water service because the Flint River water was corroding its parts.

In January 2015, the City issued a notice that the drinking water violated standards, but that it was safe to drink. In February 2015, further water testing indicated high levels of contaminants such as lead and total trihalomethane. The Defendants state that the City conducted its two required rounds of sampling to determine lead levels, from July to December 2014 and January to June 2015, but the results did not exceed the SDWA Lead and Copper Rule's "action level." The results did indicate that corrosion control treatment measures were needed to counteract lead levels, which "had risen since switching to the Flint River." In March 2015, the Flint City Council voted to reconnect with DWSD rather than continuing to use the Flint River water supply, but the City government's vote was overruled by the Emergency Manager.

Over the next few months, the City issued instructions to residents on their use of water, including advising them to "pre-flush" taps prior to use or to stop drinking the water altogether. In June 2015, the EPA warned of high lead levels in the water. In response, officials provided consumers with water filters, which the Plaintiffs state did not substantially improve the water quality and were incapable of filtering out known contaminants.

In October 2015, Genesee County declared a public health emergency in Flint, advising residents not to drink the water. That same month, the Emergency Manager ordered that Flint reconnect to DWSD. By that point, however, the protective coating in the water supply pipes had been damaged by water from the Flint River, and until the coating could "buil[d] up to appropriate levels," the water would continue to have elevated lead levels. The EPA issued an advisory to Flint residents in February 2016, warning them that unfiltered water was not safe and advising the use of bottled water, especially for young children and pregnant women....

Flint residents have been billed continuously for their water services since April 2014. The City of Flint has engaged in collection efforts when payments have not been made, including disconnecting water service altogether and issuing liens against real property. The Defendants state that Michigan is providing funds for the reimbursement of water bills, as well as making other efforts to ameliorate the effects of the water crisis.

On January 25, 2016, the Michigan Civil Rights Commission passed a resolution to hold a series of hearings to determine the impact of the Flint water contamination crisis on the civil rights of Michigan's citizens. The Commission, appointed by the Governor, held three hearings that included "expert testimony focusing on the history of Flint's economy and housing, environmental justice, and the application of the ... emergency manager law." Michigan Civil Rights Commission, *The Flint Water Crisis: Systemic Racism Through the Lens of Flint* iii (Feb. 17, 2017). The Commission's 130-page report determined that the response to the Flint water crisis was "the result of systemic racism," *Id.* at 2, and that its finding was "based on a plethora of events and policies that so racialized the structure of public policy that it systemically produced racially disparate outcomes adversely affecting a community that is primarily made up of people of color."

B. Procedural History of *Boler v. Earley*

Plaintiffs Beatrice Boler, Pastor Edwin Anderson and Mrs. Alline Anderson, and EPC Sales, LLC, a Flint business, brought a class action on behalf of purchasers of Flint water. They brought suit against Darnell Earley and Gerald Ambrose, both former emergency managers of Flint; Dayne Walling, the former mayor of Flint; the City of Flint; Governor Rick Snyder; the State of Michigan; the Michigan Department of Environmental Quality (MDEQ); and the Michigan Department of Health and Human Services (MDHHS).

The Plaintiffs filed suit in the Eastern District of Michigan on January 31, 2016, alleging twelve causes of action, five of them pursuant to 42 U.S.C. § 1983: (1) impairment of the constitutional right to contract; (2) deprivation of substantive and procedural due process; (3) breach of the duty to protect against state-created danger; (4) breach of the Equal Protection Clause; and (5) deprivation of property interest without due process or just compensation....

The Plaintiffs filed a motion for a preliminary injunction, seeking to enjoin the defendants from billing and collecting money from Flint residents for water.... The court subsequently dismissed the case for lack of subject matter jurisdiction, finding that the Plaintiffs' § 1983 claims were precluded by the SDWA, leaving only state law claims over which the court did not have jurisdiction.... This appeal followed...

II. ANALYSIS

A. Preclusion of § 1983 Claims by the Safe Drinking Water Act

The district court's SDWA preemption analysis drew from *Middlesex County Sewerage Authority v. National Sea Clammers Association*, 453 U.S. 1 (1981), in which the Supreme Court found that the § 1983 claims presented were preempted by the statutes alleged. The court primarily relied on the First Circuit's determination that the SDWA foreclosed other federal remedies for an alleged right to "safe and potable water." The Plaintiffs argue that this is not the proper focus of their claims, and more importantly, that the district court misapplied the standard enunciated by the Supreme Court in its line of cases that began with *Sea Clammers* and concluded with *Fitzgerald v. Barnstable School Committee*, 555 U.S. 246 (2009).

The provisions of 42 U.S.C. § 1983 may serve as a vehicle for a plaintiff to obtain damages for violations of the Constitution or a federal statute. Section 1983 provides in part:

> Every person who, under color of any statute, ordinance, regulation, custom, or usage, of any State or Territory or the District of Columbia, subjects, or causes to be subjected, any citizen of the United States ... to the deprivation of any rights, privileges, or immunities secured by the Constitution and laws, shall be liable to the party injured in an action at law, suit in equity, or other proper proceeding for redress....

In *Sea Clammers*, the Court examined claims—brought under the [Clean Water Act], 33 U.S.C. § 1251, and the Marine Protection, Research, and Sanctuaries Act (MPRSA), 33 U.S.C. § 1401, as well as under § 1983—alleging violations of those statutes as a result of damage to fishing grounds from pollution. Focusing on Congress's intent in enacting [CWA] and MPRSA and finding that they provide "unusually elaborate enforcement mechanisms," the Court held that the plaintiffs could not use § 1983 to enforce their rights under those pollution statutes. The Court compared § 1983 to [CWA] and MPRSA, primarily examining the extensiveness of the remedial scheme and its relationship to congressional intent: "[w]hen the remedial devices provided in the particular Act are sufficiently comprehensive, they may suffice to demonstrate congressional intent to preclude the remedy of suits under § 1983." Based on these statutory provisions, the Court found it "hard to believe that Congress intended to preserve the § 1983 right of action" for violations of the statute....

In the most recent Supreme Court authority on these issues, *Fitzgerald*, the Court explained the distinction between § 1983 claims premised on constitutional violations and those based on statutory violations in determining whether a § 1983 claim is precluded. "In those cases in which the § 1983 claim is based on a statutory right, evidence of such congressional intent may be found directly in the statute creating the right, or inferred from the statute's creation of a comprehensive enforcement scheme that is incompatible with individual enforcement under § 1983." The Court then explained:

> In cases in which the § 1983 claim alleges a constitutional violation, lack of congressional intent may be inferred from a comparison of the rights and protections of the statute and those existing under the Constitution....

... Based on the case authority set out above, the Plaintiffs in *Boler* and *Mays* aver that they do not "invoke[] § 1983 ... as a vehicle to enforce the substantive federal law found in [the SDWA], but as a vehicle to recover for alleged violations" of various constitutional provisions, including the Contract Clause, Equal Protection Clause, and Due Process Clause—allegations that they state would be actionable even if Congress had never enacted the SDWA. Plaintiffs argue that the fact that Congress "created a set of substantive statutory requirements, and adopted a set of procedures for enforcing *those* requirements, does not ... suggest that Congress intend[ed] to foreclose a Section 1983 remedy for the violations of independent rights that find their source, not in laws passed by Congress, but in the Constitution itself."

The focus of our inquiry on this question is congressional intent.

... Having resolved that there is no textual indication in the SDWA that Congress expressly chose to preempt § 1983 claims and that the provisions of the remedial scheme do not demonstrate such an intention, we also find that the contours of the rights and protections found in the constitutional claims diverge from those provided by the SDWA such that we infer lack of congressional intention to foreclose § 1983 claims. The Defendants have not demonstrated that "Congress intended to abandon the rights and remedies set forth in Fourteenth Amendment equal protection jurisprudence" when it enacted the SDWA. Under the governing precedent, primarily that of the Supreme Court, the Defendants have not carried their burden and the Plaintiffs may thus move forward with their cases. We find that the SDWA does not preclude § 1983 claims as pled by the *Boler* and *Mays* Plaintiffs, and reverse the district court's dismissal of their Complaints on that basis....

Notes and Questions

1. **§ 1983 vs. the Safe Drinking Water Act.** As noted by the Sixth Circuit, the Safe Drinking Water Act (SDWA), like most of the federal environmental statutes, has citizen suit provisions allowing private individuals to bring civil actions to "enforce ... any requirement" established under the SDWA. As with many other environmental statutes, violations of the SDWA are generally subject to strict liability. § 1983 claims, on the other hand, may present plaintiffs with much more challenging proof standards, such as the Substantive Due Process standard that a state actor acted with "deliberative indifference." Why then would a private individual like Beatrice Boler bring an action under § 1983 instead of under the SDWA citizen suit provision? In fact, private individuals (including Melissa Mays (from *Mays v. Governor*) did file a citizen suit under the SDWA. *See Concerned Pastors for Social Action v. Khouri*, 217 F.Supp.3d 960 (E.D. Mich. 2016) (granting plaintiffs' motion for preliminary injunction). What are the relative advantages of each approach for both a private individual and the affected community?

2. **Preclusion?** As noted in the Sixth Circuit's opinion, the district court originally dismissed the § 1983 action relying on the U.S. Supreme Court's decision in *Middlesex County Sewerage Authority v. National Sea Clammers Association*, 453 U.S. 1 (1981). As described by the Sixth Circuit, *Sea Clammers* "determined that the statutory remedies at issue" in that case, including under the Clean Water Act, "were sufficiently comprehensive to evince congressional intent to preclude § 1983 claims for *violations of the statute*" (emphasis in original). In dismissing the § 1983 claims by the Flint plaintiffs, the district court seemed to assume that the entire case depended on *violations of the statute*—specifically, in this case, violations of the Safe Drinking Water Act. The district court asserted, "Indeed, here the crux of each of Plaintiffs' constitutional claims is that they have been deprived of 'safe and potable water.' Plaintiffs' allegations are addressed by regulations that have been promulgated by the EPA under the SDWA." *Boler v. Earley*, 2016 WL 1573272 (E.D. Mich. 2016). How accurate do you find that characterization of plaintiffs' constitutional claims? After infants and children have been exposed to high doses of lead in drinking water and suffered neurological impairment, is it realistic to believe that a potential lifetime of adverse consequences will be "addressed by regulations that have been promulgated by the EPA under the SDWA," as the district court suggests?

3. **A [Not Very] Hypothetical.** Imagine that you lived in a small town with a large percentage of low-income residents and people of color. Your local water authority provides semi-annual reports identifying chronic violations of standards under the Safe Drinking Water Act. According to the water authority, the violations may affect the taste and smell of your water, but are not expected to affect human health. The water authority, like the rest of your local government, is struggling financially, but it is slowly making upgrades to water infrastructure. The upgrades are expected to fix the SDWA violations, but at the current pace of funding and construction, completion of the upgrades may take 20 years or more. Meanwhile, you learn that the next town over,

with a predominantly white and middle-class population, is making similar upgrades but expecting to complete its construction within three years, given proportionally greater funding by the state government. In this scenario, if you wanted to ensure the protection of drinking water in your community, would you prefer to file civil litigation under the Equal Protection Clause, an administrative complaint under Title VI, or a claim for damages under § 1983? What are the pros and cons of each legal strategy?

Chapter 5

Environmental Regulations

A. Introduction

The major federal environmental laws, including the Clean Air Act (CAA), Clean Water Act (CWA), Resource Conservation and Recovery Act (RCRA), Safe Drinking Water Act (SDWA), and Toxic Substances Control Act (TSCA), usually require agencies such as the U.S. EPA and state regulators to promulgate regulations for implementation. These rules will determine, for example, how much ozone should be allowed in the ambient air in a metropolitan area and how many days a typical auto repair shop may store hazardous waste on-site before sending it away for proper disposal. These rules are important for regulated parties (e.g., small businesses and large industries) to understand in order to ensure compliance. For many reasons, these rules are also important for community advocates to comprehend. For example, while environmental regulations are usually enforceable by regulatory agencies, as discussed in Chapter 7 (Government Enforcement), they may also be enforceable by impacted individuals, as discussed in Chapter 12 (Citizen Enforcement and Common Law Remedies).

Compliance with environmental regulations, however, will not necessarily ensure protection of human health and the environment. Environmental regulations, as currently established, may fail to protect "all people," leading to environmental injustice in some communities. For example, standards for lead in drinking water may be established to protect an average adult, failing to protect children, whose developing brains may be more affected by lead exposure. Air quality standards may be set to protect healthy adults, but fail to protect adults with asthma. Air quality standards may be established for large geographic airsheds, but fail to ensure safe air for an elementary school across the street from an industrial facility.

Science is continually evolving, and often standards set in the past fail to keep up with the latest understandings of chemical toxicity. Very often, even when the science is clear, political or legal opposition succeeds in stalling, blocking, or reversing environmental regulations needed to ensure the protection of human health and the environment. In one egregious case, the Canadian asbestos industry succeeded in challenging an EPA rule banning asbestos manufacturing, allowing asbestos—whose deadly effects on human health had been known for millennia—to remain legal for industrial use in the United States for more than 30 years until finally banned *again* in 2024. *Corrosion Proof Fittings v. EPA*, 947 F.2d 1201 (5th Cir. 1991); *Asbestos Part 1; Chrysotile Asbestos; Regulation of Certain Conditions of Use Under the Toxic Substances Control Act (TSCA)*,

89 Fed. Reg. 21970 (March 28, 2024). In June 2025, the Trump administration suggested it may reopen that rule and make asbestos legal again. Hiroko Tabuchi, *E.P.A. Plans to Reconsider a Ban on Cancer-Causing Asbestos*, N.Y. Times, June 16, 2025.

Because environmental regulations on the books today may or may not be sufficient to protect every member of every community, it is important for EJ advocates to understand how environmental rules are made, how they may be challenged, and how they may—or may not—allow for meaningful community involvement. Section B will begin with some law and policy governing federal rulemaking, including recent developments from the U.S. Supreme Court. Section C will take a closer look at the process for federal rulemaking in the United States. Section D will consider opportunities for more protective standards set by states and tribes. Section E will conclude with a case study examining major concerns for environmental injustice in communities of Louisiana's "Cancer Alley" and recent rulemaking to address some of these concerns.

B. Statutory Authority and Policy Approaches to Environmental Regulations

Development of environmental regulations by agencies such as EPA and state commissions often involves significant policy choices. For example, which chemicals should be subject to restriction in drinking water and at what levels? Should regulations for reducing air pollution require the use of certain technologies or allow flexibility in meeting air quality objectives? How should costs and benefits of environmental regulations be considered? Should regulations attempt to embrace market forces or correct for market failures?

While agencies continue to engage in such policy considerations, agency discretion has become increasingly constrained, at least on the federal level. Within federal agencies, environmental regulations may often reflect concerns for political feasibility, especially considering what rules can be completed within the four years of a given administration. In 2025, the second Trump administration raises a different question: *How many rules can be eliminated in four years? See, e.g.,* U.S. EPA, *EPA Launches Biggest Deregulatory Action in U.S. History*, March 12, 2025 (announcing plans to roll back 31 new EPA rules designed to protect human health and the environment).

In both supportive and hostile regulatory climates, community engagement can be meaningful. In a supportive climate, community advocates may find more access to policymakers and more willingness of policymakers to consider the needs of individual communities. In hostile climates, community advocates can (and do) challenge agency efforts to roll back environmental regulations. In the first Trump administration, community advocates were, in fact, highly successful in challenging efforts to roll back environmental protection, prevailing in court most of the time. According to the NYU Institute for Policy Integrity, over the course of the first Trump administration, the administration "prevailed less than 10 percent of the time when its federal agency actions have been challenged in court." Institute for Policy Integrity, https://www

.epa.gov/system/files/documents/2025-01/guidelines-for-cumulative-risk-assessment-planning-and-problem-formulation_0.pdf.

As will be explored further in Chapter 12 (Citizen Enforcement), judgments against federal agencies can both stop deregulation and require affirmative regulation, often on schedules specified in enforceable consent decrees. Negotiation of consent decrees and schedules can provide community advocates with significant leverage for achieving environmental regulations to protect overburdened communities. For example, litigation against the Trump EPA resulted in a court order in 2018 mandating that EPA move forward with a new rule under the Clean Air Act Section 112r, Risk Management Program (RMP), to enhance the safety of chemical facilities and fence-line communities. *Air Alliance Houston v. U.S. EPA*, 906 F.3d 1049 (D.C. Cir. 2018). Under the court deadline, the Biden EPA proceeded to promulgate the new RMP rule, known as the *Safer Communities by Chemical Accident Prevention* rule. 89 Fed. Reg. 17622 (March 11, 2024). The new rule was embraced broadly by EJ advocates, including petitioners concerned about the potential for industrial accidents within Houston's sprawling petrochemical corridors. In March 2025, the second Trump EPA announced its intent to reconsider the 2024 RMP rule. Citizen litigation to defend the 2024 RMP rule may be anticipated.

Even if a statute allows flexibility in regulatory design, environmental regulations must be grounded in statutory authority. Early on, legal scholars recognized that statutes like the Clean Air Act and Clean Water Act provided broad legal authority for addressing concerns for environmental justice, as the excerpt below attests.

Richard J. Lazarus & Stephanie Tai, *Integrating Environmental Justice into EPA Permitting Authority*

26 Ecology L.Q. 617 (1999)

Clean Air Act

The Clean Air Act (CAA) presents EPA with more opportunities to integrate environmental justice concerns into the Act's substantive standards than the Agency has utilized. The national ambient air quality standards (NAAQS) that serve as the Act's cornerstone are illustrative. Pursuant to the CAA, EPA administrators must promulgate NAAQS to protect "public health" with an adequate margin of safety. It is well settled that Congress intended for EPA to consider especially sensitive subpopulations in determining what pollutant levels would meet the "public health" standard. Pollutant levels that pose no health hazard to average healthy individuals may nonetheless present significant hazards to some individuals who, because of preexisting physical conditions, have heightened vulnerabilities. The Act, accordingly, instructs EPA in developing the "air quality criteria" upon which the NAAQS are based to include information on "those variable factors . . . which of themselves or in combination with other factors may alter the effects on public health or welfare."

EPA's statutory authority in this respect is also of a continuing nature. It does not end once a NAAQS is first promulgated. Pursuant to CAA Section 109(d), EPA is required to revise air quality criteria and standards at a minimum of every five years or as needed to ensure their adequacy in light of new information and changing circumstances....

Section 112 [dealing with controls for hazardous air pollutants] also includes two other subsections relevant to environmental justice priorities. Section 112(c)(3) and Section 112(k) both authorize EPA to consider the aggregate effects of multiple sources of hazardous air pollutants, especially those emitted in urban areas....

Clean Water Act

... The water quality standard provisions of the [Clean Water Act (CWA)] offer another opportunity for EPA to exercise its authority to consider and address environmental justice concerns. Under the CWA, states must establish water quality standards applicable to waters within the states' borders. Unlike the CAA's NAAQS, which are nationally uniform, these state water quality standards may not only vary between states, but need not be uniformly applied to all water bodies within any one state. A state may legitimately apply different levels of water quality protection to different water bodies depending on the specific uses (for example, recreation, transportation, or industry) the state designates for each body of water. EPA oversees a state's promulgation of water quality standards primarily to ensure that the standards are consistent with the state's "designated uses" but also to ensure compliance with EPA's nondegradation policy, which guards against unwarranted degradation of existing uses of water and associated water quality. CWA permits must ensure compliance not only with the Act's various technology-based effluent limitations, but also with the state water quality standards....

The water quality program is especially relevant to environmental justice because it involves EPA and the states making a series of judgments with clearly distributional consequences. For instance, EPA's nondegradation policy, which protects "existing uses" of water, should provide protection to such existing uses by environmental justice communities, including those that are economically or culturally dependent on the subsistence use of water....

Federal Insecticide, Fungicide, and Rodenticide Act

The Federal Insecticide, Fungicide, and Rodenticide Act (FIFRA) confers substantial authority on the EPA Administrator to address environmental justice concerns. EPA's principal responsibility in administering FIFRA is its registration of pesticides to guard against "unreasonable adverse effects on the environment." Environmental justice advocates are interested in FIFRA's administration for many reasons, one of which is the substantial threat to the health of farmworkers posed by the unreasonably dangerous use of pesticides. FIFRA provides EPA with significant authority to eliminate these unreasonable risks through tactics as varied as use restrictions, disposal restrictions, labeling requirements, registration denials, and conditional registrations....

Notes and Questions

1. Decline of agency deference. While statutes such as the Clean Air Act, Clean Water Act, and FIFRA provide agencies like EPA with significant authority to promulgate implementing regulations, those regulations may be subject to immediate challenge in court and subject to increasing judicial scrutiny. For forty years, one of the most cited Supreme Court cases was *Chevron v. NRDC*, 467 U.S. 837 (1984), a case in which an environmental organization, the Natural Resources Defense Council, challenged EPA regulations under the Clean Air Act that favored industry. In upholding the Reagan EPA regulations, the Supreme Court established a principle that came to be known as *Chevron* deference. As explained by the Court:

> When a court reviews an agency's construction of the statute which it administers, it is confronted with two questions. First, always, is the question whether Congress has directly spoken to the precise question at issue. If the intent of Congress is clear, that is the end of the matter, for the court, as well as the agency, must give effect to the unambiguously expressed intent of Congress. If, however, the court determines Congress has not directly addressed the precise question at issue, the court does not simply impose its own construction on the statute.... Rather, if the statute is silent or ambiguous with respect to the specific issue, the question for the court is whether the agency's answer is based on a permissible construction of the statute.

Id. at 843–44. Under *Chevron*, federal courts afforded EPA and other agencies considerable deference when interpreting regulations grounded in federal statutes that the agency administered. However, in recent years, members of the Supreme Court began questioning the wisdom of *Chevron* deference, suggesting among other things that judicial deference may interfere with the separation of powers, limiting the independent role of the judiciary. After years of such signals and more changes to the Supreme Court membership, the Supreme Court in 2024 overruled *Chevron*, abolishing *Chevron* deference. *Loper Bright Enterprises v. Raimondo*, 603 U.S. 369 (2024).

The *Loper Bright* decision came as little surprise to anyone watching, including federal agencies who anticipated the decision and began to eschew reliance on *Chevron* deference. In the end, *Loper Bright* may not effect a major shift in the standard for judicial review of agency actions. *See* Dan Farber, *Judicial Review After Loper Bright*, Legal Planet, July 2, 2024.Writing for the majority, Chief Justice Roberts suggested that agencies were still entitled to some level of respect and deference within their areas of expertise: "[A]lthough an agency's interpretation of a statute 'cannot bind a court,' it may be especially informative 'to the extent it rests on factual premises within [the agency's] expertise.' Such expertise has always been one of the factors which may give an Executive Branch interpretation particular 'power to persuade, if lacking power to control.'" *Id.* at 402 (citations omitted). One year later, Justice Kavanaugh, writing for the majority, accorded the federal Surface Transportation Board substantial deference in a NEPA determination, observing that under the "arbitrary and capricious" standard of the Administrative Procedure Act (discussed below), "a court asks not whether it agrees with the agency decision, but rather only whether the agency action was reasonable and reasonably explained...." *Seven County Infrastructure Coalition v. Eagle County, Colorado*, 145 S. Ct. 1497, 1511 (2025).

What will *Loper Bright* mean to EJ advocates supporting progressive regulation or opposing deregulation? While the end of *Chevron* deference was largely bemoaned by environmental advocates, can EJ advocates find upsides to its demise?

2. The "Major Questions Doctrine." In addition to diminishing deference to agencies, the increasingly conservative Supreme Court recently embraced a new doctrine aimed at limiting agency ability to address "major questions" through regulatory authority. The Supreme Court announced the major questions doctrine in the majority opinion for *West Virginia v. EPA*, 597 U.S. 697 (2022). In *West Virginia*, coal-producing states challenged EPA's exercise of Clean Air Act authority to promulgate a regulation known as the "Clean Power Plan," designed to reduce greenhouse gas emissions from fossil fuel-fired power plants. Although the Clean Power Plan never went into effect, the Court proceeded to the merits, finding, "Precedent teaches that there are 'extraordinary cases' in which the 'history and breadth of the authority that [the agency] has asserted,' and the 'economic and political significance' of that assertion, provide a 'reason to hesitate before concluding that Congress' meant to confer such authority." In such a "major questions case," according to Chief Justice Roberts, "the agency must point to 'clear congressional authorization' for the authority it claims." *Id.* at 700. In other words, if a regulation crosses some unknown threshold of economic or political significance, the agency may not be allowed to regulate at all unless Congress explicitly says so.

Courts and legal scholars will necessarily grapple with the implications of the major questions doctrine for years to come. For an entry into emerging scholarship in this area, *see* Daniel E. Walters, *The Major Questions Doctrine at the Boundaries of Interpretive Law*, 109 Iowa L. Rev. 465, 510 (2024) (identifying the major questions doctrine as "extreme on every dimension," with the "potential to make major regulation by agencies impossible or at least fraught with peril"); Michael D. Ramsey, *An Originalist Defense of the Major Questions Doctrine*, 76 Admin. L. Rev. 817, 849 (2024) (major questions doctrine "is consistent with early judicial practice" and "operates to protect against costly judicial error in applying ambiguous statutes"); Daniel T. Deacon & Leah M. Litman, *The New Major Questions Doctrine*, 109 Virginia L. Rev. 1009, 1057–58 (2023) ("The focus in the new major questions doctrine on whether an agency policy is 'politically controversial' ... allows political activity outside of formal lawmaking channels to affect the outcome of cases").

What does the major questions doctrine mean for communities experiencing the disproportionate impacts of environmental pollution? Would agency efforts to address diminished quality of life or differences in life expectancy constitute matters of "economic and political significance"? On the other hand, could agency efforts to roll back environmental regulations, freeze federal funding, or abolish enforcement, be subject to challenge under the major questions doctrine?

C. Rulemaking Processes

The federal process for creating new rules can be extremely complex and lengthy, often requiring years—and sometimes decades—of determined effort. The rulemaking process is regularly a major subject studied in law school courses on Administrative Law, highly recommended for any future EJ advocates. For those unable to take such a course, or perhaps in need of a primer or refresher, this section provides a basic introduction to federal rulemaking processes, beginning with key provisions of the major federal statute governing federal rulemaking, the Administrative Procedure Act (APA).

Administrative Procedure Act

5 U.S.C. § 553

(a) This section applies, according to the provisions thereof, except to the extent that there is involved—

(1) a military or foreign affairs function of the United States; or

(2) a matter relating to agency management or personnel or to public property, loans, grants, benefits, or contracts.

(b) General notice of proposed rule making shall be published in the Federal Register, unless persons subject thereto are named and either personally served or otherwise have actual notice thereof in accordance with law. The notice shall include—

(1) a statement of the time, place, and nature of public rule making proceedings;

(2) reference to the legal authority under which the rule is proposed;

(3) either the terms or substance of the proposed rule or a description of the subjects and issues involved; and

(4) the Internet address of a summary of not more than 100 words in length of the proposed rule, in plain language, that shall be posted on [www.regulations.gov].

Except when notice or hearing is required by statute, this subsection does not apply—

(A) to interpretative rules, general statements of policy, or rules of agency organization, procedure, or practice; or

(B) when the agency for good cause finds ... that notice and public procedure thereon are impracticable, unnecessary, or contrary to the public interest.

(c) After notice required by this section, the agency shall give interested persons an opportunity to participate in the rule making through submission of written data, views, or arguments with or without opportunity for oral presentation. After consideration of the relevant matter presented, the agency shall incorporate in the rules adopted a concise general statement of their basis and purpose. When rules are required by statute to be made on the record after opportunity for an agency hearing, sections 556 and 557 of this title apply instead of this section.

(d) The required publication or service of a substantive rule shall be made not less than 30 days before its effective date, except—

(1) a substantive rule which grants or recognizes an exemption or relieves a restriction;

(2) interpretative rules and statements of policy; or

(3) as otherwise provided by the agency for good cause found and published with the rule.

(e) Each agency shall give an interested person the right to petition for the issuance, amendment, or repeal of a rule.

* * *

The process described above is sometimes referred to as "notice-and-comment rulemaking" or "informal rulemaking." "Formal rulemaking" generally requires a hearing on the record before a presiding official, following procedures specified in 5 U.S.C. §§ 556–557. Informal rulemaking is intended to be more streamlined, depending primarily on submission of written comments submitted to the agency. In practice, however, informal rulemaking is usually a very formal and laborious process. The public process may begin with a Notice of Proposed Rulemaking (NPRM) published in the Federal Register to solicit public comment on a proposed rule. Alternatively, the process may begin with Federal Register publication of an Advance Notice of Proposed Rulemaking (ANPRM) to solicit data or other information to help inform agency development of a proposed rule. In both cases, agencies should consider all comments received on the proposals and provide responses to substantive comments along with any final rule that may follow from the process.

The final rule then usually becomes subject to judicial review as provided in the APA for "final agency action." 5 U.S.C. § 704. In particular, the APA, 5 U.S.C. § 706, provides that a reviewing court shall

(1) compel agency action unlawfully withheld or unreasonably delayed; and

(2) hold unlawful and set aside agency action, findings, and conclusions found to be—

(A) arbitrary, capricious, an abuse of discretion, or otherwise not in accordance with law;

(B) contrary to constitutional right, power, privilege, or immunity;

(C) in excess of statutory jurisdiction, authority, or limitations, or short of statutory right;

(D) without observance of procedure required by law;

(E) unsupported by substantial evidence in a case subject to [formal rulemaking]; or

(F) unwarranted by the facts to the extent that the facts are subject to trial de novo by the reviewing court.

In making the foregoing determinations, the court shall review the whole record or those parts of it cited by a party....

In addition to the public processes required by the APA, federal rulemaking is heavily influenced by a process almost entirely invisible to the public. Executive Order 12866, signed by President Clinton in 1993, established a process of "Regulatory Planning and Review" internal to the federal government. Most substantively, EO 12866 requires that "Each agency shall assess the costs and the benefits of the intended regulation and, recognizing that some costs and benefits are difficult to quantify, propose or adopt a regulation only upon a reasoned determination that the benefits of the intended regulation justify its costs." EO 12866 at (b)(6).

EO 12866 also creates a process of inter-agency review of potential agency actions subject to supervision of the White House Office of Management and Budget (OMB). Within OMB, the Office of Information and Regulatory Affairs (OIRA) is supposed to provide "meaningful guidance and oversight so that each agency's regulatory actions are consistent with applicable law, the President's priorities, and ... do not conflict with the policies and actions of another agency." OIRA's review process is supposed to ensure that all interested federal agencies and White House offices have an opportunity to provide input on proposed regulatory actions before they go out for public review and comment.

Until a proposed rule is released for public comment, EO12866 allows limited opportunity for public involvement. Each October, OIRA is supposed to publish a Unified Regulatory Agenda, publicly identifying the priority regulatory actions of each agency for the coming fiscal year. EO 12866 allows "persons not employed by ... the Federal Government" to petition for a meeting with OIRA "regarding the substance of a regulatory action under OIRA review." In 2023, President Biden attempted to reform this system, directing OIRA to "[p]rovide information to facilitate the initiation of meeting requests regarding regulatory action under OIRA review from potential participants ... who have not historically requested such meetings, including those from underserved communities...." EO 14094, *Modernizing Regulatory Review*, April 6, 2023. Unfortunately for supporters of meaningful engagement, the OIRA reform effort embodied by EO 14094 was revoked by President Trump immediately upon taking office in January 2025.

While EO 12866 remains in place, OIRA's review process is supposed to be completed within strict timelines. For a Notice of Proposed Rulemaking, OIRA is directed by EO 12866 to conclude its review "within 90 calendar days" from the date it receives the proposed action from the agency. EO 12866 at Sec. 6(b)(2). In exceptional cases, "The review process may be extended (1) once by no more than 30 calendar days upon the written approval of the [OIRA] Director and (2) at the request of the agency head." *Id.*

In reality, OIRA may honor these timelines more in the breach. As one observer noted from experience within the Obama EPA: "OIRA's actual practice in reviewing agency rules departs considerably from the structure created by the executive order.... The distribution of decision-making authority is ad hoc and chaotic ... there are no longer any meaningful deadlines for OIRA review...." Lisa Heinzerling, *Inside EPA: A Former Insider's Reflections on the Relationship Between the Obama EPA and the Obama White House*, 31 PACE ENVTL. L. REV. 325, 326 (2014). In the Biden administration, OIRA did not appear more responsive or observant of deadlines. While the review process itself remains outside of the public eye, a publicly accessible dashboard, www.reginfo.gov, allows for public tracking of when agency proposals are submitted to OIRA for review and when they are finally released by OIRA for the agency to move the proposal forward for publication in the Federal Register. For one example from reginfo.gov, see Figure 5-1 below.

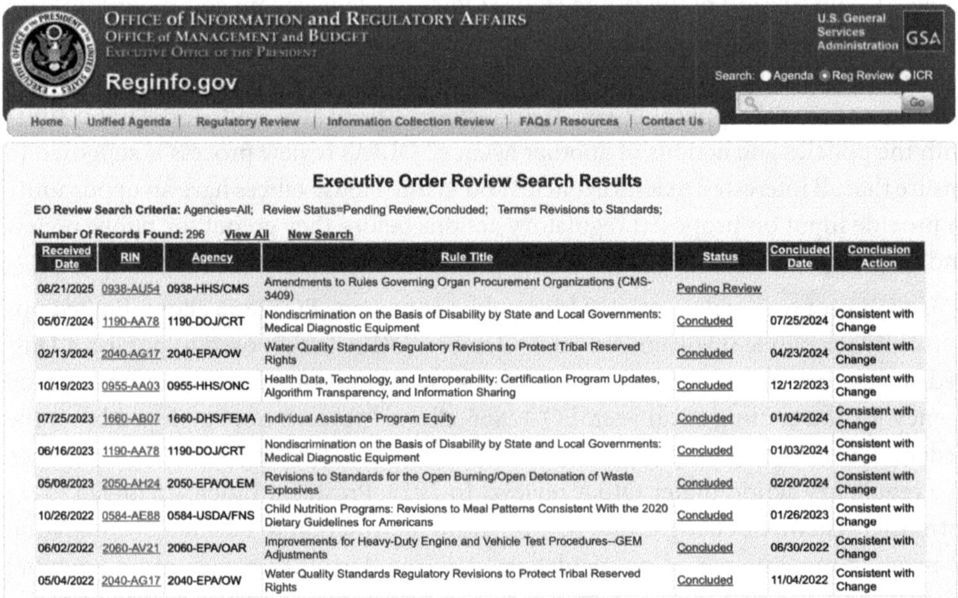

Executive Order Review Search Results

EO Review Search Criteria: Agencies=All; Review Status=Pending Review,Concluded; Terms= Revisions to Standards;

Number Of Records Found: 296 View All New Search

Received Date	RIN	Agency	Rule Title	Status	Concluded Date	Conclusion Action
08/21/2025	0938-AU54	0938-HHS/CMS	Amendments to Rules Governing Organ Procurement Organizations (CMS-3409)	Pending Review		
05/07/2024	1190-AA78	1190-DOJ/CRT	Nondiscrimination on the Basis of Disability by State and Local Governments: Medical Diagnostic Equipment	Concluded	07/25/2024	Consistent with Change
02/13/2024	2040-AG17	2040-EPA/OW	Water Quality Standards Regulatory Revisions to Protect Tribal Reserved Rights	Concluded	04/23/2024	Consistent with Change
10/19/2023	0955-AA03	0955-HHS/ONC	Health Data, Technology, and Interoperability: Certification Program Updates, Algorithm Transparency, and Information Sharing	Concluded	12/12/2023	Consistent with Change
07/25/2023	1660-AB07	1660-DHS/FEMA	Individual Assistance Program Equity	Concluded	01/04/2024	Consistent with Change
06/16/2023	1190-AA78	1190-DOJ/CRT	Nondiscrimination on the Basis of Disability by State and Local Governments: Medical Diagnostic Equipment	Concluded	01/03/2024	Consistent with Change
05/08/2023	2050-AH24	2050-EPA/OLEM	Revisions to Standards for the Open Burning/Open Detonation of Waste Explosives	Concluded	02/20/2024	Consistent with Change
10/26/2022	0584-AE88	0584-USDA/FNS	Child Nutrition Programs: Revisions to Meal Patterns Consistent With the 2020 Dietary Guidelines for Americans	Concluded	01/26/2023	Consistent with Change
06/02/2022	2060-AV21	2060-EPA/OAR	Improvements for Heavy-Duty Engine and Vehicle Test Procedures--GEM Adjustments	Concluded	06/30/2022	Consistent with Change
05/04/2022	2040-AG17	2040-EPA/OW	Water Quality Standards Regulatory Revisions to Protect Tribal Reserved Rights	Concluded	11/04/2022	Consistent with Change

Figure 5-1. Graphic adapted from reginfo.gov.

In this example, the seventh line reflects a rule that EPA sought to promulgate in order to strengthen regulation of open burning and open detonation (OB/OD) of waste military explosives in the United States. As indicated, OIRA "received" the proposed rule on May 8, 2023, so that OIRA's review should have been completed no more than 90 days later, approximately August 8, 2023. However, OIRA did not complete its review until February 20, 2024, approximately 282 days later. After OIRA finally completed its review, EPA published the proposed rule in the Federal Register on March 20, 2024. Revisions to Standards for the Open Burning/Open Detonation of Waste Explosives, 89 Fed. Reg. 19952, Mar. 20, 2024. At that point, the public finally had a chance to see and comment on the proposed rule. Unfortunately, after the close of the comment period, insufficient time remained for finalizing and publishing the final rule during the Biden administration, and the OB/OD rule effectively died.

The demise of the OB/OD rule perpetuates environmental injustice for fence-line communities where OB/OD activities continue, including on the Pacific island of Guam, a U.S. territory and home of Andersen Air Force Base. The health impacts of open burning of munitions are unfortunately grave and well-known. In 2022, Congress passed the Honoring our PACT Act, which identified some two dozen cancers and other illnesses that may be presumptively associated with exposure to toxic fumes from burn pits operated by the U.S. military forces overseas. *See* 38 U.S.C. § 1120. While the PACT Act may assist military veterans with obtaining benefits following exposures to toxic burn pits, no such benefits are extended to civilian neighbors in communities who continue to host these hazardous facilities.

Notes and Questions

1. Except for good cause? From the APA provisions excerpted above, note the exception from rulemaking procedures for the circumstance "when the agency for good cause finds ... the notice and public procedure [] are impracticable, unnecessary, or contrary to the public interest." 5 U.S.C. § 553(b)(B). What kind of circumstances do you imagine would be appropriate for dispensing with public procedures for rulemaking? The APA itself provides several explicit exceptions, including "military or foreign affairs," "interpretive rules, general statements of policy, [and] rules of agency organization...." As such, the "good cause" exception must mean something more than that. But what?

In April 2025, President Trump issued a memorandum directing federal agencies to "finalize rules without notice and comment, where doing so is consistent with the 'good cause' exception in the Administrative Procedure Act." Directing the Repeal of Unlawful Regulations, Presidential Memoranda, April 9, 2025. The memorandum asserts that "[r]etaining and enforcing facially unlawful regulations is clearly contrary to the public interest" and that "notice-and-comment proceedings are 'unnecessary' where repeal is required as a matter of law to ensure consistency with a ruling of the United States Supreme Court," citing several recent decisions including *Loper Bright* and *West Virginia*.

Do you agree that recent Supreme Court decisions make any specific environmental regulations "facially unlawful"? Note that in *Loper Bright*, Chief Justice Roberts, writing for the majority, expressly observed that, by overruling *Chevron*, "we do not call into question prior cases that relied on the *Chevron* framework. The holdings of those cases that specific agency actions are lawful—including the Clean Air Act holding of *Chevron* itself—are still subject to statutory stare decisis despite our change in interpretive methodology." 603 U.S. 369, 412. As for *West Virginia*, the Supreme Court left significant room and uncertainty in defining the scope of the major questions doctrine and its application beyond the scope of the Clean Power Plan regulation that was the subject of that decision. For an argument approving of President Trump's use of the

APA's "good cause" exception for bypassing notice and comment procedures, see Eli Nachmany, *"Good Cause" to Deregulate*, Notice & Comment, Yale J. on Regulation, April 21, 2025. For a counterargument, urging agency caution, see Cary Coglianese & Daniel E. Walters, *Did* Loper Bright *Also Overturn Notice-and-Comment Rulemaking Procedure?*, Notice & Comment, Yale J. on Regulation, April 11, 2025. Coglianese and Walters remind policymakers on either end of the political spectrum to "be careful what one wishes for." Most saliently, they observe:

> If *Loper Bright*'s majority thought it was moving to limit agencies from going their own way in interpreting their statutes, it is remarkable to see the Court's decision now invoked as a justification for a bold assertion of executive power to effectuate sweeping regulatory change based on agencies' own statutory interpretations—and without even going through the notice-and-comment process.

If courts allow President Trump to use the APA's "good cause" exception to eliminate environmental regulations without notice-and-comment rulemaking, should courts also allow a future administration to restore environmental regulations without notice and comment procedures? If so, what would remain of meaningful involvement in environmental regulation?

For a thorough examination of the APA "good cause" exemption generally, urging careful and judicious application, see Mark Squillace, *Best Practices for Agency Use of the Good Cause Exemption for Rulemaking* (Oct. 4, 2024) (draft report to the Admin. Conf. of the U.S.), available at https://www.acus.gov/sites/default/files/documents/Best%20Practices%20for%20Agency%20Use%20of%20the%20Good%20Cause%20Exemption%20for%20Rulemaking%20%28Draft%20Report%20for%20Committee%29.pdf.

2. Cost-benefit analysis. As indicated above, in 1993, Executive Order 12866 required federal agencies to "assess the costs and the benefits of the intended regulation," even while acknowledging that "some costs and benefits are difficult to quantify..." The conduct of cost-benefit analysis (CBA) quickly leads to complicated questions of environmental economics, which begins with an objective to express both costs and benefits in monetary units. In order to transform societal or individual values into monetary units, economists seek to determine individual and collective "Willingness to Pay" for environmental goods and services (e.g., clean air or water) and "Willingness to Accept" the loss of environmental goods and services (e.g., wetlands buffers against storm surge). To calculate the costs and benefits associated with regulation of toxic chemicals, economists may refer to the "value of statistical life" (VSL), a measure of the willingness to pay for reductions in risk of premature death. As of 2022, federal agencies "typically utilize central estimates of VSL between $10 million to $12 million." OMB Circular No. A-4, Nov. 9, 2023, at 49–50.

While EO 12866 and the CBA requirement for regulatory analysis remain in place, methods of conducting this analysis have evolved over time, guided by OMB Circular A-4 and advancements in economic theory and practice. In 2023, OMB revised Circular A-4 for the first time since 2003, among other things recommending adjustments to the discount rate that agencies use to account for the effects of inflation over time. Based upon more accurate data collected since 2003, the 2023 guidance recommended lowering the default discount rate from three percent to two percent. By lowering the discount rate, greater weight may be given to long-term benefits of environmental regulations, including benefits associated with climate change mitigation and benefits associated with cleanup of radioactive contamination.

Shortly after taking office in January 2025, President Trump directed OMB to rescind the 2023 update to Circular A-4 and reinstate the 2003 version. *Unleashing Prosperity Through Deregulation*, Executive Order 14192 Sec. 6(b), Jan. 31, 2025. However, such recission may be subject to legal requirements established by Congress, including "independent and external peer review." Regulatory Right-to-Know Act, Pub. L. No. 106-554, § 624(d) (2000). For further discussion, see Max Sarinsky & Jason A. Schwartz, *The Legal Dynamics of Rescinding the Circular A-4 Update*, Institute for Policy Integrity (Feb. 2025).

Political dynamics aside, how does cost-benefit analysis work in the practice of environmental rulemaking? While it will never be perfect, CBA analysis has benefited from increasingly sophisticated techniques in environmental economics and can be a useful tool for supporting the value of environmental regulations. For example, in 2024, the Biden EPA announced a new final rule that would control 90 percent of carbon emissions from coal-fired and gas-fired power plants. New Source Performance Standards for Greenhouse Gas Emissions from New, Modified, and Reconstructed Fossil Fuel-Fired Electric Generating Units, 89 Fed. Reg. 39798, May 9, 2024. In support of this final rule, the EPA estimated net benefits with a present value of $370 billion, to include health benefits from reducing air pollutants such as ozone and climate benefits such as reducing property damage from increased flood risk. *Id.* at 40007–08.

While estimating the "social cost of carbon" and the attendant value of reducing greenhouse gas emissions may be tricky business, many if not most environmental regulations raise challenging questions for cost-benefit analysis. Imagine the following scenario. Scientists discover that Chemical X, in widespread commercial use, has extremely toxic effects on human health and is highly persistent in the environment. EPA proposes to promulgate a regulation that would require cleanup of Chemical X to certain standards wherever it may be found in the United States. However, EPA has no information on how many sites in the United States are currently contaminated with Chemical X. Nor does EPA have any reliable estimate of how much it will cost to clean up all these unknown sites, as the technology needed to safely extract Chemical X from contaminated soil and groundwater is still developing. Can EPA still proceed with a rulemaking to require cleanup of Chemical X despite these limitations on estimating cleanup costs for purposes of cost-benefit analysis? If you were representing a community impacted by Chemical X contamination in municipal drinking water, how would you advocate for proceeding with such regulation?

D. State and Tribal Regulations

With passage of federal environmental legislation including the Clean Air Act in 1970 and Clean Water Act in 1972, Congress preserved significant roles for states and later tribes. In general, EPA would establish national standards for concerns such as air quality and hazardous waste, and states or tribes would be responsible for devising plans for meeting those standards. States or tribes might also retain authority for addressing environmental concerns not otherwise addressed by federal requirements. Especially in an era of federal deregulation, state and tribal authorities may prove essential for ensuring continued progress toward the aims of environmental justice. This section provides examples of state and tribal regulations that promote environmental protection beyond the requirements of federal regulation. The section begins with a case decided by the Missouri Court of Appeals, reviewing state rules for air emissions from animal feeding operations.

Friends of Agriculture for the Reform of Missouri Environmental Regulations ("FARMER") v. Zimmerman

51 S.W. 3d 64 (W.D. Mo. Ct. Apls. 2001)

I. INTRODUCTION

A. Background

... With the Clean Air Amendments of 1970, Congress enacted a comprehensive national program that made the federal government partners with the states in the fight against air pollution, requiring the Environmental Protection Agency (the EPA) Administrator to promulgate national ambient air quality standards (NAAQS) for certain pollutants. Shortly thereafter, each state was to submit a state implementation plan (SIP) for each designated "air quality control region" within their borders for the implementation, maintenance, and enforcement of the NAAQS. The SIP must specify emission limitations and other measures necessary for that region to meet and maintain the required NAAQS. Finally, the EPA was required to act upon a proposed SIP within four months. After a public notice and comment period, the Administrator was directed to approve the SIP if he determined that it met various substantive requirements under the Act.

With the Clean Air Act, Congress intended to promote federalism and encourage experimentation in environmental regulation. Under the federal law, the standards set forth are only minimum standards, and the states remain free to impose more stringent standards with or without EPA approval. This frees the states to carry out the important role of laboratories in our federal system.

This state enacted the Missouri Air Conservation Law in 1965. Section 643.030 created the Missouri Air Conservation Commission (Commission) "to maintain purity of the air resources of the state ... through the prevention, abatement and control of air pollution by all practical and economically feasible methods." With this purpose, the Commission is vested with rulemaking authority under Section 643.050.... Currently, the first subsection states:

> In addition to any other powers vested in it by law the commission shall have the following powers:
>
> (1) Adopt, promulgate, amend and repeal rules and regulations consistent with the general intent and purposes of sections 643.010 to 643.190, chapter 536, RSMo, and Titles V and VI of the federal Clean Air Act, as amended, 42 U.S.C. § 7661, et seq., including but not limited to:
>
> (a) Regulation of use of equipment known to be a source of air contamination;
>
> (b) Establishment of maximum quantities of air contaminants that may be emitted from any air contaminant source; and
>
> (c) Regulations necessary to enforce the provisions of Title VI of the Clean Air Act, as amended, 42 U.S.C. § 7671, et seq., regarding any Class I or Class II substances as defined therein.

When faced with the possibility of losing federal highway funds, the legislature passed § 643.055 in 1979 to insure compliance with the federal act. At the same time, however, the statute prohibits the Commission from adopting rules or regulations that are either stricter than required by federal law or enforceable sooner than federal law. The statute provides, in relevant part:

> Other provisions of law notwithstanding, the Missouri air conservation commission shall have the authority to promulgate rules and regulations, pursuant to chapter 536, RSMo, to establish standards and guidelines to ensure that the state of Missouri is in compliance with the provisions of the federal Clean Air Act, as amended (42 U.S.C. § 7401, et seq.). The standards and guidelines so established shall not be any stricter than those required under the provisions of the federal Clean Air Act, as amended; nor shall those standards and guidelines be enforced in any area of the state prior to the time required by the federal Clean Air Act, as amended.

B. Missouri Hospital Association

Our first occasion to address the Commission's rulemaking authority under the Missouri Air Conservation Law was in *Missouri Hospital Association.* The case stemmed from two rules promulgated by the Commission pertaining to waste incinerators. The circuit court found both rules to be void on two grounds: (1) the Commission failed to comply with the provisions of § 536.200 and § 536.205, in promulgating and adopting the rules, and (2) because the Commission's rulemaking power was constrained by § 643.055, the Commission was therefore without adequate legislative authorization to adopt the two rules. For these reasons, the circuit court declared both rules void.

1. Fiscal Notes, § 536.200, and § 536.205

Addressing the trial court's first ground (the "fiscal notes"), we explained:

> In 1978, the General Assembly added an important element to the rulemaking process called the "fiscal note." There are two types of fiscal notes: one for rules requiring public funds to be spent or redirected, governed by § 536.200; and one for rules requiring an expenditure of funds by private persons or entities, governed by § 536.205.
>
> If a state agency proposes to adopt, amend or rescind a rule which will "require or result in an expenditure of public funds by or a reduction of public revenues for that agency" or any other state agency or political subdivision, a fiscal note is required if the change is estimated to cost "any category" of such public entities more than $500 in the aggregate. § 536.200.1....
>
> Although its provisions are somewhat different, § 536.205 reflects a similar concern about the economic impact of rules on the private sector. It requires state agencies to file a fiscal note with the Secretary of State along with the notice of proposed rulemaking if the rule change "would require an expenditure of money by or a reduction of income for any person, firm, corporation, association, partnership, proprietorship or business entity of any kind or character" of more than $500 in the aggregate. § 536.205.1. The note must contain an estimate, by class, of the number of persons, firms, etc. which would likely be affected; a classification by type of business entity so as to give reasonable notice of the number and kind of businesses which would likely be affected; and an estimate of the aggregate cost of compliance for the likely affected entities. §§ 536.205.1(1)–(3). If a fiscal note is required due to the proposed rule's aggregate effect on private finances, § 536.205.2 mandates that the fiscal note itself be published contemporary with and next to the notice of proposed rulemaking in the Missouri Register. If the state agency fails to publish the fiscal note, "any rule promulgated thereunder [is] void and of no force and effect."

We found that the Commission failed to comply with both § 536.200 and § 536.205 in adopting the first of the rules at issue. The Commission failed to comply with § 536.200 because it filed neither a fiscal note nor an affidavit after a previously-filed fiscal note was officially withdrawn before the promulgation of a newer version of the rule. The fiscal note was deficient under § 536.205 because there was no estimate of the number of persons, firms, corporations, etc. by class that might have been affected by adoption of the rule; there was no classification of the types of business entities that could be affected; and there was no fiscal note published in the Missouri Register contemporary with and adjacent to the notice of proposed rulemaking....

Concluding our discussion of the fiscal notes at issue, we explained the dual purpose that fiscal notes serve:

Sections 536.200 and 536.205 are clearly designed to require agencies to take reasonable steps to consider and identify all public and private entities significantly affected by any proposed rule, and to investigate, consider and comprehensively estimate the full range of costs involved. As one commentator has observed:

> The object of the fiscal note requirement is assurance that state agencies and, in turn, the legislature and the public are aware of the economic costs as well as the benefits of rulemaking actions. To achieve this, fiscal notes are required when the effect of rulemaking includes a material economic impact on public and private expenditures, public revenues and private incomes.

These requirements are not trivial. They are necessary to ensure that any agency proposing a rule adequately considers the private and public entities it will affect. At the very least, the fiscal note "force[s] the agency to think about the economic consequences of its rulemaking." Fiscal notes also serve another important purpose: to give potentially affected entities notice of the estimated financial impact a given rule might have on them. In fact, § 536.205.1(2) explicitly requires that private entities be classified "in such manner as to give reasonable notice of the number and kind of businesses which would likely be affected" by a given rule. Indeed, as our Supreme Court recently noted while discussing the general notice and comment procedures contained in § 536.021, RSMo Supp.1992:

> The very purpose of the notice procedure for a proposed rule is to allow opportunity for comment by supporters or opponents of the measure, and so to induce a modification.... To neglect the notice ... or to give effect to a proposed rule before the time for comment has run ... undermines the integrity of the procedure.

If an entity potentially affected by a proposed rule sees a public notice of rulemaking reflecting no cost or minimal cost of compliance, that entity may choose not to participate in the rulemaking process. If, on the other hand, the entity anticipates substantial compliance costs, it will be far more inclined to get involved. With such participation, state agencies are more likely to adequately consider the economic impact of their rulemaking activities, better rules are adopted, and public support for such rules is generated.

2. Obiter Dicta and § 643.055

Noting that our holding that the rules were void was dispositive of the appeal, we went on to conclude that the Commission's rulemaking power under § 643.050, was limited by § 643.055, thus leaving the Commission without the authority to adopt the two rules. Using fundamental principles of statutory construction, we determined "that the true intention of the General Assembly in adopting § 643.055 was to direct the Commission to make sure that Missouri was in compliance with the federal Clean Air Act...." We reasoned:

> As noted earlier, the limitation on the Commission's rulemaking authority is contained in the second sentence of § 643.055.1. The first sentence of the section requires the Commission to adopt standards and guidelines to ensure that Missouri is complying with the federal Clean Air Act. The second sentence says, in effect, that such standards and guidelines cannot be any stricter or be enforced sooner than those required by federal law. The meaning and effect of this provision can only be that the General Assembly has chosen to allow federal law to preempt the Commission's rulemaking authority as to areas covered by the Clean Air Act. In other words, if Congress has spoken on a particular issue in the federal Clean Air Act, the Commission is prohibited from adopting rules or regulations on that issue that are either stricter than federal law or enforceable sooner.... The Commission continues to have rulemaking authority to regulate Missouri air quality in all ways, and in all areas, not covered by the federal Clean Air Act....
>
> It is only in areas where Congress has acted that the Commission will be implementing the EPA programs; in all other areas of air quality, the Commission will still act independently....

D. Procedural History

With this milieu, the instant case arose as a result of several regulations promulgated by the Commission in 1999. The Commission promulgated 10 CSR 10–2.070, 10 CSR 10–3.090, 10 CSR 10–4.070, and 10 CSR 10–5.160 (the "Odor Rules"); 10 CSR 10–6.010; and 10 CSR 10–6.065(4). These rules differ from federal regulations in the following ways: (1) the EPA has not implemented any federal regulations under the federal Clean Air Act imposing any regulatory requirements on odor and odorous emissions; whereas the Commission has promulgated the Odor Rules, which impose regulatory requirements concerning odors and odorous emissions from Class IA animal feeding operations; (2) the EPA has established ambient air quality standards for six compounds, but has not established an ambient air quality standard for hydrogen sulfide; whereas the Commission has adopted 10 CSR 10–6.010, which establishes an ambient air quality standard for hydrogen sulfide; and (3) the EPA requires states to require any source that has the potential to emit greater than 100 tons per year (tpy) of non-hazardous air pollutants or greater than 10 tpy of hazardous air pollutants to obtain an air operation permit, but, if a source has the potential to emit less than these thresholds, the EPA does not compel states to require the source to obtain any air operating permit; whereas the Commission has adopted 10 CSR 10–6.065(4), which requires a source that has the potential to emit less than the EPA thresholds to obtain a "basic state operating permit."

Friends of Agriculture for the Reform of Missouri Environmental Regulations (FARMER) filed its Petition in Cole County Circuit Court on August 11, 1999, challenging the validity of the Odor Rules, the ambient air rule for hydrogen sulfide, and the basic state operating permit rule.... The circuit court entered partial summary judgment on four of five counts in favor of the Commission pursuant to Rule 74.01(b). This appeal follows.

III. LEGAL ANALYSIS

FARMER contends that in promulgating the Odor Rules, setting an air quality standard for hydrogen sulfide and requiring a source that has the potential to emit less than the EPA thresholds to obtain a basic state operating permit, the Commission has exceeded its authority under § 643.055. We will address these points in turn, but first we address the point FARMER raises about the fiscal note published for 10 CSR 10-3.090.

A. The Fiscal Note

When an agency intends to adopt, amend or repeal a rule that "would require an expenditure of money by, or a reduction in income for, any person, firm, corporation, association, partnership, proprietorship or business entity of any kind or character which is estimated to cost more than five hundred dollars in the aggregate," the agency must file a fiscal note along with the notice of proposed rulemaking. The statute specifically sets out the contents for a valid fiscal note:

> (1) An estimate of the number of persons, firms, corporations, associations, partnerships, proprietorships or business entities of any kind or character by class which would likely be affected by the adoption of the proposed rule, amendment or rescission of a rule;
>
> (2) A classification by types of the business entities in such manner as to give reasonable notice of the number and kind of businesses which would likely be affected;
>
> (3) An estimate in the aggregate as to the cost of compliance with the rule, amendment or rescission of a rule by the affected persons, firms, corporations, associations, partnerships, proprietorships or business entities of any kind or character.

Here, the rule amendment to 10 CSR 10-3.090 first appeared in the Missouri Register on December 1, 1998. The private entity fiscal note was filed with the initial version of the rule (along with the public entity fiscal note). It declared that twenty Class 1A concentrated animal feeding operations, consisting of thirteen swine, six poultry and one dairy, would be affected by the adoption of the proposed rule. It gave an estimate of the private entity cost of compliance of $10,967,200 in the aggregate and calculated for a period of five years and in 1998 dollars, even though the life of the rule was expected to be more than five years. After the notice and comment period, revised fiscal notes were published with the final order of rulemaking in the Missouri Register on June 1, 1999. The rule was effective on July 30, 1999. The revised private entity fiscal note declared that the proposed rule would affect only nineteen Class 1A concentrated animal feeding operations—thirteen swine, five poultry and one dairy—with an estimated cost of $25,378,490 with the same qualifications on the estimate.

The validity of the public entity fiscal note is not disputed. Instead, FARMER argues that 10 CSR 10–3.090 is void on its face because the revised private entity fiscal note published in the Missouri Register did not comply with § 536.205. FARMER contends that the private entity fiscal note for 10 CSR 10–3.090 failed to make a reasonable estimate in the aggregate of private entity compliance costs as required by § 536.205. Instead of making a reasonable effort to investigate, consider and comprehensively estimate the full range of costs involved for the poultry and dairy industries as required, FARMER advances that the Commission merely assumed that the costs were similar to those estimates associated with the swine industry....

FARMER presented no evidence in challenging the private entity fiscal note. Rather, FARMER claims that the fiscal note is facially invalid. The circuit court was provided with an affidavit by Paul Myers, the environmental specialist who prepared the challenged fiscal note, and ultimately concluded that the administrators responsible for preparing the fiscal note made a comprehensive and diligent attempt to identify and list all affected private entities and made a reasonable, good faith effort to estimate the cost to those entities of compliance with the rule so long as the rule may be in effect. The evidence supports this conclusion.

Mr. Myers' affidavit showed that he made a comprehensive and diligent attempt to identify and list all affected private entities and that he made a reasonable, realistic, good faith effort to estimate the cost to those entities of compliance with the rule so long as the rule may be in effect. His investigation was thorough. He attempted to obtain cost information specific to the poultry and dairy industries, but persons he contacted were apparently not forthcoming. The studies he reviewed that provided information concerning the costs of odor controls for concentrated animal feeding operations did not distinguish between the types of animals being raised. The available studies focused on the swine industry, which, to him, appeared to provide the best information on the subject.

Although affected industries were provided three public hearings and an opportunity to submit written comments, no comments about the accuracy of the fiscal note were offered by the poultry or dairy interests. The reason for having notice and comment requirements is to provide both supporters and opponents with the opportunity for comment on a proposal and to encourage the free exchange of ideas so that the agency may become well informed on the issues. FARMER agrees in its reply brief that notice and comment rulemaking is founded upon "public input and participation to produce the best possible rule." Mr. Myers relied upon the comments submitted on behalf of the swine industry to publish a more accurate fiscal note with the final order of rulemaking, as required by § 536 .215, and estimated the cost of compliance in the aggregate for the foreseeable future. Because the accuracy of a fiscal note is only as good as the information available, we believe that the estimate was reasonable and the product of a reasonable effort to investigate, consider and comprehensively estimate the full range of costs involved for the poultry and dairy industries. The record does not reflect that appellants suffered any detriment in their ability to participate in or react to the rulemaking process.

FARMER also contends that the Commission violated § 536.205 by merely assuming that the costs were similar to those estimates associated with the swine industry. FARMER, however, presented no evidence to the circuit court to challenge that assumption, and somehow expects us to infer that the estimates associated with the swine industry are in reality not similar to the costs involved for the poultry and dairy industries. The studies used by Mr. Myers drew no distinction between different types of concentrated animal feeding operations, and we see no need to make that distinction on our own....

We find that the state agency administrators here, Mr. Myers in particular, prepared cost estimates that comply with both the letter and spirit of § 536.205. The point is denied.

B. The "Odor Rules"

In February 1980, the EPA issued a report to Congress as "the response of the Environmental Protection Agency (EPA) to Section 403(b) of the 1977 Clean Air Act Amendments (P.L. 95–95), which require[d] a study of the effects of odors and odorous emissions on public health and welfare and an analysis of strategies or authorities available or appropriate under the Clean Air Act for abating such emissions." After finding the authority to regulate odors, the report concluded that federal regulatory involvement was unwarranted because "[l]ocal and state odor control procedures appear to be generally adequate and are probably more cost effective than a uniform national regulatory program under the Clean Air Act." To be sure, the study concluded that "Federal regulatory involvement in odor control [did] not appear to be warranted since local and State odor control procedures appear[ed] to be generally adequate."

Contrary to the EPA's blessing, however, FARMER asserts that the Commission is statutorily prohibited from regulating odorous emissions because the EPA elected to not regulate the same. FARMER focuses on the second sentence of § 643.055.1, which provides that "[t]he standards and guidelines so established shall not be any stricter than those required under the provisions of the federal Clean Air Act, as amended; nor shall those standards and guidelines be enforced in any area of the state prior to the time required by the federal Clean Air Act, as amended." FARMER submits that the Odor Rules are stricter than the standards and guidelines adopted under the federal Clean Air Act, reasoning that the EPA's decision to not regulate odor "sets the bar at zero" and, thus, binds the Commission under § 643.055.1 to follow suit. FARMER insists that the EPA's decision not to regulate is a "guideline" under the statute. A guideline is defined as "an indication or outline of future policy or conduct (as of a government)." Consequently, FARMER frames the issue as "whether the Odor Rules promulgated by the Commission are more 'stringent in requirements or controls' than any 'outline of policy or conduct' issued by [the] EPA under the Clean Air Act." Since the EPA has outlined a policy of not regulating odors, under FARMER's line of reasoning, the Commission is statutorily bound to follow the same course by not regulating odors....

In enacting § 643.055.1 and requiring compliance with the federal Clean Air Act, the Missouri General Assembly did not adopt the Act, but rather the statute merely reflects an intention that Missouri should follow the EPA's lead in the areas that are regulated under the Clean Air Act. The General Assembly's intention was gleaned from the text of the statute in *Missouri Hospital Association:*

> The meaning and effect of this provision can only be that the General Assembly has chosen to allow federal law to preempt the Commission's rulemaking authority as to areas covered by the federal Clean Air Act. In other words, if Congress has spoken on a particular issue in the federal Clean Air Act, the Commission is prohibited from adopting rules or regulations on that issue that are either stricter than federal law or enforceable sooner....

We are left then with the issue of whether Congress has directly spoken on the precise issue of odors and odorous emissions. It is clear that the conscious decision at the federal level to not regulate odors is no federal mandate, and it therefore does not bind the Commission under § 643.055. Congress did speak on the issue, but the conclusion was that local and state odor control procedures appeared to be generally adequate. If Missouri law was to mirror every aspect of the Clean Air Act, both with the presence and absence of regulation, Missouri law in this area would be merely duplicative and largely unnecessary.

We believe that, by the legislature's choice of words in the statute such as "required" and "compliance," the General Assembly was focusing on affirmative regulation under the Clean Air Act. The terms connote as much. This understanding was implicit when we stated "the General Assembly has chosen to allow federal law to preempt the Commission's rulemaking authority as to areas covered by the federal Clean Air Act." We do not believe that odors and odorous emissions qualifies as an area covered by the Act solely because of a report concluding that regulation of odors is better off being left to the state and local governments.

In other words, where there is affirmative regulation under the Clean Air Act, Congress has directly spoken as to the specific topic of that particular regulation, and § 643.055.1 is triggered. For example, in *Corvera Abatement Technologies, Inc. v. Air Conservation Commission,* the Commission had promulgated a regulation concerning asbestos abatement projects, while the EPA had adopted regulations which imposed requirements on asbestos abatement in demolition projects. Our Supreme Court reiterated that § 643.055 .1 prohibits regulations containing provisions stricter than their federal counterparts and remanded for a determination as to what portions of the Commission's regulations were stricter than the federal requirements. Here, however, there is no federal counterpart, and there are no standards or guidelines required for conformity with the Clean Air Act....

The Commission has the broad authority to promulgate rules to implement the state air conservation law. "The Commission continues to have rulemaking authority to regulate Missouri air quality in all ways, and in all areas, not covered by the federal Clean Air Act." "It is only in areas *where Congress has acted* that the Commission [must implement the] EPA programs; in all other areas of air quality, the Commission will still act independently." Because Congress has not acted, rather it has chosen a course of *in* action, the promulgation of the Odor Rules was a valid exercise of the Commission's power. The point is denied.

C. Hydrogen Sulfide

In federal regulations under the Clean Air Act, the EPA has established NAAQS for sulfur oxides, particulate matter, carbon monoxide, ozone, nitrogen dioxide, and lead. FARMER suggests that any air quality standard for hydrogen sulfide is prohibited by § 643.055.1 because the EPA has not created a standard for this compound. Because the EPA has established ambient air quality standards for only six compounds, which do not include hydrogen sulfide, FARMER insists that the Commission's ambient air quality rule for hydrogen sulfide in 10 CSR 10–6.010 is stricter than the federal standards....

Again, we must ascertain whether Congress has spoken. Where there is affirmative regulation under the Clean Air Act, Congress has spoken as to the specific topic of that particular regulation, and § 643.055.1 is triggered. Here, there is affirmative regulation for six compounds, but hydrogen sulfide has been left unregulated under the Clean Air Act. Congress has not directed the EPA to create a standard for hydrogen sulfide. Therefore, the Commission is not required to comply with any regulations pertaining to hydrogen sulfide, Congress has not spoken, and "[t]he Commission continues to have rulemaking authority to regulate Missouri air quality in all ways, and in all areas, not covered by the federal Clean Air Act." The point is denied.

D. Basic State Operating Permits

[With similar reasoning, the Court of Appeals affirmed Missouri's regulations requiring air permits for facilities not addressed by the federal Clean Air Act. "The key question is once again whether Congress has spoken."]

IV. CONCLUSION

After a thorough review of the record, we conclude the circuit court's ruling on the partial summary judgment is affirmed.

Notes and Questions

1. Cost-benefit analysis? Note the court's discussion of the "dual purpose" of the fiscal note requirements. How would you summarize these purposes? How do these purposes compare to the requirements for cost-benefit analysis as discussed earlier in this chapter for federal rulemaking?

2. Odor control. In many rural communities, air and water quality may be severely impacted by the kind of swine, dairy, and poultry operations targeted by the Missouri regulation. In the absence of state or federal regulations addressing impacts such as odors, can community advocates use common law or other authorities to find relief? For one example of a rare victory in a nuisance suit against commercial hog farmers, see *McKiver v. Murphy-Brown, LLC.*, 980 F.3d 937 (4th Cir. 2020). Prevailing on common law claims in this area may be particularly difficult for impacted communities because most states have passed "Right-To-Farm" legislation that creates legal immunities or higher burdens of proof for would-be plaintiffs. For a collection and analysis of recent Right-To-Farm legislation across the states, see Kitt Tovar, *Update on Right-To-Farm Legislation, Cases, and Constitutional Amendments*, Iowa State University, Center for Agricultural Law and Taxation, May 28, 2019, https://www.calt.iastate.edu/article/update-right-farm-legislation-cases-and-constitutional-amendments.

3. Identical twins? If air regulations in the State of Missouri must meet the minimum requirements of the federal Clean Air Act, but by state law "shall not be any stricter than those required under the provisions of the federal Clean Air Act," does that leave room for any differences between federal and state requirements? The formulation reflected in the Missouri air statute ("no less and no more strict than federal standards") is commonly found in the environmental statutes of other states. *See, e.g.*, Idaho Solid Waste Facilities Act, I.C. § 39-7404 (state board prohibited from promulgating "any rule pursuant to this act that would impose conditions or requirements more stringent or broader in scope than the referenced RCRA regulations of the United States environmental protection agency").

Some states, however, have created procedural requirements allowing promulgation of state standards that *are* more strict than federal standards. In Florida, for example, the Environmental Regulation Commission "shall have a study conducted of the economic and environmental impact which sets forth the benefits and costs to the public of any proposed standard that would be stricter or more stringent than one which has been set by federal agencies pursuant to federal law or regulation." F.S.A. § 403.804(2).

Still other states have signaled greater openness to standards more stringent than federal requirements. In 2019, New Jersey, for example, issued an executive order declaring that "if New Jersey is to remain a leader in environmental protection, including by taking up the mantle relinquished by the federal government when necessary, agencies enacting rules must at times exceed federal standards." Such affirmative state regulation may be particularly appropriate to ensure protection of "low-income communities [who] are often subjected to further disadvantages by the lack of attention towards 'Environmental Justice.'" New Jersey accordingly rescinded prior orders requiring state standards no more stringent than federal standards. The order also pointedly provided, "When the federal government repeals or rolls back prior protections for public health, welfare, safety, or the environment, State entities should evaluate actions New Jersey might take to restore those protections at the state level. . . ." Exec. Order No. 63, April 2, 2019.

As illustrated by the state court decision in *FARMER v. Zimmerman*, states generally have significant authority to establish environmental regulations that exceed federal standards or address concerns beyond the scope of federal regulation. Tribal governments may have such authority as well, either as delegations from the federal government or as a matter of tribal sovereignty. These authorities will be explored further in Chapter 9. For now, consider the following case involving an upstream city's

Figure 5-2. The Rio Grande between Albuquerque, New Mexico, and the Pueblo of Isleta. Photo: Cliff Villa, 2025.

challenge to a downstream tribe's water quality standards that were more stringent than analogous state standards.

City of Albuquerque v. Browner

97 F. 3d 415 (10th Cir. 1996)

McKay, Circuit Judge:

... This case involves the first challenge to water quality standards adopted by an Indian tribe under the Clean Water Act amendment.

The Rio Grande River flows south through New Mexico before turning southeast to form the border between Texas and Mexico. Plaintiff City of Albuquerque operates a waste treatment facility which dumps into the river approximately five miles north of the Isleta Pueblo Indian Reservation. The EPA recognized Isleta Pueblo as a state for purposes of the Clean Water Act on October 12, 1992. The Isleta Pueblo adopted water quality standards for Rio Grande water flowing through the tribal reservation, which were approved by the EPA on December 24, 1992. The Isleta water quality standards are more stringent than the State of New Mexico's standards.

The Albuquerque waste treatment facility discharges into the Rio Grande under a National Pollutant Discharge Elimination System [NPDES] permit issued by the EPA. The EPA sets permit discharge limits for waste treatment facilities so they meet state water quality standards. Albuquerque filed this action as the EPA was in the process of revising Albuquerque's NPDES permit to meet the Isleta Pueblo's water quality standards....

Albuquerque argues that [33 U.S.C.] § 1377 does not expressly permit Indian tribes to enforce effluent limitations or standards under § 1311 to upstream point source dischargers outside of tribal boundaries.... Under the statutory and regulatory scheme, tribes are not applying or enforcing their water quality standards beyond reservation boundaries. Instead, it is the EPA which is exercising its own authority in issuing NPDES permits in compliance with downstream state and tribal water quality standards. In regard to this question, therefore, the 1987 amendment to the Clean Water Act clearly and unambiguously provides tribes the authority to establish NPDES programs in conjunction with the EPA.... [T]he EPA has the authority to require upstream NPDES dischargers, such as Albuquerque, to comply with downstream tribal standards.

... Under the water quality standards provisions of the Clean Water Act, it is the states and tribes which conduct rulemaking proceedings. This is in accord with Congress's intent to preserve a primary role for the states and tribes in eliminating water pollution. The results of state and tribal rulemaking proceedings are then presented to the EPA for approval. The Fourth Circuit has explained the EPA's limited role in reviewing water quality standards proposed by states, stating:

> EPA sits in a reviewing capacity of the state-implemented standards, with approval and rejection powers only....
>
> *[S]tates* have the primary role, under § 303 of the CWA (33 U.S.C. § 1313), in establishing water quality standards. EPA's sole function, in this respect, is to review those standards for approval....

Albuquerque also claims that the EPA's approval of the Isleta Pueblo standards was unsupported by a rational basis on the record and was therefore arbitrary and capricious. Albuquerque argues that the EPA was required to reject the Isleta Pueblo's water quality standards unless the EPA had established its own record based on a sound scientific rationale for each particular provision.

The EPA, however, reviews proposed water quality standards only to determine whether they are stringent enough to comply with the EPA's recommended standards and criteria. If the proposed standards are more stringent than necessary to comply with the Clean Water Act's requirements, the EPA may approve the standards without reviewing the scientific support for the standards. Whether the more stringent standard is attainable is a matter for the EPA to consider in its discretion; sections 1341 and 1342 of the Clean Water Act permit the EPA and states to force technological advancement to attain higher water quality. The EPA's letter approving the Isleta Pueblo standards explains that it is approving the standards, despite their departure from the EPA's guidelines, based on the Tribe's authority to adopt standards more stringent than the minimum requirements of the Clean Water Act.

The EPA considered Isleta Pueblo's rationale for each of the standards challenged by Albuquerque, and the tribe's record contains detailed responses to all of the criticisms expressed by the EPA and Albuquerque. The record contains a detailed explanation of the Isleta Pueblo's scientific, technical, and policy reasons for choosing to establish more stringent standards. For example, the Isleta Pueblo stated that stringent standards are justified because of prevailing drought conditions and the need to protect sensitive subpopulations. The EPA concluded that the standards were consistent with the Clean Water Act's requirements and should therefore be approved. The arbitrary and capricious review standard is very deferential; "an agency ruling is 'arbitrary and capricious if the agency has ... entirely failed to consider an important aspect of the problem.'" Albuquerque has not shown that the EPA failed to consider an important aspect of the Isleta Pueblo's water quality standards....

In its next claim, Albuquerque argues that the Isleta Pueblo criteria approved by the EPA are not stringent enough to protect the Tribe's designated use standard described as primary contact ceremonial use. The Tribe describes primary contact ceremonial use as involving the "immersion and intentional or incidental ingestion of water." Albuquerque argues that this requires the river water quality to meet the standards of the Safe Drinking Water Act, 42 U.S.C. § 300f, and the Isleta Pueblo's water quality criteria approved by the EPA fail to protect water used under the ceremonial use standard.

As the district court stated:

> This argument seems far-fetched. The primary contact ceremonial use appears to resemble a fishable/swimmable standard, which assumes the ingestion of some water, more than it resembles a safe drinking water standard, which assumes the ingestion of a volume of water daily.

Albuquerque [*v. Browner*, 865 F. Supp. 733, 740 (D.N.M. 1993)]. The federal drinking water standards apply only to a "public water system," which is defined as a system supplying piped water for human consumption serving at least twenty-five persons or having at least fifteen service connections. 42 U.S.C. § 300f(4). The Isleta Pueblo's ceremonial use standard does not convert the Rio Grande River into a public water system. The EPA considered and approved this aspect of the Isleta Pueblo water quality standards. We decline to second-guess the EPA's technical determination, which is entitled to substantial deference, that the Isleta Pueblo's water quality criteria adequately protect its ceremonial designated use standard....

Albuquerque next claims that the EPA's approval of the Pueblo's ceremonial use designation offends the Establishment Clause of the First Amendment. The First Amendment provides in relevant part: "Congress shall make no law respecting an establishment of religion...." U.S. Const. amend. I. Government action does not violate the Establishment Clause if "[t]he challenged governmental action has a secular purpose, does not have the principal or primary effect of advancing or inhibiting religion, and does not foster an excessive entanglement with religion."

The EPA approved Isleta Pueblo's promulgation of "Primary Contact Ceremonial Use" as a designated use of the Rio Grande River within the boundaries of the Indian reservation. The tribe defines "Primary Contact Ceremonial Use" as "the use of a stream, reach, lake, or impoundment for religious or traditional purposes by members of the PUEBLO OF ISLETA; such use involves immersion and intentional or incidental ingestion of water." Albuquerque argues that the EPA's approval of this standard violates all three aspects of the Establishment Clause under *Lemon* [*v. Kurtzman*, 403 U.S. 602 (1971)].

First, Albuquerque argues that the reason for the designated use is explicitly sectarian. The secular purpose requirement does not mean that a law's purpose must be unrelated to religion because that would require "'that the government show a callous indifference to religious groups,' ... and the Establishment Clause has never been so interpreted." The EPA's approval of the primary contact ceremonial use designation serves a clear secular purpose: promotion of the goals of the Clean Water Act. The EPA's purpose in approving the designated use is unrelated to the Isleta Pueblo's religious reason for establishing it. The Isleta Pueblo's designation of a ceremonial use does not invalidate the EPA's overall secular goal.

Second, Albuquerque claims that the EPA's action has a primary effect of advancing religion. We disagree. The EPA is not advancing religion through its own actions, and it is not promoting the Isleta Pueblo's religion. The primary effect of the EPA's action is to advance the goals of the Clean Water Act.

Third, Albuquerque asserts the designated use results in excessive governmental entanglement with religion because the Pueblo and the EPA must inquire on an ongoing basis whether the standards adequately protect religious uses of the river water. This argument is meritless. "There is no genuine nexus between" the EPA's approval of the ceremonial use standard "and establishment of religion," and the EPA's approval of the standard provides only an incidental benefit to religion. The EPA's approval of the ceremonial use standard does not require any governmental involvement in the Isleta Pueblo's religious practices. Excessive governmental entanglement will not result when the EPA incorporates the Isleta Pueblo's water quality standards in issuing future NPDES permits....

Notes and Questions

1. Victory. As the first challenge to water quality standards adopted by an Indian tribe under the Clean Water Act, the outcome of *City of Albuquerque v. Browner* was widely celebrated as a victory for environmental regulation by federally recognized tribes. Why might this win have been so important to tribes generally and to the Pueblo of Isleta in particular? What distinguished Isleta's requirements downstream from the state's requirements for the same river upstream? To what extent did the outcome of the case depend on understanding of the Tribe's "ceremonial" use of the river water?

2. Framing the issue. Shortly before the above opinion was issued, Professor Denise Fort published an article on the dispute. In the article, she discussed a variety of important factual questions that this controversy raised:

> ... [I]n any dispute over water quality standards, the underlying factual questions are likely to be persuasive in how one views the merits of the dispute. For example, are tribal standards unreasonably strict, or are the state's unreasonably lax? How expensive will it be for upstream dischargers to comply with the standards? Should a tribe be allowed to continue its historic use of a river for ceremonial purposes, involving drinking from the river, when alternative water supplies are available, and if the answer is affirmative, should upstream taxpayers bear the cost of making a river safe for those practices? Should upstream polluters be allowed to endanger those who depend on a river, and, is it relevant that those uses predate the upstream discharge? One's views of the legal merits may vary with the answers to these questions. It is noteworthy that a state's standards provide the lens through which these questions are viewed; if tribes were to adopt standards identical to those of the surrounding states, dischargers would have no grounds to object. The Pueblo of Isleta's standards were at issue in the *Browner* case, not the standards set by the State of New Mexico.

Denise D. Fort, *State and Tribal Water Quality Standards Under the Clean Water Act: A Case Study*, 35 NAT. RESOURCES J. 771, 775–76 (1995).

As with other cases raising EJ concerns, the legal issues in this dispute were framed with reference to the dominant population. Does framing environmental justice issues as deviations from an existing norm affect the analysis? If so, why did the tribe prevail in this case? In what ways is the case helpful in resolving environmental justice disputes outside the context of tribal sovereignty?

E. Addressing Air Toxics in "Cancer Alley"

> From her front porch in Reserve, Louisiana, Mary Hampton looks in every direction and sees ghosts. To her left is her brother Fred's home. He died from cancer. On the right is another brother's home. His wife, Olga Mae, she died from cancer too. Across the street? A neighbor who died from cancer just a couple of months ago. The list goes on and on.

Jamiles Lartey & Oliver Laughland, *'Almost Every Household Has Someone That Has Died from Cancer,'* GUARDIAN, May 6, 2019.

In this town along the Mississippi River between New Orleans and Baton Rouge, it is evident how the region earned the infamous title of "Cancer Alley." Surrounded by the sprawling infrastructure of the petrochemical industry, residents of the majority Black communities in this corridor breathe toxic air day and night. In Reserve, Louisiana, cancer rates may be the highest in the country, 50 times the national average. *Id.* One major cause of cancer in the Reserve area may be exposure to chloroprene, identified by the EPA as a likely human carcinogen. Chloroprene has historically been emitted by the neighboring Denka Performance Elastomer plant in the production of neoprene, a synthetic rubber. In 2016–2017, air monitoring at the nearby Fifth Ward

Figure 5-3. Denka Performance Elastomer plant, St. John the Baptist Parish, Louisiana. Photo: Cliff Villa, 2025.

Elementary School indicated chloroprene levels in excess of 300 times the EPA's level of concern, exposing hundreds of schoolchildren to significant health risks. Approximately 29,000 people live within five km of the plant. Of this surrounding population, the percent living below the poverty level is almost double the national average. Even more extreme, the percent of the surrounding population that is Black is more than four times the national average. 89 Fed. Reg. 43047.

In February 2023, the U.S. Department of Justice filed a lawsuit against Denka and a subsidiary of DuPont, alleging that operations of the Denka facility "present an imminent and substantial endangerment to public health and welfare" and seeking injunctive relief under the Clean Air Act "requiring that Denka immediately reduce its chloroprene emissions to levels that no longer cause or contribute to unacceptably high cancer risks within the communities surrounding the Facility." United States of America v. Denka Performance Elastomer LLC and DuPont Specialty Products USA, LLC, Civil Action N. 2:23-cv-735 (Feb. 28, 2023). While the lawsuit brought hope for community members, the Trump administration dismissed the complaint soon after taking office. *Justice Department Dismisses Suit Against Denka, Delivering on President Trump's Mandate to End Radical DEI Programs*, Press Release, Mar. 7, 2025. Even so, Denka, a Japanese chemicals company, announced in May 2025 that it was shutting down its Louisiana facility after recording "an extraordinary loss in its financial results." Denka, Announcement Concerning the Recording of Extraordinary Losses of a U.S. Subsidiary of the Company and the Suspension of Chloroprene Rubber Production, May 13, 2025.

In addition to chloroprene from the Denka facility, communities in Cancer Alley have been exposed to "a whole soup of chemicals" from surrounding industry. However, according to one recent report from researchers at Johns Hopkins University, approximately 68 percent of the total health hazard from industrial air emissions in the region traces to one air toxic in particular: ethylene oxide. Ellis S. Robinson et al., *Ethylene Oxide in Southeastern Louisiana's Petrochemical Corridor: High Spatial Resolution Mobile Monitoring during HAP-MAP*, 58 Envtl. Sci. & Tech. 11084 (2024). Ethylene oxide (EtO) is "a volatile organic compound (VOC) used as a petrochemical feedstock for commercial chemicals ... as well as a sterilizing and fumigating agent for medical equipment and food safety." EtO is a "known human carcinogen associated with a variety of cancers (leukemia, myeloma, lymphoma, and breast cancer) and is also considered mutagenic." *Id.* EtO is also "extremely carcinogenic" compared to other hazardous VOCs, with an EPA level of concern as low as 10.9 parts per *trillion*. *Id.*

The Johns Hopkins researchers found that "A number of the largest EtO emitters in the U.S. are located in southeastern Louisiana." However, "analytical challenge[s]" had resulted in a "dearth of reported ambient EtO concentrations." *Id.* at 11085. To address this challenge, the researchers developed mobile monitoring techniques to produce faster and more accurate results. The results found far more EtO in the ambient air than previously measured, with approximately 75 percent of samples across the industrial corridor exceeding EPA action levels. *Id.* at 11090.

To address concerns for EtO, chloroprene, and other air toxics, EPA developed a new regulation under the Clean Air Act. On March 3, 2024, according to reginfo.gov, EPA submitted the proposed rule for review by OIRA pursuant to the process established by Executive Order 12866. After timely clearance by OIRA, EPA published the proposed rule in the Federal Register the next month. 88 Fed. Reg. 25080, April 25, 2023. Consistent with APA requirements, EPA invited public comments on the proposed rule and EPA extended the public comment period until July 7, 2023. 88 Fed. Reg. 41369, June 26, 2023. During the comment period, EPA received 2,647 comment letters, including 2,086 individual letters. U.S. EPA, *Summary of Public Comments and Responses* (March 2024). After consideration of comments, in May 2024, EPA published in the Federal Register the final regulation which came to be known as the "HON rule" (for Hazardous Organic NESHAPs). 89 Fed. Reg. 42932, May 16, 2024.

EPA estimated that full implementation of the HON rule would reduce more than 6,200 tons a year of over 100 air toxics. This would include a reduction of nearly 54 tons of EtO emissions per year and 14 tons of chloroprene per year—a reduction of nearly 80 percent of each chemical each year. *EPA Issues Final Rule to Reduce Toxic Air Pollution from the Synthetic Organic Chemical Manufacturing Industry and the Polymers and Resins Industries*, EPA Fact Sheet (undated). The reductions would result from a range of requirements, "including requirements to improve the efficiency of flares that are used to control pollution from emissions sources." *Id.* The new rule would remove general exemptions from control requirements during periods of startup and shut-down, and would establish requirements for fence-line monitoring, with data reported quarterly to EPA.

Based upon a first-of-its-kind community risk assessment, EPA estimated that the new HON rule would reduce the number of people who have elevated risk of cancer from air toxics by 96 percent. This risk reduction would provide particular benefits to people of color and low-income residents, who are disproportionately represented in fence-line communities surrounding the regulated facilities. The new rule would also benefit children by reducing their exposure to air toxic emissions which can damage DNA.

Consistent with requirements of EO 12866, EPA estimated the costs and benefits associated with implementation of the HON rule. Measurable benefits included improvements in human health from reducing short-term and long-term ozone exposure, amounting to a present value of approximately $64 million per year. The present value of estimated costs for implementing the rule amounted to approximately $150 million per year. In conclusion, EPA observed, "Most of the facilities covered by the final rule are owned by large corporations. The cost of implementing the final rule is less than 1 percent of their annual national sales." *Id.* at 4.

Unsurprisingly, the second Trump administration announced an intent to "reconsider" the HON rule along with many other regulations promulgated during the Biden administration. U.S. EPA, *Trump EPA Announces Reconsideration of Air Rules Regulating American Energy, Manufacturing, Chemical Sections (NESHAPs)*, Mar. 12, 2025. Time will tell whether such reconsideration becomes effective and withstands judicial review, particularly against the diminishing agency deference established by *Loper Bright* and other recent decisions by the U.S. Supreme Court. For now, the HON rule stands as an important example of the potential for environmental regulations to contribute significantly to environmental justice.

Chapter 6

Environmental Permits

A. Introduction

As we saw in Chapter 1 with the case of the PCBs landfill in Warren County, many environmental justice challenges appear in the context of facility permitting. There are good reasons why this occurs. First, consider the immediacy of the adverse impacts on a local level, such as toxic air emissions, chemicals that are discharged into waterways, dust, increased truck traffic through neighborhood streets, noise, odor, and at times increased vermin and rodents. Understandably, residents in overburdened communities often view a new facility or a facility expansion as the proverbial straw that breaks the camel's back. Pollution permit proceedings also raise concerns about whether the facility operator will comply with the permit terms, thus injecting into permit proceedings issues such as subsequent enforcement and potential contamination. In a sense, the permit is the gateway to environmental inequity that may stem from inadequacies that may exist in rulemaking, enforcement, and even cleanup activities.

Often, community members are not made aware of pollution sources until public notice requirements of permit proceedings have been triggered. At that point, a community will be placed in a reactive position. They may attempt to challenge a plan for siting a new facility, or to seek concessions through more protective permit terms, mitigation measures beyond those directly required by existing regulations, or public benefits. This often pits community groups against the facility sponsor and permitting officials—both of whom may have become committed to issuing the permit—and may unfairly cause community groups to be characterized as anti-development or "NIMBY" (Not In My Back Yard) oriented.

This chapter explores both the legal authority under environmental statutes to impose additional permit conditions (or to deny the permit altogether), as well as the difficulties encountered in attempting to change the permitting status quo to better respond to environmental inequities. Few states have legislation specifically addressing environmental justice in permit proceedings, although that number is growing (see Chapter 10). At the federal level, environmental laws provide significant authority to incorporate environmental justice in both rulemaking and in the development of permit conditions. Additionally, civil rights legislation and cases explicitly prohibit discrimination related to pollution permitting, ranging from the selection of sites to the provision of environmental services by states and municipalities. This chapter will examine how federal and state permitting officials have responded to environmental justice claims based on these provisions. Other sources of legal authority, such as provisions under constitutional provisions or environmental review statutes, are explored in Chapters 4 and 11, respectively.

B. Federal Authorities to Ensure Environmental Justice in Facility Permitting

As you read the following short excerpt, isolate the precise statutory language that you, as a lawyer, would use to argue that the permitting official may legally consider a community's claims that it is already unfairly overburdened with environmental pollution, risk, and nuisance impacts, and that the permit should contain additional requirements or be denied altogether.

Richard J. Lazarus & Stephanie Tai, *Integrating Environmental Justice into EPA Permitting Authority*

26 Ecology L.Q. 617 (1999)

Background: The Meaning of "Environmental Justice" in the EPA Permitting Context

... In the context of an EPA permitting decision, the core expression of environmental justice is that EPA should take into account the racial and/or socioeconomic makeup of the community most likely to be affected adversely by the environmental risks of a proposed activity. This involves two steps: the identification of the environmental justice community and the incorporation of that community's concerns into the permitting process. Taking into account the makeup of the community does not mean that EPA must automatically deny a permit solely because the affected area is a community of color or low-income. The Agency's inquiry into these characteristics of the community is, however, necessary to allow the Agency to make an informed permitting decision regarding the actual environmental and health effects of a permit applicant's proposed activity....

Some of the environmental justice concerns that can be addressed through permit conditions are discussed below. They include the enhancement of a community's capacity to participate in environmental enforcement and compliance assurance, assessment of risk aggregation or cumulative risk, and identification of disproportionality in risk imposition. The relevance of each of these concerns to the permitting process is fairly clear. What is less clear to those officials responsible for issuing the permits is whether they have the necessary authority to consider such concerns and to take actions, including the imposition of permit conditions, based upon those concerns....

Survey of Federal Statutory Provisions Authorizing Permit Conditions or Denials Based on Environmental Justice

The history of environmental law is replete with instances when broadly worded statutory language or regulations have been successfully enlisted in support of arguments that the federal government has authority or obligations beyond those initially contemplated by the regulated entities, environmentalists, affected communities, or even the government itself....

The [Clean Air] Act's nonattainment provisions provide [] potential environmental justice opportunities. [Nonattainment means an airshed that does not meet national air quality standards for certain pollutants. Eds.] Section 173 describes the requirements for a nonattainment permit. An explicit permit requirement in the Act mandates that [a permit cannot be granted unless] "an analysis of alternative sites, sizes, production processes, and environmental control techniques for such proposed source demonstrates that benefits of the proposed source significantly outweigh the environmental and social costs imposed as a result of its location, construction, or modification." The references to both "social costs" and "location" serve as strong bases for EPA's assertion of statutory authority to take environmental justice concerns into account in evaluating the "location" of a facility seeking a nonattainment permit....

In the context of permitting, the CAA provisions of greatest interest are those that may allow EPA (or a state permitting authority that has assumed permitting responsibility pursuant to CAA Section 502) greater discretion in using the permitting process to increase community participation and build community enforcement capacity. Section 504 would seem to confer on EPA just such authority. Subsection (a) provides that "[e]ach permit issued under this subchapter shall include ... such other conditions as are necessary to assure compliance with applicable requirements of this chapter...." A major component for achieving compliance assurance under the CAA is the citizen suit provision of that statute. Without that provision acting as a credible enforcement threat, there is no assurance of compliance. Therefore, Section 504(a) may authorize EPA to impose upon those receiving CAA permits the condition that they take certain steps to enhance the affected community's ability to ensure that the permitted facility complies with applicable environmental protection laws. Such conditions could range from simply providing more ready access to the information necessary to overseeing the permitted facility's operation and compliance to working to increase the resources of citizen groups participating in environmental oversight and compliance assurance.

To that same effect, Section 504(b) authorizes EPA to prescribe "procedures and methods for determining compliance," and Section 504(c) requires that each permit "set forth inspection, entry, monitoring, compliance certification, and reporting requirements to assure compliance with the permit terms and conditions." There is nothing on the face of the statute to preclude either Section 504(b)'s "procedures and methods" or Section 504(c)'s "requirements to assure compliance" from extending to permit conditions that enhance the community's own capacity to oversee the permitted facility's compliance....

Section 402 of the [Clean Water Act] ... is likely the most significant potential source of permit conditioning authority [under that statute]. Section 402 provides that the Administrator may issue a permit for the discharge of any pollutant: "upon condition that such discharge will meet either (A) all applicable requirements under [various sections of the CWA], or (B) prior to the taking of necessary implementing actions relating to all such requirements, such conditions as the Administrator determines are necessary to carry out the provisions of this chapter." A broad construction of clause (B) could confer on the Administrator wide ranging authority to impose permit conditions promoting environmental justice....

Notes and Questions

1. EJ Legal Tools. As early as 2000, EPA's Office of General Counsel (OGC) prepared a lengthy memo that similarly found significant authority under numerous statutory provisions for addressing environmental justice issues in the permitting process, including Clean Air Act Section 504, discussed by Professors Lazarus and Tai. In 2011, during the Obama administration, EPA OGC published the legal memo and made it available to the public. EPA OGC, PLAN EJ 2014, LEGAL TOOLS (Dec. 2011). The agency updated that analysis in 2022, publishing EPA, LEGAL TOOLS TO ADVANCE ENVIRONMENTAL JUSTICE (May 2022), hereinafter "EJ Legal Tools," available online at the companion website: www.environmentaljusticebook.org/chapter-materials-chapter-6/.

At more than two hundred pages, *EJ Legal Tools* provides a broad review of many existing legal authorities that could contribute to pursuits for environmental justice, including the CAA, CWA, SDWA, RCRA, CERCLA, FIFRA, TSCA, and other authorities in addition to research grants, and tribal consultation. In the particular context of Clean Air Act permitting, *EJ Legal Tools* provides numerous insights on state obligations and EPA authority. We provide two examples under the CAA below:

> EPA's opportunities to advance environmental justice on the basis of NSR [New Source Review] permitting program authorities in the CAA and EPA regulations differ depending on whether EPA or the state is the permitting authority. When EPA is the permitting authority, the Agency determines, consistent with applicable regulations, both the content of the permit and the permit review process. The latter gives EPA opportunities to enhance environmental justice by facilitating increased public participation in the formal permit consideration process (e.g., by granting requests to extend public comment periods, holding multiple public meetings, or providing translation services at hearings in areas with limited English proficiency). EPA can also take informal steps to enhance participation earlier in the process, such as inviting community groups to meet with EPA and express their concerns before a draft permit is issued. When making permitting decisions, the Agency has the legal authority described below to consider potential disproportionate environmental burdens on a case-by-case basis, without issuing or amending regulations or guidance documents. EPA has followed this case-by-case ap-

> proach in issuing NSR permits for nearly 30 years, consistent with the legal authority under the CAA provisions and NSR regulations discussed below. When a state is the permitting authority, EPA's role includes commenting on individual permits during the comment period. This presents an opportunity for EPA to advance environmental justice by focusing the state's consideration on potential disproportionate environmental burdens in determining that the permits comply with applicable requirements. EPA can offer comments to states regarding disproportionate burdens arising from permits. EPA routinely comments on proposed permits....
>
> The requirements that an applicant must meet to obtain a nonattainment NSR [New Source Review] permit are reflected in § 173 of the CAA. Section 173(a)(5) requires a permitting authority reviewing a nonattainment NSR permit to determine whether "an analysis of alternative sites, sizes, production processes, and environmental control techniques for such proposed source demonstrates that benefits of the proposed source significantly outweigh the environmental and social costs imposed as a result of its location, construction, or modification." Thus, this provision calls for consideration of siting issues. The term "social costs" is not defined in the CAA, but may be interpreted to cover a broad range of impacts on communities with environmental justice concerns. EPA's regulations governing state nonattainment NSR programs do not establish criteria or procedures for conducting the analysis required by CAA § 173(a)(5).163. EPA could advance environmental justice in the nonattainment NSR program by emphasizing the need to address this requirement and helping states understand the nature of this requirement and how it can be implemented, including the consideration of environmental justice concerns in the analysis as appropriate.

EJ Legal Tools at 38 and 48.

2. EPA policies for EJ in permitting. In addition to *EJ Legal Tools*, recognizing broad legal authorities to address EJ in permitting, some EPA guidance documents also encouraged consideration of EJ issues in permitting as a matter of agency policy. *See, e.g., EPA Activities to Promote Environmental Justice in the Permit Application Process*, 78 Fed. Reg. 27220 (May 9, 2013). The EPA's policy statement on EJ in permitting appeared in EPA's EJ 2020 ACTION AGENDA (2016). For EJ in permitting, the *EJ 2020 Action Agenda* established two basic objectives:

> The first is that environmental justice is routinely considered in EPA permitting in all appropriate circumstances. This means that in initiating a permitting action, EPA permit writers will consider whether there are environmental justice concerns present in the community affected by the permit. [Further,] EPA will establish appropriate permit terms and conditions to address environmental justice concerns to the extent supported by the relevant information and law.

> ... The second objective is to build, through engagement in "mutual learning" with state and local co-regulators and other stakeholders, a shared set of tools, best practices and approaches for considering environmental justice concerns in permitting. These tools, practices and approaches will help overburdened communities know how to advocate their concerns and help permitting agencies consider and address them in an appropriate manner.

Id. at 16–17.

The most recent EPA statement on EJ in permitting was in the 2022 *EPA Interim Environmental Justice and Civil Rights in Permitting Frequently Asked Questions*. The document was directed toward "federal, state, and local environmental permitting programs to help them meet their responsibilities to integrate environmental justice (EJ) and civil rights into relevant environmental permitting processes." One of many stand out features in the FAQ is the discussion of Health Impact Assessments (HIAs) as a valuable tool for EJ analysis in permitting:

> One promising practice for conducting EJ analyses is the Health Impact Assessment (HIA), which systematically evaluates how a proposed action may impact health and well-being. HIAs explicitly consider potential distributive effects (e.g., whether there will be disproportionate impacts) and inform decision-makers of potential outcomes before the decision is made. HIAs generally:
>
> - Determine the potential effects of a proposed decision on the health of a population and the distribution of those effects within the population;
> - Consider input from stakeholders, including those impacted by the decision;
> - Use different types of qualitative and quantitative evidence and analytical methods;
> - Are flexible based on available time and resources; and
> - Provide evidence and recommendations to decision-makers in a timely manner.
>
> A permitting program may find it helpful to organize an EJ analysis by applying HIA practice standards and elements, including by adapting the six key steps that guide the HIA process:
>
> 1. Screening. Determines the need for and value of an HIA ...
> 2. Scoping. Identifies the project partners, health and social impacts requiring assessment, methodology for the analysis, and a work plan.
> 3. Assessment. Provides an analysis of existing conditions; an assessment of the policy, plan, project, or program under study; and an evaluation of the potential impacts of the policy, plan, project, or program on existing conditions.
> 4. Recommendations. Develops a set of recommendations for maximizing health outcomes.

5. Reporting. Develops a report and communicates findings and recommendations.
6. Monitoring. Tracks the impact of the HIA on the proposed policy, plan, project, or program and the impacts of the final policy, plan, project, or program on existing conditions.

Id. at 25–27.

Later in the chapter, we examine the use of an HIA in a controversial permit dispute regarding General Iron (dba Southside Recycling), a large-scale metal shredding operation in Chicago, Illinois. HIAs move from general environmental protection to a more community-based approach that accounts for additional pollution exposures and existing health vulnerabilities in assessing the suitability of pollution permit conditions and the particular harms pollution exposure may cause.

3. The Environmental Appeals Board. Professors Lazarus and Tai also note the willingness of the Environmental Appeals Board (EAB) to endorse conditioning permits on environmental justice grounds:

> The evolving perspective of the Environmental Appeals Board on EPA's authority to base permits on environmental justice grounds can be seen in a series of decisions beginning in September 1993 and continuing to [1999]. Although the Executive Order on Environmental Justice [EO 12088 (1994)] expressly did not enlarge any agency's permitting power, the Order has had a marked effect on the Board's interpretation of the scope of authority available to permitting agencies. Prior to the Order, the Board rejected an environmental justice community's claim that environmental justice concerns should be considered in an air quality permitting process. The Board held instead that permitting agencies lacked environmental justice authority because they were limited to considering whether a facility would meet federal air quality requirements.
>
> After the Order was issued, the Board seemed to accord increasingly more acceptance to the contention that permitting agencies were able to condition permits on environmental justice grounds.... The net effect of the Order may have been to draw attention to existing areas of authority that the Board had previously overlooked so that agencies had the means to actually comply with the Order.

Richard J. Lazarus & Stephanie Tai, *Integrating Environmental Justice into EPA Permitting Authority*, 26 Ecology L.Q. 617, 655–56 (1999).

4. The executive orders. Although it appears that broadly worded clauses in federal environmental statutes grant authority to condition or deny permits on environmental justice grounds, the willingness of permitting authorities to use their legal authority is critically important. In order to prompt federal agencies to take more aggressive action to address environmental inequities, in 1994 President Clinton issued Executive Order 12898, requiring federal agencies to "make achieving environmental justice part of [the agency's] mission by identifying and addressing, as appropriate, disproportionately high and adverse human health or environmental effects of its programs, policies and activities. . . ." (See Chapter 10). Moreover, on April 21, 2023, President Joe Biden issued Executive Order 14096, *Revitalizing Our Nation's Commitment to Environmental Justice for All.* In section 3, it provided the following:

> Sec. 3 . . .
>
> (ii) evaluate relevant legal authorities and, as available and appropriate, take steps to address disproportionate and adverse human health and environmental effects (including risks) and hazards unrelated to Federal activities, including those related to climate change and cumulative impacts of environmental and other burdens on communities with environmental justice concerns . . .
>
> (vi) evaluate relevant legal authorities and, where available and appropriate, consider adopting or requiring measures to avoid, minimize, or mitigate disproportionate and adverse human health and environmental effects (including risks) and hazards of Federal activities on communities with environmental justice concerns, to the maximum extent practicable, and to address any contribution of such Federal activities to adverse effects—including cumulative impacts of environmental and other burdens—already experienced by such communities.

Available online at: https://www.federalregister.gov/documents/2023/04/26/2023-08955/revitalizing-our-nations-commitment-to-environmental-justice-for-all.

Executive Order 14096 expanded on Executive Order 12898, among other things, by including climate change and cumulative impacts unrelated to federal activities and the "cumulative impacts of environmental and other burdens of federal activities."

With particular relevance to permitting, Executive Order 14096 communicated the intention that the federal executive branch should use existing authorities "to consider adopting or requiring measures to avoid, minimize, or mitigate disproportionate and adverse human health and environmental effects (including risks) and hazards." As you read the following decision by the Environmental Appeals Board, consider whether it supports the status quo or encourages the development of more protective permitting approaches.

In re Shell Gulf of Mexico, Inc. & *In re* Shell Offshore, Inc. (Frontier Discoverer Drilling Unit)

U.S. EPA Envtl. Appeals Board *15 E.A.D. 103 (EAB 2010)*

[This case arose out of plans by Shell Oil to engage in oil exploration in the Arctic Ocean, specifically in the Chukchi Sea on the west and the Beaufort Sea to the east, within the Outer Continental Shelf of the United States. Operation of Shell's massive drill rigs would require permits under the Clean Air Act program for Prevention of

Significant Deterioration (PSD). While the drill rigs would operate offshore, residents of Alaska's North Slope, including Alaska Native villages, expressed concern about potential impacts of the drill operation in their communities. Represented by Earthjustice and other legal counsel, concerned community members filed challenges to the Clean Air Act permits written by the EPA, resulting in the following decision on appeal to the EPA Environmental Appeals Board (EAB).]

... The Board has held that environmental justice issues must be considered in connection with the issuance of PSD permits. *In re* Prairie State Generating Co., 13 E.A.D. 1, 123 (EAB 2006), *aff'd sub nom. Sierra Club v. U.S. EPA*, 499 F.3d 653 (7th Cir. 2007); *In re* AES Puerto Rico, *L.P.*, 8 E.A.D. 324, 351 (EAB 1999), *aff'd sub nom. Sur Contra la Contaminación v. EPA*, 202 F.3d 443 (1st Cir. 2000); *In re* Knauf Fiber Glass GmbH, 8 E.A.D. 121, 174–75 (EAB 1999) ("*Knauf I*"); *In re* EcoElectrica, L.P., 7 E.A.D. 56, 67–69 (EAB 1997).

In the present case, AEWC [Alaska Eskimo Whaling Commission and Inupiat Community of the Arctic Slope] and the Region agree that the North Slope communities potentially impacted by Shell's proposed operations include a "significantly high percentage of Alaskan Natives, who are considered a minority under [Executive Order] 12898." ... AEWC contends that the Region clearly erred when it concluded that compliance with the existing annual NO2 NAAQS demonstrates compliance with the Executive Order.

AEWC's Assertions and Region's Response

... Specifically, AEWC argues that the Region neglected to conduct an environmental justice analysis notwithstanding evidence of existing health disparities between Inupiat Eskimos and other U.S. populations, and despite AEWC's requests for such an analysis in its comments on both permits.... AEWC argues that relying on compliance with the applicable NAAQS as evidence of fulfilling the Executive Order means that no PSD permit will ever trigger the requirements of the Executive Order because no permit can be issued if there is a predicted violation, and further, that because EPA recently updated the NO2 NAAQS, there is evidence that the NO2 NAAQS applicable at the time the Region issued the Permits is not sufficient to protect public health....

The Region responds that its environmental justice analysis was adequate, arguing that it "engaged in extensive outreach" with affected communities to evaluate possible effects on minority or low-income communities, aided by the recently developed North Slope Communication Protocol ("NSCP").... In summarizing the analyses of the potential effects the Permits will have on air quality, the Region states that because operation of the Frontier Discoverer and the Associated Fleet will not cause or contribute to a NAAQS violation, it "means that it will not have a significant adverse impact, much less a disproportionately high and adverse human health or environmental effect, on minority or low-income populations." ... and further argues that because the Region has "determined that no such adverse effects will result from the issuance of the permits in this case, the EAB need not address the AEWC Petitioners' argument regarding the sufficiency of Region 10's environmental justice analysis." ...

Analysis

... The Region's adherence to prior Board precedent stating that compliance with the NAAQS is sufficient to demonstrate compliance with the Executive Order is misplaced. In the context of PSD permit challenges, the Region correctly states that the Board has accepted compliance with the NAAQS as sufficient to demonstrate that emissions from a proposed facility will not have disproportionately high and adverse human health or environmental effects on a minority or low-income population. *See, e.g., Knauf II*, 9 E.A.D. at 15–17; *In re Sutter Power Plant*, 8 E.A.D. 680, 692 (EAB 1999) (describing the NAAQS as the "bellwether of health protection"). However, the Region ignores the unusual context of this case, as well as the reasons that underlie the Board's precedent of looking in part to NAAQS compliance to satisfy the Executive Order.

The cases the Region cites as support for its decisions in the Chukchi and Beaufort Permits, in which the Board upheld a permit issuer's environmental justice analysis based on demonstrated compliance with the NAAQS, do not support the Region's position in this case. *See Shell*, 13 E.A.D. at 405; *Knauf II*, 9 E.A.D. at 16–17; *Ash Grove Cement*, 7 E.A.D. at 414; *see also* Region's Resp. at 99. First and foremost, in each of the cases the Region cites, no party argued that a later-in-time standard had been proposed or finalized prior to the permit issuer's decision, and thus application of the then-effective standard was not an issue raised in any of the petitions. In addition, in each of the cases cited, the permit issuer provided some analysis or record evidence to demonstrate compliance with the Executive Order that the Board could look to in evaluating Petitioners' claims regarding environmental justice. *See Shell*, 13 E.A.D. at 404–05 (citing statement in the response to comments document that compliance with the NAAQS and additional permit requirements were expected to provide verifiable means of ensuring Shell's drilling project would comply with the CAA and operate in a manner to protect the health and welfare of Native Villages); *Knauf II*, 9 E.A.D. at 16–17 (upholding Region's environmental justice analysis based on inclusion in the record of two memoranda, made available for public comment when the revised permit was issued pursuant to a remand, analyzing demographics of the areas surrounding the proposed facility and assessing whether emissions from the proposed facility would have a disproportionately high and adverse impact on human health or the environment); *Ash Grove Cement*, 7 E.A.D. at 413–14 (upholding Region's finding of no disproportionately high and adverse human health or environmental effects based on the Region's documented analysis of demographic data for the areas surrounding the proposed facility, as well as the Region's decision not to conduct a quantitative risk assessment based on its conclusions that minority and/or low-income populations identified were outside the area principally impacted by Ash Grove emissions). Thus, the cases the Region cites to support its argument that compliance with the then-applicable NAAQS also indicates de facto compliance with the Executive Order are all distinguishable from the Petitions at issue here. Further, the Region's arguments belie the basis upon which the Board relies on the Agency's NAAQS decisions....

The Board's concerns in this case lie with the Region's stated reliance on its demonstration of compliance with the NAAQS in effect at the time of the Permits' issuance despite the fact that the Administrator had finalized the new 1-hour NO2 NAAQS prior to the issuance of the Permits, and thus the Administrator had already concluded, prior to the issuance of the Permits, that the annual NO2 NAAQS alone did not provide requisite protection of the public health.... Despite the Administrator's unequivocal determination, made prior to the issuance of either final Permit, that the annual NO2 NAAQS alone was not requisite to protect the public health with an adequate margin of safety, the Region nonetheless solely relies on compliance with the then-applicable annual NO2 NAAQS to demonstrate that Alaska Natives living in North Slope communities will not experience disproportionately high and adverse human health or environmental effects.

For the reasons set forth below, the Board remands the Chukchi and Beaufort Permits for the Region to reconsider the adequacy of its environmental justice analysis....

Notes and Questions

1. Compliance with the NAAQS? Compare this decision of the EAB with the EPA's decision in the *Select Steel* case (discussed in Chapter 4). Both cases query whether the proposed operations will result in violations of the Clean Air Act's National Ambient Air Quality Standards (NAAQS). In neither case is there any showing of likely NAAQS violations. And yet, the two cases result in markedly different outcomes. What can explain these differences? Is the EAB in *Shell Oil* (twelve years after *Select Steel*) still convinced that compliance with the NAAQS confirms the absence of disproportionate impacts on minority or low-income communities?

2. Environmental justice precedent. In 2011, EPA completed its environmental justice analysis for the Shell permits. On remand, in part because of EPA's air impacts analysis that correctly applied the revised NO2 NAAQS standard, and rejecting other objections to the environmental justice analysis, the EAB "decline[ed] to review the Region's compliance with the Executive Order and applicable Board precedent." *In re* Shell Gulf of Mexico, Inc. & Shell Offshore, Inc., 15 E.A.D. 470, 504 (EAB 2012). Nevertheless, the 2010 EAB decision established precedent for the Board to consider environmental justice in permitting. Consider how the next case further illustrates the outer bounds of regulatory discretion to condition or deny a permit based upon environmental justice considerations.

In re Avenal Power Center, LLC

U.S. EPA Envtl. Appeals Board, *15 E.A.D. 384 (EAB 2011)*

[In this case, the Avenal Power Center, LLC, sought approval to construct and operate a new 600-megawatt natural gas-fired power plant in the Central Valley of California, near the communities of Avenal, Huron, and Kettleman City. In support of the project, the EPA issued a permit under the Clean Air Act PSD program. The permit was challenged by concerned members of organizations including El Pueblo Para El Aire y Agua Limpio ("El Pueblo"), Greenaction for Health and Environmental Justice ("Greenaction"), and the Center for Biological Diversity. On review of the permit, the EAB issued the following decision.]

... El Pueblo, Sierra Club, and Greenaction challenge the Agency's environmental justice analysis and argue instead that the proposed facility will have disproportionately high and adverse human health or environmental effects on residents of Avenal, Huron, and Kettleman City, the three communities in closest proximity to the proposed facility. The Agency argues that the environmental justice analysis itself and the conclusions the Agency made based on that analysis comply with Executive Order 12898.... Thus, the central question the Board must resolve is: did the Agency meet its obligation to comply with the Executive Order? ...

AGENCY'S ENVIRONMENTAL JUSTICE ANALYSIS

The Agency included in the Supplemental Statement of Basis a thirty-one page environmental justice analysis that collected and analyzed demographic, health-related, and air quality data.... The demographic analysis indicates that the communities of Avenal, Huron, and Kettleman City contain minority and low-income populations that may be impacted by emissions from the proposed facility....

After the demographic analysis, the Agency described the status of air quality in the area, explaining that it is designated as extreme nonattainment for ozone and as nonattainment for PM2.5, and that it is designated in attainment or unclassifiable for PM10, annual average NO2, carbon monoxide, SO2, and lead.... The Agency next addressed the limited availability of hourly NO2 monitoring data from Agency-approved monitoring sites, and explained that it decided to use hourly NO2 monitoring information from Hanford and Visalia, the two closest EPA-approved monitors located twenty-eight and forty-six miles from the proposed facility, respectively, to analyze background levels of hourly NO2 at the project site....

In the first part of its environmental justice analysis, the Agency determined that the proposed facility's projected emissions for NO2 (annual average), carbon monoxide (1-hour and 8-hour average), and PM10 (24-hour average) will not cause or contribute to a violation of the applicable NAAQS. The Agency concluded that compliance with these NAAQS is sufficient to demonstrate that the proposed emissions for these pollutants over these averaging times will not result in disproportionately high and adverse human health or environmental effects on minority and low-income populations residing near the proposed facility.

In the second part of its environmental justice analysis, the Agency considered the hourly impacts of NO2 concentrations.... The Agency briefly reiterated its previous conclusion that the limited data available from the Hanford and Visalia monitors located closest to the proposed facility indicate that background levels of hourly NO2 "are on par with measured levels of NO2 statewide," and thus background levels of hourly

NO2 in the general area of the facility are not disproportionately high as compared to communities throughout the state....

... Contrary to the lack of an environmental justice analysis and the failure to consider short-term impacts of NO2 emissions in *Shell II*, the Agency in this instance provided a thirty-one page environmental justice analysis coupled with a reasoned explanation for why it concluded that the limited information available prevented it from making a determination regarding potential disproportionate impacts caused by short-term NO2 emissions. The Board did not address in *Shell II* whether a permit issuer must make a determinative conclusion after analyzing available, valid data in response to an environmental justice concern. Here, however, the Board finds the Agency's inability to conclude whether short-term NO2 emissions have a disproportionate impact on the populations surrounding the proposed facility is permissible, particularly in light of the facts of this case and the discretion afforded to federal agencies under the Executive Order. The Executive Order does not mandate that the Agency reach a determinative outcome when it conducts an environmental justice analysis, especially when the available valid data is not sufficient to support a determinative outcome. Thus, El Pueblo's and Sierra Club's attempt to selectively interpret the Executive Order and Board precedent to require more must fail. Where, as here, the Agency conducts a substantive environmental justice analysis that endeavors to include and analyze data that is germane to the environmental justice issue raised during the comment period, *see Shell II*, 15 E.A.D. at 160 n.87, and the permit issuer demonstrates that it exercised its considered judgment when determining that it could not reach a determinative conclusion due to the insufficiency of available valid data, the Board will decline to grant review of the environmental justice analysis. *See, e.g., In re Ash Grove Cement Co.*, 7 E.A.D. 387, 417–18 (EAB 1997)....

Notes and Questions

1. Postscript. After the EAB's decision above, the plaintiffs sought judicial review in the Ninth Circuit Court of Appeals, arguing among other things that the EPA failed to include in Avenal's Clean Air Act permit applicable conditions including recently updated NAAQS for NO2 and SO2. The Ninth Circuit agreed with plaintiffs, vacating the Avenal permit and remanding it back to the EPA in order to fix the permit conditions. *Sierra Club v. U.S. EPA*, 762 F.3 971 (9th Cir. 2014).

2. Right to appeal. What provisions confer rights of appeal to the EAB? *See generally*, 40 C.F.R. Parts 71 (Clean Air Act Title V operating permits) and 124 (most other EPA permits). For a useful overview of EAB functions and authorities, *see* EPA, A CITIZEN'S GUIDE TO EPA'S ENVIRONMENTAL APPEALS BOARD (July 2018). What if the EPA removed the ability of individuals or community advocates to appeal EPA-issued permits before the EAB? Would the ability to challenge EPA permits in federal court provide the same level of protection and access to justice for minority or low-income communities? Does this hypothetical affect your analysis of the above cases?

3. Outer bounds? At a minimum, the *Avenal* case affirmed the precedent for requiring an environmental justice analysis as part of the permitting process. Together, these EAB permitting cases illustrate the tension, on appeal, between the principle of deference to agencies embodied in an abuse of discretion review standard and the counter-balancing policy, embodied in the federal executive order and recognized by the EAB, that discretion should be exercised in a more protective manner where impacts affect vulnerable communities. The EAB's approach has been to resolve this tension by a more probing review of procedural matters, requiring a detailed environmental justice analysis and good evidentiary support for a claim of disparate impact. As methodologies advance and more specific criteria are developed, by statute or rule, reviewing bodies may have a better basis to evaluate the adequacy of a permitting authority's response to environmental justice concerns. Given the need to substantially improve conditions in overburdened communities, while at the same time affording permit applicants fairness and certainty in the permitting process, how would you devise a more protective permitting scheme that accomplishes these goals?

4. Legal authority without EJ executive orders. Executive Order 12898, issued by President Bill Clinton in 1994 (discussed above), directed agencies to identify and address disproportionately high and adverse environmental effects on low income and minority populations. Executive Order 14096, issued by President Joe Biden in 2023, directed agencies to use existing legal authority to address environmental justice. Does President Trump's rescission of the executive orders above affect federal agencies' legal authority to address these issues broadly?

5. NEPA's EJ analysis in the permitting context. Environmental review laws, including NEPA, are more fully discussed in Chapter 11. These laws often offer a source of leverage for EJ advocates in environmental permitting. A notable D.C. Circuit opinion concerning the controversial Dakota Access Pipeline (DAPL) addresses such issues. *Standing Rock Sioux Tribe v. U.S. Army Corps of Engineers*, 255 F. Supp. 3d 101 (D.D.C. 2017).

> ... [T]he D.C. Circuit has permitted challenges to environmental justice analyses under NEPA and the APA, citing *Communities Against Runway Expansion, Inc. v. F.A.A.*, 355 F. 3d 678, 689 (D.C. Cir. 2004) ("The [agency] exercised its discretion to include the environmental justice analysis in its NEPA evaluation, and that analysis therefore is properly subject to arbitrary and capricious review under the APA.").

Standing Rock Sioux Tribe, supra, at 136.

The opinion subsequently rejected the Corps of Engineers' Environmental Assessment (EA) under NEPA for failing to provide an adequate environmental justice analysis—it had only analyzed impacts of construction, and not spills.

> "The purpose of an environmental justice analysis is to determine whether a project will have a disproportionately adverse effect on minority and low income populations." *Allen v. Nat'l Institutes of Health*, 974 F. Supp. 2d 18, 47 (D.

Mass. 2013) (quoting *Mid States Coal. for Progress v. Surface Transp. Bd.*, 345 F.3d 520, 541 (8th Cir. 2003)). The EA takes some steps toward satisfying this purpose. It acknowledges that Standing Rock, a community with a high percentage of minorities and low-income individuals, is based downstream of the Oahe crossing and could be affected by an oil spill, and it observes—without providing any specifics—that a non-tribal community's drinking-water intake is closer to the Oahe crossing than is Standing Rock's. But these statements are not enough to reasonably support the conclusion that the Tribe will not be disproportionately affected by an oil spill in terms of adverse human health or environmental effects.

The EA is silent, for instance, on the distinct cultural practices of the Tribe and the social and economic factors that might amplify its experience of the environmental effects of an oil spill. Standing Rock provides one such example in its briefing: many of its members fish, hunt, and gather for subsistence. Losing the ability to do so could seriously and disproportionately harm those individuals relative to those in nearby non-tribal communities.

The Corps need not necessarily have addressed that particular issue, but it needed to offer more than a bare-bones conclusion that Standing Rock would not be disproportionately harmed by a spill. Given the cursory nature of this aspect of the EA's analysis, the Court agrees with the Tribe that the Corps did not properly consider the environmental-justice implications of the project and thus failed to take a hard look at its environmental consequences....

Id. at 140. Compare the court's review of environmental justice analyses with the EAB's review in the above decisions.

6. The states. Several states have passed EJ legislation guiding agencies on its incorporation into environmental decision-making (Chapter 10). In those states and others, courts have turned to their state constitutions and statutory authorities to address environmental justice concerns in the permitting process. The following cases illustrate this approach.

C. Environmental Justice Claims in State Permit Proceedings

In the Matter of: Passaic Valley Sewerage Commission Title V Air Operating Permit Modification

New Jersey Dept. of Envtl. Protection, July 18, 2024

The Passaic Valley Sewerage Commission (PVSC or Applicant) comes before the New Jersey Department of Environmental Protection (Department) in the above-referenced matter for a determination of its compliance with the environmental justice review process set forth in Department Administrative Order No. 2021-25 (AO)....

The AO requires an applicant to undertake enhanced community engagement, assess facility impacts to environmental and public health stressors, and implement appropriate control measures to avoid or minimize adverse impacts from covered facilities that are proposed to operate in overburdened communities.

PVSC's application was deemed complete for Department review on July 2, 2021, environmental justice review in accordance with the AO has been completed, and this decision follows.

1. BACKGROUND

PVSC operates one of the largest sewer systems in the United States, including a secondary wastewater treatment plant situated along Newark Bay at 600 Wilson Avenue in the City of Newark, Essex County, New Jersey. The treatment plant handles sewage generated in the PVSC district comprised of forty-eight municipalities across five counties in northeastern New Jersey. In short, PVSC provides daily sewage treatment by separating and disposing of biosolids, treating reclaimed wastewater to applicable water quality standards, and discharging the treated wastewater into Newark Bay and New York Harbor. This critical infrastructure is subject to Department regulation and oversight as the proper treatment of sewage is vital to preventing disease, improving public and environmental health, and maintaining the recreational, commercial, and natural resource benefits of waterways into which sewage treatment plant effluent is discharged.

In the present application, PVSC seeks to amend its Title V Air Operating Permit to authorize the construction and operation of an on-site emergency standby power generating facility, the pursuit of which was motivated by PVSC's experience during Superstorm Sandy in 2012.

Superstorm Sandy resulted in severe flooding of the sewage treatment plant and caused PVSC to lose both primary and backup power from its utility provider, PSE&G. Without power, the sewage treatment plant could not process wastewater flows or pump out floodwaters, triggering a diversion of approximately 840 million gallons of raw sewage into the Passaic River and Newark Bay and reports of sewage backups in nearby residences. Such a considerable discharge increases public health risks due to the numerous pathogens found in raw sewage, and such discharges exacerbate environmental and public health stressors known to adversely affect overburdened communities.

PVSC estimates that if it were forced to shut down again due to loss of power during a similar storm event, street-level flooding of raw sewage will likely occur in Newark, Bayonne, and Jersey City, potentially impacting thousands of residents....

On January 27, 2020, PVSC applied to the Department to modify its existing permit to authorize the construction and operation of the proposed SPGF. The SPGF would, in the event of a major storm event threatening energy reliability, ensure that the sewage treatment plant can continue to operate with full treatment capabilities to ensure it: (1) meets its permit conditions; (2) prevents backup of raw wastewater in the collection systems of PVSC's forty-eight member communities; and (3) avoids discharging untreated wastewater to nearby waterways.

PVSC subsequently withdrew and resubmitted applications on February 4, 2020, January 14, 2021, and June 10, 2021, modifying the project to reduce air emissions and improve efficiency. On July 2, 2021, PVSC submitted the present application, which was then declared complete for review.

2. EJ REVIEW APPLICABILITY

Consistent with the EJ Law, the environmental justice review process under the AO applies where three specific criteria are present: (1) the proposed new or existing facility is one of eight (8) specific facility types identified in the rules (*e.g.*, major air sources, solid waste facilities); (2) the applicant seeks an individual permit under applicable Department regulations; and (3) the facility is located or proposed to be located, in whole or in part, in an overburdened community.

Here, the proposed project is subject to environmental justice review because the facility is: (1) a major air source; (2) seeking to modify its Title V Permit; and (3) is located in an overburdened block group due to percentage of population that qualifies as low income and minority as shown on the Department's Environmental Justice Mapping, Assessment and Protection Tool (EJMAP)....

5. DEPARTMENT REVIEW AND DECISION

Analysis

As explained above, PVSC's 2021 application preceded the Department's 2023 adoption of the EJ Rules, which direct applicants to consider initial screening criteria as presented below. As a factual matter, however, the Department notes that the host overburdened community is subject to adverse cumulative environmental and public health stressors, including a density of permitted air pollution sites more than five times greater than the relevant point of geographic comparison and adverse stressors related to concentrated areas of air pollution, as each are defined by the EJ Rules.

In reviewing PVSC's submission pursuant to the AO, the Department evaluated whether PVSC has taken measures sufficient to: (1) avoid adverse impacts to environmental and public health stressors from the proposed facility while achieving its primary purpose; (2) minimize adverse impacts that could not be fully avoided while achieving the primary purpose of the proposed facility; and (3) reduce other existing environmental and public health stressors affecting the overburdened community through additional on-site or off-site actions that improve environmental or public health conditions....

Conclusion

The Department has reviewed the information provided by PVSC and third parties throughout the environmental justice review process, including, but not limited to, PVSC's Compliance Statement, public comments, PVSC's Response to Comments, details provided in response to the Department's requests for clarification, and other

Figure 6-1. The Ironbound community of Newark, New Jersey. Home to some fifty thousand residents, the Ironbound today reflects waves of migration from Western and Eastern Europe, from the Jim Crow South, and from Central and South America. As its name suggests, the Ironbound remains encircled by railroad lines, turnpikes, the Passaic River to the north, and Newark Airport to the south. Photo: Cliff Villa, 2023.

information relevant to this decision. Based upon the record presented, the Department finds that the SPGF as originally proposed would increase the emission of air pollutants from the PVSC facility, which could exacerbate adverse cumulative environmental and public health stressors affecting the host overburdened community. The Department also finds that, the foregoing avoidance and minimization measures, together with the on-site mandatory emission reductions detailed above, a net overall reduction in facility-wide emissions of air pollutants would be achieved under regular operating conditions.

The Department acknowledges that, in the event of a storm that triggers emergency operation of the SGPF, and depending upon the extent of emergency operations, a net overall reduction in facility-wide emissions of air pollutants may not be achieved. Such conditions would necessarily be time limited. The Department also acknowledges that PVSC's stated commitments to transition to low- or zero-carbon fuels at the facility may further reduce overall greenhouse gas emissions from its operations.

Lastly, the Department recognizes the Ironbound Community Corporation, New Jersey Environmental Justice Alliance, and Earthjustice letter of June 15, 2023, asserting that Departmental approval of the SPGF could constitute discrimination on the basis of race, color or national origin in violation Title VI of the federal Civil Rights Act of 1964. As discussed above, the Department has taken care to thoroughly evaluate, avoid, and minimize potentially adverse impacts of its decision upon the host overburdened community, including any potential disparate impacts upon protected classes of persons consist with Title VI requirements. As explained herein, should PVSC proceed with its proposed permit modification, the Department's environmental justice review has ensured the imposition of special conditions that results in a net overall reduction of facility-wide emissions of air pollutants under regular operating conditions. These special conditions would be indefinite in their effect, and subject to routine Department enforcement.

Notes and Questions

1. **New law, old result or modest step forward?** The department approved the permit application as complying with the EJ Law requirements (see Chapter 10 for discussion of the law). The administrative decision recognized that the hosting community was already overburdened with air pollution but still approved the permit with the inclusion of special conditions to decrease facility emissions and adverse impacts on the community. Does this approach further environmental justice based on the enhanced public participation process and more stringent permit conditions that were required? Numerous political leaders across the state, including Ras Baraka, the mayor of Newark, where pollution impacts will be felt, decried the decision as contrary to environmental justice. Protests against the permit conditions, as well as the permit itself, may be anticipated from both the project proponents and opponents.

2. **The bounds of state permitting authority.** For one early evaluation of environmental justice and state permitting, *see* NAACP—Flint Chapter v. Engler, Genesee (Michigan) County Circuit Court (Transcript of Ruling, May 29, 1997). In the opinion, Judge Hayman for the trial court expresses concern that the economic benefits of the plant flowed to persons who lived outside the neighborhood, while residents of the impacted area were unable to obtain jobs from the plant. What is the legal relevance of this finding? The court also found problematic the fact that the impacts of the projects would be felt largely by persons outside the permitting agency's jurisdiction, in the next town. If this is an inevitable consequence of the local nature of most permitting decisions, how should the permitting agency account for this complication? Are there mitigation requirements that it should consider, or should it deny the permit altogether if the impacts reach a particular magnitude?

3. **Postscript.** On appeal, the court of appeals reversed the ruling by Judge Hayman in an unpublished decision, ruling that Judge Hayman had improperly granted relief based on claims that plaintiffs had not pleaded or raised at trial. *See* NAACP—Flint Chapter v. Engler, No. 205264 (Mich. Ct. App. Nov. 24, 1998). Judge Hayman's opinion nevertheless detailed a recurring theme: whether an agency has the authority to consider environmental justice impacts where an applicant meets all other technical permitting requirements. Consider the next case.

Figure 6-2. Sunset in Chaparral, New Mexico. One of the more developed *colonias* along the U.S.-Mexico border, the unincorporated community of Chaparral remains 66 percent Latino and ranks in the 96th percentile nationwide for ozone pollution. Photo: Cliff Villa, 2022.

Colonias Dev. Council v. Rhino Envtl. Services Inc.

138 N.M. 133 (2005)

BACKGROUND

On September 10, 2001, more than 250 people packed the middle school cafeteria in Chaparral, New Mexico, for a public hearing. The purpose of the meeting was to review an application by Rhino Environmental Services, Inc. (Rhino) for a permit to put a landfill in Chaparral pursuant to the [New Mexico] Solid Waste Act.

Even though the September 11 terrorist attack on the World Trade Center in New York City disrupted the public hearing, emptying chairs the day after the attack, more than 300 people eventually came forth between September 10 and 19, with about sixty actively testifying or conducting cross-examination. Some community members attended the sessions during the day. Others came at night, after driving home from jobs across the border in Mexico and El Paso, Texas. People brought their children and crying babies. They held press conferences. They tried to hang banners protesting the landfill. Some spoke in Spanish, through a translator provided by the Department.

Although a few community members supported the landfill during the hearing, the vast majority did not. Many testified that they did not understand why another landfill had to be placed just a couple of miles from Chaparral, an unincorporated community that lacks infrastructure, political representation, and medical facilities. As a border community consisting primarily of low-income, minority residents, Chaparral has been called New Mexico's largest *colonia* [*Colonias* are rural settlements, usually along the United States-Mexico border, that lack safe housing, potable water, wastewater treatment, drainage, electricity, and paved roads. Eds.]....

Despite the overwhelming community opposition, the Secretary, acting through the Director of the Water and Waste Management Division, granted the permit for a period of ten years subject to a list of twenty conditions....

CDC [Colonias Development Council, a nonprofit dedicated to improving conditions in New Mexico *colonias*] appealed that decision to the Court of Appeals, which affirmed the Department's approval of the landfill permit. On certiorari to this Court, CDC acknowledges that community members were given an opportunity to speak but claims the hearing officer erred by interpreting the Department's role too narrowly. In CDC's view, the hearing officer perceived her duty as strictly confined to overseeing the technical requirements of the permit application. As a result, the Secretary approved the landfill permit based on an erroneous assumption that the Department was neither required nor allowed to consider the impact of the proliferation of landfills on a community's quality of life. This perception, CDC contends, ultimately undermined any influence the public's nontechnical testimony could have on the decision to grant a landfill permit....

CDC further contends that the hearing officer erred in refusing to consider testimony regarding the adverse cumulative effects caused by the proliferation of landfills and other industrial sites. CDC claims there are four waste disposal facilities and three industrial sites near Chaparral....

DISCUSSION

CDC argues that the impact of the landfill on the community's quality of life, and the general concerns of community members opposed to the landfill, were not considered in determining whether to grant the solid waste permit. It contends that such considerations are required by the Environmental Improvement Act, the Solid Waste Act, and the regulations adopted pursuant to the acts. CDC does not challenge the technical issues addressed in the permitting process....

The Solid Waste Act directs "the establishment of a comprehensive solid waste management program." One purpose of the act is to "plan for and regulate, in the most economically feasible, cost-effective and environmentally safe manner, the reduction, storage, collection, transportation, separation, processing, recycling and disposal of solid waste." Another important purpose is to "enhance the beauty and quality of the environment; conserve, recover and recycle resources; and protect the public health, safety and welfare."

... In issuing [regulations under the Solid Waste Act], the Board is required to "assure that the relative interests of the applicant, other owners of property likely to be affected and the general public will be considered prior to the issuance of a permit for a solid waste facility." In addition, the Board is required to adopt procedural regulations providing for notice and a public hearing on permit actions.

Pursuant to this statutory authority, the Board adopted regulations providing technical siting criteria. The Board also adopted regulations governing permitting procedures, which encourage public participation.

... [T]he regulations regarding permit issuance state: "The Secretary *shall* issue a permit if the applicant demonstrates that the other requirements of this Part are met *and* the solid waste facility application demonstrates that neither a hazard to public health, welfare, or the environment nor undue risk to property will result."

... Pursuant to the authority delegated by the enabling statutes, and the regulations adopted to implement those statutes, CDC urges this Court to conclude that the Secretary is required to allow testimony regarding the impact of a proposed landfill on a community's quality of life. Such consideration is required, CDC argues, in order to realize the general purposes of the statutes to confer optimum social well-being, to protect public health, safety and welfare, and to assure that "relative interests" of all parties are considered.

In the view of Rhino and the Department, on the other hand, the purposes of the enabling statutes to promote public welfare and social well-being are addressed in the implementing regulations. Concerns such as landfill proliferation are not mentioned in the regulations, they assert, and cannot be an independent factor in considering whether to issue a solid waste facility permit. The Department sees its role as dictated by the technical regulations. If the siting criteria is met, they argue, the Department has no discretion to deny a permit or impose conditions on one. The Court of Appeals agreed, stating, "[The Department] cannot reasonably be expected to weigh sociological concerns, which it has no expertise in doing. Its role is to pass judgment on the technical aspects of a solid waste site, a subject within its expertise and which it was designed to do." Thus, the Court of Appeals determined that the hearing officer could properly limit evidence relating to "social impact" because the term is not mentioned in the statutes or regulations, and therefore is legally irrelevant.

We think the Court of Appeals' view of the Department's role is too narrow and has the potential to chill public participation in the permitting process contrary to legislative intent. The Solid Waste Act is replete with references to public input and education. The process of applying for a landfill permit attempts to facilitate public participation in several ways. First, the applicant submits an application for a permit, which includes all the technical information required to support the permit, and files notice to the public and affected parties. The Department solicits comments, and once the application is complete, conducts a public hearing, which provides the public and interested parties an opportunity to comment and present evidence. By directing the Department to adopt procedural regulations to provide all persons with a reasonable opportunity to be heard, the Legislature has clearly indicated its intent to ensure that the public plays a vital role in the hearing process....

In finding public participation and the hearing requirement central to the Solid Waste Act, our courts have protected and promoted the role of public input in the Department's decision to issue a permit. In our view, the Legislature did not limit the Department's role to reviewing technical regulations. Instead, our courts have acknowledged that the Secretary must use discretion in implementing the Solid Waste Act and its regulations in order to encourage public participation in the permitting process.

Given the Legislature's goal to involve the public in the permitting process to the fullest extent possible, we do not agree with the Court of Appeals that the Secretary was not allowed to consider testimony relating to the community's quality of life. The Legislature clearly believed public participation is vital to the success of the Solid Waste Act. Members of the public generally are not technical experts. The Legislature did not require scientific evidence in opposition to a landfill permit, but instead envisioned that ordinary concerns about a community's quality of life could influence the decision to issue a landfill permit. While testimony relating to something as broad as "social impact" may not require denial of a permit, the hearing officer must listen to concerns about adverse impacts on social well-being and quality of life, as well as report them accurately to the Secretary. In reviewing the hearing officer's report, the Secretary must consider whether lay concerns relate to violations of the Solid Waste Act and its regulations. Therefore, the Secretary should consider issues relating to public health and welfare not addressed by specific technical regulations....

Proliferation

Although we hold that the Department must allow testimony regarding the impact of a landfill on a community's quality of life, we agree with the Department that its authority to address such concerns requires a nexus to a regulation. Like the Court of Appeals, we are not persuaded that the general purposes of the Environmental Improvement Act and the Solid Waste Act, considered alone, provide authority for requiring the Secretary to deny a landfill permit based on public opposition. The purposes of the enabling acts, which include the goal of protecting the "public health, safety and welfare," are designed to invoke the general police power of the state. This general expression of legislative police power, without more, does not create a standard for protecting "public health, safety and welfare." Thus, the Court of Appeals was correct to reject CDC's reliance on the purposes of the acts as a statutory mandate to respond to issues that fit ever so loosely under the umbrella of "sociological concerns." Such a broad mandate would offer no guidance to the Department, and violate the well-settled principle that a legislative body may not vest unbridled or arbitrary power in an administrative agency.

Unlike the Court of Appeals, however, we do find that quality of life concerns expressed during the hearing bear a relationship to environmental regulations the Secretary is charged with administering. Although both parties refer to the issues on appeal in a wide variety of ways, including "social impact," "sociological concerns," "social well-being," and "environmental justice," we believe there are legitimate concerns at the core of CDC's claim that are within the purview of the Secretary's oversight role. Contrary to the Department's position, the impact on the community from a specific environmental act, the proliferation of landfills, appears highly relevant to the permit process....

Landfill opponents presented testimony that Chaparral is a residential, low income border community that is being overrun by industrial sites including numerous pre-existing landfills. If this is true, we think it is reasonable for the Department to consider whether the cumulative effects of pollution, exacerbated by the incidences of poverty, may rise to the level of a public nuisance or hazard to public health, welfare, or the environment. If proliferation has an identified effect on the community's development and social well-being, it is not an amorphous general welfare issue, but an environmental problem. The adverse impact of the proliferation of landfills on a community's quality of life is well within the boundaries of environmental protection. Thus, the testimony regarding the impact of the proliferation of landfills is relevant within the context of environmental protection promised in the Solid Waste Act and its regulations. For that reason, the Secretary must evaluate whether the impact of an additional landfill on a community's quality of life creates a public nuisance or hazard to public health, welfare, or the environment.

The Department concluded as a matter of law that granting the permit would not result in a public nuisance or a hazard to public health, welfare or the environment. These conclusions, however, were made only after the Department incorrectly found that lay testimony relating to living near multiple disposal facilities was beyond the scope of the Secretary's authority for granting or denying a landfill. In our view, the Department's own regulations not only allow, but require consideration of the cumulative effect of large-scale garbage dumps and industrial sites on a single community.

As the regulations indicate, the Department cannot ignore concerns that relate to environmental protection simply because they are not mentioned in a technical regulation. The Department has a duty to interpret its regulations liberally in order to realize the purposes of the Acts. Because the impact of the proliferation of landfills and industrial sites on a community is relevant to environmental protection, we conclude that the Solid Waste Act and its regulations require the Department to consider whether evidence of the harmful effects from the cumulative impact of industrial development rises to the level of a public nuisance or potential hazard to public health, welfare or the environment.

Remedy

Because of the potential chilling effect of the hearing officer's error, we direct the Secretary to afford CDC a reasonable opportunity at a limited public hearing to tender additional evidence regarding the impact of proliferation.... Rhino shall have a reasonable opportunity to respond. We further instruct the Secretary to reconsider the public testimony opposing the landfill and explain the rationale for rejecting it, if the Secretary decides to do so. We are not suggesting that the Secretary must reach a different result, but we do require, as the Act itself requires, that the community be given a voice, and the concerns of the community be considered in the final decision making....

Notes and Questions

1. **The meaning of *Rhino*.** The *Rhino* decision by the New Mexico Supreme Court represented a landmark for the jurisprudence of environmental justice, the first state decision requiring consideration of "non-technical" factors such as socioeconomic status of the surrounding population and cumulative impacts from existing facilities. Consider for a moment, however, had the decision gone the other way. If you were the officer presiding over this hearing, could you explain to the hundreds of community members who showed up to attend the public hearing (even during the national trauma of 9/11) that nothing they might say would matter to your decision unless it concerned the technical specifications for the proposed landfill? As technical comments could perhaps more easily be submitted in writing, what then would be the purpose of any public hearing? Fortunately, the hearing officer's disregard for community input was rejected by the highest court in the state, establishing not just a new precedent for the State of New Mexico but also a model for other states to follow.

2. **Codification of *Rhino*.** In the wake of the *Rhino* decision, the New Mexico Environment Department promulgated regulations enumerating factors to be considered if a community impact assessment is applicable to permit proceedings under the State's Solid Waste Act. *See* N.M. Code R. § 20.9.3.8 D(2)(a)–(j). For a discussion of this case, *see* Kristina G. Fisher, *The Rhino in the Colonia: How* Colonias Development Council v. Rhino Environmental Services, Inc. *Set a Substantive Standard for Environmental Justice*, 39 Envtl. L. 397 (2009).

3. **The benefits and burdens test.** Following *Rhino*, the Pennsylvania Supreme Court reached a similar conclusion and upheld environmental justice criteria for waste siting established by the Pennsylvania Department of Environmental Protection despite the absence of any specific statutory mandate. Pennsylvania took a different approach, however, requiring among other things, that the project proponent of a waste disposal facility demonstrate that the project's benefits, including social and economic benefits, clearly outweigh its burdens, including social and economic harms. In *Eagle Envtl. II, L.P. v. Commonwealth Dept. of Envtl. Protection*, 584 Pa. 494, 884 A.2d 867 (Pa. 2005), a landfill permitting case, the state supreme court endorsed this "benefits and burdens" test and rejected the argument that Pennsylvania's police power was exceeded because police power only protects the public against harm and does not extend to providing public benefits. In that case, the benefits and burdens were described as follows:

> Eagle cited the following potential short term benefits: disposal of debris in the event of a disaster; payments for health and safety training courses for landfill operators; and use of coal excavated from the site. Eagle identified additional real short term economic benefits: jobs for local residents at the landfill; increased employment at businesses associated with or located near the landfill; increased local, state and federal income taxes as a result of increased employment; higher real estate taxes; a $2 dollar per ton host fee to the township (as specifically authorized by [Pennsylvania law]); and provision of a recycling drop-off center. Eagle further noted real long term benefits of the project: re-

> placement of wetland acreage (although the project would disturb .17 acres of wetlands, the disturbed wetland would be replaced with .42 acres of wetlands); improvement of the roads leading to the landfill; benefit to wetlands in the form of landfill runoff and reduced erosion; reclamation of a strip mine, and the resulting visual enhancement and increased soil fertility.
>
> In contrast, Eagle identified harms resulting from the landfill and described how those harms could or could not be mitigated. The potential harm of a malfunction of the leachate treatment plant could be mitigated by proper operation of the plant and utilization of a leachate storage tank Eagle recognized the potential negative impact on the residents of the area but concluded that any impact would largely be anticipatory and could be alleviated by working with the residents. Eagle acknowledged sediment-laden runoff as a harm but asserted that it could be mitigated by erosion and sedimentation control features, and various measures relating to sediment required by other regulations. Furthermore, the resulting sedimentary ponds would be beneficial to aquatic life and migratory birds. Eagle observed that an increased risk of fires, emergencies, and accidents that could result from the project would burden the local emergency services, but could be mitigated by contingency planning, fire protection measures, and payments to the local fire departments to cover the increased burden. Eagle further noted the short term harms caused by waste hauling trucks which include fumes, visual impact, noise, spills, and odors. Eagle offered to mitigate these harms by insuring that the trucks are well maintained and that other measures would be employed to reduce the dust, noise, and odors resulting from the site.
>
> Eagle acknowledged the long term harms of the project. After closure of the landfill, the land, which is currently woodland, would be converted to grassland. Eagle argued that, although the conversion could be viewed as a harm, it could also be seen as a benefit because it would increase species diversity in the area. Another long term harm is the negative aesthetic aspect of the landfill, however, Eagle planned to mitigate this by planting vegetation around the perimeter of the landfill.

Id. at 501–02, 871–72.

Based upon the foregoing, how would you decide whether the permit should be issued? Would an impact assessment approach change your determination?

4. Comparing the states. The cases adjudicating environmental justice claims in permit and related proceedings under state laws by no means uniformly provide remedies to affected communities. Some state courts have been reluctant to find environmental justice requirements in statutes that do not expressly include them. *See, e.g.*, *Pine Bluff for Safe Disposal v. Ark. Pollution Control & Ecology Comm'n*, 354 Ark. 563, 127 S.W.3d 509, 521–22 (2003) (in connection with an air and hazardous waste permit, finding no adverse health effects to *any persons* will result from the Facility's emissions); *Hinds County v. Mississippi Com'n on Environmental Quality*, 61 So.3d 77 (Miss.

Sup. Ct. April 14, 2011) (finding no obligation to perform an in-depth environmental justice review and deferring consideration to the Permit Board).

On the other hand, where statutes specifically require consideration of environmental justice or environmental equity, state courts will enforce those requirements. *See, e.g.*, *Hartford Park Tenants Ass'n v. R.I. Dep't of Envtl. Mgmt.*, No. C.A. 99-3748, 2005 WL 2436227 (R.I. Super. Ct. Oct. 3, 2005) (provisions under the state's Industrial Property Remediation and Reuse Act, a cleanup statute). However, even in these instances, state courts will often defer to agency interpretations of how extensive the considerations must be and will narrowly interpret statutory mandates. *See, e.g.*, *Harrelson Materials Mgmt. v. La. Dept. of Envtl. Quality*, No. 2006 CA 1822, 2007 WL 1765563 (La. Ct. App. June 20, 2007) (demolition, debris, and landfill permit); *In re* Gaeta Recycling Co., 2007 WL 609161 (N.J. Super. Ct. Mar. 1, 2007); *Bronx Envtl. Health & Justice, Inc. v. N.Y. City Dept. of Envtl. Protection*, No. 25754/04, 2005 WL 1389360 (N.Y. Sup. Ct. May 11, 2005) (solid waste facility permit); *City of Brockton v. Energy Facilities Siting Bd.*, 469 Mass. 196, 14 N.E.3d 167 (Mass. Sup. Ct. July 31, 2014) (finding it appropriate for judicial review of application of environmental justice policy, but deferring to agency determination to not apply heightened review under the policy).

5. Informed decision-making. Some successful attempts to add additional permit conditions have targeted another key aspect of permitting: information disclosure laws. In *Communities for a Better Environment v. City of Richmond*, 184 Cal. App. 4th 70 (2010), community groups successfully challenged the City of Richmond's approval of a permit to allow the refining of a heavier, and more polluting, crude oil feedstock at the Chevron Richmond Refinery. While Chevron denied this was a central purpose of their permit, the company had filed Securities and Exchange Commission forms identifying the central purpose of their project to enable this crude switch. Consequently, the California Court of Appeal held that Chevron's informational document was deficient under the California Environmental Quality Act and failed its informational purpose. For a discussion of how this permitting challenge contributed to community organizing that tilted the balance of power in Richmond, California, *see* Steve Early, REFINERY TOWN: BIG OIL, BIG MONEY, AND THE REMAKING OF AN AMERICAN CITY (Beacon Press 2017).

6. Remedies? How would you assess the overall approach to environmental justice claims in the permitting context? Do claims reflect concerns for both procedural justice and distributive justice? What kinds of remedies are available to address each concern? Does it matter whether the claims are premised upon state law or federal law?

7. The permit applicant's perspective. If you were the lawyer for a permit applicant, how would you advise your client regarding the inherent uncertainty and potential delay associated with addressing environmental justice concerns? Former developers' lawyer and now Professor Michael Gerrard stresses involvement of the community at an early (pre-application) stage:

> At this early stage, a little bit of community opposition can go a long way. If the sponsor has several different options for where to site the project, protests in

> one community and silence in another may point to the path of least resistance. If it is the type of project that a community might accept if it were modified in certain ways, at this preliminary stage modifications are often rather easy, before heavy investments have been made in design and engineering.

Michael B. Gerrard, *Stopping and Building New Facilities*, in THE LAW OF ENVIRONMENTAL JUSTICE 511 (Michael B. Gerrard & Sheila R. Foster eds., 2d ed. 2008). For additional suggestions for the permit applicant, *see* Clifford J. Villa, *No "Box To Be Checked": Environmental Justice in Modern Legal Practice*, 30 N.Y.U. ENVTL. L.J. 157 (2022); EPA, *Promising Practices for Permit Applicants Seeking EPA-Issued Permits: Ways to Engage Neighboring Communities*, 78 Fed. Reg. 27220, 27226 (May 9, 2013).

D. Environmental Justice in Municipal Permits

General Iron (dba Southside Recycling) operated a metal shredding facility in the Lincoln Park neighborhood of Chicago where 80 percent of residents are white. The company sought to move the operation to the Southeast Side of Chicago, where more than 80 percent of residents are Black or Hispanic. Although the request was initially welcomed by Chicago Mayor Lori Lightfoot, consultation with EPA Administrator Michael Regan resulted in the city deciding that additional study of the proposed location was necessary before rendering a decision. After conducting a Health Impact Assessment [HIA] in conjunction with the EPA, the Commissioner for the Chicago Department of Public Health (CDPH) denied the permit request based on the HIA results. The decision was subsequently challenged by General Iron. The city administrative law judge hearing the case reversed the commissioner's decision and directed the city to issue the permit. The city appealed the decision to the Cook County Circuit Court which issued the following opinion.

CDPH v. Chicago Dept. of Administrative Hearings

Case No. 2023 CH 06165

MEMORANDUM OPINION AND ORDER

This matter is before the Court on Plaintiff, City of Chicago Department of Public Health's Complaint for Administrative Review. For the following reasons, the Decision of the City of Chicago Department of Administrative Hearings is reversed.

BACKGROUND

Plaintiff, City of Chicago Department of Public Health ("CDPH"), is an administrative agency charged with the administration of various public health issues and programs throughout the City of Chicago, including determining the issuance and denial of recycling facility permits for large recycling facilities in Chicago. Chapter 11-4 of the Chicago Municipal Code ("MCC") and City of Chicago Rules for Large

Recycling Facilities ("Rule") govern the CDPH's authority and procedures in the permit application process.

On February 18, 2022, a CDPH Commissioner denied Defendant General III, LLC, doing business as SSR ("SSR"), an application for a Large Recycling Facility ("LRF") permit at 11600 S. Burley Avenue (the "Burley Campus"). The denial was based on the Commissioner's conclusions that: (1) SSR's proposed facility would negatively affect the residents of the Southeast Side, a population identified by the CDPH's Health Impact Assessment ("HIA") as having significant health vulnerabilities; (2) the past and present compliance history of SSR and related entities support a denial; and (3) additional facilities operated by RMG d/b/a SSR lacked transparency, and SSR's responsiveness was inadequate throughout and leading up to the permit process. *Id.* On March 2, 2022, SSR appealed the Commissioner's decision and filed its Demand for Hearing in the City of Chicago Department of Administrative Hearings ("DOAH").

On June 1, 2023, the Administrative Law Judge ("ALJ") of the DOAH vacated the Commissioner's denial. The ALJ found that the Commissioner lacked the authority to rely on the three stated grounds for denying the LRF permit. The ALJ (1) concluded that the findings of the HIA used to deny the permit were not consistent with the findings made earlier by the Chicago Zoning Board of Appeals ("ZBA"), Illinois Environmental Protection Agency ("IEPA"), Chicago Department of Buildings ("DOB") and CDPH, (2) determined RMG's noncompliance concerns were contradicted by several inconsistent statements made earlier by CDPH, and (3) rejected CDPH's claim that RMG entities lacked transparency or responsiveness during the permitting process.

CDPH subsequently filed a Complaint for Administrative Review arguing that the ALJ's decision was legally erroneous and against the manifest weight of the evidence. SSR and DOAH filed briefs in opposition and requested this Court to direct CDPH to issue the permit. Both CDPH's Complaint for Administrative Review and SSR's request for an order are presently before the Court....

DISCUSSION

[T]he Court must decide whether the Municipal Code grants the Commissioner the authority or discretion to require a HIA as part of the LRF permit application process, even though an environmental justice report such as the HIA is not explicitly mandated by the code. Specifically, the issue is whether the implementation of the HIA constitutes a new policy or requirements for the LRF permit application process....

Substantive Findings of the HIA

Having determined that conducting the HIA did not establish new standards for the permit process, the Court now examines the findings of the HIA to assess whether the Commissioner's denial based on the HIA should be upheld. In evaluating whether the Commissioner's denial should be upheld, it is essential to consider both the legal framework and the substantive findings of the HIA itself. The Court has already established that conducting the HIA did not create new standards for the permit process but rather operated within the existing regulatory framework. This determination affirms that the HIA was a proper tool for assessing potential health impacts, and its use does not conflict with the MCC's provisions.

Given that the ALJ's findings regarding the HIA are legal in nature, this Court is required to conduct a *de novo* review. This means that the Court must independently evaluate the legal conclusions drawn from the HIA without deferring to the ALJ's judgment. Upon such review, the Court assesses whether the HIA's findings provide a rational basis for the Commissioner's decision to deny the permit.

The findings of the HIA highlighted significant health risks associated with the proposed facility. The Southeast Side is particularly susceptible to the potential health impacts that a large metal shredding facility like SSR would pose, given the area's dense concentration of industrial facilities. For instance, in 2020, one-third of all air toxic releases in Chicago originated from facilities on the Southeast Side. As of 2018, the Southeast Side had higher rates of chronic conditions in adults compared to the Chicago average. Moreover, the population living near the proposed facility is predominantly low-income, composed largely of people of color, and includes individuals with limited English proficiency and education levels below high school. The Commissioner's decision to deny the permit, therefore, was not arbitrary but grounded in the substantive data and analysis presented in the HIA.

Additionally, the Court does not find that the findings of the HIA are necessarily inconsistent conclusions reached by the ZBA [Chicago Zoning Board of Appeals], IEPA [Illinois Environmental Protection Agency], DOB [Chicago Department of Buildings], or even the CDPH in its earlier assessments. Each of these agencies conducted their evaluations based on specific regulatory frameworks and criteria, which differ from the public health focus of the HIA.

For instance, the ZBA's determination that SSR's proposed facility complies with the Chicago Zoning Ordinance and would not have a significant adverse impact on the general welfare of the community was based on land use and zoning considerations. The IEPA's finding that the facility met all applicable state and federal air pollution emissions standards and would not adversely affect the nearby community was rooted in compliance with environmental regulations concerning air quality. The DOB issued building permits for the facility based on structural and construction standards. Similarly, the CDPH's earlier draft permit issuance letter was prepared in anticipation of meeting general regulatory requirements.

The HIA, on the other hand, was specifically conducted to assess the potential health impacts of the proposed facility on the local population, particularly in an area already burdened with significant environmental and health challenges. The HIA's focus on public health risks provides a distinct but complementary perspective that does not negate the findings of the other agencies but rather adds a critical layer of analysis that is essential for a comprehensive decision-making process.

While the other agencies confirmed compliance with their respective standards, the HIA highlighted potential public health risks that might not have been fully captured by those regulatory frameworks. The differences in purpose and scope between the HIA and the assessments conducted by the ZBA, IEPA, and DOB underscore the benefit of considering health impacts as part of the permit review process. Therefore, denying the permit based on the HIA's findings is not inconsistent with the other agencies' conclusions; rather, it reflects the broader, multi-faceted approach required to safeguard public health in the context of a heavily industrialized area.

In conclusion, the Commissioner's decision to deny the permit, grounded in the findings of the HIA and supported by legal authority under the MCC, is upheld as a valid exercise of administrative discretion aimed at safeguarding public health. This Court thereby reverses the ALJ's decision to disregard HIA as part of the permit review process.

Notes and Questions

1. Health matters. The city based its decision on a close review of the specific health impacts the facility would cause on the local community. The court found that the health assessment did not contradict previous determinations but added an additional layer of analysis. Does this additional layer of analysis correct a major concern of EJ advocates that, without consideration of environmental justice or cumulative impacts, regulatory processes disregard the actual pollution burdens community members live with every day and the harms they cause?

E. Case Study: State Permits in Federal Court

As the material above indicates, increasing attention to environmental justice is being considered in permitting decisions. Relatively few of these cases have proceeded to appeals in federal court and the kind of published decisions students often see in casebooks. The following decision is one of these rare cases. As you read this case, consider what arguments seemed most persuasive on behalf of the plaintiffs and what law ultimately grounded the decision.

Friends of Buckingham v. Virginia Air Pollution Control Bd.

947 F.3d 68 (4th Cir. 2020)

Friends of Buckingham and the Chesapeake Bay Foundation, Inc. (collectively, "Petitioners") challenge the Virginia Air Pollution Control Board ("Board")'s award of a permit for construction of a compressor station on behalf of Intervenor Atlantic Coast Pipeline, LLC ("ACP") in the historic community of Union Hill in Buckingham County, Virginia (the "Compressor Station"). The Compressor Station is one of three such stations planned to support the transmission of natural gas through the ACP's

600-mile pipeline (the "Pipeline"), which is projected to stretch from West Virginia to North Carolina....

Petitioners filed this petition for review against the Board and its chairman, and the Virginia Department of Environmental Quality ("DEQ") and its director (collectively, "Respondents"), raising two assignments of error. First, Petitioners contend the Board erred in failing to consider electric turbines as zero-emission alternatives to gas-fired turbines in the Compressor Station. Second, they contend the Board erred in failing to assess the Compressor Station's potential for disproportionate health impacts on the predominantly African-American community of Union Hill, and in failing to independently evaluate the suitability of that site.

As explained below, we agree with Petitioners and vacate and remand to the Board....

Pursuant to Virginia's SIP [State Implementation Plan], all new stationary sources, whether major or minor, are subject to BACT [Best Available Control Technology] review. *See* 9 Va. Admin. Code § 5-50-260(B) ("A new stationary source shall apply best available control technology for each regulated pollutant for which there would be an uncontrolled emission rate equal to or greater than the levels in 9 Va. Admin. Code § 5-80-1105 [providing charts of exemption levels in tons per year for various pollutants]."). This is so even though *federal* law does not require a BACT analysis of minor sources....

In addition to the SIP, Virginia law also contains a Commonwealth Energy Policy, which "[e]nsure[s] that development of new, or expansion of existing, energy resources or facilities does not have a disproportionate adverse impact on economically disadvantaged or minority communities." Va. Code Ann. § 67-102(A)(11). Likewise, one of the "[e]nergy objectives" of the Commonwealth Energy Policy is to "[d]evelop[] energy resources and facilities in a manner that does not impose a disproportionate adverse impact on economically disadvantaged or minority communities."

... The Board is a seven-member citizen board selected by the Governor "from the Commonwealth at large on the basis of merit without regard to political affiliation." The Board is empowered to "make, or cause to be made, such investigations and inspections and do such other things as are reasonably necessary" to discharge its duties. For example, the Board may "call upon any state department or agency for technical assistance" in performing its duties.

The Board often calls upon DEQ to provide technical support and help the Board to fulfill its obligations. In general, DEQ can review permit applications, prepare draft permits and related documents, review and respond to comments from the public, and hold public hearings. Either the Board or DEQ can issue minor source Article 6 Permits, but when the Board does so, as in this case, it must consider:

> (i) the verbal and written comments received during the public comment period made part of the record, (ii) any explanation of comments previously received during the public comment period made at the Board

> meeting, (iii) the comments and recommendation of [DEQ], and (iv) the agency files.

Va. Code Ann. § 10.1-1322.01(P). If the Board adopts the recommendation of DEQ, it "shall provide in writing a clear and concise statement of the legal basis and justification for the decision reached." Likewise, if the Board's decision varies from DEQ's recommendation, the Board must "provide a clear and concise statement explaining the reason for the variation and how the Board's decision is in compliance with applicable laws and regulations." . . .

Because natural gas transported through the Pipeline must remain pressurized, ACP sought to construct three compressor stations in different locations along the Pipeline—one in West Virginia, one in Virginia (the Buckingham County location at issue here), and one in North Carolina.

ACP claims the Compressor Station site in Buckingham County is "the only feasible location" because: (1) "it allows the ACP to interconnect with the existing Transco pipeline"; (2) "it was available for [ACP] to purchase commercially"; and (3) "the Federal Energy Regulatory Commission ('FERC') ruled out the only other site that met the previous two criteria. . . .

After the Permit application was complete, DEQ provided several comment periods. On August 16, 2018, at the beginning of the first 30-day comment period, DEQ held an informational session for the residents of Buckingham County. DEQ representatives stated that, before the Board would take final action on the permit application, it would consider all comments. They also assured all public commenters that they could address the Board at a public meeting. After the comment period closed, DEQ conducted a public hearing on September 11, 2018, and heard proposed comments. Almost 200 people attended, and 60 people made oral comments. DEQ extended the comment period by 10 days. Over the 40-day comment period, DEQ received more than 5,300 comments. "Many comments" expressed "concerns about the potential for disproportionate impacts of the proposed facility on the African American population in Union Hill."

On November 8, 2018, the seven-member Board held its first public hearing. DEQ presented its summary of public comments from the 40-day comment period for the Board's consideration. These comments included concerns such as whether the "[f] acility should use electric turbines" instead of natural gas turbines, criticism that EPA's "[a]ir quality standards [are] not adequately protective," and "[e]nvironmental [j]ustice" and "[s]ite suitability issues." More than 80 people spoke at the hearing, and the Board made the following statements to and inquiries of DEQ officials:

- "[W]hat can you tell me about the demographics of Union Hill? I'd like to know about the community. I'd like to know about the race, the age distribution, anything you know about the health status of the community."
- "I thought [DEQ presented] a very narrow construction of what environmental justice means, and the reason I feel it's important for me to point that out is be-

cause I do think that site suitability and environmental justice are wrapped up together."

- "[H]ow is it that DEQ interprets [the Commonwealth Energy Plan] with respect to its obligations to consider environmental justice?"

Based on these concerns, the Board deferred consideration of the Permit. One week later, Governor Ralph Northam removed two Board members who had voiced concerns about the disproportionate harm to Union Hill and replaced them with two new members....

On January 8, 2019, the Board held its final meeting. A DEQ official made a brief presentation, [] stating that "[r]egardless of the demographics of the area surrounding the compressor station, [it] will not cause a disproportionate adverse impact to the community" for two reasons: first, the residents surrounding the Compressor Station site "are already breathing air that is cleaner than the air breathed by 90% of the residents of Virginia"; and second, although "air modeling does indicate... a slight increase in air pollution concentration [from the Compressor Station], the increase is slight."

The [Board] voted unanimously on January 8, 2019, to adopt DEQ's recommendation and approve the Permit. In doing so, individual Board members made statements on the record. Specifically, the Board Chairman stated, "For purpose of my review, I have assumed that [the community around the Compressor Station] may be an E[nvironmental] J[ustice] community." Another member said the same. ("I... have assumed that the community at issue is an environmental justice community."). The Board as a whole issued a one-page Decision Statement the same day, stating simply that the Permit was "prepared in conformance with all applicable statutes, regulations, and agency practices"; the limits and conditions in the permit "have been established to protect public health and the environment"; and "all public comments relevant to the permit [were] considered."... The Permit was issued the following day.

Petitioners filed this timely petition for review of the grant of the Permit. We possess jurisdiction pursuant to the Natural Gas Act, 15 U.S.C. § 717r(d)(1) (providing the "United States Court of Appeals for the circuit in which a [natural gas] facility ... is proposed to be constructed ... or operated shall have original and exclusive jurisdiction over any civil action for the review of an order or action of a ... State administrative agency acting pursuant to Federal law to issue ... any permit ... required under Federal law")....

Union Hill is a historic community with a high population of African-Americans whose ancestors established the community in the aftermath of the Civil War. Community members founded the Union Hill Baptist Church, as well as the Union Grove Missionary Church, and have buried their dead there for generations. In 2015, ACP bought a neighboring 68.5-acre plot of land and chose that site for the placement of the Compressor Station.

According to the ACP permit application, the Compressor Station's four turbines, with a combined 58,162 horsepower, would burn gas 24 hours a day, 365 days a year.

Together, the turbines' combustion of gas accounts for 83% of the facility's projected nitrogen oxide emissions and 95% of its emissions of particulate matter (PM, PM2.5, and PM10), and also generates emissions of toxic materials such as formaldehyde and hexane. FERC determined that the Compressor Station will increase the area's amount of nitrogen oxide pollution and fine particle (PM2.5) pollution, and emit known carcinogens into the community. FERC likewise recognized that pollutants from compressor stations "are known to increase the effects of asthma and may increase the risk of lung cancer."

Friends of Buckingham, Inc., a group of Buckingham County citizens, conducted a demographic survey (the "Friends of Buckingham Survey"). According to Petitioners:

> The study indicated that about 84% of [Union Hill] residents are nonwhite, most of African-American descent—a percentage far higher than the county-wide percentage of African Americans (34.7%). Of the 67 households for which a full set of responses exists, 42 (or 62.6%) are known descendants of formerly enslaved people from area plantations. Eight households reported unmarked slave and Freedmen graves on their property or nearby. An independent analysis found that the area within one mile of the proposed Compressor Station has a population density 51% higher than the county average—and 77% higher than either [ACP] or DEQ identified in community profiles they prepared during the Compressor Station permitting process.
>
> The Friends of Buckingham study also revealed a prevalence of health conditions consistent with national data showing higher rates of respiratory sickness among the African-American population. Thirty-five households reported pre-existing medical diagnoses, chiefly respiratory and heart conditions. Residents of Union Hill, including many elderly residents, reported suffering from chronic ailments including asthma, chronic obstructive pulmonary disease, chronic bronchitis and pneumonia, heart disease, and other conditions that would make them particularly susceptible to air pollution from the Compressor Station.

Petitioners contend that the Board (and to the extent its recommendations were adopted, DEQ), violated Virginia law by "failing to assess the Compressor Station's disproportionate health impacts on the predominantly African-American Union Hill community and the suitability of the site." These arguments are grounded in a Virginia statute, which provides:

> The Board in ... approving ... permits ..., shall consider facts and circumstances relevant to the reasonableness of the activity involved and the regulations proposed to control it, including:
>
> 1. The character and degree of injury to, or interference with, safety, health, or the reasonable use of property which is caused or threatened to be caused;
> 2. The social and economic value of the activity involved;
> 3. The suitability of the activity to the area in which it is located; and

4. The scientific and economic practicality of reducing or eliminating the discharge resulting from such activity.

Va. Code Ann. § 10.1–1307(E). Petitioners argue the Board failed to consider the potential for disproportionate health impacts under (E)(1), and made an incomplete and misinformed site suitability determination under (E)(3).

We conclude that the Board thrice erred in performing its statutory duty under sections 10.1–1307(E)(1) and (E)(3): (1) it failed to make any findings regarding the character of the local population at Union Hill, in the face of conflicting evidence; (2) it failed to individually consider the potential degree of injury to the local population independent of NAAQS and state emission standards; and (3) DEQ's final permit analysis, ostensibly adopted by the Board, relied on evidence in the record that was incomplete or discounted by subsequent evidence.

Before delving into these issues, we begin with a discussion of environmental justice ("EJ").

"As Justice Douglas pointed out nearly [fifty] years ago, '[a]s often happens with interstate highways, the route selected was through the poor area of town, not through the area where the politically powerful people live.'" Jersey Heights Neighborhood Ass'n v. Glendening, 174 F.3d 180, 195 (4th Cir. 1999) (King, J., concurring) (quoting Triangle Improvement Council v. Ritchie, 402 U.S. 497, 502 (1971) (Douglas, J., dissenting)); *see also* Nicky Sheats, *Achieving Emissions Reductions for Environmental Justice Communities Through Climate Change Mitigation Policy*, 41 Wm. & Mary Envtl. L. & Pol'y Rev. 377, 382 (2017) ("There is evidence that a disproportionate number of environmental hazards, polluting facilities, and other unwanted land uses are located in communities of color and low-income communities."). "The purpose of an environmental justice analysis is to determine whether a project will have a disproportionately adverse effect on minority and low income populations." Mid States Coal. for Progress v. Surface Transp. Bd., 345 F.3d 520, 541 (8th Cir. 2003). "Although the term 'environmental justice' is of fairly recent vintage, the concept is not." *Jersey Heights*, 174 F.3d at 195 (King, J., concurring).

Of note, on August 16, 2018, Governor Northam's own Advisory Council on Environmental Justice recommended suspending the permitting decision for the Compressor Station "pending further review of the station's impacts on the health and the lives of those living in close proximity."

Indeed, under Virginia law, the Board is *required* to consider "character and degree of injury to ... health," and "suitability of the activity to the area." Va. Code Ann. § 10.1–1307(E). Both Respondents and ACP acknowledge that Virginia law—including the Commonwealth Energy Policy and factors outlined in § 10.1-1307(E)(3)—"require[s] the Board to consider the potential for disproportionate impacts to minority and low income communities." In fact, no party argues that the Board was excused from considering EJ in its analysis. Therefore, we accept that the Board was required to consider EJ in the Compressor Station Permit approval process. Underpinning Petitioners' arguments here is the idea that not only did the Board consider EJ separate and apart from site suitability, it did not give this point enough consideration.

As explained below, it is clear to us that the Board's EJ review was insufficient, which undermines the Board's statutory duties and renders the Board's Permit decision arbitrary and capricious, and unsupported by substantial evidence.

To begin, Petitioners contend, "Despite access to a wealth of information, the Board failed to make any findings regarding the demographics of Union Hill that would have allowed for a meaningful assessment of the likelihood of disproportionate harm." We agree. The Board was presented with conflicting evidence about whether and how Union Hill was a "minority" EJ population, and it made no finding as to its resolution of this conflict. This is improper under both federal law, and Virginia administrative law.

Throughout the public comment period and public meetings, one of the main points of dispute was whether the Union Hill community could be deemed a "minority" EJ community. As noted by the Board and ACP, the Board deferred its vote twice in order to obtain more information on this issue. Yet in the end, it did not even bother to make a finding on this issue. Rather, at least two Board members "assumed" that Union Hill was an EJ minority community without performing further analysis on what that means.

The minority EJ community designation is important because, if Union Hill is considered a minority EJ community, then information about "African-American populations hav[ing] a greater prevalence of asthma" and other health issues is an important consideration. For example, FERC's analysis in the EIS—upon which DEQ originally relied—outlined all the risks to African Americans from the Compressor Station, e.g., increased risk of asthma and lung cancer, and even noted that African Americans were an "especially sensitive" community for these conditions. But because the African-American population around the Compressor Station did not "exceed the threshold[] for environmental justice populations," it was of no moment. Id. at 2373; *see also id.* at 2372 ("None of the three census tracts within 1 mile of the [Compressor Station] are designated minority [EJ] populations [based on a methodology involving 2013 census data].").

There are multiple pieces of conflicting evidence about the minority population of Union Hill in this record, presented to DEQ and the Board:

- FERC's analysis, which is based on 2013 census data, states that in Virginia, "minorities comprise 30.8 percent of the total population." However, on December 9, 2018, DEQ told the Board that Virginia has an average 37% minority.
- FERC stated that "[n]one of the three census tracts within 1 mile of the [Compressor Station] are designated minority environmental justice populations." But the Friends of Buckingham Study (also called the Fjord Study or Household Study) demonstrates that "the area surrounding the [Compressor Station] is clearly an environmental justice area for minority population." Indeed, a September 2018 version of this Study found that, in an actual door-to-door house-

hold survey, minorities make up 83% of residents, with African Americans comprising around 62%. After more households were reached, in January 2019, the percentage of minorities increased to 83.5%.

- DEQ also presented an "EJSCREEN" study from the EPA that "found the minority population around the compressor station to be in the range of 37 to 39%." Yet at an earlier presentation, a DEQ staff member had told the Board, "I wouldn't really rely on" EJSCREEN.

DEQ's final permit analysis submission to the Board says nothing further about EJ. And of course, the Board's decision is only one page long, says nothing about EJ or which stud(ies) it relied on, and even adds a provision in handwriting, professing that "[T]he Board does not adopt any legal views expressed by DEQ regarding the Board's authority under Va. Code Ann. Section 10.1–1307.E," without further explanation.

The Board acted arbitrarily in failing to provide *any explanation* regarding the EJ issue, which makes its extensions of public comments and additional meetings ring hollow. Moreover, under Virginia law, the Board's factfinding would fail under a substantial evidence standard of review because there is conflicting evidence in the record that the Board did not resolve. Virginia law is clear: "It is not unusual for there to be conflicting evidence in contested cases, and it is the job of the agency, as factfinder, to resolve those conflicts." Virginia Ret. Sys. v. Blair, 772 S.E.2d 26, 32 (Va. Ct. App. 2015) (emphasis in original).

... If the area around the Compressor Station is indeed an EJ minority community, the demographic and statistics change regarding whether this is [an] "especially sensitive" community for certain conditions. Rather than take this into account in its assumption, the Board merely falls back on NAAQS and state air quality standards not tailored to this specific EJ community....

The Board's reliance on air quality standards led it to dismiss EJ concerns. Even if all pollutants within the county remain below state and national air quality standards, the Board failed to grapple with the likelihood that those living closest to the Compressor Station—an overwhelmingly minority population according to the Friends of Buckingham Survey—will be affected more than those living in other parts of the same county. The Board rejected the idea of disproportionate impact on the basis that air quality standards were met. But environmental justice is not merely a box to be checked, and the Board's failure to consider the disproportionate impact on those closest to the Compressor Station resulted in a flawed analysis....

For these reasons, we conclude that the Board failed in its statutory duty to determine the character and degree of injury to the health of the Union Hill residents, and the suitability of the activity to the area. We vacate and remand for the Board to make findings with regard to conflicting evidence in the record....

Notes and Questions

1. Local health impacts. The court emphasized that the Board decision neglected the actual health impacts on the local community. Granular data revealed greater risk to community residents' health than recognized by the state evaluation. Like the General Iron case considered above, this case found that official's knowledge of health impacts were proper considerations in permitting decisions.

2. "Not merely a box to be checked." From the excerpt, where does it appear that the Fourth Circuit derives the notion that "environmental justice is not merely a box to be checked"? Does it come exclusively from the Virginia permitting statute, or does it reflect the development of broader legal principles? If the latter, what are the sources of these legal principles?

3. "EJ minority community"? What is the legal significance of whether or not the "area around the Compressor Station is indeed an EJ minority community"? If the EPA has defined "environmental justice" to apply to "all people," shouldn't it be enough that some people in the area of the Compressor Station would be disproportionately impacted by the facility operations? How does the Court frame its considerations of race in its legal reasoning?

4. Litigation strategy. How did the community advocates in this case position themselves for this legal victory? Do there appear to be strategies here that would work in different states or under different environmental statutes?

5. Better advice? Note that the Virginia DEQ in this case made the same major mistake that the EPA made in the *Select Steel* case, conflating compliance with national air quality standards and protection of local communities. If you had been the legal advisor to the DEQ in this case, how might you have counseled your clients to proceed with this permitting process and reach a result that would withstand judicial review?

6. The Atlantic Coast Pipeline. The Atlantic Coast Pipeline (ACP) was proposed to run six hundred miles across three states of the Southeast, raising many concerns for environmental injustice, including its potential impacts on racial minorities, low-income communities, and tribes and Indigenous peoples. Given the vigorous community opposition and numerous delays to the project, proponents canceled the ACP proposal in 2020. *See* Ivan Penn, *Atlantic Coast Pipeline Canceled as Delays and Costs Mount*, N.Y. TIMES, July 6, 2020.

Chapter 7

Government Enforcement

Figure 7-1. Removal of rail cars after train derailment in East Palestine, Ohio. March 2023. Photo: U.S. EPA.

A. Introduction

At 8:54 pm on February 3, 2023, Norfolk Southern Railway Train 32N derailed while traveling eastbound through the Village of East Palestine, Ohio, just shy of the Pennsylvania state line. The derailment consisted of 38 railcars, including 11 tank cars carrying hazardous materials. Fires sparked by the derailment eventually spread to 35 railcars and were fueled by hazardous materials that spilled from the cars, including butyl acrylate and ethylene glycol. At 8:56 pm, the first 911 call came in and all available fire and emergency medical service units were dispatched. As local responders began fighting the fire, it continued to grow in size and intensity, and the deputy fire chief ordered an evacuation of approximately two thousand residents within one mile of the derailment site.

The next day, responders became concerned that a pressure relief valve on one of the tank cars containing vinyl chloride might fail and result in a catastrophic explosion. To address this danger, on February 6, the local fire chief authorized a "vent and burn" procedure for the railcars containing vinyl chloride. The evacuation zone was extended to additional residents of Ohio and Pennsylvania, and the "controlled burn" procedure commenced, generating a persistent plume of smoke. Two days later, the fires were extinguished and residents were allowed to return home.

After returning home, many residents discovered odors and became concerned for their health. In the months following the derailment, "hundreds of people" reported experiencing health impacts including headaches, nausea, nosebleeds, and respiratory problems. Many families also experienced mental trauma and financial distress that was particularly challenging for low-income families and rural residents of the impacted area. Norfolk Southern established a program offering temporary relocation to impacted residents, providing reimbursement for hotels. For many families, personal health and financial concerns continued after the relocation ended. *See, e.g.*, Emily Baumgaertner, *One Family's Toxic Train Wreck Ordeal: Illness, Exile, and Debt*, N.Y. Times, Aug. 21, 2023.

Meanwhile, along with local fire and other emergency personnel, EPA responders arrived onsite the night of the derailment and remained for more than 20 months. During the first few weeks, EPA conducted air monitoring in and around the site and assisted with environmental response efforts conducted by Ohio EPA and Norfolk Southern. On February 21, after determining that hazardous substances released at the site posed an imminent and substantial threat to public health and the environment, EPA issued an administrative order under CERCLA directing Norfolk Southern to clean up the contamination. Under the CERCLA order, with EPA oversight, Norfolk Southern removed and disposed of more than 219,000 tons of contaminated soil and some 73 million gallons of wastewater. By October 2023, most of this soil cleanup was complete, but an oily sheen in nearby creeks prompted EPA to issue a second order under the Clean Water Act to address contaminated sediments.

EPA also continued indoor and outdoor air monitoring in and around the area of the derailment, ultimately collecting more than 115 million data points, and consistently finding no chemicals of concern "at levels anticipated to be harmful to health." *See, e.g.*, U.S. EPA, Frequently Asked Questions: "Is the air monitoring equipment detecting chemicals of concern?" (April 10, 2024), https://www.epa.gov/east-palestine-oh-train-derailment/air-monitoring-equipment-detecting-chemicals-concern.

In March 2023, while cleanup work in East Palestine was ongoing, the U.S. Department of Justice filed a civil complaint against Norfolk Southern, alleging claims under CERCLA and the Clean Water Act, and seeking relief including penalties, additional cleanup, and reimbursement of response costs. In May 2024, the parties released for public comment a proposed settlement valued at over $310 million. By the time the settlement was announced, cleanup work at East Palestine had already exceeded $780 million, and completion of work under the settlement was expected to push the total cleanup over $1 billion.

The settlement also included rail safety enhancements valued at more than $200 million; $25 million for a 20-year community health program to include medical monitoring and mental health services for impacted residents and responders; a $15 million civil penalty for violations of the Clean Water Act; and $15 million for long-term monitoring of groundwater and surface water. *United States Reaches Over $310 Million Settlement with Norfolk Southern to Address Harms Caused by East Palestine Train Derailment*, May 23, 2024, https://www.epa.gov/newsreleases/united-states-reaches-over-310-million-settlement-norfolk-southern-address-harms.

One powerful and direct means of pursuing environmental justice (EJ) is through enforcement of environmental laws and regulations by government agencies. Activists and academics often overlook government enforcement, perhaps because it rarely draws public attention or results in appellate decisions you find in a typical casebook. Compared to citizen suits (discussed in Chapter 12), government agencies (federal, state, local, tribal) bring far more cases each year to address environmental violations, but as with East Palestine, almost all of these cases settle at some point, often outside the spotlight. From the outside, this can be frustrating for some EJ advocates who feel their voices may be ignored in the enforcement process. From the inside of an agency, however, EJ advocates may find tremendous authority and opportunity for taking action to protect vulnerable communities. In this chapter, we will explore these opportunities and authorities, helping EJ advocates collaborate with enforcement agencies by identifying violations, supporting investigations, shifting agency priorities, and suggesting more appropriate enforcement resolutions. Through this process, this chapter may also encourage EJ advocates to consider public service themselves to further the pursuit of environmental justice.

B. Historical Critiques

Early concerns for environmental racism included allegations of discrimination in the way that the U.S. EPA enforced federal environmental laws. In 1992, the *National Law Journal* (NLJ) conducted an investigation to determine whether in fact EPA's environmental enforcement was discriminatory. *See* Marianne Lavelle & Marcia Coyle, *Unequal Protection: The Racial Divide in Environmental Law*, Nat. L.J., Sept. 21, 1992, at S1–S12. The report reviewed civil judicial enforcement cases resolved by EPA from 1985 to 1991. It also looked at EPA responses to contaminated sites under the Superfund program established by the federal Comprehensive Environmental Response, Compensation, and Liability Act (CERCLA). The report examined all sites listed on CERCLA's National Priorities List (NPL) from 1980 to 1992. The study classified zip codes around the facilities and waste sites into four quartiles, ranging from those with the highest white population and highest income to those with the lowest white population and lowest income.

The NLJ study found that penalties for violations of federal environmental laws were substantially lower in minority communities than in white communities. The overall average penalty for all environmental statutes was 46 percent lower in minority communities than white communities ($153,067 vs. $105,028). With respect to the effect of a community's income on penalties, the picture was less clear. The report found that the average penalty for all violations was significantly lower in poor communities than in wealthy areas: $95,664 per case compared to $146,993. But this result varied considerably by individual statute. Penalties under four statutes—the Clean Air Act, the Safe Drinking Water Act (SDWA), Superfund, and RCRA—were higher in poor areas, ranging from 3 percent (RCRA) to 63 percent (SDWA) greater than in wealthy areas. On the other hand, in Clean Water Act cases average penalties in low-income communities were 91 percent lower than in upper income areas, and in multi-media cases, the average fine in high-income areas was $315,000 compared to $18,000 in low-income communities. The study concluded that the pattern of penalties varied so markedly depending upon the particular law involved that income was not a reliable predictor of the size of penalties.

The NLJ study also found racial disparities in EPA's response to Superfund sites. In particular, it found that "abandoned hazardous waste sites in minority areas take 20 percent longer to be placed on the National Priorities List than those in white areas" (5.6 years from the date of discovery until its listing on the NPL vs. 4.7 years). The report found that by the time cleanup commenced, this gap had narrowed and minority sites were only 4 percent behind white sites (10.4 years vs. 9.9 years), although in half of the EPA regions this difference was 12 percent to 42 percent. The NLJ study also found that EPA chose less protective cleanup remedies at minority sites, opting for "containment" (the capping or walling off of a waste site) 7 percent more frequently than permanent treatment methods that reduce or eliminate the volume or toxicity of hazardous substances. At sites located in white communities, EPA ordered permanent treatment 22 percent more often than containment.

The NLJ study, published more than 30 years ago, has been criticized on a number of methodological grounds. Critics have argued that the study's use of quartiles to divide cases into white and minority areas resulted in areas being classified as "minority" even though they were not in fact predominantly minority; that the disparities reported were not statistically significant; and that the NLJ study failed to control for other variables that might affect penalties.

Two later examinations of the NLJ study questioned its conclusions. Professor Evan Ringquist found that the results varied depending on how one grouped the historical data. Professor Ringquist first confirmed the study's findings that penalties from 1985 to 1991 were higher in white communities. However, when Ringquist further examined civil judicial enforcement actions dating back to 1974, he found that from 1974 to 1985, penalties were actually *higher* in minority and poor communities, and that during the entire period from 1974 to 1991, there was little difference in average fines between white and minority communities (and that penalties were higher in poor communities). After controlling for other factors that could influence penalties, Ringquist concluded that "minorities are not disadvantaged by case outcomes in environmental protection, and the case for class bias in these outcomes is weak." Evan J. Ringquist, *A Question of Justice: Equity in Environmental Litigation, 1974–1991*, 60 J. Pol. 1148, 1162 (1998).

Researcher Mark Atlas also reevaluated the cases analyzed by the NLJ study using some different methodologies, such as geographic concentric rings around facility locations as the units of analysis (rather than facility zip codes), and correcting for mistakes in EPA's original enforcement database. Atlas found that the income level of an area had no meaningful effect on penalties, and that while a community's race affected penalties, it was in the opposite direction of what the NLJ study found; penalties *increased* as the proportion of minorities in a community increased. Atlas also concluded that factors which influenced penalties the most were the specific characteristics of the case, such as the types of violations involved and how recently the case was resolved. Mark Atlas, *Rush to Judgment: An Empirical Analysis of Environmental Equity in U.S. Environmental Protection Agency Enforcement Actions*, 35 LAW AND SOC'Y REV. 633 (2001).

In his critique of the NLJ report, Mark Atlas also noted other possible explanations for variations in penalty amounts. For example, under agency policy, EPA may lower a penalty to reflect a defendant's limited ability to pay; in a minority community, this may help avoid driving a minority-owned business into bankruptcy. Discussed later in this chapter, EPA may also lower penalties if the defendant agrees to undertake a "supplemental environmental project," bringing environmental benefits to a local community instead of sending penalty payments to the U.S. Treasury.

More recent studies appear to confirm the criticism of the NLJ study and the conclusions of Ringquist and Atlas. *See, e.g.*, Spencer Banzhaf, Lala Ma, & Christopher Timmins, *Environmental Justice: The Economics of Race, Place, and Pollution*, 33 J. ECON. PERSPECTIVES 185, 202 (2019) (concluding that while a community's "potential for collective action [is] an important determinant[] of enforcement activities, [] race does not have an independent effect and [] the effect of income is mixed").

On the other hand, Professor David Konisky and colleagues, after more than a decade of empirical research, have concluded that there are "meaningful disparities in environmental enforcement" of standards designed to address air pollution, water pollution, and hazardous waste management. David M. Konisky, Christopher Reenock & Shannon Conley, *Environmental Injustice in Clean Water Act Enforcement: Racial and Income Disparities in Inspection Time*, 16 ENVT. RESEARCH LETTERS 2 (2021). These findings are "not homogenous," however, and often defy generalizations. In one substantial study, Konisky et al. examined data concerning more than 123,368 inspections of approximately 6,700 facilities across the United States operating between 2001 and 2017 and holding discharge permits under the federal Clean Water Act. Most of these inspections were conducted by state agencies delegated authority to implement the federal statute, subject to EPA guidance that each permitted facility should be inspected at least once every two years. After crunching the numbers, Konisky concluded that "on average, state agencies take longer—on the order of a couple weeks—to inspect facilities in Black and Hispanic neighborhoods." As for distinctions based upon income, "CWA facilities in neighborhoods with large poor population are likely to be targeted by state inspectors *more rapidly*." Konisky et al. at 6–7 (emphasis added).

Notes and Questions

1. The takeaway? After all of the attention that the NLJ report received, were you surprised by the subsequent critiques and Banzhaf's conclusion that "race does not have an independent effect" on government enforcement? Does a delay of inspections by "a couple weeks" matter for protection of minority communities? At the very least, the Konisky (2021) study suggests a loss of opportunity for regulators to accelerate environmental improvement. After classifying permitted facilities as either in "compliance" or "noncompliance" before the inspection, Konisky found that "in heavily Hispanic neighborhoods, noncompliant facilities wait the same amount of time for their next inspection as compliant ones," a finding also reached for Black communities. This suggests that regulators could, if they choose, focus more inspections on noncompliant facilities in Black and Hispanic neighborhoods in order to bring these facilities back into compliance faster.

2. Enforcement bias? Even if empirical results are "not homogenous," isn't it still possible that some underserved communities are adversely impacted by bias and discrimination in environmental enforcement? One recent study of EPA data collected over ten years concluded that "[s]ignificant disparities exist in the median penalties imposed from state to state, between the states and the EPA, and among the various EPA regional offices." Jerry L. Anderson & Amy Grace Vaughan, *Environmental Penalties: Discretion and Disparities*, 42 STAN. ENVTL. L.J. 3 (2023). While there may be many explanations for such disparities, institutional racism and other forms of bias embedded in local and regional enforcement agencies may be one of them. For one detailed analysis of this potential for bias, including bias in favor of business interests and bias against political controversies, *see* Robert R. Kuehn, *Bias in Environmental Agency Decision Making*, 45 ENVTL. L. 957 (2015).

On an individual level, agency staff—like everyone else—have personal prejudices that could affect their enforcement work. But against this potential for prejudice, however, imagine this scenario. You are an enforcement attorney in EPA Region 5, based in Chicago. Your regional office has enforcement jurisdiction in Minnesota, and your supervisor assigns you a case concerning leaking drums discovered in a vacant lot in Richfield, Minnesota. What do you know at this moment about the demographics of Richfield, Minnesota? If you know nothing about these demographics, would you take time to investigate this? If you discovered an elementary school next to the vacant lot or a high population of Latino residents in the neighborhood, would that information affect your legal analysis of the possible violations related to the leaking drums or your strategy for how to resolve this case?

In reality, busy, overworked enforcement staff often have little or no understanding of the demographics of a community affected by environmental violations. This is both good and bad. It may be good in confirming the empirical finding that racial discrimination is not a significant factor in enforcement decisions. However, it also represents a missed opportunity for promoting environmental justice. If you are a busy, overworked enforcement attorney, would you rather invest your time seeking monetary penalties for violations in wealthy, white communities or seeking to fix serious health threats in poor, minority communities? To a significant extent, enforcement staff often do have these choices and opportunities for pursuing environmental justice within government agencies, consistent with the concept of enforcement discretion, discussed below.

3. Squeaky wheels? Note that one "important determinant" for enforcement activities, according to empirical studies, is the "potential for collective action." What does that mean? In simplest terms, it may reflect the old adage, "The squeaky wheel gets the grease." As Professor Richard Lazarus further elaborated: "Those who complain, who have greater access, who know how to tweak their Congresspeople to do something, are more likely to get the attention of very busy people. And the people with greater know-how are generally those with greater political and economic resources, who tend to be white." Richard Lazarus, quoted in *Unequal Protection: The Racial Divide in Environmental Law*, NAT. L.J., Sept. 21, 1992, at S3. Of course, from the Civil Rights Movement of the 1960s, we know that political and economic resources are not the only factors in determining "collective action." From the historic March on Washington with Martin Luther King, Jr. in 1963 to the nationwide protests in 2020 following the murder of George Floyd in Minneapolis, organized communities and masses have learned and demonstrated the power of "collective action" even without the benefits of wealth and political access.

4. Citizen complaints. In the 30-plus years since the observation above by Professor Lazarus, there have certainly been some improvements in access to government. Citizen complaints of suspected environmental violations may always be made to any authorities in person or via telephone. With the advent and increasing accessibility of the Internet, community activists can also file reports online. *See, e.g.*, https://echo.epa.gov/report-environmental-violations (EPA violations reporting website). Reports submitted through the EPA website are assigned tracking numbers to ensure response by the appropriate federal, state, or local authorities. What do you imagine are the advantages and limitations of filing reports online versus in person or on the phone? Do any of these systems work? In one case responding to a tip from "anonymous informants," EPA discovered and removed more than one hundred containers with pesticide residue buried illegally in an agricultural area with a heavy concentration of migrant farmworkers. *See* Double H Pesticide Burial Site, https://response.epa.gov/site/site_profile.aspx?site_id=4851.

C. Enforcement Purposes

Perhaps the most significant problem with the 1992 National Law Journal report was its limited focus on one narrow category of enforcement action (civil litigation) by one government agency (the U.S. EPA). In reality, there are many forms of environmental enforcement, including administrative actions, civil litigation, and criminal prosecution. By far the most common form of enforcement is administrative action, which may include things such as warning letters or agency orders issued without judicial intervention. Notably, the most common environmental enforcement agency is not the U.S. EPA but agencies of the states, tribes, territories, and local governments. Environmental enforcement can be complex, sometimes the subject of a full three-credit course in law school. Nevertheless, this section will provide a quick, analytical framework to explain *why* enforcement response may be important to address certain situations. Once we understand the three broad purposes of enforcement discussed below, we can then move on to considering specific legal authorities providing how environmental justice may be achieved through environmental enforcement.

Much of the above discussion about penalties for environmental violations assumes that penalties are a measure of environmental protection, such that lower penalties produce lower protection and higher penalties provide greater protection. In reality, penalties are simply one method of many for addressing violations of environmental law. Which method is most appropriate in a given case depends in part on consideration of three major purposes for environmental enforcement, which may be described as follows: (1) fix the problem; (2) deter future violations; and (3) level the playing field. To understand these three purposes, imagine that you are still that enforcement attorney for EPA Region 5 in Chicago, which has enforcement jurisdiction in the State of Michigan. In February 2015, you learn through an elevator conversation that an EPA chemist in your building has identified extremely high levels of lead in the drinking water of your hometown of Flint, Michigan. With this information, if you could advise your agency clients on a course of action, what would that be? Would you recommend preparing a civil complaint to file in federal court to seek an assessment of civil penalties? Or would you advise more immediate action to stop people from drinking contaminated water?

In this scenario, the most urgent need may be to "fix the problem," which suggests not years of civil litigation for penalties but an administrative order requiring immediate compliance with drinking water standards (which was actually issued by EPA on January 21, 2016). In time, once safe drinking water is provided (even temporarily with bottled water), the enforcement purpose of "deter future violations" may suggest the agency should seek penalties to punish the violator and encourage future compliance with drinking water regulations; in the most egregious cases, such as Flint, deterrence may even include criminal prosecution and jail time for offenders who put people in danger. Finally, if the violator benefited from the violation (e.g., saving money on water treatment), "level the playing field" suggests additional penalties should be recovered so that no other party that incurs the costs of compliance would be placed at a competitive disadvantage for playing by the rules.

For any violation of environmental requirements, enforcement action may be appropriate to serve one, two, or all three of these purposes. The purpose which must be served, or served *first*, may thus dictate the choice or sequence of enforcement tools, whether administrative, civil, criminal, or other action.

Notes and Questions

1. Enforcement discretion. Enforcement agencies generally have broad discretion to choose which violations will become the subject of a government enforcement action. To some activists and commentators, this enforcement discretion may seem alarming. As Professor Kuehn observed in the early years of concern for environmental justice, "In fact, the conditions that give rise to the discriminatory impact of environmental hazards may be even greater when the government acts as enforcer, since few areas of the law invest more discretion in agency employees or are more hidden from the public's view and oversight than an agency's enforcement actions." Robert R. Kuehn, *Remedying the Unequal Enforcement of Environmental Laws*, 9 St. John's J. Legal Commentary 625 (1994).

Under the concept of enforcement discretion, the potential for discriminatory enforcement is certainly real, as courts consistently decline to review cases where agencies refuse to take enforcement action. As the U.S. Supreme Court explained in *Heckler v. Chaney*, 470 U.S. 821 (1985), agency decisions whether to take enforcement action in response to a certain violation require a "complicated balancing of factors." These factors include whether the agency has sufficient resources to undertake the action, whether the agency would be likely to succeed on the merits, and whether agency resources would be best spent on this particular violation instead of other competing concerns. Consistent with this Supreme Court guidance, environmental organizations have occasionally challenged EPA's failure to take an enforcement action, but they have rarely prevailed. *See, e.g.*, *Sierra Club v. Whitman*, 268 F.3d 898 (9th Cir. 2001) (dismissing citizen suit seeking to compel EPA to respond to 128 documented violations of a Clean Water Act permit for a treatment plant in Arizona). In this Arizona case, does EPA's refusal to enforce the Clean Water Act necessarily mean there could be no enforcement to address these 128 violations of the Clean Water Act? What other enforcement options might the Sierra Club or other concerned citizens have considered in this case?

2. Enforcement and compensation. Look again at the three broad purposes of environmental enforcement articulated above. How do these three purposes of enforcement align with the four dimensions of justice (distributive, procedural, corrective, and social) discussed in Chapter 1? Can enforcement by the government serve all four of these justice dimensions? Consider just the dimension of corrective justice, which according to the reading in Chapter 1 includes "retributive justice," "compensatory justice," "restorative justice," and "commutative justice." Within this framework, one may see how criminal environmental enforcement, for example, could serve interests in retributive justice. Similarly, Superfund enforcement—focused on cleaning up contaminated sites—may serve interests in restorative justice. Enforcement concepts of the "level playing field" may serve interests in commutative justice. But can government enforcement serve interests in compensatory justice, directing resources to public and private parties who have suffered financial or other injuries from environmental violations?

While government enforcement can serve many dimensions of justice, government enforcement may not be able to serve *every* dimension of justice. Consider the case study of the Duwamish Waterway explored in the next chapter (Chapter 8). If pollution in your local waterway prevents you from eating crabs, shellfish, or flounder, you may feel that you have suffered a loss for which compensation is due. This may be particularly true if you are a subsistence fisher and depend on fish and shellfish to feed your family. But in general, violations of environmental law do not give rise to private rights for compensation. The fact that the Duwamish River, in this case, may exceed water quality standards under the Clean Water Act does not mean that fishers have rights to compensation under the Clean Water Act for losses due to CWA violations.

Penalties for violations of the Clean Water Act typically go to the U.S. Treasury, not to the communities harmed by violations of the Clean Water Act. So too with violations of the Clean Air Act, RCRA, and most other federal statutes.

CERCLA is primarily a remedial, not regulatory, statute, designed to remedy past releases of hazardous substances. Even so, the Comprehensive Environmental Response, Compensation, and Liability Act (CERCLA), like other federal environmental statutes, provides little "compensation" for personal injuries. *See Exxon Corp. v. Hunt*, 475 U.S. 355, 360 (1986) ("Superfund money may not be used to pay for injury to persons or property caused by hazardous wastes").

One exception to this general rule comes under CERCLA § 107(a), which allows statutory claims for **natural resource damages (NRD)**. Under an NRD action, natural resource trustees (designated entities of federal, state, and tribal governments) may sue for restoration of impaired resources and damages for lost uses. 42 U.S.C. § 9607(a)(4)(C) (authorizing damage claims for "injury to, destruction of, or loss of natural resources"). Expanding on CERCLA's NRD concept, the Oil Pollution Act § 1002(b) provides a laundry list of possible damage claims for injuries related to oil spills. 33 U.S.C. § 2702(b)(2) (authorizing damage claims for injuries to natural resources, real and personal property, subsistence uses, tax revenues, profits and earnings, and public services). This OPA authority was the primary legal basis for many of the damage claims associated with the BP Deepwater Horizon oil spill in the Gulf of Mexico in 2010.

Another exception to the general rule against compensation through enforcement actions is the possibility of restitution as part of a criminal sentencing. For many convictions under federal law, the U.S. Sentencing Guidelines provide, "In the case of an identifiable victim, the court shall ... enter a restitution order for the full amount of the victim's loss. ..." U.S. Sentencing Guidelines Manual § 5E1.1(a) (2023). Victims of environmental crimes, including crimes in vulnerable communities, may thus find another pathway through environmental enforcement for seeking compensation for their injuries. In 2023, for example, a worker at an aluminum plant in The Dalles, Oregon, was awarded restitution of $213,000 for injuries that led to charges under the Clean Air Act for negligent endangerment involving a hazardous air pollutant. In addition to restitution, the company was also required to pay a criminal fine of $550,000. See https://www.justice.gov/usao-or/pr/criminal-fine-and-restitution-ordered-company-operating-aluminum-processing-facility.

Despite narrow exceptions like criminal restitution and natural resource damages, the general rule remains that government enforcement will not result in compensation for public or private losses. If compensation is not available through government enforcement, are there other legal avenues for seeking compensation for injuries? We will return to this question in Chapter 12, when we consider the authorities for citizen suits and common law remedies.

D. Enforcement Authorities to Protect Vulnerable Communities

As suggested so far in this chapter, diligent government enforcement of federal pollution control laws, including the Clean Air Act, Clean Water Act, RCRA, CERCLA, and the Safe Drinking Water Act, could go a long way toward achieving the objectives of environmental justice. Many of these federal statutes, and state and local counterparts, share structural similarities as well as subtle differences. As you review the key provisions presented below, consider how you might use these provisions in order to protect the health and environment of underserved communities.

Clean Air Act § 113 (42 U.S.C. § 7413)

(a)(1) Whenever, on the basis of any information ... [EPA] finds that any person has violated or is in violation of any requirement or prohibition of an applicable implementation plan or permit, [EPA] shall notify the person and the State in which the plan applies of such finding. At any time after the expiration of 30 days following the date on which such notice of a violation is issued, [EPA] may ... (A) issue an order requiring such person to comply with the requirements or prohibitions of such plan or permit, (B) issue an administrative penalty order ... or (C) bring a civil action....

(b) Civil judicial enforcement. [EPA] shall, as appropriate ... commence a civil action for a permanent or temporary injunction, or to assess and recover a civil penalty of not more than $25,000 per day for each violation, or both....

(c) Criminal penalties. (1) Any person who knowingly violates any [specified] requirement or prohibition ... shall, upon conviction, be punished by a fine ... or by imprisonment for not to exceed 5 years, or both.... (4) Any person who negligently releases into the ambient air any hazardous air pollutant ... and who at the time negligently places another person in imminent danger of death or serious bodily injury shall, upon conviction, be punished by a fine ... or by imprisonment for not more than 1 year, or both.... (5)(A) Any person who knowingly releases into the ambient air any hazardous air pollutant ... and who knows at the time that he thereby places another person in imminent danger of death or serious bodily injury shall, upon conviction, by punished by a fine ... or by imprisonment of not more than 15 years, or both....

(e) Penalty assessment criteria. (1) In determining the amount of any penalty to be assessed under this section ... [EPA] or the court, as appropriate, shall take into consideration (in addition to such other factors as justice may require) the size of the business, the economic impact of the penalty on the business, the violator's full compliance history and good faith efforts to comply, the duration of the violation ..., the economic benefit of noncompliance, and the seriousness of the violation....

Clean Water Act § 309 (33 U.S.C. § 1319)

(a)(1)–(3) Whenever ... [EPA] finds that any person is in violation of any condition or limitation [of specified CWA provisions], [EPA] shall ... notify the person in alleged violation and such State of such finding [or] [EPA] shall issue an order requiring such person to comply with such section or requirement, or [EPA] shall bring a civil action....

(c) Criminal penalties. (1) Any person who—(A) negligently violates [specified CWA sections] shall be punished by a fine of not less than $2,500 nor more than $25,000 per day of violation, or by imprisonment for not more than 1 year, or by both.... (2) Any person who—(A) knowingly violates [specified CWA sections] or any permit condition or limitation ... shall be punished by a fine of not less than $5,000 nor more than $50,000 per day of violation, or by imprisonment for not more than 3 years, or by both.... (3)(A) Any person who knowingly violates [specified CWA sections] and who knows at that time that he thereby places another person in imminent danger of death or serious bodily injury, shall, upon conviction, be subject to a fine of not more than $250,000 or imprisonment of not more than 15 years, or both....

(g) Administrative penalties. (1) Whenever [EPA] finds that any person has violated [specified CWA sections], [EPA] ... may ... assess a class I civil penalty [not to exceed $25,000] or a class II civil penalty [not to exceed $125,000].... (3) In determining the amount of any penalty assessed under this subsection, [EPA] shall take into account the nature, circumstances, extent and gravity of the violation, or violations, and with respect to the violator, ability to pay, any prior history of such violations, the degree of culpability, economic benefits or savings (if any) resulting from the violation, and such other matters as justice may require....

Resource Conservation and Recovery Act (RCRA)

RCRA § 3008 (42 U.S.C. § 6928). (a)(1) [W]henever on the basis of any information [EPA] determines that any person has violated or is in violation of any requirement [concerning the handling of hazardous waste], [EPA] may issue an order assessing a civil penalty for any past or current violation, requiring compliance immediately or within a specified time period, or both, or [EPA] may commence a civil action in the United States district court ... for appropriate relief, including a temporary or permanent injunction....

(e) Knowing endangerment. Any person who knowingly transports, treats, stores, disposes of, or exports any hazardous waste ... in violation of [paragraph (d)] who knows at that time that he thereby places another person in imminent danger of death or serious bodily injury, shall, upon conviction, be subject to a fine of not more than $250,000 or imprisonment for not more than fifteen years, or both....

RCRA § 7003 (42 U.S.C. § 6973). (a) Notwithstanding any other provision of this chapter, upon receipt of evidence that the past or present handling, storage, transportation or disposal of any solid waste or hazardous waste may present an imminent and substantial endangerment to health or the environment, [EPA] may bring suit on behalf of the United States in the appropriate district court.... [EPA] may also, after notice to the affected State, take other action under this section, including, but not limited to, issuing such orders as may be necessary to protect public health and the environment.

Comprehensive Environmental Response, Compensation, and Liability Act (CERCLA)

CERCLA § 106 (42 U.S.C. § 9606). (a) In addition to any other action taken by a State or local government, when [EPA] determines that there may be an imminent and substantial endangerment to the public health or welfare or the environment because of an actual or threatened release of a hazardous substance from a facility, [EPA] may require [DOJ] to secure such relief as may be necessary to abate such danger or threat.... [EPA] may also, after notice to the affected State, take other action ... including, but not limited to, issuing such orders as may be necessary to protect public health and welfare and the environment.

CERCLA § 107 (42 U.S.C. § 9607). (c)(3) If any person who is liable for a release or threat of release of a hazardous substance fails without sufficient cause to properly provide removal or remedial action upon order of [EPA] ..., such person may be liable to the United States for punitive damages in an amount at least equal to, and not more than three times, the amount of any costs incurred by [EPA] as a result of such failure to take proper action....

Oil Pollution Act [Clean Water Act § 311] (33 U.S.C § 1321)

(e) In addition to any action taken by a State or local government, when [EPA or the Coast Guard] determines that there may be an imminent and substantial threat to the public health or welfare of the United States, including fish, shellfish, and wildlife, public and private property, ... because of an actual or threatened discharge of oil ... from a vessel or facility, [EPA or the Coast Guard] may—(A) require the Attorney General to secure any relief from any person ...; or (B) after notice to the affected State, take any other action under this section, including issuing administrative orders, that may be necessary to protect the public health and welfare.

Federal Insecticide, Fungicide, and Rodenticide Act (FIFRA)

§ 13 (7 U.S.C. § 136k). (a) Stop sale orders. Whenever any pesticide or device is found by [EPA] ... in any State and there is reason to believe on the basis of inspection or tests that such pesticide or device is in violation of any of the provisions of this subchapter, ... [EPA] may issue a written or printed "stop sale, use, or removal" order to any person who owns, controls, or has custody of such pesticide or device....

§ 14 (7 U.S.C. § 136*l*). (a) Civil penalties. (1) Any registrant, commercial applicator, wholesaler, dealer ... or other distributor [of pesticides] who violates any provision of this subchapter may be assessed a civil penalty by [EPA] of not more than $5,000 for each offense. (2) Any private applicator ... who knowingly violates any provision of this subchapter subsequent to receiving a written warning from [EPA] ... may be assessed a civil penalty ... of not more than $1,000 for each offense....

(b) Criminal penalties. (1)(A) Any registrant ... or producer [of pesticides] who knowingly violates any provision of this subchapter shall be fined not more than $50,000 or imprisoned for not more than 1 year, or both ... (B) Any commercial applicator of a restricted use pesticide ... who knowingly violates any provision of this subchapter shall be fined not more than $25,000 or imprisoned for not more than 1 year, or both. (2) Any private applicator ... who knowingly violates any provision of this subchapter shall be fined not more than $1,000 or imprisoned for not more than 30 days, or both.

Toxic Substances Control Act § 16 (15 U.S.C. § 2615)

(a) Civil. (1) Any person who violates [select provisions of TSCA] shall be liable to the United States for a civil penalty in an amount not to exceed $37,500 for each such violation. Each day such a violation continues shall ... constitute a separate violation....

(b) Criminal. (1) Any person who knowingly or willfully violates any [select provision of TSCA] shall ... be subject, upon conviction, to a fine of not more than $50,000 for each day of violation, or to imprisonment for not more than one year, or both. (2) Any person who knowingly and willfully violates any [select provisions of TSCA] and who knows at the time of the violation that the violation places an individual in imminent danger of death or serious bodily injury, shall be subject on conviction to a fine of not more than $250,000, or imprisonment for not more than 15 years, or both.

Safe Drinking Water Act § 1414 (42 U.S.C. § 300g-3)

(a)(1)(A) Whenever [EPA] finds ... that any public water system ... does not comply with any national primary drinking water regulation in effect ... [EPA] shall so notify the State and such public water system and provide such advice and technical assistance to such State and public water system as may be appropriate to bring the system into compliance with such regulation or requirement by the earliest feasible time.

(a)(1)(B) If, beyond the thirtieth day after [EPA's] notification ..., the State has not commenced appropriate enforcement action, [EPA] shall issue an order ... requiring the public water system to comply with such regulation or requirement or [EPA] shall commence a civil action...

Notes and Questions

1. Notice of violation. The Notice of Violation (NOV)—also known as a Notice of Noncompliance and other terms—is to an environmental violator as a warning from a traffic cop might be to a speeding driver: there is a message delivered, but no penalty to pay. How could this kind of agency action help address concerns for environmental justice? Does this minimal action just let violators continue to violate? As one response to this question, consider that enforcement agencies almost never have sufficient resources to fully investigate and prosecute every environmental violation that comes to their attention. An NOV offers an efficient way of drawing attention to a problem and giving the violator an opportunity to fix it. It also documents the existence of a violation, which may figure into a future penalty calculation considering a history of noncompliance. Is the issuance of an NOV always required before further agency enforcement action? Compare Clean Air Act § 113(a)(1) with Clean Water Act § 309(a)(1)–(3). What do you find? Also consider the NOV provisions of FIFRA § 14(a)(2) and Safe Drinking Water Act § 1414(a)(1). What policy choices do you see in these unique provisions?

2. Administrative orders. As noted above, most federal environmental statutes authorize EPA or other agencies to issue orders requiring immediate compliance with specific environmental requirements. What are the differences between an administrative order and injunctive relief available through a court? Which one is likely to provide a quicker response to environmental problems? An administrative order is not necessarily "self-enforcing;" that is, if the recipient of an order chose to disobey it, the agency may have to go to court to compel compliance with it. So why wouldn't the recipient of an administrative order simply ignore it and wait to see if the agency does go to court to enforce it? In answering this question, look closely at CERCLA § 107(c)(3). Do you see why now?

In practice, few recipients of administrative orders simply choose to ignore them. For example, in January 2011, when EPA discovered crude oil leaking from the head of the Trans-Alaska Pipeline near Prudhoe Bay, EPA issued an administrative order within 24 hours under the Oil Pollution Act [Clean Water Act § 311], requiring the pipeline company to fix the problem. Rather than spend time and money fighting the order, the pipeline company chose to comply with the order and had the leak repaired within a week. U.S. EPA Region 10, In the Matter Of: Trans-Alaska Pipeline System, Pump Station 1, Prudhoe Bay, Deadhorse, Alaska, Docket No. CWA-10-2011-0035, Unilateral Administrative Order for Removal Activities, Jan. 11, 2011.

In the relatively rare case where the recipient of an administrative order refuses to comply with it, the order may usually be enforced by the issuing agency and also by concerned citizens. *See, e.g.*, CERCLA § 310(a)(1) (authorizing citizen suits "against any person ... who is alleged to be in violation of any ... order which has become effective pursuant to this chapter"). In one epic saga, an EPA order against a Canadian mining company under CERCLA § 106 became the subject of a citizen suit filed by an affected tribe in 2004. For backstory on the case, *see* Michael Robinson-Dorn, *The Trail Smelter: Is What's Past Prologue? EPA Blazes a New Trail for CERCLA*, 14 N.Y.U. Envtl. L.J. 233 (2006). For a later development after 15 years of litigation, *see Pakootas v. Teck Cominco Metals, Ltd.*, 905 F.3d 565 (9th Cir. 2018) (affirming award of attorney fees to Tribe for prevailing in their action).

3. Penalty calculations. Recall the early concern about lower penalty assessments in minority communities. Is there a necessary connection between the level of penalties and the level of environmental protection in a community? Look again at some of the statutory factors for calculating penalties, including gravity of the harm, ability to pay, and "such other matters as justice may require." How would you balance these factors in a case like the drinking water contamination in Flint, Michigan (see discussions in Chapters 3–4), where actions by a municipality on the brink of bankruptcy contributed to the gravest of harms to human health? For efficiency and consistency, EPA and states often use written penalty policies to determine proposed penalties. *See, e.g.*, EPA, RCRA Civil Penalty Policy, June 2003; EPA, Public Water System Supervision Program Settlement Penalty Policy for Civil Judicial Actions and Administrative Complaints for Penalties, May 25, 1994. Nevertheless, consistent with the concept of enforcement discretion, much flexibility may go into any penalty calculation—creating opportunities for pursuing "justice," however agency staff may choose to define it.

4. Penalty adjustments. While the basic structures of the federal environmental statutes have not changed for decades, the maximum penalty amounts specified in the individual statutes have been adjusted over time to reflect inflation, consistent with federal law. Federal Civil Penalties Inflation Adjustment Act, 28 U.S.C. § 2461 note, Pub. L. 114-74 (2015). For example, the maximum penalty of $5,000 per violation specified in FIFRA § 14 became a maximum penalty of $24,255 per violation in 2023. Similarly, the $25,000 maximum penalty per day under Clean Air Act § 113(b) became a maximum penalty per day of $57,617 in 2023. EPA, Civil Monetary Penalty Inflation Adjustments, 88 Fed. Reg. 89312 (Dec. 27, 2023). How do these adjustments reflect the purposes of environmental enforcement and opportunities for pursuing environmental justice?

5. Criminal prosecution. Look again at the maximum criminal penalties in the environmental statutes excerpted above. Did you know that people can go to jail for breaking environmental laws? How could the threat of imprisonment contribute to achieving environmental justice in minority or low-income communities?

In one egregious case leading to criminal prosecution, the owner of a fertilizer company near Soda Springs, Idaho, ordered four workers to enter a large, 25,000-gallon tank to clean out sludge from the bottom of the tank. On this hot summer day in 1996, the workers entered the tank through a 22-inch manhole at the top and reported experiencing sore throats and other health effects from the air inside. The owner, Allen Elias, failed to provide the workers with any safety equipment or training, and ordered the workers to continue their work. The next day, one of those workers, Scott Dominguez, collapsed inside the tank. The fire department had to cut a hole in the tank to reach Dominguez and rush him to the hospital. Elias denied knowledge of any toxic materials in the tank, but in fact it contained the byproduct of a cyanide leaching process that Elias had patented. Elias was later charged with a four-count indictment for RCRA violations and 18 U.S.C. § 1001 for making false statements to federal officers. Elias was convicted on all counts, which included the first federal conviction for knowing endangerment under RCRA. *U.S. v. Elias*, 269 F.3d 1003 (9th Cir. 2001). While the victim in this tragic case unfortunately suffered permanent brain injury, the conviction did send a strong signal to all other business owners and operators about the potential consequences for disregarding the value of worker lives. For the full story behind the Allen Elias case, and the criminal agents and prosecutors who pursued it, *see* Joseph Hilldorfer & Robert Dugoni, The Cyanide Canary (2004).

Less dramatically, federal, state, and local prosecutors may pursue cases that never draw public attention but may have significant potential to promote environmental justice. In one series of cases, for example, prosecutors in Oregon and Washington charged building contractors under Clean Air Act § 113(c), 42 U.S.C. § 7413(c), for violations of rules governing the safe handling of asbestos-containing materials. *See* 40 C.F.R. § 61.145 (Standards for Demolition and Renovation). By failing to provide proper safety equipment, among other things, the contractors endangered the health of demolition workers, many of whom were low-income day laborers and immigrants. *See, e.g., U.S. v. Pearson*, 274 F.3d 1225 (9th Cir. 2001) (affirming conviction and sentencing for asbestos violations during renovation project on U.S. Navy base).

In addition to charges under specific environmental statutes, criminal prosecutions often include charges under general criminal statutes, such as those prohibiting false statements (18 U.S.C. § 1001) and obstruction of justice (18 U.S.C. § 1505). Depending on the circumstances, state and local prosecutors might consider more extraordinary charges. For example, in response to the Flint drinking water contamination, prosecutors obtained indictments against at least nine state and local officials, including employees or former employees of the former Michigan Department of Environmental Quality [now Michigan Department of Environment, Great Lakes, and Energy (EGLE)]. Charges in this case included misconduct in office, willful neglect of duty, and involuntary manslaughter, recognizing the suspected link between the drinking water contamination and multiple deaths due to Legionnaire's Disease.

6. Pesticides regulation. While often overshadowed by the attention and resources dedicated to other environmental statutes, the Federal Insecticide, Fungicide, and Rodenticide Act (FIFRA) may offer powerful enforcement authorities for protecting the health of farmworkers or other community members facing disproportionate exposure to pesticides. Major requirements of FIFRA include federal registration of pesticide products and the handling and use of registered pesticide products in a prescribed manner.

Under FIFRA, the distribution of unregistered pesticides may result in "Stop Sale" orders and civil penalties. In one interesting case, EPA issued Stop Sale orders and administrative penalties against Amazon.com for the distribution of unregistered pesticides. U.S. EPA, In the Matter of: Amazon Services LLC, Consent Agreement and Final Order, Docket No. FIFRA-10-2018-0202, Feb. 14, 2018. In this administrative case, EPA alleged that Amazon had committed nearly four thousand violations of FIFRA in the previous five years. EPA alleged that many of these violations particularly endangered Asian immigrants, who were more likely to use certain unregistered pesticides and less likely to be able to read warning labels printed in English. In settlement of this case, Amazon agreed to pay penalties of $1,215,700 and conduct a "supplemental environmental project" that would provide free online education about FIFRA requirements in English, Spanish, and Mandarin.

Beyond pesticide registration, FIFRA requires the safe use and handling of pesticides as well as protection of workers who may be exposed to pesticides on farms, forests, nurseries, and other agricultural workplaces. The FIFRA Worker Protection Standard, 40 C.F.R. Part 170, aims to protect agricultural workers through such measures as personal protective equipment, posted pesticide information, worker safety training, and restricted entry to fields immediately after pesticides have been applied. Farmworkers represent the population segment most at risk from pesticides, with reported pesticide poisonings among farmworkers 25 times higher than the general population (and unreported poisonings potentially vastly higher). Requirements of the Worker Protection Standards were updated in the Biden administration particularly to enhance protection of farmworkers through measures including expanded exclusion zones after pesticide application. 89 Fed. Reg. 80767 (Oct. 4, 2024). In one recent case, EPA Region 7 filed an administrative complaint against a pesticide applicator in Lincoln, Nebraska, where evidence indicated that aerial application had resulted in pesticides landing on a neighbor's apple tree and on the neighbor's shirt worn at the time of application. The complaint was eventually settled with the respondent agreeing to pay a penalty of two thousand dollars. In the Matter of: Emrich Aerial Spraying LLC, Docket No. FIFRA-07-2022-0133 (Jan 29, 2024).

If a neighbor's aerial application of pesticides resulted in you or your family members getting sprayed by dangerous chemicals, would you find justice in your neighbor's agreement to pay a penalty of two thousand dollars? Would this penalty serve any of the purposes of environmental enforcement? Unfortunately, for purposes of environmental justice, FIFRA has been recognized as "the weakest federal environmental statute" when it comes to enforcement provisions. Michael J. McClary & Jessica B. Goldstein, *FIFRA at 40: The Need for Felonies for Pesticide Crimes*, 47 Envtl L. Rep. News & Analysis 10767, 10770 (2017). Compare the criminal provisions of FIFRA with those of the Clean Air Act, Clean Water Act, RCRA, or TSCA excerpted above. What is missing from FIFRA? Notice in particular the maximum criminal penalty for a "private applicator," which may include the owner of a large farm. Based upon the maximum jail sentence and fine provided by FIFRA, "a private applicator who knowingly violates a FIFRA requirement and causes the death or serious injury of another person, has committed [only] a 'petty offense.'" *Id.* at 10769. Are the FIFRA enforcement provisions a comment by Congress on the value of farmworker lives? Or on the power of agricultural or chemical lobbies? If FIFRA's criminal enforcement authorities remain weak, could more active use of administrative authorities enhance protections for farmworkers and other vulnerable communities?

7. Toxic substances. Like FIFRA, the Toxic Substances Control Act (TSCA) is often overshadowed and under-resourced for enforcement purposes, yet may offer significant authority for pursuing environmental justice in certain cases. In general, TSCA focuses on designated categories of toxic chemicals, which EPA may ban or restrict if they are found to pose an unreasonable risk to human health. Since 1976, when Congress passed the original legislation, TSCA has consisted mostly of a grab bag of regulatory programs addressing a handful of toxic substances. One such TSCA program concerns the use, distribution, and disposal of items containing polychlorinated biphenyls (**PCBs**). 40 C.F.R. Part 761. PCBs are often found in old transformers or other electrical equipment, posing particular risks to workers who may be engaged in building maintenance or equipment salvage activities. Another, far broader program for TSCA enforcement concerns required notices that sellers or landlords must provide to prospective home buyers or renters about the potential for lead-based paint in a given housing unit. 40 C.F.R. Part 745. Regular enforcement of the TSCA lead-paint disclosure rules may help address chronic problems with lead poisoning from older housing stock in urban areas.

In 2016, Congress amended TSCA substantially, requiring EPA, among other things, to review additional substances for potential restriction. Frank R. Lautenberg Chemical Safety Act, Pub. L. 114–182 (June 22, 2016). EPA responded to this Congressional charge in the Biden administration by establishing regulatory bans on toxics substances including **chrysotile asbestos**, which, despite possessing toxic properties known for *centuries*, was still unrestricted for import, processing, and distribution in the United States until 2024. 89 Fed. Reg. 21970 (March 28, 2024). Under "New TSCA," the Biden EPA also banned most manufacturing, processing, and distribution of trichloroethylene (TCE), an extremely toxic chemical in wide commercial use. 89 Fed. Reg. 102568 (Dec. 17, 2024).

As with the other federal statutes, most government enforcement of TSCA is administrative and results in a settlement. *See, e.g.*, U.S. EPA Region IX, In the Matter of: McNamara Realty, Consent Agreement and Final Order, Docket No. TSCA-09-2018-0007, Dec. 26, 2018 (administrative settlement requiring payment of $32,000 penalty for alleged violations of TSCA lead disclosure rules). Unlike FIFRA, TSCA has criminal provisions that include felonies such as "knowing endangerment," added by the 2016 TSCA amendments. It remains to be seen whether this enhanced enforcement authority and broader suite of regulations under New TSCA will be implemented vigorously for the benefit of potentially impacted communities.

8. Federalism. Under most federal environmental statutes, including the Clean Air Act, Clean Water Act, RCRA, FIFRA, and the Safe Drinking Water Act, states and tribes may seek and receive authorization to implement the federal program within their jurisdiction. This includes the authority to issue permits and take enforcement action for violations. All states and a growing number of tribes now have authority to implement Clean Air Act programs. Almost every state is now authorized to carry out the Clean Water Act and the Safe Drinking Water Act. State enforcement is essential to the success of most environmental programs, as states contribute enforcement resources, innovation, industry insights, and community sensitivities beyond the capability of the federal government. Environmental groups, however, worry that states are more susceptible to industry capture and that, absent federal controls, states will engage in a "race to the bottom" to attract industry by lowering environmental standards. States (like the federal government) may also become directly responsible for environmental violations in some cases, as with the drinking water contamination in Flint, Michigan.

What balance of state or federal primacy would best serve the interests of vulnerable communities such as the poor and minority communities of Flint? The State of Michigan is authorized to carry out and enforce requirements of the federal Safe Drinking Water Act. In Flint, the Michigan Department of Environmental Quality (MDEQ) clearly failed to do its job enforcing the Safe Drinking Water Act. So too did EPA Region 5, which has oversight authority in the State of Michigan. Of course, agencies can act only through the people within them. Employees within EPA Region 5 and state agencies sounded alarms when they discovered the drinking water contamination in Flint, but unfortunately, agency management failed to support staff concerns. Eventually, both the EPA Regional Administrator and the Director of MDEQ resigned under political pressure. For deeper background and insight into the dynamics (and moral failings) leading to the "Flint Water Crisis," see Clifford J. Villa, *Don't Blame the Flint River*, 52 ENVTL L. 241 (2022).

If you were senior leadership for EPA or the State of Michigan when the drinking water contamination in Flint came to light, what conflicting pressures would you expect to encounter and how might you resolve them? Is it possible that agency heads who fail in their duties to the public could become liable to injured parties?

E. Enforcement Strategies to Promote Environmental Justice

In addition to the statutory authorities discussed above, government agencies may be able to make use of various policies and administrative tools in order to pursue environmental justice through enforcement activity. Some of these policies are longstanding. In 1995, for example, as part of its initial Environmental Justice Strategy, EPA indicated that it would use its enforcement discretion to focus on environmental justice issues raised by violations in communities disproportionately harmed by environmental pollution. Soon after, EPA began to encourage use of specific enforcement authorities to achieve environmental justice. *See, e.g.*, U.S. EPA, Guidance on Use of Section 7003 of RCRA (1997) ("When prioritizing actions to be taken under Section 7003 ..., the Regions should give particular consideration to sites and facilities that pose environmental justice concerns").

Under the Obama administration, EPA refocused attention to EJ concerns through its "Plan EJ 2014" initiative. Among other things, Plan EJ 2014 established a three-year plan "to fully integrate consideration of environmental justice concerns into the planning and implementation of [enforcement] program strategies, case targeting strategies, and development of remedies in enforcement action to benefit these [overburdened] communities." EPA Office of Environmental Justice, Plan EJ 2014 at 57 (Sept. 2011). Plan EJ 2014 was superseded by EPA's EJ 2020 Action Agenda, which among other things promised to "direct[] more enforcement resources to the most overburdened communities and strengthen the role of environmental justice in EPA's compliance and enforcement work." EPA, EJ 2020 Action Agenda at 19 (Oct. 2016).

Similarly, at the outset of Biden administration, EPA made environmental justice a top priority for its enforcement programs, issuing a series of strategies in 2021:

- *Strengthening Enforcement in Communities with Environmental Justice Concerns* (April 30, 2021)
- *Strengthening Environmental Justice Through Criminal Enforcement* (June 21, 2021)
- *Strengthening Environmental Justice Through Cleanup Enforcement Action* (July 1, 2021)
- *Using All Appropriate Injunctive Relief Tools in Civil Enforcement* (April 26, 2021).

In the second Trump administration, one may expect less emphasis on enforcement actions to promote environmental justice. However, recall that most environmental enforcement in the United States is actually done by states, tribes, territories, and local government. Accordingly, enforcement actions by state agencies and other bodies may provide substantial opportunities to help address environmental injustice, with or without leadership on the federal level. In 2023, for example, the Maryland Department of the Environment, in coordination with the Environmental Crimes Unit of the Maryland Attorney General's Office, secured a $1.7 million criminal fine against a biomedical waste incinerator operating in Baltimore City. The incinerator facility, operating in the Curtis Bay neighborhood with some 59 percent people of color, had been charged with forty criminal counts including improper handling of medical waste and concealment of an unpermitted discharge outlet. *State of Maryland v. Curtis Bay Energy, LP* (May 23, 2023) (plea agreement).

Maryland's successful conclusion of the Curtis Bay investigation reflected a state policy "to implement environmental laws and programs wherever possible in a manner that reduces existing inequities and avoids the creation of additional inequities in communities with EJ concerns." Maryland Dept. of the Environment, *Environmental Justice Policy and Implementation Plan* (Nov. 1, 2022). Of course, while such policies may be embraced by EJ advocates, they remain far from legal mandates. As researchers have observed:

> An ineffective agency policy would not be a shocking thing. After all, we can all imagine situations where policies are declared simply to take a stance on an issue or recognize the plight of a particular demographic group without actually addressing the problem. In our research, we have found that policies on environmental justice, generally, are more effective at recognizing the plight of minority and low-income communities in regards to adverse environmental conditions than they are at actually addressing the problem. By creating a policy on environmental justice, a state's policymakers not only publicly recognize the plight of traditionally disempowered groups, but affirmatively take a stance

> on the side of protecting these communities. The provisions of environmental justice policies are most often incapable of actually addressing the problem at hand, essentially making these policies more symbolic than authentic.

Tonya Lewis & Jessica Owley, *Symbolic Politics for Disempowered Communities: State Environmental Justice Policies*, 29 BYU J. Pub. L. 183, 186 (2014).

So, beyond symbolism, do agency policies on EJ and enforcement offer any real potential for environmental improvements in underserved communities? This concluding section of the chapter will examine three authentic and demonstrated opportunities for pursuing environmental justice goals through enforcement policies: (1) enforcement targeting, (2) equitable remedies, and (3) supplemental environmental projects.

1. Enforcement Targeting

Enforcement targeting involves how an agency should direct its limited enforcement resources, including field inspectors, legal counsel, travel budget, and laboratory support. Flowing from the concept of enforcement discretion, enforcement agencies have substantial flexibility to determine where and what kind of enforcement actions to bring in response to environmental violations. To address concerns for environmental justice, should agencies devote more enforcement resources to industries with higher rates of regulatory violation? Or to communities where there is a higher share of polluting facilities? Or to communities with higher proportions of minority or low-income residents? Or to communities with higher proportions of adverse health impacts?

In order to answer any of these questions, agencies need access to ready and reliable data, including the locations of polluting facilities, the presence of minority populations, and the incidence of adverse health impacts. While all of this data may exist, it may be spread across myriad databases controlled by disparate agencies and organizations. A continual challenge has been the integration of such information to allow enforcement personnel—and concerned community members—to prioritize local areas or facilities for possible enforcement action. Toward that end, EPA and regulatory agencies of many states, including California, Illinois, Maryland, Massachusetts, Michigan, New York, and Washington, have worked to develop a series of tools using Geographic Information System (GIS) technology. Over time, these GIS tools have carried different names, added more GIS layers, and become easier for both government personnel and community members to use. EPA's main GIS tool for this purpose is known as **EJSCREEN**. After being removed from the EPA website in February 2025, EJSCREEN remains preserved by external websites, including the companion website for this book: www.environmentaljusticebook.org (see "GIS Tools").

As described by EPA:

> EJScreen is an environmental justice mapping and screening tool that provides EPA with a national consistent dataset and approach for combining environmental and demographic indicators. EJScreen users choose a geo-

> graphic area; the tool then provides demographic and environmental information for that area. All of the EJScreen indicators are publicly available data. EJScreen simply provides a way to display this information and includes a method for combining environmental and socioeconomic indicators into EJ indexes.
>
> Environmental indicators incorporated in EJSCREEN include data on local traffic; toxic air pollutants; proximity to hazardous waste facilities and designated Superfund sites; and older housing stock (indicating potential for lead-based paint). Socioeconomic indicators include population data on "people of color, "low income," "limited English speaking," and "over age 64." More recent data sets provide information on climate risks, such as risks of fire, flood, or extreme heat, and information on health disparities, such as asthma, cancer, and low-life expectancy....

Using these GIS tools, inspectors may be able to identify areas for targeted inspections in order to protect vulnerable communities. Where environmental violations are suspected or identified by any means, enforcement personnel can gather information quickly about potentially impacted communities in order to help the agency decide whether to take enforcement action and what kind of action might be most appropriate to protect the community. Within EPA, information from EJSCREEN may also help convince the U.S. Department of Justice or a local prosecutor's office to accept an enforcement case for civil litigation or criminal prosecution. At the same time, concerned citizens can use GIS tools to identify vulnerable communities, suggest facilities for inspection and enforcement, and potentially focus their own resources for citizen litigation (discussed in Chapter 12).

Notes and Questions

1. **Return to Richfield.** Consider the scenario suggested earlier in this chapter, where a pile of leaking drums is discovered in a vacant lot in Richfield, Minnesota. Using EJSCREEN, what can you learn now about potential impacts to vulnerable populations in Richfield? What additional information would you like to know about the location of the drums before making any enforcement recommendation?

2. **Other targeting tools.** Besides EJSCREEN, what other tools may be available to government agencies or the general public for use in identifying violations and prioritizing areas for enforcement action? Government agencies may have access to law enforcement databases not generally available to the public. But many other enforcement resources are publicly available, including the EPA's Enforcement and Compliance History Online (ECHO) database, available at https://echo.epa.gov/. Through ECHO, members of the public may search the compliance and enforcement history of regulated facilities across the country. Of course, government enforcers also use many of the same online tools available today to anyone with Internet access. How might you use a program such as Google Earth (https://www.google.com/earth/) for identifying potential environmental concerns in your community?

2. Equitable Remedies

Recalling the three broad purposes of environmental enforcement discussed earlier in this chapter, we can see that administrative, civil, or criminal fines may contribute to the purposes of deterring future violations and creating a "level playing field" for regulated parties. But for members of overburdened communities, the most important objective may be the first purpose of enforcement: "fix the problem." In many cases, violators may correct problems promptly and voluntarily upon discovery through a facility inspection or a written Notice of Violation. In other cases, however, regulatory agencies may need to take affirmative measures to compel violators to comply with environmental requirements. Authority to require such measures may be provided expressly to regulatory agencies through applicable legislation or may reside inherently in judicial powers to fashion equitable remedies. But what is the breadth of a court's equitable powers? Can courts use equitable powers to require a violator to go beyond a return to compliance and provide for mitigation of past harms? For an examination of equitable powers in the context of the federal Clean Air Act and Clean Water Act, the two statutes most commonly enforced by federal agencies, consider the following excerpt.

Sara A. Colangelo, *Forging Complete Justice: Equitable Relief in Environmental Enforcement*

46 Harvard Envtl. L. Rev. 315 (2022)

The principles of equity and its historical roots are likely known to most readers. A few foundational aspects and maxims of equity are summarized here to provide an analytical grounding for the argument that a court may award mitigation as a form of equitable relief. Article III of the U.S. Constitution grants federal judicial power to "all Cases, in Law and Equity, arising under this Constitution, [and] the Laws of the United States." As summarized by the Federal Judicial Center:

> Equity was a centuries-old system of English jurisprudence in which judges based decisions on general principles of fairness in situations where rigid application of common-law rules would have brought about injustice. Judges exercised equitable jurisdiction based on a distinct set of procedures and remedies....

In their earliest years, some states "followed the English tradition of maintaining separate courts for law and equity" and others provided courts with both types of jurisdiction.

In the Process Act of 1792, Congress directed that the Supreme Court should supply rules for equity procedure and that cases should be governed "according to the principles, rules and usages which belong to courts of equity." Courts were to look to the English Court of Chancery for such principles and rules. In the mid-nineteenth century, some states began dissolving the formal divide between courts of equity jurisdiction and common law. The 1938 Federal Rules of Civil Procedure codified this evolution. The rules formally combined both equity and law into a single type of case: a civil action.

Today, both federal and state courts still intone several foundational principles when analyzing requests for equitable relief. A primary maxim is that equity will be invoked when there is no adequate remedy at law. Other principles focus on the preservation of the *status quo* or return to the *status quo ante*—the condition prior to the illicit conduct. And others emphasize that "it would be inequitable that [a wrongdoer] should make a profit out of his own wrong."

What, then, is an equitable remedy? In his anthology of the evolution of remedies as a legal field, Professor Douglas Laycock describes the modern vision of a remedy as "what the court will do to correct or prevent the violation of legal rights that gives rise to liability." Thus, when a court sits in equity, "equitable remedies usually contain a coercive or injunctive element." They force the defendant to either do something or to stop doing something....

Courts possess the equitable authority to order mitigation in a CAA or CWA enforcement matter once a violation that caused harm is established. The analyses in *Porter v. Warner Holding Co.* and *Mitchell v. Robert De Mario Jewelry, Inc.*, non-environmental enforcement cases, shed light on the CAA and CWA because they interpret similar language. They confirm that the language of the CAA and CWA invokes the full equitable discretion of district courts with their authorization to restrain violations, require compliance, and award any other appropriate relief. Further, a district court's inherent discretion, at its height when the public interest is involved, is curtailed neither by a "clear ... command" nor an "inescapable inference" from Congress in the Acts. Awarding mitigation also furthers the purposes of both Acts....

The CAA stationary source provisions grant district courts "jurisdiction to restrain [a] violation [of the CAA], to require compliance, to assess [a] civil penalty, to collect any fees owed the United States ... and award any other appropriate relief." Under the CWA, the United States may seek "appropriate relief" and district courts are empowered to "restrain such violation and to require compliance. As the Ninth Circuit in *United States v. Holtzman* explained, "most cases interpreting statutes with similar jurisdictional grants have interpreted *the power to restrain as including the power to enjoin*." Under the background law described below, these grants of jurisdiction to district courts invoke the full scope of their inherent equitable authority to order restorative injunctive relief....

The Supreme Court's decisions in *Porter v. Warner Holding Co.* and *Mitchell v. Robert De Mario Jewelry, Inc.* supply the framework for this analysis. In *Porter*, the Court examined whether section 205(a) of the Emergency Price Control Act of 1942 authorized a district court to order restitution of rents collected in excess of statutory maximums. While the statute did not expressly list restitution, it authorized several types of remedies, including ones in equity: the Administrator of the Office of Price Administration is authorized to seek a "permanent or temporary injunction, restraining order, or other order."

In *Porter*, the Court held that when Congress invokes the equity jurisdiction of courts in a statute, "all the inherent equitable powers of the [courts] are available." Only by a "clear and valid legislative command" or "necessary and inescapable inference" does Congress restrict the "complete exercise of that jurisdiction." Restitution was thus authorized under the Emergency Price Control Act because section 205(a) invoked a court's equity jurisdiction and nothing in the statute precluded the award of such equitable relief. The Court added that because the public interest was involved, the courts' "equitable powers assume[d] an even broader and more flexible character than when only a private controversy is at stake."

... As evidenced by the Court's holding in *Mitchell*, however, such broad statutory language is not required to invoke equitable authority. This time, the Court interpreted language empowering district courts to "restrain violations." In *Mitchell*, the Court held that the Fair Labor Standards Act ("FLSA") authorized courts to award reimbursement of lost wages caused by discharges in violation of the Act. The FLSA provided "jurisdiction ... for cause shown, to restrain violations" of the Act. The Court again rejected the argument that Congress must expressly or impliedly grant equitable authority. It confirmed that "[u]nless otherwise provided by statute, all the inherent equitable powers for the District Court are available for the proper and complete exercise of that jurisdiction."

... The language of the CAA and CWA invokes a district court's equitable authority without limitation. When a court sits in equity, it possesses authority to order "categories of relief that were typically available in equity." That authority includes the ability to enjoin otherwise lawful conduct or to order an equitable adjunct to address past harm from statutory violations. Neither Act contains limitations on this authority. Instead, the authorizing language is unmistakably broad and multiple confirm it to invoke such jurisdiction.

Section 13(b) of the CAA invokes a district court's inherent equitable authority with three phrases. An order for mitigation is appropriate under the language authorizing courts to "restrain" a "violation," "require compliance," or order "any other appropriate relief." The phrase "award any other appropriate relief" is broad, and the word "any" suggests an expansive meaning. Indeed, when the Supreme Court analyzed the words "any other final action" in a different section of the CAA, it emphasized that in the absence of contradictory legislative history, "any" meant exactly what it said, "namely, *any* other final action." ...

The CWA similarly authorizes the United States to seek "appropriate relief" and courts to "restrain such violation and to require compliance." Many courts affirm the authority of courts to order restorative relief in CWA enforcement cases from permit violations to wetlands restoration, and by both governmental and private enforcers.... For example, in a citizen suit arising in the District of Maine, the court ordered defendants to remediate the pollution illegally discharged prior to their application for a permit. The First Circuit affirmed the district court's authority to order injunctive relief in the form of permit limitations that were more stringent than those mandated by the state permit obtained during the pendency of the suit:

> [T]he court may grant additional injunctive relief governing the post-permit operations of the companies insofar as the court is remedying harm caused by their past violations ... Conventionally, a court's equitable power to enforce a statute includes the power to provide remedies for past violations—an area in which the courts have settled authority and competence....

Courts have also determined that they could order a defendant to pay into a remedial fund to redress harm from their illicit pollution. Indeed, the Volkswagen settlement contained this type of "mitigation trust."

Notes and Questions

1. The *Volkswagen* settlement. In 2015, information came to light that Volkswagen, then the largest automobile manufacturer in the world, had been installing "defeat devices" in their diesel vehicles for many years in order to falsify emissions ratings, in violation of the Clean Air Act. Civil and criminal investigations by EPA and DOJ that followed resulted in penalties and other relief exceeding 20 billion dollars, the most in the history of CAA enforcement. For background on this extraordinary case, *see* John C. Cruden et al., *Dieselgate: How the Investigation, Prosecution, and Settlement of Volkswagen's Emissions Cheating Scandal Illustrates the Need for Robust Environmental Enforcement*, 36 Virginia Envtl. L.J. 118 (2018).

As noted in the Colangelo excerpt above, the *Volkswagen* settlement included establishment of a "mitigation trust." With initial funding of $2.7 billion, the mitigation trust would allow beneficiaries, including states and federally recognized tribes, to fund projects to reduce nitrous oxides emissions, mitigating the environmental impacts from Volkswagen's emissions cheating. Eligible projects could include charging stations for electric vehicles; electrifying heavy-duty vehicles, school buses, forklifts, and other cargo handling equipment; and providing connections to shore power for ocean-going vessels in port. The net effect of such measures might help significantly improve air quality in communities around ports, freeways, distribution centers, and other areas frequently impacted by environmental injustice. For more on potential benefits of the Volkswagen mitigation trust, see Gina Allery, *The Volkswagen Settlement: An Opportunity for Tribes to Mitigate Nitrous Oxide Emissions in Indian Country*, 64 Fed. Lawyer 12 (2017).

2. Restitution vs. mitigation. In the excerpt, Colangelo emphasizes mitigation as an equitable remedy available to address violations of the Clean Air Act and Clean Water Act. How does mitigation relate to the equitable remedies of restitution or disgorgement? If restitution is available for resolution of criminal prosecution under the Clean Air Act or Clean Water Act, is it also available for resolution of civil actions under these statutes? Why or why not?

3. Mitigation and RCRA. While the Colangelo article focuses on under the Clean Air Act and Clean Water Act, it acknowledges that mitigation may not be broadly available under all environmental statutes, including RCRA. In 1996, the U.S. Supreme Court held that a private party, bringing an action under the citizen suit provisions of RCRA, cannot recover cleanup costs for wholly past violations of RCRA that no longer pose an imminent and substantial danger of public health or the environment. *Meghrig v. KFC Western, Inc.*, 516 U.S. 479 (1996). The decision is significant, among other reasons, because neither citizens nor the government may sue under CERCLA for cleanup of petroleum contamination due to CERCLA's "petroleum exclusion" (see Chapter 8). How might community advocates faced with petroleum contamination from a neighborhood gas station address this potential gap in federal regulation?

4. Mitigation policies. The "2012 EPA Mitigation Memo" issued during the Obama administration "strongly encourage[d] case teams to seek mitigation, where appropriate, as a component of the injunctive relief they seek in civil judicial enforcement cases." The memo defined "mitigation" as "injunctive relief sought by the government to remedy, reduce, or offset past (and in some cases ongoing) harm caused by the alleged violations in a particular case. It also provided examples, to include—

- Cleaning up illegally emitted or discharged pollutants from the environmental media affected by the violation; [and]
- Limiting the amount of future pollutants emitted (more stringently than legal limits) to address past excesses.

Enforcement emphasis diminished in the first Trump administration but returned with the Biden administration. In 2021, EPA issued a new memo, *Using All Appropriate Injunctive Relief Tools in Civil Enforcement Settlements* (April 26, 2021). The 2021 memo provided that, "Through enforcement . . . , we strive not only to return facilities to compliance but also to tailor the relief to address the underlying causes of the violations to prevent reoccurrence and, in appropriate cases, mitigate the harm to the communities impacted by noncompliance." The 2021 memo further expanded upon the definition of "mitigation," clarifying that mitigation "is not focused on preventing future violations and does not require proof that a defendant is currently violating the law. Rather, mitigation is intended to redress harm from ongoing and past violations."

In the second Trump administration, environmental enforcement may once again diminish at the federal level. However, mitigation should remain an available equitable remedy for pursuing environmental justice in appropriate circumstances.

5. Mitigation and East Palestine. As noted in the Introduction, the East Palestine train derailment required a billion-dollar cleanup under EPA oversight, but also resulted in a settlement providing for potentially groundbreaking mitigation to address some (but not all) harms and to prevent future rail accidents.

As described by DOJ, "The proposed Consent Decree incorporates (making enforceable) and enhances certain rail safety measures undertaken by Norfolk Southern following the derailment." Memorandum in Support of United States of America's Motion to Enter Consent Decree, Civil Case No. 23-cv-517, Oct. 10, 2024. Such rail safety measures included more detectors and more frequent monitoring on major routes to identify overheated wheel bearings, improved procedures for emergency coordination, specific training requirements in the Incident Command System (discussed in Chapter 15), and new rules for building long trains. *Id.*

Mitigation measures also included the creation of a $25 million dollar Community Health Fund to provide for medical monitoring and mental health services for qualified residents and responders, for up to 20 years. In support of these measures, and consistent with the analysis of Professor Colangelo above, DOJ observed that the Clean Water Act enforcement provisions "allow for expansive injunctive relief." But DOJ also acknowledged that the scope of this potential relief was not unlimited, observing, "The stated objective of the CWA, however, is to 'restore and maintain the chemical, physical, and biological integrity of the Nation's waters.'" *Id.* at 23. DOJ continued:

> To date, the United States has not sought healthcare services under these provisions to the extent requested by some commenters and therefore no court has yet granted such relief. The CWA is not a personal injury statute and Sections 309 and 311 do not explicitly provide for individualized, personal-injury type remedies.... When negotiating the Consent Decree, the United States considered the litigation risk in establishing that healthcare is appropriate relief for the alleged CWA violations ... and recognized the potential challenges in obtaining an order requiring Norfolk Southern to provide more extensive healthcare services given the facts of this case.... *Id.* at 24.

Compared to the Clean Water Act, DOJ recognized that CERCLA has broader objectives for protecting "the public health or welfare." However, DOJ also noted that "provision of individual healthcare is not a specifically identified statutory goal" of CERCLA, suggesting that injunctive relief available under CERCLA is not unbounded.

Addressing broader public concerns for personal injuries and losses as a result of the East Palestine train derailment, DOJ noted a "recent $600 million class action settlement, which has been widely accepted among potential class members," as well as claims that continued to be pursued by the State of Ohio. *Id.* at 26.

3. Supplemental Environmental Projects

As noted previously, penalties collected for environmental violations typically go into the U.S. Treasury or a state's general fund, not to individuals impacted by the violation. As an alternative, EPA and state policies for **supplemental environmental projects (SEPs)** allow violators to reduce penalties in exchange for undertaking environmentally beneficial projects such as projects to prevent or reduce pollution from ongoing operations, or projects to remedy harms caused by a violation. Such projects can include wetlands restoration, establishment of health clinics, additional air monitoring, reduction of emissions beyond required levels, and so forth.

For communities impacted by environmental violations, SEPs can bring substantial resources toward restorative justice, on the scale of hundreds of thousands or even millions of dollars. There are many inspiring stories of success with SEPs across the country. However, to date, SEPs have not been used as broadly and effectively as they might be to achieve EJ goals in underserved communities. On the federal level, support for SEPs—and enforcement generally—has waxed and waned with changes in administration. Beyond politics, obstacles to greater use of SEPs include legal requirements, technical challenges, public information deficits, and lack of transparency in the enforcement process. Such obstacles and also opportunities for greater use of SEPs are explored in the following article.

Patrice L. Simms, *Leveraging Supplemental Environmental Projects: Toward an Integrated Strategy for Empowering Environmental Justice Communities*

47 Envtl. Law Rep. News & Analysis 10511 (2017)

... II. The Unrealized Potential of SEPs

State and federal environmental enforcement authorities initiate thousands of actions each year in the United States. Environmental enforcement, as a result, is one of the most influential activities when it comes to polluter behavior. And the vast majority of these cases end in settlement agreements, which not only assess penalties but also specify injunctive relief (such as the installation of emission control technology), and often direct violators to undertake remedial steps to address the impacts of their noncompliance (by, for example, performing environmental cleanups). Under the right conditions, the potential for local benefits from such environmental enforcement actions is considerable. Whether this happens or not can be influenced by the degree to which affected communities themselves are involved in selecting the violators' remedial obligations.

While in most cases local communities will not be in a position to directly participate in settlement proceedings in a meaningful way—except where local groups are actually *parties* to the enforcement action—SEPs may offer a tool for such groups, by proxy, to play a significant role. In order to empower local communities in this manner, two things will be necessary: (1) the proper policy architecture to provide communities with access to the settlement process, and (2) access to legal and technical expertise to develop locally valuable off-the-shelf SEPs. For this to happen, states, NGOs, academic institutions, and federal enforcement authorities, with meaningful support from the funding community, will need to cooperate to build an effective and sustainable model for engagement.

A. Understanding SEPs: A Basic Primer

SEPs are enforcement-related tools through which defendants in environmental enforcement cases can mitigate monetary penalties by agreeing to undertake environmentally beneficial projects that they would not otherwise be obligated to perform. As EPA explains in its SEP policy guidance document:

> SEPs are projects or activities that go beyond what could legally be required in order for the defendant to return to compliance, and secure environmental and/or public health benefits in addition to those achieved by compliance with applicable laws.... The primary purpose of [EPA's] SEP Policy is to encourage and obtain environmental and public health protection and benefits that may not otherwise have occurred in the settlement of an enforcement action.

EPA further explains, "[a] primary incentive for a defendant to propose a SEP is the potential mitigation of its civil penalty." That is, a defendant who voluntarily elects to undertake a qualifying SEP may end up paying a lower enforcement-related monetary penalty.

> Settlements that include a SEP must always include a settlement penalty that [in the aggregate] recoups the economic benefit a violator gained from non-compliance with the law, as well as an appropriate gravity-based penalty reflecting the environmental and regulatory harm caused by the violation(s).... [A] violator's commitment to perform a SEP is a relevant factor for the EPA to consider in establishing an appropriate settlement penalty.

Thus, when a defendant elects to undertake a SEP, EPA may rely on that fact as a mitigating circumstance to impose a lower final monetary penalty.

At least in the federal context, there are significant limitations imposed on the availability of SEPs, which constrain the extent to which federal agencies can rely on them. As EPA explains:

> To include a proposed project in a settlement as a SEP, Agency enforcement and compliance personnel should—
>
> 1. Ensure that the project conforms to the basic definition of a SEP ...;
> 2. Ensure that all legal guidelines are satisfied ...;
> 3. Ensure that the project fits within one (or more) of the designated categories of SEPs ...;
> 4. Determine the appropriate amount of penalty mitigation to reflect the project's environmental and/or public health benefits using the evaluation criteria ...; and
> 5. Ensure that the project satisfies all of the EPA procedures, settlement requirements and other criteria.

Additionally, SEPs cannot involve activities that defendant entities would otherwise be legally required to perform. And SEPs must involve projects that have some nexus to the violation that gave rise to the enforcement action. In this regard, "[p]rojects must relate to the underlying violation(s) at issue in the enforcement action." That is, they must be designed to reduce:

> a) Likelihood that similar violations will occur in the future;

> b) The adverse impact to public health and/or the environment to which the violation at issue contributes; or
>
> c) The overall risk to public health and/or the environment potentially affected by the violation at issue....

SEPs are available not just in federal enforcement proceedings, however, but are recognized tools in the context of most state enforcement regimes as well. And in the context of such state programs, they are considerably more flexible—as most of the federal legal and policy limitations do not apply to states....

SEPs mostly derive from administrative enforcement cases as opposed to judicial enforcement. State and federal environmental enforcement actions, in turn, mostly derive from three statutes: the Clean Air Act (CAA), the Clean Water Act (CWA), and the Resource Conservation and Recovery Act (RCRA). According to a study of enforcement over a 12-year period from 2001 to 2012, the CAA had the highest number of enforcement cases overall, followed by the CWA and RCRA. For each type of action, states brought significantly more cases than did the federal government.

Indeed, according to one study, states are generally responsible for between 80% and 90% of all environmental enforcement actions. However, when considering total penalties collected from such cases, despite the lower numbers of cases, the federal enforcement actions resulted in substantially higher aggregate penalties. The highest penalties were under the CWA, followed by RCRA and then the CAA. For example, federal enforcement of the CWA resulted in more than $500 million in penalties over the time period studied, while state enforcement of the CAA netted only about $100 million.

In light of the large number of enforcement cases and high aggregate dollar value, it seems clear that the opportunities for restorative benefits are rich. However, SEPs continue to be underutilized as a mechanism to address the array of environmental challenges that marginalized communities face. The reasons for this, ultimately, are identifiable, and steps could be taken to empower communities to take greater advantage of SEP-related opportunities....

A. Clarifying the Impediments to Full Community Participation in SEP Development

The necessary first step to empowering communities to participate more fully in the development and utilization of SEPs is understanding the source of their current disenfranchisement. Here, the underutilization, or ineffective deployment, of SEPs in service of community-driven objectives can be conceptualized as a problem with three relatively distinct components: (1) a process failure (the absence of institutionalized prompts in the enforcement process to reliably ensure that SEPs are consistently explored as an option); (2) an informational failure (a lack of knowledge on the part of communities about SEPs in general, and about the existence of particular enforcement actions that might provide opportunities to realize SEP-related benefits); and (3) a resource failure (a deficiency in technical, science, health, and legal expertise, available to communities, to develop meaningful projects that best reflect community priorities).

... [T]he environmental enforcement process is not designed to be an inclusive affair. There are serious confidentiality-related concerns that restrain enforcement authorities from disclosing ongoing enforcement activities, and violators are often unwilling to invite the direct participation of community groups for fear of complicating the enforcement proceedings. The issue of confidentiality in civil settlements is certainly not without its critics—indeed some have more generally advocated for broader transparency, and EPA itself acknowledges the importance of sharing SEP development information with affected communities. However, there is continued resistance to what is perceived as "attempts to transform the court into an advocate ... or an information clearinghouse."

In the end, because of limited access to the process, and relatively short settlement time lines once information does become available, it is simply too late to begin the process of considering SEPs, informing the affected community, and locating and deploying resources to develop community-driven project proposals, after enforcement officials have already effectively completed settlement negotiations with the defendant. Therefore, in order to make full and most effective use of SEPs for the benefit of communities, the structural mechanisms to allow for meaningful participation must be fully in place in *anticipation of* (not in reaction to) the emergence of enforcement-related SEP opportunities.

More important perhaps, enforcement officials typically do not reach out to potentially affected communities in advance of initiating enforcement, even in ways that might protect the identity of the alleged violators. Nor do agencies typically routinize proactive outreach to communities in advance of geographically focused, or industry-specific, enforcement initiatives—where it might be possible to predict with some accuracy which communities are likely to be affected based on region or on the type of industry subject to enforcement efforts (which, in turn, would provide insights into the kinds of SEPs that might be most promising). In these and other ways, the enforcement process itself is not structurally optimized to facilitate consideration of community-driven SEPs, or generally to maximize community involvement.

In addition to these process flaws, there are some very basic informational impediments to effective community participation. Among these is the fact that marginalized communities are often unaware that SEPs are even an available mechanism for obtaining restorative environmental benefits. And even when communities do know about SEPs generally, they are likely to have little access to information about how to engage with enforcement officials, how to find out about enforcement cases, or how to effectively offer input regarding enforcement-related options.

As a result, even when a community might be inclined to participate, it may never find out about enforcement cases, or even if it does, it may not know how to appropriately engage in order to advocate for a SEP, to offer up its own views about what the community needs, or to otherwise meaningfully participate in SEP development.

In order to participate, communities must have access to information regarding what SEPs are and how they work. They must also have access to accurate and usable information about the enforcement process, about how to work with enforcement officials, and about what kinds of enforcement actions are underway or anticipated, or at least what types of enforcement actions are reasonably likely to arise in the future (and therefore what kinds of SEPs are likely to be viable).

Finally, even in the absence of the process- and information-related barriers discussed above, communities will often lack the resources to access the science, health, technical, and legal expertise necessary to meaningfully advocate for particular SEP approaches that would best reflect community priorities. SEP development can be a technically burdensome, procedurally complicated, and legally nuanced undertaking, and may be out of the reach of many communities without professional assistance. The process often involves multiple layers of scientific, legal, and economic analyses, and sometime delicate dealings with enforcement agencies and implementing defendants.

Thus, in order to meaningfully contribute to SEP development efforts, in the absence of some kind of supportive infrastructure, communities may need to independently access and manage a substantial suite of resources. An inability to do so thus may stand as an effective obstacle to meaningful engagement. Accordingly, empowering communities in the context of SEP participation will require mustering resources to put to work on their behalf.

Notes and Questions

1. **SEP policy.** EPA's SEP policy has evolved and expanded over time. Any party interested in a SEP as part of an EPA enforcement action should be sure to study the latest version of the EPA SEP policy. As of 2025, the latest policy update (2015) appeared online at the link below: https://www.epa.gov/sites/default/files/2015-04/documents/sepupdatedpolicy15.pdf.

2. **Nexus.** As noted in the article, a SEP cannot be something already required. However, every SEP approved for a settlement with EPA and most states must have sufficient *nexus* to the underlying environmental requirement. In other words, a SEP project must be close—but not *too close*—to the underlying violation. How do you determine that? One factor for determining sufficient nexus is whether the proposed project will reduce "[t]he adverse impact to public health or the environment to which the violation at issue contributes." EPA, Supplemental Environmental Projects Policy, 2015 Update at 7. The EPA SEP policy further offers that nexus will be "easier to establish if the primary impact of the project is at the site where the alleged violation occurred ... or within the immediate geographic area." For this purpose, the policy defines "immediate geographic area" as "generally ... the area within a 50-mile radius of the site on which the violations occurred." *Id.* n.9.

While "nexus" for purposes of the EPA SEP policy may remain somewhat amorphous, it is clear that SEPs must in some way benefit the particular community

Figure 7-2. Bike trail through South Valley of Albuquerque, supported in part by a SEP resolving Clean Water Act violations at a nearby wastewater treatment plant. Photo: Cliff Villa, 2025.

impacted by the violation. Thus, SEPs may not include simple cash donations to an alma mater or national environmental organization. As such, SEPs may offer unique opportunities for local groups and grassroots organizations to help direct resources towards unmet needs in their communities.

3. Categories. In addition to the nexus requirement, the EPA SEP policy generally requires that an approved SEP fall within at least one of seven defined project categories:

1. Public Health
2. Pollution Prevention
3. Pollution Reduction
4. Environmental Restoration and Protection
5. Assessments and Audits
6. Environmental Compliance Promotion
7. Emergency Planning and Preparedness

SEPs in any of these categories may certainly help communities overburdened with pollution.

For example, under the Public Health category, EPA Region 5 in 2024 reached an administrative settlement with a real estate company for alleged violations of TSCA's Lead Disclosure Rule at residential properties in Chicago. The settlement required the company to pay a $40,000 penalty and to spend at least $384,350 for projects to abate lead hazards in residential properties and child-occupied facilities in the Chicago area. The SEP may include removal of lead-based paint and lead dust, including from window trim and sills, "which may require replacement of the window, using energy efficient windows that meet EPA Energy Star requirements." U.S. EPA Region 5, In the Matter of: Pangea Real Estate, Consent Agreement and Final Order, Docket No. TSCA-05-2024-0024, Sept. 19, 2024.

Under the category of Environmental Restoration and Protection, EPA Region 6 settled an administrative penalty in 2016 for violations of the Clean Water Act at the wastewater treatment plant in Albuquerque, New Mexico. In this settlement, the water utility agreed to spend at least four hundred thousand dollars to construct a waterline from the treatment plant to the nearby Valle de Oro National Wildlife Refuge. The new waterline would provide reclaimed water for wetlands habitat at the urban refuge and also for landscaping along a new bike trail that will allow the nearby Latino neighborhood to reach the refuge safely within a surrounding industrial corridor. (*See* Figure 7-2.) U.S. EPA Region 6, In the Matter of: Albuquerque Bernalillo County Water Utility Authority, Consent Agreement and Final Order, Docket No. CWA-06-2015-1777, Mar. 17, 2016.

Under the category of Emergency Planning and Preparedness, EPA Region 10 settled an administrative penalty in 2013 for violations of the Emergency Planning and Community Right-to-Know Act (EPCRA) in Pierce County, Washington. In this settlement, an oil storage company agreed to provide a rural fire district with an upgrade to a "hazardous materials ID processor" and other emergency response equipment. U.S. EPA Region 10, In the Matter of: Targa Sound Terminal LLC, Consent Agreement and Final Order, Docket No. EPCRA-10-2013-0061, Sept. 18, 2013.

For a comprehensive catalog of EPA SEP projects, under both administrative and civil settlements, see the EPA SEP website and/or the EPA ECHO database.

4. SEPs vs. mitigation. What is the relationship between SEP projects and mitigation projects? Both kinds of projects may be included in settlements under the federal environmental statutes. SEPs, however, are only available for settlements involving penalties, and only authorized for federal settlements where the project meets the additional criteria discussed above. Mitigation, on the other hand, may be more flexible, but dependent on the equitable powers of a court. There may also be overlap of projects approvable as either SEPs or mitigation. For example, the "Community Health" mitigation program funded under the East Palestine settlement may be very similar to a "Health Care" project funded as a SEP under a settlement with W.R. Grace related to asbestos contamination in Libby, Montana. In this settlement, the company agreed to establish a public health clinic in Libby and provide the clinic with "$2,750,000 in funding … to pay for medical care for asbestos-related illnesses…." *United States v. W.R. Grace & Company*, Consent Decree, Civ. No. 00-167-M-DMW, May 3, 2002.

5. State enforcement and citizen suits. As noted in the article, the EPA SEP policy only applies to enforcement actions brought by EPA. Almost all states have some version of their own SEP policy, most with analogous provisions to the EPA SEP policy, plus minor variations. The SEP policy for Rhode Island, for example, defines eight categories of SEPs, including a unique category for "Outreach and Education." Rhode Island Dept. of Environmental Management, Policy on Supplemental Environmental Projects (July 15, 2004). Michigan's SEP policy requires "adequate nexus," providing that a SEP project "must take place within the state of Michigan," and with "strong preference" for "geographic proximity to the violation(s)." Michigan Dept. of Environment, Great Lakes, and Energy, Supplemental Environmental Projects for Penalty Mitigation (August 7, 2020). Texas, by statute, authorizes SEPs "with activities in the United Mexican States if the project substantially benefits territory in this state...." Texas Water Code § 7.067 (2015). New Mexico requires "nexus to the violation," but for violations of the state's Hazardous Waste Act, defines a SEP narrowly as a project that "occurs within the fence line of the violator's facility, or at facilities that are functionally related to the violating facility and under common operational control." NM Envt Dept., Hazardous Waste Bureau, Hazardous Waste Act Civil Penalty Policy, Rev. 1 (March 2017).

SEPs may also be used to settle citizen suits under environmental statutes. The EPA SEP policy does not specifically apply to SEPs resolving citizen suits, so some greater flexibility may be found for SEPs in this context. However, citizen suits settled in the form of a consent decree under certain federal statutes may be subject to review by the U.S. Department of Justice. *See, e.g.*, Clean Water Act § 505, 33 U.S.C. § 1365(c)(3) ("No consent judgment shall be entered in an action in which the United States is not a party prior to 45 days following the receipt of a copy of the proposed consent judgment by the Attorney General and the [EPA] Administrator"); Clean Air Act § 304, 42 U.S.C. § 7604(c)(3) (same). DOJ can and does file objections with the court to some proposed citizen suits, including on the basis that the SEP does not conform to the EPA SEP policy. *See, e.g.*, *Luke Delgadillo Garcia v. Miller Castings, Inc.*, United States' Statement of Concern, Case No. 2:17-cv-07408-AB-AGR at 29 (C.D. Cal. May 18, 2018) (submitting that proposed consent decree under the Clean Water Act "appears to have no nexus to the violations alleged"). To avoid potential DOJ objections and judicial delay of entry for a proposed settlement, counsel for citizen plaintiffs may seek to ensure that any proposed settlement including a SEP does comport with the EPA SEP policy.

Notwithstanding these potential constraints, SEPs as part of citizen suit settlements have provided substantial benefits for communities with environmental justice concerns.

6. Public involvement in government enforcement. Law enforcement, including environmental enforcement, is not typically a public process. As the Simms article acknowledges, "There are serious confidentiality-related concerns that restrain enforcement authorities from disclosing ongoing enforcement actions...." Confidentiality may be essential to maintain the integrity of enforcement processes, to include protecting the presumption of innocence, preserving grand jury deliberations, and preventing political interference in prosecutorial decisions. Confidentiality may also pose particular challenges for the environmental justice principle of meaningful involvement for affected communities. How might one who is dedicated equally to both law enforcement and environmental justice balance enforcement confidentiality and meaningful public involvement? What does Mr. Simms recommend for ensuring opportunities for public engagement in the particular context of SEPs?

Affected communities may play an important role in identifying potential environmental violations. Community members may also be needed as witnesses or sources of information to support enforcement investigations and prosecution. If at some point the enforcement process proceeds into a "black box," where enforcement personnel engage in investigations outside the public eye, opportunities for meaningful involvement may reemerge with opportunities for public comment on proposed civil settlements or plea agreements.

Like the settlement for East Palestine, most civil settlements entered in federal court will allow for public comment between the time a proposed consent decree is lodged with the court and the time the court signs and enters the decree. In contrast with civil settlements entered in court, administrative settlements under federal environmental laws may or may not require an opportunity for public comment before the agreement becomes final. Administrative settlements under TSCA, for example, require no opportunity for public comments. On the other hand, proposed administrative settlements under the Clean Water Act and Safe Drinking Water Act do require an opportunity for public comment and even allow members of the public to request a hearing where they may present evidence and cross-examine witnesses. 40 C.F.R. § 22.45.

Where proposed settlements may be subject to public review and comment, the public obviously has some opportunity for engagement in the enforcement process. However, even where a settlement requires no public comment, some public involvement may still be allowed. For example, as noted in the Simms article, enforcement staff or defendants involved in settlement negotiations may invite community suggestions for supplemental environmental projects to include in a settlement. To find such opportunities for public input, settlement-savvy EJ advocates will watch for public notices through conventional channels, but also cultivate relationships with agency staff, industry counsel, nonprofit leaders, elected officials, media members, and other information networks.

Chapter 8

Environmental Justice and Contaminated Sites

Figure 8-1. EPA contractors excavating contaminated soil from residential yard within Westside Lead Superfund Site, Atlanta, Georgia. Photo: U.S. EPA, 2023.

A. Introduction

In 2018, a doctoral student from Emory University presented data to the U.S. Environmental Protection Agency (EPA) indicating elevated levels of lead in soils collected from Atlanta's Westside, northwest of downtown. Emory's data convinced EPA to conduct its own investigation, which began later that year. EPA's investigation confirmed the presence of high levels of lead throughout the mostly residential area, with the contamination reflecting a legacy of historic industrial activities to include metal foundries and ammunitions manufacturing.

In 2020, EPA began to address the lead contamination under authority of a federal law known as the Comprehensive Environmental Response, Compensation, and Liability Act (CERCLA), better known as "Superfund." The CERCLA removal action involved excavating contaminated soils from residential properties and backfilling with clean materials. In spring 2022, as this early cleanup work proceeded, EPA listed the Westside Lead Superfund Site on the National Priorities List (NPL). 87 Fed. Reg.

14805 (Mar. 16, 2022). Later that same year, after public comment and coordination with the Georgia Department of Environmental Protection, EPA selected a final remedy for the Westside Lead Superfund Site, which called for substantial expansion of the excavation, backfilling, and revegetation of disturbed areas. The total cost of this cleanup was estimated at over $49 million dollars, requiring six years for construction. As of January 2025, 606 individual properties had been identified as requiring cleanup and 333 properties of those properties had cleanup completed.

The Westside Lead Superfund Site is unusual in some respects, including extraordinarily speedy action from site discovery to cleanup action. But the Westside Lead Site is also typical in that disproportionate impacts of a contaminated site fall upon racial minorities and low-income people. According to EPA data, the Westside Lead area northwest of downtown Atlanta was 77 percent "people of color" and 63 percent "low income." For all Superfund sites nationwide, according to data published by the U.S. EPA in 2017, minorities comprised almost half (49.3 percent) of the population within one mile of a Superfund site, despite comprising closer to a third (38.4 percent) of the U.S. population. U.S. EPA Office of Land and Emergency Management, Population Surrounding 1,836 Superfund Remedial Sites (2017). Within the same mile from any Superfund site, compared to their general populations within the United States, the Latino population is approximately 45 percent higher, the Asian population is approximately 63 percent higher, and linguistically isolated households are approximately 62 percent higher.

Designated Superfund sites and tens of thousands of other contaminated properties across the country clearly pose serious challenges for environmental justice (EJ). Part B of this chapter will explore some of the legal authorities for addressing contaminated sites in the United States. Part C will then investigate the opportunities available for EJ advocates to ensure that cleanup processes provide fair treatment and meaningful involvement for all affected communities. Part D will conclude the chapter by considering a case study from Seattle, Washington, where community members engaged in innovative efforts to address a major Superfund site in their own backyard.

B. Legal Authorities for Cleaning Up Contaminated Sites

For most lawyers and academics in the United States, the first (and often only) legal authority they will associate with the cleanup of contaminated sites is the Comprehensive Environmental Response, Compensation and Liability Act (CERCLA). Known commonly as "Superfund," CERCLA is the primary federal statute governing the remediation of spills or releases of hazardous substances. The prime directive of CERCLA is to protect "human health and the environment." CERCLA § 121(b), 42 U.S.C. § 9621(b). If every cleanup met this directive, for *every* "human," we might go a long way toward achieving environmental justice in this country.

CERCLA is not, however, the only federal statute that addresses spills and releases of hazardous materials in the United States. Different kinds of contamination may require the application of different statutes, including the Resource Conservation and Recovery Act (RCRA) for "hazardous waste" and "solid waste." Different statutes, in turn, may provide different legal authorities and opportunities for community engagement. We will begin by considering the different triggers for each statute, followed by a review of the various sources of funding for cleanup, and the processes under CERCLA for selecting cleanup actions.

1. Jurisdictional Triggers for Cleanup Statutes

CERCLA § 104 (42 U.S.C. § 9604):

(a)(1) Whenever (A) any hazardous substance is released or there is a substantial threat of such a release into the environment, or (B) there is a release or substantial threat of release into the environment of any pollutant or contaminant which may present an imminent and substantial danger to the public health or welfare, the [EPA] is authorized to act, consistent with the national contingency plan, to remove or arrange for the removal of, and provide for remedial action relating to such hazardous substance, pollutant, or contaminant at any time....

CERCLA § 101 (42 U.S.C. § 9601):

(14) The term "hazardous substance" means [any "hazardous waste" under RCRA, any "hazardous air pollutant" under the Clean Air Act, any "toxic pollutant" under the Clean Water Act, and any substance designated as a CERCLA "hazardous substance" by the National Contingency Plan.] The term does not include petroleum, including crude oil or any fraction thereof....

(33) The term "pollutant or contaminant" shall include, but not be limited to, any element, substance, compound, or mixture, including disease-causing agents, which after release into the environment and upon exposure, ingestion, inhalation, or assimilation into any organism ... will or may reasonably be anticipated to cause death [or] disease, ... except that the term shall not include petroleum, including crude oil or any fraction thereof....

RCRA § 3008(h) (42 U.S.C. § 6929(h)):

Whenever on the basis of any information the [EPA] determines that there is or has been a release of hazardous waste into the environment from a facility authorized to operate [under interim status before obtaining a final permit for a treatment, storage, or disposal facility], the [EPA] may issue an order requiring corrective action ... or the [EPA] may commence a civil action in the United States district court ... for appropriate relief, including a temporary or permanent injunction.

RCRA § 7002 (42 U.S.C. § 6972):

(a) ... [A]ny person may commence a civil action on his own behalf ... (B) against any person, including the United States, and any other governmental instrumentality or agency, ... and including any past or present generator, ... who has contributed or is contributing to the past or present handing, storage, treatment, transportation, or disposal of any solid or hazardous waste which may present an imminent and substantial endangerment to health or the environment....

RCRA § 1004 (42 U.S.C. § 6903):

(27) The term "solid waste" means any garbage, refuse, ... or other discarded material, including solid, liquid, semisolid, or contained gaseous material resulting from industrial, commercial, mining, and agricultural operations, ... but does not include solid or dissolved material in domestic sewage, or solid or dissolved materials in irrigation return flows or industrial discharges which are point sources subject to permits under [the Clean Water Act].

Clean Water Act § 311 (33 U.S.C. § 1321)
(as amended by the Oil Pollution Act of 1990):

(b)(3) The discharge of oil ... (i) into or upon the navigable waters of the United States [or] adjoining shorelines ... in such quantities as may be harmful ... is prohibited....

(c)(A) The President shall, in accordance with the National Contingency Plan and any appropriate Area Contingency Plan, ensure effective and immediate removal of a discharge ... of oil ... (i) into or on the navigable waters; [or] (ii) on the adjoining shorelines to the navigable waters....

Notes and Questions

1. Test your understanding. Given the jurisdictional triggers above, which cleanup statute would appear most appropriate in the following circumstances:

- Two fifty-five-gallon drums containing human waste appear one morning along a county road through the Winnebago Indian Reservation in Nebraska.
- Five million gallons of jet fuel are discovered to have leaked over a 20-year period from storage tanks on an Air Force base in Ohio, creating a plume of contaminated groundwater beneath a largely Black neighborhood.
- A fishing vessel sinks off the Georgia coast, discharging an estimated 2,200 gallons of diesel fuel and contaminating the shoreline of a Gullah community on a nearby island.
- Residents of a poor, rural county in Texas near the border with Mexico supplement their income by picking through an illegal dumpsite in order to salvage metals including cadmium, copper, nickel, and zinc.
- A newly constructed pipeline transporting crude oil from North Dakota to Illinois develops a leak and spills more than 100,000 gallons of oil on an Iowa cornfield.

In the scenarios above, do you find that the jurisdictional elements would be triggered for at least one of the statutes we have considered so far? Do you find that more than one statute may apply in these cases? If so, how would you determine which statute would best support the interests of the local community? In part, the answer may lie in a deeper understanding of each statute, an objective beyond the scope of this book but addressed in other available resources. *See, e.g.*, Robert Percival et al., Environmental Regulation: Law, Science, and Policy (10th ed. 2024). However, another part of the answer may depend on the unique needs and interests of the local community, a fundamental consideration for environmental justice. For example, even if the Georgia spill impacts fishery resources, could the Gullah community still reject a major federal cleanup operation in favor of protecting the community's privacy on the island?

2. RCRA vs. CERCLA. One common question for cleaning up contaminated lands is whether to apply RCRA or CERCLA authorities. As noted above, a RCRA "hazardous waste" is also by definition a CERCLA "hazardous substance." However, a RCRA "solid waste" may extend jurisdiction to materials beyond CERCLA jurisdiction, such as piles of used tires (a hazard due to flammability as well as breeding grounds for mosquitoes if they collect water). On the other hand, CERCLA jurisdiction may reach categories of contamination that RCRA cannot, such as radioactive materials (included on CERCLA's list of hazardous substances at 40 C.F.R. Table 302.4, App. B) and mining wastes (excluded from RCRA regulation by the RCRA Bevill Amendment, 42 U.S.C. § 6921(b)(3)(A)(ii)).

For an active facility with financially capable owners or operators, a facility may undergo cleanup through the RCRA **corrective action** process. In some cases, RCRA corrective action may be the only cleanup authority available, as for sites contaminated only with petroleum products, which would be subject to the CERCLA **petroleum exclusion** noted above. In other cases, a facility may proceed with cleanup under the RCRA corrective action process because of a history of RCRA regulation at the site.

3. National Contingency Plan. Note the references to the "National Contingency Plan" in both CERCLA and the Clean Water Act. Does that sound like a—plan? In fact, the National Contingency Plan (NCP) is a set of regulations guiding the cleanup of both oil and hazardous substances in the United States. More formally, it is the National Oil and Hazardous Substances Pollution Contingency Plan, 40 C.F.R. Part 300. In a twist upon the usual sequence of a statute followed by implementing regulations, the NCP actually predated both CERCLA and the modern Clean Water Act but was embraced by Congress when it passed both statutes. Today, the NCP continues to provide the applicable rules for the cleanup of oil and hazardous substances in the United States and should be consulted regularly when engaged in related activities.

2. Paying for Site Investigation and Cleanup

The investigation of a site where contamination is suspected, and cleanup of contamination where it is needed, may entail widely varying costs, from a few hundred bucks for removal of cracked car batteries to billions of dollars for restoration of watersheds impacted by industrial activities. Each of the federal statutes noted above begins with the "**polluter pays principle**," presuming that costs of site investigation and cleanup will be performed by parties legal responsible for the contamination. The federal statutes generally reflect schemes of strict liability for pollution; that is, liability in general does not depend on any proof of intent to cause a spill or release. Rather, liability may be established simply by a party's act causing a spill or even by a party's status within certain categories, such as the past or present owner or operator of a facility from which a release occurred. *See* CERCLA § 107(a), 42 U.S.C. § 9604(a) (establishing four categories of liable parties under CERCLA). The polluter pays principle has proven a powerful instrument for achieving cleanup actions under CERCLA since the statute was passed in 1980. According to one study of data from the 1990s, some three-quarters of remedial actions at designated Superfund sites were in fact conducted or funded by responsible parties. Katherine N. Probst & David M. Konisky et al., SUPERFUND'S FUTURE: WHAT WILL IT COST? at 43 (2001).

Most remedial work under CERCLA is performed by "**potentially responsible parties**" (PRPs) under agreements with the EPA, without the need for litigation. *See* CERCLA § 122, (d), 42 U.S.C. § 9622(d). Cleanups may also be conducted under administrative order from an authorized agency. CERCLA § 106(a), 42 U.S.C. § 9606(a). For example, as noted in Chapter 7, the billion-dollar cleanup following the East Palestine train derailment is being conducted by Norfolk Southern under administrative order from EPA.

In some cases, EJ advocates may question whether a party responsible for polluting a site may be trusted with cleaning it up. In such cases, it is important to note that cleanup agreements must be subject to agency oversight, with penalties available for violations of an agreement. CERCLA § 122(k), 42 U.S.C. § 9622(k). Cleanup agreements and orders may also be subject to direct citizen enforcement. CERCLA § 310, 42 U.S.C. § 9659. *See, e.g.*, *Pakootas v. Teck Cominco Metals, Inc.* (*Pakootas I*), 452 F.3d 1066 (9th Cir. 2006) (Colville Indian Tribe enforcing EPA CERCLA order against Canadian mining company).

In the case of a liable party who is able but refuses to pay for cleanup, the EPA may pay for cleanup actions from the Superfund trust fund and then seek to recover its cleanup costs through subsequent legal action. CERCLA § 107(a), 42 U.S.C. § 9607(a). States, tribes, and other parties may also seek to recover cleanup costs from responsible parties, *id.*, but they do not have access to the Superfund to pay for cleanup actions up front

Under CERCLA, there are two broad categories of cleanup (or "response") actions: (1) **removal actions**; and (2) **remedial actions**. Removal actions are generally discrete, short-term responses for relatively smaller problems. *See* CERCLA § 101(23), 42 U.S.C. § 9601(23) (defining "removal"). A removal action might include, for example, a two-hour operation to pick up a pile of cracked car batteries discovered along a bike trail on a Sunday morning. Remedial actions, by contrast, are typically long-term responses for larger problems. *See* CERCLA § 101(24), 42 U.S.C. § 9601(24) (defining "remedial action"). A remedial action might include, for example, excavating a million tons of contaminated soil or pumping and treating contaminated groundwater over a period of years. Funding from the Superfund for removal actions is generally capped at $2 million. CERCLA § 104(c), 42 U.S.C. § 9604(c)(1). Exceptions to this cap may be made for removal actions "immediately required to prevent, limit, or mitigate an emergency...." *Id.* For remedial actions, the CERCLA statute places no limitations on Superfund expenditures, where the site has been included on the **National Priorities List (NPL)**. Such designated "Superfund sites" may potentially receive hundreds of millions of dollars from the Superfund trust fund for major cleanups, limited only by the availability of funds in any year and competition from other Superfund sites in need of funding.

The Superfund, or more formally, the **Hazardous Substance Superfund**, was established by Congress through CERCLA § 111, 42 U.S.C. § 9611. Originally financed by an excise tax on certain petroleum and chemical industries, the "Superfund" tax expired in 1995, but the trust fund was sustained for decades by congressional appropriations and recovery of costs from responsible parties. In a surprising turn, the Superfund tax on chemicals was reinstated in 2021 for a period of ten years through passage of the Bipartisan Infrastructure Law, Pub. L. No. 117-58. The tax on petroleum was reinstated indefinitely in 2022 through the Inflation Reduction Act, Pub. L. No. 117-169.

The **Bipartisan Infrastructure Law** also provided an additional $3.5 billion for Superfund remedial actions. Allocated over three fiscal years during the Biden administration, the additional funding allowed EPA to clear a backlog of NPL sites that had been awaiting funding and also to accelerate cleanup at hundreds of other sites across the country. One of the Superfund sites benefiting from BIL funding was the Westside Lead Site in Atlanta, Georgia, which moved in record time from discovery to initiation of cleanup.

In contrast with Superfund, administered largely by EPA, the **Brownfields program** takes a different approach, driven largely by community organizations. The EPA Brownfields program, as well as state and tribal analogues, allows local entities and nonprofit organizations to apply for grants, loans, and technical assistance for designated purposes including site assessment, cleanup, community planning, and job training. Through Brownfields programs, abandoned properties have been brought back to life across the country. Vacant lots become urban gardens. Old railyards become parks and playgrounds. Heavy industry makes room for small businesses and clean energy. In Pennsylvania, a $2 million Brownfields grant from EPA to the Urban Redevelopment Authority of Pittsburgh in 2024 will help fund cleanup of an old slag disposal site and conversion to solar farm and recreational space. In Puerto Rico, a $1 million Brownfields grant from EPA will help a community organization assess, clean up, and convert a former convent into community assets including affordable housing for seniors. See Figure 8-2 below.

The EPA Brownfields program was created, in part, by amendment to CERCLA. CERCLA defines the term "brownfield site" to mean "real property, the expansion, redevelopment, or reuse of which may be complicated by the presence or potential presence

Figure 8-2. Chapel on former convent in San Juan, Puerto Rico. Photo: U.S. EPA, 2023.

of a hazardous substance, pollutant, or contaminant." 42 U.S.C. § 9601(39)(A) (2002). The EPA estimates there are at least 450,000 brownfield sites across the U.S., to include former gas stations, drycleaners, and old industrial properties all across the country.

Where contamination is suspected, Brownfields funding allows community organizations, including EJ advocates, direct opportunity to plan and prioritize actions for site assessment, cleanup, and redevelopment. The Brownfields program is particularly suited for pursuing environmental justice because the authorizing statute provides a rare example of legal authority directed expressly at reducing threats to "the health or welfare of children, pregnant women, minority or low-income communities, or other sensitive populations." CERCLA § 104(k), 42 U.S.C. § 9604(k)(6)(C)(x) (Application ranking criteria).

There are obviously many advantages to be gained from redeveloping brownfields, but there are also concerns, as noted in the excerpt below from one early commentator.

> [B]rownfield redevelopment can take advantage of existing urban infrastructures. A brownfield site often features excellent water and sewer systems, and rail and highway access to the metropolitan area, the region, and outlying areas. Densely concentrated urban areas offer better accessibility to workers and other advantages. Other potential benefits include aesthetic qualities such as waterfront access and views, proximity to downtown business districts, public tax and financing initiatives to support development, access to major universities and medical centers, and ancillary benefits of spending by rejuvenated industries and their workers on local goods and services....

> Despite these potential advantages, brownfields remain abandoned or underutilized. In the eyes of many, this is due to widespread fears of brownfield developers ... that the cost of cleaning brownfield sites to meet government standards is both so uncertain and so high that it might outweigh the sites' market value.... A developer must also be concerned about the uncertainties caused by state hazardous waste cleanup programs, because it cannot predict at the outset whether it will be subjected to state or federal regulation. The states have primary responsibility for sites that do not rise to the threshold for federal action and for sites that states have decided to regulate in the absence of federal requirements...

Joel B. Eisen, *Brownfields of Dreams?: Challenges and Limits of Voluntary Cleanup Programs and Incentives,* 1996 U. ILLINOIS L. REV. 883, 894–900 (1996).

The **Brownfields Job Training Program** deserves special attention from community advocates. As one of the co-authors of this book enthused in a speech at the University of Memphis:

> For over twenty years, the EPA has given grants under the Brownfields program to states, tribes, local governments, and nonprofit organizations to assess, clean up, and revitalize communities across the country. But one of the coolest of the coolest is the Brownfields Job Training Program, which provides funding to nonprofit organizations who train community members to do environmental work in their communities. In December 2022, [former EPA] Deputy Administrator Janet McCabe and I attended a ceremony in Chicago to celebrate one of these graduating classes and it was one of the most moving experiences of my life. Imagine if you could create a program that would help improve the environment and also provide good, stable jobs for many Americans, including people reentering the workforce after incarceration. Through the Brownfields Job Training Program, we are doing that.

Clifford J. Villa, *A New Day for Environmental Justice at the U.S. EPA*, 54 U. MEMPHIS L. REV. 867 (2024).

In FY24, for example, the Brownfields Job Training Program awarded a $500,000 grant to Santa Fe Community College to provide four years of environmental job training for largely low-income workers and tribal members in northern New Mexico. In FY25, EPA awarded 16 Brownfields Job Training grants, including one for nearly $500,000 dollars to the Workforce Alliance of South Central Kansas in Wichita, which provides job training services for workers including justice involved individuals.

In addition to direct grants to local organizations, EPA provides grants to many state and local authorities to capitalize **Revolving Loan Funds (RLF)**. RLF programs enable many state and local governments and development authorities to provide low-interest loans for brownfields cleanup and redevelopment.

Over time, the EPA Brownfields program has proven a success. According to the EPA, as of January 2025, the Brownfields program had leveraged creation of 279,884 new jobs and provided a return on investment of $20.45 for every dollar awarded through Brownfields funding. *See* https://www.epa.gov/brownfields. The Brownfields program also enjoys strong bipartisan support, reflected in an additional $1.5 billion allocated for Brownfields through the Bipartisan Infrastructure Law. Through BIL funding, EPA has allocated approximately $300 million a year in additional funding since FY23. In May 2024, for example, EPA announced Brownfields grants totaling $233 million for 180 communities plus $68 million in supplemental funding for 31 Revolving Loan Funds. *Biden-Harris Administration Announces More Than $300 Million in Brownfield Grants Through Investing in America Agenda to Rehabilitate and Revitalize Communities*, May 20, 2024.

While EPA Brownfields funding has helped support community projects in every state, there remain serious **geographic inequities** in the distribution of funding. For example, over the first three years of BIL funding for Brownfields (FY22–24), the State of Maine, followed by Massachusetts, received the largest amount of Brownfields funding, totaling almost $40 million dollars each. Over the same time period, at the very bottom of EPA Brownfields funding, was the State of New Mexico, with only $500,000. It is no coincidence that New Mexico is also one of the poorest states in the country. Significant resources may be required to successfully apply for and manage Brownfields grants. Brownfields grants typically require applicants to provide matching funds of at least 20 percent of the project cost. CERCLA § 104(k), 42 U.S.C. § 9604(k)(10)(B)(iii). To address this concern, Brownfields grants funded by BIL waived this matching requirement. Pub. L. No. 117-58, 135 Stat. 429, 1403 (Nov. 15, 2021). The Brownfields program provides free technical assistance to help prospective applicants navigate the application process. See EPA's **Technical Assistance to Brownfields (TAB)** program for additional information. The Brownfields program also makes contractor resources available for *free, non-competitive assistance* with site assessment and planning under the **Targeted Brownfields Assessment (TBA)** program.

Unlike CERCLA removals and remedial actions, EPA Brownfields grants are *not* subject to the CERCLA petroleum exclusion, so they can be used, for example, to clean up former gas stations. Most brownfield cleanups are also guided not by federal law, but by state cleanup statutes. Most states have enacted provisions specifically directed at brownfield sites. Many states encourage cleanup of sites through voluntary cleanup programs. Voluntary cleanup programs are a popular means for achieving relatively quick and uncomplicated site cleanups. However, a lack of agency oversight and enforceable cleanup standards may leave some communities uncertain whether cleanup measures will genuinely protect their health. For a review of one local brownfields program, noting both successes and continuing challenges, *see* Jessica Higgins, *Evaluating the Chicago Brownfields Initiative: The Effects of City-Initiated Brownfield Redevelopment on Surrounding Communities*, 3 Northwestern J. L. & Social Pol'y 240 (2008).

For cleanup of **oil spills**, the Oil Pollution Act of 1990 (OPA), passed in the wake of the *Exxon Valdez* spill in 1989, created a liability and funding program modeled upon CERCLA. OPA added authorities to Clean Water Act § 311 authorizing the EPA (for inland waters) and the U.S. Coast Guard (for marine waters) to issue orders for cleanup of oil spills. *See* 33 U.S.C. 1321(c)(1). Analogous to CERCLA's Superfund, OPA also created an Oil Spill Liability Trust Fund, to be used by the EPA or the Coast Guard where responsible parties are unable or unwilling to perform cleanup actions themselves. OPA § 1012, 33 U.S.C. § 2712. With lessons from the impacts to fisher families and Native Alaskans after the *Exxon Valdez*, OPA also greatly expanded upon the scope of liability for damages from oil spills, to include possible claims for lost profits, lost subsistence uses, and injuries to private or public property. OPA § 1002(b)(2), 33 U.S.C. § 2702(b)(2). This expanded scope of liability became particularly crucial after the BP Deepwater Horizon oil spill in 2010, allowing injured communities including Vietnamese American fisher folks a means to pursue restorative and compensatory justice from BP. For more on the impacts of the BP spill to this community, *see* Chapter 15 (Disaster Justice).

3. Superfund Listing

When people speak of "Superfund sites," they usually mean contaminated sites that EPA has included on the CERCLA National Priorities List (NPL). EPA defines the NPL as a "list of sites of national priority among the known releases or threatened release of hazardous substances, pollutants, or contaminants throughout the United States, and its territories." Most sites go on the NPL through use of the Hazard Ranking System (HRS). Through HRS, the EPA generates a numerical score for an individual site based upon factors such as releases of contamination to soil, groundwater, and surface water, the size of the population at risk, the potential for contaminating water supplies, the potential for public contact, and the possibility that damage to natural resources might affect the human food chain. *See* CERCLA § 105(c), 42 U.S.C. § 9605(c). Sites that score above 28.5 generally qualify for NPL listing, although the final decision by the EPA whether to list any particular site often follows a protracted, political process, including seeking concurrence on the listing decision from the governor of the affected state.

In 2024, for example, with concurrence from the State of Washington, plus support from the Spokane and Colville Tribes, EPA added to the NPL the "Upper Columbia River," a stretch of the river in northeastern Washington contaminated by metals including lead and mercury largely from a smelter ten miles north of the border in Canada. 89 Fed. Reg. 100751 (Dec. 13, 2024). See *EPA Adds Upper Columbia River Site to the Superfund National Priorities List to Protect Public Health from Metals Contamination*, Dec. 13, 2024. In 2024, with support from tribal government, EPA also added the Lukachukai Mountains Mining District to the NPL, ensuring resources to address a significant area of uranium contamination on the Navajo Nation. 89 Fed. Reg. 16463 (March 7, 2024). *EPA Adds Sites to the Superfund National Priorities List, including the Lukachukai Mountains Mining District in Navajo Nation*, March 5, 2024.

Once a site goes on the NPL, it generally proceeds through phases of site investigation, remedial action, and then monitoring to ensure that objectives for soil, groundwater, surface water, or other targets have been met. Sites can go on the NPL when they require cleanup, and then come off the NPL when all remedial actions have been completed—a process known as **deletion**.

As of March 2025, there were 1,340 sites on the NPL, 458 sites deleted from the NPL, and 42 new sites proposed for the NPL. One of the sites proposed for NPL listing is Exide Technologies—Vernon, with lead contamination from a former battery recycling facility impacting a heavily Spanish-speaking neighborhood south of downtown Los Angeles. 89 Fed. Reg. 72356 (Sept. 5, 2024).

Due to the challenges posed by extensive contamination, some sites may remain on the NPL for a long time. Many sites currently on the NPL today were part of the first listing of NPL sites in 1983. In September 2024, EPA deleted from the NPL one of the original sites listed in 1983—and one of the most notorious: the Lipari Landfill in Pittman, New Jersey. The Lipari Landfill, once listed as Number 1 on the NPL, had been contaminated by dumping of household trash as well as chemical wastes and industrial materials starting in 1958. Contaminants seeped into nearby aquifers and marshlands, requiring decades of cleanup effort. Today, the former Superfund site has been transformed into valuable community assets, featuring a revitalized Alcyon Lake as well as recreational facilities supporting boating and fishing, walking trails, and minor league baseball.

Importantly, even before a site is fully deleted from the NPL, when units of a site have had all physical actions completed and only a period of monitoring remains, the site may be designated as "**construction complete**." By 2025, 1,246 NPL sites had reached "construction complete" status over the life of the Superfund program.

4. Removal Actions

While designated "Superfund sites" such as Love Canal and the Lipari Landfill often garner the most attention from the mass media, academic literature, and the legal community, far more contaminated sites are addressed each year under Superfund without NPL listing. In FY2024, 203 removal actions were completed across the United States and its territories under EPA's Superfund authority.

Removal actions are usually conducted by the EPA through a corps of credentialed officers known as **on-scene coordinators** (OSC). Based in EPA regional and field offices across the country, OSCs have the training, authority, and resources to respond to spills, abandoned drums, and other discoveries of contaminated sites, potentially deploying on a moment's notice. Beyond the EPA, OSCs may be designated by the U.S. Coast Guard and other federal agencies within the scope of their respective jurisdictions. State and tribal governments may also designate OSCs through state or tribal law.

EPA OSCs must operate within the limitations established by Congress. As noted above, the EPA generally has authority under CERCLA to spend up to $2 million from the Superfund trust fund for sites not included on the NPL. CERCLA also establishes a presumption that all removal actions will be completed within 12 months or less. CERCLA § 104(c)(1), 42 U.S.C. § 9604(c)(1). For emergency situations and other extraordinary circumstances, as noted above, removal actions may continue beyond 12 months and in some cases for many years. *See, e.g.*, *United States v. W.R. Grace & Co.*, 429 F.3d 1224 (9th Cir. 2005) (approving EPA removal expenditures of more than $50 million over three years where evidence indicated devastating health impacts from asbestos contamination in Libby, Montana).

Removal actions at extraordinary sites such as Libby, Montana, may involve massive excavation of contaminated soils. At other sites, removal actions may require only a few hours to retrieve and safely discard a pile of abandoned drums. In cases of more significant contamination, where long-term remediation may eventually be required, removal actions may include the provision of bottled water or the **temporary relocation** of residences or businesses. For more on temporary relocation, *see infra* (note on Relocation). For a deeper analysis of the potential for Superfund removal actions to address a variety of environmental justice concerns, see Clifford J. Villa, *Beyond Bake Sales: Environmental Justice through Superfund Removal Actions*, 52 Envtl. L. Rep. 10784 (2022).

5. Remedial Actions

Where a contaminated site appears to require more attention than may be addressed through removal authorities, the EPA may embark on the CERCLA remedial process. Under CERCLA, the remedial process generally includes the following major elements:

- **Remedial Investigation (RI):** a study of the nature and the extent of contamination at a site, along with assessment of attendant risks to human health and the environment. An RI may include soil sampling, air monitoring, and groundwater monitoring; collection of blood samples and fish tissues; quantitative assessment of risks to ecological receptors such as fish, birds, and mammals; and quantitative assessment of health risks to children, pregnant women, subsistence fishers, and other vulnerable human populations.
- **Feasibility Study (FS):** an evaluation of alternatives to address unacceptable risks to human health and the environment identified in the RI. The FS may consider treatment options such as incineration or solidification; engineering controls such as constructed landfills and water filtration systems; and institutional controls such as deed restrictions to prevent certain land uses.
- **Proposed Plan:** an agency proposal for addressing contamination at a remedial site, drawing upon the conclusions of an RI/FS, identifying a preferred alternative, and submitted for public review and comment.
- **Record of Decision (ROD):** a document identifying the selected remedy for a site, including supporting analysis and a response to comments on the proposed plan.
- **Remedial Design (RD):** a collection of engineering plans, architectural drawings, and other specifications necessary to construct the remedy selected in the ROD.
- **Remedial Action (RA):** actual implementation of a selected remedy, which may include excavation of contaminated soil; dredging of contaminated sediments;

treatment of contaminated water; temporary or permanent relocation of residents or businesses; establishment of deed restrictions or other institutional controls; and monitoring for a period of years to ensure a remedy is operating properly and successfully.

The remedial investigation and feasibility study are usually conducted simultaneously, with each process helping to inform the other. Hence, they are routinely referred to collectively as the "**RI/FS**." An RI/FS may be conducted by the EPA or by potentially responsible parties (PRPs) under agreement with the EPA. *See* CERCLA § 104(a), 42 U.S.C. § 9604(a)(1) (EPA may allow a PRP to conduct an RI/FS "when such action will be done properly and promptly" by such party). Whether by the EPA or PRPs, an RI/FS will be overseen by an EPA **remedial project manager** (RPM). 40 C.F.R. § 300.120(f). The RPM must ensure the RI/FS is conducted according to criteria established by the CERCLA statute plus implementing rules in the NCP. CERCLA § 121, 42 U.S.C. § 9621; NCP at 40 C.F.R. § 300.430.

Under the statute, CERCLA establishes an overall command that remedial actions "shall attain a degree of cleanup of hazardous substances ... which assures protection of human health and the environment...." 42 U.S.C. § 9621(d)(1). A second command is that any remedial action must ordinarily comply with any applicable or relevant standard set by other federal or state environmental laws. *Id.* § 9621(d)(2). Such **applicable or relevant and appropriate requirements** (**ARARs**) commonly include standards for water quality under the Clean Water Act, standards for drinking water under the Safe Drinking Water Act, and standards for treatment and disposal of hazardous waste under RCRA.

The NCP expands upon these statutory commands by establishing **nine criteria** for remedy selection: overall protection of human health and the environment; compliance with ARARs; long-term effectiveness and permanence; reduction of toxicity, mobility, or volume through treatment; short-term effectiveness; implementability; cost; state government acceptance; and community acceptance. 40 C.F.R. § 300.430(e)(9)(iii). According to EPA, the first two of these (protection of health human and environment and compliance with ARARs) operate as "threshold" criteria: only those alternatives that satisfy these criteria will be among those considered. The next five serve as "primary balancing" criteria, providing the technical bases for choosing among the alternatives remaining on the table. Finally, the last two (state and community acceptance) serve as "modifying" criteria, suggesting ways in which aspects of the preferred alternative might be modified. U.S. EPA, The Feasibility Study: Detailed Analysis of Remediation Alternatives at 2 (1990).

With all the criteria that must be considered, supported by all the data that often must be collected, an RI/FS is often a major undertaking. For so-called "mega-sites," where total cleanup exceeds $50 million, the average time to complete an RI/FS may be five years. Katherine N. Probst & David M. Konisky, Superfund's Future: What Will It Cost? at 52 (2001). For big sites, an RI/FS may take considerably longer. For example, the RI/FS culminating in the 2001 ROD to address contaminated sediments in 40 miles of the Hudson River took 12 years to complete. About the same length of time was required to complete the 2014 ROD for Seattle's Lower Duwamish Waterway, discussed at the end of this chapter.

Many large Superfund sites are administratively divided into **operable units** (OUs) to facilitate more efficient investigation and cleanup. According to the NCP, "Sites should generally be remediated in operable units ... when phased analysis and response is necessary or appropriate given the size or complexity of the site...." 40 C.F.R. § 300.430(a)(1)(ii)(A). Each OU may get its own RI/FS, leading to the potential for multiple RODs at a single large site.

Despite the enormous effort that may go into completing an RI/FS and ROD for a site, a need for changes may always arise based upon new site information or other factors. If the changes are relatively minor, they may be documented through an **explanation of significant differences (ESD)**. CERCLA § 117(c), 42 U.S.C. § 9617(c). If, on the other hand, the proposed changes will "fundamentally alter the basic features of the selected remedy," then the ROD must be amended, triggering essentially the same process required for developing a ROD. 40 C.F.R. § 300.435(c)(2).

The need for an ESD or ROD amendment may be triggered by the findings of a **five-year review**. CERCLA requires these reviews no less often than every five years for any site where contamination remains at the site. CERCLA § 121(c), 42 U.S.C. § 9621(c). Five-year reviews are intended "to assure that human health and the environment are being protected by the remedial action being implemented." *Id.* Where such protection cannot be assured, then the EPA may find that additional actions are appropriate, and the EPA "shall take or require such action." *Id.*

Five-year reviews may become increasingly important for ensuring environmental justice as we learn more about risks to human health from environmental contamination. For example, as part of its decades-long cleanup of mining contamination in Butte, Montana, EPA Region 8 proposed in October 2024 to lower its cleanup level for lead from 1,200 parts per million (ppm) to 175 ppm. EPA estimated that the lowered level will require expansion of cleanup work to include an additional 7,253 homes in the Butte area. *The EPA Proposes New Lead Cleanup Level for Butte*, Oct. 16, 2024. The new cleanup level for Butte follows from action by EPA in January 2024, updating guidance on lead toxicity that had remained in place for 30 years.

Where investigations find that no further response actions are required at a site to meet the cleanup objectives, the Remedial Project Manager may document that finding through an RA report. The RA report, in turn, may be used to support subsequent determinations of **construction complete** and **deletion** (or partial deletion) of the site from the NPL.

Notes and Questions

1. **How clean is clean?** Perhaps the most vexing question in the CERCLA cleanup process is *How clean is clean?* In other words, how much cleanup should be required

for any particular contaminated site? In some cases, this may not be a hard question, as where a dozen drums of waste have been dumped in a field and not yet leaked into the ground. In this hypothetical case, just pick up the drums safely, dispose of them properly, and you're done. Most contaminated sites, however, are not like this. In an urban environment like Los Angeles, Chicago, Cleveland, or Newark, for example, lead from an old industrial facility may be mingled in the soil with lead from paint in older housing stock plus lead from decades of leaded gasoline. In a rural context like the Coeur d'Alene Basin of northern Idaho, lead from old mills and smelters may be mingled with lead that is naturally occurring in the geology that attracted the mining industry in the first place. In these two scenarios, where human health may be significantly impacted by lead exposure, once you begin remediation, how will you ever know when you are done?

CERCLA itself provides little guidance. The prime directive of CERCLA § 121 to "assure[] the protection of human health and the environment" does nothing to suggest any particular degree of protection. The NCP fills in this blank with at least some guideposts. In general, no cleanup action is suggested where the contamination presents a risk of less than one "excess" case of cancer in one million people. This is often expressed as a 10-6 cancer risk. On the other hand, cleanup action is recommended where contamination presents a risk of cancer greater than one in ten thousand (10-4). In between these two posts, cleanup actions may be discretionary, depending on factors including technical uncertainty. 40 C.F.R. § 300.430(e)(2)(A).

For noncancer impacts, such as the effects of lead exposure on neurological development in children, the NCP provides that "acceptable exposure levels shall represent concentration levels to which the human population, including sensitive subgroups, may be exposed without adverse effect during a lifetime or part of a life, incorporating an adequate margin of safety." *Id.* Quantitatively, noncancer risks are often expressed through calculation of a **hazard quotient (HQ)**, with an HQ below 1 considered not likely to result in an adverse health impact and an HQ above 1 increasing in the risk of adverse health impacts.

Based upon your understanding of quantitative risk assessment from Chapter 3, how confident would you feel about using these risk calculations to determine "how clean is clean" in your community? What vulnerabilities do you see in this approach to determining the appropriate level of cleanup for site? On the other hand, what alternatives to this approach do you see, particularly where a site may be situated in an area with multiple sources of contamination?

2. Institutional controls. According to the NCP, while CERCLA establishes a preference for treatment of contaminated materials, the EPA also "expects to use a combination of methods ... to achieve protection of human health and the environment," including "institutional controls such as water use and deed restrictions ... to prevent or limit exposure to hazardous substances. ..." 40 C.F.R. § 300.430(a)(1)(iii). The use of institutional controls has been promoted by the EPA, private industry, and some community representatives as an efficient, relatively low-cost means for protecting human

Figure 8-3. Public warning signs along Houston Ship Channel. Photo: Cliff Villa, 2017.

health while at the same time accelerating efforts to return contaminated properties to economic reuse. *See, e.g.*, U.S. EPA, Land Use in the CERCLA Remedy Selection Process (May 1995). Institutional controls may include a range of administrative devices designed to guide human behavior in order to prevent exposure to contamination that may remain at a site. Institutional controls may include proprietary controls, such as easements, equitable servitudes, and restrictive covenants; governmental controls, such as zoning and other municipal regulation of land uses; and informational devices, such as warning signs against eating fish from a contaminated waterway. *See, e.g.*, Figure 8-3 above.

While some intentions behind the use of institutional controls may be laudable, simultaneously promoting community development and the protection of human health, in practice, institutional controls may also prove challenging to implement and even inappropriate as a matter of law and policy. Through the history of the EPA's experience with contaminated sites, three generations of perspectives on institutional controls may be discerned.

In the first generation, the EPA often invoked institutional controls as if the phrase itself would bring the restriction into being. In 1979, for example, near the town of Klamath Falls in southern Oregon, the EPA caught a developer in the act of demolishing old military buildings in violation of rules for asbestos abatement. The EPA ordered the developer to cease the demolition immediately and place restrictions on the contaminated property to prevent use for residential purposes. The developer quickly agreed and then proceeded to do the exact opposite, completing the demolition and then building homes directly on top of the asbestos contamination. Endangering the lives of some two dozen families for more than a decade, the asbestos contamination finally came to light in 2002. When it became apparent that the problem could not be fixed readily, community members were relocated in 2005 and the site resembled a ghost town until remedial construction at the North Ridge Estates Superfund Site was completed in 2018. *See* www.epa.gov/superfund/north-ridge-estates. For further examples and analysis of institutional control failures in the CERCLA program, *see* Catherine A. O'Neill, *No Mud Pies: Risk Avoidance as Risk Regulation*, 31 Vt. L. Rev. 273, 313–14 (2007).

In the second generation, the EPA began to recognize that institutional controls such as deed restrictions were not subject to magic incantations and, in fact, might not be enforceable at all under controlling state law. Students of property law may recall a general reluctance of law to support endless restrictions on the use of property (among other things, giving us the famous Rule Against Perpetuities). But what if you really needed to ensure such restrictions in perpetuity? To make certain, for example, that an asbestos disposal cell in your neighborhood would never be used for residential homes? One answer was development of the Uniform Environmental Covenants Act (UECA) in 2003, which has since been adopted by at least half of the states, *not* including some of the most populous states such as California, Texas, Florida, and New York. For the text of UECA and tracking of states and territories where it has been adopted, *see* https://www.uniformlaws.org/committees/community-home?CommunityKey=ce3a1f73-4bc5-4de2-82a9-f4f54ce70294.

In states and territories where UECA or similar legislation has been adopted, property restrictions may be established and enforceable by third parties including the EPA or relevant state agencies, with careful drafting and attention to applicable requirements. For one thoughtful critique of UECA and other institutional controls in the particular context of environmental justice, *see* Andrea Ruiz-Esquide, *The Uniform Environmental Covenants Act: An Environmental Justice Perspective*, 31 Ecology L.Q. 1007 (2004) (suggesting that reliance on land-use restrictions "leads minority inner-city communities to accept disproportionately higher health risks in exchange for the possibility of jobs and economic development").

In the third generation of perspectives on the matter, the very concept of institutional controls became subject to increasing scrutiny. For example, even if state law allowed perpetual restrictions on land use, is it still a good idea to leave an asbestos dump near a residential neighborhood, tying up use of the land and creating the risk that someone, someday will disturb it? To take another example, imagine if the government said that instead of cleaning up an industrial waterway, it would simply ban all fishing in the waterway, with restrictions to be enforced in perpetuity by local law enforcement. Do you believe that would stop all people from fishing in the waterway forever? Would it stop children? The homeless? Members of Asian-Pacific Islander communities with cultural connections to fishing? Members of federally recognized tribes with treaty rights to take fish from the waterway? If the restrictions did stop all these groups from fishing in the waterway, would that constitute environmental justice? Does fair treatment permit banning every member of a community from fishing? Would meaningful involvement allow elected officials to enact a ban on fishing that would bind future generations who could not have voted for it? Keep these questions in mind as you consider the case study on the Lower Duwamish Waterway cleanup in the concluding section of this chapter.

3. Relocation. In addition to the use of institutional controls, CERCLA response actions may include the movement of people away from contaminated sites, an action known as **relocation**. CERCLA removal actions may include **temporary** relocation of residents and businesses while remedial actions may provide for **permanent** relocation.

Permanent relocation is exceedingly rare, often considered a remedy of last resort, with many perils including the disruption and possible destruction of community bonds and cultural roots. Uranium contamination on the Navajo Nation, for example, has required relocation of tribal members for years, disrupting tribal lifeways and access to native foods. Another concern with permanent relocation is appraisal of property values that may already be depressed by contamination or other features of urban blight. If the government must pay for the property it takes through relocation, how should it determine a fair value: by the market value for the property as contaminated, or the property value as may appear after cleanup?

Most relocations under CERCLA are voluntary; that is, no resident should be compelled to leave against their will in order to avoid site contamination. For contaminated sites in Indian country, Congress added the provision that no tribal members shall be permanently relocated without the concurrence of the affected tribal government. 42 U.S.C. § 9626(b). In any relocation circumstance, there may be individuals who decline to leave. For example, in the case of North Ridge Estates noted above, although 22 families chose immediate evacuation in 2005, two households chose to remain in a residential development that came to resemble an empty movie set. What reasons can you imagine people would give for refusing relocation away from contamination? Are there any circumstances you can imagine where relocation should ever be mandatory to protect public health?

Now consider the opposite problem: where community members *want* relocation but the government does not believe the contamination warrants relocation. If risk calculations remain imprecise, are the subjective concerns of community members enough to warrant relocation? Should community concerns such as anxiety about contamination or the inability of children to play outside safely ever go into a government decision whether to offer relocation to residents? What if it turns out that the government has underestimated the risks and the community concerns are well-founded? For an account of one deeply disturbing, but ultimately successful community effort to obtain permanent relocation from a highly contaminated site in Portsmouth, Virginia, *see* Armen H. Merjian, Washington Park Lead Committee, Inc. v. United States Environmental Protection Agency: *Helen Person and the Landmark Struggle Against Environmental Injustice*, 30 CHICANA/O-LATINA/O L. REV. 65 (2011).

One of the EPA's early experiences with permanent relocation concerned residents affected by contamination from the Escambia Wood Treating Company (ETC) Superfund Site in Pensacola, Florida. Decades of wood treatment activities at the ETC site threatened the health of the predominantly Black community with exposure to toxic pollutants including dioxin, creosote, and pentachlorophenol. Through formation of a community organization, Citizens Against Toxic Exposure, residents advocated for relocation, which the EPA agreed to provide in a pilot project in 1995. In all, a total of 358 households were relocated in the ETC action. Years later, the EPA collected feedback from relocated residents, identifying a number of areas for improvement and suggestions for future relocations under CERCLA. *See* U.S. EPA, Escambia Wood Treating Company (ETC) Superfund Site Permanent Relocation: Focus Groups Summary Report 3 (undated document).

Any relocation by the federal government, including temporary and permanent relocation under CERCLA, will trigger rights to assistance under the Uniform Relocation Assistance and Real Property Acquisition Act ("**Uniform Relocation Act**" or URA), 42 U.S.C. §§ 4601 *et seq*. Relocation assistance may include rent, per diem for meals and personal items, moving expenses, utility costs, insurance premiums, transportation to school, boarding of animals, and other out-of-pocket expenses necessitated by the relocation. For comprehensive information on temporary relocation under CERCLA, including checklists and template relocation agreements, *see* U.S. EPA, Superfund Response Actions: Temporary Relocations Implementation Guidance (2002). Advocates for community members facing relocation (temporary or permanent) should also be sure to carefully review provisions of the URA itself and implementing regulations at 40 C.F.R. Part 24.

4. Debunking "Superfund stigma." Proposals for listing a site on the National Priorities List sometimes draw opposition arguing "Superfund stigma"—the concern that designation of a Superfund site will lower property values in a surrounding community. These concerns are not, however, generally supported by empirical studies of housing prices in relation to NPL listing and site remediation; many studies, in fact, find the opposite.

One study published in 2014 examined neighborhoods near 29 NPL sites in the Los Angeles area, measuring the effects on housing prices from specific phases of the Superfund remedial process. According to this study, placing a site on the NPL resulted in an *increase* in housing values averaging 1.6 percent. The same study found that a site designation of "construction complete" raised prices an average of 2.8 percent while site deletion raised prices an average of 7.3 percent. Ralph A. Mastromonaco, *Hazardous Waste Hits Hollywood: Superfund and Housing Prices in Los Angeles*, 59 Environ. Resources & Econ. 207 (2014). Consistent with these findings, a more recent study of 103 hazardous waste sites in the Twin Cities of Minneapolis and Saint Paul, Minnesota, flatly found "little evidence of stigma effects once a hazardous waste site is remediated." Laura O. Taylor et al., *Disentangling Property Value Impacts of Environmental Contamination from Locally Undesirable Land Uses: Implications for Measuring Post-Cleanup Stigma*, 93 J. Urban Econ. 85 (2016).

Figure 8-4. Gowanus Canal Superfund Site, Brooklyn, NY. Photo: Cliff Villa, 2022.

A third study helps to explain the findings of the two studies noted above. According to this third study, "Proposal of a site to the NPL may reduce neighborhood housing prices *when this action provides new information* to the housing market that contamination is severe enough to warrant the potential listing...." Shanti Gamper-Rabindran & Christopher Timmins, *Does Cleanup of Hazardous Waste Sites Raise Housing Prices? Evidence of Spatially Localized Benefits*, 65 J. Envtl Econ. & Mgmt. 345, 347 (2013) (emphasis added). In most communities concerned with environmental injustice, the presence of serious contamination in their midst will hardly represent "new information" to the local housing market. Accordingly, for communities already concerned about pollution in their neighborhood, listing a contaminated site on the NPL may "increase housing prices by signaling that a site has been placed on the path towards remediation." *Id.* Moreover, the same study also indicated that the strongest increases in property values after cleanup are homes associated with the lowest income brackets. In this study, homes at the 10th percentile appreciated an average of 24.4 percent post-remediation, compared to homes in the upper 90th percentile, which appreciated 18.7 percent post-remediation. *Id.* at 346. In short, poor homeowners may have the most to gain from NPL listing, in protection of their health as well as in increases in wealth represented by the value of their homes. For one of the latest studies on stigma, largely confirming prior conclusions, see Michael R. Greenberg, *Stigma as a Multispatial-Scale Process: Revisiting the Worst US Superfund Sites*, 43 Risk Analysis 1811 (2023) (finding that only about one-third of older NPL sites continued to "fit the stereotype of stressed areas with environmental injustice challenges").

5. Gentrification and anti-displacement. It should be no surprise when cleanup of contaminated sites leads to rising property values. But there are downsides to this, including problems of gentrification. In the Brooklyn neighborhood of Park Slope, for example, evidence of gentrification is striking, even as cleanup of the adjacent Gowanus Canal Superfund Site remains years away from completion. See Figure 8-4.

In neighborhoods experiencing gentrification, renters may feel any hope of purchasing a home slip away and may even find themselves priced out of their neighborhood by rising rents. Rising rents may also create greater challenges for the homeless to find a stable home. Even for current homeowners themselves, who may enjoy an increase in home equity, rising home values may mean rising property taxes as well, which some people on fixed incomes—particularly the elderly—may not be able to afford.

EPA has defined "gentrification" as "the process of neighborhood change that occurs as places of lower real estate value are transformed into places of higher real estate value." The EPA definition draws upon the work of scholars and community leaders including participants on the National Environmental Justice Advisory Council in the 1990s, who produced a report, ENVIRONMENTAL JUSTICE, URBAN REVITALIZATION, AND BROWNFIELDS: THE SEARCH FOR AUTHENTIC SIGNS OF HOPE (Dec. 1996). In this influential report, instead of a focus on combatting gentrification, the NEJAC focused on promoting what it called "urban revitalization."

> Urban revitalization is a bottom-up process. It proceeds from a community-based vision of its needs and aspirations and seeks to build capacity, build partnerships, and mobilize resources to make the vision a reality. Revitalization, as we define it, does not lead to displacement of communities through gentrification that often results from redevelopment policies. Governments must not simply view communities as an assortment of problems but also as a collection of assets. Social scientists and practitioners have already compiled methodologies to apply community planning models.

Authentic Signs of Hope at 12. In the decades since this influential NEJAC report, methodologies for preventing displacement have been refined and deployed to assist communities across the country. For a quick review of some of these tools, see the notes below.

Community Benefit Agreements (CBA). A Community Benefit Agreement often takes the form of a contract between community organizations and a private developer, requiring the developer to provide specific benefits to the community, often in exchange for community support (or non-opposition) to a proposed development. CBAs may be voluntary or legally mandated. In San Francisco, a city notorious for gentrification and astronomical housing prices, the cleanup of the Hunters Point Naval Shipyard Superfund Site presents an extraordinary opportunity for benefiting residents in an historically Black community. While the U.S. Navy continues cleanup of the site, a redevelopment plan calls for construction of 10,500 housing units, plus recreation areas and commercial centers, potentially creating up to 20,000 jobs. Under a CBA between developers and local nonprofits, 32 percent of the housing is to be designated as affordable, including downpayment assistance, with the developer also contributing $8.5 million in job training for local residents. For more on CBAs, see Chapter 10 (Private Governance).

Community Land Trusts (CLTs). Most commonly, Community Land Trusts are nonprofit organizations that purchase land with public or private funds and then lease parcels of that land on a long-term basis to homeowners and tenants. Homes built on the land are more affordable because the land is not sold. The homes can often be passed down to family members, building generational wealth, or may be sold at restricted prices to preserve affordability. In Denver, Colorado, the Vasquez Boulevard and I-70 Superfund Site reflects the legacy of metal smelting activities that contaminated soil and groundwater of six neighborhoods, including low-income communities of color. As the site is being cleaned up, the GES Land Trust is working to preserve existing affordable housing, create new affordable housing, and develop additional community amenities including a "community food forest."

Tax Abatement. Tax abatements are financial programs designed to ease property taxes for low- and moderate-income homeowners, particularly in areas experiencing increasing property taxes due to rising property values. Tax abatement programs are administered by local jurisdictions and vary in the amount of tax relief provided. The City of Cleveland, Ohio, for example, has a residential tax abatement program which eliminates 100 percent of tax associated with new developments and remodeling projects for 15 years. For rehabilitation of existing homes, homeowners pay only the amount of taxes based upon the home's value before renovation. Tax abatement strategies may also assist with economic redevelopment. For example, in South Point, Ohio, tax abatement strategies have contributed to revitalization efforts at the South Point Superfund Site, facilitating conversion of the site to a new 185-acre industrial park.

For additional information on anti-displacement strategies, see the website maintained by Smart Growth America: https://smartgrowthamerica.org/tag/anti-displacement/. The website for EPA's **Superfund Redevelopment Program** is also an outstanding resource, providing plentiful case studies of successful efforts to transform contaminated sites to accessible housing and other community assets. *See* https://www.epa.gov/superfund-redevelopment. Among the robust body of scholarly work on gentrification and anti-displacement strategies, *see, e.g.*, Kristin King-Ries, *Advocating for Community Land Trusts*, 31 J. Affordable Housing & Community Dev. L. 365 (2023); Sarena Malsin, *Unveiling the "Trojan Horses" of Gentrification: Studies of Legal Strategies to Combat Environmental Gentrification in Washington, D.C. and New York, N.Y.*, 38 Pace Envtl. L. Rev. 147 (2020).

C. Fair Treatment and Meaningful Involvement in Site Cleanup

Advocates for environmental justice might read a statute like CERCLA from end to end and find nothing that requires fair treatment or promotes the values of meaningful involvement. In fact, throughout the CERCLA remedial process, where a site might take a decade or more to reach a selected remedy in a Record of Decision, the only explicit requirement for public involvement in the statute follows completion of an RI/FS when the lead agency must "[p]rovide a reasonable opportunity for submission of written and oral comments and an opportunity for a public meeting at or near the facility at issue regarding the proposed plan…." CERCLA § 117(a)(2), 42 U.S.C. § 9617(a)(2). The statute also, however, requires the EPA to promulgate regulations "to provide for the participation of interested persons" in the selection of removal and remedial actions. 42 U.S.C. § 9613(k). The regulations appear in the National Contingency Plan (NCP), 40 C.F.R. Part 300, and will be considered in this section. Importantly, this section will also examine other opportunities for public involvement in cleanup that appear nowhere in the statutes or regulations but exist nonetheless for advocates who take initiative to find them. To begin this section, we will consider the meaning of "fair treatment" in the cleanup context, where remedy decisions are intended to respond to the unique conditions of each individual site but may sometimes fail to meet objectives for protecting human health or the environment.

1. Fair Treatment and Contaminated Sites

As noted in the prior section, the overall command for CERCLA response actions is the protection of human health and the environment. This standard, of course, is highly contextual and often dependent on unique factors at a given site, such as the demographics of the surrounding community and the presence of additional sources of pollution. With such variability, what constitutes "fair treatment" in any individual circumstance may be difficult to define. And yet, in most cases, we may truly "know it when we see it."

Consider this scenario. Two contaminated sites in the same state are discovered in the same year: 1991. The source of contamination for both sites is also the same: old drycleaner facilities. The same contaminants, trichlorethylene (TCE) and perchloroethylene (PCE), are found in soils and groundwater underlying neighborhoods that surround the old facilities. In 2001, EPA issued a CERCLA Record of Decision (ROD) for both sites, selecting final actions to clean up the groundwater contamination. However, the selected remedies for the two sites are strikingly different.

The ROD for Site A called for construction and operation of a conventional "pump and treat" system, through which contaminated groundwater is pumped to the surface, treated with filters, and then reinjected into the aquifer. Construction and operation of the treatment system cost approximately $11.5 million. By all accounts, the system worked. Within five years, the pump and treat system had met remedial objectives.

Within ten years, a portion of the site had been redeveloped into affordable housing and other uses.

By contrast, the ROD for Site B, located 60 miles north, called for "enhanced bioremediation." The bioremediation remedy involved the injection of organic materials (such as vegetable oil) into the groundwater to encourage microorganisms to grow and break down the contamination. The advantage of this "in-situ" technology is that it is cheaper than pump and treat, with an estimated cost of $5.8 million. After 20 years of bioremediation efforts, however, the groundwater still had not met remedial objectives; in fact, in some places, contamination appeared to be increasing.

What can explain the fate of these two sites, so similarly situated in 1991, yet so widely divergent 20 years later? There could, of course, be important differences in geology, hydrology, or other physical conditions. But what if the difference appears related to demographics, with the community surrounding Site B substantially higher in low-income population and people of color than the community surrounding Site A?

Cases like the one above (not very hypothetical) appear across the United States. Look around and chances are you may find cases of what looks like unfair treatment for a contaminated site near you. You may know discrimination when you see it, or when you *feel* it, but as discussed in Chapter 4, discrimination is notoriously hard to prove.

Notes and Questions

1. **What now?** Rather than leaping first to an Equal Protection case, guaranteeing years of litigation and the challenging proof requirement, how might effective advocates for environmental justice begin to address evident cases of unfair treatment? Recall that for sites where contamination remains in place, CERCLA generally requires EPA to conduct a **five-year review**, which will likely be made available for public review and comment. *See, e.g.*, U.S. EPA Region 2, Final Third Five-Year Review Report for the Hudson River PCBs Superfund Site, Jan. 15, 2025 (final report issued following 120-day public comment period). The review may indicate that minor changes to the remedy are appropriate, which may be made through an Explanation of Significant Differences (ESD). Or the five-year review report could call for an amended ROD or a new ROD altogether, both actions requiring opportunities for public engagement.

2. **The "blunt withdrawal" of jurisdiction.** What if, even after admitting the failure of a selected remedy, the EPA simply refuses to engage in selecting a new remedy? In this case, effective advocates will find many avenues for advocacy, including within executive and legislative branches of government. As lawyers (or future lawyers), we know there must be options for judicial action as well. Under CERCLA, however, there are express limitations for challenging a selected remedy. CERCLA § 113(h) presumptively bars federal courts from reviewing "challenges to any removal or remedial actions" selected under the statute until the cleanup work is actually completed. 42 U.S.C. § 9613(h)(4) (authorizing challenges to removal or remedial actions only once

the actions are "taken"—past tense). Courts have recognized that this language effects a "blunt withdrawal of federal jurisdiction," *see, e.g.*, *McClellan Ecological Seepage Situation v. Perry*, 47 F.3d 325, 328 (9th Cir. 1995). This "blunt withdrawal" serves the congressional intent of CERCLA to provide for expeditious cleanup of contaminated sites without the delay of litigation—a policy described colloquially as "shovels first, lawyers later."

3. Constitutional challenges? For contaminated sites where the § 113 bar may apply, such as any site receiving ongoing active remediation under CERCLA, challenge to the selected remedy may be tougher, though not impossible. As the plaintiffs in the Portsmouth, Virginia, case pointed out, while § 113(h) may bar challenges under the CERCLA statute, it might not bar challenges under the U.S. Constitution itself. Courts appear split on the question of whether § 113(h) may preclude constitutional challenges to CERCLA remedies. *See* Robert G. Ruggieri, Broward v. Environmental Protection Agency: *CERCLA's Bar on Pre-enforcement Review of EPA Cleanup Under Section 113(h)*, 13 Vill. Envtl. L.J. 375 (2002). In the Portsmouth case, the federal court allowed the constitutional challenge, observing that if the § 113(h) bar applied, plaintiffs "could not raise their constitutional claims until the cleanup was concluded," at which point "the case would be moot." *Washington Park Lead Comm. v. U.S. EPA*, 1998 WL 1053712 at 9 (E.D. Va. Dec. 1, 1998).

Surviving the § 113(h) bar, of course, plaintiffs bringing an Equal Protection challenge to a CERCLA remedy must still prove defendant's intent to discrimination in order to prevail on the merits. While this may be a high burden of proof, the Supreme Court has provided guidance identifying a range of factors from which discriminatory intent may be inferred. *See Village of Arlington Heights v. Metropolitan Housing Development Corp.*, 429 U.S. 252 (1977). Among the factors identified in *Arlington Heights* are "a clear pattern, unexplainable on grounds other than race...." *Id.* at 266. In the Portsmouth case, plaintiffs seeking to challenge the EPA's denial of permanent relocation for the largely Black community introduced evidence that of the 19 permanent relocations that had taken place at NPL sites as of 2000, 16 had been in predominantly white communities. Merjian, *supra*, at 94–95. Only three relocations had taken place in predominantly Black communities, one of which was based upon an act of Congress and another (the Portsmouth case) the result of litigation. Whether this evident pattern would be enough to support a judicial finding of intentional discrimination, we do not know. We do know, however, that it was enough to induce the EPA (and the U.S. Department of Justice) to settle the Portsmouth case and provide the permanent relocation that the residents sought through the litigation.

4. Natural resource damages. Beyond remedial actions to address contamination directly, CERCLA and the Oil Pollution Act (OPA) further authorize legal actions to restore natural resources, such as groundwater, surface water, wetlands, and other wildlife habitats that may be injured by contamination. *See* CERCLA § 107(a), 42 U.S.C. § 9607(a)(4)(C); OPA § 1002, 33 U.S.C. § 2702(b)(2)(A). In one settlement for **natural resource damages** resulting from mining contamination in the Clark Fork

River Basin of western Montana, the Confederated Salish and Kootenai Tribes (CSKT) of the Flathead Reservation received $18.3 million for restoration projects in the Clark Fork River Basin. Funded CSKT projects include $6.4 million for restoration of up to 800 acres of wetlands and $1.5 million for measures to restore the local population of native bull trout, a threatened species under the Endangered Species Act and a traditional food source for the Tribes.

5. State authorities. Of course, where community members remain unsatisfied with remedies for contamination under federal law, additional remedies may be found under applicable state, tribal, or local authorities. Like many states, the State of Washington, for example, has its own version of Superfund, the Model Toxics Control Act (MTCA), 70.105D RCW. Among other distinct features, MTCA rejects the CERCLA petroleum exclusion, providing a possible remedy for soils contaminated by mismanaged gas stations and other potential sources of petroleum pollution. As another example, the Minnesota Environmental Response and Liability Act (MERLA), Minn. Stat. § 115B, establishes a Harmful Substance Compensation Program to compensate persons who suffer certain kinds of injury or property damage from contamination in Minnesota. Claims for personal and economic injuries under MERLA may be combined with common law tort claims such as trespass, negligence, nuisance, and ultra-hazardous activity. *See* Madeline Gallo, *From Wood Treatment to Unequal Treatment: The Story of the St. Regis Superfund Site*, 29 L. & Inequality 175, 184 (2011).

One possible limitation on the use of state or other non-federal authorities is an argument based upon federal preemption by CERCLA. In one recent case, landowners near the former Anaconda Smelter in Montana filed suit in state court, asserting claims for trespass, nuisance, and strict liability in order to compel the responsible party, Atlantic Richfield, to conduct actions beyond EPA's cleanup plan. In its defense, Atlantic Richfield pointed to CERCLA § 113(b), which provides in part that "the United States district courts shall have exclusive original jurisdiction over all controversies arising under this chapter..." 42 U.S.C. § 9613(b). Upon reaching the U.S. Supreme Court, Chief Justice Roberts, writing for the majority, observed that the landowners' claims were not "arising under" CERCLA, but found a legal basis under Montana law. *Atlantic Richfield Co. v. Christian*, 590 U.S. 1 (2020). Writing separately, Justice Gorsuch observed, "Everything in CERCLA suggests that it seeks to supplement, not supplant, traditional state law remedies." *Id.* at 36. The landowners' claims were thus allowed to proceed in state court.

2. Meaningful Involvement with Contaminated Sites

As noted at the beginning of the section, the CERCLA statute requires little in terms of public participation—and nothing like modern understandings of "meaningful involvement." That said, this section will outline areas of the CERCLA process where community advocates should expect and may demand public involvement. For cleanup in the RCRA corrective process, even less is required for public involvement (there is no equivalent of the NCP for RCRA corrective action), but nonbinding agency policies may help establish some best practices. *See, e.g.*, U.S. EPA, Resource Conservation and Recovery Act Public Participation Manual (Jan. 11, 2017). Of course, state, tribal, and local cleanup authorities may always establish greater requirements for public participation and should always be consulted as appropriate.

CERCLA requires opportunities for public involvement in three general contexts: proposals for amending the National Contingency Plan; proposals for settlement; and proposals for response actions. Each context will be considered with more detail below.

a. Public comment on the National Contingency Plan (NCP). As noted earlier in this chapter, the National Contingency Plan, in a twist on administrative law, represents a set of regulations that came before the statutes they would implement. With the passage of CERCLA in 1980, Congress required the EPA to revise the NCP, and the EPA in fact continues to revise the NCP regularly. The most frequent NCP revisions, approximately twice a year, are updates to the National Priorities List, to which new sites are regularly added and from which completed sites may be deleted. *See, e.g.*, 89 Fed. Reg. 100751 (Dec. 13, 2024) (final NPL listing for the Upper Columbia River in Washington State).

Under CERCLA, any legal challenges to the NCP, including challenges to proposed NPL listings or proposed NPL deletions, must proceed through the D.C. Circuit Court of Appeals, within 90 days of the rule promulgation. CERCLA § 113(a), 42 U.S.C. § 9613(a). Any failure to observe this jurisdictional rule may result in dismissal of the challenge. *See, e.g.*, *United States v. Asarco Inc.*, 214 F.3d 1104 (9th Cir. 2000) (dismissing challenge to scope of NPL listing for the "Bunker Hill Mining Site," as all challenges to NPL listing remain within exclusive jurisdiction of the D.C. Circuit Court of Appeals). While environmental justice advocates clearly may challenge NPL listings and NPL deletions, may they also challenge EPA *refusals* to list a site? What does CERCLA § 105(d) plus CERCLA § 310(a)(2) tell you?

b. Public comment on settlements. With the general understanding that community advocates should have a "seat at the table" for deliberations that may affect their communities, one exceptional circumstance may be settlement negotiations, where government lawyers and potentially responsible parties (PRPs) often meet in closed-door sessions to hammer out the terms of a proposed agreement. Due to the nature of many negotiations, the law generally supports limited protections for "settlement confidentiality." *See, e.g.*, Federal Rules of Evidence 508: Compromise Offers and Negotiations. Closed-door sessions, however, may give rise to community concerns that the government may engage in less than "arms-length" negotiations and provide "sweetheart deals" to favored parties, at the expense of public interests.

Against such concerns, CERCLA provides specific opportunities for public review and comments on proposed settlements for both cleanup actions and cost recovery. Public comments on a proposed settlement with a PRP may convince a government agency (e.g., EPA or a state) or a reviewing court to modify or reject the settlement. In addition to the (rather vague) standard of "inappropriate, improper, or inadequate" specified in CERCLA § 122(i), federal courts have established a more articulate standard for reviewing CERCLA settlements. "In order to approve a CERCLA consent decree, a district court must conclude that the agreement is procedurally and substantively 'fair, reasonable, and consistent with CERCLA's objectives.'" *State of Arizona v. City of Tucson*, 761 F.3d 1005, 1011–12 (9th Cir. 2014), *citing United States v. Montrose Chem. Corp. of Cal.*, 50 F.3d 741, 747 (9th Cir. 1995). In the *Arizona* case, the City of Tucson and other intervenors challenged settlements proposed by the State of Arizona where the State asserted that the settling defendants were only responsible for less than 0.2 percent of $75 million in remediation costs at the Broadway-Patano Landfill (a state Superfund site). Agreeing with the intervenors, the Ninth Circuit vacated the district court's order approving the consent decrees, finding that the court "failed to independently scrutinize the terms of the agreements, … and in so doing, afforded undue deference to the [Arizona Department of Environmental Quality]." *State of Arizona* at 1010.

Given the prospect that trial courts or appellate courts may reject a proposed CERCLA settlement for insufficient basis to conclude the agreement is "procedurally and substantively 'fair, reasonable, and consistent with CERCLA's objectives,'" how might a community advocate argue that community concerns should be addressed at the outset of settlement negotiations rather than the tail-end when the product of negotiations is presented to the court for approval?

c. Public comment on response actions. The most common opportunity for public engagement within the CERCLA program is commenting on proposals for CERCLA removals and remedial action. While CERCLA § 117 provides explicit opportunities to comment on proposed remedial actions, the statute leaves comment opportunities in the removal context entirely up to the NCP to define. Look closely at the sliding scale for public involvement in removal actions defined by 40 C.F.R. § 300.415(n). Does a removal action that can be completed within 30 days require any opportunity for public comment? Noting the NCP's frequent use of "as appropriate," when, if ever, would it be "appropriate" to hold a public comment period on an action that has already been completed?

Whenever public comments are collected on a proposed cleanup action, CERCLA and the NCP require a written response to all "significant comments." CERCLA § 117(b), 40 C.F.R. 415(n)(2)(iii). What are "significant" comments? Significance depends at least in part on the scope of the given comment period. A proposal to clean up an illegal dumpsite in a city park, for example, may have little relation to whether people drive too fast on the road in front of the park. EJ advocates may assist community members with understanding the scope of any particular comment period and finding more appropriate venues for other community concerns.

Perhaps the most important question concerning public comment on proposed response actions is this: *Do public comments ever make any difference in the final remedy selected?* The answer to this question is *Yes*. But much may remain at the discretion of individual agency decisionmakers. For example, in the final days of the Biden administration, EPA and the Navajo Nation selected a cleanup plan for one of the largest uranium mine sites on the Navajo reservation. Under the plan, EPA will remove over one million cubic yards of contamination from the mine site, for proper disposal in a landfill on private land in New Mexico. *EPA and Navajo Nation Select Cleanup Plan to Remove Waste at Quivira Mines Site*, Jan. 7, 2025. Removal of this waste had been specifically urged by members of the nearby Red Water Pond Road Community, which had lived in the shadow of this waste pile for generations. *See* MASE Supports EPA Decision That Will Protect Uranium Impacted Communities, Jan. 7, 2025 (quoting one community member: "I feel as though our community finally has something of a win").

Of course, community members may not always—or often—feel they get "something of a win" from the CERCLA remedy selection process. The lengthy time required to reach a final cleanup decision, measured in years or even decades, may itself be a form of environmental injustice, even if the outcome is one that the community desires. As a community advocate, what might you do to help accelerate this process?

d. Additional public involvement tools. For all remedial actions, and for removal actions expected to continue for more than 120 days, the NCP at 40 C.F.R. § 415(n)(3) establishes a number of specific requirements to promote public involvement besides public comment periods. These include community interviews, a community relations plan, a local information repository, and—for NPL sites—technical assistance grants. For sites included on the NPL, most of these functions may be handled or managed by a **community involvement coordinator** (CIC), who may serve as a liaison beyond community members and the on-scene coordinator (OSC) or remedial project manager (RPM), who may be more focused on field work or technical analyses. Each of these community involvement functions will be considered briefly in the notes below.

Community interviews. Direct contact between community members and agency staff may be an essential means for an agency to understand the diverse perspectives and needs of a community. Among other things, community interviews may identify the various languages that must be accommodated in public meetings and written materials. Community meetings may also identify the best means of communicating with community members (email? printed factsheets? radio broadcasts? personal appearances in farmers markets or faith-based organizations?). In a community with a high level of distrust of the government, how might you design these interviews for maximum usefulness?

Community involvement plans. Information from community interviews and other resources will help the lead agency develop the required community relations plan, known more commonly now as a community involvement plan. The community involvement plan documents important information about a community such as languages spoken, educational levels, preferred means of communication, and possible meeting venues. As indicated by the NCP at 40 C.F.R. § 300.435, the community involvement plan should be updated from time to time, particularly following completion of the remedy selection process and before construction activities begin. For an

Figure 8-5. Navajo tribal member Mable Franklin (right) and EPA environmental engineer Angie Villa (left). Navajo Nation near Cameron, Arizona. Photo: U.S. EPA, 2024.

excellent example, *see* the Community Involvement Plan for the USS Lead Superfund Site in East Chicago (EPA 2018), available online.

Technical Assistance Grants. Given the enormous data analysis and technical complexities associated with most Superfund sites, Congress through CERCLA § 117 (e) established the availability of technical assistance grants (TAGs) for community organizations. TAGs are generally capped at $50,000, but may be renewed over the life of the CERCLA process. In addition to TAGs, further technical assistance for community advisory groups may be available through EPA contracts for Technical Assistance Services for Communities (TASC). Through TASC, EPA may provide considerably more funding than a TAG grant, retaining scientists, engineers, and other professionals to assist communities with certain projects at no cost to the communities. For a comprehensive collection of policies and regulations on TASC and TAG grants, *see* www.epa.gov/superfund/technical-assistance-grant-tag-program.

3. Further Opportunities for Public Engagement on Contaminated Sites

In addition to all the specific requirements for public involvement identified in the preceding section, there remain many more opportunities for community advocates to engage meaningfully in cleanup processes. Reflecting these additional opportunities, EPA during the Biden administration began emphasizing a shift from "meaningful involvement" to meaningful *engagement*. In August 2024, EPA released a new guidance document, *Achieving Health and Environmental Protection Through Meaningful Engagement Policy*. The 2024 *Meaningful Engagement Policy* offers a compendium of legal authorities and best practices that may prove useful in many contexts, including work on contaminated sites. For example, in 2024, and consistent with authorities identified in the *Meaningful Engagement Policy*, EPA provided compensation to tribal members who traveled to a listening session in Arizona that EPA organized for purposes of gathering information about uranium contamination on the Navajo Nation.

Beyond practices identified in the 2024 *Meaningful Engagement Policy*, determined community advocates may also consider the following suggestions.

a. Get a job. Ironically, this may be the most overlooked suggestion in academia, as many students invest in education specifically to seek employment after graduation. But for aspiring EJ advocates, employment—*where?*

Imagine that you genuinely cared about protecting human health in a community with a new NPL site, and you had an opportunity to shape an RI/FS for that site from the very start. There are people who get paid to do that, including attorneys in the regional offices of the U.S. EPA. If this interests you, consider applying to the various EPA regional offices and headquarters offices, which independently hire entry-level attorneys most years through honors attorney programs. Consider applying to the U.S. DOJ Environment and Natural Resources Division, where you also may find more litigation experience. Consider applying to other federal agencies who may have more opportunity to promote environmental justice than you suspect: agencies such as the U.S. Department of Agriculture, U.S. Department of the Interior, and the Army Corps of Engineers.

In light of recent attacks on the federal workforce by the second Trump administration, you might alternatively consider applying to state agencies, including environmental departments and state AG offices. Consider tribal agencies, local governments, nongovernmental organizations, and private firms of all sizes. What could you do to effect positive change in each capacity?

b. Get involved. Short of going to work for an agency or organization directly involved in the cleanup of a contaminated site, you may find other opportunities to get involved in the cleanup process, such as participation through a community advisory group, a neighborhood association, or a faith-based organization. Engage in a community interview with an EPA community involvement coordinator and put your name on an email list for regular site updates. Attend a public meeting when you can, provide a thoughtful public comment when the opportunity presents, and invite your neighbors to join you. Agency staff should understand that they work for you, but they won't know what you want unless you tell them.

c. **Make a phone call.** The most powerful phone call you can probably ever make is to this phone number: **1-800-424-8802.** This is the phone number for the **National Response Center (NRC)** in Washington, D.C., staffed around the clock by the U.S. Coast Guard. Dial it if you witness an oil spill or a chemical release anywhere in the United States. Within minutes, your call will be routed to the proper authorities for response in the local area, likely to include a member of the EPA regional response team and state or tribal counterparts. Do not dial this number to report the existence of a stable, designated Superfund site. But dial it in case of a sudden, unexpected release from a Superfund site.

Reporting to the NRC is mandatory for "[a]ny person in charge of a ... facility" where there has been a release of a hazardous substance above a "reportable quantity." CERCLA § 9603(a), 42 U.S.C. § 9603(a). *See* NCP at 40 C.F.R. Table 302.4 for list of reportable quantities by hazardous substance.

In addition to NRC reporting, citizen tips and complaints about pollution and contaminated sites may also be made online through EPA and state agency websites. Reporting may also be made anonymously if preferred.

D. Case Study: The Lower Duwamish Waterway Superfund Site

For many people, the Duwamish River holds special meaning as Seattle's only river, flowing from the south to the north to empty into Elliott Bay. On modern maps, however, the Duwamish River does not exist. In fact, it has not existed for a long time. In 1913, the Corps of Engineers went to work on the Duwamish River, deepening its channels, straightening its meanders, and transforming it into the Duwamish *Waterway.* A century of urban runoff plus heavy industrial activity, including cement production, airplane manufacturing, auto shredding, and metals recycling, fouled the waterway with a variety of toxins, much in the way of urban waterways across the United States. While industrial practices and water quality improved with environmental regulations in the 1970s, the sediments at the bottom of the Duwamish Waterway remain contaminated with pollutants including arsenic and polychlorinated biphenyls (PCBs), a human carcinogen now banned from production due to its toxic effects. Driven by concern for PCBs in the fish, the EPA added the Lower Duwamish Waterway (LDW) to the National Priorities List in 2001, beginning a long process of Superfund investigation and remediation. Meanwhile, the Duwamish Waterway continues in active industrial use, flanked by diverse neighborhoods impacted by the pollution. In this

Figure 8-6. Duwamish River, Seattle, Washington. Photo: Cliff Villa, 2015.

concluding section of the chapter on contaminated sites, we will consider the case of the Lower Duwamish Waterway to understand continuing challenges for environmental justice plus emerging solutions to these challenges.

As the waterway cuts diagonally across former mudflats and farmland, the Georgetown neighborhood sits to the north and east, with the South Park neighborhood to the south and west. Both neighborhoods are more diverse and low-income than Seattle overall, with South Park one of the most diverse neighborhoods in the county. Of some 4,264 people living in South Park, approximately 25 percent were born outside of the United States, with high populations of Latinos and Asian-Pacific Islanders. At the one public elementary school in the community, 83 percent of students qualify for free or reduced price lunch. The community also includes populations of Native Americans, with three federally recognized tribes holding treaty rights to the river plus the Duwamish Tribe, which remains unrecognized by the federal government but an important presence in the community. Stakeholders in the cleanup of the Lower Duwamish Waterway further include members of more than 20 ethnic groups across the Seattle area who fish the river and engage in other activities to include picnicking and boating. Subsistence fishers who eat resident fish are most likely to come from Asian-Pacific Islander communities and multi-racial backgrounds. *See* U.S. EPA Region 10, *Fishing in the Duwamish River: What Did We Learn and What Do We Do Next?* (Feb. 2017).

Threats from contamination in the Duwamish Waterway led the state health department to issue advisories against eating clams, crabs, and resident fish such as perch and flounder, while promoting salmon as a healthier choice. In a prior era of environmental thought, this might have been considered enough to address concerns for pollution in urban waterways. In time, government agencies began to recognize the need for actual cleanup of such contamination, as urged by the work of scholars and activists in environmental justice. *See, e.g.*, National Environmental Justice Advisory Council, FISH CONSUMPTION AND ENVIRONMENTAL JUSTICE (Nov. 2002); Catherine O'Neill, *Variable Justice: Environmental Standards, Contaminated Fish, and "Acceptable" Risk to Native Peoples*, 19 STAN. ENVTL. L.J. 3 (2000). With the NPL listing of the Lower Duwamish Waterway in 2001, the EPA recognized the need for inclusive processes to address community concerns throughout the phases of Superfund cleanup. The EPA met the minimum requirements of CERCLA and the NCP. For example, the EPA established a local information repository at the South Park Branch Public Library, prepared an original community involvement plan in 2002, and held a public comment period for the LDW proposed plan in 2013. But the EPA also went farther to promote meaningful involvement for this diverse community—in some cases farther than ever before.

In addition to inviting comments on the proposed plan in 2013 (a requirement of CERCLA § 117), the EPA held public meetings and collected public comments on draft documents throughout the RI/FS process. Public comments on the RI report, for example, encouraged the EPA to begin a series of early cleanup actions in five areas of the waterway with the most contamination. The five early action areas were substantially completed in 2015, reducing PCBs concentrations in the waterway by half even before the final remedy would begin in earnest in 2024.

During the comment period on the FS, community members requested that the EPA conduct an **environmental justice analysis** on the proposed cleanup alternatives. While EJ analyses have become increasingly common in other contexts such as NEPA reviews, no EJ analysis had ever been done in the context of CERCLA remedy selection. The EJ analysis for the Lower Duwamish Waterway became the first. Predictably, potentially responsible parties (PRPs) questioned the role of this EJ analysis in the LDW remedy selection. In response, EPA agreed "that an EJ analysis is not a separate criterion for CERCLA remedy selection." But EPA maintained that it was appropriate to consider EJ as part of the NCP **nine criteria**, which includes "overall protection of human health and the environment." 40 C.F.R. §300.430(e)(9). *See* U.S. EPA, LOWER DUWAMISH WATERWAY SUPERFUND SITE RECORD OF DECISION—PART 3: RESPONSIVENESS SUMMARY at 125 (Nov. 2014).

Throughout the Superfund process for the Lower Duwamish Waterway, community involvement was enhanced through the engagement of a **community advisory group** now known as the Duwamish River Community Coalition (DRCC). Founded in 2001, the DRCC convened interests from neighborhood, environmental, tribal, and small business organizations in order to advocate for community concerns with respect to the Duwamish River. With support from EPA **technical assistance grants** and other sources, the DRCC contracted their own technical advisor to interpret and explain technical reports, site conditions, and cleanup proposals and decisions, thereby facilitating community input into the Superfund planning process. The DRCC also continues to support related programs such as river tours, educational forums, habitat restoration activities, an annual river festival, and other neighborhood events.

In 2013, the DRCC took a lead role in facilitating community comments during the official comment period on the **proposed plan** for the Lower Duwamish Waterway. The proposed plan generally recommended a mix of dredging some contaminated sediments from the riverbed and capping other contaminated sediments in place, for an estimated total cost of $305 million. During this comment period, the EPA held five formal comment meetings, including one in the South Park neighborhood conducted entirely in Spanish. Due to significant public interest in the cleanup, the EPA extended the comment period from the 30 days required by the NCP to 105 days. By the end of this extended comment period, the EPA had collected 2,327 written and oral submissions, in ten different languages. Comments from the DRCC and tribes generally supported the proposed cleanup and advocated for expanded cleanup measures. Comments from PRPs generally advocated for less cleanup and for waiving applicable or relevant and appropriate requirements (ARARs) for sediment cleanup standards. In the final Record of Decision, released in November 2014, no commenter received everything they wanted. However, the EPA did reject the ARARs waiver requested by the PRPs and did agree to expand the scope of cleanup by 25 percent, from 84 acres of dredging as proposed to 105 acres of dredging as selected, at a total final estimated cost of $342 million. U.S. EPA, Lower Duwamish Waterway Record of Decision, Fact Sheet on the Final Cleanup Plan (Nov. 2014).

Since the EPA released the final ROD in 2014, community members have remained engaged in the LDW Superfund process. 187 community members contributed comments for an update of the community involvement plan for the Lower Duwamish Waterway released in 2016. Among other creative ideas captured in the updated plan, community members suggested holding information sessions during soccer practices within the Latino community; coordinating through churches, youth organizations, and karaoke nights within the Vietnamese community; and working with community services for recent immigrants from Somalia, Sudan, Kenya, and other East African nations. The EPA continues to collaborate with agency partners on all levels of government in order to ensure efficient and effective cleanup actions and to avoid overloading community members with repeated requests for input. U.S. EPA, Lower Duwamish Waterway Superfund Site: Community Involvement Plan (Oct. 2016). One particularly fruitful collaboration between the EPA and the local health department resulted in the training and engagement of more than 20 "Community Health Advocates," who help explain technical information and promote safe fish consumption within their own communities.

After ten years of additional studies, designs, engineering, and negotiations, remedial dredging of the Lower Duwamish Waterway finally began in November 2024 and is expected to conclude in February 2027. The cleanup work will be performed by local contractors, providing employment opportunities for local workers. Cleanup progress may be followed at www.ldwg.org. Meanwhile, as the cleanup proceeds, new parks have already opened and new opportunities will continue to unfold for the people of the South Park community.

Notes and Questions

1. **Community involvement tools.** Of all the tools for promoting community involvement identified in this case study, which ones seemed most meaningful to you? What other tools, not identified here, would help reach underserved people in your community? Consider, for example, how you would best reach children, seniors, or homeless populations. What might you hope to learn from each of these groups that could assist in developing a more protective remedy or a remedy most likely to receive community support?

2. **EJ analysis.** For a contaminated site in a community such as South Park with a large population of low-income people and people of color, how would you evaluate the argument for conducting an EJ analysis under CERCLA, given that "environmental justice" is not one of CERCLA's **nine criteria** for remedy selection?

3. **Opposition?** Imagine if most community members opposed cleanup, perhaps concerned that gentrification might consume the last affordable neighborhood in Seattle. If so, should EPA still proceed with cleanup to protect human health?

4. **Georgia on my mind.** From the opening vignette of this chapter, recall the Westside Lead Superfund Site in Atlanta, which moved with extraordinary speed from site discovery to NPL listing to the start of cleanup. Can speedy cleanup be reconciled with EJ mandates for meaningful community involvement? If so, how? Are there also circumstances where a delay in cleanup may be justified by the need for additional community involvement?

Chapter 9

Environmental Justice for Indian Tribes and Indigenous People

> *There is just no getting around the fact that applying the concept of environmental justice to situations that affect the communities of Indian reservations is tricky. If environmental justice problems are characterized by disproportionate impacts on communities of color or low-income, then almost every environmental issue in Indian country is an environmental justice issue.*

Dean B. Suagee, *Environmental Justice and Indian Country*, 30 HUMAN RIGHTS 16 (2003).

A. Introduction

As observed above by the late distinguished lawyer and Indian law scholar Dean Suagee, applying environmental justice concepts in Indian country and among Indigenous peoples in the United States can be "tricky" for many reasons. Among other things, "disproportionate impacts" on "low-income communities" could implicate almost every Indian reservation, where poverty rates are almost three times higher than elsewhere in the United States and health disparities across a range of ailments are pronounced. *See, e.g.*, Indian Health Service, INDIAN HEALTH DISPARITIES (April 2018). Native Americans (to include Alaska Natives and Native Hawaiians) and other Indigenous peoples may share many of the environmental challenges and burdens of other communities of color and low-income populations, including disproportionate pollution of air, water, and land. Some environmental burdens, however, fall heavily and uniquely on Indigenous communities. By way of example, historic uranium mining in the American Southwest has left a legacy of devastating health impacts to citizens of the Navajo Nation and other nearby tribes. *See* Eric Jantz, *Environmental Racism with a Faint Green Glow*, 58 NAT. RESOURCES J. 247, 251 (2017) ("During the uranium boom of the 1950s to 1980s, 80–90 percent of uranium extraction occurred on or adjacent to indigenous lands").

Tribes have borne an especially heavy burden associated with U.S. energy infrastructure, whether related to nuclear power, hydroelectric dams, coal mining, oil and gas pipelines, or electricity transmission. Dam projects have heavily affected tribes both by flooding tribal lands and disrupting resources, such as Pacific salmon, upon which Native people have relied on since time immemorial and still use today, many in exercise of treaty-reserved rights. Margaret Schaff, *Indian Country and the American*

Energy Economy, 36 NAT. RESOURCES & ENVT. 9 (2021). Oil and gas pipelines have met heavy resistance from tribes, including protests led by the Standing Rock Sioux Tribe against the Dakota Access Pipeline, and more recently opposition to pipeline projects in the Great Lakes and Boundary Water regions of the Midwest. *See, e.g.*, Elizabeth Ann Kronk Warner, *Tribal Treaty Rights: A Powerful Tool in Challenges to Energy Infrastructure*, 51 CONN. L. REV. 843 (2019); Rebecca Solnit, *Standing Rock Protests: This Is Only the Beginning*, THE GUARDIAN, Sept. 12, 2016. Tribes are a major voice in conversations about lithium and other mineral extraction projects, mineral processing (like copper smelting), offshore wind, and new power transmission projects—all issues that arise as a result of the movement toward clean energy. *See, e.g.*, Lisa Benjamin, *EVs As EJ?*, 47 HARV. ENVTL. L. REV. 347, 376 (2023) (discussing recent litigation related to lithium mining involving the Fort McDermitt Paiute and Shoshone Tribes).

Tribes have special concerns and interests with respect to climate change, including issues like heat waves, land loss due to erosion, water availability in the West, more frequent and intense storms along the Gulf Coast, melting permafrost and retreating ice cover in the Arctic, and climate impacts on culturally important species, just to name a few. *See, e.g.*, Elizabeth Ann Kronk Warner, *Indigenous Adaptation in the Face of Climate Change*, 21 J. ENVTL. & SUSTAINABILITY L. 129 (2015); U.S. GLOBAL CHANGE RESEARCH PROGRAM, FOURTH NATIONAL CLIMATE ASSESSMENT, Chap. 15: *Tribes and Indigenous Peoples* (2018).

Questions of environmental justice in Indian country also require unique considerations of history, culture, tribal sovereignty, and political identity. "Indian country" is a legal term of art—defined by Congress to include "all land within the limits of any Indian reservation," together with "all dependent Indian communities" within the United States and "all Indian allotments." 18 U.S.C. § 1151. In more colloquial usage, however, "Indian country" may sweep across broader landscapes, from the Arctic coastal plain of the Inupiat people on the North Slope of Alaska to the hardwood forests of the Menominee Tribe in Wisconsin to the high desert Pueblo communities of New Mexico. Some tribal lands, such as the Wind River Reservation in Wyoming, stretch across vast open spaces. Other tribal lands, however, lie within urban or suburban environs. In Florida, the Fort Lauderdale metropolitan area includes the Hollywood Reservation of the Seminole Tribe. In Massachusetts, the rich and famous share Martha's Vineyard with the Mashpee Wampanoag Tribe. The metro area of Tulsa, Oklahoma, occupies land of the Osage Nation, Muskogee Nation, and Cherokee Nation, and is home for members of many other tribes.

As of 2025, in the United States, there were 574 tribes recognized by the federal government across 35 states. In addition to these federally recognized tribes, other tribes may be recognized only by state governments. These include the Elnu Abenaki Tribe in Vermont; the Ramapough Lenape Nation in New Jersey; and the Duwamish Tribe, whose homeland includes present-day Seattle. Of course, enrolled tribal members and other Indigenous people may live anywhere they choose, on or off tribal lands, while retaining strong connections to ancestral landscapes. As such, environmental justice for Indian tribes and Indigenous peoples must always consider the unique environments and individual interests that each case may present.

Pathfinder on Environmental Justice in Indian Country

Comprehensive background on Indian law is provided in COHEN'S HANDBOOK OF FEDERAL INDIAN LAW (Nell Jessup Newton & Kevin R. Washburn, eds., 2024 Edition). Matthew L.M. Fletcher's FEDERAL INDIAN LAW (2016) is a hornbook intended to guide students through this complex field. An introduction to many environmental issues in Indian country can be found in the treatise, William H. Rodgers, Jr. & Elizabeth Burleson, ENVIRONMENTAL LAW IN INDIAN COUNTRY (2005–2025). More contemporary cases and analyses may be found in the latest edition of the casebook, Judith V. Royster, Michael C. Blumm, Elizabeth Kronk Warner & Monte Mills, NATIVE AMERICAN NATURAL RESOURCES LAW: CASES AND MATERIALS (5th ed. 2023). A detailed discussion of tribal governments' authority to manage environmental matters within their jurisdiction and under federal environmental statutes can be found in James M. Grijalva, CLOSING THE CIRCLE: ENVIRONMENTAL JUSTICE IN INDIAN COUNTRY (2008). Some key federal documents include Indian Sacred Sites, Exec. Order No. 13007, 61 Fed. Reg. 26,771 (May 29, 1996); Consultation and Coordination with Indian Tribal Governments, Exec. Order No. 13175, 65 Fed. Reg. 67,249 (Nov. 9, 2000); Memorandum of Understanding Regarding Interagency Coordination and Collaboration for the Protection of Tribal Treaty Rights and Reserved Rights, (Nov. 15, 2021); the EPA Policy for the Administration of Environmental Programs on Indian Reservations (Nov. 8, 1984) ("1984 Indian Policy"); the EPA Policy on Consultation and Coordination with Indian Tribes (Dec. 7, 2023); and the EPA's Policy on Environmental Justice for Working with Federally Recognized Tribes and Indigenous Peoples (July 24, 2014).

In addition to the sources cited or excerpted in this chapter, other articles on environmental justice concerning Indian country and Indigenous peoples include Dean B. Suagee, *Turtle's War Party: An Indian Allegory on Environmental Justice*, 9 J. ENVTL. L. & LITIG. 461 (1994); John P. LaVelle, *Achieving Environmental Justice by Restoring the Great Grasslands and Returning the Sacred Black Hills to the Great Sioux Nation*, 5 GREAT PLAINS NAT. RESOURCES J. 40 (2001); Jana L. Walker et al., *A Closer Look at Environmental Injustice in Indian Country*, 1 SEATTLE J. SOC. JUST. 379 (2002); Elizabeth Kronk Warner, *Application of Title VI in Indian Country: The Key Is Tribal Sovereignty*, 6 FLA. A&M U. L. REV. 215 (2011); Rebecca Tsosie, *Climate Change and Indigenous Peoples: Comparative Models of Sovereignty*, 26 TULANE ENVTL. L.J. 239 (2013); D. Dapua 'ala Sproat, *An Indigenous People's Right to Environmental Self-Determination: Native Hawaiians and the Struggle Against Climate Change Devastation*, 35 STAN. ENVTL. L.J. 157 (2016); Hillary M. Hoffmann, *Fracking the Sacred: Resolving the Tension Between Unconventional Oil and Gas Development and Tribal Cultural Resources*, 94 DENVER L. REV. 319 (2017). A wealth of information about environmental issues facing Native Americans and Indigenous peoples can be found on the website of the Indigenous

Environmental Network, a national grassroots network of Indigenous groups working on environmental issues, available at ienearth.org. Another excellent resource on a broader range of legal issues in Indian country may be found on the blog Turtle Talk, available at turtletalk.blog.

B. Special Factors for EJ in Indian Country

While effective advocates must always consider the individual circumstances of any particular matter, many common interests and concerns may be discerned when it comes to environmental justice for Indian tribes and Indigenous peoples. In the excerpt that follows, Elizabeth Kronk Warner, a law school dean and legal scholar who writes at the intersection of Indian law and environmental law, sets the stage for this chapter by examining several special factors to consider for the pursuit of environmental justice in Indian country.

Elizabeth Kronk Warner, *Environmental Justice: A Necessary Lens to Effectively View Environmental Threats to Indigenous Survival*

26 Transnat'l L. & Contemp. Probs. 343 (2017)

... [I]ndigenous communities are often environmental justice communities. Although there are many similarities, environmental justice claims arising in Indian country within the United States differ from indigenous communities elsewhere throughout the world. These differences include considerations of tribal sovereignty (where applicable), unique obligations owed by the domestic state to indigenous communities (such as the federal trust responsibility in the United States), and the unique connection between many indigenous communities and their environment, as well as potential international considerations. Each of these considerations are discussed in detail below.

A. Tribal Sovereignty

Indigenous communities differ from other environmental justice communities due to their status as sovereign governments within some domestic nation states, such as the United States. While other environmental justice communities typically come together as informal groups whose legal rights flow from environmental laws, the legal rights of indigenous communities, with sovereign status, flow from their sovereignty and their related historical management of the land and resources. For example, in the United States, Native nations exist as entities separate from state and federal governments.

A myriad of historical legal developments led to this separateness. American Indian tribes are extra-constitutional, meaning that tribes exist apart from the U.S. Constitution. In the early 19th Century, the U.S. Supreme Court affirmed the separateness of Native nations. In *Cherokee Nation v. Georgia*, the U.S. Supreme Court held that American Indian tribes were "domestic dependent nations," highlighting their separateness from both state and federal governments. In *Worcester v. Georgia*, the U.S. Supreme Court further clarified the separateness of American Indian tribes, finding that the laws of the states are "void, and of no effect" within the exterior boundaries of American Indian tribal territory.

Although the federal government's perception of tribal sovereignty has ebbed and flowed significantly since the Court released the *Worcester* decision, "[i]n the modern era, as tribes have increasingly assumed governmental functions formerly performed by the Bureau of Indian Affairs and Indian Health Service, the relationship between the federal government and the tribes is often described as a government-to-government relationship." Moreover, Congress has indicated its recognition of tribal sovereignty by passing the Indian Self-Determination and Education Assistance Act and by subsequently amending various federal statutes to allow for increased tribal governance.

Accordingly, environmental justice claims arising in Indian country within the United States differ from claims arising elsewhere given the inherent sovereignty still possessed by Native nations. Environmental justice claims raised by Native nations "must be consistent with the promotion of tribal self-governance." This is because environmental justice claims arising from within Indian country include not only racial considerations but also political considerations. The additional consideration of tribal sovereignty is crucial to any discussion of environmental justice claims arising in Indian country. Specifically, an environmental injustice occurs if courts fail to consider the sovereignty of Native nations, because Native nations cannot meaningfully participate in the legal process if courts fail to consider something so essential to Native nations as their sovereignty. Moreover, the government-to-government relationship with American Indian tribal nations forces "the federal government [to] be prepared to defend vigorously the environmental self-determination that tribes already have." Therefore, courts consider Native nations' sovereignty when evaluating claims in order to ensure an environmentally just result as well as a trust relationship between Native nations and the federal government.

B. Federal Trust Relationship with Native Nations

Beyond the consideration of tribal sovereignty, indigenous communities must also incorporate special obligations owed by the domestic nation to them in their environmental justice claims. Thus, indigenous communities within the United States have a unique trust relationship with the federal government. Consequently, "the United States has a trust responsibility to each tribal government that includes the protection of the sovereignty of each tribal government." The trust relationship between the Native nations and the federal government emerged from the many cessions of both land and external sovereignty. The U.S. government owes federally recognized Native nations fiduciary obligations related to the management of tribal trust lands and resources. Today, Native nations may regularly assume governmental functions that were previously held by the federal government.

To better understand the trust responsibility that the federal government owes to Native nations, it is helpful to look to the history between the sovereigns. The federal trust responsibility doctrine has been the subject of many court decisions related to Indian country over the past two centuries. The doctrine originated from Chief Justice Marshall's opinion in *Cherokee Nation v. Georgia*. With the emergence of the federal trust responsibility doctrine, the federal government began to hold lands in trust for tribal governments. Five decades later, the Court reaffirmed its commitment to this doctrine in *United States v. Kagama*. In the 20th Century, the Court used the federal trust responsibility doctrine to define the scope of review of congressional legislation related to Indian country. Thus, Congress must act as a trustee when taking action within Indian country. Furthermore, "because of the trust responsibility, it is well settled that statutes affecting Indians 'are to be construed liberally in favor of the Indians, with ambiguous provisions interpreted to their benefit.'"

Recognition of the federal trust responsibility is not limited to the courts. President Nixon recognized the federal trust responsibility in his 1968 Special Message to Congress on the Problems of the American Indian:

> The special relationship between Indians and the Federal government is the result of solemn obligations which have been entered into by the United States Government. Down through the years, through written treaties and through formal and informal agreements, our government has made specific commitments to the Indian people. For their part, the Indians have often surrendered claims to vast tracts of land and have accepted life on government reservations.

Subsequent administrations have reaffirmed and expanded upon Nixon's recognition of the federal trust responsibility doctrine.

In sum, any Indian environmental justice claim should be considered under the federal trust responsibility doctrine. Failure to include consideration of this responsibility again results in Native nations being deprived of meaningful participation in the consideration of claims.... Under the federal trust responsibility doctrine, the federal government owes to Native nations a duty that ensures natural resources are sustained. This obligation extends to the federal government as a whole and should be upheld by the federal judiciary. In evaluating an environmental justice claim arising in Indian country, federal courts must be mindful of, and uphold, the federal government's trust responsibility to Native nations. Failure to do so results in an environmental injustice.

C. Unique Tribal Connection to the Land and Environment

Indigenous communities' claims differ from many other environmental claims because many indigenous cultures and traditions are tied to the environment in a manner that traditionally differs from that of the dominant society. As Frank Pommersheim points out, land "is important to Indian people in a multitude of ways: beyond subsistence, land is the source of spiritual origins and sustaining myth which in turn provides a landscape of cultural and emotional meaning. The land often determines the values of [their] human landscape." Analogous connections to the environment and the land among indigenous communities stem from the fact that many indigenous cultures are "land-based," meaning that they are connected to a certain location or area. Many individual indigenous people and communities also possess a spiritual connection with land and the environment. These communities

> continue to have a deep relationship with ancestral homelands for sustenance, religious communion and comfort, and to maintain the strength of personal and interfamiliar identities. Through language, songs, and ceremonies, tribal people continue to honor sacred springs, ancestral burial places, and other places where ancestral communities remain alive.

The spiritual connection between many Native nations and their surrounding environment is crucial to the self-determination of these communities.

Therefore, many communities facing environmental challenges may also encounter devastating impacts to their culture, spirituality, and traditions. Such spiritual, cultural, and historical connections to the affected land play an important role in any environmental justice claim arising in indigenous territory because land, identity, and sovereignty/self-determination are uniquely connected within indigenous communities. Failure to consider these interconnections will negatively impact the quality of the indigenous community's participation in the legal process.

D. International Considerations

Beyond domestic legal considerations, principles of international law should also be considered when evaluating the environmental justice matters impacting indigenous communities. As a starting point, there are some principles under international law applicable to all people that are helpful when discussing indigenous rights from an environmental justice perspective. For example, domestic states have an obligation to respect the human rights of individuals subject to their authority. Moreover, OAS [Organization of American States] Member States recognize the right to hold property as a human right under both Article 21 of the American Convention on Human Rights and Article 17 of the Universal Declaration of Human Rights. The right of development was also recognized in 1986 by the U.N. General Assembly via the Declaration on the Right to Development ("Declaration"), which is important for indigenous peoples because it refers to both persons and peoples as rights holders.

International law also contains provisions that are specific to indigenous peoples. Adopted in 1989, the International Labour Organization's Convention Concerning Indigenous and Tribal Peoples in Independent Countries ("ILO 169") is a foundational document on the rights of indigenous peoples. Notably, ILO 169 recognizes the right of indigenous peoples to "exercise control ... over their own economic, social and cultural development" and participate in development that "may affect them directly." Furthermore, Article 14 of the Convention guarantees that indigenous peoples' "rights of ownership and possession ... over the lands which they traditionally occupy shall be recognized," and Article 16 states that indigenous peoples "shall not be removed from the lands which they occupy."

Building on ILO 169, the U.N. Declaration on the Rights of Indigenous Peoples (UNDRIP) was adopted by the U.N. General Assembly in 2007. This international declaration supports and reaffirms the rights of indigenous peoples. On December 16, 2010, former president Barack Obama announced that the United States endorsed the UNDRIP. UNDRIP's articles pertaining to Indigenous self-determination, property, and redress are of particular importance. UNDRIP Article 3 states "Indigenous peoples have the right to self-determination." Article 8 states "Indigenous peoples and individuals have the right not to be subjected to forced assimilation or destruction of their culture." Article 10 states "Indigenous peoples shall not be forcibly removed from their lands or territories. No relocation shall take place without the free, prior and informed consent of the indigenous peoples concerned and after agreement on just and fair compensation and, where possible, the option to return." Article 26 states "Indigenous peoples have the right to the lands, territories and resources which they have traditionally owned, occupied or otherwise used or acquired.... States shall give legal recognition and protection to these lands, territories and resources." Finally, Article 28 states that "Indigenous peoples have the right to redress, by means that can include restitution or, when this is not possible, just, fair and equitable compensation, for the lands, territories and resources which they have traditionally owned or otherwise occupied or used, and which have been confiscated, taken, occupied, used or damaged without their free, prior and informed consent."

... In conclusion, environmental justice requires that courts consider the unique aspects of environmental justice communities to ensure adequate access to substantive or procedural justice. Environmental justice issues arising in Indian country encapsulate considerations that differ from claims arising from other environmental justice communities. These considerations include tribal sovereignty, the obligations of domestic states to indigenous communities including the federal trust responsibility owed by the United States toward Native nations, international legal considerations, and the unique cultural and spiritual connection many indigenous communities have with their land.

* * *

Unique historical experience. Consider that American Indians, as distinct from other "minority" groups in the United States, were the original human inhabitants of the continent, with deep histories and complex cultures, thriving here for many thousands of years before the arrival of European colonizers. The experience of American Indians after European arrival was extremely complicated, but was punctuated by persecution, genocide, forced removal from historic lands, coercive assimilation, and social, political, legal, and economic oppression. This experience is very different from the equally traumatic experiences of African people who were kidnapped and enslaved by European traffickers and profiteers, and the experience of immigrants from around the world who were subject to economic exploitation and oppression in various ways.

How do you think the unique experience of Indigenous American peoples might influence how they view the idea of environmental justice? Consider these excerpts from Bethany R. Berger, *Red: Racism and the American Indian*, 56 UCLA L. REV. 591 (2009) (offering a detailed examination of how American Indians have experienced racism in the U.S., and how it has differed from the experience of African Americans):

> European Americans were not primarily concerned with using Indian people as a source of labor, and so did not have to theorize Indians as inferior individuals to justify the unfair terms of that labor. Rather, colonists' primary concern with respect to Indians was to obtain tribal resources and use tribes as a flattering foil for American society and culture. It was therefore necessary to theorize tribal societies as fatally and racially inferior while emphasizing the ability of Indian individuals to leave their societies and join non-Indian ones.
>
> ... There are of course situations in which discrimination against American Indians accords with classical paradigms of racism. Indians have been denied the right to vote, attend schools with or marry whites, eat at restaurants, stay at hotels, or get jobs because of their race. Like African Americans, native people have been lynched, raped, and had their homes burnt out from under them because of their race.
>
> ... English overseas efforts were spurred by the desire to prove England's superiority to Spain. Stories of Spanish cruelty to the natives were popular national propaganda, justifying English desires to appropriate the lands for themselves. The first schemes to stake English claims to North American land were conceived of as a kind of tri-racial liberation movement, joining runaway African Cimarrons and oppressed Indians to fend off Spanish conquistadores.
>
> ... While these visions were short lived, the fiction of benefit to native peoples remained part of the Anglo-American nationalist myth. English colonization was justified because the English would bring the Indians true religion, would acquire land only by purchase, and would teach Indians how to use their land to ensure prosperity. The faith in the inferiority of the Indian community, the attractiveness of the English, and the malleability of the individual Indian were thus placed at the heart of the fledgling North American colonies. All three were challenged on arrival, but were replaced or reinforced with notions of the inherent inferiority of Indian tribes.
>
> Although religious superiority was the earliest and the most fervent of the initial justifications for colonization, the religious mission of the early colonies also made it easy to see God's will in the acquisition of Indian bodies (through death) as well as souls. Governor John Winthrop's letters are the infamous example of this, referring to smallpox epidemics as the means by which "God hath[ ] ... cle[a]red our title to this place," and a sign that the Lord was "pleased with our inheriting these parts ... taking[ ] it from a people who had long usurped upon him, and abused his Creatures." ...

These dynamics went on to inform the development of early American law. For example, "Locke's image of 'the wild Indian' who could not feed his com-

> munity and had not established any property rights in America for 'want of improving it by labor' became a convenient foil for the Anglo Saxon notion of property rights. In 1758, Emmerich de Vattel built this perception into an explicit justification for North American colonization, arguing that although it was unjust to colonize Latin America, where the indigenous peoples had cultivated the soil, it was right to claim North America, where they had not."

Treaty rights. Another unique aspect of environmental justice in Indian country is the legal authority of tribes as sovereign governments under the U.S. Constitution to enter into treaties with the United States. Professor Matthew Fletcher explains:

> The original legal relationships between Indian nations and the United States were established and governed by treaties. Indian treaties negotiated by the Executive branch and ratified by the Senate are the supreme law of the land under the Constitution's Supremacy Clause. From the point of view of Indian nations, Indian treaties are sacred, often familial arrangements that cannot be broken.... Hundreds of Indian treaties remain extant, and still form the foundational basis of federal Indian law.

FLETCHER, FEDERAL INDIAN LAW at 212–13.

In many of these treaties, Indian nations ceded vast expanses of their aboriginal homelands, while nonetheless reserving certain lands and resources, as well as various off-reservation rights, such as rights to fish, hunt, and gather. Although on their face the treaties guarantee access to these resources in perpetuity, the treaties themselves have not stopped the degradation of these resources. *See, e.g.,* Wenona T. Singel & Matthew L.M. Fletcher, *Indian Treaties and the Survival of the Great Lakes*, 2006 MICH. ST. L. REV. 1285 (2006) (noting that "in the early years of the twenty-first century, the inland seas known as the Great Lakes are all but depleted [of fish].... And what fish are harvested cannot be consumed in great (or subsistence) quantities because of contamination by pollutants such as mercury and dioxin").

In the Pacific Northwest, many tribes retain rights to natural resources including salmon under treaties with the U.S. Government. These include the treaties negotiated in 1854–1855 by Territorial Governor Isaac Stevens. Under the **Stevens Treaties**, tribes often retained rights to fishing and food gathering "at all usual and accustomed grounds." *Washington v. Washington State Comm'l Passenger Fishing Vessel Ass'n*, 443 U.S. 658 (1979). In the famous *Boldt* decision, U.S. District Court Judge George Boldt determined that the Stevens treaty language reserving the tribal rights to take fish "in common with" white settlers meant that treaty tribes could "shar[e] equally the opportunity to take fish." *United States v. Washington*, 384 F. Supp. 312, 338 (1974), *aff'd*, 520 F.2d 676 (9th Cir. 1975).

After confirming the right to 50 percent of the fish harvest, both on and off-reservations, the tribes next pursued a right to protection of fish habitats. In 1980, the district court agreed, finding that "[t]he fundamental prerequisite to exercising the right to take fish is the existence of fish to be taken." *United States v. Washington*, 506

F. Supp. 187 (W.D. Wash. 1980), *vacated*, 759 F.2d 1353 (9th Cir. 1985). For almost 50 years, the right to protection of fish habitat remained the subject of epic litigation that came to be known as the *Culverts Case*. In 2007, the U.S. district court in the *Culverts Case* found that highway culverts constructed and maintained by the State of Washington obstructed fish migration in violation of the tribal treaty rights to fish. *United States v. Washington*, 2007 WL 2437166 (W.D. Wash. 2007). In 2017, the Ninth Circuit Court of Appeals affirmed, 827 F.3d 836 (9th Cir. 2016), and in 2018, the U.S. Supreme Court affirmed 4–4 by a divided court. *Washington v. United States*, 584 U.S. 837 (2018). For a thorough review of the history, holdings, and theoretical underpinnings in the *Culverts Case*, see CHARLES WILKINSON, TREATY JUSTICE: THE NORTHWEST TRIBES, THE BOLDT DECISION, AND THE RECOGNITION OF FISHING RIGHTS (2024).

Following the *Culverts Case*, the U.S. Supreme Court has continued to demonstrate strong support for enforcing tribal treaty rights. *See, e.g., McGirt v. Oklahoma*, 591 U.S. 894 (2020) ("Today we are asked whether the land these treaties promised [to the Creek Nation] remains an Indian reservation for purposes of federal criminal law. Because Congress has not said otherwise, we hold the government to its word"); *Wyoming v. Herrera*, 587 U.S. 329 (2019) (Crow Tribe's 1868 federal treaty right to hunt on "unoccupied lands of the United States" continued beyond Wyoming statehood in 1890); and *Washington State Dept. of Licensing v. Cougar Den, Inc.*, 586 U.S. 347 (2019) (Washington State fuel tax preempted by right-to-travel provision of 1855 treaty with Yakama Nation).

Notes and Questions

1. Fish—and people? As demonstrated by judicial decisions including the *Culverts Case*, assertion of treaty rights can provide advocates with powerful authority for protecting natural resources in Indian country. Can the same powerful authority for protecting fish, for example, also help to protect *people*—the traditional focus of environmental justice? How might you frame such arguments? Is the traditional EJ focus on people still appropriate when considering the values associated with *Indigenous* people?

2. Environmental justice or not? Given the discussion above, how closely should tribes align themselves with other environmental justice interests? Consider, as President Trump began efforts in 2025 to eliminate federal investment and engagement in environmental justice and "DEI," a coalition of tribal leaders and Native organizations sent a letter to Trump, congressional leaders, and Interior Secretary Doug Burgum, warning against misclassifying tribal programs as diversity or environmental justice initiatives. Letter, "*RE: Status of Tribal Nations as Political Entities in the Implementation of the President's New Executive Orders*" (Feb. 2, 2025).

3. More on tribal sovereignty. Perhaps the most defining distinction for environmental justice in the tribal context follows from tribal sovereignty. Among a sovereign's prerogative is the right to make laws and be ruled by them, i.e., "self-government." In its 1984 Indian Policy, the U.S. EPA acknowledged, "In keeping with the principle of Indian self-government, the [EPA] will view Tribal Governments as the appropriate non-Federal parties for making decisions and carrying out program responsibilities affecting Indian reservations, their environments, and the health and welfare of the reservation population." While this acknowledgment may seem unremarkable now after the passage of decades, at one time states broadly assumed jurisdiction for all environmental regulation within their state borders, even on tribal lands. *See Washington Dept. of Ecology v. EPA*, 752 F.2d 1465 (9th Cir. 1985).

4. Tribal consultation. In recognizing tribes as "the appropriate non-Federal parties" for making decisions concerning tribal lands, the EPA also recognized the obligation to engage with tribes in **"government-to-government consultation"** on matters affecting tribes. In 2000, President Clinton signed Executive Order No. 13175 "to strengthen the United States government-to-government relationships with Indian tribes" and "to establish regular and meaningful consultation ... with tribal officials...." Consultation and Coordination with Indian Tribal Governments, Exec. Order No. 13175, 65 Fed. Reg. 67,249 (Nov. 9, 2000).

The federal duty to engage in tribal consultation has never been fully satisfactory, and tribes have long sought to make the process more meaningful. Consider the following from Elizabeth Kronk Warner, *Sovereignty over Box Checking: Effective Tribal Consultation Leading to Consent*, 38 J. LAND USE & ENVTL. L. 131, 141–49 (2023):

> ... In a presidential memorandum dated January 26, 2021, President Biden stated that "regular, meaningful, and robust consultation with Tribal Nations" was a priority of his Administration. Additionally, under the Biden Administration, the federal government has engaged tribes to obtain feedback on existing consultation processes, and even released a plan for improving upon the status quo. To start, the Department of the Interior (DOI) sent out a framing paper that asked four questions: "(1) Does the input in 2009 still reflect tribal views about consultation today?... (2) Should Interior include the actions recommended by the January 2017 report in its plan to improve consultation? (3) Are there additional steps Interior could take to improve tribal consultation and make it more meaningful? (4) What actions to improve tribal consultations should be made the top priorities in Interior's plan?"
>
> The tribal responses overwhelmingly suggest that tribal leaders are frustrated with existing ineffective consultation. For example, ... Michael Chavarria, Governor of the Santa Clara Pueblo, explained, "as a matter of environmental justice[,] all federal agency officials should use their inherent authority and discretion to deny any projects that virtually impact culture resources when there is no way to mitigate those environmental justice impacts." [Brian Vallo, Governor of the Pueblo of Acoma, went on to explain that] "unfortunately, consultation is often still a process in checking the box. And meaningful consultation consistent of a two-way dialog and joint [decision-making] at a nation to nation level is still lacking.... Here federal agencies are beholden to limited timeframes for a consultation as a result of

industry-initiated expressions of interest or applications for permits.... Compounding this lack of meaningful consultation is the lack of consistency between different federal agencies...."

Manuel Heart, Chairman for the Ute Mountain Ute Tribe, suggested that "Interior should offer a method of—or a process in which[]tribes can request consultation on issues that affect them, giving tribes an opportunity to request consultation rather than tribes waiting for the interior to reach out to them."

... Aaron Payment, then Chairman of the Sault Ste. Marie Tribe of Chippewa Indians, ... suggested that a curriculum should be developed to help educate federal officials about effective consultation and the government-to-government relationship.

... Terri Parton, President for Wichita and Affiliated Tribes, ... explained that there should be some sort of follow up on consultations to make sure that such consultations were not just talk without action.... Tina Abrams, Councilor from the Seneca Nation of Indians, made several poignant points, including "[r]ather than being a mere box-checking activity, consultation must be an ongoing nation-to-nation process that treats native nations as sovereign governmental entities." Additionally, she argues that consultation should last as long as necessary suggesting that there is not a specific "consultation window."

Following the consultations with tribes on improving consultations, the Department of the Interior released *A Detailed Plan for Improving Interior's Implementation of E.O. 13175*. The foreword by Secretary Deb Haaland notes that "[t]ribes are not interest groups. Tribes are sovereign entities with indigenous perspectives and knowledge that can improve the quality of Federal decisions and result in better outcomes for all affected communities." The Plan is premised on the input from tribes that "unanimously echoed that their prior input was still applicable, making clear that in some cases, Interior and its bureaus and offices have missed the mark on even meeting a baseline for meaningful consultation."...

The Plan then details how DOI has or will respond to the comments by tribes. The two items DOI has already responded to are: (1) reconstituting the White House Council on Native American Affairs; and (2) revoking several ... policies regarding ... consultation [issued during the first Trump administration]. DOI notes several actions that it could not take due to legal, resource, or policy constraints. One such action was the codification of Executive Order 13175 to prevent shifts between administrations. DOI then provides six action items that it will implement: (1) a centralized consultation website; (2) identify technology to improve notice to tribes; (3) update consultation policy; (4) educate interior officials and staff on tribes; (5) establish a Secretary's Tribal Advisory Committee; and (6) review policies that inhibit consultation. Finally, DOI provides timelines for the implementation of the action items.

> At the end of 2022, the Biden Administration took additional steps forward to improve the federal government's consultation processes with tribes. On November 30, 2022, the White House released the "Memorandum on Uniform Standards for Tribal Consultation," intended for heads of executive departments and agencies. The 2022 Memorandum builds on the 2021 Executive Order, explaining that "[t]he purpose of this memorandum is to establish uniform minimum standards to be implemented across all agencies regarding how Tribal consultations are to be conducted."

While Professor Kronk Warner notes that the Department of Interior's response "acknowledges that the current system of consultation is not meeting expectations ... [and] goes a long way toward addressing many of the concerns surrounding the federal government's consultation with tribes," she also notes that "it is but one federal agency," and that the November 2022 Presidential Memo "falls short of the necessary binding changes." *Id.* at 141–49; *see also* Elizabeth Kronk Warner et al., *Changing Consultation*, 54 U.C. Davis L. Rev. 1127 (2020).

On the question of what decisions should trigger tribal consultation, agencies may have published guidance indicating "non-exclusive" categories of actions appropriate for government-to-government consultation. The EPA, for example, has identified a "non-exclusive list of EPA activity categories [] normally appropriate for consultation if they may affect a tribe." Such activities include regulations, policies, permits, budget planning, legislative comments, civil enforcement, emergency response, state or tribal program authorization, and implementation of international treaty. *See* EPA Policy on Consultation with Indian Tribes at 5–6 (Dec. 7, 2023). It remains unclear what changes might occur to tribal consultation under the second Trump administration, or whether the administration will significantly pull back from the commitments made during the Biden administration. However, the second Trump administration's intense focus on rapid fossil fuel energy development seems at odds with the goal of meaningful engagement with tribes, who often find their lands and resources in peril from such projects.

Considering the categories of activities that are subject to consultation obligations, imagine a proposal to construct a gas refinery on tribal lands. Then imagine a deadly explosion at this refinery five years after it begins operations. In these two contexts, what EPA activities might trigger government-to-government consultation and how might such consultation support (or hinder) the aims of environmental justice?

On the question concerning who speaks for the tribal government, regular phone calls or email exchanges between staff for tribal and federal agencies may certainly be encouraged to resolve technical questions on a draft document, for example. However, just as some decisions may only be made by designated officials of state or federal government, some decisions concerning tribal interests may only be made by designated tribal authorities, such as a tribal council or a tribal governor or chairperson. On this point, EPA's guidance observes, "The appropriate level of interaction" may vary according to factors including "the continuing dialogue between EPA and Tribal government...." *Id.* at 1. How helpful does this guidance seem to you? What are the potential consequences for a failure to consult with the appropriate tribal officials? If you were a federal attorney for the Army Corps of Engineers considering approval of a new oil pipeline crossing a river near tribal lands, what steps might you take to ensure the "appropriate level of interaction" for your particular case?

5. Federal trust relationship. Professor Kronk Warner asserts that "any Indian environmental justice claim should be considered under the federal trust responsibility doctrine." What do you understand that to mean? How do "fair treatment" and "meaningful involvement," hallmarks of EPA's definition of environmental justice, compare to the federal trust responsibility? Do we need another definition of environmental justice for application in Indian country? Compare the EPA definition of "tribal consultation" to the EPA definition of "meaningful involvement" for purposes of the EPA's conception of "environmental justice" as presented in Chapter 1. Does "tribal consultation," for purposes of satisfying the federal trust responsibility, mean anything more than the "meaningful involvement" of tribes? If so, how?

Substantively, the federal trust responsibility requires federal agencies to affirmatively protect the interests of tribes whenever the federal agency undertakes any action. Courts describe this responsibility as the federal government "charg[ing] itself with moral obligations of the highest responsibility and trust," *Seminole Nation v. United States*, 316 U.S. 286, 297 (1942), to be judged by "the most exacting fiduciary standards." *Cobell v. Norton*, 391 F.3d 251, 257 (D.C. Cir. 2004). At the same time, the federal government "has an 'overriding duty ... to deal fairly with Indians.'" *Id.*, quoting *Morton v. Ruiz*, 415 U.S. 199, 236 (1974). Is this federal duty to "deal fairly with Indians" the same duty of "fair treatment" required by the EPA's previous standard for environmental justice? Should it be more?

While recognizing the federal trust responsibility owed to tribes, courts have limited the scope of remedies for trust violations. In a string of cases, the U.S. Supreme Court has held that damages for violations of the trust duty may only be obtained where the federal government agreed to accept affirmative management responsibility through a specific "rights-creating statute or regulation." *U.S. v. Navajo Nation*, 537 U.S. 488, 503 (2003); *U.S. v. White Mountain Apache*, 537 U.S. 465, 475 (2003); *U.S. v. Jicarilla Apache Nation*, 564 U.S. 162, 174 (2011).

In addition to denial of damages for violation of the federal trust responsibility, courts have also denied injunctive relief. In the lawsuit by the Standing Rock Sioux Tribe challenging completion and operation of the Dakota Access Pipeline, amici including the Association on American Indian Affairs argued that the federal trust responsibility supported the Tribe's request for injunctive relief "based upon the heightened fiduciary duties of the trust doctrine." Brief of *Amici Curiae* Association on American Indian Affairs, In Support of Plaintiff Standing Rock Sioux Tribe's Motion for Summary Judgment, Case No. 1:16-cv-1534-JEB, Feb. 21, 2017, at 15. Without reaching this argument, the district court did find that the Corps of Engineers in this case violated legal mandates flowing from the standard definition of environmental justice, as will be discussed further in Chapter 11 (Information Disclosure and Environmental Review). *Standing Rock Sioux Tribe v. U.S. Army Corps of Eng'rs*, 255 F.Supp.3d 101, 140 (D.D.C. 2017). Unfortunately for the plaintiff tribes, in denying the requested injunctive relief, the court allowed Dakota Access to complete construction of the pipeline and put the pipeline into operation.

In denying the requested injunctive relief, did the court apply the wrong standard for an environmental justice claim in Indian country? How might you have ruled on this question, and why?

6. Tribal connections to land. Professor Kronk Warner observes that "many indigenous cultures ... are tied to the environment in a manner that traditionally differs from that of the dominant society." She specifically notes unique connections to land for purposes of sustenance, family identities, and cultural and spiritual practices. For one colorful illustration of this "unique tribal connection to the land," law professor Jeanette Wolfley, an enrolled member of the Shoshone-Bannock Tribes, offered this anecdote:

> In the summer of 2008, the Yellowstone National Park (YNP) cultural anthropologist contacted me to request information about the cultural significance of certain sites in the YNP. She asked if some Shoshone and Bannock elders would be willing to make a trip to YNP and visit certain sites and advise the park officials about the areas. About twenty elders from Fort Hall and I took several trips to meet with the YNP officials.
>
> Several events during the trips remain with me. First, the NPS's recognition that the Shoshone and Bannock were original inhabitants of YNP, and the desire of the park officials to seek tribal ecological knowledge, place names, and wisdom about cultural areas. Second, the recitation of the official YNP policy declaration to the elders advising them that the park's resources were federal property and were not to be removed, disturbed, or impacted in any manner.[2] Third, many elders' telling me that they had never been to the YNP as they were told they were prohibited. Fourth, the beginning of a collaborative and cooperative relationship with park officials that remains today.
>
> [Footnote 2]: This declaration [of federal property] fell on deaf ears who either did not hear the declaration, did not understand the detailed English rules, or preferred an elder's interpretation who told the others in the Shoshone language that the park was Shoshone and Bannock lands, and they were welcome to gather what they wished on the trip. The third version was preferred by all, and when the bus stopped at the first park site and the elders pulled out their gathering bags, the cultural anthropologist was horrified. And so, the YNP and tribal relations began.

Jeanette Wolfley, *Reclaiming a Presence in Ancestral Lands: The Return of Native Peoples to the National Parks*, 56 NAT. RESOURCES J. 55, 56 (2016).

In fact, the western tradition of "fortress conservation" that forcibly separates lands from their Indigenous inhabitants is the subject of scrutiny both in the U.S. and abroad.

Consider the following excerpt from Kekek Jason Stark et al., *Re-Indigenizing Yellowstone*, 22 Wyo. L. Rev. 397 (2022):

> Tribal connections to the area now known as "Yellowstone" are numerous, varied, and have existed since time immemorial. The creation of Yellowstone National Park a century and a half ago marked an unprecedented approach to preserving the natural and geologic wonders of the region. Yellowstone's creation also resulted in the physical, legal, and actual exclusion of Indigenous peoples from these spaces. While certain inroads breaking down those barriers have been made, tribal members may still feel like visitors in the park—a deeply tragic state of affairs given long-standing tribal connections throughout the area.
>
> In recent years, tribal leaders and their allies have sparked a broader movement to engender restorative justice across the American landscape. Fueled by high-profile conflicts over tribal interests in sacred waters, Supreme Court victories upholding and re-validating historic treaty promises, and a coalescence of conservation, recreation, and other interest groups behind tribal proposals to protect sacred areas, a national reckoning with the history of tribal dispossession has ensued, resulting in a variety of demands to redress that legacy. Fundamentally, this movement seeks greater respect for tribal values in and connections to lands and resources from which Indigenous peoples have been separated.... At their core, calls for #Landback, tribal co-management, or the use of tribal knowledge and wisdom are all rooted in the desire to ensure that peoples indigenous to these lands can restore and invigorate their vital historical, cultural, and other meaningful connections to the places and resources taken from them....
>
> Over the past 30 years or so, from the early 1990s up to the sesquicentennial [in 2022], federal-tribal relations at Yellowstone have changed considerably—drastically, really, when compared to where things stood a century prior.... The Park Service and Yellowstone-associated tribes have sought connection.... In this way, "[t]he long-standing tradition of American Indian groups being affected by management policies instituted at Yellowstone but not having any influence over those policies themselves has ... evidently started to change...."
>
> At its most aggressive forefront, the modern movement in support of tribal resource management demands the return of all lands taken from Indigenous peoples. "#Landback" is a commonly repeated phrase in popular culture that frequently appears on social media but, like "co-management," the term carries a kaleidoscope of meanings and often the baggage of mis-understanding.... For some, #Landback is a simple and sometimes provocative expression to call out the injustice of colonization with no real thought given to a strategic action. For others, land back carries its literal meaning and represents a call for the undoing of the large-scale displacement of tribes from their lands and the

> returning of the legal title of all previously Native lands to tribes and Indigenous people.

Id. at 429–30, 445–46, 497–99.

For more discussion of the idea of "fortress parks" and the interests of tribes in national parks, and the **Landback movement,** *see* David Hales, *Changing Concepts of National Parks, in* CONSERVATION FOR THE TWENTY-FIRST CENTURY at 142 (David Western & Mary C. Pearl eds., 1989); Nazune Menka, *The Landback Movement: Native Nations and the Restoration of Ancestral Lands*, 39 NAT. RESOURCES & ENVT. 23 (2025); and David Treuer, *Return the National Parks to the Tribes,* THE ATLANTIC (Apr. 12, 2021).

Where Indigenous people maintain "unique connections" to certain lands, what does the EJ principle of "fair treatment" require? Would fair treatment sustain a flat ban on all gathering at Yellowstone National Park? Or would fair treatment recognize the historical ties of the Shoshone-Bannock people to the land now designated as Yellowstone National Park and allow for limited gathering by certain individuals? Would truly "fair treatment" require something more? If the question were presented to you as a federal judge, how might you weigh a National Park Service ban on hunting, fishing, and gathering in a national park against a tribal member's treaty-reserved rights to engage in the same?

Besides matters of sustenance, how might other unique connections to land be served by applications of federal environmental law? As we have seen already in Chapter 5 (Environmental Regulations), the federal Clean Water Act can be used to set standards for surface water to protect uses including cultural or religious practices by an Indian tribe. *See City of Albuquerque v. Browner*, 97 F.3d 415 (10th Cir. 1996) (upholding EPA's approval of water quality standards established by the Isleta Pueblo to protect "religious or traditional" uses of water flowing in the Rio Grande through the Isleta Pueblo Indian Reservation). Likewise, the federal Comprehensive Environmental Response, Compensation, and Liability Act (CERCLA) may be used to clean up contaminated sites for designated tribal uses. For example, at the Midnite Mine on the Spokane Indian Reservation of eastern Washington, the EPA selected a remedy of more than $150 million to address uranium contamination and protect future traditional uses defined by the Spokane Tribe. EPA, Midnite Mine Superfund Site, Record of Decision (Sept. 2006) at 2–36, 2–95. EPA has also embraced the use of CERCLA authorities to support tribal treaty rights and other unique considerations for cleanup in the tribal context (like special considerations for calculating risk). *See*, EPA, *Consideration of Tribal Treaty Rights and Traditional Ecological Knowledge in the Superfund Remedial Program* (Jan. 17, 2017).

What about other statutes like the Toxic Substances Control Act (TSCA)? Consider the following passage from Sean Dixon & Kelsey Furman, *Beyond PFAS: What's Up with Emerging Contaminant N-(1,3-Dimethylbutyl)-N'-Phenyl-P-Phenylenediamine (6ppd)?*, ABA TRENDS, March/April 2024, at 1, 3–4.

> On August 1, 2023, the Yurok, Port Gamble S'Klallam, and Puyallup Tribes petitioned the EPA under section 21 of [TSCA] ... to "establish regulations prohibiting the manufacturing, processing, use, and distribution of 6PPD in and for tires," with such regulation "to take effect as soon as practicable, in order to eliminate the unreasonable risk 6PPD in tires presents to the environment." ... The petitioning Tribes rely upon salmon and other aquatic species experiencing devastating impacts from the ubiquitous nature of 6PPD/q. The petition argues that the "extraordinary toxic effects" of 6PPD/q are "precisely what TSCA was designed to address" and asserts that 6PPD/q's toxicity and ubiquity present a level of risk to aquatic organisms that EPA has previously characterized as "unreasonable."

TSCA could also be a tool to address the special vulnerability of Indigenous communities who rely on subsistence hunting and fishing, and who therefore experience much higher exposure to persistent hazardous chemicals like per- and polyfluoroalkyl substances (PFAS) especially in places like the Arctic where such chemicals concentrate in fish and game. *See* Rainer Lohmann et al., *Cross-cutting studies of per- and polyfluorinated alkyl substances (PFAS) in Arctic wildlife and humans,* 954 SCIENCE OF THE TOTAL ENVIRONMENT 176274 (Dec. 2024).

In addition to CERCLA, TSCA, and the Clean Water Act, how might other environmental laws support the "unique connections" between certain tribes and lands? Could the Clean Air Act, for example, be used to compel stronger protections for viewsheds in sacred landscapes? On the flip side, could tribal industries demand special relief from federal land disposal requirements?

7. International law. Beyond the consideration of domestic laws such as CERCLA and the Clean Water Act, Kronk Warner suggests that some "principles of international law" may be "helpful when discussing Indigenous rights from an environmental justice perspective." Principles of international law may derive from "hard law" such as treaties and customary international law as well as "soft law" such as nonbinding rules and declarations. One source of hard law cited by Kronk Warner is the American Convention on Human Rights, a treaty ratified by most nations in the Western Hemisphere, but not including Canada and the United States. The 2007 UN Declaration on the Rights of Indigenous Peoples (UNDRIP) is an example of "soft law" that is not, of itself, intended to bind nation-states. Over time, soft law may develop into hard law through administrative practice, judicial decisions, and other future developments. For a comprehensive review of related principles of international law, *see* EDITH BROWN WEISS ET AL., INTERNATIONAL LAW FOR THE ENVIRONMENT 146 (2016).

Principles of international law, as Kronk Warner suggests, may help to identify certain norms and expectations for conduct between sovereign entities. Violations of these norms may be discussed and addressed through formal and informal mechanisms where parties are committed to acting in good faith. Where such commitment is lacking, however, principles of international law may be difficult to enforce. In 2011, for example, Navajo tribal members ("Diné") filed a petition with the Inter-American

Commission on Human Rights (IACHR), a body charged with investigating alleged violations of human rights by parties of the Organization of American States (OAS). In the petition, the Diné petitioners alleged that the United States had violated their rights under the 1948 American Declaration of the Rights and Duties of Man by subjecting the Diné to continued exposure to radioactive contamination from uranium mining and processing. *See* Petition, *Eastern Navajo Diné Against Uranium Mining et al. v. United States of America*, Inter-American Commission on Human Rights, Organization of American States (2011). On March 28, 2021, the IACHR issued Report No. 67/21 and found the case against the U.S. government admissible, announcing that it would schedule a merits hearing. IACHR, Report No. 67/21, Petition 654-11 Admissibility: Navajo Communities of Crownpoint and Church Rock, United States of America (2021). In 2023, members of the IACHR made a "promotional visit" to Church Rock and Crownpoint to see conditions on the ground first-hand. The IACHR later held a "thematic hearing" on February 28, 2024, in Washington, D.C. *See* Indigenous Environmental Network, *IACHR Grants Thematic Hearing on Impacts to Indigenous Peoples' Human Rights from Uranium Exploitation*, ienearth.org/iachr-grants-thematic-hearing-on-impacts-to-indigenous-peoples/. For a video recording of the IACHR hearing, featuring testimony from tribal members (plus one co-author of this book), see the following link: oas.org/en/iachr/sessions/hearing.asp?Hearing=3702.

Since the adoption of UNDRIP in 2007, advocates for Indigenous rights have increasingly sought to address their concerns through international mechanisms. In the protests against the Dakota Access Pipeline, for example, the Chairman of the Standing Rock Sioux Tribe traveled to Geneva, Switzerland, to testify before the UN Human Rights Council on September 20, 2016. Nine days later, the Human Rights Council directed the Special Rapporteur on the rights of Indigenous peoples to extend her charge "To examine ways and means of overcoming existing obstacles to the full and effective protection of the rights of indigenous peoples...." UN Human Rights Council, Resolution 33/12: *Human rights and indigenous peoples; mandate of the Special Rapporteur on the rights of indigenous peoples* (Sept. 29, 2016).

Responding to this charge, in early 2017, the UN Special Rapporteur engaged in a fact-finding mission to the United States, with the purpose "to assess the impacts of energy development projects ... on Indian tribes living both within and outside of reservations." In this mission, which included visits with Indian tribes in Arizona and New Mexico, "Special attention was paid to the Dakota Access Pipeline and its impact on indigenous peoples, including the Standing Rock Sioux Tribe and other tribes indirectly affected by the pipeline." In her final report, the Special Rapporteur identified many concerns regarding the federal government's approval of energy development projects in the West, the Dakota Access Pipeline in particular. She also emphasized that "Consent, not consultation, should be the policy to allow for the government-to-government relationship necessary to fulfill the principles set forth in [UNDRIP]." Recognizing that the Dakota Access Pipeline had already become operational, she could only commit to "continue to monitor the situation...." UN Human Rights Council, *Report of the Special Rapporteur on the rights of indigenous peoples on her mission to the United States of America* (Aug. 9, 2017).

8. Tribes and energy infrastructure. As previously noted, energy extraction, production, and infrastructure often have profound implications for and impact on tribes and tribal lands. This has been the case for coal mining, uranium processing, oil and gas pipeline construction, dam operations, and fossil fuel electricity production and transmission. As the country continues to transition toward clean energy, it will also be true for critical mineral mining and processing, wind and solar development, and clean energy transmission. Consider the following from Margaret Schaff, *Indian Country and the American Energy Economy*, 36 Nat. Resources & Envt. 9 (2021):

> The U.S. Department of Energy estimates that Indian country has 6.5% of the country's utility-scale renewable energy potential, including 7.8% of the technical potential for wind and 5.4% for utility-scale photovoltaic solar. Wind power from tribal lands could satisfy 32% of total U.S. electricity demand, and tribal solar resources could generate twice the total amount of energy needed to power the country.

Hydroelectric projects in particular have had a devastating impact on tribes. Margaret Schaff observes:

> Common to almost all of the projects was the systematic taking and use of Indian lands for dams, reservoirs, facilities, and rights of way for transmission lines. Because many tribes traditionally used the rivers and adjacent areas for access to fresh water, fishing, agriculture, and cemeteries, reservations were often on rivers.... Looking at a map of dams and Indian reservations, one can note that dams were often sited to purposely flood reservation lands. Many traditional Indian villages and cultural sites, such as Celilo Falls on the Columbia River and the town of Sanish on the Fort Berthold Reservation on the Missouri River, were inundated for dams. The dams also impeded treaty protected salmon migration and caused other severe environmental damages.

Today, in addition to multiple pipeline related fights, several tribes are engaging in challenges to "clean energy" related projects, including offshore wind production and lithium mineral extraction. With the push in Trump's second term to rapidly and dramatically expand fossil fuel energy production and infrastructure, it seems likely that energy-related development will continue to create challenges for tribes and tribal communities. These challenges will likely involve both fossil fuels and clean energy related projects. For more on the intersection of energy and tribes, *see* Robin Kundis Craig, *Tribes and Water in the Wake of Navajo Nation and Sackett: Treaties, Winters, Montana, and Rights of Nature*, 48 Wm. & Mary Envtl. L. & Pol'y Rev. 687 (2024); Michael C. Blumm & Dara Illowsky, *The World's Largest Dam Removal Project: The Klamath River Dams*, 101 Or. L. Rev. 1 (2022); Ann M. Eisenberg & Elizabeth Kronk Warner, *The Precipice of Justice: Equity, Energy, and the Environment in Indian Country and Rural Communities*, 42 Energy L.J. 281 (2021); Elizabeth Ann Kronk Warner, *Tribal Treaty Rights: A Powerful Tool in Challenges to Energy Infrastructure*, 51 Conn.

L. REV. 843 (2019); Rebecca Tsosie, *Climate Change, Sustainability and Globalization: Charting the Future of Indigenous Environmental Self-Determination*, 4 ENVTL. & ENERGY L. & POL'Y J. 188 (2009).

C. Tribes as Resource Managers

Indian tribes own approximately 56.6 million acres of land in the lower 48 states. Some of these lands are rich in hard rock minerals, timber, oil, natural gas, wildlife, and other natural resources. For instance, according to one report, underlying Indian reservations is approximately half of all uranium deposits, one-third of all western low-sulfur coal, and 20 percent of all known oil and natural gas reserves in the United States. Mary Christina Wood, *Indian Land and the Promise of Native Sovereignty: The Trust Doctrine Revisited*, 1994 UTAH L. REV. 1471, 1481 (1994). The following excerpt from 1996 considers the issues raised by the status of tribes as governments with management authority over tribal lands and resources, recognized by the federal policy of tribal "self-determination" that emerged in the 1970s.

Rebecca Tsosie, *Tribal Environmental Policy in an Era of Self-Determination: The Role of Ethics, Economics and Traditional Ecological Knowledge*

21 VERMONT LAW REVIEW 225 (1996)

As Indian nations assume greater responsibility for managing tribal lands under the rubrics of tribal sovereignty and the federal self-determination policy, they are able to exercise more autonomy over environmental decision-making. That decision-making process, however, raises significant legal issues, ethical conflicts, and economic considerations.... [T]ribal environmental policy must be responsive to the interacting forces of traditional ecological knowledge, western science, economics, and tribal ... ethics....

Tribal Environmental Authority in the Era of Self-Determination

... In 1970, President Richard Nixon called for a new federal policy of self-determination for American Indians. The self-determination policy represented a welcome change from the previous federal policy of "termination," which sought to abolish the federal trusteeship over Indian tribes, dismantle the reservations, and end the Indian tribes' unique status as "domestic, dependent nations." The self-determination policy, intended to "strengthen the Indian's sense of autonomy without threatening his sense of community," encouraged tribes to assume control over many of the federal programs being administered on the reservation....

The federal policy of self-determination has also encouraged tribes to ... exercise control over their natural resources, thereby reversing earlier federal policies that placed control over land and resources with the Bureau of Indian Affairs, often to the clear detriment of the tribes. These newer policies are significant because natural resource development has long been a predominant means of economic development on many reservations. In particular, the extractive industries, such as coal, uranium, oil, and gas, have played a major role in reservation economic development. Along with their fiscal contributions, however, the extractive industries have brought mining, milling, and smelting operations to Indian lands, causing pollution of reservation lands, waters, and air....

The Role of Indigenous Land Ethics in Guiding Tribal Environmental Law and Policy

The diversity among American Indian people makes defining an "indigenous land ethic" somewhat difficult. Nevertheless, the similarities among indigenous world views regarding the environment cannot be discounted....

Professor Ronald Trosper has drawn on several tribal traditions to construct a model of "traditional Indian world views" premised on four basic principles: "community," "connectedness," "the seventh generation," and "humility." ... Trosper's model of traditional world views, as affirmed by other scholarship, has several important aspects: a perception of the earth as an animate being; a belief that humans are in a kinship system with other living things; a perception of the land as essential to the identity of the people; and a concept of reciprocity and balance that extends to relationships among humans, including future generations, and between humans and the natural world.

The Role of Indigenous Ethics in Guiding Tribal Environmental Policy

The influence of traditional ethics and environmental knowledge on contemporary tribal policy cannot be underestimated. Indeed, there are many examples of successful implementation of traditional ethics in contemporary tribal environmental management. However, there are also many examples of tribal policy built on what appear to be Anglo-American norms, particularly in the case of industries such as mining and waste disposal, which also serve non-Indian interests....

Incorporation of Traditional Values into Environmental Policy

Notably, there are several examples of indigenous communities successfully applying traditional norms and values to community development projects. For example, the Zuni Pueblo instituted a comprehensive agricultural project that restores community control over food production and implements traditional methods consistent with the Zuni's unique environment such as "field rooting" and "dry farming." Jim Enote, the director of the Zuni Conservation Project, describes the goals of the project as being based on traditional Zuni knowledge: "Reaching a modern vision of Zuni sustainability requires developing full partnerships with the Zuni people and promoting the status of Zuni values, traditional knowledge, and resource management practices." ...

The Confederated Salish and Kootenai Tribes of the Flathead Reservation in Montana have developed a comprehensive environmental regulatory and land use management scheme that rests heavily on traditional values. For example, the Salish and Kootenai Natural Resources Department developed the "Mission Mountains Tribal Wilderness Management Plan" ("Wilderness Plan") to prescribe how the Tribe will manage natural resources and human uses within the Wilderness. In the Plan's statement of policy, the Tribal Council acknowledges that:

> Wilderness has played a paramount role in shaping the character of the people and the culture of the Salish and Kootenai Tribes; it is the essence of traditional Indian religion and has served the Indian people of these Tribes as a place to hunt, as a place to gather medicinal herbs and roots, as a vision-seeking ground, as a sanctuary, and in countless other ways for thousands of years.

An important part of the Wilderness Plan is the preservation of cultural and historical resources. The Flathead Culture Committee was given a critical role in determining specific policies and actions to govern specific sites. In some cases this has resulted in barring public access to certain ceremonial and religious sites.

Tribal Environmental Policy That Departs from Traditional Norms

There are several categories of land use that appear to be inconsistent with the traditional environmental norms that we have explored, including coal strip-mining, uranium mining, and siting solid, hazardous, or nuclear waste repositories on tribal land. Both the mining industry and the waste industry carry the potential of severe environmental degradation and, as a result, would appear to be diametrically opposed to traditional indigenous land ethics. Yet both industries have found homes on some Indian reservations.

Why? [T]o a large extent, all Indian nations have been subjected to successive federal policies which encouraged the exploitation of mineral resources on Indian lands. In the late nineteenth century and early twentieth century, Indian treaty lands were often removed from Indian ownership and trust status to facilitate mineral exploitation. For example, the Crow Reservation once encompassed 39 million acres, including vast stores of coal, oil, and natural gas. After several land cessions, the Crow Reservation now encompasses only 2.2 million acres, although the Tribe has reserved mineral rights in certain of the ceded lands. Other lands remained in tribal ownership but were leased out for mineral development by BIA officials convinced, as was Commissioner of Indian Affairs Cato Sells, that it is "an economic and social crime ... to permit thousands of acres of fertile land belonging to the Indians and capable of great industrial development to lie in unproductive idleness." ...

Concluding Thoughts

... Tribal governments who depart from traditional norms to engage in nontraditional economic development are responding to a complex history and set of realities.... These departures may be caused by a lengthy history of competing values imposed by federal policy, by values formulated as a protective response to ensure the continuation of tribal sovereignty, by values stemming from economic dependency on earlier development decisions, and by the cultural loss that has become endemic to many reservations as a result of loss of traditional lands, resources, and a certain measure of sovereignty....

Notes and Questions

1. **Indigenous land ethic.** Professor Rebecca Tsosie recognizes that the diversity among American Indian peoples makes any definition of an "indigenous land ethic" difficult. Even so, she cites the work of Professor Trosper and others to identify a number of common Indigenous values toward land and natural resources. How might these common values apply to each of the cases noted below concerning tribal management of natural resources?

2. ***Nance v. U.S. EPA.*** In some instances, tribes may appear on opposite sides of environmental issues and litigation. In a case referenced by Professor Tsosie, federal courts upheld EPA's approval of the Northern Cheyenne Tribe's redesignation of its reservation from Class II to Class I (pristine) air quality standards, over objections from the neighboring Crow Tribe, whose "primary concern ... was clearly the potential impact of such a redesignation on their ability to mine coal...." *Nance v. U.S. EPA*, 645 F.2d 701, 711 (9th Cir. 1981), *cert. denied sub nom Crow Tribe of Indians v. U.S. Environmental Protection Agency*, 454 U.S. 1081 (1981). How should the EJ dimensions of distributive justice and procedural justice apply in the case of an environmental dispute between tribes? Are there more appropriate procedural mechanisms than federal court? Years after the *Nance* case concluded, the Northern Cheyenne's Class I redesignation resulted in substantial impacts to off-reservation industry, including abandonment of a coal-fired power plant project by the upwind Crow Tribe. Is this the right result for purposes of environmental protection? For Indigenous rights? What common elements of "Indigenous land ethics" would be supported (or aggrieved) by the outcome of this case?

3. **National Bison Range Management.** For generations, tribes have acted as managers of natural resources, including fish and wildlife, in accordance with their particular systems of law and custom. *See, e.g.*, Joseph C. Dupris et al., The Si'lailo Way: Indians, Salmon, and Law on the Columbia River (2006) (detailing the extensive history of Indian management respecting salmon in the Columbia River Basin). Recent efforts have included extensive habitat restoration and wildlife management on the Flathead Indian Reservation in western Montana by the Confederated Salish and Kootenai Tribes (CSKT). Under auspices of the Tribal Self-Governance Act, 25 U.S.C. §§ 458aa, the CSKT have managed their own conservation areas and also petitioned to assume management of the National Bison Range, a 19,000-acre national wildlife refuge in the heart of the Flathead Reservation. Bison on the range today descended from wild bison saved from extinction by tribal members at the turn of the century. For background on the CSKT quest to manage the National Bison Range, *see* Brian Upton, *Returning to a Tribal Self-Governance Partnership at the National Bison Range Complex: Historical, Legal, and Global Perspectives*, 35 Pub. Land & Resources L. Rev. 51 (2014); *see also* Patrick J. White, *Co-Stewardship in Practice: Yellowstone Bison*, 47 Pub. Land & Resources L. Rev. 127 (2024). The CSKT proposal was supported by the Obama administration in 2016 but rejected by the Trump administration in 2017. With the arrival of the second Trump administration in 2025 this progress could be

Figure 9-1. Bison (with calves) on National Bison Range, Flathead Reservation, Montana. Photo: Cliff Villa, 2019.

in jeopardy again. With your understanding of Indigenous land ethics and traditional ecological knowledge, what arguments could you make for or against future management of the National Bison Range by the CSKT?

D. Tribes as Environmental Regulators

Beyond management of land, wildlife, and other natural resources in Indian country, there is the question of who will regulate concerns such as air emissions, water pollution, and contaminated sites in Indian country. As we have seen, the major federal pollution control laws in the United States, such as the Clean Air Act and the Clean Water Act, primarily adopt the model of **cooperative federalism**, under which the federal government (largely, the U.S. EPA) sets national standards for other governments (largely, states) to implement. When Congress passed the original versions of the pollution control laws (e.g., the Clean Air Act in 1970 and the Clean Water Act in 1972), Congress supported state roles in environmental regulation, but for the most part failed to consider the proper role of tribes in the same.

Initially, states may have simply assumed that they had jurisdiction to regulate all environmental matters within their state lines, to include tribal lands within their borders. After this assumption was rejected by courts, *see Washington Dept. of Ecology v. EPA*, 752 F.2d 1465 (9th Cir. 1985), many states and tribes entered cooperative arrangements to ensure environmental protection across respective lands and resources. However, it also became clear that some major pollution concerns fell within regulatory gaps, to be filled either by the tribes themselves or by the U.S. EPA. In the Pacific

Northwest, for example, the absence of air quality regulations established by individual tribes compelled the EPA in 2005 to promulgate the Federal Air Rules for Indian Reservations ("the FARR"). The FARR established air quality rules applicable to 39 Indian reservations across Oregon, Washington, and Idaho, setting some of the first reservation standards for public health and welfare concerns such as agricultural burning, particulate matter, and visibility. For general background on the FARR and links to specific regulations, *see* epa.gov/farr. The FARR is directly enforceable by the EPA; however, tribal employees may receive (and have received) credentials to carry out FARR inspections on their reservations. *See generally*, U.S. EPA, *Guidance for Issuing Federal EPA Inspector Credentials to Authorize Employees of State/Tribal Governments to Conduct Inspections on Behalf of EPA*, Sept. 30, 2004. For a thorough and timely examination of the challenges for regulating air pollution on Indian reservations, *see* Arnold Reitze, Jr., *The Control of Air Pollution on Indian Reservations*, 46 Envtl. L. 893 (2017).

As for environmental regulation by tribes themselves, tribal authority in Indian country generally stems from two sources. "First, Indian tribes possess inherent powers to govern their territories. Although those powers may be limited by federal law in certain respects, tribes nonetheless retain substantial authority over matters affecting tribal health and welfare." Cohen § 14.01[1]. Within this realm, tribes may enact tribal environmental codes and provide for enforcement through tribal agency proceedings and in tribal court. "Second, Indian tribes may exercise powers authorized by Congress. In the environmental context, Congress has authorized tribes to assume primary regulatory authority, or primacy, for administering most federal environmental programs in Indian country." *Id.* Congress established this authority through a series of statutory amendments by which tribes, upon application to EPA, may seek and obtain status for "treatment in the same manner as a state" (TAS).

Typical TAS provisions are illustrated in the following example from Section 301(d) of the Clean Air Act:

> (1) [T]he [EPA]—(1) is authorized to treat Indian tribes as States under this chapter ...
>
> (2) ... Such treatment shall be authorized only if—
>
>> (A) the Indian tribe has a governing body carrying out substantial governmental duties and powers;
>>
>> (B) the functions to be exercised by the Indian tribe pertain to the management and protection of air resources within the exterior boundaries of the reservation or other areas within the tribe's jurisdiction; and
>>
>> (C) the Indian tribe is reasonably expected to be capable, in the judgment of the Administrator, of carrying out the functions to be exercised in a manner consistent with the terms and purposes of this chapter....

42 U.S.C. § 7601(d). Boiling down the requirements above, tribes generally must establish in their TAS application that they (1) are federally recognized; (2) have legal authority for implementing the desired program (e.g., with appropriate regulatory

codes); and (3) are logistically capable of carrying out the desired program (e.g., with inspection resources).

Beyond the Clean Air Act, for TAS provisions in other statutes, see the following—

- Clean Water Act: Sec. 518(e), 33 U.S.C. § 1377(e)
- Safe Drinking Water Act: Sec. 1451, 42 U.S.C. § 300j-11
- CERCLA: Sec. 126(a), 42 U.S.C. § 9626(a)
- Federal Insecticide, Fungicide, and Rodenticide Act (FIFRA): Sec. 23, 7 U.S.C. § 136u

Oddly, Congress never included TAS amendments in the Resource Conservation and Recovery Act (RCRA), regulating the treatment, storage, and disposal of hazardous wastes. For those concerns, tribes may need to rely upon either direct enforcement by the EPA or exercise of their "inherent powers to govern their territories." COHEN § 14.01[1].

As tribes have built capacity for implementing environmental programs over time, the question has arisen how tribes will ensure environmental justice for tribal members and others subject to the tribe's environmental authority. As we have already seen in this chapter, tribes may bring different perspectives to the EJ principles of "fair treatment" and "meaningful involvement," for example. To the extent that a tribe's perspective differs from EPA definitions and expectations, could that difference endanger a tribe's TAS application or program implementation? On the other hand, could there be consequences if a tribe deliberately conforms its views to established criteria? Professor Darren Ranco points to a crucial paradox facing tribes as they contemplate seeking TAS status: "the more closely a tribal program resembles a federal or state program, the more likely it is to survive litigation; but the more a tribe tries to build a program that reflects its own cultural values, the greater the risk to its own tribal sovereignty...." Darren Ranco, *Models of Tribal Environmental Regulation: In Pursuit of a Culturally Relevant Form of Tribal Sovereignty*, 56 FED. LAWYER 46 (2009).

Confronting this seeming paradox, Emerita Professor Jeanette Wolfley searches for and suggests resolutions in the excerpt that follows.

Jeanette Wolfley, *Tribal Environmental Programs: Providing Meaningful Involvement and Fair Treatment*

29 J. ENVTL. L. & LITIGATION 389 (2014)

Over the past two decades, Indian tribes throughout the United States have begun to develop and implement tribal environmental programs based on their inherent sovereignty and amendments in federal environmental laws. Tribal governments are directly responsible and accountable for the health and welfare of their people and reservation residents and are in the best position to meet their people's needs and community interests. Accordingly, tribes are in the process of defining their tribal authority by planning and developing the basic frameworks and institutions for protecting air quality, preserving water quality, and managing contamination and hazardous and solid waste pollution caused by industrial society. Regulating polluting activities and other threats to lands, waters, and vital cultural resources is imperative for tribes to continue their way of life and maintain a homeland in which present and future generations of the tribe may flourish.

As tribes begin administering their environmental programs, including establishing boards, commissions, and drafting codes and regulations, they must weigh carefully the concepts of public participation, meaningful involvement, and due process in decision-making affecting Indian and non-Indian reservation citizens, industry, and state interests....

This Article proposes that there must be an understanding of, or reference to, the tribal values of due process within the tribal culture and context. And a tribal institution—through rulemaking or review by a tribal administrative agency, dispute resolution board, or tribal court—must be given the opportunity to articulate the cultural and social norms of due process. It is through the tribal process that tribes can best preserve, strengthen, and incorporate native concepts of equity and justice, and build communication, cooperation, and support within the tribal community. This represents tribal sovereignty in action. Indeed, due process, if premised on the native way of life, may well introduce the "genius of tribally held values" to a majority society....

Policies Supporting Meaningful Involvement and Fair Treatment

At the time a tribe assumes authorization to develop and implement a federal environmental program, the tribal environmental program should simultaneously seek ways to provide for due process and public participation.... This Section presents three policy reasons supporting the establishment of participation and due process procedures including: (1) promoting good governance, (2) respecting the interests of community members, and (3) protecting and promoting tribal sovereignty....

A. Providing Good Governance

... Governments have a broad set of responsibilities including protecting the health and safety of its citizens or members, improving the community's quality of life through education, planning, property protection, and securing a viable economic future. With this wide range of responsibilities, governments are frequently tasked with balancing competing interests, particularly in the environmental area. Governments often mediate conflicts between those concerned with protecting the environment and those seeking to ensure long-term economic stability through development and use of natural resources, or between individual landowner interests and the interests of the greater community.

To be credible, government officials must demonstrate transparency and accountability in their decision-making. This "[t]ransparency minimizes the opportunity for preferential treatment and the advancement of private interests over public good." Transparency means that information should be provided in easily understandable forms and media. It should be freely available and directly accessible to those who will be affected by governance laws, regulations, and policies and procedures, as well as the outcomes resulting therefrom. "Consolidating and then openly sharing processes and procedures assures citizens that decisions are made fairly." ...

The fundamental exercise of sovereignty by a government includes not only power but also the responsibility to establish a governmental infrastructure and institutions that provide for sound decision-making. These institutions create avenues for the public and local community to participate in policymaking and establish mechanisms for consultation with the community. It also requires the implementation of the laws and regulations in a manner that recognizes the interest of its citizenry and in the case of tribal governments, tribal members and nonmembers residing on the reservation....

Providing opportunities for public participation can strengthen tribal government and sovereignty, improving the tribes' relations with the rest of the community and with off-reservation communities. Participation by the local community and the public is a key cornerstone of good governance. Participation needs to be informed and organized. Support from the community, by recognizing the legitimacy of tribal institutions, increases a tribe's ability to exercise its sovereignty and authority and will likely result in less interference from external parties. In turn, a tribe is better able to protect and preserve its resources, land base and homeland.

Of course, it should be clear that good governance is an ideal that is difficult to achieve in its totality. But still, these ideals are viewed as legitimate and if governments seek to attain such goals their actions will be perceived as fair and just. Fairness, in turn, is equated with procedural regularity, adequate opportunity to be heard, and nondiscriminatory treatment.

B. Respecting the Interests of Community Members

Tribal environmental program decisions affect the entire social, cultural, and spiritual beliefs as well as the political fabric of a community because such decisions impact communal rights to live on, use, harvest, conserve, and transfer lands within the reservation, and the land, itself, as community. Accordingly, tribal members have a legitimate stake in the decisions affecting the environment and land base in which they hold a communal interest....

Tribal leaders, in addressing the myriad of important issues pertaining to running a government, must also be cognizant of the traditional values of respect, reciprocity, humility, and connectedness as they relate to land and tribal members. Often, certain individuals, traditional and religious tribal leaders, advocate the critical importance of cultural integrities to preserve the beauty and stability of the community, to protect the health and welfare of the residents, and to plan for future generations. These voices, comments, and opinions serve an important role in the tribal institutional setting.

Tribal leadership often calls upon federal agencies to recognize tribal interests and to consult with them on federal decisions based upon the trust obligations owed to the tribes. Similarly, tribal members expect and request their tribal leadership to recognize, as many tribal leaders do, the responsibilities they have to the membership....

Community members do not always expect to get everything they want, but they do expect to be heard, taken seriously, and informed of tribal council decisions and processes. Indeed, the impetus for establishing tribal environmental programs is to clean up contamination, confront ecological degradation, improve the overall quality of life for tribal community members, and preserve the treaty-reserved homelands.

Moreover, tribal decision-making seeks to reflect the history, experience, culture, and wishes of the unique people and community it serves. Tribal members share culture, customs, traditions, kinships, and history with the tribal leaders that are elected or appointed as part of the established tribal government. Governance structures and issues differ from reservation to reservation; therefore, the solutions to governance matters must be tailored individually. Traditionally, tribal decisions were not taken lightly in Indian societies but were carefully deliberated, sometimes for days or weeks, by kinship-clan groups, elders, spiritual leaders, and tribal leaders. The groups varied from tribe to tribe. Building consensus and gaining community support were priorities before tribal leadership took action. Today, as part of this deliberative process, tribal environmental institutions should seek out comments and opinions of elders, culture committees, individuals impacted, and the community as a whole.

C. Protecting and Promoting Tribal Sovereignty

Tribal sovereign autonomy and self-government, a principled foundation for Indian law, has weathered over 150 years of U.S. jurisprudence, and indeed, insulating tribes against the passage of time is a consistent theme in the law. Additionally, tribal separatism remains both a focal point for modern Indian policy and for tribes themselves. A priority implicit in tribal separatism is maintaining a homeland in which both present and future generations of the tribe may live. A viable tribal land base is the linchpin to other attributes of sovereignty. The tribal territory forms the geographical limits of the tribe's jurisdiction, supports a residing population, is the basis of the tribal economy, and provides an irreplaceable place for cultural traditions often premised on the sacredness of land. Through control over Indian lands and resources, Indian nations maintain a degree of economic self-sufficiency necessary to Indian self-determination.

... Land and natural-cultural resources will always occupy an important place in Indian cultures. Accordingly, tribes have a vital stake in resource and environmental management to preserve their homelands and their sovereignty.

Similarly, tribes should be aware of public perceptions about the role of tribal government in providing fundamental fairness to all residents of the reservation. To many non-Indians, the reservation remains a foreign place and the governmental structure is a mystery. While territorial jurisdiction is a vital aspect of self-government, policy makers have noted, "[i]n most cases, non-Indians vigorously reject any type of regulation by the tribe." Some states voice concerns about law and order and the efficiency of government, and view tribal regulation as unduly lax in comparison to their own programs. There are also questions about the ability of tribal governments to guarantee due process and fairness. Many of these criticisms are based upon a lack of knowledge and understanding of the structures of tribal governments, anecdotal evidence, unwillingness to recognize tribal institutions, and outright prejudice. Whether they are unfounded or not, the public and community perception of tribal institutions and their environmental programs should be recognized by tribal governments. Tribes should work to address these misconceptions.

... Institutional support needs to come from both the Indian and non-Indian communities as well as the regulated industry. Non-Indian companies that pursue mineral or other natural resource development affecting the tribal environment are accustomed to deriving some regulatory certainty from written laws and regulations. The establishment of advisory committees or boards can also lend support to a fair and meaningful system. Dialogue among the tribes and industry can foster mutual understanding of the need to define and make known specific environmental concerns. Importantly, these forms of public involvement enable the tribes to obtain sound input and receive information that can assist the tribe in its thoughtful deliberations and decision-making. A structured, open process can instill a careful weighing of concerns and issues by tribal program officers, council members, and community members. This approach is similar to existing traditional tribal processes.

Some tribes have already instituted these types of measures to defray the disapproval of, and challenges to, tribal authority, and to allay the concerns of EPA and state interests. Tribes define for their community what due process means based upon their traditions and how due process should be implemented to meet the needs of their community, protect their lands and people, and ultimately protect their sovereignty....

Notes and Questions

1. The "paradox." In the excerpt above, how does Professor Wolfley respond to the seeming paradox suggested by Professor Ranco? Can tribal governments implement environmental programs on their lands while harmonizing the interests of both tribal sovereignty and environmental justice? What steps does Professor Wolfley suggest to resolve potential conflicts?

2. Defining EJ principles for tribes. Professor Wolfley continues in the article to suggest a number of available authorities—beyond EPA criteria—which tribes may consult for articulating their own understanding of principles such as fair treatment and meaningful involvement. These available sources include oral traditions, tribal constitutions and codes, the Indian Civil Rights Act, federal environmental statutes, federal common law, and principles of administrative law. What advantages might each of these authorities offer as tribes seek to define environmental justice terms for themselves?

3. TAS today. Despite the concerns noted above, tribal governments have invested substantial time and effort to obtain TAS approvals. The process for obtaining TAS approval can be onerous. For one tribal perspective on this process, *see* Jill Elise Grant, *The Navajo Nation EPA's Experience with "Treatment as a State" and Primacy*, 21 NAT. RES. & ENVT. 9 (2007). Recent reforms by the EPA may bring some relief from TAS application requirements. *See, e.g.*, 81 Fed. Reg. 30,183 (May 16, 2016) (eliminating certain application requirements for obtaining TAS for water quality standards). As of early 2025, EPA identified 107 TAS approvals to implement regulatory programs under Clean Air Act, Clean Water Act, Safe Drinking Water, and Toxic Substances Control Act. Of these 107 TAS approvals, most of them (84) authorize tribes to establish their own water quality standards under the Clean Water Act. EPA, Tribes Approved for Treatment as a State (TAS), epa.gov/tribal/tribes-approved-treatment-state-tas. It is unclear, however, what impact policies of the second Trump administration might have on the rate of TAS approvals.

For Professor Grijalva, the bottom-line on TAS appears to be this:

> We might hope the time comes when the preservation of American indigenous culture needs no federal agency, court or legislative body. Until that day, tribal primacy for federal environmental programs may well be the most effective means for addressing environmental injustice in Indian country because it can be conducted in a culturally relevant manner, as defined by the culture itself.

Grijalva, *supra*, at 200.

4. Open dumps. As noted above, Congress never managed to amend the Resource Conservation and Recovery Act (RCRA) to add TAS provisions authorizing tribes to assume primacy for programs in hazardous waste treatment, storage, and disposal. Partly as a result of this congressional failure, partly a consequence of poverty on many Indian reservations, and partly due to the opportunities presented by large, rural landscapes, illegal dumping has been a pervasive problem in Indian country. In 1994, Congress acknowledged the problem with the Indian Lands Open Dump Cleanup Act, 25 U.S.C. §§ 3901–3908, which noted the existence of "at least 600 open dumps on Indian and Alaska Native lands...." To address this problem, the Indian Health Service (IHS), directed by statute, maintains an inventory of open dumps on reservations lands.

In 2021, the Bipartisan Infrastructure Law provided $3.5 billion to IHS for the development of water infrastructure, to include drinking water and sanitation, plus solid waste disposal facilities across Indian country. This significant funding boost may allow closure of many open dumps that have lingered on Indian lands for generations. EPA's Tribal Waste Management Program may also provide support through policy direction, technical assistance, and education and outreach to tribes on sound waste management practices. For additional information, *see* U.S. EPA, Tribal Waste Management Program, epa.gov/tribal-lands/tribal-waste-management-program.

Chapter 10

Public and Private Initiatives to Promote Environmental Justice

A. Introduction

In addition to considering environmental justice in the context of core governmental functions such as rulemaking, permitting, enforcement, and cleanup, governmental agencies at all levels have attempted to address environmental inequities through a wide range of broader initiatives. In the previous chapter, we considered how tribal governments may seek to address environmental concerns and inequities. In this chapter, we focus on how environmental justice concerns have been addressed at federal and state levels. We observe how federal initiatives have supported environmental justice—and reversed. We observe how a few states, such as California and New York, have enacted robust environmental justice legislation. We also provide a brief introduction to private governance, potentially filling regulatory gaps and providing advocates with new tools for pursuing environmental justice.

B. Federal Initiatives

In the United States, as early as 1971, the White House Council on Environmental Quality issued an annual report acknowledging that racial discrimination adversely affects the urban poor and the quality of their environment. However, it was not until the early 1990s that a concerted effort was undertaken to address this and other disparities in environmental protection. In 1992, the U.S. EPA released the first governmental report comprehensively examining environmental justice. Shortly thereafter, the EPA established what later became the Office of Environmental Justice and convened a 25-member National Environmental Justice Advisory Council (NEJAC) to the EPA. In 1994, the first formal policy directive was issued by the White House requiring all federal agencies to take actions in support of environmental justice, as discussed below.

1. Executive Orders on Environmental Justice

Executive Order 12898, *Federal Actions to Address Environmental Justice in Minority Populations and Low-Income Populations*, was issued on February 11, 1994. In it, President Bill Clinton directed each agency, among other things, to identify and address "disproportionately high and adverse human health and environmental effects of its programs, policies, and activities" on minority and low-income populations. During the three decades Executive Order 12898 remained in force, environmental justice grew into a federally recognized concern and a global framework for understanding environmental issues. President Joe Biden built on Executive Order 12898 through the issuance of two additional Executive Orders: 14008, *Tackling the Climate Crisis at Home and Abroad* (2021), and 14096, *Revitalizing Our Nation's Commitment to Environmental Justice for All* (2023). EO 14008 stood out for its creation of the Justice40 program. Justice40 promised to direct at least 40 percent of the benefits of investments under the Bipartisan Infrastructure Law, the Inflation Reduction Act, and the American Rescue Plan to disadvantaged communities. The implementation guidelines provided the following examples for climate change:

Example Benefits for Disadvantaged Communities

- Reduction of greenhouse gas emissions and local air pollutants
- Creation of community resilience plans that specifically address needs of disadvantaged communities
- Increased technical assistance and community engagement of disadvantaged communities
- Increased flood mitigation benefits
- Hectares of floodplain restored
- Hectares of wetlands restored
- Green stormwater infrastructure
- Urban flood risk mapping addressing the distribution of socially vulnerable communities and risks
- Increased urban heat island effect mitigation benefits
- Increased acres of greenspace restored
- Increased tree cover and sustainable shade coverage
- Increased availability of public health warnings (e.g., weather preparedness) translated into multiple languages

The Council on Environmental Quality (CEQ) developed a publicly available Climate and Economic Justice Screening Tool (CEJST) to assist agencies in identifying "disadvantaged communities" under the Justice40 initiative. The CEQ geospatial mapping tool highlighted census tracts "marginalized by underinvestment and overburdened by pollution" as disadvantaged for purposes of investment under the initiative. The CEJST tool was subsequently removed from federal websites by the Trump administration, but has been preserved by institutions including Harvard University and remains available at the following link: https://ndcpartnership.org/knowledge-portal/climate-toolbox/climate-and-economic-justice-screening-tool-cejst.

Beyond CEJST developed by CEQ, many other EJ GIS mapping tools have been created by other entities, including academic and community organizations. For example, led by Dr. David Padgett of Tennessee State University, a technical team funded by the Bullard Center for Environmental Justice developed an HBCU Climate Environmental Justice Screening Tool (HCEJST). Significantly, the HCEJST tool incorporates race and other data layers not found in federal GIS tools. The HCEJST tool is available at https://cdu-gis.maps.arcgis.com/apps/instant/basic/index.html?appid=de6aa42f3ce24fb7999f2af01540be9f&center=-95.1024;29.7719&level=7.

Notes and Questions

1. Shared leadership. Under the original and subsequent executive orders, the president set a policy direction for the federal government to follow in applying its existing legal authority. Over the years, states have developed both laws and policies on environmental justice while businesses and many other institutions domestically and internationally have created a vast infrastructure of practices to address the issue.

2. Limitations. An important limitation of the Executive Order on Environmental Justice (EO 12898) was section 6-609, an express provision stating that the executive order does not create any new rights enforceable at law or equity, a provision common to such executive orders. What practical value is an executive order given this limitation? In fact, EO 12898 has been cited by courts and administrative boards as authority for requiring agency action. *See, e.g., Standing Rock Sioux Tribe v. U.S. Army Corps of Engineers*, 255 F.Supp.3d 101, 136 (D.D.C. 2017); *In re* Shell Gulf of Mexico, Inc., 15 E.A.D. 103 (EAB 2010). How have courts found related agency duties despite the express provision that the order does not create any new enforceable rights?

2. Government Use of Race Classifications

The Trump administration's change in approach in 2025 took place in the wake of a reversal of constitutional jurisprudence in the area of equal protection law under a pair of decisions in 2024 by the U.S. Supreme Court: *Students for Fair Admissions v. Harvard* and *Students for Fair Admissions v. UNC*. These cases involved equal protection challenges to the consideration of race in admissions decisions at Harvard College and the University of North Carolina at Chapel Hill for the purpose of promoting a diverse student body. Although the case was decided in a context different from environmental protection, in reading the following excerpt of the decision, consider how the case bears upon the actions of the Trump administration in revoking Executive Orders 12898 and 14008 on environmental justice and "terminating 'environmental justice' offices and positions."

Students for Fair Admission v. Harvard

600 U.S. 181 (2023)

ROBERTS, Chief Justice:

Because "[r]acial discrimination [is] invidious in all contexts," we have required that universities operate their race-based admissions programs in a manner that is "sufficiently measurable to permit judicial [review]" under the rubric of strict scrutiny, *Fisher v. University of Tex. at Austin*, 579 U.S. 365, 381 (2016) (*Fisher II*). "Classifying and assigning" students based on their race "requires more than ... an amorphous end to justify it." *Parents Involved*, 551 U.S., at 735

Respondents have fallen short of satisfying that burden. First, the interests they view as compelling cannot be subjected to meaningful judicial review. Harvard identifies the following educational benefits that it is pursuing: (1) "training future leaders in the public and private sectors"; (2) preparing graduates to "adapt to an increasingly pluralistic society"; (3) "better educating its students through diversity"; and (4) "producing new knowledge stemming from diverse outlooks." UNC points to similar benefits, namely, "(1) promoting the robust exchange of ideas; (2) broadening and refining understanding; (3) fostering innovation and problem-solving; (4) preparing engaged and productive citizens and leaders; [and] (5) enhancing appreciation, respect, and empathy, cross-racial understanding, and breaking down stereotypes."

Although these are commendable goals, they are not sufficiently coherent for purposes of strict scrutiny. At the outset, it is unclear how courts are supposed to measure any of these goals. How is a court to know whether leaders have been adequately "train[ed]"; whether the exchange of ideas is "robust"; or whether "new knowledge" is being developed? Even if these goals could somehow be measured, moreover, how is a court to know when they have been reached, and when the perilous remedy of racial preferences may cease? There is no particular point at which there exists sufficient "innovation and problem-solving," or students who are appropriately "engaged and productive." Finally, the question in this context is not one of *no* diversity or of *some*: it is a question of degree. How many fewer leaders Harvard would create without racial preferences, or how much poorer the education at Harvard would be, are inquiries no court could resolve.

The race-based admissions systems that respondents employ also fail to comply with the twin commands of the Equal Protection Clause that race may never be used as a "negative" and that it may not operate as a stereotype.

First, our cases have stressed that an individual's race may never be used against him in the admissions process. Here, however, the First Circuit found that Harvard's consideration of race has led to an 11.1% decrease in the number of Asian-Americans admitted to Harvard. And the District Court observed that Harvard's "policy of considering applicants' race ... overall results in fewer Asian American and white students being admitted."

Respondents nonetheless contend that an individual's race is never a negative factor in their admissions programs, but that assertion cannot withstand scrutiny. Harvard, for example, draws an analogy between race and other factors it considers in admission. "[W]hile admissions officers may give a preference to applicants likely to excel in the Harvard-Radcliffe Orchestra," Harvard explains, "that does not mean it is a 'negative' not to excel at a musical instrument." But on Harvard's logic, while it gives preferences to applicants with high grades and test scores, "that does not mean it is a 'negative'" to be a student with lower grades and lower test scores. This understanding of the admissions process is hard to take seriously. College admissions are zero-sum. A benefit provided to some applicants but not to others necessarily advantages the former group at the expense of the latter.

Respondents also suggest that race is not a negative factor because it does not impact many admissions decisions. Yet, at the same time, respondents also maintain that the demographics of their admitted classes would meaningfully change if race-based admissions were abandoned. And they acknowledge that race is determinative for at least some—if not many—of the students they admit. How else but "negative" can race be described if, in its absence, members of some racial groups would be admitted in greater numbers than they otherwise would have been? The "[e]qual protection of the laws is not achieved through indiscriminate imposition of inequalities."

Respondents' admissions programs are infirm for a second reason as well. We have long held that universities may not operate their admissions programs on the "belief that minority students always (or even consistently) express some characteristic minority viewpoint on any issue." *Grutter*, 539 U.S., at 333 (internal quotation marks omitted). That requirement is found throughout our Equal Protection Clause jurisprudence more generally. *See, e.g., Schuette v. BAMN*, 572 U.S. 291, 308 (2014) (plurality opinion) ("In cautioning against 'impermissible racial stereotypes,' this Court has rejected the assumption that 'members of the same racial group—regardless of their age, education, economic status, or the community in which they live—think alike...."

Yet by accepting race-based admissions programs in which some students may obtain preferences on the basis of race alone, respondents' programs tolerate the very thing that *Grutter* foreswore: stereotyping. The point of respondents' admissions programs is that there is an inherent benefit in race *qua* race—in race for race's sake. Respondents admit as much. Harvard's admissions process rests on the pernicious stereotype that "a black student can usually bring something that a white person cannot offer." *Bakke*, 438 U.S., at 316 (opinion of Powell, J.). UNC is much the same. It argues that race in itself "says [something] about who you are."

We have time and again forcefully rejected the notion that government actors may intentionally allocate preference to those "who may have little in common with one another but the color of their skin." The entire point of the Equal Protection Clause is that treating someone differently because of their skin color is *not* like treating them differently because they are from a city or from a suburb, or because they play the violin poorly or well. "One of the principal reasons race is treated as a forbidden classification is that it demeans the dignity and worth of a person to be judged by ancestry instead of by his or her own merit and essential qualities." But when a university admits students "on the basis of race, it engages in the offensive and demeaning assumption that [students] of a particular race, because of their race, think alike,"—at the very least alike in the sense of being different from nonminority students. In doing so, the university furthers "stereotypes that treat individuals as the product of their race, evaluating their thoughts and efforts—their very worth as citizens—according to a criterion barred to the Government by history and the Constitution. Such stereotyping can only "cause[ ] continued hurt and injury," contrary as it is to the "core purpose" of the Equal Protection Clause, *Palmore*, 466 U.S. at 432.

Notes and Questions

1. Zero-sum? According to Chief Justice Roberts, "College admissions are zero-sum," asserting that, "A benefit provided to some applicants but not to others necessarily advantages the former group at the expense of the latter." If this observation is true, how does it compare to the distribution of environmental benefits? If today a predominantly white community has clean air and a neighboring community of color has heavily polluted air, would efforts to reduce air pollution in the community of color "necessarily" advantage one group at the expense of the other?

2. "Ending Radical and Wasteful Government DEI Programs and Preferencing." On his first day in office in 2025, President Trump issued Executive Order 14151, purporting to end diversity, equity, and inclusion (DEI) programs. The order directs the Office of Management and Budget (OMB), with the assistance of the Attorney General and the Office of Personnel Management (OPM), to oversee the termination of DEI "mandates, policies, programs, preferences, and activities ...," ultimately directing the review and revision of all existing federal employment practices, union contracts, and training policies or programs. Although focused on employment-related matters, it includes the following provision:

> Each agency, department, or commission head, in consultation with the Attorney General, the Director of OMB, and the Director of OPM, as appropriate, shall take the following actions within sixty days of this order:
>
> (i) terminate, to the maximum extent allowed by law, all DEI, DEIA, and "*environmental justice*" offices and positions (including but not limited to "Chief Diversity Officer" positions); all "equity action plans," "equity" actions, initiatives, or programs, "equity-related" grants or contracts; and all DEI or DEIA performance requirements for employees, contractors, or grantees. [Emphasis added.]

Recall from Chapter 1 EPA's longstanding definition of environmental justice applying to "all people." Considering this definition of environmental justice and its historical development, would you consider it to be a DEI program? In what ways does it differ from the employment and education programs typically associated with DEI? How is it similar?

3. Supreme Court influence. President Trump's advisors may have been influenced or emboldened by the decision in *SFFA v. Harvard*. The decision related exclusively to consideration of race in the admissions programs of colleges and universities. Does the identification of the socio-economic status, tribal identity, and racial or ethnic makeup of neighborhoods to assess and address pollution burdens in certain areas fall within the express prohibition presented by the Court? The excerpt also includes the primary reasoning for finding that the admissions programs were unconstitutional. Do those reasons apply to any of the environmental justice programs you have read about so far?

4. Race, income, exposure, and health matters. When research shows that siting and permitting decisions associated with pollution exposures and adverse health risks correlate to the income status or the tribal or racial identity of residents, to what extent does this allow government action to address these disparities? Assuming that racial disparities do in fact continue today, is it likely or possible for a strategy that does not explicitly consider race to alleviate these disparities? Does environmental justice for "all people" differ in any meaningful way from the EPA's general mission to protect human health and the environment?

Alternatively, can the EPA use racial criteria to *evaluate* whether its general strategy is, in fact, alleviating racial disparities (even if not explicitly considered in the strategy itself)? Would the use of race for agency action be more problematic than consideration of race in evaluation of the status quo? Would it be better to adopt a more conservative approach (and avoid litigation) or adopt a more aggressive approach and take the position that we need race-conscious strategies in order to alleviate racial disparities?

Since income is not a suspect classification, can (and should) the agency take targeted initiatives in low-income communities? Will that likely alleviate racial disparities as well?

3. Federal Initiatives for Promoting Cleanup of Alaska Native Claims Settlement Act (ANCSA) Contaminated Lands

One unique area of federal responsibility for environmental justice is addressing the hundreds—if not thousands—of sites in Alaska contaminated by federal activities including historic defense operations. The nature, extent, and gravity of these contaminated sites is outlined in the excerpt below from Alaska's U.S. Senator Lisa Murkowski, who has championed federal legislation and action to address these concerns.

Lisa Murkowski, *Alaska's Contaminated Lands Are an Environmental Injustice*

62 ABA Judges' Journal 17 (2023)

In 1971, Congress passed the Alaska Native Claims Settlement Act (ANCSA), which settled the aboriginal land claims of Alaska Natives in exchange for $962.5 million and fee simple title to approximately 45.7 million acres of land. ANCSA's nontreaty model has produced notable results over the past half century. More than 44 million acres of land have now been conveyed to the Alaska Native Corporations (ANCs) it chartered. Many of those ANCs have become economic engines providing benefits to their Tribal members, villages, cities, regions, and the state as a whole. Yet, there is also a deep stain on ANCSA's legacy, in the form of a shocking environmental injustice. Under this landmark law, the federal government has conveyed lands with hundreds of significantly contaminated sites to Alaska Natives. The extent of this contamination has never been fully inventoried, but it is extensive, involving lands, facilities, and equipment previously utilized by the Department of Defense and other federal agencies. The state of Alaska has estimated that some level of contamination could affect up to 17.6 million acres, or 40 percent of what has been conveyed under ANCSA.... [T]his is not the "eight stars of gold on a field of blue" we celebrate on Alaska's flag—these are a thousand points of blight damaging the natural environment and the health of people across our state. Some contamination is occasionally visible, including leaking barrels, corroding fuel tanks, and unexploded ordnance from World War II. But much of it cannot be easily detected because it is either buried or harmful even in small quantities. That list includes arsenic, asbestos, mercury, toxic metals, and polychlorinated biphenyls.... Over the years, examples of contamination on ANCSA lands have become well known.... At a field hearing I held in Unalaska last year, Hallie Bissett, the executive director of the Alaska Native Village Corporation Association (ANVCA), testified about contaminated drinking water in communities such as Utqiagvik and Unalakleet, where leaking jet fuel was the source.

The mayor of Unalaska, Vincent Tutiakoff, testified about the sustained loss of fish populations and clam beds and how local residents unknowingly used contaminated materials from infrastructure left on conveyed lands to help weatherize their homes. Alaska news organizations have also reported on contamination found in berries, which are an important subsistence food.... Contaminated sites have led to a slowdown in ANCSA conveyances and the loss of economic opportunities those lands were meant to provide. But nothing compares to the physical impacts of exposure, which are often horrific and can result in toxic poisoning. In humans, the effects have ranged from hair loss, skin burns, and illnesses to clusters of Parkinson's disease, cancer, and untimely death. This crisis is not getting better with time. As climate change accelerates, erosion and other factors are literally bringing old contamination to the surface. As that occurs,

Figure 10-1. Nome, Alaska, one of many communities in Alaska where historic federal activities have left a legacy of contamination impacting Alaska Natives and requiring assessment and cleanup. Photo: Carlton Waterhouse, 2022.

decades of burying and abandoning equipment and waste are proving to be anything but a "best practice." So, what is being done to remedy this historic injustice?...

[A]mid the national push for environmental justice, there is renewed hope for a more sustained effort to address ANCSA-contaminated lands. At the Unalaska field hearing I held last year, the Department of the Interior was once again unwilling to take the lead to address this longstanding issue, but the EPA has agreed to step in to facilitate the federal response. The revived Arctic Executive Steering Committee, which is composed of senior officials from numerous federal agencies, is making this a priority.

Congress is also taking action through both oversight and legislation. I established the Contaminated ANCSA Lands Assistance Program at the EPA to offer both technical assistance and grants to tribal entities in Alaska to empower them to help clean up their own lands. Congress approved $20 million for this new program in fiscal year 2023. The first grants were announced in August 2023, and I have included $30 million for the program in the Senate's fiscal year 2024 appropriations bills. These are all positives, but the situation demands perspective. Today's funding levels are a pittance compared to what is needed for full remediation, which is expected to cost billions of dollars. It could take hundreds of years to complete full remediation at the current pace. Given the scale of contamination on some lands, it's also important to recognize that funding is only one part of a more comprehensive solution. In some instances, land exchanges and other options will need to be on the table to help make Alaska Natives whole. Looking ahead, we need to pay special attention to the recommendations made by ANVCA, AFN [the Alaska Federation of Natives], the State of Alaska, and other stakeholders. We need to do more to prioritize cleanup, including the completion of a full inventory of contaminated lands, the designation of responsible federal parties, and detailed plans to remediate each site. We also need to continue increasing federal appropriations for this purpose because cleanups cannot consist of roping off areas and telling those who live nearby, "Just don't go there."... Ultimately, more administrative, legislative, and judicial action will be needed to fully remedy this longstanding environmental injustice. That is the only way forward to remove the stain on ANCSA's legacy and fully protect the health, safety, and well-being of Alaska Natives.

Notes and Questions

1. Site inventory. Since Senator Murkowski published this article in 2023, significant steps have taken place. The first step included development of a shared platform that could be used by all agencies and interested parties for tracking site assessment and remediation. In partnership with other agencies, EPA created this platform, known as the Contaminated ANCSA Sites Common Operating Picture, which is available now at the link below: https://experience.arcgis.com/experience/51479962643a49368433f43204d493e3.

This fully searchable web-based mapping platform includes a fully searchable inventory of sites, their stages of completion, lead agencies, and associated Alaska Native Village Corporations. As of June 2025, the platform reflected an inventory of 1,284 contaminated ANCSA sites.

2. Grant funding. The Contaminated ANCSA Lands Assistance Program, noted by Senator Murkowski, has empowered Native corporations, villages, and other organizations to participate in land identification and remediation. Early rounds of grant funding have helped address, for example, concerns for asbestos at a former Naval Public Works Building on Adak Island and concerns for PCBs contamination in soils near a former World War II-era warehouse in Dutch Harbor. For an engaging resource providing additional information on projects funded by this grant program, see the EPA's Contaminated ANCSA Lands Program StoryMap at https://storymaps.arcgis.com/stories/09dd21b44b8349fe9cac37bce01e76bf.

4. Recent Federal Strategies for Promoting Environmental Justice Across the United States

During the Biden administration, there was an unprecedented level of federal action on environmental justice. Co-authors Carlton Waterhouse and Cliff Villa oversaw or participated in some of those actions. Space does not allow full coverage of the range of recent activities across the federal government, so this section provides a few highlights of activities with special emphasis on the EPA. Among other things, the Biden administration substantially elevated environmental justice in the federal government through the creation of new offices and a new federal advisory council.

Pursuant to Executive Order 14008, *Tackling the Climate Crisis at Home and Abroad*, President Biden created the White House Environmental Justice Advisory Council (WHEJAC). The council brought together advocates, scholars, community leaders and others from across the country to participate in the federal advisory committee on environmental justice. The WHEJAC was the first federal advisory committee uniquely tasked with providing advice and recommendations to the White House on how to address environmental injustice. In Executive Order 14096, *Revitalizing Our Nation's Commitment to Environmental Justice for All*, President Biden established a White House Office of Environmental Justice within the Council of Environmental Quality. Through the order, the President Biden also established a Chief Environmental Justice Officer to "advance environmental justice initiatives" and coordinate policy and program development in accordance with the order. Along with the White House, the administration created a new Office of Environmental Justice in the Justice Department to oversee and coordinate environmental justice policies across its divisions and with other federal agencies.

American Rescue Plan and IRA Grants. The American Rescue Plan, signed into law in 2021, provided one hundred million dollars to EPA to address health outcome disparities from pollution and the COVID-19 pandemic. It provided millions of dollars to states and municipalities under EPA's State Environmental Justice Cooperative Agreement program. Funded projects ranged from air quality outreach and education to health worker training to environmental justice mapping tool development. The Inflation Reduction Act allocated $2.8 billion in community level environmental and climate justice grants. A significant amount of these funds went to community-based groups to address environmental and climate-based issues.

EPA OEJECR. Within EPA, the Office of Environmental Justice was combined with the agency's external civil rights office and elevated to become the Office of Environmental Justice and External Civil Rights—one of a handful of national EPA program offices. In turn, staffing was substantially increased in the headquarters office in Washington, DC and in the ten regional offices across the country. (OEJECR was dissolved by the second Trump administration in 2025.)

Journey to Justice. President Biden's EPA Administrator Michael Regan personally elevated environmental justice in the EPA by conducting a tour across the country that included many communities overburdened by pollution. The "Journey to Justice" tour included visits with impacted communities in Puerto Rico, in Louisiana's "Cancer Alley," and in coal country of West Virginia. After his visits, Administrator Regan directed agency staff to act within their authority to address critical issues facing the communities he visited and encouraged state and local leaders to use their authority in collaboration with EPA to address longstanding pollution problems and health concerns.

Civil Rights Act Title VI. The Biden EPA significantly increased its enforcement and compliance capacity under President Biden to address longstanding concerns that the agency failed to provide timely and substantive response to administrative complaints filed under Civil Rights Act Title VI. While EPA worked to review and clear the backlog of complaints, one complaint investigation, as noted in Chapter 4, resulted in a permanent injunction against EPA from applying its Title VI disparate impact regulations in Louisiana.

Figure 10-2. EPA Administrator Michael Regan speaks with community member in Mossville, Louisiana, during "Journey to Justice" tour in 2021. Photo: U.S. EPA.

Federal legislation. Do we need new federal legislation to address concerns for environmental justice? Do you believe such legislation would help moderate the flip-flopping on EJ we have seen recently with changes in presidential administrations? Environmental justice attorney and scholar Jeremy Orr in 2018 observed the importance of the codification of environmental justice protections by federal statute. Orr notes:

> There have certainly been various environmental justice bills introduced in both chambers of Congress over the past three decades, but none of them have ever made it out of committee and to the floor for a vote. The most notable of past environmental justice bills was the Environmental Justice Act of 1992, sponsored by civil rights activist and U.S. Representative John Lewis. It was the first federal bill directly aimed at eradicating racial inequalities in the application of environmental laws and policies.

Jeremy Orr, *Environmental Justice Act of 2017: A Fighting Chance for Frontline Communities*, 24 Hastings Envtl L.J. 303 (2018).

U.S. Senator Cory Booker and the late U.S. Representative Raúl Grijalva introduced the Environmental Justice Act of 2017. The latest iteration introduced by Congressional Democrats in 2020 would have mandated consideration of the cumulative impacts of the Clean Air Act and the Clean Water Act with respect to permitting decision. In addition, the 2020 bill would have established a fund for fossil fuel communities to transition from greenhouse gas-dependent economies. The bill would also have broadened rights for communities with environmental justice concerns and develop new federal grants and program authority to address environmental and public health concerns.

Actions to limit federal initiatives. As the pendulum swings wildly back in the second Trump administration, will the environmental justice movement survive? Consider that leadership and governance in environmental justice is inherently a shared enterprise, so that when federal initiatives decline, initiatives at other levels of government and non-governmental action may expand to continue the movement. Significant authorities for promoting environmental justice remain at the state and local levels of government, which the following section examines.

C. State Initiatives

State efforts to address environmental justice have grown substantially since the first edition of this book was published in 2002. At that time, only a small number of states had environmental justice laws or policies. Today, the opposite is true. Now, many if not most states have some environmental justice policy or legislation. As discussed below, New Jersey, New York, and California deeply embed environmental justice into their environmental protection programs, and many other states have taken action to address environmental injustice. Policies and legal enactments in other states include the creation of advisory bodies, improved community engagement requirements, the development of mapping tools, and requirements for assessing and considering disproportionate or cumulative impacts during the permit review process. While a state-by-state survey of environmental justice laws, policies, and programs is beyond the scope of this book, a valuable tool created by environmental justice scholars and practitioners is available online at Environmental Justice State by State at https://ejstatebystate.org/.

1. New Jersey Environmental Justice Law

In 2020, New Jersey enacted a groundbreaking environmental justice law. N.J. Stat. Ann. §§ 13:1D-157–161 (2020). Unlike prior environmental justice laws, it allows state regulators to deny a pollution permit in an "overburdened community" where the permitted action would "cause or contribute to adverse cumulative environmental or public health stressors" in that community "that are higher than those borne by other communities within the State, county, or other geographic unit in facility permitting decisions." New Jersey supported the law with the following finding:

> The Legislature finds and declares that all New Jersey residents, regardless of income, race, ethnicity, color, or national origin, have a right to live, work, and recreate in a clean and healthy environment; that, historically, New Jersey's low-income communities and communities of color have been subject to a disproportionately high number of environmental and public health stressors, including pollution from numerous industrial, commercial, and governmental facilities located in those communities; that, as a result, residents in the

State's overburdened communities have suffered from increased adverse health effects including, but not limited to, asthma, cancer, elevated blood lead levels, cardiovascular disease, and developmental disorders; that children are especially vulnerable to the adverse health effects caused by exposure to pollution, and that such health effects may severely limit a child's potential for future success; that the adverse effects caused by pollution impede the growth, stability, and long-term well-being of individuals and families living in overburdened communities; that the legacy of siting sources of pollution in overburdened communities continues to pose a threat to the health, well-being, and economic success of the State's most vulnerable residents; and that it is past time for the State to correct this historical injustice.

Notes and Questions

1. **Historical environmental injustice acknowledgement.** New Jersey prefaced their decision to prevent additional stressors in overburdened communities with a finding that New Jersey residents in those communities already suffer from "asthma, cancer, elevated blood lead levels, cardiovascular disease, and developmental disorders" and other adverse effects that "impede the growth, stability, and long-term well-being of individuals and families." How compelling are these findings?

2. **Compelling exception?** The New Jersey law creates a notable exception for new facilities "that will serve a compelling public interest in the community where it is to be located." By requiring that new facilities permitted under the exception serve the interest of the overburdened community, does the law adequately protect the community against future environmental injustices? Recall from Chapter 6 the local concern for backup power to maintain sewage treatment capacity in the event of a disaster like Superstorm Sandy in 2012. Is that a "compelling public interest" in your view?

2. New York Initiatives

Michael Gerrard & Edward McTiernan, *New York Adopts Nation's Strongest Environmental Justice Law*

NEW YORK LAW JOURNAL, May 10, 2023

On March 3, New York Gov. Kathy Hochul signed the strongest environmental justice (EJ) law in the United States. While federal guidelines and the laws of some other states—notably California, Massachusetts, and Washington—require analysis, disclosure and consideration of EJ issues, only a New Jersey law adopted in 2020 imposed substantive limitations, as we discussed in our May 12, 2021, column. New York's new law—building on enactments in 2019 and 2020—is even more restrictive. The new law—which we'll call the EJL—provides that the Department of Environmental Conservation (DEC) "shall not issue an applicable permit for a new project if it determines that the project will cause or contribute more than a de minimis amount of pollution to a disproportionate pollution burden on the disadvantaged community." Environmental Conservation Law (ECL) Sec. 70-0118.

With some exceptions discussed below, DEC may not approve a permit modification if "the issuance of the permit would significantly increase the existing disproportionate pollution burden." A similar bar applies to permit renewals, though it is not clear how this applies to permit renewals that do not involve modifications. The EJL also provides that DEC "shall require actions to implement any appropriate operational changes that would reduce the pollution burden on the disadvantaged community as a condition of an applicable permit, only if such actions are reasonable and practicable, as determined by the department." In enacting the EJL, the Legislature "declare[d] that there has been an inequitable pattern in the siting of environmental facilities in minority and economically distressed communities, which have borne a disproportionate and inequitable share of such facilities." All in all, the EJL addresses the longstanding concern of EJ advocates that the cumulative impacts of multiple pollution sources have not been adequately addressed in the environmental review and permitting processes, and that certain communities are overburdened by pollution.

Notes and Questions

1. Similar but distinct approaches. The New York law requires the denial of permits for new projects that will "contribute more than a de minimis amount of pollution to a disproportionate pollution burden on a disadvantaged community." Contrast that standard with the New Jersey law's focus on denying permits in overburdened communities that will "cause or contribute to adverse cumulative environmental or public health stressors" higher than those borne by other communities. Can you tell the difference between them? Is one more protective than the other?

2. Considering the exceptions. Later in the article, the authors maintain that the New York law is stronger than the New Jersey law since the New York law provides no exception for new facilities. They note that New York allows permit renewals and permit modifications to take place in covered communities but only when they "serve an essential environmental, health or safety need of the disadvantaged community for which there is no reasonable alternative."

3. State definitions of environmental justice. Note that while the Trump administration repealed executive orders defining "environmental justice" on a federal level, definitions of environmental justice remain established as a matter of state law and policy. In 2019, the State of New York, for example, passed legislation that, among other things, established a statewide policy "that all people, regardless of race, color, religion, national origin or income, have a right to fair treatment and meaningful involvement in the development, implementation and enforcement of laws, regulations and policies that affect the quality of the environment." N.Y. Envtl Conserv. L. § 48-0101 (2019). Similarly, the State of Washington, in the 2021 Healthy Environment for All (HEAL)

Act, defined "environmental justice" to mean "the fair treatment and meaningful involvement of all people regardless of race, color, national origin, or income with respect to the development, implementation, and enforcement of environmental laws, rules, and policies." RCW 70A.02.010 (2021). How do these state definitions compare to the definition long held by EPA, as discussed in Chapter 1?

3. California Initiatives

California has (with considerable sustained effort) enacted multiple environmental justice bills. California's first major statute, SB 115, requires the California Environmental Protection Agency (Cal/EPA) to follow principles that closely parallel the provisions of President Clinton's Executive Order 12898. SB 115 was passed in 1999 after five other environmental justice bills were vetoed by former Governor Pete Wilson in the prior seven years. Under the bill, Cal/EPA is required to promote enforcement of health and environmental statutes and conduct its programs and policies "in a manner that ensures the fair treatment of people of all races, cultures, and income levels." It is also required to develop a model environmental justice mission statement for its constituent departments. *See* Cal. Gov't Code § 65040.12 (1999); Cal. Pub. Res. Code §§ 72000–01 (1999). Subsequent legislation also requires Cal/EPA to ensure that environmental justice considerations are addressed in carrying out reviews by the agency under the California Environmental Quality Act (the state's version of NEPA), and to make recommendations for ensuring that public documents, notices, and hearings are understandable and accessible to the public, including translation for limited-English-speaking populations. *See* Ellen M. Peter, *Implementing Environmental Justice: The New Agenda for California State Agencies*, 31 Golden Gate U. L. Rev. 529 (2001). California's climate change legislation, AB 32 and subsequent policies, incorporate environmental justice considerations into regulations adopted to reduce greenhouse gas emissions, *see* Chapter 14 (Climate Justice).

AB 32, also known as the Global Warming Solutions Act, spurred significant debate over its established cap-and-trade program, and arguably revealed a split in the environmental and environmental justice movements. The following article by policy expert and strategist on building an equitable green economy, Vien Truong, illustrates the investments in environmental justice, or "disadvantaged" communities, as a result of SB 535, a statute designed to further implement the Act.

Vien Truong, *Addressing Poverty and Pollution: California's SB 535 Greenhouse Gas Reduction Fund*

49 Harvard Civil Rights-Civil Liberties L. Rev. 493 (2014)

... Immediately after the passage of SB 535, the Greenlining Institute and others began organizing to ensure that the goals of SB 535 and AB 1532 would be realized and translated into jobs and investments in priority disadvantaged communities.

Advocates formed the appropriately named "SB 535 Coalition," led by the Greenlining Institute, the Asian Pacific Environmental Network, the Coalition for Clean Air, and Public Advocates. The SB 535 Coalition created webinars to inform leaders across the country about the new laws and their potential impact, as well as the new investments they would bring to disadvantaged communities. The Coalition also created online surveys for community leaders about what investments would have the greatest effect in their communities. Respondents listed programs that they believed would reduce GHG emissions, as well as those that would create jobs, improve the quality of life in the community, and support local economies. The Coalition continued to inform the broad public about the new laws, the cap-and-trade program, and how they could participate....

Allocating Funds to Disadvantaged Communities

SB 535 requires that the cap-and-trade revenues be allocated so that 25% of funds benefit disadvantaged communities and 10% are invested inside the geographic boundaries of disadvantaged communities. The law directs CalEPA to identify the State's most disadvantaged communities for investment opportunities by looking at their geographic, socioeconomic, public health, and environmental-hazard problems. The statute gives CalEPA some criteria for identifying disadvantaged communities—such communities may be (1) areas disproportionately affected by pollution and other hazards that can lead to negative public health effects, exposure, or environmental degradation; or (2) areas with a concentration of people who are of low income and suffer from high unemployment rates, low levels of homeownership, high rent burden, or low levels of educational attainment.

CalEPA's Office of Environmental Health Hazards Assessment ("OEHHA") created a screening methodology to help identify the areas disproportionately harmed by environmental and socioeconomic burdens. This unprecedented tool allows the State to scientifically identify the disproportionate environmental harms, which contributes to a better understanding of the relationship between race/ethnicity and the pollution burdens facing communities in California. Under the direction of CalEPA, OEHHA conducted a series of regional public workshops to get input on a draft cumulative impacts screening tool. The screening tool, named "CalEnviroScreen," was released in 2012. The tool maps the environmental, health, demographic, and socio-economic data of various areas (currently by zip code, but future versions will use census tracts) to create a screening score for communities across the state. These maps show which areas of the state have the highest pollution burdens and vulnerabilities. CalEnviroScreen guides investments under SB 535 but also helps the State and other stakeholders identify areas that have the most need for assistance....

Benefits of SB 535

Cap-and-trade auction revenues offer California the opportunity to further the State's climate, air-quality, public-health, and economic goals. If used as intended, strategic investments may not only accelerate the State's transformation in GHG-emissions-reducing sectors, but also revitalize areas that have been historically underserved....

Figure 10-3. Former Exide Recycling Center in Vernon, California, south of Downtown Los Angeles, and surrounded by residential community impacted by lead contamination from former industrial operations. One of California's "disadvantaged communities" according to analysis from CalEnviro-Screen 4.0. Photo: Cliff Villa, 2022.

... Thanks to cap-and-trade revenues, California, for the first time, has significant funding to directly aid disadvantaged communities. The Governor's proposed budget for 2014–2015 estimates that cap-and-trade revenues will be $850 million: $225 million of which would be directed to programs that benefit disadvantaged communities. And this is only the first year of allocations. While future revenue is unpredictable, cap-and-trade revenues are likely to be high. In fact, some have deemed these revenues "California's new gold."

SB 535, through its goals of investing in programs that provide co-benefits, helps California move toward an equitable green future. Creating a green economy is beyond a political or legislative challenge; it is a moral challenge. The challenge is whether the State will create greener, more sustainable communities for the wealthy few, or make such improvements a reality for those who need them most. There are areas in California that have suffered disproportionate levels of pollution, poverty, and unemployment; in allocating the funds captured by cap-and-trade, we can and should make sure that those areas are prioritized.

Limits of SB 535

... First, SB 535 provides only a floor for investments in disadvantaged communities. The State must invest much more than this minimum—10% of revenue generated by cap-and-trade auctions—to counter the decades of pollution in low-income communities and communities of color....

... Second, policymakers must better define the requirement that 25% of investments "benefit" disadvantaged communities. Under the current law, "benefit" can be interpreted broadly....

... Third, policymakers must use a consistent metric to allocate the cap-and-trade funds via the budget process every year. Reallocation each year creates uncertainty about which programs will be funded and for how many years. Funds are then also subject to some additional unpredictability because they are distributed through agencies before going to the community....

... Fourth, SB 535 implementation should include an explicit role for community members and other stakeholders to guide and shape the allocation of revenue. Those who work or live in the community know best what the community needs....

... In 2013, the Public Policy Institute of California found that 52% of Californians agreed that it was very important to spend cap-and-trade revenues in low-income or disadvantaged communities (31% agreed that it was somewhat important to spend this money in low-income communities). SB 535 is a popular policy, but it must be implemented to fulfill its intent and requirements if it is to continue garnering support from disadvantaged communities. If there is not evidence of a growing green economy in disadvantaged communities, these communities will see the hope of a green economy as mere hype.

Notes and Questions

1. **Real benefits.** As of December 2024, proceeds from cap-and-trade in California were reported to have generated more than $31.4 billion. Of that, projects approved and implemented by the funds total $12.8 billion, with $9.2 billion (73 percent) benefiting priority populations. https://www.caclimateinvestments.ca.gov/about-cci.

As just one example, $9 million of these proceeds were reportedly dedicated to cleanup of a brownfields site in National City, San Diego County, allowing for construction of a 201-unit affordable housing complex. *See* Charles Lee, *A Game Changer in the Making? Lessons from States Advancing Environmental Justice Through Mapping and Cumulative Impact Strategies*, 50 Envtl L. Rep. 10203, 10210 (2020).

2. **Investments in disadvantaged communities.** Several California programs, outside of SB 535, have also targeted "green" investments in disadvantaged communities. AB 523 directs at least 25 percent of California Energy Commission Technology Demonstration and Deployment funding to projects located in and benefitting disadvantaged communities. AB 2672 required the California Public Utilities Commission to analyze solutions to provide San Joaquin Valley disadvantaged communities access to affordable energy. Implementation of the bill resulted in the Commission's approval of a $56 million investment for pilot projects in 11 San Joaquin Valley communities, providing energy-efficiency upgrades, solar benefits, and job training, while reducing energy costs and pollution. *See* Martha Guzman Aceves, *CPUC Provides San Joaquin Valley Residents with Cleaner and Safer Energy Options*, Working for California,

A Monthly Newsletter from the CPUC (Jan. 2019). California's targeted investment focus has even reached the local level: California enacted SB 1000 (2016), which required all cities and counties to include climate adaptation and resiliency strategies in the safety elements of their general plans. SB 1000 has four core requirements: identify disadvantaged communities; identify objectives and policies to reduce the unique or compounded health risks in disadvantaged communities; identify objectives and policies to promote civil engagement in the public decision-making process, and identify objectives and policies that prioritize improvements and programs that address the needs of disadvantaged communities.

3. Revisiting race. What theories of justice does California's definition of "disadvantaged community" and distribution of cap-and-trade revenues raise? Are there other benefits or drawbacks to such designation for "environmental justice" communities? What are the limitations imposed by the U.S. Supreme Court decision in *Grutter* and now *SFFA*? CalEnviroScreen currently does not factor in race/ethnicity due to California's Proposition 209, which banned affirmative action by amending the California Constitution to prohibit state institutions from discriminating on the basis of race, sex, or ethnicity. Cal. Const. art. I, § 31.

4. Another game changer? In the brief excerpt below, Charles Lee argues that the creation of comprehensive environmental justice mapping tools like those used in New Jersey, New York, and California is critical for addressing environmental injustice because it provides decisionmakers with the comprehensive data needed to address disproportionate environmental impacts. Do you agree?

> Identifying communities that suffer greater pollution burden and population vulnerability is a fundamental first step for integrating EJ in government decision making. In order to focus attention and resources on the most disproportionately impacted areas, one must know where they are located. Recent advances in EJ practice have made this possible by revealing a basic architecture for operationalizing disproportionate impacts. Because tools and methods now exist that map the distribution of greater pollution burden and population vulnerability, we can readily identify such disproportionately impacted areas. Over time, our ability to do so will become more sophisticated and accurate. Essentially, EJ at its core is about the spatial distribution of environmental burdens and benefits.

Charles Lee, *Confronting Disproportionate Impacts and Systemic Racism in Environmental Policy*, 51 Envtl. L. Rep. 10207 (2021).

5. State GIS tools. Noted in Chapter 2 and further discussed in Chapter 11, EPA has developed a GIS tool known as EJSCREEN to provide easy access to environmental and demographic information for all areas of the United States. Many states have developed similar tools, including the State of California's EJ screening tool known as CalEnviroScreen: https://oehha.ca.gov/calenviroscreen. Colorado created a Colorado EnviroScreen: https://www.cohealthmaps.dphe.state.co.us/COEnviroscreen_2/. Maryland maintains an MDEnviroScreen Tool: https://mde.maryland.gov/Environmental

_Justice/Pages/MDEnviroScreen.aspx. Illinois established an Environmental Justice Communities Map, available at https://www.illinoissfa.com/environmental-justice-communities-map/. How do these and other state GIS tools compare to EJSCREEN for data sets and reliability? Pick one place you know and check results under EPA and state tools. What similarities or differences do you see?

6. "Protecting American Energy from State Overreach." In Executive Order 14260, President Trump directed the U.S. Attorney General to identify state and local laws, policies and practices "burdening the identification, development, siting, production, or use of domestic energy resources" that the Attorney General believes could be unconstitutional, preempted under federal law, or unenforceable. The order directed the U.S. Attorney General to prioritize the identification of such laws purporting to address "environmental justice" in addition to those related to climate change and environmental, social, and governance (ESG) initiatives. Upon identification, the U.S. Attorney General is directed to "expeditiously take all appropriate action to stop the enforcement" of such laws. If you were a state attorney working for the AG's office in one of these states who have developed EJ laws, policies, and screening tools, how might you advise responding?

One powerful response was demonstrated by a statement issued in June 2025 by a coalition of 13 state Attorneys General lead by California, Massachusetts, and New York. *See* Multi-State Guidance Affirming the Importance and Legality of Environmental Justice Initiatives (June 17, 2025). In direct response to allegations of the Trump administration used to support reversal of federal initiatives on environmental justice, the coalition observed that "simply calling these practices 'illegal' does not make it true. Environmental justice does not constitute illegal discrimination.... To the contrary, environmental justice activities help public and private entities avoid and prevent unlawful discrimination and remediate its impacts." The coalition further observed, pointedly, "The President cannot unilaterally prohibit lawful state, Tribal, and local policies, programs, and activities to advance environmental justice."

D. Private Initiatives

As indicated in the preceding section, many states—especially in the absence of federal leadership—have taken substantial measures to promote environmental justice for their citizens. Unfortunately, at least as many states have taken measures opposing environmental justice, as seen in the Chapter 4 discussion of Louisiana's aggressive attack on EPA rules implementing Civil Rights Act Title VI. When community advocates experience any and all levels of government as dead-ends, environmental injustice may still be addressed through private initiatives. Consistent with the EJ philosophy of "We speak for ourselves," community advocates may "speak" for themselves through many channels, including citizen litigation as explored in Chapters 11 and 12. This concluding section of Chapter 10 takes a brief, but important, look at another channel for pursuing environmental justice, known generally as "private governance."

Legal scholarship on private governance has grown rapidly over the last two decades, accelerated in 2007 with an influential article by Professor Michael Vandenbergh, who announced—

> A new form of governance is emerging that achieves traditionally public ends through private contracting. In response to a variety of social, economic, and legal incentives, many of the largest firms in developed countries are imposing private contractual environmental requirements on suppliers and other contractors in developing countries. Nongovernmental organizations (NGOs), rather than lobbying national or international governmental bodies to generate public requirements, are using consumer pressure to demand that corporations engage in this form of private regulation.

Michael P. Vandenbergh, *The New Wal-Mart Effect: The Role of Private Contracting in Global Governance*, 54 U.C.L.A. L. Rev. 913, 914 (2007). Since publication of this article, scholars have advanced private governance theory. *See, e.g.*, Tracey M. Roberts, *Innovations in Governance: A Functional Typology of Private Governance Institutions*, 22 Duke Envtl. L. & Pol'y Forum 67 (2011) (identifying governance institutions including education, codes of conduct, contractual arrangements, and environmental management systems); Michael P. Vandenbergh, *Private Environmental Governance*, 99 Cornell L. Rev. 129 (2013) (describing a new model of "private environmental governance" with potential for addressing environmental concerns including climate change and emerging issues such as fracking and nanotechnology); Joshua Ulan Galperin, *Board Rooms and Jail Cells: Assessing NGO Approaches to Private Environmental Governance*, 71 Arkansas L. Rev. 403 (2018) (developing a framework to assess the engagement of NGOs in private environmental governance).

While the literature suggests that private governance schemes can help address a spectrum of environmental concerns, opportunities for addressing environmental justice in particular are beginning to receive greater consideration, as indicated in the excerpt below:

Seema Kakade, *A Contractual Relationship with Environmental Justice*

73 American U. L. Rev. 343 (2023)

[C]orporations are waking up to justice issues . . . , increasingly focusing attention on elements of justice within "corporate social responsibility ("CSR") and "environmental, social, governance" ("ESG") frameworks. With surveys indicating that eighty-one percent of Americans want CEOs to do more on justice and inequality, it is no wonder corporations are upping their game.

At the same time, there is reason to caution against relying on corporations to achieve much by way of environmental justice. Some argue that claims by corporations regarding ethical and responsible practices towards marginalized communities are greenwashing. Others assert that CSR is simply "soft law" that lacks the teeth of real accountability that exists within "hard law." Research has shown that business "codes of conduct" in the space of social justice and human rights have largely failed to benefit marginalized communities due in part to lack of oversight mechanisms....

This Article asserts that in a world where corporations, nonprofit organizations, and the government intend to advance environmental justice, private-ordering tools provide a vehicle to get there. Agreements between corporations and community-based organizations have been around for decades as "community benefit agreements" ("CBA") or "good-neighbor agreements" ("GNA").... These types of agreements stipulate that corporations provide environmental benefits to a community in exchange for the community's commitment to resolve opposition (or provide support for) the corporation's permitting and licensing a new or expanded facility. Some legal scholars tout corporate-community agreements as proof of an available mechanism to advance environmental justice when government decision-making does not suffice. Other legal scholars express concerns with corporate-community agreements related to unequal bargaining positions between the entities that are party to the agreement. Yet, scholars seem to agree there is a great potential for corporate-community agreements to be better, particularly through an assembly of best practices and lessons learned, and the development of model draft agreements.

This Article calls for a heightened role for environmental nonprofit organizations to support corporate-community agreements through the development of environmental transactional practice groups within their organizations. Environmental nonprofit organizations are increasingly prioritizing justice within their core missions, actively pledging to protect environmental rights, pursuing solutions to advance equity, and confronting systemic racism and oppression. The funders of environmental nonprofits are also emphasizing giving to those organizations that prioritize justice work. To meet the growing justice work, environmental nonprofit organizations should also expand the tools used in their work. The same litigation and policy focused tools that inherently focus on government decision-making remain critical. However, adding private-ordering tools that focus on corporate decision-making helps to complete the environmental justice toolbox.

Notes and Questions

1. Community benefits. As noted by Professor Kakade, the idea of community benefit agreements has been around for decades. *See, e.g.*, Michael P. Vandenbergh, *The Private Life of Public Law*, 105 Columbia L. Rev. 2029, 2064 (2005) (estimating that "good neighbor agreements" number "at least several dozen in the United States"). Vandenbergh observed that such agreements may require firms to "provide information to the local community beyond that required by law," "reduce emissions below legal requirements," or "provide local subsidies, such as public health clinics or park facilities." *Id.* In reviewing decades of such agreements, Kakade reported such agreements "in a variety of areas, including real estate development, mining operations, and wind energy projects." Kakade, *supra*, at 371. For example, Kakade identified a 2008 agreement "that included housing and local hiring benefits" to garner local support for the development that now includes the Barclays Center in Brooklyn, though Kakade noted these intended benefits had "yet to come to fruition as of 2022." *Id.* at 377. If you represented an EJ group interested in entering a community benefit agreement with a prospective developer, how would you know what benefits to seek and how would you seek to ensure delivery of those benefits?

2. In your community. Are there examples of community benefit agreements in your community? What benefits do they seek to provide? How would you find an example of such an agreement?

3. Contract law? Professor Kakade discusses contract law as an underappreciated legal tool for environmental justice. Law students: recall your 1L course in Contracts. What elements of contract law seem most relevant for community benefit agreements? What additional courses might help strengthen your skills as an EJ advocate?

Chapter 11

Information Disclosure and Environmental Review

A. Introduction

> "I do not say this lightly, but it must be said. This case reeks of environmental racism. . . ."
>
> ***Center for Community Action & Environmental Justice v. Federal Aviation Admin.***, 61 F.4th 633, 655 (9th Cir. 2023) (Rawlinson, J., dissenting)

The strong words above from Judge Rawlinson reflect a particularly egregious case of environmental injustice arising from a proposal to establish a new air cargo facility—an "Amazon project"—at the San Bernardino airport in Southern California. The 658,000-square-foot building for sorting and distributing cargo to and from the airport would potentially draw 3,823 daily truck trips through a community, 73 percent Latino and 13 percent Black, that has already long suffered some of the worst air pollution in the country. Even so, the FAA declined to conduct an Environmental Impact Statement under the National Environmental Policy Act (NEPA), instead issuing a Finding of No Significant Impact. The Ninth Circuit Court of Appeals affirmed the FAA's decision, over Judge Rawlinson's blistering dissent.

For more than half a century, information generation, analysis, and disclosure to the public has been a cornerstone of environmental law in the United States. In theory, this legal commitment to environmental transparency undergirds legal mechanisms designed to ensure informed decision-making, promote meaningful public participation, and provide remedies for noncompliance with environmental laws. As such, environmental policymaking embraces the oft-quoted observation from Justice Brandeis that "sunlight is the most powerful disinfectant." Access to accurate and timely environmental information is particularly important for environmental justice. Such information can be a catalyst for social change and is central to the advocacy work that is the foundation of environmental justice. Access to information facilitates effective community participation in rulemaking and lays the groundwork for citizen suits, as explored further in Chapter 12. Unfortunately, as demonstrated by Judge Rawlinson's dissent, access to good information does not always lead to good decisions.

Professor Sarah Lamdan had this to say about the centrality of environmental information:

> In our modern-day world, environmental information is the backbone of environmental law and regulation, playing a critical and necessary role at every level of environmental decision-making. Navigating this arena and dealing with the divergent interests of the different groups that participate in environmental activities and policymaking can often make accessing environmental information a very thorny and complicated venture....
>
> EPA is often put in a difficult position, information-wise, recognizing both the importance of protecting the privacy of information that polluters report to the agency and also the key role of public participation in the Agency's programs. EPA recognizes that every environmental issue and effort benefits from public participation, and that environmental information access is vital to that participation. Citizen awareness is crucial to all facets of environmental preservation and the progress on environmental safety and welfare.

Sarah Lamdan, ENVIRONMENTAL INFORMATION: RESEARCH, ACCESS & ENVIRONMENTAL DECISIONMAKING 1–3 (2017).

Professor Browne C. Lewis made the case that "in order to effectively combat environmental discrimination, people must have access to quality information." She argued that a primary driver of disproportionate placement of environmental hazards in minority and low-income communities is the residents' lack of information about potential risk. If she is correct, access to environmental information must be part of the solution to remedy environmental injustice. Access to environmental information can educate community members, empowering them both to successfully oppose new projects in their neighborhoods that present environmental hazards, and to advocate for removing existing hazards from environmental justice communities. Browne C. Lewis, *What You Don't Know Can Hurt You: The Importance of Information in the Battle Against Environmental Class and Racial Discrimination*, 29 WM. & MARY ENVTL. L. & POL'Y REV. 327, 328 (2005).

While the second Trump administration has backtracked on the commitment to consider environmental justice in federal decision-making, including under NEPA, environmental review laws continue to have potential value as a tool to advance environmental justice goals. This chapter will describe the access to information laws that environmental justice advocates have relied on to organize for social and political change as well as to bring lawsuits challenging governmental and/or private action. The chapter will also identify how these laws have been subject to political pendulum swings, how they have recently come under attack in the courts, in Congress, and in broader policy debates, and why information availability as a tool for advancing environmental justice, while still vital, has significant gaps and may be in jeopardy moving forward.

B. The National Environmental Policy Act

1. Introduction to NEPA

NEPA is the oldest and best-known environmental disclosure statute. Generally characterized as a "look before you leap" statute, NEPA plays a critical role in gathering information about the potential environmental impacts of proposed agency actions. In adopting NEPA in 1969, Congress declared that "it is the continuing policy of the Federal Government, in cooperation with State and local governments, and other concerned public and private organizations, to use all practicable means and measures, including financial and technical assistance, in a manner calculated to foster and promote the general welfare, to create and maintain conditions under which man and nature can exist in productive harmony, and fulfill the social, economic, and other requirements of present and future generations of Americans." 42 U.S.C. § 4331(a).

Section 102(c) of NEPA requires that "all agencies of the Federal Government shall ... include in every recommendation or report on proposals for legislation and other major Federal actions significantly affecting the quality of the human environment, a detailed statement by the responsible official on—

> (i) the environmental impact of the proposed action,
>
> (ii) any adverse environmental effects which cannot be avoided should the proposal be implemented,
>
> (iii) alternatives to the proposed action,
>
> (iv) the relationship between local short-term uses of man's environment and the maintenance and enhancement of long-term productivity, and
>
> (v) any irreversible and irretrievable commitments of resources which would be involved in the proposed action should it be implemented."

42 U.S.C. § 4332(c).

NEPA cuts across the entire federal government, requiring that every federal agency perform an environmental review known as an **Environmental Impact Statement (EIS)** for "major Federal actions." Actions subject to this requirement include many permit decisions, adoption of agency policy, formal planning, agency projects, and a slew of other actions potentially of interest to environmental justice communities.

Until recently, the Council on Environmental Quality (CEQ), a small agency within the Executive Office of the President, was widely accepted as having authority to issue rules under NEPA that direct how federal agencies comply with the law. As discussed more fully in Section 3 below, at least two federal courts have seemingly repudiated CEQ's authority to issue binding rules under NEPA, and CEQ has begun the process of rescinding its regulations. *See Iowa v. Council on Env't Quality*, 765 F. Supp. 3d 859 (D.N.D. 2025); *Marin Audubon Soc'y v. Fed. Aviation Admin.*, 121 F.4th 902 (D.C. Cir. 2024) (both cases rejecting CEQ authority to issue legally binding rules as opposed to nonbinding guidelines for agencies); *Removal of National Environmental*

Policy Act Implementing Regulations, 90 Fed. Reg. 10610 (Feb. 25, 2025) (direct final rule to rescind CEQ's NEPA rules). Nonetheless, CEQ's longstanding NEPA rules can be instructive for understanding how NEPA has functioned for decades, and how environmental justice considerations have and may yet play a role in environmental decision-making. Accordingly, all citations to CEQ regulations in this chapter are to those regulations as in effect immediately prior to rescission in 2025. It is likely that the NEPA landscape will continue to evolve quickly, so students should take care to research the current state of play.

In addition to CEQ's NEPA regulations, most agencies have adopted their own NEPA implementing procedures pursuant to CEQ guidelines, and many of the features of CEQ's NEPA rules live on in these agency-level rules, at least for now. That said, the substance of these agency rules may also change in response to directives from President Trump in 2025. *See* Executive Order 14154, *Unleashing American Energy* (Jan. 20, 2025) (among other things, directing that "the Chairman of CEQ shall convene a working group to coordinate the revision of agency-level implementing regulations ... [to] expedite permitting approvals.... Consistent with applicable law, all agencies must prioritize efficiency and certainty over any other objectives ... that could otherwise add delays and ambiguity to the permitting process).

A Supreme Court case decided in June 2025 might represent a first judicial step toward a substantial, across-the-board narrowing of NEPA analysis. It also raises serious questions about the longstanding approach to environmental review that has been embodied in CEQ's and individual agency regulations (and practice) for many decades. *See Seven County Infrastructure Coalition v. Eagle County, Colorado*, 145 S. Ct. 1497 (2025) (discussed in more detail in Section 3 below).

There remain, however, important windows for public participation in NEPA proceedings. CEQ regulations and guidance called on agencies to seek public input at various points in the NEPA process, such as when determining the *scope* of matters to be included in an EIS, after issuing a *draft EIS,* and after issuing a *final EIS* but before final decisions have been made about the project. *See* 40 C.F.R. § 1502.9. Agencies also were expected to hold public hearings when there is substantial controversy surrounding a project or substantial interest in a hearing. And the NEPA rules required agencies to respond to all significant public comments submitted on a draft EIS.

The CEQ's rules also included various provisions about the nature of the required review that were helpful for encouraging more meaningful analysis that could encompass environmental justice concerns. For example, for purposes of assessing the "impact of a proposed action" pursuant to NEPA, the regulations long defined "effects" or "impacts" to include "ecological ... aesthetic, historic, cultural, economic, social or health, whether direct, indirect, or cumulative." 40 C.F.R. § 1508.8. Moreover, over the years, CEQ had adopted guidelines for how to consider things like environmental justice and climate related impacts in the context of the NEPA review process. As of June 2025, it remains unclear what aspects of NEPA will survive the second Trump administration and how long it might take to repair any damage done. In fact, there has never been a moment of greater uncertainty for NEPA, both with regard to environmental review generally and with respect to the value of NEPA as a tool for advancing environmental justice goals.

Pathfinder on NEPA

In addition to the various sources quoted and cited in this chapter, the following materials may be instructive for a more complete understanding of NEPA and its implications for environmental justice. For a thorough overview of the NEPA statute, regulations, and case law, readers may consult one of many excellent casebooks on environmental law, including Robert v. Percival et al., Environmental Regulation: Law, Science, and Policy (10th ed. 2024) at Chap. 8. For general background on NEPA and environmental justice, *see* Uma Outka, *NEPA and Environmental Justice: Integration, Implementation, and Judicial Review*, 33 B.C. Envtl. Aff. L. Rev. 601 (2006); Browne C. Lewis, *What You Don't Know Can Hurt You: The Importance of Information in the Battle Against Environmental Class and Racial Discrimination*, 29 Wm. & Mary Envtl. L. & Pol'y Rev. 327 (2005). The regulations implementing NEPA, which at least until recently were considered binding on other federal agencies, can be found at 40 C.F.R. §§ 1500–1518. For a discussion of the extent to which NEPA may require consideration of environmental justice issues, *see* U.S. EPA, *Final Guidance for Incorporating Environmental Justice Concerns in EPA's NEPA Compliance Analyses* (1998); CEQ, *Environmental Justice Guidance Under the National Environmental Policy Act*; Alan Ramo, *Environmental Justice as an Essential Tool in Environmental Review Statutes: A New Look at Federal Policies and Civil Rights Protections and California's Recent Initiatives*, 19 Hastings W.-N.W. J. Envtl. L. & Pol'y 41, 49 (2013).

2. Understanding the Environmental Review Process

NEPA review occurs in a stepwise fashion. In a very general sense, it follows these steps:

- NEPA review begins when a designated "**lead agency**" (the federal entity most directly involved in the qualifying action—*see* 40 C.F.R. § 1501.7) **identifies a project or action** that it wants or needs to take, approve, or financially support in some way (say the funding of a new highway project, the issuance of a permit to fill wetlands, or the granting of a lease for extraction of resources on federal land).
- The federal entity then determines whether the action is **likely to have significant environmental impacts**; if not, it excludes the action from environmental review. Agencies sometimes exempt entire classes of actions from NEPA review. By issuing what is known as a **Categorical Exclusion** ("CatEx"), an agency may find that a class of actions will not individually or cumulatively have a significant effect on the human environment.
- If it is unclear whether the action might have significant environmental impacts, the federal entity may perform a nominally less comprehensive analysis called

an **Environmental Assessment (EA)** to determine if significant environmental impacts are likely. *See* 40 C.F.R. § 1508.9(a). This is generally at least a two-step process involving the preparation of both a draft EA and a final EA. If the federal entity determines that the action will not have significant environmental impacts, it will issue a **Finding of No Significant Impacts (FONSI)** along with the final EA. An agency's issuance of a FONSI is final agency action for purposes of the Administrative Procedure Act (APA).

- If it is clear from the start, or if the EA finds that the action will have significant environmental impacts, the federal entity should prepare a more comprehensive **EIS** that must fully satisfy the requirements of section 102(c).

The preparation of an EIS itself has several stages, including:

- ***Scoping***: The publication of a Notice of Intent in the Federal Register describes the upcoming EIS process and kicks off an exchange in which the federal agency, with public input, defines the range of issues and potential alternatives to be addressed in the EIS. A lead agency must also consult and coordinate with other federal agencies with relevant jurisdiction or special expertise. *See* NEPA section 102(c).
- ***Draft EIS***: Once the scope of the analysis has been decided upon, the federal entity prepares its initial environmental analysis, addressing each of the issues required by NEPA section 102.
- ***Final EIS***: After receiving and responding to public comments on the Draft EIS, the federal entity makes changes and/or incorporates additional analysis and issues into a final EIS. The final EIS triggers a thirty-day "wait period" during which the agency cannot make a final decision on the proposed action. Importantly, A final EIS is also a final agency action subject to judicial review under the APA.
- ***Record of Decision***. The EIS process formally ends with the issuance of the Record of Decision (ROD). The ROD explains the agency's decision, in light of the EIS, about how to proceed on the underlying action, describes the alternatives the agency considered and which alternative it selected, and discusses the agency's plans for mitigation, if any.

When changes to a proposed action, or comments on a draft or final EIS (or some other information) lead to a major change in a federal entity's environmental review, the agency must issue what is called a **Supplemental EIS**. When an agency decides to supplement its EIS, it prepares, publishes, and files the supplemental EIS in the same fashion as a draft or final EIS. In some instances, agencies might undertake a "**Programmatic EIS**"—that is, an environmental review to address the environmental issues relating to broad decisions, such as those establishing policies, plans, programs, or a suite of projects, and that might inform many related individual decisions in the future that might also be subject to their own action-specific environmental reviews.

In some recent efforts to address the perception of NEPA as cumbersome and time consuming, Congress amended the statute by, among other things, requiring a single lead agency to coordinate review, and by adding time and page limits to the environmental review processes. *See* Fiscal Responsibility Act of 2023, Pub. L. 118-5, 137 Stat. 10 (June 3, 2023). Specifically, NEPA now calls on agencies to conduct EA's within one year and EIS's within two years. It additionally limits the length of NEPA documents to 75 pages for an EA and 150 pages for an EIS (with up to 300 pages allowed for projects of extraordinary complexity), not including tables and appendices. *Id.* At a policy level, NEPA has been a political football, and the details of NEPA review have varied from administration to administration. As one group of authors explained in a 2024 article:

> Over the past few years, the NEPA regulations and statute have undergone a series of substantial changes. In 2020, the [first] Trump administration released the first comprehensive revisions to the original 1978 NEPA regulations in more than 40 years. The Biden administration rolled back three key elements of the regulations in the 2021 Phase 1 Rule. In 2023, Congress made the first substantial changes to the statute in more than 50 years as part of the Fiscal Responsibility Act. [Then], on May 1, 2024, the Biden administration released a more comprehensive rewrite of the regulations in the "Phase 2 Rule," which went into effect on July 1, 2024. These rapid changes have left many struggling to keep up and understand the current state of NEPA law and practice.

Temple Stoellinger & Dessa Reimer, *Navigating the New NEPA Landscape: An Overview of the 2024 Phase 2 Regulations and Recent Statutory Changes,* 61 FOUND. J. FOR NAT. RESOURCES & ENERGY L. 223, 224 (2024).

For a basic summary of the NEPA process from 2023, *see* Congressional Research Service, NATIONAL ENVIRONMENTAL POLICY ACT: AN OVERVIEW (2023), https://www.congress.gov/crs-product/IF12560. EPA also has a NEPA page that may contain helpful materials. EPA, NATIONAL ENVIRONMENTAL POLICY ACT REVIEW PROCESS, https://www.epa.gov/nepa/national-environmental-policy-act-review-process.

Some aspects of NEPA review seem particularly well-suited to addressing or advancing procedural and distributive justice goals. For example, NEPA generally contemplates robust public engagement that seeks to truly scrutinize the impacts of federal decisions that might otherwise go unrecognized until too late. And substantively, unlike most pollution control statutes, NEPA review has historically required evaluation of indirect and cumulative impacts, and of the socioeconomic consequences of proposed projects. Read broadly and executed well, such analysis could sweep in many issues important to environmental justice advocates, including for example the impact of pre-existing concentrations of industrial facilities, occupational health risks, access to medical care, and environmental exposures in a community.

However, NEPA has a number of important features that can limit its effectiveness as a tool for environmental justice. First, NEPA applies only to "federal actions"—that is, actions carried out by, funded by, or with some regulatory nexus to the federal government. Most pollution control permits are issued not by EPA, but by states (or in some instances tribes) that have been granted authority to implement federal environmental programs in lieu of EPA. To fill this gap, 16 states plus Puerto Rico, the District of Columbia, and many tribes have enacted their legislation requiring environmental review. These statutes, known generally as State Environmental Policy Acts (SEPAs) or Tribal Environmental Policy Acts (TEPAs), govern projects approved by state, local, or tribal authorities. *See, e.g.*, Washington State Environmental Policy Act, RCW 43.21C; California Environmental Quality Act, Cal. P.R.C. §§ 21000; Swinomish Indian Tribal Community, Tribal Environmental Policy Act, Title 19, Ch. 1 (2003). They impose analogous information and participation requirements on state, local, and tribal environmental decision-making. Increasingly, states require that the SEPA reviews include an assessment of potential climate impacts, and they can encompass EJ as well. SEPAs /TEPAs may be of growing importance moving forward if federal environmental review laws are further weakened by the executive, by the courts, and/or by Congress.

Second, NEPA's broad public participation requirements do not apply unless the agency decides that it may be required to prepare an EIS. However, the overwhelming majority of projects subject to NEPA do not involve the preparation of an EIS. Most now either result in a FONSI following completion of an EA or are excluded from the NEPA process from the start because of a categorical exclusion. In fact, categorical exclusions have been used to exclude some major issues of concern like noise from FAA flight paths or the proposed border wall and associated infrastructure on the United States-Mexico border. Alarmingly, the former Marine Minerals Service used a categorical exclusion to exempt from NEPA the construction of deepwater wells in the Gulf of Mexico—including the Deepwater Horizon, which led to the worst oil spill in U.S. history. *See* Oliver A. Houck, *Worst Case and the Deepwater Horizon Blowout: There Ought to Be a Law*, 40 Envtl. L. Rep. News & Analysis 11033 (2010).

Even when an agency prepares an EIS, that does not ensure actual protection for communities with environmental justice concerns. Federal courts have interpreted NEPA as imposing only procedural rather than substantive requirements on federal agencies. Agencies thus fulfill their NEPA obligations when they consider and fully disclose the environmental impacts of proposed projects. NEPA does *not* require that agencies select less environmentally harmful alternatives, nor does it require that agencies actually adopt *any* of the mitigation measures they might identify. NEPA "merely prohibits uninformed—rather than unwise—agency action." *Robertson v. Methow Valley*, 490 U.S. 332, 351 (1989); *Seven County Infrastructure Coal. v. Eagle County, Colorado*, 145 S. Ct. 1497, 1510 (2025). SEPAs vary in this regard; while many are similarly procedural, several require that state agencies minimize or avoid significant adverse impacts (for example, Minnesota, New York, and California).

Further narrowing NEPA's scope, federal courts have ruled that EPA does not have to comply with NEPA when the environmental assessment and public participation procedures required by other regulatory provisions are "functionally equivalent" to those mandated by the NEPA process. EPA thus does not comply with NEPA, when, for example, it issues hazardous waste permits under the Resource Conservation and

Recovery Act (RCRA) and therefore is not required to engage in NEPA's more robust public participation processes, or consider socioeconomic impacts, project alternatives, or other NEPA-specific factors. Congress has also created express statutory exemptions from NEPA for a number of EPA programs, such as all actions under the Clean Air Act and many under the Clean Water Act. (CWA § 404 dredge and fill permits, issued by the Army Corp of Engineers, remain subject to NEPA and frequently give rise to legal disputes like the one at the heart of the Dakota Access Pipeline fight).

Notes and Questions

1. Value? Although NEPA is often criticized as weak because it does not impose any substantive requirements on federal agencies, many scholars contend that it can nonetheless be of considerable value to communities with environmental justice concerns because it serves as an information-gathering, educational, and organizational tool. For example, mandated disclosure of alternatives and mitigation measures can leave the agencies more vulnerable to criticism and result in pressure for them to take steps to mitigate adverse project impacts they might have otherwise overlooked. Likewise, the environmental review process can create important opportunities for organizing community opposition and ensuring community comments are included in the administrative record—to be used for judicial review of final agency action or as ammunition for political advocacy. What do you think about the value of a law that only requires analysis and not action? In what ways can this information be valuable even if NEPA does not compel action?

2. The "Mitigated FONSI." For advocates of environmental justice, another important opportunity to engage in the NEPA process might come before an agency issues a FONSI. In reaching a finding that a proposed action will not significantly affect the environment, agencies have relied on mitigation measures to avoid an adverse effect. Thus, many EAs will conclude with a "mitigated FONSI." One example is the mitigated FONSI for the Dakota Access Pipeline, which, according to the Corps of Engineers, was the result of "over 250 interactions" between the Corps, Dakota Access, and "consulting parties" including tribal governments, historic preservation officers, and other "interested parties." The DAPL mitigated FONSI also followed a public comment period on the draft EA and, according to the Corps, "formal government-to-government consultation with tribal representatives." Following all this process, the DAPL FONSI provided the following:

> The majority of potential impacts would be mitigated by [Horizontal Directional Drilling (HDD) beneath river crossings], by which Dakota Access would install the pipeline beneath sensitive resources without surface disturbance, and allow pipeline construction to proceed with the fewest possible impacts. Additional mitigation measures are set out in the Environmental Construction Plan; the Stormwater Pollution Prevention Plan; the Spill Prevention, Control, and Countermeasure Plan, ... Unanticipated Cultural Resources Discovery Plan; and the Geographical Response Plan....

Figure 11-1. The Dakota Access Pipeline just north of the Standing Rock Sioux Reservation in North Dakota. Oil began flowing through the underground pipeline in 2017, continuing to threaten contamination of the land and water of the Standing Rock Sioux. Photo: Cliff Villa, 2020.

U.S. Army Corps of Engineers, *Mitigated Finding of No Significant Impact, Environmental Assessment, Dakota Access Pipeline Project* at 3 (July 25, 2016).

Given all this evident process and apparent mitigation of anticipated impacts, why do you imagine the Standing Rock Sioux Tribe and other parties remained so concerned about completion and operation of the Dakota Access Pipeline? Is it a question of procedural justice? distributive justice? both?

3. Hard look. One rule of NEPA review, long established by precedent of the U.S. Supreme Court, is that agencies must "take a 'hard look' at environmental consequences" of their proposed actions. *Robertson v. Methow Valley Citizens Council*, 490 U.S. 332, 350 (1989), quoting *Klepp v. Sierra Club*, 427 U.S. 390, 410 n.21 (1976). In a new NEPA case, courts reviewed an EIS prepared by the federal Surface Transportation Board (STB) to evaluate potential impacts from a proposed rail-line that would allow transportation of crude oil from Utah, through Colorado, to refineries in Texas and Louisiana. Upon review, the D.C. Circuit Court of Appeals found that the STB's EIS failed to take the requisite "hard look" in several ways. According to the D.C. Circuit, the EIS failed to consider the potential impacts of "tens of thousands of additional barrels of oil shipments daily" for processing in "locales with known, disproportionate exposure to pollution already." *Eagle County, Colorado v. Surface Transportation Board*,

82 F.4th 1152, 1177 (D.C. Cir. 2023). The EIS also failed, among other things, to take a "hard look" at the increased potential for wildfires and rail accidents associated with the new railway. In reversing the D.C. Circuit, as discussed later in this chapter, the U.S. Supreme Court suggested new standards for the scope of potential impacts that must be addressed in an EIS. Nevertheless, the Court left undisturbed the rule of NEPA that whatever impacts must be addressed by an EIS, must be subject to "hard look" review. *Seven County Infrastructure Coalition v. Eagle County, Colorado*, 145 S. Ct. 1497, 1509 (2025).

4. NEPA victories. As indicated by the D.C. Circuit's decision in *Seven County*, discussed above, advocates for environmental justice do win NEPA cases in court. While the increasingly conservative U.S. Supreme Court has upended law in many ways (e.g., reversing the D.C. Circuit's decision in *Seven County*), students should recognize that the U.S. Supreme Court accepts far fewer cases than are decided by district or appellate courts. For example, in the 2023–24 term, the U.S. Supreme Court received some 7,000 petitions for review and agreed to hear 62 of them. This means that most cases will be decided by lower courts, presenting greater opportunities for environmental victory.

One notable victory, at least on the merits, involved the legal challenge by the Standing Rock Sioux Tribe to construction of the Dakota Access Pipeline. After the massive protests against the pipeline in 2016, the Tribe, represented by Earthjustice, continued to litigate under legal authorities including NEPA, challenging the "Mitigated FONSI" by the Corps of Engineers. After initial setbacks, the U.S. District Court for the District of Columbia found that the Corps of Engineers had failed to satisfy its "environmental-justice responsibilities under NEPA." *Standing Rock Sioux Tribe v. U.S. Army Corps of Eng'rs.*, 255 F. Supp. 3d 101, 140 (D.D.C. 2017). In particular, the district court found that the EJ analysis from the Corps "covers only *construction* impacts, not *spill* impacts." *Id.* at 139 (emphasis in original). The district court subsequently granted the Tribe's petition to vacate the Corps approval for pipeline construction and ordered the Dakota Access Pipeline to be "shut down within 30 days." 471 F. Supp. 3d 71, 75 (D.D.C. 2020). On appeal, the D.C. Circuit upheld the vacatur but reversed the order to shut down the pipeline. 985 F.3d 1032 (D.C. Cir. 2021). While failing to stop the pipeline in the end, it was at least a moral victory for the Tribe and a legal victory setting precedent for continued advocacy for environmental justice.

Many other victories through NEPA and environmental review never result in published decisions. For example, after repeated legal challenges to the proposed Byhalia Pipeline in Tennessee (see Chapter 2) and the Atlantic Coast Pipeline in Virginia (see Chapter 6), proponents of these projects withdrew their support and both pipelines were defeated.

5. The EIS goes global. The impact assessment approach pioneered by NEPA has been widely emulated around the world. In the vernacular of international environmental law, "Environmental Impact Assessments" (EIAs) have found their way into international agreements like the Convention on Environmental Impact Assessment in a Transboundary Context (Espoo Agreement); the Madrid Protocol to the Antarctic Treaty of 1991; the Convention on Biological Diversity; and the North American Agreement on Environmental Cooperation. Supporters claim that these measures promote environmental democracy and ensure deliberate and transparent analysis of the consequences of environmental decision-making. Indeed, in its 2010 decision concerning Pulp Mills on the River Uruguay (*Argentina v. Uruguay*), the International Court of Justice found that the practice of environmental assessments "in recent years has gained so much acceptance among States that it may now be considered a requirement under general international law." [2010] ICJ Rep. 14 ('Pulp Mills'), ¶ 204. What do you think accounts for the singular attractiveness of this approach? Do you see any concerns?

3. NEPA and Aspirations for Environmental Justice

Advocates have, at times, held high hopes for NEPA as a tool for helping to advance the goals of environmental justice. This is true for addressing both procedural and distributive aspects of environmental injustice at the federal level. However, realizing progress on environmental justice in NEPA review has been frustratingly inconsistent, and subject to sometimes dramatic political swings. In the wake of President Clinton's executive order in 1994 (EO 12898) it seemed possible that NEPA might be able to deliver on its promise. However, in the intervening years, and across successive presidential administrations—George W. Bush (2001–2009); Barack Obama (2009–2017); Donald Trump (2017–2021); and Joe Biden (2021–25)—each with a different commitment to environmental justice (or lack thereof), it was difficult to build momentum. And because the environmental justice movement itself was still relatively new as an organized political force (consider the discussions of the movement's origins from Chapter 1), it was difficult to overcome other political pressures and to make environmental justice a consistent priority for executive branch policymakers. Perhaps the most promising moments came with President Biden and Vice President Harris, for whom environmental justice was an explicit campaign priority. Ultimately, however, at the start of second Trump administration, things took an alarmingly negative turn as that administration specifically targeted federal environmental justice efforts for elimination—including under NEPA. The discussion that follows identifies some of the major touchpoints for environmental justice in NEPA review throughout this political history.

Public Participation. Not surprisingly, *public participation* has been a central feature of NEPA review. CEQ's NEPA regulations outlined public engagement expectations for NEPA reviews, *see* 40 C.F.R. §§1501.9, 1503, and called for public notice and comment early and frequently in the NEPA process, including upon issuance of an EA, at the scoping stage of an EIS, upon issuance of both Draft and Final EIS's, and for any Supplemental EIS. *See id.* and 40 C.F.R. §§1502.4, 1502.9. Additionally, CEQ rules have tasked the lead agency with convening public hearings when there is substantial controversy surrounding a project or substantial interest in a hearing. For obvious reasons, if well executed, robust public participation can help to address procedural injustice.

CEQ guidance issued in 1997, three years after issuance of President Clinton's (now rescinded) Executive Order on Environmental Justice (EO 12898), had the following to say about the intersection of NEPA and procedural environmental justice:

> Early and meaningful public participation in the federal agency decision making process is a paramount goal of NEPA. CEQ's regulations require agencies to make diligent efforts to involve the public throughout the NEPA process. Participation of low-income populations, minority populations, or tribal populations may require adaptive or innovative approaches to overcome linguistic, institutional, cultural, economic, historical, or other potential barriers to effective participation in the decision-making processes of Federal agencies under customary NEPA procedures. These barriers may range from agency failure to provide translation of documents to the scheduling of meetings at times and in places that are not convenient to working families.

Council on Environmental Quality, *Environmental Justice Guidance Under the National Environmental Policy Act* at 13 (Dec. 10, 1997). The guidance went on to identify steps that might be considered in developing innovative public participation strategies, including coordination with community-based individuals, institutions, or organizations; translation of major documents (or summaries), provision of translators or other language access steps; opportunities for participation through means other than written communication (such as personal interviews or audio or video recording); periodic newsletters or summaries to provide updates; different meeting sizes or formats better tailored to the particular community; specialized materials that reflect local concerns and sensitivities (e.g., for subsistence consumers of fish, vegetation, or wildlife); locations and facilities that are local, convenient, and accessible; and assistance for hearing-impaired or sight-impaired individuals. *Id.* As discussed in the following section, the Trump administration also rescinded this guidance in 2025.

The progressive thinking reflected in CEQ's 1997 guidance was welcomed by EJ advocates and regarded as a necessary first step toward a more inclusive and responsive environmental review process. But the kinds of practices contemplated by the guidance were not consistently employed by federal agencies. Even had they been, there are structural aspects of NEPA review that present persistent obstacles. Consider Professor Uma Outka's observations from 2006:

> [G]iven the limited amount of public participation that takes place at the EA stage, these [comment] opportunities come late in the decisionmaking process. Notice and comment offers an opportunity for the public to learn and express opinions about a proposed project, and for the agency to see which alternatives are politically sensitive; there is only a negligible chance that an agency will choose the no action alternative at this stage. Naturally, an agency will not be inclined to let the time, effort, and expense that went into a draft EIS go to waste because the investment and institutional momentum are powerful forces behind the project. As one commentator has observed, "the agency usually ends up defending its plan instead of taking citizens' comments and

> actually formulating a plan based on the citizen concerns ... [T]here is no way for the agency and the public to develop any sort of meaningful discourse."
>
> Therefore, the value of public involvement in NEPA is significantly limited by the structure and timing of its public participation provisions. The minimal outreach at the crucial EA stage, combined with a project's momentum by the notice and comment stage, creates an impression that the public is appeased rather than an actual part of the decisionmaking process. This is particularly limiting in the environmental justice context; mistrust of government is common, and agency understandings have historically lacked depth. The CEQ Guidance documents recognize the inadequacy of typical government outreach methods and recommend a range of new approaches that, if used, will be a step in the right direction. Nevertheless, it is important to understand the limitations of the overall structure in which these approaches will be applied.

Uma Outka, *NEPA and Environmental Justice: Integration, Implementation, and Judicial Review*, 33 B.C. Envtl. Aff. L. Rev. 601, 609–10 (2006).

What else do you think communities might need to facilitate more meaningful and more influential involvement in environmental decisions? Given Professor Outka's views, might one missing element be better relationships with agency decisionmakers, which might lead to earlier engagement and more thorough integration into agency decision-making processes?

As Professor Skinner-Thompson points out, "[a]chieving environmental justice ... requires providing impacted communities not just the formal right, but the substantive ability, to participate as equal partners at every level of environmental decisionmaking." This means providing them "with the consultation and technical expertise needed to bolster the authority of their lived experiences in order to substantively influence regulatory outcomes." Jonathan Skinner-Thompson, *Procedural Environmental Justice*, 97 Wash. L. Rev. 399 (2022). He then highlights Superfund's Technical Assistance Grant (TAG) that Congress created in 1986. As Professor Skinner-Thompson notes:

> TAGs are awarded to qualifying non-profit community groups to contract with independent advisors to help those groups understand technical information about a Superfund site. Importantly, TAGs can be used to interpret technical information *and* "comment on site-related information and decisions." Although TAGs cannot be used to underwrite legal actions or be used to pay attorney fees, "any information developed through grant assistance may be used ... in a court of law." Between 1988 and 2019, a total of 307 TAGs have been awarded. And, as of December 2019, there are forty-four active TAGs.

Id. 439–40 (also describing a TAG for the Duwamish River Cleanup Coalition in Seattle, Washington, discussed further in the case study concluding Chapter 8).

What might it look like if communities had access to assistance to participate in NEPA processes? While not specifically intended as NEPA-related resources, might the "Thriving Communities Technical Assistance Centers" that EPA created during the

Biden administration have improved community level capacity in the NEPA context? If so, how? For more on TCTACs, *see* Clifford J. Villa, *A New Day for Environmental Justice at the U.S. EPA*, 54 U. Memphis L. Rev. 867 (2024).

4. EJ and Substantive NEPA Review

Notionally, the kind of review that has been the bread and butter of NEPA for nearly half a century is very much in line with what many frontline communities are often demanding—analysis that looks at the direct, indirect, and cumulative impacts of environmental decision-making, and that identifies alternatives and mitigation strategies that could avoid those impacts.

Thus, not surprisingly, many commentators have not just identified NEPA as a potentially powerful tool, but have also argued for a broader reading of NEPA to address substantive environmental justice issues. After **President Clinton** issued EO 12898, federal agencies sought to some degree to adapt the NEPA process to take into account environmental justice concerns. The Executive Order included two key information gathering and disseminating directives. Section 3 of the Executive Order specifically recognized the importance of research, data collection, and analysis, particularly with respect to the multiple and cumulative exposures to environmental hazards that environmental justice communities face, and Section 5 of the Executive Order required that agencies work to ensure effective public participation and access to information about environmental justice issues. Specifically, Section 5-5(b) of the Executive Order suggested that each federal agency may "wherever practicable and appropriate, translate crucial public documents, notices and hearings, relating to human health or the environment for limited English speaking populations," and Section 5-5(c) directed that agencies "work to ensure that public documents, notices, and hearings relating to human health or the environment are concise, understandable, and readily accessible to the public."

CEQ's 1997 *Environmental Justice NEPA Guidance* was intended to implement EO 12898 and offered strategies not just for participatory improvements (as noted above) but also for delivering better substantive analysis in NEPA reviews. To that end, the CEQ guidance identified core environmental justice information that should be considered as part of NEPA analyses, including the demographic composition of the affected area; health data addressing multiple or cumulative exposure to environmental hazards; and social, economic, or other factors that might amplify the environmental effects of the proposed agency action. Where NEPA documents had traditionally analyzed impacts on broadly defined affected areas and populations, the CEQ guidance called on agencies to determine whether an area impacted by a proposed project includes low-income populations, minority populations, or Indian tribes, and whether the proposed action is likely to have a disproportionately high and adverse human health or environmental impact on these populations. Agencies were also directed to consider the potential for multiple or cumulative exposure, historical patterns of exposure to environmental hazards, and cultural differences which may lead certain communities to experience impacts more severely than the general population. For example, the guidance notes, "data on different patterns of living, such as subsistence fish, vegetation, or wildlife consumption and the use of well water in rural communities may be relevant to the analysis." *Id.* at 14.

With respect to NEPA's alternatives analysis, the CEQ guidance instructed that the distribution and magnitude of any disproportionate adverse effects should be a factor in the agency's identification of the "environmentally preferable alternative" for a project (which agencies are required to identify in a Record of Decision following preparation of an EIS). *Id.* at 15. Moreover, in developing mitigation measures, the CEQ guidance directed agencies to solicit views from the affected populations throughout the public participation process and proposed that mitigation measures should reflect the views of affected low-income populations, minority populations, or Indian tribes to the maximum extent practicable. However, the CEQ guidance made it clear that identifying disproportionate impacts did not "preclude a proposed agency action from going forward, nor does it necessarily compel a conclusion that a proposed action is environmentally unsatisfactory" The CEQ guidance also clarified that the Executive Order "does not change the prevailing legal thresholds and statutory interpretations under NEPA and existing case law." *Id.* at 9.

During the **Obama administration**, EPA issued two key guidance documents for incorporating environmental justice into agency decision-making. U.S. EPA, Final Guidance on Considering Environmental Justice During the Development of an Action (2015); and U.S. EPA, Final Technical Guidance for Assessing Environmental Justice in Regulatory Analysis (2015). EPA described these guidance documents as an effort "to advance environmental justice and to protect the health and safety of the historically underrepresented in the environmental decision-making process—minority, low-income, and indigenous populations, and tribes—who are often most at risk from environmental hazards." The guidance documents provided direction on when environmental justice should be considered during rulemaking, and on how to do so in an analytical fashion.

In 2015, EPA released **EJSCREEN**, an environmental justice mapping and screening tool intended, among other things, to help the agency meet its responsibilities related to the protection of public health and the environment. EJSCREEN created a nationally consistent data set and Geographical Information System (GIS) tool for combining environmental and demographic indicators in maps and reports. EPA intended EJSCREEN to both be a tool that would assist agency decisionmakers in implementing the environmental justice guidance documents and a resource for states, researchers, and community advocates.

EJSCREEN pulled together data from the Clean Air Act, the Resource Conservation and Recovery Act, the Clean Water Act, the Emergency Planning and Community Right-to-Know Act, and other key federal statutes. It drew demographic information obtained from sources including the U.S. Census Bureau's American Community Survey (ACS). EJSCREEN then paired this demographic information with environmental

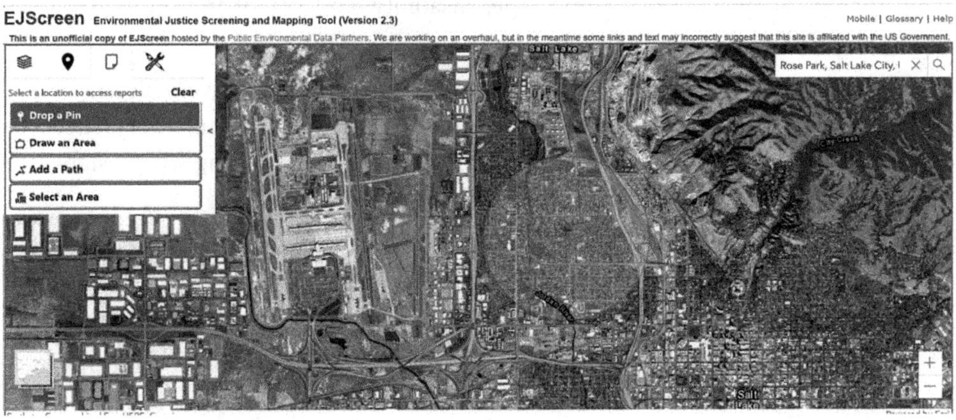

Figure 11-2. Screenshot from EPA EJSCREEN 2.3 (2025), centered on Rose Park neighborhood of Salt Lake City, Utah. Rose Park and other Westside communities were subject to redlining and cut off from the rest of the city by I-15. Now sandwiched between I-15 and the SLC airport, the community has more than double the percent Latino population of the rest of Utah and ranks in the top 90th percentile statewide for Superfund Proximity, Traffic Proximity, Diesel Particulates, and Air Toxics.

hazard exposure data, evaluating factors including air pollution, traffic, lead hazards, waste sites, and wastewater discharges.

EJSCREEN allowed environmental justice advocates, regulators, and others to easily connect environmental and demographic characteristics of any specific location in the United States. As noted below, in the first weeks of the second Trump administration, EJSCREEN was taken down. As of mid-2025, it is not available on any federal platform, although it remains available on other platforms including one established by Harvard University.

The **Biden administration** took significant additional steps to advance environmental justice, including the issuance of two executive orders that provided specific direction to agencies: *Revitalizing Our Nation's Commitment to Environmental Justice for All* (EO 14096, April 21, 2023) and *Tackling the Climate Crisis at Home and Abroad* (EO 14008, Jan. 27, 2021).

Specifically with regard to NEPA, EO 14096 provided that each agency shall, as appropriate and consistent with applicable law—

> (ix) carry out environmental reviews under [NEPA], 42 U.S.C. 4321 et seq., consistent with the statute and its implementing regulations and through the exercise of the agency's expertise and technical judgment, in a manner that:
>
> > (A) analyzes direct, indirect, and cumulative effects of Federal actions on communities with environmental justice concerns;
> >
> > (B) considers best available science and information on any disparate health effects (including risks) arising from exposure to pollution and other environmental hazards, such as information related to the race, national

origin, socioeconomic status, age, disability, and sex of the individuals exposed; and

(C) provides opportunities for early and meaningful involvement in the environmental review process by communities with environmental justice concerns potentially affected by a proposed action, including when establishing or revising agency procedures under NEPA.

With regard to information disclosure, EO 14096 provided that each agency shall—

> (xi) ensure that the public, including members of communities with environmental justice concerns, has adequate access to information on Federal activities, including planning, regulatory actions, implementation, permitting, compliance, and enforcement related to human health or the environment, when required under the Freedom of Information Act, 5 U.S.C. 552, the Government in the Sunshine Act, 5 U.S.C. 552b, the Clean Air Act ..., the Clean Water Act ..., the Emergency Planning and Community Right-to-Know Act ..., or other environmental statutes with public information provisions.

Notes and Questions

1. Looking back. Looking back at previous administrations, are there things that they could or should have done to deliver more durable benefits for environmental justice? What else, if anything, could prior administrations have done to improve NEPA reviews in enduring ways? If an opportunity were to arise, how might you change the NEPA statute?

2. Lost in translation? Can continuing obligations under federal laws like Title VI of the Civil Rights Act help NEPA review improve outcomes in distributive or procedural justice? For example, might EPA and other agencies sometimes be required to translate NEPA documents if a project will impact a community that has a significant percentage of members who do not speak English? How large a percentage should this be? What if there are numerous, monolingual subpopulations within the affected community—should agencies be required to translate documents into multiple languages? Should entire documents be translated, or only summaries and/or important documents? (As noted, EISs and even EAs can sometimes be several hundred pages long.) What other legal obligations might you argue are required under NEPA that might address environmental justice concerns?

C. NEPA Under Assault

In 2025, with Donald Trump's second term, NEPA is suffering a barrage of setbacks and sustained criticism—in the courts, in Congress, and from the executive branch. It is no surprise that major industries, including the fossil fuel industry, continue to regard NEPA with distain and have found deregulatory allies in President Trump, the conservative majority in the 119th Congress, and a Supreme Court with a right-leaning supermajority. However, the landscape is uniquely complicated at this moment due in part to the perception by some in the climate movement that robust NEPA review stands as an obstacle to rapid deployment of clean energy, and a resulting reluctance to aggressively defend the integrity of the statute and its implementation. For one timely and thoughtful defense of NEPA to critics across the political spectrum, *see* Alejandro E. Camacho & Robert L. Glicksman, *NEPA: The Accepted Lies and Mistakes About This Critical Environmental Law*, THE REVELATOR, June 27, 2025 (NEPA "known as the 'Magna Carta' of global environmental law"). And yet, those "lies and mistakes" about NEPA continue to inspire a lot of activity now across all branches of government, as indicated below.

1. NEPA in the Courts

Several recent cases have taken a swipe at NEPA in ways that will likely have significant ongoing consequences and might signal a new judicial hostility to the law. The D.C. Circuit decided a case in late 2024 in which Judge Raymond Randolph (in a 2–1 split decision) took the remarkable step of concluding that CEQ lacks the authority to issue NEPA regulations at all (which it has been doing since the late 1970s). *Marin Audubon Soc'y v. Fed. Aviation Admin.*, 121 F.4th 902 (D.C. Cir. 2024). The case was brought by California environmental organizations challenging an Air Tour Management Plan that governed tourist flights over four national parks near San Francisco, and which the Federal Aviation Administration (FAA) and National Park Service (NPS) had approved without environmental analysis under NEPA. The case centered on whether the agencies had complied with CEQ regulations. Both sides in the case took for granted CEQ's authority to issue binding NEPA regulations; however, considering the question *sua sponte*, Judge Randolph concluded that "the CEQ regulations, which purport to govern how all federal agencies must comply with [NEPA], are *ultra vires*." *Id.* at 908. After examining the statute, and CEQ's history of issuing regulations under NEPA, Randolph concluded that "[n]o statutory language states or suggests that Congress empowered CEQ to issue rules binding on other agencies—that is, to act as a regulatory agency rather than as an advisory agency," and that "NEPA contains nothing close to the sort of clear language Congress typically uses to confer rulemaking authority." *Id.* at 912. Randolph further found that a 1977 Carter administration Executive Order 11991, 42 Fed. Reg. 26,967 (May 25, 1977), was insufficient to convey rulemaking authority, explaining that "[i]f all federal agencies are bound by the CEQ regulations and must follow them in carrying out their obligations under NEPA, and if the regulations are enforceable by courts, then those regulations cannot be justified solely as an exercise in a President's oversight of his Administration." *Id.* at 913. Randolph therefore concluded that CEQ "had no lawful authority to promulgate these regulations." *Id.* at 914.

In a subsequent District Court decision in 2025, a North Dakota Federal District Court looked at the same issue in connection with a direct challenge by several states to CEQ's 2024 "Phase II" NEPA rulemaking that, among other things, incorporated the new time and page limitation requirement of the Fiscal Responsibility Act of 2023 (discussed above), adjusted factors that define the level and scope of environmental analysis, and integrated environmental justice considerations. *Iowa v. Council on Env't Quality*, 765 F. Supp. 3d 859 (D.N.D. 2025). Judge Daniel Traynor, in granting the states' motion for summary judgement, similarly concluded that "NEPA is not ambiguous. The plain text of the statute does not give CEQ authority to issue binding regulations. NEPA only authorizes CEQ to make recommendations to the President. Therefore, the Court finds that CEQ does not have authority under NEPA to issue regulations." *Id.* at 878. In doing so, the Court vacated only CEQ's "Phase II" NEPA regulation as *ultra vires*, while acknowledging that this holding also calls all CEQ rules into question.

In yet another case, decided in June 2025, the U.S. Supreme Court took a big swing at NEPA, in a case related to oil extraction in Utah's remote Uinta Basin. *Seven County Infrastructure Coalition v. Eagle County, Colorado*, 145 S. Ct. 1497 (2025). In order to bring these fossil fuels to market, a coalition of counties supported by industry proposed to build an 88-mile stretch of railroad that would connect the Uinta Basin to other rail networks. In conducting its NEPA analysis related to its approval of the rail project, the Surface Transportation Board (STB) ignored the fact that the only purpose of the railway would be to facilitate the extraction of oil in the Basin and transport that oil to specific refineries near the Gulf of Mexico. In so doing, the STB failed to consider foreseeable environmental impacts, like environmental degradation in the Basin from expanded drilling and more air pollution in communities around the receiving refineries. Several environmental groups challenged the STB's decision, as did the Colorado county through which the railway would run. The D.C. Circuit had held that the NEPA analysis was fatally inadequate and had vacated the STB's EIS and the approval of the rail line. The Supreme Court granted certiorari and reversed the D.C. Circuit's ruling, based on two major objections: (1) the circuit court failed to extend the appropriate deference to the agency conducting the NEPA review; and (2) the circuit court erred in requiring the STB to consider the effects of activities that were "separate in time or place from the construction and operation of the railroad line."

In examining the issue of whether the STB was required to consider **indirect upstream and downstream impacts** from the rail project (like increased oil drilling and increased refining activities) the Court observed as follows:

> [T]he EIS explained why further analysis of those "potential future, as yet unplanned, oil and gas development projects" was not needed.... Moreover, the Board possesses "no authority or control over potential future oil and gas development" in the Basin. Future projects would be "subject to the approval processes of other federal, state, local, and tribal agencies." In any event, the environmental effects of future oil and gas development in the Basin are "speculative" and attenuated from the project at hand.
>
> ... As for ... downstream oil refining projects, the Board recognized that "trains originating on the proposed rail line would transport crude oil to markets in other regions of the United States," such as Louisiana and Texas, and

that oil refining (and the associated effects on the environment) could increase in those locations as a result. But the identity of specific destinations "would depend on the ability and willingness of refineries in other markets to receive rail cars carrying Uinta Basin crude oil and process the oil in their refineries." Moreover, the Board "would have no role in approving or regulating the production, refining, or use" of Uinta Basin crude oil....

The Board's EIS explained that the "proposed rail line and any future oil and gas development projects are not two phases of a single action," but "separate, independent projects." Those other projects, the Board reasoned, should not be considered "part of the proposed action assessed in the EIS."...

[Thus, court reasoned that] ... when the effects of an agency action arise from a separate project—for example, a possible future project or one that is geographically distinct from the project at hand—NEPA does not require the agency to evaluate the effects of that separate project.... [Although,] the environmental *effects* of the project at issue may fall within NEPA even if those *effects* might extend outside the geographical territory of the project or might materialize later in time—for example, run-off into a river that flows many miles from the project and affects fish populations elsewhere, or emissions that travel downwind and predictably pollute other areas. Those so-called indirect effects can sometimes fall within NEPA.

But if the project at issue might lead to the construction or increased use *of a separate project*—for example, a housing development that might someday be built near a highway—the agency need not consider the environmental effects *of that separate project*. To put it in legal terms, the separate project breaks the chain of proximate causation between the project at hand and the environmental effects of the separate project.... [That] effects ... may be factually foreseeable ... does not mean that those effects are relevant to the agency's decisionmaking process or that it is reasonable to hold the agency responsible for those effects....

Moreover, and importantly, the Board here possesses no regulatory authority over those separate projects.... The Board approves railroad lines.... [I]n the NEPA canon, "where an agency has no ability to prevent a certain effect due to its limited statutory authority over the relevant actions, the agency cannot be considered a legally relevant 'cause' of the effect."... In other words, agencies are not required to analyze the effects of projects over which they do not exercise regulatory authority. For that reason as well, there is no "reasonably close causal relationship" between the 88-mile railroad project at hand and the environmental effects of the separate oil drilling and oil refining projects....

Under NEPA, it also bears emphasis, a mere "'but for' causal relationship is insufficient to make an agency responsible for a particular effect."... The agency may draw what it reasonably concludes is a "manageable line"—one that encompasses the effects of the project at hand, but not the effects of proj-

> ects separate in time or place.... An agency need not assess the environmental effects of other separate projects simply because those projects (and effects) might not materialize but for the project at hand, or are in some sense foreseeable....
>
> [E]ven if the reviewing court in such a case might think that NEPA would support drawing a different line, a court should defer to an agency so long as the agency drew a reasonable and "manageable line."...
>
> In this case, in any event, the NEPA question is not close. The Board did not need to evaluate potential environmental impacts of the separate upstream and downstream projects....

For additional discussion of the "causal connection" requirement in NEPA review, *see* Eric G. Biber & Daniel A. Farber, *The* Seven County *Case and the Limits of Causation Under NEPA*, 10 Admin. L. Rev. 1 (2025).

The *Seven County* decision also offered a significant new take on **deference** to agency expertise in the context of NEPA review. The Court said:

> As a general matter, when an agency interprets a statute, judicial review of the agency's interpretation is *de novo* [citing *Loper Bright Enterprises v. Raimondo*, 603 U.S. 369 (2024)]. But when an agency exercises discretion granted by a statute, judicial review is typically conducted under the Administrative Procedure Act's deferential arbitrary-and-capricious standard. Under that standard, a court asks not whether it agrees with the agency decision, but rather only whether the agency action was reasonable and reasonably explained....
>
> When a party [challenges] ... an EIS, the reviewing court must account for the fact that NEPA is a *purely procedural statute*. Under NEPA, an agency's only obligation is to prepare an adequate report. So ... "the only role for a court" is to confirm that the agency has addressed environmental consequences and feasible alternatives as to the relevant project.... [Thus] the adequacy of an EIS is relevant only to the question of whether an agency's final decision (here, to approve the railroad) was reasonably explained.
>
> In short, when determining whether an agency's EIS complied with NEPA, a court should afford substantial deference to the agency.
>
> ... The agency is better equipped to assess what facts are relevant to the agency's own decision than a court is. As a result, "agencies determine whether *and to what extent* to prepare an EIS based on the usefulness of any new potential information to the decisionmaking process."... So the question of whether a particular report is detailed enough in a particular case itself requires the exercise of agency discretion—which should not be excessively second-guessed by a court....
>
> The EIS also must identify significant environmental impacts and feasible alternatives. But there too, an agency exercises substantial discretion. An agency must make predictive and scientific judgments in assessing the rele-

> vant impacts ... and alternatives.... [W]hen an agency makes those kinds of speculative assessments or predictive or scientific judgments, and decides what qualifies as significant or feasible or the like, a reviewing court must be at its "most deferential."
>
> In analyzing [an agency's EIS], it is critical to disaggregate the agency's role from the court's role. So long as the EIS addresses environmental effects from the project at issue, courts should defer to agencies' decisions about where to draw the line—including (i) how far to go in considering indirect environmental effects from the project at hand and (ii) whether to analyze environmental effects from other projects separate in time or place from the project at hand.
>
> ... [F]or purposes of NEPA, an agency will invariably make a series of fact-dependent, context-specific, and policy-laden choices about the depth and breadth of its inquiry—and also about the length, content, and level of detail of the resulting EIS. Courts should afford substantial deference and should not micromanage those agency choices so long as they fall within a broad zone of reasonableness.... [W]e doubly underscore again today, "inherent in NEPA ... is a 'rule of reason,' which ensures that agencies determine whether and to what extent to prepare an EIS based on the usefulness of any new potential information to the decisionmaking process."... A reviewing court may not "substitute its judgment for that of the agency as to the environmental consequences of its actions."

It remains to be seen where the potentially paradigm-shifting decisions outlined above will lead in the long run, but it is evident that NEPA review as we have known it for many decades is likely to change markedly.

Notes and Questions

1. **What are indirect impacts?** The Court in *Seven County* seems to suggest that effects that extend outside the geographical territory of a project like run-off into a river that flows many miles from the project and affects fish populations elsewhere, or emissions that travel downwind and predictably pollute other areas, are "indirect effects." Do you agree? Are these effects really "indirect" or are they just geographically distant direct effects? How important do you think indirect impacts are for getting at environmental justice issues in NEPA cases? Are there instances where such impacts might look more like the kinds of effects the Court says *are* within NEPA's scope?

2. **What role for foreseeability?** The *Seven County* court says just because indirect effects are entirely foreseeable does not mean that courts should "hold the agency responsible for those effects." Does this framing make sense to you? What does it mean to hold an agency "responsible" under NEPA? Isn't the agency's "responsibility" to understand and make public the full suite of environmental consequences of federal actions? Does it make sense to selectively ignore some entirely foreseeable (and undisputed) consequences just because they relate to actions that will be taken by others?

What do you think about the Court's discussion of the "but for" test? Are there examples where you would disagree?

3. What is fully informed? The *Seven County* Court also says "NEPA's procedural mandate helps 'to insure a fully informed and well-considered decision....'" How instructive is the Court's opinion about what constitutes "fully informed decision-making" under NEPA? Notably, the Court does not grapple meaningfully with the underlying purpose or history of NEPA. Do you think that was an oversight?

2. NEPA in Congress

Like the courts, Congress is more actively engaged in scrutinizing NEPA than it has been perhaps since the law's adoption. In 2023, we saw the first substantive amendments to NEPA, with Fiscal Responsibility Act of 2023, Pub. L. 118-5, 137 Stat. 10 (June 3, 2023), largely codifying rules adopted during the Biden administration reflecting its desire to make NEPA review more efficient and faster on clean energy development. In the wake of the 2022 Inflation Reduction Act (IRA), we have also seen repeated attempts in Congress to advance "permitting reform" that includes changes to NEPA review. *See, e.g.*, David E. Adelman et al., *Dispelling the Myths of Permitting Reform and Identifying Effective Pathways Forward*, 55 Envtl. L. Rep. (ELI) 10038 (2025).

The legislative threat to NEPA is exacerbated by the ambivalence among progressive policymakers and some environmental advocates rooted in a sense of urgency to deploy clean energy infrastructure. The danger, however, is that, in the face of current political realities, "in order to buy the cow those looking to compromise may have to give up the farm." Adelman et al. present the dilemma this way:

> On the left, recent support for permit reform is founded on a fear that federal environmental laws are stifling efforts to address climate change. In short, they believe that environmental regulations are preventing rapid deployment of renewable energy projects, electrical transmission lines, and other critical infrastructure. As legal scholar Michael Gerrard put it, "[s]ociety has run out of time to save everything we want to save, and to mull things over for years."
>
> The narrative that regulations cause delay resonates, because everyone has experienced permit-related frustration. Whether it is waiting for a building permit that took months to issue, wandering through bureaucratic hallways to obtain a business license, or watching a local infrastructure project mired in obscure government processes, we have all been there. The mere mention of permitting evokes images of sticky red tape and unhurried, out-of-touch bureaucrats. The solution, in this light, is obvious—cut procedures and relax protections.
>
> While this sense of urgency is understandable, the focus on deregulation is grounded on four myths that are distorting public perceptions and policymaking. The four myths embody a zero-sum mentality that pits essential environmental procedures and protections against the exigency of addressing climate

> change. The four myths are that: (1) federal environmental permitting is a rigid monolith with the National Environmental Policy Act (NEPA) at its center; (2) federal environmental reviews and permitting are the primary reason that infrastructure projects are delayed or cancelled; (3) environmental laws are systematically weaponized against the construction of new infrastructure via obstructive litigation in federal courts; and (4) federal environmental procedures and standards must be sacrificed for the green energy transition to proceed at the scale and speed required to address climate change.
>
> Each of these myths is premised on misperceptions of the law, the facts, or both. The available empirical record shows that environmental reviews and permitting rarely delay or block utility-scale renewable energy projects, that environmental litigation (outside specific locations and types of projects) is seldom a factor, and that permitting reform does not have to occur at the expense of environmental procedures and standards. While environmental laws certainly play a role in shaping the pace and scale of infrastructure development, in practice, they are one among many factors, and rarely the rate-limiting one. Indeed, the fixation on environmental laws often obscures other more important challenges, such as the growing patchwork of state and local regulations that make development difficult to navigate, unpredictable, or impossible. Local opposition is fueling this gridlock and exposing tensions in our federal-state system, which recent U.S. Supreme Court decisions limiting agency authority will exacerbate.

David E. Adelman et al., *Dispelling the Myths of Permitting Reform and Identifying Effective Pathways Forward*, 55 Envtl. L. Rep. (ELI) 10038, 10038–39 (2025); *see also* (Climate Justice Alliance letter) Letter: Environmental Groups Oppose Sweeping Detrimental Changes to the National Environmental Policy Act (Sept. 10, 2024) (a letter from a collection of EJ and environmental groups opposing Congressional gutting of NEPA), https://climatejusticealliance.org/NEPA/. Many have observed that the "sacrifice of environmental procedures and standards" that Adelman et al. mention would fall most heavily on already overburdened communities where the most harmful infrastructure has been and would likely continue to be built. *See, e.g.*, California Environmental Justice Alliance, Energy Justice, at https://ceja.org/what-we-do/energyequity/. Adelman et al. also acknowledge that "permitting reform should not lose sight of the values served by permitting and the risks associated with compromising those values. First, hasty permitting reforms, especially those aimed at NEPA, risk eliminating public involvement. Without public involvement, it is inevitable that environmental justice and tribal communities will be disadvantaged." 55 Envtl. L. Rep. at 10055.

In 2025, as the second Trump administration is pursuing an agenda of massive fossil fuel expansion and open hostility to clean energy, we are seeing more vigorous efforts from Congress to cut NEPA off at the knees (or perhaps at the neck). Currently, some of the most extreme proposals are emerging as part of the ongoing budget reconciliation process, in legislation that Trump has ironically dubbed the "Big Beautiful Bill." One of the most extreme features of this bill would involve "[c]reating a 'pay-to-play' NEPA scheme to allow natural gas infrastructure projects to pay the lesser of $10 million or 1 percent of a project's projected capital cost to receive expedited permitting, which would be insulated from judicial review...."

Whether these current efforts might be successful (either now or later through some other legislative vehicle), and to what degree, is uncertain, but they appear to signal a new era of Congressional willingness to fundamentally reconsider bedrock environmental laws like NEPA. While NEPA may never have lived up to its full promise as a tool for environmental justice, it is clear that eliminating (or severely curtailing) environmental review would leave environmental justice communities in harm's way. This is especially true for communities that bear the greatest burden from fossil fuel and petrochemical infrastructure, including many communities in the Gulf South. These communities would feel the biggest impact from Congressional efforts to pave the way for unchecked fossil fuel expansion with minimal environmental review and regulatory oversight.

Notes and Questions

1. Permitting reform or not? What do you think about the tension that Adelman et al. mention around permitting and NEPA "reform," and its connection to both protecting people and advancing climate solutions? What do you think this says about how far the mainstream environmental movement has come (or not) with respect to understanding, respecting, and fully engaging with environmental justice issues? Is a winning solution likely to emerge if the mainstream and environmental justice movements don't work together? What would you suggest as a path forward?

3. NEPA & EJ in the Second Trump Administration

From the beginning, the second Trump administration expressed open hostility to both environmental review and environmental justice. Specific to NEPA, environmental review, and environmental justice, Trump directed that:

> (a) The heads of all agencies shall review all existing regulations, orders, guidance documents, policies, settlements, consent orders, and any other agency actions ... to identify those agency actions that impose an undue burden on the identification, development, or use of domestic energy resources—with particular attention to oil, natural gas, coal, hydropower, biofuels, critical mineral, and nuclear energy resources....
>
> (b) Within 30 days of the date of this order, the head of each agency shall ... develop and begin implementing action plans to suspend, revise, or rescind all agency actions identified as unduly burdensome under subsection (a) of this section, as expeditiously as possible and consistent with applicable law.

EO 14154, *Unleashing American Energy*, Section 3 (Jan. 20, 2025). The same EO also directed CEQ to "expedite and simplify the permitting process, within 30 days of the date of this order, provide guidance on implementing [NEPA], and propose rescinding CEQ's NEPA regulations...." Making good on Trump's plan, CEQ took action to rescind its NEPA regulations by "interim final rule" on February 25, 2025. In the Federal Register notice, CEQ explained:

> The [CEQ] ... is issuing this interim final rule to remove the existing implementing regulations for [NEPA] ..., in response to [President Trump's] Executive Order (E.O.) 14154, *Unleashing American Energy*. Among other things, E.O. 14154 rescinds [President Carter's] E.O. 11991, Relating to Protection and Enhancement of Environmental Quality, which amended [President Nixon's] E.O. 11514, Protection and Enhancement of Environmental Quality, and directed CEQ to promulgate regulations for implementing NEPA and required Federal agencies to comply with those regulations. E.O. 14154 also directs CEQ to issue guidance on implementing NEPA and to propose rescinding the NEPA implementing regulations. This interim final rule carries out President Trump's latter instruction.... CEQ has also concluded that it may lack authority to issue binding rules on agencies in the absence of the now-rescinded E.O. 11191 ... and CEQ therefore has determined that it is appropriate to remove its regulations from the Code of Federal Regulations.

Removal of National Environmental Policy Act Implementing Regulations, 90 Fed. Reg. 10610-01 (Feb. 25, 2025). Trump also directed CEQ to rescind its 1997 guidance on the consideration of EJ in NEPA review, which CEQ did. Moreover, CEQ issued an Interagency Memorandum, citing EO 14148 and EO 14173, and advising agencies "not [to] include an environmental justice analysis" in NEPA documents moving forward, "to the extent that this approach is consistent with other applicable law." *CEQ, Memorandum for Heads of Federal Departments and Agencies Re: Implementation of the National Environmental Policy Act* (Feb. 19, 2025).

The combined threats from the courts, Congress, and the Trump administration do not bode well for NEPA in the long run, or for the ongoing availability of environmental review as an effective and reliable tool for environmental justice advocacy. That said, EJ advocates will continue to fight to preserve NEPA, and to limit the damage from judicial, executive, and legislative incursion. In the more immediate term, NEPA may already be a much more difficult legal resource for EJ communities given the obvious federal agency hostility and given the strong signal from the Supreme Court regarding deference to agency decision-making and limitations on the scope of review that NEPA requires. This will likely make it harder for communities to demand analysis of the kinds of impacts (especially indirect impacts) that would be most valuable for environmental justice advocacy.

Notes and Questions

1. Surviving hostile administrations. What options do environmental justice advocates have in the face of such open hostility on the part of the federal government? To what extent is there power in numbers? Consider how willing you would be to stand up and make your voice heard if you were an EJ activist involved in a NEPA dispute given the possibility of retaliatory action—from industry or from the federal government itself?

2. Judicial review of NEPA EJ analyses. Very few cases have addressed either the impact of environmental justice executive orders, or the role that the CEQ and EPA guidance on environmental justice should play in decisions under NEPA. As an initial matter, since Section 6-609 of EO 12898 provides that it does not create any private right of action to judicial review, some courts have held that they lack jurisdiction to consider challenges to environmental justice analyses carried out under the Order. *See Citizens Concerned About Jet Noise, Inc. v. Dalton*, 48 F. Supp. 2d 582, 604 (E.D. Va. 1999). Other courts treat environmental justice analyses like any other agency decision-making process in the EIS, finding that such an analysis is reviewable under an arbitrary and capricious standard. *See Sierra Club v. Federal Energy Regulatory Commission*, 867 F.3d 1357, 1369 (D.C. Cir. 2017). Under such a review, the agency's analysis

> must be reasonably and adequately explained, but the agency's choice among reasonable analytical methodologies is entitled to deference. As always with NEPA, an agency is not required to select the course of action that best serves environmental justice, only to take a "hard look" at environmental justice issues.

Id. at 1369. *See also, Latin Americans for Social and Economic Justice v. Administrator of the Federal Highway Administration*, 765 F.3d. 447, 475 (6th Cir. 2014); *Communities Against Runway Expansion, Inc. v. Federal Aviation Administration*, 355 F.3d 678, 688 (D.C. Cir. 2004); *Senville v. Peters*, 327 F. Supp. 2d 335 (D. Vt. 2004). For further consideration of the role of EO 12898 in judicial review, *see* Clifford J. Villa, *"No Box To Be Checked": Environmental Justice in Modern Legal Practice*, 30 N.Y.U. ENVTL. L.J. 157, 180 (2022).

Most of the rulings that reach the question of whether the environmental justice analysis is adequate have, under principles of deference to the agency, upheld the agency decision. One early instance in which a NEPA environmental justice analysis was more fully explored involved the Nuclear Regulatory Commission (NRC), an independent regulatory agency not technically covered by the Executive Order, but that voluntarily agreed to be bound by it. In 1997, the Atomic Safety and Licensing Board (Board) of the NRC heard a challenge to a Final Environmental Impact Statement (FEIS) prepared for a proposal by Louisiana Energy Services to build an $855 million uranium-enrichment facility (the Claiborne Enrichment Center) in the midst of two historically Black communities in Claiborne Parish, Louisiana. The Board issued a detailed ruling from a hearing in which Dr. Robert Bullard compellingly testified. For more, *see In the Matter of Louisiana Energy Services, L.P.*, 45 N.R.C. 367 (1997).

D. Information Disclosure & the Emergency Planning and Community Right-to-Know Act

Over the past four decades, information-disclosure and right-to-know statutes have become increasingly popular as an alternative to conventional regulation. These laws serve numerous objectives. One, they improve the efficient functioning of the market by remedying information gaps facing consumers and workers. Such laws also are premised on an entitlement rationale; the underlying notion is that members of the public have a "fundamental right to know" what chemicals are "out there," to which they are being exposed. These laws also promote citizen power and advance democratic decision-making. Armed with more information, citizens can make better-informed decisions and are thus in a better position to bargain with private corporations and the government. Finally, such measures provide indirect incentives for industry to undertake self-regulation and thereby reduce risky activities, help avoid accidents and facilitate emergency planning, and add to the database that helps government agencies determine the need for additional regulation.

The most well-known federal information disclosure law is the **Freedom of Information Act (FOIA)**, 5 U.S.C. § 552, originally established by Congress in 1966. As amended, FOIA generally requires that "Each agency shall ... upon any request for records which (i) reasonably describes such records and (ii) is made in accordance with published rules ..., shall make the records promptly available to any person." 5 U.S.C. § 552(a)(3)(A). As described by Justice Stevens, FOIA was intended to implement "a general philosophy of full agency disclosure" of agency documents. "If an agency improperly withholds any documents, the district court has jurisdiction to order their production." FOIA also "expressly places the burden on the agency to sustain its action and directs the district courts to determine the matter de novo." *U.S. Dept. of Justice v. Reporters Comm. for Freedom of the Press*, 489 U.S. 749, 755 (1989) (internal citations omitted). Agency failure to respond timely to a FOIA request or to otherwise invoke at least one of nine exemptions (e.g., national defense; trade secrets; personnel, financial, or medical records) may be subject to judicial review.

Advocates for environmental justice make regular use of FOIA requests (and state analogues) for collecting agency information about their communities. For further background on FOIA theory and practice, *see* David J. Sheffner & Congressional Research Service, The Freedom of Information Act (FOIA): A Legal Overview (2020). For specific information about how to submit a FOIA request and access to a portal for submitting a FOIA request online, see https://www.foia.gov/.

Another federal statute requiring information disclosure, specifically in the context of environmental pollution, is the **Emergency Planning and Community Right-to-**

Know Act (EPCRA), 42 U.S.C. §§ 11001–11050. Section 313 of EPCRA authorizes EPA to establish and maintain a Toxic Release Inventory (TRI) of facilities that manufacture, import, process, or use certain types of chemicals. Section 313(d) outlines the criteria by which chemicals are added to the TRI, including chemical toxicity, potential adverse impacts on human health if exposure were to occur, and certain types of illnesses or health conditions that may be associated with potential exposure to the chemical. Section 313(f) establishes a general reporting threshold of 10,000 pounds for toxic chemicals used at a facility during a calendar year, and 25,000 pounds for toxic chemicals manufactured, imported, or processed at a facility during a calendar year. This data is then shared with the public via an EPA website. For reporting year 2020, the TRI covered 770 individual chemicals and 33 chemical categories. Additional chemicals are added regularly to the TRI list, including nine PFAS chemicals added to the list for reporting year 2025. For the history and policy behind TRI reporting under EPCRA, see the excerpt below.

Sarah Lamdan & Rebecca Bratspies, *Taking a Page from the FDA's Prescription Medicine Information Rules: Reimagining Environmental Information for Climate Change*

40 U. Ark. Little Rock L. Rev. 573 (2018)

... EPCRA emerged in response to two Union Carbide chemical disasters: one in Bhopal, India, and another in Institute, West Virginia. In 1984, faulty operations at a Union Carbide pesticide manufacturing plant in Bhopal, India, led to a massive explosion. Over half a million people were exposed to airborne toxic chemicals; tens of thousands died or suffered severe injuries. Less than a year later, a storage tank exploded at another Union Carbide plant, this one in Institute, West Virginia. The resulting toxic cloud injured scores of nearby residents.

In both Bhopal and Institute, residents were caught unaware and unprepared. First responders faced added dangers because they lacked knowledge about the chemical substances at issue and thus could not take appropriate protective measures. Doctors treating the injured had no idea what symptoms to expect or what treatments would be effective. These chemical disasters became human disasters, and lack of information magnified the harms.

In November 1986, less than two years after the Bhopal disaster, Congress enacted EPCRA to respond to the need for accurate, timely information about chemical risks.... [EPCRA] included sweeping public information access provisions. Through these provisions, EPCRA ... sought to transform industrial chemical practices "from a secretive alchemy to a publicly posted overload of papers, training materials and neighborhood emergency maps." The resulting ... regulatory schemes provided for information disclosure to make public the chemical hazard data needed to improve awareness, planning, and preparation for potential disasters....

EPCRA governs local and state emergency planning for potential disasters involving hazardous chemicals, the right of the public to access information on chemical hazards in their community, and the reporting responsibilities for facilities that use, store, and release hazardous chemicals. The law has four major provisions: emergency planning obligations; emergency release notifications; reporting requirements for hazardous chemical storage; and the creation of a toxic chemical release inventory. These provisions are markedly different from more traditional "command and control," "end of pipe" governance that limit hazardous discharge. Instead, EPCRA uses regulation to proactively promote chemical disaster awareness and preparation. The theory behind EPCRA is that public access to data helps communities make informed decisions about the chemical hazards in their midst. The law prioritizes public participation (hence the "right-to-know" language in its title). Indeed, EPCRA is the only U.S. environmental law that arguably creates a stand-alone right of environmental information access. EPCRA mandates the public availability of two major types of information: (1) emergency plans and (2) information about toxic releases....

The most well-known information access provision in EPCRA is the one that requires the EPA to create and maintain an inventory of toxic chemicals, or Toxics Release Inventory (TRI). The TRI has been credited with reducing chemical emissions in the United States by twenty-one percent since 2006. While these reductions are highly significant, the TRI has also produced a less concrete but equally important outcome in the context of information policy, "serv[ing] as a constant example of the vital role information plays in a democracy, and the importance of the public's right to know." Beyond the TRI, which reports on past releases, EPCRA also helps communities plan for future emissions by providing information to the public through Local Emergency Planning Committees (LEPCs). LEPCs are composed of local participants including elected officials; police, fire, civil defense, and public health professionals; environmental, transportation, and hospital officials; facility representatives; members of the media; and community groups who develop and review local emergency response plans and disseminate disaster preparation information to the public....

Unfortunately, ... [EPCRA is] plagued with implementation issues on local, state, and federal levels. EPCRA ... mandated programs are typically low priorities, thinly staffed with small budgets. Violations often go unchecked, and fines for noncompliance are light and sparsely enforced. Worse, many states actively restrict access to the chemical data that EPCRA was designed to make public, citing fears about unintended uses of the information to promote terrorism or interfere with trade secrets.

Notes and Questions

1. TRI tensions. What are the tensions between disclosure and corporate privacy with regard to toxic releases? How should regulators resolve legitimate disagreements between these public and private interests?

2. TRI supporters. Supporters such as Bradley Karkkainen claim that the TRI is a "watershed, pioneering the systematic use of performance monitoring and benchmarking as regulatory tools," that can "push in the direction of continuous improvement as facilities and firms endeavor to leapfrog over their peers to receive credit for larger improvements or superior performance." Bradley C. Karkkainen, *Information as Environmental Regulation: TRI and Performance Benchmarking, Precursor to a New Paradigm?* 89 GEORGETOWN L.J. 257, 260–262 (2001).

3. TRI doubters. Kathryn E. Durham-Hammer suggests that TRI's success is overstated and that "the assumption that companies will change their use and release of hazardous waste because they are ashamed of being flagrant polluters in comparison to their competitors ... is not based on convincing empirical evidence ... [and] is pure speculation." She contends that, "Communities cannot safely rely on EPCRA and TRI data because EPCRA allows facilities to report their own data, and requires only an estimate if a true measurement is not feasible. EPCRA establishes no means for communities or the EPA to confirm facilities' self-made reports." Kathryn E. Durham-Hammer, *Left to Wonder: Reevaluating, Reforming, and Implementing the Emergency Planning and Community Right-to-Know Act of 1986*, 29 COLUM. J. ENVTL. L. 323, 337–38, 347–48 (2004).

4. Inequities. Studies using TRI data have documented that reporting facilities are disproportionately sited in poor communities and communities of color. Ryan Johnson, Kim Ramsey-White, & Christina H. Fuller, *Socio-demographic Differences in Toxic Release Inventory Siting and Emissions in Metro Atlanta,* 13 INT. J. ENVIRON. RES. PUBLIC HEALTH 747 (2016); Kerry Ard, *Trends in Exposure to Industrial Air Toxins for Different Racial and Socioeconomic Groups: A Spatial and Temporal Examination of Environmental Inequality in the U.S. from 1995 to 2004*, 53 SOCIAL SCI. RES. 375 (2015). Is an information disclosure law like TRI likely to be useful in remedying these disparate environmental burdens? Who is most likely to access and use the information made available through the TRI? Are such laws best as a complement to strong pollution control laws? Environmental justice activists generally support the TRI program (including expanding and strengthening its provisions).

Chapter 12

Citizen Enforcement and Common Law Remedies

A. Defining Citizen Enforcement

The law plays an important role in advancing environmental justice, and communities can and do turn to the courts to help achieve their environmental justice goals. It is helpful to unpack, at least a little, what we mean when we refer to "citizen enforcement" in the context of environmental protection. In the narrowest sense, "citizen enforcement" could refer to the policing of regulated entities for compliance with environmental standards—for example, a refinery's compliance with air pollution emission limitations. In this sense, citizen enforcement occurs when private individuals or organizations stand in the shoes of public enforcement authorities to prosecute violations of environmental laws. (Agency enforcement is discussed in detail in Chapter 7.)

In a broader sense, "citizen enforcement" might also be understood to encompass litigation directed at ensuring that *government entities* live up to their legal responsibilities. This kind of citizen enforcement might involve, for example, a private lawsuit that seeks to *compel* agency action (like the promulgation of a rule that is required by statute) or that challenges the *adequacy or legality* of an agency decision (like the stringency of a regulation or the content of an environmental permit). (Agency rulemaking is discussed in more detail in Chapter 5 and permits are discussed in Chapter 6.) This chapter focuses primarily on the narrower understanding of citizen enforcement but also touches on the other kinds of litigation.

Citizen enforcement can offer an opportunity for environmental justice advocates to obtain enforceable court orders that compel positive action or that prevent harmful activities. Or it can result in settlements that offer similar benefits. However, as discussed below, litigation is not a panacea. It comes with its own limitations, complexities, biases, and risks.

This chapter looks first at the question of how lawyers should think about their own role and the role of litigation in environmental justice advocacy. It then discusses some of the practical aspects of citizen enforcement, and some of the longstanding and emerging challenges, and finally concludes with a short discussion of the role that common law can play in advancing environmental justice.

B. The Role of the Lawyer and Litigation

Before we consider specific enforcement tools, it is important to consider how and why environmental justice advocacy calls for a special kind of lawyering. Recall that as a political movement, environmental justice is premised on the principle that affected communities should speak for themselves and community empowerment is central. Considering this, to what extent should environmental justice activists rely on legal strategies at all? When is litigation appropriate, and what is the proper role of the lawyer in environmental justice disputes?

The fact is that environmental justice activists may have an ambivalent relationship with the legal system and with lawyers, and often for good reason. On the one hand, legal representatives can play a powerful and essential role in advocating on behalf of communities. In addition, many lawyers working with community groups are (or have been) activists in their own right and are deeply committed to the principles and goals of environmental justice. On the other hand, many activists and community residents distrust lawyers and the legal process. In their view, not only has past reliance on legal processes and procedures resulted in the inequitable distribution of environmental harms, but the legal system has often fundamentally failed communities in other ways (such as by over-policing, discriminatory criminalization, and mass incarceration). And community members' past interactions with the law, and with courts, may be overwhelmingly negative.

Additionally, when lawyers arrive they may look at the advocacy landscape with an exclusively legal lens, taking over disputes from community leaders and framing issues in narrow legal terms that do not fully address the community's concerns. Moreover, communities will rarely, if ever, be able to match the legal resources of the government or of private entities.

This is all complicated further by the problematic behavior of many "big green" organizations in the past. These mainstream environmental organizations, who have often invested in building significant legal capacity, have a history of "parachuting in," bringing lawsuits, and then disappearing again with little regard for ongoing community interests. Many of these organizations are now more aware of their responsibilities in this regard and getting better and showing up as partners in ways that value and respect community knowledge, leadership, and self-determination. However, the history and power-dynamics that inform these relationships are important for any student of environmental justice to understand and keep in mind.

Finally, we are in a particular political moment in 2025 with the second Trump administration. The political leadership at agencies like EPA, for example, are proudly declaring their intent to pursue massive and sweeping environmental deregulation, with the intent of wiping away rules that provide widespread benefits, including to frontline communities. At the same time, the federal government (and many states) plan to dramatically ramp-down environmental enforcement, and Congress appears unlikely to take action to preserve environmental protections that might be in danger.

At times like these, the courts are often a powerful and necessary tool to advance the interests of overburdened communities. Nonetheless, when lawyers show up, it necessarily changes the nature of community advocacy, and it is critical that lawyers and community advocates alike appreciate this and keep it in mind as they pursue their environmental justice goals.

1. Environmental Justice Lawyering

The following article from 1994 was written by a long-time community organizer in Oakland, California. How much of the perspectives shared here do you believe prevail today?

Francis Calpotura, *Why the Law?*

THIRD FORCE (May/June 1994)

I was once told by an organizer friend of mine that lawsuits are a tactic to be used during a fight when you want to (a) end the campaign and move on to another issue, (b) inspire your members by showing that you are not afraid to take on these bastards, or (c) force the hand of your opposition to react to your initiative during a stalemate.

In none of these instances, I remember, is a lawsuit a strategy for winning a fight. It is always a tactical move. So where does this penchant for legal strategies come from? Indigenous community organizations normally don't have lawyers (some don't even have paid staff) on their payroll; environmental organizations do. I would argue that the alliance of community organizations with the proliferating Environmental Law Centers around the country has resulted in legal strategies for winning environmental justice fights, to the detriment of direct-action, community-oriented strategies.

The political implications are serious. A legal strategy affects how the issues that confront a community are understood. For example, the fight by [activists in the Georgia Sea Islands against development] was framed as a "preservation" issue in order to employ a variety of zoning and endangered species laws to delay development. This cut on the issue fails to show the racial and class character of the developer's strategy, something organizing for community control and equitable development would do to a much greater extent.

In addition, a legal strategy takes the fight away from arenas in which people can have some direct influence—their politicians, local development company offices, residences of the CEO, bank offices, etc.—to a place where they don't, i.e., in some chamber controlled by a judge where only the lawyers are allowed to speak (and only in English)....

Notes and Questions

1. **The effect(iveness) of litigation.** Do you agree with Mr. Calpotura's misgivings about relying on legal strategies? From the perspective of community groups, is it true

that a lawsuit is never a strategy for winning a fight but is always a tactical move? Professors Gregg Macey and Lawrence Susskind explore the impact on the West Dallas Coalition for Environmental Justice of turning from an approach with community organizing at its center to one focused on litigation in *The Secondary Effects of Environmental Justice Litigation: The Case of West Dallas Coalition for Environmental Justice v. EPA*, 20 VA. ENVTL. L.J. 431 (2001). They note that the group's emphasis shifted from cumulative exposure stories that had prompted many residents to join the coalition, to scientific testing and gathering evidence to support the litigation. As a result, "the perceived need for protests, meeting attendance, testimony at hearings, and picketing around industrial land uses (as well as the use of stories of long-term exposure) diminished." *Id.* at 454.

2. What role should lawyers play with regard to representing communities in environmental justice controversies? Does the late attorney/activist Luke Cole, whose excerpt follows, differ from Mr. Calpotura in his view of the role that a lawyer can take in an environmental justice battle?

Luke W. Cole, *Empowerment as the Key to Environmental Protection: The Need for Environmental Poverty Law*

19 ECOLOGY L.Q. 619 (1992)

Client Empowerment

"Client empowerment" occurs when a lawyer's practice helps clients realize and assert greater control over decisions which affect their lives. Empowerment is also a process which enables individuals to participate effectively in collective efforts to solve common problems.... Client empowerment is about creating in the client community the dynamics of democratic decision making, accountability, and self-determination—ideals which one would like to create in society.

In the environmental poverty law context, empowerment means enabling those who will have to live with the results of environmental decisions to be those who actually make the decisions. "Community-based" and "community-led" are key descriptive and prescriptive phrases for the environmental poverty lawyer, who should seek to decentralize power away from herself and to her clients. The client empowerment model is thus the reverse of the legal-scientific mode of lawyering used by mainstream environmental groups. Rather than solving a problem *for* a community, the empowerment model calls upon attorneys to help community members solve their own problems.

"Empowerment law" is more a *method* than a *product*, a practice through which the lawyer helps the group learn empowering methods of operation. Empowerment of clients is the answer to the political organizers' eternal question: "What happens when we go away?" By helping people take control over the decisions which affect their lives, an attorney leaves the community stronger than when she arrived....

Law as a Means, Not an End....

While our first instinct as lawyers might be to use legal tactics, they may not achieve the results our clients desire. Other tactics may be more useful in generating public pressure on an unresponsive bureaucracy or polluting corporation: tactics such as community organizing, administrative advocacy, or media pressure. Because environmental problems are political problems—some government official is allowing one actor to pollute the neighborhood of another—non-legal tactics often offer the best approach. As is so often the case, there may not even *be* a legal solution to the problem faced by the community. Or, the legal approach may radically disempower a client community and thus should be avoided. Translating a community's problems into legal language may render them meaningless.... Finally, lawsuits take fights into the arena most controlled by the adversary and least controlled by the community....

Three Questions for Effective Advocacy

Activists for social change have long relied on [the following] three questions in evaluating prospective strategies and tactics. These three questions parallel the three tenets of environmental poverty law: ....

Will the strategy educate people? This broad question fits the empowerment model of legal services because education is a key to empowerment. Environmental poverty lawyers must broadly construe their concept of "education"—it should encompass education of a client or client group by the lawyer, education of policymakers or decisionmakers, and education of the public. Further, the educational process should be two-way: a lawyer must not only educate her clients, but also be educated by them. By increasing the community's knowledge, and others' knowledge of the community's problems, the community's persuasive power is necessarily strengthened.

Will it build the movement? Group representation is a self-conscious strategy to build local movements by developing local community groups. Community groups and their lawyers should look for tactics that draw new members into a group, rather than alienate potential supporters. An environmental poverty law model which is based on community education and empowerment will necessarily "build the movement," while a narrow legal approach will almost certainly fail to build anything.

Does the strategy address the cause rather than the symptoms of a problem? Environmental issues—like most legal services issues such as housing, health care access and (un)employment—are systemic. The disproportionate burden borne by poor people is a direct result of the system of economic organization in the United States and the corresponding inequities in the distribution of political power. Legal solutions to the environmental problems faced by poor people most often treat only the symptom, the environmental hazard itself. Embracing non-legal approaches, and legal approaches which treat the law as a means rather than an end, can help environmental poverty lawyers attack the root cause of the environmental problems faced by their clients, political and economic powerlessness....

Figure 12-1. Kettleman City, California, remains severely impacted by environmental injustice. According to 2025 data in EPA's EJSCREEN, the population is 93 percent Latino and ranks nationally in the 99th percentile for Drinking Water Non-Compliance, 98th percentile for Particulate Matter, and 93rd percentile for Ozone. Photo: Cliff Villa, 2020.

What Does It Look Like? Public Participation in Kettleman City

Kettleman City is a small farmworker community located in California's San Joaquin Valley. The community is ninety-five percent Latino, and seventy percent of its 1,100 residents speak Spanish in the home. Most residents work in the agricultural fields that stretch out in three directions from the town. Many of Kettleman City's residents have lived there for years and own their own homes, purchased with low-interest loans from the Farmers Home Administration.

Kettleman City also hosts the largest toxic waste dump west of Louisiana. Established without the community's knowledge or consent in the late 1970s, Chemical Waste Management's (CWM) Kettleman Hills Facility is a Class I toxic waste landfill. Just four miles from town, it may legally accept just about any toxic substance produced.

In 1988, CWM proposed to build a toxic waste incinerator at the dump. A Greenpeace organizer tipped off the Kettleman City community about the proposal and gave residents information on toxic waste incinerators. Feeling that the incinerator would threaten their health, homes, and livelihoods, Kettleman City residents organized a community group, *El Pueblo para el Aire y Agua Limpio* (People for Clean Air and Water), held demonstrations, and pressured their local officials. In 1989, they also secured the legal representation of the California Rural Legal Assistance Foundation (CRLAF).

The young lawyer handling the case—his first—was faced with a dilemma [the lawyer was in fact the author, Luke Cole. Eds.]. The Kings County Planning Department, the local agency responsible for granting permits for the project, had issued a dense, tedious, more than 1,000-page Environmental Impact Report (EIR) on the proposed incinerator. The County had refused to translate the EIR into Spanish, despite repeated requests from Kettleman City residents. Kettleman City residents wanted to take part in the EIR process. The lawyer needed comment on the EIR, so that the administrative record would reflect the deficiencies of the document and the process. The lawyer faced a choice: the traditional mode of environmental lawyering or a new environmental poverty law approach.

Traditional approach. In the traditional model of environmental advocacy, the lawyer reads and analyzes the EIR document, shares parts of it with selected experts, and then writes extensive, technical comments on the EIR on behalf of a client group. These comments are submitted to the agency and form the basis of later lawsuits if the agency does not respond adequately.

Lawyering for social change model. The lawyer attempts to involve and educate the community while addressing the root of the problem: that the County is ignoring and dismissing the needs of Kettleman City residents without fear of repercussions because the residents are not organized.

Environmental poverty law in Kettleman City: How it worked. The lawyer chose the latter strategy. Working with several key leaders in the community, he and a CRLAF community worker held an initial series of three house meetings in Kettleman City. Each meeting was held in a different home, and all were held on the same day.

At a typical meeting, the community leaders would explain the incinerator proposal to eight to ten residents. The lawyer would then describe parts of the EIR and the County's response to the community's requests. The residents would ask questions, which the leaders and the attorney would answer to the best of their abilities. Discussions among the residents would ensue about the incinerator and why it was to be located in Kettleman City. The conversations were not limited simply to the incinerator, however. Residents would tell stories of health symptoms they had experienced (which they blamed on the existing toxic waste dump), of past dealings with County officials, and of other incidents they felt were important. Since the meetings involved almost entirely monolingual Spanish-speakers, the meetings were held in Spanish, with the community worker translating for the lawyer.

At the end of each meeting, the leaders and the attorney would ask each person present to write a letter of comment on the EIR to the Planning Commission. The letters—almost all in Spanish—questioned the Planning Commission about the incinerator, and also asked to have the EIR documents translated so that Kettleman residents could take part in the process. The meetings were as inclusive as possible: if a person was not literate, he or she would dictate a letter to a more educated Kettleman resident; children were encouraged to write as well. Out of the first three meetings, the community group generated twenty-five letters of comment on the EIR.

At the first meetings, people were asked to hold future meetings in their own homes, with five to eight of their neighbors. The community worker followed up with community leaders to ensure that the meetings continued. Over the course of the following three weeks more house meetings were held, and many more letters were written. When the EIR's public comment period closed, the record contained 162 comments from individuals—126 of them from Kettleman City residents. More importantly, 119 of the comments—seventy-five percent of all comments by individuals on the EIR—were in Spanish.

Although the results of such organizing are difficult to quantify—except, of course, for the large volume of letters—the letter-writing campaign served several important purposes. It brought Kettleman City residents together to learn about and discuss the incinerator. It allowed community leaders to bring Kettleman City residents up to date on the project. It informed the community of upcoming opportunities for participation, including a hearing before the Planning Commission. It encouraged individuals to take action—writing a letter—and to express themselves both in the house meetings and on paper. It validated residents' experiences with and concerns about the incinerator and the siting process by creating an opportunity to discuss and affirm them. People could collectively share other individual problems, tell their stories, and, through that process, see the commonality of their experiences. Lastly, the letter-writing campaign allowed residents to tell their stories to the Planning Commission, to act as "experts" in their own case.

Rather than gathering the residents' stories and translating them into narrow legal points (or even into English), the lawyer sought to facilitate the people of Kettleman City speaking for themselves. By asking others to hold meetings in their homes, the attorney and the community leaders fostered a sense of ownership of the campaign among members of the community. And finally, the letters created a stunning administrative record. The County could no longer claim that Kettleman residents and Spanish-speakers were not interested in the project: more than ten percent of the community had written letters to the Planning Commission. The attorney had helped create what he needed—the administrative record—in a way which fostered community action rather than shifting it.

The letter-writing campaign was an instance of empowering the client using group representation and non-litigation avenues. Ironically, by using tactics other than litigation, the campaign facilitated the litigation that ultimately resulted. The Kings County Board of Supervisors ultimately approved the incinerator proposal, and the environmental poverty lawyer was forced to take the County to Court. The Court overturned the County's approval, in part because of the County's exclusion of Spanish-speakers.

The letter-writing campaign also provided solid answers to the three questions environmental poverty lawyers must ask themselves. It educated people both in the community and in the County government. The campaign built the movement by bringing house meetings into new homes and involving residents who had not participated in the group to that point. Finally, it addressed the root of the problem, by using the

EIR public comment process as an organizing focus and forcing the County decision makers to listen to the people of Kettleman City.

Notes and Questions

1. **Community empowerment.** Should empowerment of communities always be the primary goal of EJ attorneys? As a tool for legal advocacy, how effective is the EJ principle that communities speak for themselves? For one perspective on these questions, from one of the true pioneers of the environmental justice movement, *see* Peggy Shepard, *Issues of Community Empowerment*, 21 FORDHAM URBAN L.J. 739 (1994). For another compelling discussion of what it means to respect community narrative, and how that principle can inform the role of a lawyer in community advocacy, *see* Helen H. Kang, *Respect for Community Narratives of Environmental Injustice: The Dignity Right to Be Heard and Believed*, 25 WIDENER L. REV. 219 (2019) (discussing experiences of community members in San Francisco's Bayview Hunter's Point neighborhood).

2. **Context and community narratives.** As the above discussions illustrate, to truly serve the interest of communities, litigation as a tool for advancing environmental justice must be deployed with care. It must be initiated in partnership with community members, it must respect and incorporate community narrative, and it must take steps to avoid interrupting community power-building.

How do each of these factors benefit a campaign? How does this holistic contextualization benefit litigation? Discuss the importance of providing a forum for listening to the narratives of environmental injustice.

3. **Relationship building.** Three community lawyers who worked on a successful effort to preserve open space in Boston's Chinatown offer the following advice about building relationships between lawyers and the communities they represent:

> *Do not assume "trust" exists simply because of shared ethnicity, race, or language ability....* Regardless of the similarities between lawyer and client, the client sees the lawyer first as a "lawyer." For many, the legal profession represents the hostile, inaccessible, and insensitive legal system that permeates and complicates their lives....
>
> *Build trust by learning about the community....* We mean learning about its history, its geography, and the various players, institutions, and organizations that constitute the community.... Such in-depth knowledge enabled us to identify what sorts of strategies, both legal and non-legal, might be viable and appropriate during the ... struggle.
>
> *Build trust by establishing a permanent presence within the community....* Besides serving on boards of community-based organizations, [community lawyers] need to volunteer their time and skills and use their legal training to further the best interests of the community on myriad issues. Examples include conducting community legal education on relevant topics such as immi-

gration, workers' rights and American government structure; mentoring community youth; and assisting community functions.

Zenobia Lai, Andrew Leong & Chi Chi Wu, *The Lessons of the Parcel C Struggle: Reflections on Community Lawyering*, 6 ASIAN PAC. AM. L.J. 1, 27 (2000). Can lawyers realistically undertake all of these various activities while also actively litigating complex cases? Or are these tasks better performed by community organizers, activists, and others, or by some combination of advocates that include lawyers? What about in situations when a lawyer represents a community group or residents that are geographically distant? Under what conditions is such "long distance" community lawyering appropriate (if ever)?

4. Ethical considerations. Lawyers engaged in community activism must keep in mind the roles they are playing and be cognizant about issues of legal ethics. For instance, before an attorney has been retained by a community group, does the duty of confidentiality apply? And once it does, to whom does it extend and under what circumstances? To whom does the attorney owe her ethical responsibility? The American Bar Association is clear that an attorney owes ethical duties to the "duly authorized constituents" of the organization represented. Model Rules of Prof'l Conduct R. 1.13. What ethical issues are raised if a grassroots organization's goal begins to deviate from that of its members?

Suppose the lawyer is privy to discussions about a planned illegal protest outside a facility? Likewise, could a lawyer who goes door-to-door organizing neighbors to oppose a power plant be accused of improperly soliciting clients? In short, how does a lawyer separate her role as an activist from her role as an "officer of the court"? For more discussion of these issues, *see* Irma Russell & Joanne Sum-Ping, *Issues of Legal Ethics in Environmental Justice Matters*, *in* THE LAW OF ENVIRONMENTAL JUSTICE: THEORIES AND PROCEDURES TO ADDRESS DISPROPORTIONATE RISKS 471 (Michael B. Gerrard & Sheila R. Foster eds., 2d ed. 2008).

2. A Note on Environmental Law Clinics

As of 2024, there were as many as 50 law schools that operate environmental law clinics throughout the country, and some of them have been at the forefront of representing community groups in environmental justice matters. Law students are often permitted to practice law under attorney supervision prior to their admission to the bar under state student practice rules, established by state bar associations or, in some instances, by state supreme courts.

With aggressive advocacy on behalf of environmental justice clients, however, the clinics themselves also have come under attack. The most prominent early example occurred in the late 1990s in Louisiana, where complaints by business organizations and then-Louisiana Governor Mike Foster against the Tulane Environmental Law Clinic led the Louisiana Supreme Court to greatly restrict the state's student practice rules. The business organizations charged, among other things, that "the individual faculty and students' legal views [at Tulane] are in direct conflict with business positions." These complaints arose from the clinic's representation of citizens living in the low-income, 84 percent Black industrial corridor town of Convent, in St. James Parish, Louisiana. The residents opposed a plan by Shintech, a multinational petrochemical firm, to build a polyvinyl chloride plant that would result in emissions of over three million pounds of air pollutants per year, including close to seven hundred thousand pounds of toxic air pollutants. (The project is discussed in more detail in Chapter 1.) As a result of administrative appeals filed by the clinic, EPA vetoed the state's proposed air permit for the facility and accepted the citizens' Title VI civil rights complaint for investigation. As the controversy over the plant grew, Shintech eventually dropped its plans to site the facility in St. James Parish and opted to build a smaller facility elsewhere in the state. *Environmental Law Clinic Raises Environmental Justice ... And a Hostile Reaction from the Governor and the Louisiana Supreme Court*, TULANE ENVTL. L. NEWS, Winter 1999 at 1.

It appears that the revised Louisiana student practice rules adopted in 1999 were designed to preclude representation of virtually all of the community and environmental organizations served by the Tulane clinic in the prior ten years. The story of the attack on Tulane's clinic is vividly recounted in Robert R. Kuehn, *Denying Access to Legal Representation: The Attack on the Tulane Environmental Law Clinic*, 4 WASH. U. J. L. & POL'Y 33 (2000). Professor Kuehn's account is replete with details of conflicts of interest, corrupt political practices, business intimidation, and unequal justice.

Academic institutions have come under even more intense, more politicized, and blatantly racialized attack in 2025 as the second Trump administration has attempted to punish universities for their perceived "liberal leanings" by threatening various political reprisals (such as withdrawal of federal funding and revocation of the right to admit foreign students). The second Trump administration has targeted "environmental justice" as well as "diversity, equity and inclusion" programs by name—ideas that the administration seems to frequently (and wrongly) conflate. We have yet to see how these attacks will ultimately play out, but in one of the most recent salvos (decidedly reminiscent of the tactics of authoritarian regimes), the administration has announced its intention to withdraw federal funding from Harvard University and ban the university from admitting foreign students. However such attacks may finally be resolved, the specter of the administration's explicit targeting of environmental justice and DEI is already having a chilling effect on universities and other kinds of institutions.

Notes and Questions

1. **How would you respond?** What would you do if the federal government were pressuring your school to suspend its environmental clinical work? What would you do if a government official pressured your school to stop teaching environmental justice? How would you want your school to respond to this kind of government intimidation? For one strong response, see the excerpt below from the Dean of Georgetown Law School to Trump's Interim U.S. Attorney for the District of Columbia:

> Your letter challenges Georgetown's ability to define our mission as an educational institution. It inquires about Georgetown Law's curriculum and classroom teaching, asks whether diversity, equity, and inclusion is part of the curriculum, and asserts that your office will not hire individuals from schools where you find the curriculum "unacceptable." The First Amendment, however, guarantees that the government cannot direct what Georgetown and its faculty teach and how to teach it. The Supreme Court has continually affirmed that among the freedoms central to a university's First Amendment rights are its abilities to determine, on academic grounds, who may teach, what to teach, and how to teach it.... This is a bedrock principle of constitutional law....

William M. Treanor, Dean and Executive Vice President, Georgetown University Law Center, to Edward R. Martin, Jr., Interim U.S. Attorney, District of Columbia (Mar. 6, 2025).

2. What would you have done? Environmental law clinics at Tulane University, the University of Oregon, and many other schools have come under political pressure. For instance, in 2010, lawmakers debated a measure to cut money for the University of Maryland's law clinic if it did not provide details to the legislature about its clients, finances, and cases. *See* Hope M. Babcock, *How Judicial Hostility Toward Environmental Claims and Intimidation Tactics by Lawyers Have Formed the Perfect Storm Against Environmental Law Clinics: What's the Big Deal about Students and Chickens Anyway?*, 25 J. ENVTL. L. & LITIG. 249 (2010).

More recently, the Trump administration has engaged in direct attacks on individual law firms. *See, e.g.*, Presidential Actions, *Addressing Risks from Perkins Coie LLP*, Mar. 6, 2025 (alleging that "The dishonest and dangerous activity of the law firm Perkins Coie LLP ... has affected this country for decades"). After legal challenge, U.S. District Court Judge Beryl Howell granted summary judgement for Perkins Coie, finding that Trump's order amounted to "unconstitutional retaliation and viewpoint discrimination, plain and simple." In a 102-page order, Judge Howell noted, "No American President has ever before issued executive orders like the one at issue in this lawsuit.... [T]his action draws from a playbook as old as Shakespeare, who penned the phrase: 'The first thing we do, let's kill all the lawyers.'" *Perkins Coie v. U.S. Dept. of Justice*, 783 F. Supp. 3d 105, 118-19 (D.D.C. 2025).

Is it ethical for attorneys and public officials to attack law firms and law clinics for representing unfavored clients? For discussion of this issue in a much different political climate, *see* Robert R. Kuehn, *Shooting the Messenger: The Ethics of Attacks on Environmental Representation*, 26 HARV. ENVTL. L. REV. 417 (2002). For a broader review of attacks on law clinics generally, with suggestions for avoiding undue interference, *see* Robert R. Kuehn & Bridget M. McCormack, *Lessons from Forty Years of Interference in Law School Clinics*, 24 GEO. J. LEGAL ETHICS 59 (2011).

C. Private Enforcement: Citizen Suits

1. Sources of Authority to Litigate

When community groups decide to turn to the courts, there are several ways that this can happen. Citizen enforcement is authorized by many of the major environmental statutes. Among other things, these statutes incorporate discrete "citizen suit" provisions that "deputize members of the public to function as private attorneys general." For example, the federal Clean Air Act, 42 U.S.C. § 7604, provides the following:

> **(a) Authority to bring civil action; jurisdiction** ... any person may commence a civil action on his own behalf—
>
> > (1) against any person ... who is alleged to have violated ... or to be in violation of (A) an emission standard or limitation under this chapter or (B) an order issued by the [EPA] Administrator or a State with respect to such a standard or limitation ...
> >
> > (3) against any person who proposes to construct or constructs any new or modified major emitting facility without a permit [required by specific sections of the Clean Air Act] ... or who is alleged to have violated ... or to be in violation of any condition of such permit.

As you can see, and for obvious reasons, this provision (and others like it) only authorizes *civil actions*, not criminal prosecution. This kind of citizen suit provision is fairly common for federal pollution statutes and reflects Congressional recognition that public enforcement authorities cannot be everywhere all the time. Considering this, Congress did not want to leave the public without recourse under the law in the face of environmental violations.

In general, these statutes allow citizens to sue without demonstrating discrete economic injury or specific harm to the environment. Private plaintiffs in these cases can obtain *penalties* and *injunctive relief* directing a polluter to comply with the law. However, they cannot recover *damages* for any harm suffered. Importantly, these laws also often provide for the recovery of attorney fees and costs if the suit is successful. In allowing the recovery of fees in these cases, Congress recognized that (1) members of the public are unlikely to pursue enforcement if they must bankroll the litigation themselves and (2) that people who bring such suits are serving a public interest that is worthy of encouraging. Some state environmental statutes also have citizen suit provisions, but they are far less common than under federal law.

In addition to authorizing litigation to enforce environmental laws against violators, environmental statutes often also authorize private individuals to sue the government for failure to properly implement federal law. The Clean Air Act citizen suit provision quoted above also includes the following language:

> **(a) Authority to bring civil action; jurisdiction** ... any person may commence a civil action on his own behalf ...

> (2) against the [EPA] Administrator where there is alleged a failure of the Administrator to perform any act or duty under this chapter which is not discretionary with the Administrator . . .

For example, when EPA is directed by statute to take a specific action within a specified time frame or by a date certain (say, promulgate emission standards for a particular category of stationary sources), if EPA fails to do so, private parties can rely on this authority to compel the agency to take the required action. However, such litigation (often referred to as a "deadline suit" or "mandatory duty" suit) will not compel a *particular outcome*—that is, it will not define the *stringency* of an emissions standard that EPA is required to promulgate. It will simply compel the agency to perform the nondiscretionary duty that it failed to complete.

Finally, the public can also challenge the *substance* of agency final decisions (like rulemakings and environmental permits), either under the Administrative Procedure Act (APA) or under the specific judicial review provisions that Congress has incorporated into many environmental statutes. In these "petitions for review" of agency actions, petitioners *can challenge the particular outcome* of an agency decision-making process (like the stringency of an emission standard) and ask the court to vacate the agency's action.

With respect to the substantive review of agency final actions, the APA provides that:

> **§ 702. Right of review**
>
> A person suffering legal wrong because of agency action, or adversely affected or aggrieved by agency action within the meaning of a relevant statute, is entitled to judicial review thereof. . . .
>
> **§ 706. Scope of review**
>
> To the extent necessary to the decision and when presented, the reviewing court shall decide all relevant questions of law, interpret constitutional and statutory provisions, and determine the meaning or applicability of the terms of an agency action. The reviewing court shall—
>
> (1) compel agency action unlawfully withheld or unreasonably delayed; and
>
> (2) hold unlawful and set aside agency action, findings, and conclusions found to be—
>
> (A) arbitrary, capricious, an abuse of discretion, or otherwise not in accordance with law;
>
> (B) contrary to constitutional right, power, privilege, or immunity;
>
> (C) in excess of statutory jurisdiction, authority, or limitations, or short of statutory right;
>
> (D) without observance of procedure required by law;
>
> (E) unsupported by substantial evidence in a case subject to sections 556 and 557 of this title or otherwise reviewed on the record of an agency hearing provided by statute; or

> (F) unwarranted by the facts to the extent that the facts are subject to trial de novo by the reviewing court.
>
> In making the foregoing determinations, the court shall review the whole record or those parts of it cited by a party, and due account shall be taken of the rule of prejudicial error.

Individual environmental statutes can also have their own administrative procedure provisions that address judicial review. To this end, for example, the CAA provides:

> A petition for review of action of the [EPA] Administrator in promulgating any national primary or secondary ambient air quality standard, [or any emission standard, requirement, determination, control, prohibition, or rule under specified sections of the CAA], or any other nationally applicable regulations promulgated, or final action taken, by the Administrator under this chapter may be filed only in the United States Court of Appeals for the District of Columbia.... Any petition for review under this subsection shall be filed within sixty days from the date notice of such promulgation, approval, or action appears in the Federal Register, except that if such petition is based solely on grounds arising after such sixtieth day, then any petition for review under this subsection shall be filed within sixty days after such grounds arise.

42 U.S.C. §7607(b)(1).

With respect to challenges to EPA rules, the CAA's procedural provisions go on to say that the "record for judicial review will consist exclusively of the material [included in the rulemaking record as defined in section 7606(d)]," and that "[o]nly an objection to a rule or procedure which was raised with reasonable specificity during the period for public comment ... may be raised during judicial review." 42 U.S.C. §7607 (d)(7)(B).

Upon review, the CAA provides that:

> [T]he court may reverse any such action found to be—
>
> (A) arbitrary, capricious, an abuse of discretion, or otherwise not in accordance with law;
>
> (B) contrary to constitutional right, power, privilege, or immunity;
>
> (C) in excess of statutory jurisdiction, authority, or limitations, or short of statutory right; or
>
> (D) without observance of procedure required by law ...

Each of these litigation pathways can be a powerful resource for environmental justice advocacy. However, before environmental justice attorneys apply litigation as a tool in a campaign to further the environmental justice objectives, they must be aware of the complexities involved in bringing such suits.

2. Legal Requirements for Filing Suit

In order to initiate a citizen suit alleging a violation of federal environmental law, plaintiffs must satisfy various threshold procedural requirements. For a more detailed discussion *see* Ellen P. Chapnick, *Access to the Courts*, *in* THE LAW OF ENVIRONMENTAL JUSTICE: THEORIES AND PROCEDURES TO ADDRESS DISPROPORTIONATE RISKS 395 (Michael B. Gerrard & Sheila R. Foster eds., 2d ed. 2008).

Plaintiffs must first demonstrate that they have a right to sue under the statute that they are seeking to enforce. Virtually all of the major federal pollution-control and waste statutes contain a citizen suit provision authorizing suits by "any person" or "any citizen." *See, e.g.*, Clean Air Act § 304, 42 U.S.C. § 7604 (reproduced above); Clean Water Act § 505, 33 U.S.C. § 1365; RCRA § 7002, 42 U.S.C. § 6972; CERCLA § 310, 42 U.S.C. § 9659; Safe Drinking Water Act § 1449, 42 U.S.C. § 300j-8; Endangered Species Act § 11(g), 16 U.S.C. § 1540(g).

Notice of intent to sue. Virtually all of the citizen suit provisions require that at least sixty days before filing an enforcement action, plaintiffs must provide notice to government enforcement agencies and the alleged violator of their intent to sue. *See, e.g.*, RCRA § 7002, 42 U.S.C. § 6972(b)(1)(A). For potential consequences of failure to provide proper notice of intent to sue, see *Hallstrom v. Tillamook County*, 493 U.S. 20 (1989) (citizen suit under RCRA dismissed after pending in court for eight years due to attorney's failure to provide proper notice to EPA and state before filing original complaint).

Diligent prosecution. Citizen suits may be precluded when the government is "diligently prosecuting" an action against the violator. *See*, e.g., RCRA § 7002, 42 U.S.C. § 6972(b)(1)(B). Not infrequently, citizens will file suit where the government has taken some enforcement action, but citizens contend it is too weak or ineffectual to constitute "diligent prosecution." Court decisions on the issue of "diligent prosecution" are divided between those finding "diligent prosecution" and precluding citizen enforcement and those rejecting it and allowing citizen suits to proceed. For one infamous example of what diligent prosecution is *not*, see *Friends of the Earth v. Laidlaw Environmental Services*, 528 U.S. 167, 178 (2000) (no "diligent prosecution" where defendant drafted the state complaint and settlement agreement, paid the filing fee, and set a low penalty). Even so, for argument that courts frequently accord more deference to government prosecutions than Congress intended, *see* Jeffrey G. Miller, *Theme and Variations in Statutory Preclusions Against Successive Environmental Enforcement Actions by EPA and Citizens: Part One: Statutory Bars in Citizen Suit Provisions*, 28 HARV. ENVTL. L. REV. 401, 466 (2004).

Past violations. The Supreme Court significantly limited the reach of some citizen enforcement actions in *Gwaltney of Smithfield Ltd. v. Chesapeake Bay Foundation*, 484 U.S. 49 (1987), holding that the wording of the citizen suit provision of the Clean Water Act does not allow citizens to sue defendants for wholly past violations of that law. The *Gwaltney* decision had far-reaching implications because the great majority of environmental citizen suits are filed under the Clean Water Act and because other federal statutes have similarly worded citizen suit provisions (although not the Clean Air Act, which authorizes citizen suits for *repeated* past violations).

Sovereign immunity. In addition, citizen suits against federal, state, and tribal governments may be barred by sovereign immunity. *See, e.g., DOE v. Ohio,* 503 U.S. 607 (1992) (Congressional waiver of sovereign immunity for federal agencies must be "unequivocal" in order to sustain penalties under RCRA and Clean Water Act); *Seminole Tribe v. Florida*, 517 U.S. 44 (1996) (Congress lacks authority to abrogate states' Eleventh Amendment immunity from private suits in federal court); CERCLA § 101(21), 42 U.S.C. § 9601(21) (tribes not "persons" subject to suit under CERCLA).

Final agency action. In challenging agency actions, such as the adoption of regulations or the issuance of permits, certain preconditions must be met, including that the agency actions be "final," that they are "ripe for review," and that plaintiffs have exhausted administrative remedies or otherwise raised their objections in earlier proceedings before the agency. However, under the principle of enforcement discretion, agency decisions about whether or not to initiate an enforcement action are generally not reviewable by courts. *Heckler v. Chaney*, 470 U.S. 821 (1985).

Standing to sue. In addition to all preconditions, plaintiffs suing in federal court must demonstrate constitutional **standing to sue**. Questions of standing derive from Article III, section 2 of the U.S. Constitution, which limits the jurisdiction of federal courts to "cases" and "controversies." To establish constitutional standing, a plaintiff traditionally must prove (1) an **injury in fact** that is concrete, affects the plaintiff in a personal and individual way, and is actual or imminent; (2) that the injury complained of is **fairly traceable** to the actions of the defendant (causation); and (3) that an order in the plaintiff's favor will **redress** the injuries complained of (redressability). *Lujan v. Defenders of Wildlife*, 504 U.S. 555, 560–61 (1992). The Court has also imposed a "prudential limitation," one that can be altered by Congress, which requires that the plaintiff's injury arguably falls within the "zone of interest" that the statute the plaintiff is enforcing is designed to protect. In *Bennett v. Spear*, 520 U.S. 154 (1997), the Supreme Court held that citizen suit provisions authorizing "any person" to sue—language typically used in federal environmental statutes—establish the broadest possible zone of interests, authorizing any party with standing to sue. An association has standing to bring suit on behalf of its members when one or more of its members would otherwise have standing to sue in their own right, when the interests at stake are germane to the organization's purpose, and if neither the claim asserted nor the relief requested requires the participation of individual members in the lawsuit. *Hunt v. Wash. State Apple Adver. Comm'n*, 432 U.S. 333 (1977).

In its seminal decision in *Sierra Club v. Morton*, 405 U.S. 727 (1972), the Supreme Court held that injury to aesthetic and environmental values may be sufficient to establish standing, provided that the plaintiffs are among those personally injured. 20 years later, the Court issued another major decision on standing in *Lujan v. Defenders of*

Wildlife, 504 U.S. 555 (1992). Justice Scalia delivered the opinion of the Court, finding that conservation and environmental plaintiffs

> did not demonstrate that they suffered an injury in fact ... [because] they failed to show that one or more of their members would thereby be directly affected apart from the members' special interest in the subject. Affidavits of members claiming an intent to revisit project sites at some indefinite future time, at which time they will presumably be denied the opportunity to observe endangered animals, do not suffice, for they do not demonstrate an "imminent" injury. Respondents also mistakenly rely on a number of other novel standing theories. Their theory that any person using any part of a contiguous ecosystem adversely affected by a funded activity has standing even if the activity is located far away from the area of their use is inconsistent with this Court's opinion in *Lujan v. National Wildlife Federation*, 497 U.S. 871. And they state purely speculative, nonconcrete injuries when they argue that suit can be brought by anyone with an interest in studying or seeing endangered animals anywhere on the globe and anyone with a professional interest in such animals.

Id. at 562–557.

In *Citizens for a Better Environment v. Union Oil Company (Unocal) and Tosco Oil Company*, and *Communities for a Better Environment v. Exxon*, Bay Area environmental organizations and private individuals challenged Unocal's and Exxon's discharge of excessive amounts of selenium into the San Francisco Bay in violation of the oil companies' pollutant discharge permit limits. As a result of settlements reached in the two cases, the oil companies agreed to implement water treatment systems to comply with their selenium discharge permit limits and to contribute millions of dollars to local foundations to fund projects dedicated to the health of the San Francisco Bay and its ecosystem. *CBE v. Unocal* also established landmark precedent in the Ninth Circuit Court of Appeals, holding that citizens may sue polluters for violating their permit limits when previous government enforcement against those violations is inadequate. *See Citizens for a Better Environment v. Unocal Oil Co.*, 83 F. 3d 1111 (9th Cir. 1996).

In the third major standing case of the 1990s, *Steel Company v. Citizens for a Better Environment*, 523 U.S. 83 (1998), plaintiffs sued a manufacturing company for its failure to file reporting forms required under the Emergency Planning and Community Right-to-Know Act (EPCRA) from 1988 to 1995. The defendant had filed the overdue forms after receiving plaintiffs' sixty-day notice of intent to sue and before the litigation was initiated. The Supreme Court ruled that where a defendant has come into compliance at the time the complaint is filed, plaintiffs lack standing to bring a claim for civil penalties, at least where the penalties are awarded to the federal treasury, because such penalties could not redress plaintiffs' injuries. The Court held that in these circumstances plaintiffs (even those directly injured by defendant's noncompliance) share only an "undifferentiated public interest" in seeing compliance with the law.

In *Friends of the Earth v. Laidlaw Environmental Services*, 149 F.3d 303 (4th Cir. 1998), the Fourth Circuit decided an issue not addressed by *Steel Company*. If a defendant is in violation at the time a plaintiff files a complaint but comes into compliance at some other point during the litigation, does the plaintiff still have standing to sue for penalties? In *Laidlaw*, environmental groups and individual residents sued the operator of a hazardous waste incinerator for violating its Clean Water Act permit. The trial court found that Laidlaw had committed hundreds of violations through unpermitted discharges of toxic pollutants, including mercury, into the North Tyger River of South Carolina. At least 36 violations occurred after plaintiffs filed their complaint, and the court imposed a penalty of over $400,000. The trial court also found that Laidlaw had been in substantial compliance with its permit for several years by the time of the final order in the case, and denied plaintiffs' request for injunctive relief. The Fourth Circuit, relying on *Steel Company*, held that plaintiffs lacked standing to proceed because their only remaining relief requested was civil penalties paid to the federal treasury, and such penalties could not redress any injuries that plaintiffs had suffered. To the surprise of many, the Supreme Court reversed in *Friends of the Earth v. Laidlaw Environmental Services*, 528 U.S. 167 (2000). Justice Ginsburg delivered the opinion of the Court and, in particular, found "To the extent that [civil penalties] encourage defendants to discontinue current violations and deter them from committing future ones, they afford redress to citizen plaintiffs who are injured or threatened with injury as a consequence of ongoing unlawful conduct...."

In an important subsequent portion of its opinion, the *Laidlaw* Court addressed the related question of **mootness**. Defendant argued that plaintiffs' claim for penalties was moot because it had voluntarily come into substantial compliance with its permit after the complaint was filed, and later permanently closed the facility at which the violations had occurred. The Court ruled that a case "might become moot if subsequent events made it absolutely clear that the allegedly wrongful behavior could not reasonably be expected to recur," but that the "heavy burden" of demonstrating this rested with the party asserting mootness. The Court found that the effects of Laidlaw's voluntary compliance and facility closure were disputed facts that had not been litigated at the trial court, and remanded this question to the lower courts. *Id.* at 189, 193–94.

Exxon Baytown involves a citizen suit brought by Environment Texas Citizen Lobby and the Sierra Club for violations at a 3,400 acre ExxonMobil complex in Baytown, Texas. The federal district court found Exxon liable for more than 16,000 separate days of Clean Air Act violations and imposed a $20 million penalty (one of the largest civil penalties ever awarded in a Clean Air Act citizen suit). ExxonMobil never denied any of the violations but argued that civil penalties could only be imposed for *individual days* where plaintiffs could show that they had suffered actual injury on *that day.* Among the claimed injuries were various breathing difficulties and other physical symptoms, fear for their health, visual observation or smell of pollution from Exxon's plants, worry about the risk of explosions, limitation of outdoor activities, and changes in location of residences. While plaintiffs could directly correlate those experiences to several specific reportable events, they did not offer testimony to tie specific injury to every single one of the more than 16,000 violation days. Both the District Court and the Fifth Circuit found the testimony sufficient to establish standing under the prevailing case law. *Env't Tex. Citizen Lobby, Inc. v. ExxonMobil Corp.*, 968 F.3d 357, 363, 378 n.1 (5th Cir. 2020) (upheld on *en banc* review); *Env't Texas Citizen Lobby, Inc. v. ExxonMobil Corp.*, 123 F.4th 309 (5th Cir. 2024). Exxon petitioned for certiorari with the U.S. Supreme Court, supported by many states as amici. *See* Brief of Iowa, West Virginia, and 25 Other States as Amici Curiae Support Granting the Petition, *ExxonMobil Corp. v. Environment Texas Citizen Lobby Inc.*, No. 24-982 (Apr. 11, 2025)]. The U.S. Supreme Court denied the certiorari petition on June 30, 2025.

On the same day, the U.S. Supreme Court denied certiorari in another case challenging the constitutionality of certain citizen suits under the Clean Water Act. In denying the cert petition, the Court left standing a Ninth Circuit ruling in favor of citizen plaintiffs, finding the Port of Tacoma, Washington, responsible for controlling stormwater across the entire footprint of its transportation facilities. *Puget Soundkeeper Alliance v. Port of Tacoma*, 104 F.4th 95 (9th Cir. 2024). In support of the petition for certiorari, *amici curiae* alleged "serious constitutional concerns" grounded in federalism and separation of powers for allowing "private plaintiffs to bring an action in federal court against a state governmental entity for alleged violations of state law." *See Brief for the Chamber of Commerce of the United States as Amicus Curiae Supporting Petitioners, Port of Tacoma*, WL 4640259, at *5, *11–*12 (2024) (No. 24-350).

Notes and Questions

1. How important are citizen suits? If the Supreme Court were to significantly limit the availability of citizen enforcement, how big of a blow would that be to environmental justice? What do you think about the arguments that opponents have levied against citizen suits? For some additional discussion about the value of citizen enforcement as a tool for environmental justice, consider David E. Adelman & Jori Reilly-Diakun, *Environmental Citizen Suits and the Inequities of Races to the Top*, 92 U. Colo. L. Rev. 377 (2021); Bina R. Reddy, *No Accounting for Accountability? A Comment on Environmental Citizen Suits and the Inequities of Races to the Top*, 52 Envtl. L. Rep. (ELI) 10619 (2022).

2. Scalia's dissent. Dissenting from the majority's opinion in *Laidlaw*, Justice Scalia would have denied standing to sue for local residents who refused to engage in activities such as fishing and swimming in the river because of concerns for the contamination. Dismissing these community concerns as nothing but "subjective apprehensions," Justice Scalia pointed to the lack of data documenting exceedances of water quality standards in the river. 528 U.S. 167, 199 (2000). How might you respond to this argument? Can "subjective apprehensions" cause real harm—measurable, for example, in terms of physical stress or lost property values?

3. Standing as a barrier? Because environmental justice claims are often centered upon disproportionate burdens, cumulative impacts, and synergistic effects, how would you assess the ability of such plaintiffs to prove injury in fact sufficient for constitutional standing? Are worries regarding anonymity of members, for fear of retaliatory immigration action, for instance, something that attorneys or the courts can or should address? If so, how?

3. Benefits of Private Enforcement

Despite all the challenges and obstacles potentially facing citizen plaintiffs, citizen enforcement efforts can deliver discrete and significant benefits for communities experiencing environmental injustice. In the narrowest sense, enforcement actions that seek to ensure facility-level compliance can have a dramatic impact on the environmental conditions of surrounding neighborhoods and the health of the people who live there. Such suits can result in the installation of additional pollution controls, the cessation of polluting activities, adoption of cleaner practices, and the issuance of penalties that deter future violations (as endorsed by the majority in *Laidlaw*).

In many instances, especially in the context of direct enforcement against regulated entities that are in violation of the law (e.g., that are violating applicable limits or conditions included in a permit), citizen suit enforcement cases can end up in settlement. One benefit of settlement is that it can allow for the inclusion of conditions that might not otherwise be ordered by a court, including enhanced monitoring, fence-line monitoring, public availability of pollution data, and investment in beneficial community-based supplemental environmental projects ("SEPs"). For more discussion of SEPs, see Chapter 7: Government Enforcement.

Compliance and accountability. Increasingly, and often motivated by EJ concerns, enforcement efforts (and permitting and rulemaking efforts as well) are seeking specifically to improve the nature and quality of pollution monitoring. In the clean air context, for example, advocates in enforcement cases, permitting, and environmental rules have begun to focus more heavily on things like continuous emission monitoring and fence-line monitoring to enhance compliance, accountability, and information availability. Less reliable monitoring, like opacity limits or estimated emission using "emission factors," can lead to higher rates of air pollution release and make enforcement and accountability harder.

Continuous emission monitoring involves the operation of equipment that measures the rate of *pollution discharges* (e.g., from a smokestack) in real time on an ongoing basis and provides for the most reliable and consistent determination of compliance with pollution standards. Fence-line monitoring, on the other hand, for a facility that is subject to emission limitations for specific air pollutants, typically involves the installation and operation of air monitors at the *fence-line of a facility* that can detect *ambient concentrations* of the same air pollutants that are the subject of the facility's emission limits. A settlement agreement would then identify ambient "action levels"—that is, concentrations of pollutants at the fence-line that require the facility to take remedial steps (e.g., changing operational parameters, fixing leaks, or performing maintenance) to reduce the fence-line pollution concentrations. If the applicable reg-

Figure 12-2. Community members from the Birmingham, Alabama, area participating in "Smoke School," where they receive training and certification in EPA's "Method 9" for evaluating visible air emissions from local industrial facilities. Photo: Joshua Weichman, May 2025.

ulatory standard only imposes limitations on "emissions" (such as rates of pollution release from a smokestack or from fugitive emission sources like leaking pipes and valves), and does not impose "ambient concentration limits," the exceedance of a fence-line action level is not necessarily a violation of the underlying regulatory standard. But fence-line monitoring can significantly improve accountability, enhance regulatory compliance, and improve protections for surrounding communities. Additionally, the public availability of continuous emission monitoring and fence-line monitoring data can provide a powerful political tool for communities to engage in other kinds of self-advocacy, whether with local, state, or federal policymakers, or with polluting companies themselves.

For a specific example of this kind of settlement in action, consider the citizen enforcement litigation brought by East Yard Communities for Environmental Justice (represented by attorneys at Earthjustice) against two Phillips 66 refineries in Southern California. These facilities were subject to emission limitations for a host of harmful air toxics, including both smokestack and fugitive emission standards. However, East Yard's investigation in preparation for litigation demonstrated that the facilities were sometimes emitting as much as two hundred times the level of pollution allowed by their permits. The case resulted in a settlement that included:

- Adoption of a comprehensive state-of-the-art Leak Detection and Repair program at the refineries;
- Recordkeeping and reporting requirements (including submission of reports to East Yard);
- Internal and third-party auditing;
- Software and database updates for monitoring and recordkeeping; and
- Specific emission reduction projects, including paving of dirt parking lots that were producing dust, replacement of valves, and a community tree planting project.

CONSENT DECREE, *East Yard Communities For Environmental Justice v. Phillips 66 Company*, C.D. Cal. 2:21-cv-01088 (entered by Judge Fernando L. Aenlle-Rocha) (April 12, 2021).

Litigation as leverage. Returning to a central question of this chapter, after considering the barriers and practicalities of litigating cases to pursue environmental justice, is there any point? Professor Helen Kang emphasizes that litigation may be the only way for community residents to get a seat at the table with regulators and sources of pollution.

> Litigation is uniquely successful in motivating pollution sources to negotiate with community groups. Lawsuits force corporate decisionmakers to consider the merits and practicalities of their position at every stage of the case—from answering the complaint, to deciding whether to file motions to dismiss or for summary judgment, and eventually to devising positions for mandatory settlement conferences. The same is true when the lawsuit is filed against a regulator. Lawsuits force regulators to retract decisions that are without basis. In addition, where judicial decisions are necessary for statutory or regulatory interpretations, litigation is the only available recourse.

Helen H. Kang, *Pursuing Environmental Justice: Obstacles and Opportunities—Lessons from the Field*, 31 WASH. U. J. L. & POL'Y 121, 136–37 (2009).

Community groups have sometimes negotiated **"Good Neighbor Agreements"** in which industry commits to ongoing environmental improvements such as pollution prevention, emergency preparedness measures, or broader access to information for the public in exchange for the community settling ongoing challenges and ending protests or negative publicity. *See* Sanford Lewis, *Good Neighbor Agreements: A Tool for Environmental and Social Justice*, SOCIAL JUSTICE (Winter 1996). For a more recent and critical review of good neighbor agreements, examined through a case study from Portland, Oregon, *see* Thalia González & Giovanni Saarman, *Regulating Pollutants, Negative Externalities, and Good Neighbor Agreements: Who Bears the Burden of Protecting Communities?*, 41 ECOLOGY L.Q. 37 (2014).

A related approach that has become popular in recent years is a **Community Benefit Agreement (CBA)**. A CBA is a contract negotiated between a developer and a local community detailing the benefits that the developer will provide in exchange for front-end community support for a proposed project. For more detailed discussion of CBAs, see Chapter 10 (Private Governance). For scholarly analysis, *see* Seema Kakade, *A Contractual Relationship with Environmental Justice*, 73 AMERICAN U. L. REV. 343 (2023); Benjamin S. Beach, *Strategies and Lessons from the Los Angeles Community Benefits Experience*, 17 J. AFFORDABLE HOUSING 77 (Fall 2007/Winter 2008).

SLAPP suits. Community groups may encounter pressures against activism in the form of a Strategic Lawsuit Against Public Participation (SLAPP). SLAPPs are retaliatory actions filed by private developers or project applicants against organizations or individuals who oppose a project through litigation or other forms of advocacy. At their core, SLAPPs are a reaction to some political action; i.e., some effort to influence a government decision. Because they seek damages that easily can bankrupt a community or public interest group if successful, SLAPPs can chill public participation. As Professor Sheila Foster has pointed out, however, most SLAPPs are successfully defended, particularly on grounds that the underlying activity is protected by the First Amendment right to petition the government. She also notes that "the landscape of SLAPP litigation has become increasingly unfavorable to plaintiffs who bring SLAPPs, due to recent legislation that recognizes the antidemocratic nature of such lawsuits." Sheila Foster, *Public Participation, in* THE LAW OF ENVIRONMENTAL JUSTICE: THEORIES AND PROCEDURES TO ADDRESS DISPROPORTIONATE RISKS 225, 248–49 (Michael B. Gerrard & Sheila R. Foster eds., 2d ed. 2008).

Nevertheless, such aggressive strategies are still employed in response to environmental justice campaigns. In a significant recent example, in the wake of the protests and other action growing from the Standing Rock Sioux Tribe's opposition to the Dakota Access Pipeline, Energy Transfer (an owner and operator of oil pipelines that was leading the pipeline construction) filed a SLAPP suit against Greenpeace and Greenpeace International. In March 2025, a jury in Morton County, North Dakota, reached a verdict in the long-running lawsuit finding the Greenpeace entities liable for more than $660 million, based upon claims of defamation and racketeering.

Greenpeace itself stated:

> The lawsuits filed by Energy Transfer (ET) against Greenpeace International (GPI) and two Greenpeace entities in the United States (Greenpeace Inc., and Greenpeace Fund) since 2017 are clear-cut examples of SLAPPs.... Like all SLAPPs, ET's lawsuits have been an attempt to bury nonprofits and activists in legal fees, push them towards bankruptcy, and ultimately silence dissent. Not only does Energy Transfer's SLAPP attempt to erase the Indigenous leadership of the Standing Rock movement, but it poses a threat to free speech, basic expressions of solidarity, and peaceful protest.
>
> The absurd US$ 660 million jury verdict against Greenpeace entities in North Dakota made news, but this fight is bigger than the Greenpeace network. With the overwhelming support of allies all around the world, the defense against Energy Transfer's bullying tactics will continue for as long as it

> takes to secure the freedoms we all need to deliver a green, just and peaceful future for all. After nearly a decade of defending these SLAPPs, the Greenpeace Legal departments are prepared to continue as long as it takes!

See https://www.greenpeace.org/international/story/73887/greenpeace-trial-verdict-appeal-slapp-legal-process/ (April 1, 2025).

Similarly, in November 2015, Youth for Environmental Justice, South Central Youth Leadership Coalition, and the Center for Biological Diversity sued the City of Los Angeles, arguing that the City was not complying with its responsibilities under the California Environmental Quality Act and, instead, "rubber stamping" oil drilling applications. The case settled, but an oil industry trade group intervened in the case and challenged the settlement, accusing the City and nonprofits of settling the claims pursuant to a "strategy" of "secret[] and collusive negotiations." The California trial court agreed, but the Court of Appeal reversed, reasoning that the oil industry could not establish a probability of prevailing on the merits of its claim under California's anti-SLAPP statute, Code of Civil Procedure section 425.16. *Youth for Environmental Justice v. City of Los Angeles, California Independent Petroleum Association*, Super Ct. No. BC600373 (2019).

For additional insights on SLAPP suits, *see* Robert Sprague, *SLAPPed by RICO: Corporations Punishing Social Activism*, 55 Am. Bus. L.J. 763 (2018); James M. Redwine, *Does It Hurt to Get SLAPPed? A Study of the Perils of Citizen Involvement*, 32 Nat. Resources & Envt. 15 (2017); Brief of Amici Curiae Public Interest Advocacy Organizations in Support of Appellees, Morgan Banks, Plaintiffs-Appellant, v. David D. Hoffman, Defendants-Appellees., 2024 WL 5446558.

D. Common Law Remedies

Before the start of the modern environmental movement, common law actions were the primary tool for protecting the environment. Such actions would include tort claims for trespass, negligence, public and private nuisance, and ultra-hazardous activities. Although such actions largely receded into the background with the adoption of the major federal environmental laws beginning in the 1970s, they continued to be used at the local level, and have enjoyed periodic moments of resurgence of interest among practitioners in recent years. For an insightful reflection on the continuing value of common law remedies for environmental harms, *see* Michael Axline, *Differential Access to Justice in Environmental Cases Involving Private Property and Public Laws*, 27 J. Envtl. L. & Litig. 21 (2012). For a more comprehensive overview of this complex area of legal practice, *see* Robin Kundis Craig et al., Toxic and Environmental Torts: Cases and Materials (2nd ed. 2024).

Environmental plaintiffs have achieved some important successes in actions seeking damages from catastrophic spills or accidents and damages for injuries from harmful products such as asbestos. However, tort actions alleging harm from routine, ongoing environmental releases are much more difficult to win. Limited access to medical care can result in a lack of baseline health data prior to exposure. Work environments or other lifestyle factors can often be presented as alternative causal factors. A lack of scientific evidence on the causal connection between certain exposures and health problems poses a significant barrier for plaintiffs, and technical assistance with medical and scientific evidence can be costly. *See* Melissa Tofflon-Weiss & J. Timmons Roberts, *Toxic Torts, Public Interest Law, and Environmental Justice: Evidence from Louisiana*, 26 LAW & POL'Y 259 (2004); *see also* Allan Kanner, *Tort Remedies and Litigation Strategies*, *in* THE LAW OF ENVIRONMENTAL JUSTICE: THEORIES AND PROCEDURES TO ADDRESS DISPROPORTIONATE RISKS 667 (Michael B. Gerrard & Sheila R. Foster eds., 2d ed. 2008).

Notes and Questions

1. Common law and pesticides. Common law claims alleging harm from pesticide exposure have been difficult to maintain because until 2005, most appellate courts had found that the Federal Insecticide, Fungicide and Rodenticide Act (FIFRA) preempts state tort law claims related to pesticide warning and use labels. In *Bates v. Dow Agrosciences*, 544 U.S. 431 (2005), however, the Supreme Court reversed this jurisprudence, holding that common law claims for strict or negligent product liability, breach of warranty, and others were not preempted by FIFRA. It also ruled that plaintiffs' fraud and negligent failure to warn claims would not be preempted if state requirements were "equivalent to and fully consistent with" FIFRA's labeling requirements. For additional discussion of how tort claims related to pesticides can change corporate behavior, *see* Alexandra B. Klass, *Pesticides, Children's Health Policy, and Common Law Tort Claims*, 7 MINN. J.L. SCI. & TECH. 89 (2005); Valerie J. Watnick, *The "Roundup" Controversy: Glyphosate Litigation, Non-Hodgkin's Lymphoma, and Lessons for Toxics Regulation Going Forward*, 30 N.Y.U. ENVTL. L.J. 1 (2022).

2. Nuisance claims. Professor Kang has observed:

> Clients also commonly ask the clinic to file claims against pollution sources that cause a nuisance. These suits typically allege that facilities emit intense and persistent odors or contaminated dust. Our clinic has received requests to investigate or file lawsuits against a yeast manufacturing company, a Kraft pulp mill, a steel foundry, and a large construction project disturbing naturally occurring asbestos-laden rocks. The clients in these cases describe odors or dust that interrupt their lives and prevent them from fully enjoying their homes, schools, and neighborhoods. The odors and dust deter them from leaving windows open, sitting in their backyards, gardening, walking, biking, and relaxing after work. Like residents living near other sources of pollution, residents who live near a nuisance are burdened with persistent worries about their families' and their own health. Unfortunately, nuisances are not well regulated by state or federal pollution control laws....
>
> ... I argue that litigation is insufficient to address cumulative pollution or nuisance sources because, in addition to being resource intensive and difficult to pursue, it does not have the potential to cure the root cause of the problem

of cumulative pollution. In addition, while litigation may be successful in addressing particular nuisance sources, they tend to cause a nuisance wherever they operate, which suggests that broader national regulation, rather than individual litigation, is necessary to address the[se] problems....

... [T]ort litigation is difficult at best, and, even in successful cases, abatement of the problem is not a guaranteed remedy. Moreover, litigation under statutory environmental provisions can only produce relief that incidentally addresses the nuisance. For example, community members may privately enforce permit limits on volatile organic compounds and thereby reduce odors, but the limits may not be set low enough to eliminate the nuisance. In addition, there may be sources of odors other than volatile organic compounds, and a lawsuit to enforce limits on specific chemicals will not address those alternative sources. Professor Morag-Levine has also painstakingly documented that nuisance-based odor regulations administered by regional air quality districts rarely work. Such regimes rely on detection and confirmation of the complaints by government inspectors, who often cannot show up in time to make a confirmation.

Helen H. Kang, *Pursuing Environmental Justice: Obstacles and Opportunities—Lessons from the Field*, 31 WASH. U. J. L. & POL'Y 121, 135–144 (2009).

3. **"Nuisance with a twist."** Nevertheless, environmental justice advocates have successfully applied nuisance theories in campaigns. In the excerpt below, attorney Richard Drury chronicles how the residents of Huntington Park, a low-income, largely Latino community in southeastern Los Angeles, successfully used a public nuisance theory against a concrete crushing and recycling facility.

Richard T. Drury, *Moving a Mountain: The Struggle for Environmental Justice in Southeast Los Angeles*

38 ENVTL. L. REP. NEWS & ANALYSIS 10338 (2008)

In November 1993, ... [Aggregate Recycling Systems, Inc. (ARS)] approached the city of Huntington Park [California] with a proposal for a concrete recycling facility for a long-vacant lot.... ARS' owner, Sam Chew, proposed to take concrete debris and crush it for reuse as aggregate for roadbeds and for mixing with cement for new roads and structures. The city issued a permit for the facility and it opened for business....

Two months later, the Northridge earthquake [destroyed portions of the Santa Monica Freeway, just west of Huntington Park].... In its haste to [reconstruct the freeway], CalTrans [the California Department of Transportation] had left itself little time to consider how to dispose of the huge amount of debris that used to be the Santa Monica Freeway. As low bidder on the disposal contract, ARS took in much of the debris, and its formerly small recycling operation quickly became the massive La Montaña, an 80-foot-tall mountain containing 600,000 tons of concrete debris.... ARS moved its crushing equipment to the top of the mountain, and began operating the crushers around the clock in a futile attempt to keep up with the incoming loads.

The continuous crushing operations from the top of the mountain created a massive plume of particulate matter (PM) that blanketed streets up to an inch deep, and covered nearby homes, cars, furniture, food, dishes, and lawns, particularly on the downwind Cottage Street side of the facility, with a layer of sticky concrete dust. Residents of the low-income community, many without air conditioning, were forced to keep their doors and windows closed even in the squelching heat of the Los Angeles summer, and many had to abandon outdoor activities entirely. The highly caustic concrete dust caused many residents to suffer from respiratory problems, including bloody noses, sinus headaches and irritated noses, eyes, and throats. Many area children suffered increased asthma episodes, frequent bloody noses, and breathing difficulty. Some nearby businesses also experienced problems....

To remove La Montaña from Huntington Park and shut down the ARS facility, [Communities for a Better Environment (CBE), a local environmental group] undertook to organize the community, to marshal scientific evidence of the deleterious health effects of the pollution from ARS, and ultimately to take legal action....

[CBE] hire[d] veteran community organizer Alicia Rivera, ... [who] went door to door through the Cottage Street neighborhood to hear complaints directly from the people who were affected, and to encourage the neighbors to band together. In a short time, the neighbors were holding weekly house meetings.... The residents, now known as the Los Angeles Comunidades Asembleadas y Unidas para un Sostenible Ambiente, or Los Angeles Communities Assembled and United for a Sustainable Environment (LA CAUSA), decided to begin attending meetings of the Huntington Park City Council to raise their concerns [and] ... conducted pre-meeting rallies outside of City Hall.... Word of the popular uprising spread quickly, and soon local newspapers, radio, and television were covering the demonstrations outside the formerly sleepy Huntington Park City Council chambers ... [T]he community was now organized, and the issue of La Montaña had been injected into the politics of Huntington Park.

[CBE scientists] compiled a compelling mountain of evidence.... CBE retained an independent test lab to gather dust samples upwind and downwind of ARS. The company conducted polarized light microscopy on the samples, finding that 70% of the downwind samples were composed of concrete dust, while only 16% of the upwind samples were concrete.

[Huntington Park's] Mayor Loya obtained support from local doctors and the American Lung Association to test Cottage Street residents for respiratory problems. The study revealed that over one-half of the residents suffered from chronic obstructive pulmonary disease.

LA CAUSA members, supported by CBE staff, demonstrated at the South Coast Air Quality Management District (SCAQMD) to demand air testing by the agency. After meeting initial resistance, the SCAQMD agreed to conduct some tests. Despite giving

ARS advance notice of the test dates, the results of the downwind test revealed levels of total suspended particulates (TSP) higher than any ever recorded in central Los Angeles during the entire calendar year.

CBE also retained Los Angeles Unified School District atmospheric scientist Bill Piazza, who conducted sophisticated air quality modeling to demonstrate that PM levels generated by ARS were even higher than those measured by the SCAQMD....

Recognizing that the options for legal action under environmental statutes were limited, CBE's attorneys turned to the common law. The California Civil Code §§ 3479 and 3480 contain an expansive public nuisance provision. Section 3479 defines a nuisance as:

> Anything which is injurious to health ... or is indecent or offensive to the senses, or an obstruction to the free use of property, so as to interfere with the comfortable enjoyment of life or property, or unlawfully obstructs the free passage or use, in the customary manner, of any navigable lake, or river, bay, stream, canal, or basin, or any public park, square, street, or highway, is a nuisance.

Section 3480 defines a "public nuisance" to be one "which affects at the same time an entire community or neighborhood, or any considerable number of persons, although the extent of the annoyance or damage inflicted upon individuals may be unequal." CBE was aware of a long line of older California cases finding operations very similar to ARS' to be nuisances.... The common law approach was also advantageous because of the breadth and vagueness of the definition of nuisance under California law: if a nuisance action were brought in trial court, the judge would have broad discretion to determine whether the ARS facility was creating a nuisance and, if so, to balance the equities in determining the appropriate remedy.... In assessing ARS' potential defenses, CBE again saw some advantages to a common law approach. The California courts had held that a company may not claim a "permit defense." That is, a company may not create a nuisance even if it is operating its business under valid governmental permits. The courts had reasoned that a permit does not tacitly allow the company to create a nuisance even though the government has granted it a permit to operate....

The CBE legal team then discovered an interesting twist that offered the advantages of the common law of nuisance but eliminated many of the uncertainties of a nuisance lawsuit. Rather than sue ARS in California Superior Court, the residents and CBE could bring an administrative complaint for public nuisance before the city of Huntington Park. If the city could be persuaded to declare ARS to be a public nuisance, then ARS, not the residents, would have the burden of suing the city in the Superior Court to attempt to reverse the decision. But the result had some risks—the court would apply a highly deferential standard of review and likely support the city's determination either way, as long as it was supported by "substantial evidence." ...

Under [Huntington Park's] nuisance ordinance, any resident could petition to have a facility deemed a public nuisance. The matter would be assigned to an administrative law judge assigned by the city manager, and a decision could be appealed to the city council.... LA CAUSA launched a new organizing campaign to convince the city to institute a quasi-judicial administrative proceeding to determine whether ARS was creating a public nuisance pursuant to the city's nuisance ordinance.... [Thereafter] the city's attorney ... recommended that the city invoke its nuisance ordinance and commence a quasi-judicial public nuisance proceeding, as recommended by CBE and LA CAUSA.... [T]he city council agreed and retained the respected environmental lawyer Colin Lennard to preside as its hearing officer.

Lennard conducted five days of administrative hearings.... CBE's strategy was to combine real-life community experiences with scientific evidence and legal authority. CBE began the proceedings with almost a dozen area residents who testified to their personal experiences living near ARS—breathing problems, nosebleeds, asthma attacks, and hospitalizations. This testimony was supported by an atmospheric scientist, a respiratory health expert, an environmental scientist, and others who testified that ARS was the likely source of the residents' health problems and that the health problems were consistent with high-level exposure to concrete PM....

In defense, Chew primarily argued that the dust was created by Saroyan Lumber [a facility located on the other side of ARS]. His legal argument hinged almost entirely on the partial SCAQMD tests results, which found ARS not to be in violation of Air District regulations.... [H]earing officer Lennard found the SCAQMD's test results largely unpersuasive for a variety of reasons and rejected ARS' arguments.... Lennard found ARS to be creating a nuisance per se because it was violating several provisions of the Huntington Park municipal code.... He also found ARS' operations to constitute a public nuisance within the definitions of California Civil Code §§ 3479 and 3480 because its operations were injurious to the health of its neighbors, were offensive to the senses, and interfered with the comfortable enjoyment of property.

[Lennard issued an order abating the nuisance] requir[ing] ARS to render all of its equipment inoperable immediately and to cease all deliveries of new material to the site. ARS was required to hire an independent consultant to develop a plan to remove all debris from the site in an environmentally responsible manner that included controls for dust, noise, and vibrations, and which would eventually decrease the pile's height to a maximum of eight feet. ARS was to remove the debris within 60 days....

[In subsequent reviews, the city council affirmed Lennard's order and a superior court found that the city had substantial evidence to support its nuisance determination.] ARS still refused to clean up the concrete mountain, even though it had lost all of its legal challenges. The city then brought a criminal enforcement action against ARS, but the company pled poverty. ARS claimed that without any revenues from the receipt of new aggregate debris or from the sale of crushed material, it did not have funding to comply with the cleanup order....

[Epilogue: After the property sat idle for the next seven years, the city in 2004 secured $2 million in state funding to clean up La Montaña. At the urging of local community members, the city subsequently purchased the property and turned it into a park. See Figure 12-3 below.]

Figure 12-3. Raul R. Perez Memorial Park, site of the former "La Montaña" in Huntington Park, CA. Photo: Roselynn Loaiza, 2020.

Notes and Questions

1. Another tool in the toolbox? Prominent California attorney Richard Drury explains that his clients turned to nuisance law because of the weaknesses of applicable statutory remedies. Their options under the Clean Air Act were limited because the local air district had granted ARS a mobile source air permit, based on the fact that ARS used movable crushing equipment. The district's mobile source permitting rules were far more lenient than stationary source rules (on the assumption, inaccurate in the case of ARS, that a mobile source would not remain in one location for more than a few weeks). Likewise, the city had initially exempted ARS from review under California's environmental review statute, the California Environmental Quality Act, based on the company's representations that the project would have minimal impacts. In addition, the statute's very short (thirty-five day) statute of limitations for challenging that determination had long since passed. *See id.* at 182–83. What does the experience of this case suggest about the relative usefulness of common law approaches?

2. Nuisance and climate change. In a unanimous 2011 decision, the Supreme Court stated that the Clean Air Act displaced the federal common law of nuisance, leaving enforcement and regulation to the EPA. *American Electric Power v. Connecticut*, 564 U.S. 410 (2011). In 2017, cities including San Francisco and Oakland challenged oil companies, including BP, Chevron, ConocoPhillips, Exxon Mobile, and Royal Dutch Shell, attempting to use the nuisance doctrine at the state level. The cities alleged that the oil companies had long known of the climate risks posed by fossil fuels to the environment and downplayed those risks with public relations campaigns. The cities sought damages under a public nuisance theory to shift costs for adaptation projects, such as protecting coastlines from flooding, to the oil companies. The defendants removed the case to federal district court. Judge Aslup's opinion rejecting the lawsuit and motion to remand to state court held that plaintiff's nuisance claims are governed by federal common law, and reasoned "[t]he problem deserves a solution on a more vast scale than can be supplied by a district judge or jury in a public nuisance case." *City of Oakland v. BP*, 325 F. Supp. 3d, 1017, 1024–26 (N.D. Cal. 2018). The plaintiffs appealed the district court's ruling to the Ninth Circuit, which remanded concluding that the district court erred in determining that it had federal-question jurisdiction. *City of Oakland v. BP PLC*, 969 F.3d 895, 903 (9th Cir. 2020). It sent the case back to the district court to determine whether there was an alternative basis for jurisdiction.

Before the district court issued its new order in 2022, the Ninth Circuit issued two other opinions in similar actions denying removal jurisdiction. *See County of San Mateo v. Chevron Corp.*, 32 F.4th 733 (9th Cir. 2022); *City & County of Honolulu v. Sunoco LP*, 39 F.4th 1101 (9th Cir. 2022). Then in a November 2023 opinion, the court similarly ruled that the Energy Companies' removal arguments in this case also fail. *City of Oakland v. BP PLC*, No. 22-16810, 2023 WL 8179286 (9th Cir. Nov. 27, 2023).

Other cities and counties, including King County in Washington State, Rhode Island, the City of Baltimore, and Marin County, San Mateo County, and the City of Imperial Beach in California, have also mounted similar challenges against the fossil fuel industry. These various cases have been proceeding in state courts. For a more detailed discussion, and for more on other cities' application of tort theory to climate change and adaptation, *see* Albert C. Lin & Michael Burger, *State Public Nuisance Claims and Climate Change Adaptation*, 36 Pace Envtl. L. Rev. 49 (2018).

3. When to use tort law? Do you think environmental groups should rely more on tort cases as opposed to citizen enforcement actions to deter corporate noncompliance? On the one hand, damages in large tort cases (both actual and punitive damages) can sometimes far exceed the penalties imposed (or even theoretically available) in enforcement actions. On the other hand, establishing liability in a citizen enforcement case typically only requires establishing that a defendant violated a regulatory or permit requirement, and avoids complex and often insurmountable issues of causation. Which approach is preferable, and under what circumstances? For an example of a legally successful toxic tort lawsuit that failed to make the affected community feel whole, *see* Dennis Love, My City Was Gone: One American Town's Toxic Secret, Its Angry Band of Locals, and a $700 Million Day in Court (2006) (describing lawsuit against Monsanto for dumping polychlorinated biphenyls (PCBs) into Anniston, Alabama's local environment over a 40-year period, which resulted in a seven hundred million dollar settlement).

4. What would you do? If you were an attorney for community groups, what would you convey to your clients about the strengths and limitations of citizen suits and common law theories compared to regulation, governmental initiatives, and multi-party collaboration as a means of achieving environmental justice?

Chapter 13

Environmental Justice in International Law

Figure 13-1. At COP 28 in Dubai, United Arab Emirates, this pavilion mural depicts demands for systemic change over superficial fixes, centering justice, Indigenous rights, and people power. With bold messages like *"No Climate Justice Without Human Rights"* and *"No More Stolen Land,"* it captures the 2023 summit's urgent call for equity in climate solutions. COP (Conference of the Parties) is the UN's annual climate summit, bringing global leaders, activists, and scientists together to confront the climate crisis and push for meaningful, just action. Photo: Nadia Ahmad, 2023.

A. Introduction

The distribution of environmental benefits and burdens across the global community reveals patterns of inequality that mirror and reinforce existing structures of economic, political, and social marginalization. Those who contribute least to environmental degradation often bear its heaviest costs, while those who profit most from environmentally destructive activities frequently remain insulated from their consequences. This fundamental asymmetry between environmental harm and responsibility transcends national boundaries, creating what scholars have termed "environmental colonialism," the systematic exportation of environmental costs from the Global North to the Global South, from the wealthy to the poor, from the politically powerful to the marginalized. *See, e.g.*, José Arturo Maldonado Andreu, *The Legacies of Environmental Colonialism and the Legal Protection of Forests in Puerto Rico*, 93 REV. JUR. U.P.R. 289 (2024); ANIL

Agarwal & Sunita Narain, Global Warming in an Unequal World: A Case of Environmental Colonialism (1991).

International environmental justice emerges from this recognition that environmental problems cannot be understood or addressed without examining their distributional dimensions. Unlike domestic environmental justice movements that focus primarily on the disproportionate impacts of environmental burdens on local communities, international environmental justice encompasses a broader range of phenomena: the global trade in toxic waste that systematically flows from developed to developing countries; the displacement of Indigenous peoples from their traditional territories to make way for extractive industries that serve distant markets; the atmospheric appropriation by wealthy nations of the planet's carbon-absorbing capacity while externalizing the costs of global warming to vulnerable populations; and the exploitation of natural resources in politically weak states to serve the consumption patterns of affluent societies. The legal response to these patterns of environmental injustice has been fragmented, evolving across multiple international legal regimes, human rights law, environmental law, investment law, trade law, and criminal law, each with its own institutional framework, remedial mechanisms, and conceptual limitations. This fragmentation reflects deeper tensions within international law between competing values: sovereignty and accountability, economic development and environmental protection, state-centric governance and community-level justice.

This chapter examines the emergence and evolution of environmental justice as a principle of international law, tracing its development from early recognition of transboundary environmental harm through contemporary efforts to establish comprehensive frameworks for environmental rights and corporate accountability. The chapter proceeds through three interconnected parts that explore the theoretical foundations of international environmental justice, its jurisprudential development through landmark cases and institutional innovations, and the contemporary frameworks that will shape its future trajectory.

B. Theoretical Foundations and Historical Development

The theoretical foundations of international environmental justice rest upon a synthesis of distributive justice theory, human rights doctrine, and ecological jurisprudence that challenges traditional approaches to both environmental protection and international legal ordering. This synthesis has emerged from recognition that environmental degradation operates simultaneously as both cause and consequence of social inequality, creating complex patterns of harm that transcend temporal and spatial boundaries in ways that conventional legal frameworks have proven inadequate to address. International environmental justice differs fundamentally from its domestic counterpart in both scope and complexity. While domestic environmental justice movements typically focus on the discriminatory environmental burdens within single jurisdictions, international environmental justice must contend with multiple overlapping legal systems, vast disparities in economic and political power between states, and cultural and linguistic barriers that complicate community mobilization and legal advocacy. Moreover, the remedial mechanisms available in international law, primarily state-to-state dispute resolution and individual petition systems, can prove inadequate to address the collective dimensions of environmental harm or to provide effective relief to affected communities.

The theoretical framework of international environmental justice has evolved through the interaction of several intellectual traditions. Environmental justice theory reveals that environmental harms follow systematic patterns of social, economic, and political inequality rather than random distribution. Human rights law provides the normative foundation, recognizing inherent human dignity and state obligations to protect fundamental rights. Meanwhile, postcolonial analysis exposes how today's environmental inequalities echo historical colonial extraction and exploitation patterns. Ecological economics contributes crucial insights about biophysical growth limits and the urgent need for development models prioritizing both ecological sustainability and social equity.

1. Historical Emergence: From Sovereignty to Responsibility

The evolution of international environmental justice can be traced through several distinct phases, each characterized by different conceptions of the relationship between state sovereignty, environmental protection, and community welfare. The earliest phase, extending from the late nineteenth century through the mid-twentieth century, was dominated by a territorial conception of environmental harm that focused primarily on direct physical damage to state territory or economic interests. The paradigmatic case from this period, the *Trail Smelter Arbitration* between the United States and Canada (1938–1941), established the foundational principle that states may not use their territory in ways that cause significant harm to neighboring states, but paid little attention to the actual experiences of affected communities.

The second phase, beginning with the 1972 Stockholm Declaration and extending through the 1992 Rio Conference, witnessed growing recognition of the global dimensions of environmental problems and the need for international cooperation in environmental protection. However, this period remained largely state-centric in its approach, emphasizing cooperation between governments rather than protection of affected communities. The Stockholm Declaration's recognition of the human right to a healthy environment represented an important normative development but lacked the institutional mechanisms necessary for effective implementation.

The third phase, emerging in the 1990s and continuing to the present, has been characterized by the proliferation of international environmental justice claims in regional human rights systems, investment arbitration panels, and international criminal law forums. This phase has witnessed the development of more sophisticated approaches to environmental harm that integrate human rights, environmental, and development concerns, though implementation remains highly variable across different institutional contexts.

2. The 1972 Stockholm Declaration: Foundational Aspirations and Limitations

The theoretical framework of international environmental justice has evolved through the interaction of several intellectual traditions. The United Nations Conference on the Human Environment, held in Stockholm in 1972, marked the first global recognition of the interconnection between environmental quality and human welfare, establishing principles that would influence environmental law development for decades to come. Principle 1 of the Stockholm Declaration proclaimed that humans have "the fundamental right to freedom, equality and adequate conditions of life, in an environment of a quality that permits a life of dignity and well-being, [bearing] a solemn responsibility to protect and improve the environment for present and future generations."

This language represented a significant normative advance, linking environmental quality directly to human dignity and establishing the concept of intergenerational responsibility that would become central to environmental justice advocacy. However, the Declaration's impact was limited by several factors that continue to constrain international environmental justice efforts. The Declaration was framed as "soft law," politically binding but legally non-enforceable, reflecting the reluctance of states to accept binding international obligations regarding their domestic environmental policies. The Declaration's anthropocentric approach, while acknowledging the instrumental value of environmental protection for human welfare, failed to recognize the intrinsic value of natural systems or the rights of non-human nature that have become important themes in contemporary environmental justice discourse.

The Declaration's state-centric approach provided no mechanisms for affected communities to enforce their environmental rights or to participate meaningfully in international environmental governance. This limitation reflected broader tensions within international law between sovereignty and accountability that continue to complicate efforts to address environmental injustice across national boundaries. The Stockholm Declaration's legacy is thus ambivalent: while it established important normative foundations for international environmental protection, it also embedded certain limitations, state-centrism, anthropocentrism, and the absence of enforcement mechanisms that continue to constrain the effectiveness of international environmental justice advocacy.

3. Indigenous Rights and the Decolonization of International Environmental Law

International environmental justice theory has developed through interactions across multiple intellectual traditions, with Indigenous peoples' relationship to environmental law representing perhaps the most transformative development. This evolution challenges both anthropocentric environmental law and Eurocentric legal assumptions. Indigenous communities globally bear disproportionate environmental burdens from extractive industries, infrastructure projects, and conservation initiatives. Paradoxically, these same communities protect much of the world's remaining biodiversity and hold invaluable traditional ecological knowledge. International Indigenous rights law has emerged as a powerful tool for environmental justice advocacy, directly confronting the commodification of nature and the marginalization of alternative knowledge systems. Two key instruments anchor this framework: the International Labour Organization's Convention 169 (1989), which established consultation and consent principles for development projects affecting Indigenous territories, and the UN Declaration on the Rights of Indigenous Peoples (2007). Article 29 of the Declaration states that Indigenous peoples have rights to environmental conservation and protection of their lands' productive capacity, while requiring their free, prior, and informed consent before any hazardous material storage or disposal.

"Free, prior and informed consent" has become central to environmental justice advocacy, offering a framework to challenge projects imposing environmental costs without genuine community agreement. Yet implementation remains contentious, with ongoing disputes over legal status, scope, and practical requirements. Indigenous contributions extend beyond specific legal provisions to fundamental challenges of Western legal categories. Indigenous legal traditions recognize natural entities as having agency and inherent value. This perspective suggests alternative governance frameworks potentially more effective and just than state-centric approaches. The growing recognition of "rights of nature" in national legal systems reflects Indigenous concepts' influence on contemporary environmental law.

4. The Right to a Healthy Environment: Normative Development and Institutional Fragmentation

The theoretical framework of international environmental justice has evolved through the interaction of several intellectual traditions. The recognition of a human right to a healthy environment represents perhaps the most significant normative development in international environmental justice, providing a conceptual framework that links environmental protection directly to fundamental human rights principles. The development of this right has been characterized by institutional fragmentation with different international and regional bodies adopting varying approaches to its content, scope, and implementation. At the global level, the human right to a healthy environment has developed primarily through the work of UN human rights mechanisms, including special rapporteurs, treaty bodies, and the Human Rights Council. The appointment of Professor John Knox as the first UN Special Rapporteur on human rights and the environment in 2012 (initially titled "human rights obligations relating to the enjoyment of a safe, clean, healthy and sustainable environment") marked a significant institutional development, providing a focal point for developing the normative content of environmental rights and documenting violations worldwide.

In 2021, the UN Human Rights Council adopted Resolution 48/13, recognizing "the right to a clean, healthy and sustainable environment as a human right that is important for the enjoyment of human rights." The UN General Assembly followed with Resolution 76/300 in 2022, formally recognizing this right at the global level. While these resolutions are not legally binding, they provide authoritative interpretation of existing human rights obligations and create political momentum for further development of environmental rights. The normative content of the right to a healthy environment encompasses both procedural and substantive dimensions. The procedural dimensions include rights to environmental information, participation in environmental decision-making, and access to effective remedies when environmental rights are violated. These procedural rights are essential to environmental justice because they provide mechanisms through which affected communities can challenge environmental decisions and seek remedies for environmental harm. The substantive dimensions of the right include protection from environmental hazards that threaten life, health, and well-being, as well as positive obligations to maintain environmental conditions necessary for human flourishing. The scope of these substantive obligations remains contested, with ongoing debates about their extraterritorial application, the standard of environmental protection required, and the relationship between environmental rights and other human rights. Regional human rights systems have developed more detailed jurisprudence regarding environmental rights, often in cases involving marginalized communities challenging pollution or resource extraction projects. The African Charter on Human and Peoples' Rights explicitly recognizes the right to a "general satisfactory environment favorable to development," while the additional Protocol to the American Convention on Human Rights recognizes the right to a healthy environment. The European system, lacking an explicit environmental right, has developed extensive environmental jurisprudence through existing civil and political rights, particularly the right to private and family life.

Sumudu Atapattu, *The Right to a Healthy Life or the Right to Die Polluted?: The Emergence of a Human Right to a Healthy Environment Under International Law*

16 Tulane Envtl. L.J. 65 (2002)

The theoretical framework of international environmental justice has evolved through the interaction of several intellectual traditions. Several recognized procedural rights are increasingly applied in relation to environmental issues and are generally considered as forming part of environmental rights. These rights are found in international human rights law and reflected in most national constitutions. These rights include the freedom of information, the right to participate in the decision-making process, and the right to seek redress for violations of rights. The importance of these rights is that they contribute to the development of a decision-making process which is transparent and participatory and which holds the government entity in question accountable for its actions. Applied in relation to environmental issues these include: the right to have access to information affecting one's environment, the right to participate in decisions affecting the environment, and the right to seek redress in the event one's environment is impaired. While the former two rights are clear cut, it is in relation to the latter that a separate right to a healthy environment can be invaluable. While recourse may be available at the national level for public nuisance, such as damage caused by pollution, etc., the acceptance of a distinct right to a healthy environment would elevate it to the status of other fundamental rights, according it with the same importance and allowing the victims to resort to the same machinery. Without such a right, victims must rely on existing human rights such as the right to health, the right to an adequate standard of living, and the right to privacy. Additionally, the tribunal in question may or may not make the connection between the alleged human rights violation and the environmental problem in question.

Several international instruments, both binding and nonbinding, endorse environmental procedural rights. The provisions in the World Charter for Nature have already been noted. The Rio Declaration also contains several provisions on these rights....

The Draft Principles on Human Rights and the Environment appended to the Final Progress Report of the Special Rapporteur on Human Rights and the Environment, on the other hand, contain a comprehensive set of rights, both procedural and substantive. Only the procedural rights will be dealt with here.

The Draft Principles on Human Rights and the Environment specifically link environmental protection with human rights and also recognize that sustainable development links the right to development with the right to a healthy environment. The procedural rights incorporated in the Draft Declaration are wider than those which are found in instruments adopted by states. The provisions also specifically link existing human rights, such as freedom of expression and association, to environmental issues.

Part III of the Draft Principles on Human Rights and the Environment deals with procedural rights:

- Right to information concerning the environment;
- "[R]ight to hold and express opinions and to disseminate ideas and information regarding the environment";
- Right to environmental and human rights education;
- "[R]ight to active, free and meaningful participation in planning and decision-making activities." This includes the right to prior assessment of activities for

their environmental, developmental, and human rights consequences of proposed actions;

- Right to free and peaceful association for the purpose of protecting the environment or the rights of those affected by environmental harm; and
- "[R]ight to effective remedies and redress in judicial or administrative proceedings for environmental harm or the threat of such harm."

This is the first time that prior assessment of activities (i.e., the [Environmental Impact Assessment] EIA process) is embodied in rights language. In other words, the declaration provides that the prior assessment of activities is a right of everybody. This includes the assessment of environmental, developmental, and human rights consequences. As can be seen, these rights are wider than those in the instruments adopted so far by states in relation to environmental rights. They are not, however, alien to human rights law. The right to effective remedies is also wider than most formulations as it extends the right to threats of environmental harm. This right is invaluable as action can be taken before environmental harm actually takes place.

The corresponding duties on the part of States Parties to the Convention are to ensure that officials assist the public in seeking information, facilitate participation in the decision-making process, and in seeking access to justice. Furthermore, the parties are required to promote environmental education and awareness in order to promote these rights. Access to information seems to be the core right among these, without which participation in the decision-making process would be meaningless and ineffective.

Notes and Questions

1. **Environmental colonialism and distributive justice.** Analyze the concept of "environmental colonialism" and evaluate how environmental burdens are systematically transferred from the Global North to the Global South. Consider examples like the global toxic waste trade, displacement of Indigenous peoples for extractive industries, wealthy nations' carbon emissions affecting vulnerable populations, and resource extraction in weak states serving affluent consumption patterns. How do these patterns reinforce existing structures of marginalization?

2. **Sovereignty vs. accountability in environmental governance.** The text identifies a tension between state sovereignty and environmental accountability in international law. How does this tension limit environmental justice mechanisms? Why do you imagine that state-centric dispute resolution may fail to address collective environmental harms affecting marginalized communities?

3. **Indigenous rights and decolonizing environmental law.** How do Indigenous rights challenge traditional Western environmental law? Analyze concepts like "free, prior and informed consent" and "rights of nature" found in ILO Convention 169 and the UN Declaration on the Rights of Indigenous Peoples. Consider how Indigenous legal traditions that recognize natural entities as having inherent value, rather than merely instrumental value, offer alternatives to anthropocentric environmental governance.

C. Jurisprudential Development Through International Tribunals

1. Transboundary Environmental Harm: From State Injury to Community Impact

The jurisprudential development of international environmental justice has proceeded primarily through cases involving transboundary environmental harm, where pollution or resource extraction in one state causes environmental damage affecting communities in neighboring states. While these cases have established important principles regarding state responsibility for environmental harm, they have also revealed the limitations of state-centric approaches to environmental protection when addressing community-level environmental justice concerns.

2. The *Trail Smelter* Legacy: Foundational Principles and Persistent Limitations

The *Trail Smelter Arbitration* between the United States and Canada (1938–1941) established the foundational principle of international environmental law that "no State has the right to use or permit the use of its territory in such a manner as to cause injury by fumes to the territory of another." This principle, derived from domestic nuisance law, provided the first clear statement of international liability for transboundary environmental harm and continues to influence contemporary environmental law development. The factual context of Trail Smelter exemplified many characteristics that would later be recognized as environmental injustice: a Canadian smelter operation that generated significant profits for a multinational corporation while causing significant air pollution that crossed into the United States and imposed severe environmental costs on farming communities in the State of Washington. The affected farmers, predominantly of modest means, lacked the political influence to challenge the smelter's operations through domestic political processes and were forced to rely on diplomatic intervention by the U.S. government.

The arbitral tribunal's approach, while groundbreaking in establishing international environmental liability, reflected the limitations of state-centric international law in addressing community-level environmental justice concerns. The tribunal focused primarily on compensation for measurable economic losses, primarily crop damage, while paying little attention to broader environmental and health impacts on affected communities. The remedy consisted entirely of monetary compensation paid by Canada to the United States, with no guarantee that affected farmers would receive adequate compensation or that future environmental harm would be prevented.

Moreover, the tribunal's narrow focus on direct physical harm across international boundaries established a precedent that would prove inadequate for addressing many forms of environmental injustice, which often involve more subtle forms of environmental degradation or harm that occurs entirely within single states but affects internationally protected communities such as Indigenous peoples or racial minorities. The *Trail Smelter* principle has been repeatedly reaffirmed in subsequent international environmental law developments, including the Stockholm Declaration (Principle 21), the Rio Declaration (Principle 2), and numerous decisions of international courts and tribunals. However, its state-centric approach continues to limit its effectiveness in addressing environmental justice concerns, particularly those involving non-state actors or environmental harm that does not clearly cross international boundaries.

Russell A. Miller, *Pandemic as Transboundary Harm: Lessons from the Trail Smelter Arbitration*

55 N.Y.U. J. Int'l L. & Pol. (2023)

Causation was a central—maybe *the* central—factual issue in the *Trail Smelter Arbitration*.... [T]he case was concerned with harm occurring after 1932 up to the date of the Tribunal's first decision in 1938. The Tribunal's 1941 decision did not have to address the issue of causation because it found that the United States failed to prove that any serious harm had occurred in the state of Washington after 1938. To confuse matters regarding this material element of the Transboundary Harm Principle, the arbitrators' treatment of the issue of causation in the 1938 decision sometimes conflated several of the questions the tribunal was charged with answering, including the existence of a serious injury; whether the smelter in Canada was the cause of that harm; and the valuation of the indemnity, if any, that should be ordered as compensation for the harm. Often, the same evidence informed each of these inquiries.

Despite that lack of clarity, it is possible to divine the arbitrators' approach to the Transboundary Harm Principle's causation element. This consisted of the collection and independent consideration of extensive scientific data as well as lay testimony. The tribunal had the benefit of evidence developed through cooperative means, as had been mandated by the Special Agreement between the U.S. and Canada. The parties also contributed evidence—or advocated a particular interpretation of evidence—in an adversarial manner.

To begin, the arbitrators seemed to take notice of the fact that the Sulphur dioxide fumigations resulting from Trail Smelter's massive industrial activities could be the cause of property and environmental harm, especially in the form of "smoke damage" to crops and timber, as well as fungal "rusting" damage to vegetation. A primary proof of this phenomenon took the form of the smelter's seeming concession on this point in earlier proceedings (both domestic and international) in the case. The arbitrators took notice of this factual background, concluding that "from 1925, at least, to the end of 1931, damage occurred in the state of Washington, resulting from the Sulphur dioxide emitted from the Trail Smelter." From this, it seemed settled that the smelter's fumigations were injurious to property and the environment. The fact of Canada's failure to prevent the harmful activity by adequately regulating it could be taken for granted by the tribunal. The real issues of causation became whether the smelter's harmful fumigations were reaching the U.S. and to what degree the harmful effects of the smelter's smoke were mitigated by distance from the source and climatic conditions in the Columbia River valley.

The *Trail Smelter Arbitration* involved a considerable amount of new evidence relating to the causes of the serious harm it confirmed in the years from 1932 to 1938. The new evidence of causation presented to the arbitrators was extensive, varied, and complex. It included data from investigations jointly approved by the parties, such as emissions monitoring at Trail Smelter that sought to assess the nature, duration, and concentration of Sulphur fumigations. The tribunal concluded that these investigations had high "scientific value" as regards the question of causation. Other evidence of causation presented to the tribunal included expert and lay testimony. The arbitrators noted, however, that this testimony was sometimes inconclusive as the all-too-common clash of experts could point in opposite directions.

The various sources of evidence and the spotty quality or inconclusiveness of some of the science presented to the tribunal made it difficult for the arbitrators to conclude that the smelter caused the confirmed damage in the United States. The problem for the tribunal was that the evidence seemed to suggest that there had been episodic, scattered, and diminishing fumigations south of the border. This led the arbitrators to reject the theory of causation that had preoccupied both parties in the dispute. Instead of attributing the harm in the United States to Sulphur dioxide carried across the border by "surface winds," the tribunal turned its attention to evidence suggesting that the harmful smoke was carried into the United States by the "upper air currents." The arbitrators noted that fumes from the tall smoke stacks at the smelter enter "upper air currents, and are carried by these currents in a fairly continuous stream down the valley... [and] that the velocity and persistence of the upper air currents is greater than that of the surface winds." The evidence supporting this theory allowed the tribunal to conclude that "the upper air currents are a likely cause of the depositing of [harmful] Sulphur dioxide in the U.S."

But that conclusion on causation in the case was not the end of the tribunal's assessment. It went on to account for "the rate of attenuation of concentration of Sulphur dioxide with increasing distance from the smelter." The arbitrators demarcated the farthest geographic extent and the general intensity of the damage in the United States caused by the smelter's fumigations. Within these parameters, the tribunal found that the smelter's smoke was the cause of reduced crop yields in varying degrees in 1932 through 1937. Some of this damage, the tribunal concluded, rose to the level of seriousness under the Transboundary Harm Principle and therefore merited indemnification.

3. Sustainable Development and Procedural Innovation

The International Court of Justice's judgment in *Gabčíkovo-Nagymaros Project* (Hungary/Slovakia, 1997) represented a significant evolution in international environmental jurisprudence, introducing concepts of sustainable development and environmental assessment that have important implications for environmental justice advocacy. The case involved a complex dispute over a massive dam and hydroelectric project on the Danube River, with Hungary arguing that the project would cause irreversible ecological damage to the Danube ecosystem and Slovakia maintaining that the project was essential for economic development and flood control.

While the case was framed as a treaty dispute between two states, the underlying issues reflected broader patterns of environmental injustice associated with large infrastructure projects. The affected Szigetköz region was home to numerous small communities that depended on the Danube's natural flood cycles for their agricultural livelihoods and cultural practices. The proposed project would have fundamentally altered these flood patterns, potentially destroying traditional ways of life without providing corresponding benefits to affected communities. The Court's judgment established several important principles for international environmental law that have particular relevance for environmental justice advocacy. First, the Court recognized sustainable development as a concept that reconciles economic development with environmental protection, stating that "the need to reconcile economic development with protection of the environment is aptly expressed in the concept of sustainable development." This recognition provided normative foundation for challenging development projects that impose environmental costs without corresponding benefits for affected communities.

The Court emphasized the importance of environmental impact assessment (EIA) as a procedural requirement for major development projects, noting that "in the field of environmental protection, vigilance and prevention are required on account of the irreversible character of damage to the environment and of the limitations inherent in the very mechanism of reparation of this type of damage." While the Court did not explicitly require community participation in environmental assessment processes, its emphasis on prevention and precaution suggests the importance of inclusive decision-making processes that consider all potential impacts.

The Court's recognition of the principle of *intergenerational equity*, though not explicitly stated, is implicit in its emphasis on preventing irreversible environmental damage and ensuring that development meets present needs without compromising future generations' ability to meet their own needs. This principle has become central to environmental justice advocacy, particularly in cases involving Indigenous peoples whose traditional territories are threatened by extractive industries. The Court's remedial approach in *Gabčíkovo-Nagymaros* also demonstrated innovation in addressing complex environmental disputes. Rather than simply ordering cessation of unlawful conduct or payment of compensation, the Court required the parties to negotiate a comprehensive settlement that would address both environmental protection and development needs. This approach recognized that environmental disputes often require ongoing cooperation and adaptive management rather than simple legal remedies.

D. Regional Human Rights Systems

Regional human rights systems have emerged as the most important forums for developing international environmental justice jurisprudence, providing accessible venues for affected communities to challenge environmental harm and sympathetic judicial bodies willing to interpret human rights obligations in ways that protect environmental quality. The comparative advantage of regional systems lies in their ability to develop context-specific approaches to environmental justice while maintaining sufficient legal authority to create binding obligations for member states.

1. The Inter-American System

The Inter-American human rights system has developed perhaps the most sophisticated approach to environmental justice, particularly regarding Indigenous peoples' rights to traditional territories threatened by extractive industries and development projects. The system's jurisdiction over a region characterized by significant Indigenous populations, abundant natural resources, and persistent social inequality has provided opportunities to develop comprehensive approaches to environmental justice that integrate human rights law with environmental protection and development policy.

Mayagna (Sumo) Awas Tingni Community v. Nicaragua

Inter-American Court of Human Rights, 2001

The *Awas Tingni* case represented the first decision by an international human rights tribunal to recognize Indigenous peoples' collective property rights to traditional territories, establishing precedents that have influenced environmental justice advocacy worldwide. The case involved the Mayagna people's challenge to Nicaragua's granting of a logging concession covering 62,000 hectares of their traditional territory without consultation or consent. The factual pattern exemplified environmental injustice in multiple dimensions: a marginalized Indigenous community whose traditional territory was allocated to foreign corporations without consultation; environmental degradation that threatened both biodiversity and traditional ways of life; and economic benefits that flowed primarily to distant shareholders while environmental costs were borne by local communities.

The Inter-American Court's judgment established several groundbreaking principles for international environmental justice. First, the Court recognized that Indigenous peoples possess collective property rights to their traditional territories that exist independently of formal state recognition, stating: "indigenous peoples' communal property rights over lands do not require the existence of a title deed issued by the State; they require only possession of the land and use and enjoyment of it in accordance with ancestral customs."

This finding challenged fundamental assumptions about property rights in international law, which traditionally recognized only individual property rights formally recognized by states. The Court's approach acknowledged that Indigenous peoples' relationships to territory encompass cultural, spiritual, and ecological dimensions that cannot be adequately protected through individual property concepts. Second, the Court established that states have positive obligations to protect Indigenous territories from environmental degradation, including obligations to demarcate territorial boundaries, establish legal protections against encroachment, and ensure that any development projects affecting Indigenous territories receive Indigenous consent. These obligations recognize that meaningful protection of Indigenous rights requires active state intervention rather than mere non-interference. Third, the Court's remedial approach emphasized collective rather than individual relief, ordering Nicaragua to demarcate Awas Tingni territory, establish legal protections for Indigenous territorial rights, and create mechanisms for Indigenous participation in decisions affecting their territory. The *Awas Tingni* decision has influenced environmental justice advocacy far beyond the Inter-American region, providing legal precedent for Indigenous territorial rights claims in various national legal systems and inspiring similar litigation strategies in other regional human rights systems.

Saramaka People v. Suriname

Inter-American Court of Human Rights, 2007

The *Saramaka* case extended the principles established in *Awas Tingni* to address more complex issues involving extractive industries and the balance between development rights and environmental protection. The case involved the Saramaka people's challenge to Suriname's granting of logging and mining concessions covering their traditional territory without consultation or benefit-sharing. The Saramaka people, descendants of enslaved Africans who escaped plantation slavery and established autonomous communities in Suriname/s interior, faced particular challenges in asserting their territorial rights. Unlike Indigenous peoples, who often enjoy special recognition under international law, the Saramaka people were required to demonstrate that they constituted a "tribal people" deserving similar protections. The Inter-American Court found that the Saramaka people constituted a tribal community with rights to collective property over their traditional territory, extending the *Awas Tingni* precedent beyond Indigenous peoples to include other communities with special relationships to territory. This finding has important implications for environmental justice advocacy involving Afro-descendant communities, pastoralist societies, and other groups whose territorial relationships may not fit conventional Indigenous rights frameworks. More significantly for environmental justice, the Court addressed the complex issue of natural resource extraction on traditional territories, establishing detailed requirements for state obligations regarding extractive industries. The Court held that states may authorize extractive activities on traditional territories only if they:

1. Ensure effective participation of affected communities in accordance with their customs and traditions;
2. Guarantee that communities receive reasonable benefits from extractive projects; and
3. Conduct environmental and social impact assessments prior to project implementation.

These requirements represent the most detailed international legal standards for addressing environmental justice concerns related to extractive industries, providing concrete guidance for challenging projects that impose environmental costs on marginalized communities without corresponding benefits.

The Court's emphasis on benefit-sharing represents a particularly important innovation, recognizing that environmental justice requires not merely consultation about potentially harmful projects but also equitable distribution of economic benefits from natural resource extraction. This principle challenges traditional approaches to development that treat natural resources as national assets subject to state sovereignty while ignoring the rights of communities who have traditionally managed and depended upon these resources. The environmental impact assessment requirement established by the Court goes beyond technical environmental review to encompass social and cultural impact assessment, recognizing that environmental degradation often involves complex interactions between ecological and social systems. This broader approach to impact assessment reflects understanding that environmental justice requires attention to cultural and spiritual dimensions of environmental harm rather than narrow focus on physical pollution or resource depletion.

2. The African System: Environmental Rights and Resource Extraction

The African human rights system has developed important environmental justice jurisprudence addressing the intersection of environmental degradation, resource extraction, and social inequality across the continent. The African Charter on Human and Peoples' Rights, unique among regional human rights instruments in explicitly recognizing the right to a "satisfactory environment favorable to development," has provided normative foundation for addressing environmental injustice in various African contexts.

Social and Economic Rights Action Center v. Nigeria (The *Ogoni* Case)

African Commission on Human and Peoples' Rights, 2001

The *Ogoni* case represents the most significant decision in international environmental justice jurisprudence, establishing comprehensive standards for state obligations regarding environmental protection and corporate accountability. The case involved the environmental devastation of Nigeria's Niger Delta region caused by oil extraction activities conducted by Shell and other international oil companies with the support and complicity of the Nigerian government.

The factual context exemplified environmental injustice on a massive scale: the Ogoni people, numbering approximately 500,000, had experienced decades of environmental destruction that contaminated their land, water, and air while generating enormous profits for international oil companies and the Nigerian government. The complainants documented extensive pollution including oil spills, gas flaring, waste dumping, and deforestation that destroyed agricultural land, fishing areas, and drinking water sources essential to Ogoni livelihoods.

The African Commission's decision found multiple violations of the African Charter, including violations of the rights to life, health, property, food, water, and a satisfactory environment. The Commission's analysis provided sophisticated understanding of the interconnections between environmental degradation and human rights violations, recognizing that environmental destruction can violate fundamental rights even when it does not directly cause death or physical injury. Regarding the right to life, the Commission found that environmental contamination that threatens community health constitutes a violation of the right to life, stating: "The pollution and environmental degradation to a level humanly unacceptable has made living in the Ogoni land a nightmare. The survival of the Ogoni people is seriously threatened by the contamination of their environment."

This finding extends the right to life beyond protection from direct violence to encompass protection from environmental conditions that threaten community survival, providing foundation for environmental justice claims involving pollution that undermines community health and viability. The Commission also recognized violations of economic, social, and cultural rights, finding that environmental destruction that eliminates traditional livelihoods violates rights to food, water, and adequate standard of living. This approach recognizes that environmental justice involves protection of the economic foundations of community life rather than merely individual physical safety.

Perhaps most importantly, the Commission established detailed state obligations regarding environmental protection and corporate accountability. The Commission ordered Nigeria to:

- Ensure protection of the environment, health, and livelihood of the Ogoni people;

- Provide information on health and environmental risks to affected communities;
- Ensure meaningful participation in development decisions affecting Ogoni territory;
- Conduct environmental restoration of damaged areas;
- Provide adequate compensation for damages suffered; and
- Prosecute those responsible for environmental destruction.

These remedial requirements represent the most comprehensive international statement of state obligations regarding environmental justice, addressing both procedural rights (information, participation) and substantive protections (environmental restoration, compensation).

The Commission's approach to corporate accountability, while limited by its jurisdiction over states rather than corporations, established important precedents for state obligations to regulate corporate environmental conduct. The Commission emphasized that states cannot evade their human rights obligations by delegating environmental management to private corporations, stating that governments "have a duty to protect their citizens, not only through appropriate legislation and effective enforcement but also by protecting them from damaging acts that may be perpetrated by private parties."

3. The European System: Procedural Innovation and Substantive Protection

The European human rights system, while lacking an explicit environmental right, has developed extensive environmental jurisprudence through creative interpretation of existing civil and political rights, particularly the right to respect for private and family life (Article 8 of the European Convention on Human Rights). This approach has yielded important precedents for environmental justice, particularly regarding procedural rights and state obligations to protect individuals from environmental harm.

López Ostra v. Spain

European Court of Human Rights, 1994

The *López Ostra* case established foundational precedents for environmental protection under the European Convention on Human Rights, recognizing that severe environmental pollution can violate fundamental rights and that states have positive obligations to protect individuals from environmental harm. The case involved a Spanish woman's challenge to pollution from a waste treatment plant that processed liquid and solid waste from leather tanneries, causing severe odors, noise, and health problems for nearby residents.

The factual context reflected common patterns of environmental injustice involving the siting of polluting facilities in low-income neighborhoods without adequate consultation or protection measures. The affected community, consisting primarily of working-class families, lacked the political influence to prevent the facility's construction and was forced to endure severe environmental conditions that would not have been tolerated in more affluent areas.

The European Court found that Spain had violated Article 8 of the European Convention, stating: "Naturally, severe environmental pollution may affect individuals' well-being and prevent them from enjoying their homes in such a way as to affect their private and family life adversely." This finding established that environmental conditions can violate fundamental rights even when they do not cause direct physical harm, recognizing that environmental quality is essential to human dignity and well-being. The Court's approach expanded the scope of human rights protection beyond traditional civil and political rights to encompass environmental conditions necessary for human flourishing.

Perhaps more importantly, the Court established that states have positive obligations to protect individuals from environmental harm caused by private actors, stating: "the State cannot simply remain passive; it must undertake appropriate positive measures to secure the effective exercise of the right guaranteed by Article 8."

This principle of positive state obligations has become central to environmental justice advocacy in the European system and beyond, providing legal foundation for demanding state intervention to protect communities from environmental harm regardless of its source. The principle recognizes that effective human rights protection requires active government engagement rather than mere non-interference.

The Court's approach to balancing economic and environmental interests also established important precedents for environmental justice. While acknowledging that economic activities may sometimes justify environmental harm, the Court emphasized that such balancing must consider the severity of environmental impacts and the availability of less harmful alternatives: "the Court must determine whether the respondent State succeeded in striking a fair balance between the interest of the town's economic well-being—that of having a waste-treatment plant—and the applicant's effective enjoyment of her right to respect for her home and her private and family life."

This balancing approach requires states to demonstrate that environmental harm is justified by compelling public interests and that less harmful alternatives are not available, providing a framework for challenging environmental decisions that impose disproportionate burdens on vulnerable communities.

Notes and Questions

1. Scientific causation and environmental harm. How do the evidentiary challenges in *Trail Smelter* illustrate difficulties of proving environmental causation? The arbitrators struggled with "episodic, scattered, and diminishing fumigations" and rejected the parties' "surface winds" theory for "upper air currents" evidence. How might requirements for extensive scientific data and the "clash of experts" disadvantage communities lacking resources for sophisticated environmental monitoring?

2. Indigenous and community rights vs. state sovereignty. Analyze how *Awas Tingni* and *Saramaka* challenge state sovereignty over natural resources. *Awas Tingni* recognized Indigenous property rights without state-issued "title deeds," while *Saramaka* required states to ensure "reasonable benefits from extractive projects." How do these decisions address environmental justice concerns about communities bearing costs while benefits flow to "distant shareholders"?

3. Regional variations in environmental rights protection. Compare environmental rights approaches across regional systems: the African Charter's explicit "satisfactory environment" right, the Inter-American focus on territorial rights, and Europe's development through Article 8 private/family life protection. How do the *Ogoni* case's comprehensive remedies compare to *López Ostra*'s "positive state obligations"? Which approach better serves environmental justice advocacy?

4. State obligations and corporate accountability. Analyze different approaches to state obligations versus corporate conduct. The *Ogoni* decision held states "cannot evade human rights obligations by delegating environmental management to private corporations," while *Pulp Mills* focused on state-to-state obligations despite underlying corporate conduct. How do the Inter-American requirements for "effective participation" and "reasonable benefits" attempt to regulate corporate behavior through state obligations? Does this indirect approach adequately address corporate accountability for environmental injustice?

5. The United States? So which regional human rights system applies to the United States? If you guessed the Inter-American Court of Human Rights, as demonstrated in *Saramaka*, you would be forgiven, but incorrect. As with many international instruments, the United States has not ratified the American Convention on Human Rights, which came into effect in 1978 and formed the legal basis for the Inter-American Court of Human Rights, based in San José, Costa Rica. The United States does, however, participate in the non-binding investigatory work of the Inter-American Commission on Human Rights (IACHR), based in Washington, D.C. For one example of IACHR work involving the United States, responding to a complaint regarding uranium mining on the Navajo Nation, see the discussion in Chapter 9 (Environmental Justice for Indian Tribes and Indigenous People).

4. International Investment Law: Tension Between Environmental Protection and Capital Mobility

The proliferation of international investment agreements since the 1990s has introduced significant challenges for environmental justice. These agreements, designed to promote foreign investment by reducing political and regulatory risks, often establish broad legal protections for investors that can conflict with environmental regulations, particularly those intended to protect marginalized or vulnerable communities.

Investment treaties typically guarantee foreign investors' rights such as "fair and equitable treatment," protection from "indirect expropriation," and access to international arbitration. While these provisions aim to ensure stability and predictability for investors, they can undermine the regulatory autonomy of states, especially when environmental measures reduce corporate profits or disrupt extractive operations. In practice, investment arbitration panels operating under bilateral and multilateral treaties have adjudicated numerous disputes in which environmental protection efforts were challenged in ways that directly implicate environmental justice concerns.

A core structural problem is the asymmetry of investment law: foreign investors enjoy enforceable rights under these treaties, but affected communities have no comparable standing or procedural access to challenge environmental harms. As a result, environmental justice considerations, such as the disproportionate impact of pollution or climate change on low-income or Indigenous populations, are routinely excluded or marginalized in arbitration proceedings.

These concerns have led to calls for reform. Some newer international agreements, such as the United States–Mexico–Canada Agreement (USMCA), which replaced the North American Free Trade Agreement (NAFTA), and the Canada–EU Comprehensive Economic and Trade Agreement (CETA), include environmental exceptions and references to sustainable development. However, the effectiveness of such provisions remains contested. Critics argue that investor-state dispute settlement (ISDS) mechanisms continue to pose serious risks to environmental governance by allowing corporations to challenge climate and conservation policies in closed, non-transparent forums that prioritize investor interests over public welfare.

One of the most prominent examples of international investment law coming into conflict with environmental and climate goals is the Energy Charter Treaty (ECT), a multilateral agreement originally designed to protect energy investments in post-Soviet states. In recent years, the ECT has been widely criticized for enabling fossil fuel companies to sue governments over climate-related regulations, such as the phase-out of coal or the revocation of oil and gas permits. European states, in particular, have faced a wave of ISDS claims under the ECT for implementing climate transition policies. As a result, the treaty has come under intense scrutiny. In 2022, several EU member states, including Germany, France, the Netherlands, and Spain, announced their withdrawal from the ECT, citing its incompatibility with the Paris Agreement and long-term climate objectives. The backlash against the ECT underscores how investor protections embedded in older treaties can become significant legal and financial barriers to environmental justice and decarbonization.

Metalclad Corporation v. Mexico

NAFTA Chapter 11 Arbitration, 2000

The *Metalclad* case represents one of the most controversial decisions in international investment law, demonstrating how investment protections can conflict with environmental regulation designed to protect vulnerable communities. The case involved a U.S. corporation's challenge to Mexican federal and local decisions that prevented operation of a hazardous waste facility in the municipality of Guadalcázar in San Luis Potosí.

The factual context reflected typical environmental justice concerns: a multinational corporation seeking to operate a hazardous waste facility in a poor, rural community with limited political influence, where local residents opposed the facility due to concerns about groundwater contamination and health risks. The proposed facility would have processed industrial waste from throughout Mexico and potentially from the United States, concentrating environmental risks in a marginalized community while providing few local benefits. Mexican federal authorities had initially authorized the facility's construction and operation, but local authorities refused to issue required municipal permits due to environmental and health concerns. Subsequently, the state of San Luis Potosí declared the area an ecological reserve, effectively prohibiting operation of the waste facility.

Metalclad claimed that these Mexican actions violated its rights under NAFTA Chapter 11, arguing that Mexico's environmental measures constituted indirect expropriation of its investment and violated obligations to provide fair and equitable treatment. The NAFTA arbitral tribunal found in favor of Metalclad, awarding damages of over $16 million.

The tribunal's reasoning demonstrated limited consideration of environmental justice concerns, focusing primarily on Metalclad's legitimate expectations and procedural rights rather than the environmental and health impacts that motivated Mexican regulatory actions. The tribunal acknowledged that environmental protection constitutes a legitimate government objective but found that Mexico's environmental measures violated Metalclad's investor rights because they were implemented after the company had begun construction based on federal permits. This approach effectively prioritized investor rights over environmental protection, suggesting that environmental measures implemented after foreign investment begins may violate international law even when motivated by legitimate environmental concerns. The decision created "regulatory chill" effects by suggesting that environmental regulation could trigger substantial compensation obligations to foreign investors.

The *Metalclad* decision prompted significant criticism from environmental and human rights advocates, who argued that it demonstrated the need for stronger environmental protections in investment agreements and greater consideration of community rights in investment arbitration proceedings. The case became a rallying point for campaigns to reform international investment law to better accommodate environmental and social concerns. *See* William S. Dodge, *International Decisions: Metalclad Corp. v. Mexico and Mexico v. Metalclad Corp.*, 95 AM. J. INT'L. L. 910 (2001); and Marisa Yee, *Future of Environmental Regulation After Article 1110 of NAFTA: A Look at the* Methanex *and* Metalclad *Cases*, 9 HASTINGS W.-NW. J. ENVTL. L. & POL'Y 85 (2003).

E. Contemporary Frameworks and Future Trajectories

The development of international frameworks for corporate environmental accountability represents a crucial frontier in contemporary environmental justice advocacy, reflecting growing recognition that achieving environmental justice requires addressing the role of transnational corporations in creating and perpetuating environmental inequalities. Multinational corporations often play central roles in environmental injustice through their global operations, supply chain practices, and political influence, while remaining largely insulated from legal accountability through the fragmentation of international legal systems and the limitations of territorial jurisdiction. Recent developments in corporate accountability reflect multiple strategies for addressing these challenges, including the development of international soft law standards, the extraterritorial application of domestic legislation, the expansion of corporate liability theories in tort litigation, and the creation of new institutional mechanisms for corporate oversight and accountability. These developments suggest gradual evolution toward more comprehensive approaches to corporate environmental responsibility, though significant gaps remain in enforcement mechanisms and substantive protections.

1. The UN Guiding Principles on Business and Human Rights

The UN Guiding Principles on Business and Human Rights, adopted by the Human Rights Council in 2011, provide the foundational international framework for corporate human rights responsibility, including environmental rights. The Guiding Principles establish a tripartite framework consisting of the state duty to protect human rights, the corporate responsibility to respect human rights, and access to remedy for rights violations. Regarding environmental issues, the Guiding Principles require corporations to conduct human rights due diligence that identifies, prevents, and mitigates adverse human rights impacts throughout their operations and business relationships. This due diligence obligation extends to environmental impacts that affect human rights, requiring corporations to assess and address environmental risks to affected communities.

The Guiding Principles have influenced environmental justice advocacy by providing internationally recognized standards for corporate environmental responsibility and frameworks for advocacy targeting corporate conduct. However, their voluntary nature and limited enforcement mechanisms constrain their effectiveness in addressing systemic environmental injustices involving powerful transnational corporations.

2. Extraterritorial Corporate Liability

The development of extraterritorial corporate liability mechanisms represents another important strategy for addressing corporate environmental accountability, particularly regarding transnational corporations whose operations in developing countries cause environmental harm while their headquarters and primary assets remain in developed countries with stronger legal systems.

Several recent cases demonstrate the potential and limitations of extraterritorial liability approaches. In the United Kingdom, the case of *Vedanta Resources PLC v. Lungowe* involved Zambian communities' claims against a UK-based mining company for environmental damage caused by its Zambian subsidiary's copper mining operations. The UK Supreme Court allowed the case to proceed in English courts, finding that the parent company could potentially be liable for its subsidiary's environmental harm if it exercised sufficient control over the subsidiary's operations. Similar litigation has proceeded in various other jurisdictions, including the Netherlands (*Milieudefensie v. Royal Dutch Shell*), where Dutch courts have asserted jurisdiction over claims against Shell for environmental damage in Nigeria, and Canada (*Araya v. Nevsun Resources Ltd.*), involving claims against a Canadian mining company for human rights violations in Eritrea.

3. Mandatory Human Rights Due Diligence Legislation

Several states have recently adopted legislation requiring mandatory human rights due diligence that includes environmental considerations, representing significant evolution toward binding corporate obligations regarding environmental protection. France's 2017 Corporate Duty of Vigilance Law requires large French companies to adopt vigilance plans that identify and prevent human rights and environmental risks throughout their operations and supply chains. Germany's 2021 Supply Chain Due Diligence Act establishes similar requirements for German companies, while the European Union has proposed comprehensive corporate sustainability due diligence legislation that would apply throughout the EU. These developments suggest potential emergence of global standards for corporate environmental responsibility, though their effectiveness will depend on enforcement mechanisms and the scope of corporate obligations.

4. Rights of Nature and Ecocentric Approaches to Environmental Justice

The recognition of rights of nature represents perhaps the most radical development in contemporary environmental law, challenging fundamental anthropocentric assumptions about legal subjectivity and suggesting transformation toward ecocentric approaches to environmental governance that recognize the inherent value and agency of natural entities. This development has gained momentum through diverse sources, including constitutional provisions, legislative enactments, judicial decisions, and Indigenous legal traditions that offer alternative frameworks for understanding human-nature relationships.

The juridical recognition of rights of nature has proceeded through various mechanisms and contexts, reflecting adaptation to different legal systems and environmental challenges. Constitutional provisions in countries including Ecuador, Bolivia, and New Zealand have established comprehensive frameworks for rights of nature, while judicial decisions in jurisdictions including Colombia, India, and New Zealand have recognized specific natural entities as legal persons with rights to protection and restoration. These developments reflect growing understanding that anthropocentric approaches to environmental protection have proven inadequate to address the scale and urgency of contemporary environmental crises, and that effective environmental protection may require fundamental changes in legal and political frameworks that recognize non-human agency and value.

5. Constitutional Recognition of Rights of Nature

Ecuador's 2008 Constitution provides the most comprehensive constitutional framework for rights of nature, establishing that "natural communities and ecosystems possess the unalienable right to exist, flourish, maintain their vital cycles and structure, functions and their processes in evolution." The Constitution requires the state to "incentivize natural persons and collectives to protect nature, and to promote respect towards all the elements that form an ecosystem."

Bolivia's 2009 Constitution similarly recognizes rights of nature, establishing that "any person, individually or collectively, may exercise the legal actions aimed at defending the right of nature." These constitutional provisions provide normative foundation for challenging development projects that threaten ecological integrity, though their implementation has faced significant political and institutional obstacles.

New Zealand's recognition of legal personhood for the Whanganui River (2017) and Te Urewera forest (2014) demonstrates alternative approaches to rights of nature that emphasize collaborative governance between Indigenous peoples and the state. These arrangements establish legal guardianship mechanisms that represent natural entities' interests while providing ongoing roles for Indigenous communities whose traditional governance systems recognized the agency and rights of natural entities.

6. Judicial Recognition of Rights of Nature

Several recent judicial decisions have recognized rights of nature in cases involving environmental justice concerns, often in contexts where traditional environmental law approaches have proven inadequate to address systemic environmental degradation. The Supreme Court of Colombia's recognition of the Colombian Amazon as a "subject of rights" (2018) emerged from youth plaintiffs' claims regarding deforestation and climate change, reflecting judicial innovation in addressing intergenerational environmental harm.

The High Court of Uttarakhand's recognition of legal personhood for the Ganges and Yamuna rivers (2017) responded to severe pollution that threatened both ecological integrity and the spiritual and cultural practices of communities that depend on these rivers. While this decision was subsequently overturned by the Supreme Court of India, it demonstrated judicial willingness to adopt innovative legal approaches to address environmental crises. The implications of judicial rights of nature recognition for environmental justice remain uncertain and contested. While rights of nature approaches offer potential benefits for environmental protection, questions remain about how natural entities can exercise legal agency, how conflicts between different natural entities should be resolved, and how rights of nature can be integrated with existing legal and political institutions focused on human rights and welfare. For one thoughtful exploration of these questions and competing concerns, see Laura Spitz & Eduardo M. Peñalver, *Nature's Personhood and Property's Virtues*, 45 HARVARD ENVTL. L. REV. 67 (2021).

The development of international criminal law approaches to environmental destruction represents an emerging frontier in environmental justice advocacy, offering potential mechanisms for individual accountability regarding severe environmental harm that transcends national boundaries. While environmental crimes have traditionally been addressed through domestic criminal law systems, growing recognition of the global dimensions of environmental destruction and the inadequacy of existing legal frameworks has prompted efforts to develop international criminal law approaches to environmental protection.

7. Environmental War Crimes under the Rome Statute

The Rome Statute of the International Criminal Court includes provisions addressing environmental destruction in armed conflict, establishing that intentionally causing "widespread, long-term and severe damage to the natural environment which would be clearly excessive in relation to the concrete and direct overall military advantage anticipated" constitutes a war crime. This provision, based on similar language in Additional Protocol I to the Geneva Conventions, provides foundation for prosecuting environmental destruction as an international crime. The scope of this provision remains limited by its application only to international armed conflicts and its high threshold requirements for establishing environmental harm. Few cases have been prosecuted under this provision, reflecting both legal and practical limitations in applying international criminal law to environmental destruction. Recent developments suggest potential expansion of international criminal law approaches to environmental protection. The Office of the Prosecutor of the International Criminal Court has stated its intention to prioritize prosecution of crimes involving environmental destruction, while various advocacy organizations have promoted proposals for recognizing "ecocide" as a new international crime.

Giovanni Chiarini, *Ecocide in War and Peace: From the Air Pollution Consequences of the War in Ukraine to Japan's Disposal of Fukushima Water into the Ocean*

56 Case W. Res. J. Int'l. L. 242 (2024)

What is ecocide, and where does this definition come from? "Ecocide" is a "neologism derived from the Greek *oikos* (house, home) and the Latin *caedere* (destroy, kill), and essentially means the willful destruction of the environment." Criminalizing "ecocide" has been discussed by a range of experts for almost fifty years and is of increasing relevance. Starting as scientific and biological debates during the Vietnam War, ecocide arguments became foremost political and then juridical, with Richard Falk's proposal as the actual trailblazer for criminalizing ecocide in 1970. After decades of discussions, even within the United Nations, in 2021, the Stop Ecocide Foundation proposed to add ecocide as a new crime to the ICC by amending the Rome Statute. These advocates proposed amendments regarding substantive law and the structure of the crime of ecocide.

Under the definition proposed by the Stop Ecocide Foundation, ecocide, which would be classified under Article 8 of the Rome Statute, means "unlawful or wanton acts committed with knowledge that there is a substantial likelihood of severe and either widespread or long-term damage to the environment being caused by those acts." The proposed norm clarifies any definition in the second paragraph of Section II(C) of the Stop Ecocide Foundation's *Independent Expert Panel for the Legal Definition of Ecocide: Commentary and Core Text*:

a. "Wanton" means with reckless disregard for damage which would be clearly excessive in relation to the social and economic benefits anticipated;
b. "Severe" means damage which involves very serious adverse changes, disruption or harm to any element of the environment, including grave impacts on human life or natural, cultural or economic resources;
c. "Widespread" means damage which extends beyond a limited geographic area, crosses state boundaries, or is suffered by an entire ecosystem or species or a large number of human beings;
d. "Long-term" means damage which is irreversible or which cannot be redressed through natural recovery within a reasonable period of time;
e. "Environment" means the earth, its biosphere, cryosphere, lithosphere, hydrosphere and atmosphere, as well as outer space.

Introducing the crime of ecocide is essential because the existing ICC-substantive law is characterized by at least two negative traits: first, by an over-consideration, *quasi* sacralization, of the principle of military necessity, as Article 8(2)(b)(4) of the Rome Statute implicitly demonstrates; and second, by a *de facto* lack of environmental protection in the statutory law because Article 8(2)(b)(4) of the Rome Statute represents the only dedicated norm. Even though attacks against the natural environment are prohibited by the Rome Statute, the First Protocol to the Geneva Conventions, and the Convention on the Prohibition of Military or Any Other Hostile Use of Environmental Modification Techniques, the existing legal framework is insufficient to provide a solid foundation for imposing criminal responsibility for such environmental destruction. Article 8(2)(b)(4) of the Rome Statute defines the international crime as causing "long-term and severe damage to the natural environment which would be clearly excessive in relation to the concrete and direct overall military advantage anticipated."

However laudable the inclusion of this crime into this ICC statute may have been, it has two main limits. First, it is limited to international armed conflict, whilst widespread destruction of the environment occurs primarily in times of peace. Second, it can be prosecuted only if (i) the *actus reus* (criminal act) is widespread, severe and causing long-term environmental damage, (ii) the *actus reus* was not committed as a part of concrete or direct military advantage, and (iii) the *mens rea* (criminal mental state) demonstrates proof that the destruction was intentional....

The day after Russia invaded Ukraine, the Prosecutor of the ICC, Karim Khan, stated that he had been "closely following recent developments in and around Ukraine with increasing concern." Khan initiated an investigation and on February 22, 2023 submitted an arrest warrant to the Pre-Trial Chamber II against Vladimir Vladimirovich Putin, President of the Russian Federation, and Maria Alekseyevna Lvova-Belova, Commissioner for Children's Rights in the Office of the President of the Russian Federation. The warrant regarded the alleged war crime of the unlawful deportation of population (children) and the unlawful transfer of population (children) from occupied areas of Ukraine to the Russian Federation.

Without analyzing all the procedural issues connected to the ICC investigation, this Section will consider the possibility to prosecute the atmosphere pollution consequences of the Russian invasion of Ukraine under the crime of ecocide.

Indeed, it has been observed that the Russo-Ukrainian war "triggered a tsunami that dramatically impacted the world economy, geopolitics, and food security," and "due to the extreme humanitarian situation, the effects on the environment have been overlooked." However, "it is undeniable that a conflict of this scale will have enormously detrimental effects." According to several scientists, every war is, in general, "responsible for a high emission of greenhouse gases due to the inversion of military equipment heavily dependent upon oil." The impacts of warfare on the environment have been documented in numerous works.

Additionally, the United Nations Development Programme observed that "the environment will suffer," and, as other scholars have underlined, "this conflict may add pressure to other vital challenges that lay ahead, such as climate change, biodiversity loss, land degradation neutrality and ecosystems restoration, the sustainable development goals (SDG) or at the regional level European Union Green Deal." In other words, the Russian invasion of Ukraine and the subsequent war "will cause environmental damage that will be felt for generations to come." Specifically, the "emission of toxic gases in huge amounts" has been reported, in an environment (i.e., Ukraine) on which the baseline air quality was already, before the war, "among the worst in Europe."

The atmosphere consequences of the Russian invasion of Ukraine could therefore fall into the definition of ecocide as proposed by the Stop Ecocide Foundation, at least meeting both the "reasonable basis to believe" and "reasonable basis to proceed" burdens of proof set by the Rome Statute.

8. International Law, Environmental Justice, and Climate Redress

International legal frameworks recognize environmental justice principles through climate accountability mechanisms that seek to redistribute responsibility for environmental harm. The emerging architecture of climate redress, including the UN Framework Convention on Climate Change's Loss and Damage Fund, which proposed climate compensation funds and targeted reparations for egregious actors, represents an environmental justice approach that prioritizes the rights and dignity of climate-vulnerable communities. These mechanisms embody core environmental justice principles: they acknowledge that environmental harms are not distributed equally, they recognize the human rights implications of environmental degradation, and they seek to shift financial and moral responsibility to those who caused the harm. The distinction between climate compensation (for foreseeable harm from emissions) and climate reparations (for intentional disregard of vulnerable populations) reflects environmental justice's emphasis on recognizing both the material and dignitary harms that environmental injustice inflicts, particularly on communities already marginalized by historic patterns of colonialism, racism, and economic exploitation. Professor Carlton Waterhouse considers these issues related to human rights violations and international law in *Climate Redress Revisited: Loss and Damage, Compensation, and Reparations.*

Carlton Waterhouse, *Climate Redress Revisited: Loss and Damage, Compensation, and Reparations*

101 Iowa L. Rev. 2201 (2025)

In *Remedies for Human Rights Violations Caused by Climate Change*, Margaretha Wewerinke-Singh presents the case for climate change redress under international law. Without exploring the moral warrant for a reparations specific approach, the article examines remedies more broadly for human rights violations under international law. Looking to the foundation for remedies in treaties and custom, Wewerinke-Singh focuses attention on two key components for remedying human rights violations presented in the Basic Principles and Guidelines—(1) Access to justice at the state, regional, and international level; and (2) and substantive redress through restitution, compensation, and satisfaction. Wewerinke-Singh's examination discusses how climate-based harms might be addressed through individual human rights-based claims at the state, regional, and international levels of adjudication. The examination articulates the firm foundation for climate remediation in international human rights law. In doing so, it highlights important contributions of a human rights-based approach—(1) the range of available remedies to address human rights violations; and (2) the significant burden that litigation-based approaches place upon climate-vulnerable communities.

A significant benefit of examining climate redress through a human rights lens is the range of remedies recognized for human rights violations under international law. As discussed by Wewerinke-Singh and described in Basic Principles and Guidelines, restitution, compensation, and satisfaction have all been recognized as important mechanisms for remedying human rights violations. Each provides benefits to meet the differing needs of victims grounded in the distinct harms experienced. Restitution allows for the return or restoration of things lost because of the violations, while compensation provides resources that support the replacement of things lost and amends for harms caused when restitution is not possible. Satisfaction goes to mechanisms, symbolic and otherwise, that attend to victims' and the broader community's desire to understand why and how the violations took place. Apologies, truth commissions, inquiries, and reports on actions and practices causing human rights violations all sound in satisfaction-based remedial mechanisms. In the climate context, each of these approaches will be vital to provide redress for the diverse harms threatening and experienced by climate vulnerable communities. The loss of land, home, culture, political autonomy, health, well-being, family, life, and more all flow as potential and actual harms caused by climate change. A robust remedial scheme to address these is necessary to enable just responses to climate-based harms from those most responsible to those most harmed.

9. The Global Expansion of Aarhus Principles

The 1998 Convention on Access to Information, Public Participation in Decision-making and Access to Justice in Environmental Matters (Aarhus Convention) established the most comprehensive international framework for procedural environmental rights, though its geographic scope is limited to Europe and Central Asia. The Convention's three pillars, access to information, public participation, and access to justice, provide a model for procedural environmental rights that has influenced environmental law development worldwide.

The Aarhus Convention's approach to environmental information requires states to provide public access to environmental information held by public authorities, with limited exceptions for confidentiality or security concerns. This right to environmental information is essential for environmental justice because it enables affected communities to identify environmental risks and to participate meaningfully in environmental decision-making processes. The participation requirements established by the Aarhus Convention require states to provide opportunities for public participation in environmental decision-making, including decisions regarding specific projects and general environmental policies. This participatory approach recognizes that effective environmental protection requires democratic decision-making processes that include the voices of those most affected by environmental decisions.

The access to justice provisions require states to provide effective judicial and administrative procedures for challenging environmental decisions and seeking remedies for environmental harm. This right to environmental justice is crucial for environmental justice advocacy because it provides mechanisms through which affected communities can enforce their environmental rights and challenge discriminatory environmental policies. Recent developments suggest potential global expansion of Aarhus principles through regional agreements and domestic legislation. The Escazú Agreement, adopted by Latin American and Caribbean countries in 2018, establishes procedural environmental rights modeled on the Aarhus Convention while including specific protections for environmental defenders and attention to environmental justice concerns.

10. Environmental Defenders and the Right to Safe Participation

The protection of environmental defenders has emerged as a crucial issue in contemporary environmental justice advocacy, reflecting the increasing threats faced by individuals and communities who challenge environmentally destructive projects. According to Global Witness, 2021 was the deadliest year on record for environmental defenders, with 227 environmental and land defenders killed worldwide. The patterns of violence against environmental defenders reflect broader environmental justice concerns, with Indigenous peoples, women, and marginalized communities facing disproportionate risks. The targeting of environmental defenders often occurs in contexts involving extractive industries, land grabbing, and other activities that impose environmental costs on local communities while generating profits for distant actors.

International recognition of the need to protect environmental defenders has led to various initiatives, including UN Human Rights Council resolutions, regional human rights decisions, and domestic legislation establishing protection mechanisms. However, the effectiveness of these protections remains limited by inadequate enforcement and the continued impunity enjoyed by those responsible for violence against environmental defenders. The UN Human Rights Council's 2019 resolution on environmental defenders recognized the "important and legitimate role" of environmental defenders and called on states to create safe and enabling environments for their work. The resolution acknowledged the particular risks faced by women environmental defenders and Indigenous environmental defenders, reflecting an understanding that environmental justice advocacy often intersects with other forms of social marginalization.

Notes and Questions

1. **Current legal framework and limitations.** How does Article 8(2)(b)(4) of the Rome Statute currently address environmental destruction in armed conflict, and what are the two main limitations that prevent its effective application to cases like the atmospheric pollution consequences of the Russian invasion of Ukraine?

2. **Ecocide definition and real-world application.** According to the Stop Ecocide Foundation's proposed definition, analyze whether Japan's decision to release treated radioactive water from Fukushima into the Pacific Ocean could constitute ecocide. What specific elements of the proposed definition (wanton, severe, widespread, long-term) would need to be proven?

3. **Procedural environmental rights implementation.** Compare the Aarhus Convention's three pillars (access to information, public participation, and access to justice) with the Escazú Agreement adopted by Latin American and Caribbean countries in 2018. What additional protections does the Escazú Agreement provide that reflect regional environmental justice concerns?

4. **Legal reform prospects and political challenges.** Considering the ICC Prosecutor Karim Khan's arrest warrant against Vladimir Putin for war crimes related to child deportation (but not environmental crimes), what does this case reveal about the political and practical challenges of implementing ecocide as a fifth international crime under the Rome Statute?

Pathfinder on International Environmental Justice

The intersection of international law and environmental justice draws from multiple legal disciplines and theoretical traditions. For comprehensive treatments of international environmental law, see Daniel Bodansky & Harro van Asselt, Art and Craft of International Environmental Law (2nd ed. 2024); Edith Brown Weiss et al., International Law for the Environment (2nd ed. 2023); Philippe Sands et al., Principles of International Environmental Law (4th ed. 2018); Alan Boyle et al., International Law and the Environment (4th ed. 2021); Jutta Brunnée et al., International Law and the Environment (2017). The relationship between human rights and environmental protection is explored in John H. Knox & Ramin Pejan, The Human Right to a Healthy Environment (2018); Donald K. Anton & Dinah L. Shelton, Environmental Protection and Human Rights (2011); Alan Boyle, *Human Rights and the Environment: Where Next?*, 23 Eur. J. Int'l. L. 613 (2012). For theoretical perspectives on environmental justice in international law, see Sumudu Atapattu, Human Rights Approaches to Climate Change: Challenges and Opportunities (2016); Shawkat Alam et al., International Environmental Law and the Global South (2015); Balakrishna Pisupati & Willie Cordova, Sharing the Benefits of Biodiversity: The Nagoya Protocol on Access and Benefit Sharing (2016).

Key academic articles include Dinah Shelton, *Human Rights and the Environment: Jurisprudence of Human Rights Bodies,* in ENVIRONMENTAL LAW, THE ECONOMY AND SUSTAINABLE DEVELOPMENT 210 (Richard L. Revesz et al. eds., 2000); Cymie Payne, *The Norm of Environmental Integrity in Post-Conflict Legal Systems,* in Carl Bruch et al., POST-CONFLICT PEACEBUILDING AND NATURAL RESOURCE MANAGEMENT (2009); Rebecca M. Bratspies, *Human Rights and Environmental Regulation*, 19 N.Y.U. ENVTL. L.J. 225 (2012); Cinnamon Carlarne, *Delinking International Environmental Law & Climate Change*, 4 MICH. J. ENVTL. & ADMIN. L. 1 (2014); Shalanda H. Baker, *Climate Change and International Economic Law*, 43 ECOLOGY L.Q. 53 (2016).

Chapter 14

Climate Justice

Figure 14-1. On the Porcupine River above the Arctic Circle, Joe Tetlichi, son Jamie (driving boat), and nephew Shane return from a caribou hunt. Warming temperatures in the Arctic due to global climate change may increase wildfires in boreal forests and thus reduce caribou habitat and caribou herds, with disparate impacts on Indigenous subsistence hunters such as the Gwich'in people of the Yukon Territory. Photo: Subhankar Banerjee, Sept. 2001, from ARCTIC VOICES: RESISTANCE AT THE TIPPING POINT (Seven Stories Press, pbk, 2013).

A. Introduction

There is an overwhelming scientific consensus that the Earth's temperature is warming, that humans largely are responsible for this increase in temperature, and that if the world continues on its current path of energy use and economic growth, we run the risk of severe and widespread impacts from climate change. Stopping such disruptive climate change is perhaps the most daunting environmental challenge that we have ever faced.

Historical emissions dating back to the Industrial Revolution have already locked in a certain degree of climate change. That means that even if the world were to cease using fossil fuels and emitting carbon entirely, we would still have to grapple with

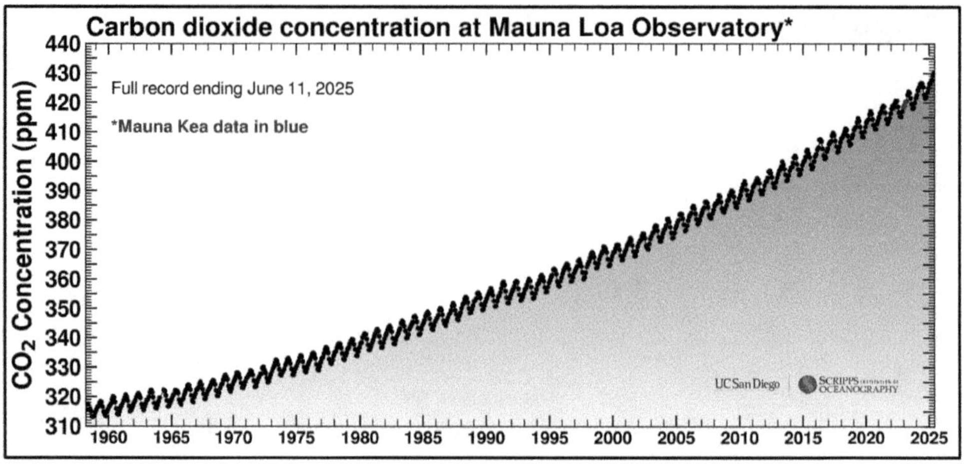

Figure 14-2. The Keeling Curve: CO2 Concentration at Mauna Loa Observatory. Source: Scripps Institute of Oceanography at UC San Diego.

the consequences of sea level rise and global warming for decades if not centuries to come. This is so for two reasons: first, because most greenhouse gas (GHG) emissions persist in the atmosphere for decades, and second, because there is a long lag time in the climate's response to the build-up of greenhouse gases in the atmosphere. The possibility of limiting global mean temperature warming to 1.5°C—a level identified in the Paris Agreement as necessary to avoid the most catastrophic impacts of climate change—hinges on radically reducing carbon emissions over a very short time period. In the fall of 2018, the Intergovernmental Panel on Climate Change (IPCC) estimated that there was an eleven-year window to make these changes.

By 2023, the IPCC was predicting that "global warming is *more likely than not* to reach 1.5°C" in the near term. IPCC, 6th Assessment Report, Summary for Policymakers 12 (2023). And in 2024, global mean temperature exceeded 1.5°C (2.7°F) above pre-industrial levels for the first time. Yet, global emissions continue to hit all-time highs.

The environmental justice ramifications of this trajectory are immense. Vulnerable communities that "have historically contributed the least to current climate change are disproportionately affected." IPCC, 6th Assessment Report, Synthesis Report 42. Their vulnerability "is exacerbated by inequity and marginalisation linked to gender, ethnicity, low income or combinations thereof, especially for many Indigenous Peoples and local communities." *Id.* at 101.

This chapter examines the disparate impacts of climate change and the legal efforts to combat problems at governance scales ranging from the international to the local. Sections B and C provide background about the nature of the problem and the international legal regime that has developed in response. Section D focuses on disproportionate impacts of climate change on marginalized communities. Sections E and F turn the focus to the United States, exploring the impacts of climate change and the array of domestic legal responses, particularly initiatives by state and local governments in the absence of federal leadership. Section G offers a brief introduction to climate litigation and Section H concludes with a quick introduction to the concept of climate adaptation, suggesting some measures that communities may take to minimize or reduce the unavoidable impacts of climate change.

Pathfinder on Climate Justice

The literature of climate change and climate justice is diverse and mature, with the disparate effects of climate change long recognized by activists, scholars, and policymakers. For the most current and authoritative science on global climate change, see the latest reports of the Intergovernmental Panel on Climate Change, available online at https://www.ipcc.ch/. For climate change science in the United States, one recent and useful resource is U.S. Global Change Resource Program, Fifth National Climate Assessment (2023).

Scholarly literature on climate justice is particularly robust. In addition to the works cited elsewhere in this chapter, *see* Camila Bustos, *Representing Climate Wreckers,* 33 N.Y.U. Envtl. L. J. 157 (2025); Sara A. Colangelo, *Bridging Silos: Environmental and Reproductive Justice in the Climate Crisis,* 112 Cal. L. Rev. 1255 (2024); Farhana Sultana, *The Unbearable Heaviness of Climate Coloniality,* 99 Political Geography 102638 (2022); Karen C. Sokol, *Seeking (Some) Climate Justice in State Tort Law,* 95 Wash. L. Rev. 1383 (2020); Carmen G. Gonzalez, *Climate Justice and Climate Displacement: Evaluating the Emerging Legal and Policy Responses,* 36 Wisc. Int'l. L.J. 366 (2019); Maxine Burkett, *Behind the Veil: Climate Migration, Regime Shift, and a New Theory of Justice,* 53 Harv. C.R.-C.L. L. Rev. 445 (2018); Atieno Mboya, *Human Rights and the Global Climate Change Regime,* 58 Nat. Resources J. 51 (2018); Uma Outka, *Fairness in the Low-Carbon Shift: Learning from Environmental Justice,* 82 Brook. L. Rev. 789 (2017); Nicky Sheats, *Achieving Emissions Reductions for Environmental Justice Communities through Climate Change Mitigation Policy,* 41 Wm. & Mary Envtl. L. & Pol'y Rev. 377 (2017); Maxine Burkett, *Climate Disobedience,* Duke Envtl. L. & Pol'y F. 1 (2016); Shalanda H. Baker, *Mexican Energy Reform, Climate Change, and Energy Justice in Indigenous Communities,* 56 Nat. Resources J. 369 (2016); Alice Kaswan, *Greening the Grid and Climate Justice,* 39 Envtl. L. 1143 (2009); Rebecca Tsosie, *Indigenous People and Environmental Justice: The Impact of Climate Change,* 78 U. Colo. L. Rev. 1625 (2007).

In addition to scholarly works, many useful materials on climate justice may be found online through various websites. Two of the most useful and reliable websites on climate justice are maintained by the NAACP: https://www.naacp.org/environmental-climate-justice-about/ and Columbia Law School's Sabin Center for Climate Change Law: https://climate.law.columbia.edu/.

Figure 14-3. Flooding after Hurricane Maria in San Juan, Puerto Rico. Sept. 20, 2017. Photo: Solmari Perez Oliveras.

B. Background on Climate Change

The summary below provides general background about climate change and is drawn largely from the IPCC's Sixth Assessment Report (2021). The IPCC is the world's most authoritative body on the science of climate change.

The primary cause of global warming is emissions of greenhouse gases stemming from human activities since pre-industrial times. The most widespread greenhouse gas is carbon dioxide, emitted as a result of combustion of fossil fuels such as coal, gasoline, natural gas, and heating oil. Other greenhouse gases include methane, primarily from agriculture and landfills, gases used in refrigerants, nitrogen oxides (also stemming largely from agriculture and fuel burning), and black carbon, a form of particulate air pollution produced by biomass burning, diesel exhaust and other sources. Since the beginning of the industrial era, atmospheric concentrations of carbon dioxide have climbed to their highest point in the last half-million years, rising from 275 parts per million (ppm) in the year 1750 to about 422.7 ppm in 2024—more than 50 percent higher than pre-industrial levels. Roughly half of this anthropogenic carbon was emitted after 1990, the year of the first IPCC Assessment Report. The IPCC projected that "rapid, deep, and ... immediate greenhouse gas emissions reductions" are necessary if we are to have a greater than 50 percent chance of keeping warming below 1.5°C and stave off catastrophic climate changes. Unfortunately, the trend is going in the other direction, with 2023 and 2024 both being record years for quantities of carbon emitted.

The impacts of climate change already are being felt. The IPCC concluded that it is "unequivocal" that human influence has warmed the atmosphere, land, and ocean. The scale and rate of these changes has been unprecedented. The current global climate is warmer than it has ever been during the past 500 years, and probably warmer than it has been for more than a thousand years. According to the World Meteorological Organization, the years between 2015 and 2024 were the ten warmest on record and in 2024 global mean temperature was 1.55°C above the 1859–1900 average. The consequences of crossing this climate threshold are still unfolding.

The rate of loss for Arctic sea ice is accelerating, and the IPCC predicts that by 2050 a large portion of the sea will be ice free in the summers. While melting sea ice does not raise sea level, losing bright white sea ice and snow cover creates a feedback loop that amplifies warming of the sea and land. As a result, Arctic surface air temperature is increasing at twice the global average, further warming the waters and melting more sea ice.

Warming is even more accelerated in the Antarctic, driving rapid environmental changes, including retreating glaciers. Greenland's ice sheets are losing mass at an accelerating rate and the melt is virtually certain to continue. The IPCC concluded it is *extremely likely* that rapid ice loss from Greenland and Antarctic ice sheets continues to increase, contributing to global sea level rise. These changes are altering biodiversity in polar marine ecosystems, posing a particular threat to charismatic Arctic mammals like the Pacific walrus and the polar bear that depend on the sea ice.

Mountain glaciers throughout the world are disappearing and their rate of retreat is increasing. Changes in winter temperatures are causing more precipitation to fall as rain rather than snow. Since snowpack can be a critical source of water supply, and feeds rivers and streams gradually, the result is less water available in the quantities and during the seasons necessary for human uses. Melting land ice and rising sea temperatures are producing rising sea levels, eroding beaches, and displacing people who live in low-lying areas and on islands.

Moreover, over the past 50 years, cold days and nights have become less frequent, while hot days and nights and heat waves have increased. It is virtually certain that there will be more frequent hot and fewer cold temperature extremes over most land areas on daily and seasonal timescales. Crops and livestock struggle when conditions become too hot, too dry, or too wet. These changes threaten livelihoods and exacerbate food insecurity.

Climate change adversely affects human health and well-being. While no individual weather event can be conclusively attributed to global warming, the IPCC has expressed very high confidence that climate change is compounding the human health risks from severe weather across the globe, and those risks will increase with further warming. Climate-related illnesses and premature deaths are increasing, particularly through heat-related mortality and vector-borne diseases. By 2050, as many as 250,000 excess deaths per year may occur because of climate change. Additionally, high temperatures can put a strain on the electricity grid and related infrastructure, sometimes causing power outages with negative human health effects.

Increases in the destructive potential of hurricanes are strongly correlated with increases in tropical sea surface temperatures that result from global warming. Global models predict that hurricanes will bring more intense rainfall and that rising seas will drive higher storm surge. While the number of storms may not change, the hurricanes that form are likely to become more intense. Events like Hurricane Katrina, which devastated the Gulf Coast in 2005, could become the norm and not the exception. Indeed, that has already happened, with Hurricane Sandy (more than double the size of Hurricane Katrina) moving up the Eastern Seaboard in 2012, Hurricanes Harvey, Irma, and Maria wreaking devastation from Houston to Puerto Rico in 2017, and Hurricane Helene and Milton creating catastrophic damage across the southeast United States in 2024. Unprecedented wildfires now burn across the western United States every year, and recent wildfires in Maui and Los Angeles devastated whole communities.

Under the current 1.1°C level of warming, climate impacts are already more widespread and severe than expected. It is impacting everyone, but those least responsible for the crisis are being hit first and hardest. Because of the persistence of greenhouse gases in the atmosphere, some of the changes to the climate system are irreversible, and the threats escalate with every tenth of a degree of additional warming. However, the IPCC predicts that aggressive mitigation and adaptation measures can avoid or mitigate many of the risks. Actions we take now (or fail to take) will dramatically affect the rate of warming in the long term.

Experts have identified an increase of 2.0°C (3.6°F) as a threshold beyond which the impacts of climate change are likely to be particularly grave. This benchmark is often cited as constituting "dangerous human interference" with the climate, a term that has legal significance under the United Nations Framework Convention on Climate Change.

C. International Law and Policy

The international community first addressed climate change with the 1992 United Nations Framework Convention on Climate Change (UNFCCC). The parties to the treaty (which now has been ratified by 192 countries, including the United States), agreed to stabilize greenhouse gas concentrations in the atmosphere with the goal of "preventing dangerous anthropogenic interference with Earth's climate system," although no numerical targets for GHG emissions reductions were set. The Framework recognizes that nations have "common but differentiated responsibilities," reflecting the view that developed countries bear a greater historical responsibility for the problem of climate change and have a greater capacity to take action. In particular, Article 3(1) of the UNFCCC provides that—

> The Parties should protect the climate for the benefit of present and future generations of humankind, on the basis of equity and in accordance with their

> common but differentiated responsibilities and respective capabilities. Accordingly, the developed country Parties should take the lead in combating climate change and the adverse effects thereof.

In late 2015, at the 21st Conference of the Parties (COP 21) to the United Nations Framework Convention on Climate Change, the international community negotiated the Paris Agreement. The Agreement's central aim is to strengthen the global response to the threat of climate change by keeping a global temperature rise this century well below 2°C above pre-industrial levels and to pursue efforts to limit the temperature increase even further to 1.5°C. The Agreement's main mechanism for achieving this goal is through nationally determined contributions (NDCs), which are specific measures to reduce greenhouse gas emissions as determined by the individual nations themselves. After publicly submitting their NDCs, all Parties to the Paris Agreement must report regularly on their emissions and on their implementation efforts. Article 14 of the Paris Agreement provides for a periodic global stocktaking "of the implementation of this Agreement to assess the collective progress towards achieving the purpose of this Agreement and its long-term goals." The Agreement specifies that this stocktaking should be done in a "comprehensive and facilitative manner, considering mitigation, adaptation and the means of implementation and support, and in the light of equity and the best available science."

The first Global Stocktake occurred in 2023. The outcome document, called the UAE Consensus because it was reached at COP 28 in Dubai, found that "despite overall progress made, Parties are not collectively on track towards achieving the purpose and long-term goals of the Paris Agreement." The Global Stocktake called for a new round of NDCs with accelerated ambition in line with the Paris Agreement 1.5°C temperature goal.

The Paris Agreement

(2015)

The Parties to this Agreement . . .

Recognizing the need for an effective and progressive response to the urgent threat of climate change on the basis of the best available scientific knowledge,

Also recognizing the specific needs and special circumstances of developing country Parties, especially those that are particularly vulnerable to the adverse effects of climate change . . .

Acknowledging that climate change is a common concern of humankind, Parties should, when taking action to address climate change, respect, promote and consider their respective obligations on human rights, the right to health, the rights of indigenous peoples, local communities, migrants, children, persons with disabilities and people in vulnerable situations and the right to development, as well as gender equality, empowerment of women and intergenerational equity . . .

Article 2

1. This Agreement, in enhancing the implementation of the Convention, including its objective, aims to strengthen the global response to the threat of climate change, in the context of sustainable development and efforts to eradicate poverty, including by:

(a) Holding the increase in the global average temperature to well below 2°C above pre-industrial levels and pursuing efforts to limit the temperature increase to 1.5°C above pre-industrial levels, recognizing that this would significantly reduce the risks and impacts of climate change;

(b) Increasing the ability to adapt to the adverse impacts of climate change and foster climate resilience and low greenhouse gas emissions development, in a manner that does not threaten food production; and

(c) Making finance flows consistent with a pathway towards low greenhouse gas emissions and climate-resilient development.

2. This Agreement will be implemented to reflect equity and the principle of common but differentiated responsibilities and respective capabilities, in the light of different national circumstances....

Article 4

1. In order to achieve the long-term temperature goal set out in Article 2, Parties aim to reach global peaking of greenhouse gas emissions as soon as possible, recognizing that peaking will take longer for developing country Parties, and to undertake rapid reductions thereafter in accordance with best available science, so as to achieve a balance between anthropogenic emissions by sources and removals by sinks of greenhouse gases in the second half of this century, on the basis of equity, and in the context of sustainable development and efforts to eradicate poverty.

2. Each Party shall prepare, communicate and maintain successive nationally determined contributions that it intends to achieve. Parties shall pursue domestic mitigation measures, with the aim of achieving the objectives of such contributions.

3. Each Party's successive nationally determined contribution will represent a progression beyond the Party's then current nationally determined contribution and reflect its highest possible ambition, reflecting its common but differentiated responsibilities and respective capabilities, in the light of different national circumstances.

4. Developed country Parties should continue taking the lead by undertaking economy-wide absolute emission reduction targets. Developing country Parties should continue enhancing their mitigation efforts, and are encouraged to move over time towards economy-wide emission reduction or limitation targets in the light of different national circumstances.

Notes and Questions

1. Differentiated responsibilities? What do you think the principle of "common but differentiated responsibilities" articulated in the U.N. Framework Convention on

Climate Change means in practice? As a general matter, do you think differentiated responsibility is a workable and desirable rule for addressing international environmental problems? Implementing this approach in the context of climate change is explored in the section below.

2. Nationally Determined Contributions. The centerpiece of the Paris Agreement is Nationally Determined Contributions (NDCs). This stands in sharp contrast to the approach of the Kyoto Protocol, where the major industrialized countries (so called "annex I" countries) had collectively committed to reducing their average annual greenhouse gas emissions between the years 2008 and 2012 to 5.2 percent below their 1990 levels. Developing countries (so-called "non-annex I" countries) were not required to limit their emissions under the Kyoto Protocol, and nearly all refused to consider such limits during the negotiations. Why do you think the international community abandoned the Kyoto Protocol approach in favor of the NDCs?

3. U.S. NDCs. The NDCs submitted by the United States in 2024 proposed to reduce carbon emissions through measures to include the following: (1) accelerated transition of the power sector, including added regulation of fossil fuel-fired power plants and investments in clean energy development; (2) "climate-smart agriculture and forestry practices," such as reforestation, wetlands restoration, and methane capture from agricultural facilities; (3) energy efficiency and technology advances in the building sector; and (4) electrification, clean fuels standards, and other measures in the transportation sector. The U.S. made some progress toward these goals under the Biden administration, assisted by resources from the Inflation Reduction Act, but the second Trump administration is doing its best to undo that progress. What are the consequences of a country failing to meet its NDCs? If there is not some international "climate police" with the authority to put a country in jail or otherwise punish violators, why would any country bother to comply with their own NDCs at all?

4. The Global Stocktake concluded that although Parties were not on track to keep global warming below 1.5°C above pre-industrial levels, full implementation of NDCs will reduce the expected global temperature increase from 4°C to 2.1–2.8°C. This is markedly better than the 3.6°C that the IPCC predicted in its 2018 *1.5°C Special Report* based on the NDCs submitted by the Parties. Does this reduction in warming represent success or failure? How much does the answer depend on which country's perspective one adopts?

* * *

Climate change will have profound implications for regional conflicts and global security, as millions of residents are displaced from their homes and conflicts develop over increasingly scarce food, water, and other natural resources. Sea-level rise, land degradation, coastal erosion, extreme temperature and other impacts from climate change can make entire areas unlivable. The 2018 Global Compact on Refugees directly addressed the way that climate change and environmental degradation "increasingly interact with the drivers of refugee movements." However, the Global Compact also asserted that climate change and environmental disasters are not "in themselves causes

Figure 14-4. Climate action sticker in New York City. Photo: Rebecca Bratspies, 2018.

of refugee movements." This assertion is based on the very narrow definition of who is a refugee under international law and seems inconsistent with the UN Institute of Migration projection that 200 million people will be displaced because of climate change by 2050. The World Bank projects that unless urgent measures are taken now, climate change will internally displace more than 140 million people in Sub-Saharan Africa, South Asia, and Latin America alone by 2050. The poorest and most climate vulnerable areas will be hardest hit. Climate-driven 'out-migration' will occur "in areas where livelihood systems are increasingly compromised by climate change impacts. These 'hotspots' are increasingly marginal areas and can include low-lying cities, coastlines vulnerable to sea level rise, and areas of high water and agriculture stress." In other words, millions of people will be forced to migrate from areas affected by rising sea levels and storm surges, as well as from areas that have become too hot or arid to support subsistence agriculture. The UN General Assembly's request for an Advisory Opinion from the International Court of Justice on the obligation of States with respect to climate change included reference to the impacts of climate "leading to the displacement of affected persons." The resulting Advisory Opinion is described in Section G below.

Notes and Questions

1. **Unjust burdens.** The disproportionate burdens that developing countries face seem particularly unjust because these countries are least responsible for climate change. What does this historical distribution suggest about how the responsibility for addressing climate change should be allocated? Should past contributions be more important than current capability (or weighted at all)?

2. **Wrongdoer identity.** Developing countries are adamant that the countries responsible for the historical stock of CO2 that is causing climate change should take the lead in emissions reductions. Developed countries, by contrast, argue that since the harmful climate change implications of carbon emissions were not widely known during the Industrial Revolution, it would be unfair to hold the present generations responsible for the "sins" of their forebearers. They instead argue that responsibility should be allocated based on current emissions, a stance that would require China and India to shoulder a large portion of the burden associated with reducing carbon emissions. Which position do you find more persuasive? Even if they had not been alive during these periods, did individuals in industrialized countries personally gain from the past activities of their countries?

3. **Kick the can down the road?** One often-repeated justification for not acting now on climate change rests on cost-benefit analysis that assumes that future generations are likely to be much richer than current ones. Do you agree with this assumption? If it is incorrect, how does it affect the underlying argument?

4. **Faith-based solutions?** In his 2015 encyclical on the environment, *Laudato Si, On the Care of Our Common Home*, Pope Francis, then-leader of more than one billion Catholics worldwide, emphasized the connection between climate change, environmental degradation, and social justice. Pope Francis wrote, "Today, however, we have to realize that a true ecological approach always becomes a social approach; it must integrate questions of justice in debates on the environment, so as to hear both the cry of the earth and the cry of the poor." After the passing of Pope Francis in 2025, Pope Leo XIV may be expected to continue his predecessor's support for climate action and social justice. *See* Kristen Toussaint, *The New Pope, Leo XIV, Has Spoken Out About Urgent Need for Climate Change Action*, Fast Company, May 8, 2025.

The Jewish religious tradition of *tikkun olam* (repair of the world) has been widely invoked to articulate a religious duty to combat climate change, with groups like Hazon integrating sustainability into Jewish practice. Islamic scholars have articulated powerful theological arguments through the *Al-Mizan: A Covenant for the Earth*, rooted in Qur'anic principles of balance (*mīzān*) and justice. The UN Environment Programme's Faith for Earth initiative also amplifies Muslim leadership alongside other faiths. Eastern religions, including Hinduism, Buddhism, and Jainism, frame ecological care as interconnected with spiritual liberation, emphasizing non-harming (*ahimsa*) and reverence for all life. Indigenous belief systems, too often marginalized, center Earth as a living being and emphasize reciprocity, kinship, and respect for ancestral ecological knowledge. Taken together, these traditions affirm that addressing climate change is a profoundly moral and spiritual imperative along with a scientific one. See *Al-Mizan: A Covenant for the Earth* (UNEP, 2022); UNEP's Faith for Earth Initiative; Hazon's Jewish Climate Leadership Coalition; *Faith and the Future of the Planet* (GreenFaith); *The Honorable Harvest*, in Robin Wall Kimmerer, Braiding Sweetgrass (2013) (Indigenous ecological ethics); and Dharma Rain: Sources of Buddhist Environmentalism, Stephanie Kaza & Kenneth Kraft, eds. (2000).

Do you think that religious traditions and practices contribute to environmental degradation? Do you think that religious teachings can offer a path out of our current environmental conundrum?

D. Climate Injustice Worldwide

Global warming's impacts, while widespread and severe, will not affect everyone equally. As the Chair of the IPCC has stated, "[i]t is the poorest of the poor in the world, and this includes poor people even in prosperous societies, who are going to be the worst hit." Similarly, the UN High Commissioner for Human Rights cautioned that "countless lives will be irreparably harmed, starting with those who already face discrimination because of their gender; because of their economic status; because they are members of Indigenous peoples or minorities; because they are migrants, or internally displaced; because of their age; or because they are people with disabilities." Indeed, the adverse impacts will fall hardest on people of color and poor people the world over because they are concentrated in areas that will bear the ecological brunt of climate change, and because they often have the least access to the resources (financial and otherwise) necessary to deal with its impacts.

For this reason, responding to climate change is often framed as a justice problem that requires ethical and political responses rather than a technical problem that calls for purely environmental or physical solutions. Indeed, the Special Rapporteur on Contemporary Forms of Racism, Racial Discrimination, Xenophobia, and Related Intolerance explained that climate justice is the attempt to respond to this inequality by "seek[ing] historical accountability from those nations and entities responsible for climate change. Climate justice also seeks radical transformation of the contemporary systems that enable global ecological crisis and distribute the suffering associated with this crisis on a racially discriminatory basis." E. Tendayi Achiume, *Ecological Crisis, Climate Justice and Racial Justice*, A/77/549 (2022).

Some countries are uniquely vulnerable to adverse climate impacts. For example, 80 percent of Bangladesh sits in a flood plain, near the rising seas. As Himalayan glaciers melt, they increase water volume in the rivers, leading to riverbank erosion. At the same time, rising sea level means that saltwater intrusions are destroying crop lands

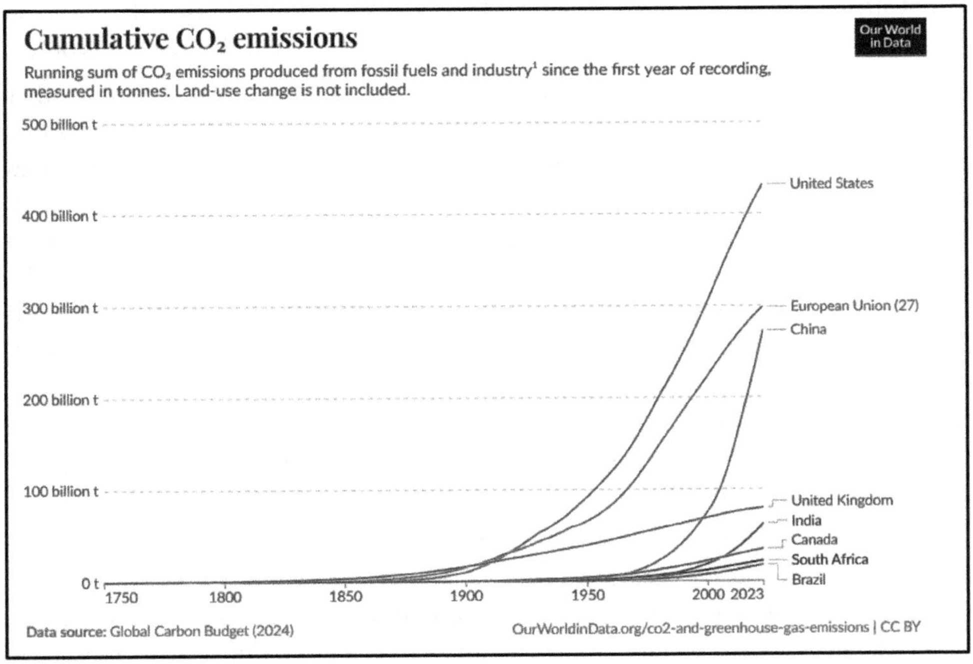

Figure 14-5. Relative contributions of CO2 emissions worldwide from fossil fuels and industry. Source: https://ourworldindata.org/grapher/cumulative-co-emissions.

and fishing areas. More extreme tropical storms and cyclones continue to hit the country. These manifestations of climate change have already forced hundreds of thousands of Bangladeshis from their homes, and the World Bank projects that number may reach 13 million by 2050.

Similarly, small island states find themselves at the frontline of climate change, with their very existence threatened by rising seas. In the Soloman Islands, five islands have already been submerged due to rising seas and erosion. In 2024, the Alliance of Small Island States issued the Declaration on Sea Level Rise and Statehood, calling attention to the existential threat to statehood, sovereignty, and UN membership that climate change poses for these states. This declaration came on the heels of the 2023 treaty between Australia and Tuvalu that provided for a "human mobility pathway" allowing citizens of Tuvalu to live, work, and study in Australia as a matter of *Falepili* (good neighborliness). Vanuatu and other small island states spearheaded the 2023 UN General Assembly resolution requesting an advisory opinion from the International Court of Justice on the obligations of states with respect to climate change.

According to the International Energy Agency, the United States alone is responsible for more than a quarter of cumulative global carbon emissions and, together with the European Union, has contributed more than half of total global emissions since the Industrial Revolution. The United States and the European Union together amount to roughly 12 percent of the world's population, so the per capita contribution disparities are even more stark. And these statistics are a significant understatement because they do not attribute to as the United States and Europe those emissions associated with the production in other countries of goods destined for markets in the United States or EU.

Climate change-driven impacts often act as a threat multiplier compounding other drivers of social and environmental vulnerability. The countries and communities that have contributed the least to global emissions and have access to the fewest resources for responding frequently find themselves on the front lines of climate disruption. This situation gives rise to calls for climate justice. The story gets more complicated because, in recent years, emissions from some developing countries, particularly India and China, have been growing rapidly. China's national carbon emissions now exceed the combined contributions of the United States and the European Union, even though per capita emissions remain far lower. The climate justice story will only get more complex. The Intergovernmental Panel on Climate Change estimates that, between the years 2000 and 2030, two-thirds to three-quarters of the projected increase in global carbon dioxide emissions will occur in developing countries.

Moreover, whatever steps we take to reduce GHG emissions will by themselves be insufficient to address the challenges of living in a warmer world. We also will have to spend vast sums of money adapting our physical infrastructure and social systems to a world altered by climate change (known as "adaptation" costs). Climate change is likely to exacerbate poverty in most developing countries and create new poverty pockets in countries with increasing inequality, in both developed and developing countries.

At the 28th United Nations Climate Change Conference of the Parties (COP 28) delegates formally agreed to create a loss and damage fund to support the most vulnerable countries as they address the impacts of climate change. As of March 2025, $765 million has been pledged to this fund. While that figure is nowhere near the amount needed, the establishment of the fund has been a long-time climate justice demand from developing countries. The materials below explore in more detail how harm from climate change is likely to be most severe for poorer countries that contributed the least to creating the problem. The first excerpt summarizes some of the major impacts projected for small island states, written by one of the scholars who helped conceive of the loss and damage fund. The second describes the situation for Indigenous peoples around the world.

Maxine Burkett, *Rehabilitation: A Proposal for a Climate Compensation Mechanism for Small Island States*

13 Santa Clara J. Int'l. L. 81 (2015)

For more than two decades, vulnerable small island states have sought a means to preserve their lives and livelihoods under threat of the impacts of climate change. Formally organized as the Alliance of Small Island States (AOSIS), small islands have been the source of many novel approaches to climate governance within the United Nations Framework Convention on Climate Change (hereinafter "Framework Convention" or

UNFCCC). Perhaps because of their unique vulnerability to its impacts, AOSIS has led a steady drumbeat for urgent and ambitious methods for arresting, and if not, adapting to climate change to survive some of the worst forecast climate phenomena....

A brief introduction to the AOSIS member states quickly reveals their heightened interest in the health and rigor of the Framework Convention. The Alliance is a "coalition of small islands and low-lying coastal countries that share similar development challenges and concerns about the environment, especially their vulnerability to the adverse effects of global climate change." Within the UN system, AOSIS functions as an ad hoc lobbying and negotiating voice for [Small Island Developing States] SIDS, advocating on behalf of roughly 59 million citizens of 44 States and observer countries from across the globe, including the Pacific, Indian, and Atlantic oceans as well as the Mediterranean, Caribbean, and South China Seas. These low-lying coastal states share similar challenges to sustainable economic development, including: geographic isolation, limited resources, dependence on international trade, and pre-existing vulnerability to natural disasters. Further, although their GDPs vary wildly in some cases, most of these countries are middle- or low-income countries, and five also rank among the least developed in the world.

AOSIS countries also have notable vulnerability to climate extremes. The Pacific islands are situated in one of the most natural disaster prone regions and are highly susceptible to—among other disasters—floods, droughts, and tropical cyclones. All SIDS are especially vulnerable to sea-level rise.

SIDS' climate vulnerability is not only the result of the unique exposure to climate extremes but also of the severe impacts that these natural hazards mete on local and national economies.... For SIDS, a single disaster has immense ripple effects, severely stressing public financial resources, if not dwarfing annual GDP.

The climate forecast for SIDS is equally troubling. Changes in the "frequency, intensity, spatial extent, duration, and timing of climate extremes" can result in "unprecedented" events. Further, "the crossing of poorly understood climate thresholds cannot be excluded, given the transient and complex nature of the climate system." In other words, scientists anticipate that the known climate-related impacts are set to shift in extreme and novel ways. And, the biggest surprises, though not fully understood, may well come to pass.... Whereas some climate impacts are avoidable, either through mitigation or adaptation, many [like sea-level rise] are no longer. These unavoidable impacts are ones that cause significant damage regardless of future measures taken to adapt. In addition to land lost to sea-level rise, for example, agricultural land lost to persistent drought, human health impacts of increasing heat events, and the entire collapse of the fishing industry due to increased ocean heat and ocean acidification all constitute unavoidable damage with which SIDS will have to contend. Not only are their territories and economic engines predicted to face significant challenges, SIDS are home to some of the most vulnerable populations—indigenous peoples, internally displaced peoples, and climate-induced migrants. In sum, there are unprecedented climate impacts that efforts to mitigate have failed to address and measures to adapt will fail to prevent or alleviate. And, there are countries and regions in the crosshairs of these impacts.

Notes and Questions

1. Small island states face the prospect that their lands may become uninhabitable within the coming decades. Absent an explicit treaty like between Australia and Tuvalu, where will the people go? What are the ramifications of declaring that the states will still exist if their population is forced by rising seas to abandon their island territory?

2. Compensation? As the readings indicate, developing countries face a double, if not triple, whammy from climate change, stemming from geography, limits in adaptive capacity, and potential impacts on the stability of their political regimes. While the costs of adaptation are uncertain and vary dramatically based on emissions scenarios, under any circumstance they are likely to be very large. The UN Environment Programme pegs these costs as between $315 and $565 billion per year by 2050. UNEP, *The Adaptation Gap Report: Status and Trends: The Adaptation Finance Gap* (2022). So far pledges to the loss and damage fund are a fraction of that amount. Is massive aid from the developed to the developing world to pay for adaptation programs likely? Do you think the recently created loss and damage fund can be successful?

Maria A. Tigre, *Climate Change and Indigenous Groups: The Rise of Indigenous Voices in Climate Litigation*

9 E-PUBLICA 214 (2022)

The Intergovernmental Panel on Climate Change (IPCC) concluded that climate change "exacerbates inequalities." These include people facing discrimination based on gender, age, race, class, caste, indigeneity, and disability. This article specifically addresses the challenges Indigenous groups face due to climate change....

There are an estimated 476 million Indigenous Peoples worldwide, representing 5 percent of the world's population. Indigenous and community lands, including those not formally recognized by governments, collectively cover 11 percent of the world's land. These include 135,400 Indigenous and community lands containing approximately 17 percent of the world's intact forest landscapes. These forests are essential sources of carbon sequestration and can significantly shift global warming trends. For example, in Brazil, Peru, Mexico, and Colombia, Indigenous and community lands sequestered more than double the amount of carbon per hectare than other areas. And although Indigenous peoples comprise less than 5 percent of the world's population, these territories contain nearly 80 percent of the Earth's biodiversity, including forests, deserts, grasslands, and marine environments. The role of Indigenous groups is, therefore, significant in climate policy, as they have proven central to climate governance.

At the same time, Indigenous and community lands are increasingly threatened, with abuses of Indigenous peoples' land rights, the expansion of agricultural land, increased hunting and trading of wildlife, and natural resources extraction and other infrastructure activities carried out within their territories without their free, prior, and informed consent (FPIC). Furthermore, the globalization of environmental challenges like climate change and of infectious diseases such as COVID-19 have significantly impacted Indigenous communities worldwide.

Indigenous groups in particular are disproportionately affected by climate change due to their connection to their land and dependence on their ecosystems. For example, in many places in Latin America, Afro-Latinos and Indigenous groups more prominently suffer from disproportionate climate effects. According to the United Nations Report of the Special Rapporteur on the Rights of Indigenous Peoples, Indigenous peoples are among those who have least contributed to the problem of climate change. Yet they are the ones who suffer most from its effects.

Indigenous groups are particularly prone to extreme weather events such as floods, droughts, heatwaves, wildfires, and cyclones. Many Indigenous peoples live in areas at greater risk of becoming uninhabitable, such as islands and coastal regions, as well as fragile polar and forest ecosystems. Effects on Indigenous food supply are particularly noteworthy for communities dependent on marine resources, considering the impact of climate change on oceans. In certain regions, this can force communities to abandon their lifestyles. Indigenous water supply is also at risk, impacting natural resources and livelihoods, cultural identity, their capacity to pass Indigenous knowledge and culture to future generations, and, at times, their survival.

Climate change also affects traditional food-gathering techniques of Indigenous communities. Rising temperatures impact frozen environments, which are integral to Indigenous culture. Glacial retreat threatens the ethnic identity of various Indigenous communities, including, for example, the Manangi community in Nepal. Furthermore, climate-related disasters will continue to worsen, significantly impacting Indigenous communities. Despite these wide-ranging effects, Indigenous groups are often left out of the political discourse and climate negotiations.

Notes and Questions

1. **Right to redress.** Article 28 of the United Nations Declaration on the Rights of Indigenous Peoples states that:

> Indigenous peoples have the right to redress, by means that can include restitution or, when this is not possible, just, fair and equitable compensation for the lands, territories and resources which they have traditionally owned or otherwise occupied or used, and which have been confiscated, taken, occupied, used, or damaged without their free, prior and informed consent.

Do the impacts of climate change trigger this provision? What about choices made to try to mitigate the impacts of climate change? Is there a way to compensate for the loss of identity and culture?

2. Risk of violence. Between 2012 and 2023, more than 2100 environmental defenders were murdered. Many of those killed were Indigenous peoples. In 2019, the United Nations Human Rights Council unanimously adopted a resolution recognizing the important and legitimate role of environmental human rights defenders in protecting the environment and in helping States fulfill their obligations under the Paris Agreement. The resolution called on States to create a safe and enabling environment for these advocates, to ensure effective remedies for human rights violations, and to combat impunity. Similarly, Article 9 of the Escazu Agreement on Access to Information, Public Participation, and Justice in Environmental Matters in Latin America and the Caribbean required member states to protect and promote the rights of environmental defenders. Yet in 2023, 196 environmental defenders were killed across the globe, the overwhelming majority within Escazu countries.

3. ***The Earth Defenders*** graphic novella depicts the struggles of Indigenous environmental defenders around the world. It is available for free download at https://www.unep.org/resources/publication/earth-defenders-graphic-novella.

E. Impacts in the United States

The Biden administration put climate justice at the center of its environmental policy. In April 2023, President Biden issued Executive Order 14096, *Revitalizing Our Nation's Commitment to Environmental Justice*, which emphasized the need for a whole of government approach to the climate crisis. This executive order built on Executive Order 14008, *Tackling the Climate Crisis at Home and Abroad*, issued his first week in office. In January 2025, President Trump withdrew both executive orders on his first day in office and has since attempted to eliminate every federal program related to energy efficiency, the transition to clean energy, or climate justice. As part of this process, the Trump administration froze all scientific research grants and community grants related in any way to climate justice, environmental justice, or equity more generally. This whipsawing jeopardized much of the environmental and climate progress achieved over the past decades.

In spring 2025, Representative Summer Lee (D-Pa.) announced plans to form a House Environmental Justice Caucus to join the Senate Environmental Justice Caucus founded in 2019. The caucus will replace the defunct House Bipartisan Climate Solutions Caucus. These legislative developments are particularly important in light of the Trump administration's avowed intention of abandoning initiatives meant to help communities responding to climate impacts and/or facing high pollution burdens.

In 2025, the Trump administration ordered the United States Department of Defense (DOD) to abandon research on the national security impacts of climate change. Yet, a decade earlier, in its 2015 *Report on National Security Implications of Climate-*

Related Risks and a Changing Climate, DOD characterized the effects of climate change as "an urgent and growing threat to our national security, contributing to increased natural disasters, refugee flows, and conflicts over basic resources such as food and water. These impacts are already occurring, and the scope, scale, and intensity of these impacts are projected to increase over time." DOD identified a variety of climate risks for military operations, missions, and installations. Of the 3,500 United States military sites around the world, roughly half are already experiencing climate-related impacts like heat, flooding, wildfire, wind, and drought. Indeed, DOD's 2019 *Report on Effects of a Changing Climate* found that "recurrent flooding, drought, and wildfires" associated with climate change jeopardize all 79 of the military installations included in the analysis. The report also identified climate change as "a source of conflict around the world." Extreme heat events are already putting U.S. soldiers at risk, with roughly 12,500 heat-related injuries between 2019 and 2023. In 2023 alone, the U.S. military reported over 2600 heat-related injuries.

Aside from the national security risks, the United States has and will continue to experience many of the same devastating impacts from climate change as other regions of the world, although these impacts will be less severe than in some parts of the world due to geographic advantages and greater resources available for adaptation. However, these impacts will hit the poor and communities of color in the U.S. the hardest. Children are particularly vulnerable, raising the concern that climate change will exacerbate existing social and economic inequalities and worsen racialized health disparities among both children and adults

Racially and socioeconomically marginalized communities in the United States are already experiencing greater impacts from storm and flood events, extreme heat, and the infectious diseases that are becoming more frequent due to climate change. A 2023 McKinsey Institute for Economic Mobility report found that "Black communities in the United States are particularly exposed and vulnerable to the impacts of climate change," exacerbating already existing racial gaps. Multiple studies have found that people of color, including Black, Latinx, Native American, Pacific Islander, and Asian communities are at higher risk of climate-related health impacts that are their white compatriots. Perhaps because climate change amplifies existing racial disparities in health, the Chicago Council on Public Affairs found that large majorities of Black, Latinx, and Asian communities view climate change as a critical threat.

In 2021, EPA produced a report on climate change and social vulnerability that documented the racialized risks that climate change imposes on Americans. Below are a few excerpts from that report.

EPA, *Climate Change and Social Vulnerability in the United States*

(2021)

A growing body of literature focuses on the impacts of climate change on socially vulnerable populations, but few studies have quantified disproportionate risks across multiple impacts and levels of global warming. This report contributes to a better understanding of the degree to which socially vulnerable populations may be more exposed to the highest impacts of climate change. . . .

Differential exposure to climate hazards can take many forms; for example, some may be more exposed to hazards due to their occupation or where they work. This report uses current data on where people live as an indicator of exposure, recognizing that demographic patterns may change in the future. Similarly, differential vulnerability can result from a wide range of social, economic, and political factors that make some populations less able to anticipate, respond to, recover from, and adapt to climate hazards. . . .

[M]inorities are most likely to currently live in areas where the analyses project the highest levels of climate change impacts with 2°C of global warming or 50 cm of global sea level rise. Black and African American individuals are 40 percent more likely than non-Black and non-African American individuals to currently live in areas with the highest projected increases in mortality rates due to climate-driven changes in extreme temperatures. In addition, Black and African American individuals are 34 percent more likely to live in areas with the highest projected increases in childhood asthma diagnoses due to climate-driven changes in particulate air pollution. Hispanic and Latino individuals are 43 percent more likely than non-Hispanic and non-Latino individuals to currently live in areas with the highest projected labor hour losses in weather-exposed industries due to climate-driven increases in high-temperature days. Hispanic and Latino individuals are also 50 percent more likely to live in coastal areas with the highest projected increases in traffic delays from climate-driven changes in high-tide flooding. American Indian and Alaska Native individuals are 48 percent more likely than non-American Indian and non-Alaska Native individuals to currently live in areas where the highest percentage of land is projected to be inundated due to sea level rise. American Indian and Alaska Native individuals are also 37 percent more likely to live in areas with the highest projected labor hour losses in weather-exposed industries due to climate-driven increases in high-temperature days.

Air Quality and Health

[S]tudies have found that minorities, individuals with lower income, and individuals with lower educational attainment are at increased risk of ambient air pollution exposure and health effects related to that exposure. Race, in particular, plays a significant role in determining one's risk of exposure to air pollution, even after controlling for other socioeconomic and demographic factors. EPA's most recent Particulate Matter Integrated Science Assessment (ISA) concludes that race and ethnicity are important factors in determining PM2.5 related risk, and that Black individuals, in particular, are at increased risk for health effects, in part due to disparities in exposure.

Extreme Temperature and Health

... Increases in extreme temperature-related premature mortality are projected to occur in many U.S. cities, but the largest increases are expected in areas with larger shares of low income and minority populations.... Black and African American individuals are 40 percent more likely than non-Black and non-African American individuals to live in areas with the highest projected increases in extreme temperature related mortality with 2°C of global warming.

Notes and Questions

1. Heat stress. As the climate continues to warm, more frequent and severe extreme heat events will disproportionately impact low-income communities, communities of color, socially isolated populations, and the elderly. Deaths caused by extremely hot weather are already a major public health concern in the United States, resulting in more deaths than any other weather-related event. There are large racial disparities in these heat-related deaths. A 2024 report from New York City found that Black New Yorkers die from heat stress at double the rate of white New Yorkers, and at a higher rate than the city's population as a whole. The report attributed this disparity to "past and current structural racism." New York City is not alone in this. Professor Maxine Burkett notes that "[h]eat stress has already been a public health nightmare for the poor and for people of color. As an example, older black males living alone with poor health status suffered a disproportionate share of excess fatalities after the 1996 heat wave in Chicago." Maxine Burkett, *Just Solutions to Climate Change: A Climate Justice Proposal for a Domestic Clean Development Mechanism*, 56 BUFF. L. REV. 169, 177 (2008). Heat-related deaths are more likely to be concentrated in urban areas because concrete and asphalt surfaces there help create the urban "heat island effect," and also because these areas often have worse air quality, and elevated pollution is often associated with heat waves. In addition, urban tree canopy is an important local mitigating factor for extreme heat. Studies in the United States have documented significant disparities in the urban tree canopy, with poor and minority neighborhoods having lower levels of tree coverage.

2. Racial disparities. As explored further in Chapter 15 (Disaster Justice), vulnerability to disasters is a function of both proximity to natural hazards and the social and economic characteristics of a community. As the readings above illustrate, the impacts of global warming experienced by minority and poor communities will be exacerbated because these groups are often the least able to adapt. Their increased vulnerability is not only a function of marginalization or poverty, but also of adaptation planning processes that perpetuate or expand their marginalization. As one social science review of vulnerability to climate change explained:

> Social processes of marginalization and disenfranchisement play important roles in creating patterns of unequal access to resources. Simultaneously, climate change will increase the exposure of populations to environmental hazards, exacerbating the existing unevenness in vulnerability across axes of social difference such as race, class, ethnicity, and gender.... Designing and implementing effective disaster risk reduction and adaptation interventions require attention to these inequalities in the context of ongoing social changes.

Kimberly Thomas et al., *Explaining Differential Vulnerability to Climate Change: A Social Science Review*, 10 WILEY INTERDISCIP. REV. CLIM. CHANGE (2019).

Structural racism, which created racial disparities in educational attainment, income, and wealth by perpetuating uneven access to resources, often means that it is more difficult for poor and minority community members to prepare for climate threats. Poor people typically have less access to health insurance, or to homeowner's and renter's insurance. The locations in which they reside are often more vulnerable to the impacts of weather and climate change. Moreover, the buildings they occupy may be poorly constructed and less able to withstand climate hazards. Poor and minority communities thus face heightened climate risks, while enjoying access to fewer preparedness resources. Color blind adaptation policies can further exacerbate inequalities in access to the resources needed to adapt to a changing climate.

3. Systemic inequities? To what extent are the disproportionate impacts from climate change part of the larger pattern of disparate environmental harms seen in Chapter 2? Beyond doubt, the climate crisis is deeply entwined with racial injustice. "Racial subjugation is commingled with environmental degradation. A look in the rearview suggests that the two have long been inextricably intertwined. Indeed, the climate crisis might not have been possible without conceptions of peoples and places that could be sacrificed for 'wealth' and 'progress.'" Maxine Burkette, *Root and Branch: Climate Catastrophe, Racial Crises, and the History and Future of Climate Justice*, 134 HARV. L. REV. 326, 333 (2021).

4. Income. White households the United States emit more carbon than their non-white counterparts. Poor Americans, regardless of race, also are far less responsible for carbon dioxide emissions than wealthier Americans, "with the average household in the wealthiest decile emitting roughly seven times as much carbon dioxide as the average household in the bottom expenditure decile." CONGRESSIONAL BLACK CAUCUS FOUNDATION, AFRICAN AMERICANS AND CLIMATE CHANGE: UNEQUAL BURDEN at 70 (2004). What implications does this have for efforts to control carbon emissions, including the likely political support for such programs?

F. Domestic Law and Policy

From the beginning of the modern era of environmental legislation in the United States, federal law has supported actions to investigate and address climate impacts from air pollution. The Clean Air Act of 1970, for example, authorized the nascent EPA to set air quality standards in order to protect "welfare," which was defined to include the effects of air pollution on "wildlife, weather, visibility, and *climate*...." Clean Air Act § 302, 42 U.S.C. § 7602(h) (emphasis added). Subsequent federal legislation, including the National Climate Program Act of 1978, the Global Climate Protection Act of 1987, and the Global Climate Change Prevention Act of 1990, emphasized the intent of Congress that the EPA and federal government broadly work to identify and avoid or mitigate the dangerous impacts of manmade climate change predicted by scientists.

The legal authority of the EPA to regulate the emission of greenhouse gases (GHG) as an air pollutant under the Clean Air Act was confirmed by the U.S. Supreme Court in *Massachusetts v. EPA*, 549 U.S. 497 (2007). The 2022 Inflation Reduction Act (IRA) further codified EPA's authority to regulate greenhouse gases under the Clean Air Act. The law was intended to reduce U.S. greenhouse gas emissions to 40 percent below 2005 levels by 2030. The IRA aimed to achieve this primarily through tax credits and subsidies to spur investment in wind, solar, and geothermal energy.

This funding and legal authority was all the more necessary because in *West Virginia v. EPA*, 597 U.S. 697 (2022), the Supreme Court dealt a blow to EPA's efforts to require carbon emission reductions under Section 111(d) of the Clean Air Act. EPA had sought to define the technology-based "best system of emissions reduction" standard to include requiring power plants to shift from gas, coal, and oil to renewable energy. As noted in Chapter 5, the Supreme Court announced that such an interpretation involved a "major question" and therefore required more explicit congressional authority. This decision did not call into question EPA's authority to regulate carbon dioxide emissions more generally.

The Trump administration in 2025 suggested that it will seek to revoke EPA's authority to regulate greenhouse gases through repeal of the 2009 endangerment finding under the Clean Air Act. However, for now it remains clear that the U.S. EPA retains legal authority under the Clean Air Act to regulate the emission of GHG whenever political will to do so returns. In the meantime, domestic GHG regulation may depend on other levels of governance, including municipal, tribal, and state governments.

In response to actions (or inaction) at the federal level, state action on climate change has been notable. Twenty-four states plus the District of Columbia, Guam, and Puerto Rico have 100 percent clean energy goals for electricity, either through legislation or executive action. Collectively these commitments cover roughly more than half of the nation's population and more than a quarter of its energy generating capacity. Hundreds of cities have embraced renewable energy and carbon reduction goals. As illustrated in the next two articles, California and New York City have been particularly ambitious.

California has been one of the states at the forefront of GHG regulation. In 2022, the legislature enacted the California Climate Crisis Act, AB 1279, which set binding 85 percent greenhouse gas emissions reductions targets and overall carbon neutrality by 2045. In this report, Professor Alice Kaswan and researcher Catalina Gonzalez analyze California's latest economy-wide climate action plan, the 2022 Scoping Plan for Achieving Carbon Neutrality, through an environmental justice lens.

Alice Kaswan & Catalina Gonzalez, *Environmental Justice in State Climate Planning: Learning from California*

Center for Progressive Reform (2024)

California's landmark climate change law, the Global Warming Solutions Act of 2006 (AB 32), tasked the California Air Resources Board (CARB) with preparing a comprehensive, economy-wide scoping plan laying out measures to achieve a 2020 emissions reduction target. CARB must update the plan every five years. After the original 2008 scoping plan, the 2013 and 2017 updates adjusted to the legislature's and the governor's increasingly ambitious targets. In step with new legislative requirements, the 2022 plan set forth paths to reduce anthropogenic emissions by 85 percent below 1990 levels and to achieve carbon neutrality by 2045.

The legislature gives CARB sole responsibility for preparing the plan but requires the agency to consult with all state agencies that have jurisdiction over GHG sources. In addition, CARB must engage with stakeholders and the public, hold public meetings, and provide a public comment period on a draft scoping plan. An Environmental Justice Advisory Committee (EJAC), drawn from residents in the state's historically marginalized communities, advises CARB staff and the Board itself on the scoping plans. The full Board ultimately votes on the final plan.... CARB must balance numerous requirements as it develops its plans. In addition to furthering environmental justice, as discussed in more detail below, AB 32 directs CARB to develop regulations that "minimize costs and maximize the total benefits to California," consider regulations' cost-effectiveness, minimize administrative implementation and compliance burdens, and minimize leakage....

The law states that, "to the extent feasible," regulations should "[e]nsure" that compliance will not "disproportionately impact low-income communities."... AB 32 also seeks to maximize economic opportunities in disadvantaged communities, stating that CARB shall, where feasible, "ensure" that its rules and programs "direct public and private investment toward the most disadvantaged communities in California" so that they have the chance to "participate in and benefit from statewide efforts to reduce greenhouse gas emissions."

AB 32 and subsequent legislation have also sought to limit the risk of pollution hot spots caused by market mechanisms like cap-and-trade. AB 32 required CARB to assess potential localized impacts, including those in "communities that are already adversely impacted by air pollution," before adopting a market mechanism. It further required that the market mechanism be designed "to prevent any increase in the emissions of toxic air contaminants or criteria air pollutants." After CARB ultimately developed a cap-and-trade program, the legislature expressed its concern with cap-and-trade by passing a law, AB 197, requiring the agency to prioritize "[e]mission reduction ... regulations that result in direct emissions reductions at large stationary sources ... and direct emission reductions from other sources." ... AB 32 required CARB to constitute an Environmental Justice Advisory Committee to advise on the scoping plans and their implementation. CARB selects members from nominees presented by environmental justice organizations and community groups.

IV. Assessment of Substantive Decisionmaking Process

A. Strength: Environmental Justice Principles

Several of the principles articulated in the 2022 Plan reflected AB 32's foundational commitment to environmental justice. AB 32 requires that measures protect low-income communities from increasing pollution, help achieve air quality standards by reducing pollution, and direct investment toward California's most disadvantaged communities. The Plan's overarching principles, like "Centering Equity," "Partnering with Tribes," "Maximizing Air Quality and Health Benefits," and "Economic Resilience," could help shape the scoping plan and the state's climate strategies more broadly. If fully implemented, they could help the state achieve multiple environmental and economic benefits for environmental justice communities and the workers and communities who currently rely on the fossil fuel industry.

In addition, the Plan's environmental justice goals in its sector-specific "Strategies for Success" could contribute to an equitable transition. Goals like making zero-emission technology affordable, funding clean trucks in the state's most polluted areas, avoiding pollution increases and reducing air pollution disparities near refineries, ensuring equitable access to new mobility options, targeting renewable energy programs to communities most at need ... would, if implemented, steer pollution-reduction and clean energy benefits to environmental justice communities.

B. Weaknesses

1. Role of Scenario Modeling

One concern is the way CARB developed its initial scenarios. We recognize that scenario development and modeling are critical. AB 32 requires these exercises, and they enable CARB to assess whether the scenarios will meet the state's transition targets and at what cost. As CARB explained in the final scoping plan, the scenarios "lay[] out the transformations needed across our society and economy to reduce emissions and reach our climate targets." However, the role and timing of the scenario and modeling exercises did not facilitate a fully deliberative process. CARB determined the "scenario inputs"—the transition goals for types of sources—early in the scoping plan process. The scenario inputs were highly abstracted.... Participants indicated that it was not always clear how or why the scenario inputs were chosen. And notably, in setting the scenario, unless the action was required by existing law, CARB did not indicate how the identified goal would be achieved....

Beginning with scenario inputs truncated the deliberative process. It was not conducive to discussions about a larger vision or guiding principles. And, because the scenario inputs were presented somewhat out of context, they did not lend themselves to a more wide-ranging discussion about the kinds of strategies that could be feasible within and across sectors. Although scenarios are necessary to engage in the modeling that helps predict whether the planned steps will meet statutory requirements, they may have emerged too soon and may have constrained the ... deliberative potential.

2. Insufficient Policy Development

As the Legislative Analyst's Office concluded in its review of the 2022 Plan, a fundamental drawback to the Plan is that, unless dictated by existing law, it does not address the specific measures and policies the state will use to achieve its intended outcomes. Consequently, the Plan does not provide a roadmap for ensuring that the stated environmental justice principles and goals will be achieved in practice. The planning process focused on needed technological and behavioral shifts and then provided a smorgasbord of potential measures—of "suggested strategies."... [M]any of the suggested strategies did not provide an implementation timeline and did not always indicate which agencies would be responsible for implementing them. In addition, in many cases, the Plan did not spell out the legal mechanisms for achieving its targeted technological and behavior shifts....

The law states that CARB should make scoping plan recommendations for "direct emission reduction measures ... market-based compliance mechanisms, and potential monetary and nonmonetary incentives for sources ... that ... [CARB] finds are necessary or desirable ... [to achieve] the maximum feasible and cost-effective reductions of greenhouse gas emissions...." AB 32 thus contemplated that CARB would set forth the policy mechanisms for achieving emission reduction goals. Although CARB sometimes made policy recommendations, in many instances, it listed a menu of options for agencies rather than providing clear policy recommendations.

From an environmental justice perspective, without knowing how a given result will be achieved, it is often not possible to know whether, or to what extent, the Plan will actually achieve the environmental justice principles it articulated or AB 32's environmental justice requirements. Principles, while important statements, cannot ensure that a state's climate policies will measure up.

Consider, for example, the industrial sector. While policymaking delays in some contexts may be understandable given the particular decarbonization challenges in some industries, others could be more easily decarbonized through a shift to clean electricity. Not only does the scoping plan scenario envision a slow transition in this sector, but CARB does not indicate how the state should accomplish the transition. The Plan does not indicate whether electrification will be achieved by new regulation, by grants, by continued reliance on the cap-and-trade program, or by some other means, leaving readers uncertain how the Plan will accomplish its stated strategy of prioritizing fuel transitions "first in communities most in need...." If by cap-and-trade, then communities face the risk that industries causing localized pollution will choose to maintain or increase their emissions, depriving that community of the benefits of the state's climate policies. That policy choice would also run counter to AB 197, the state law urging CARB to require direct emission reductions, where feasible. And, lastly, that approach would not be consistent with the Plan's goal of prioritizing reductions in the most impacted communities. Because the Plan is silent on its chosen policy mechanism, it does not enable deliberation on the policy options....

V. Participatory Processes

A. Strength: The EJAC's Role in the Scoping Plan Process

1. Valuable Role Played by the EJAC

The California experience reveals the value of having a dedicated environmental justice advisory body. As AB 32 was being debated in the legislature, environmental justice advocates foresaw the need for an Environmental Justice Advisory Committee to help the state design climate policies that would address disproportionate pollution burdens and ensure the fair distribution of climate policy benefits. The EJAC, convened to advise each scoping plan update, provides a crucial link between CARB and environmental justice communities. In a context marked by distrust between the agency and these communities, the EJAC has facilitated communication. An organized environmental justice advisory committee also provides a mechanism to channel the views of resource constrained grassroots community groups, who face greater participation challenges than other stakeholders, like industry, who are better funded and are more likely to identify specific and tangible outcomes from the planning process.

2. EJAC's Representation of Diverse Communities

One of the EJAC's strengths is the breadth of its membership, which drew from a wide range of marginalized communities across the state. The EJAC includes representatives from disadvantaged communities from both urban and rural communities and from northern, central, and southern regions of the state identified as "disadvantaged" by the state CalEnviroScreen tool. EJAC members also pushed for tribal representation on the EJAC to further enhance its capacity to reflect the state's marginalized populations....

4. Activities that Enhanced CARB's Understanding of Marginalized Communities' Priorities

Thanks in large part to the expertise, capacity, and experience that EJAC members and key support staff within CARB brought to table, the Committee played a positive role in the 2022 scoping plan process. The EJAC successfully recommended and implemented several mechanisms that further strengthened and institutionalized the participation of environmental justice communities in the state's scoping plan process.

B. Weaknesses

1. The EJAC's Role in the Scoping Plan Process

a. Timing

The EJAC was not fully constituted until the public portion of the scoping plan process was well underway....

b. Lack of Formally Structured Access to Staff and Modelers

The EJAC's ability to contribute to the scoping plan process was hampered by its lack of a systematic process for connecting committee members with ... agency staff influencing the Plan....

c. Insufficient Technical Assistance

Throughout the scoping plan process, the EJAC was frustrated by insufficient technical assistance from CARB, which hampered their ability to evaluate the scenario inputs and modeling exercises, and later the modeling results, which in turn made it difficult for them to develop recommendations for the draft scoping plan. CARB officials noted that, due to limited staff and resources, they were often unable to respond to the EJAC's questions, or were delayed in their responses, so the Committee had to use their own (minimal) resources. CARB's resource constraints meant that the EJAC did not always have the information and resources it needed....

4. Insufficient Opportunity to Participate in Scenario Development and Modeling Process

CARB began its deliberations long before the public or the EJAC had the opportunity to participate. Because the agency began the scoping plan process by developing scenarios and modeling, the parameters for selecting climate models and scenario inputs were critical. However, the EJAC did not convene and public participation did not begin until well after CARB had selected modeling tools and begun constructing and modeling potential scenarios. EJAC had no input in CARB's choice of climate models and did not have information on how the variables most important to environmental justice communities were being modeled. Fundamentally, they were unable to advocate for models that might better address the range of benefits contemplated by AB 32, like co-pollutant reductions—models that might better address the interests and concerns of the EJAC and frontline communities....

Conclusion

Good planning results cannot be achieved without good planning processes. Our analysis of the strengths and weaknesses of California's most recent scoping plan provides key lessons for ... California's future planning efforts. We demonstrate that strong background environmental justice principles and processes that promote deliberation on principles, priorities, and that articulate actual concrete policy frameworks are essential to effective planning and meaningful public participation. Multiple agencies' engagement and collaboration is essential to developing cross-sector policies that meet community needs and to having the agencies with relevant authority at the table....

Figure 14-6. Vineyards in the San Pasqual Valley, California. Grapevines are particularly vulnerable to climate change because they take years to establish—three to four seasons to bear fruit, and at least six years (and sometimes a decade) to produce high-quality berries. Photo: Nadia Ahmad, 2019.

Achieving a clean and equitable energy transition is not just about developing the right technologies. Inclusive climate action planning, planning that grapples seriously with specific policy mechanisms for achieving change, is essential to realizing deep and lasting benefits and avoiding unintentional harms. . . .

Notes and Questions

1. Scenario inputs. Kaswan & Gonzalez note as a "weakness" the lack of community involvement with developing "scenario inputs." A scenario is a forecast of what future emissions will be given implementation of certain policy measures and assumptions about market response, economic growth, technological advances, and other factors. While many of these factors may be highly technical, what input do you imagine may be valuable from a lay perspective?

2. Further opportunities for community engagement? As noted, the AB 32 Scoping Plan sets out broad goals that must be implemented by specific regulatory actions. Does the ability to engage in those processes compensate for the lack of community involvement in the development of the scenario inputs?

3. Continuing controversy. While California remains a leader in climate action, the cap and trade program remains a controversial part of its overall climate strategy. EJ advocates voice concerns about the potential for the creation of pollution hot spots, while others note (as discussed in Chapter 10) that the program has led to the investment of billions of dollars for disadvantaged communities.

Rebecca Bratspies, *Climate Justice Begins at Home*

37 New York Int'l. L. Rev. 13 (2024)

Most climate scholarship focuses on what nation-states do at international negotiations. What happens in those inter-governmental negotiations, such as the creation of international agreements, is vital to our collective future. However, international agreements are only the start. Implementing those agreements requires granular changes to a wide array of local decisions, including land-use, building standards and transit. These decisions are typically within the purview of states and cities. Thus, subnational actors play a critical role in climate mitigation and adaptation. Actions taken on the local level determine whether measures agreed to on the international sphere are actually implemented (or not). One example of this can be seen in the United States ("U.S."), where sub-national actors, including several U.S. states, can impede national commitments made on the international stage.

Consider *West Virginia v. EPA* (striking down the Clean Power Plan); *Texas v. EPA* (challenging the agency's methane rule); and *Texas v. NHTSA* (challenging stricter auto-efficiency standards). These cases reveal that when the U.S. makes a climate commitment on the international stage, that is only the start of a much larger and more complicated domestic political process. Conservative state obstruction is part of the story but looking on an even more local level—e.g. at cities—some room for hope emerges. This essay will discuss New York City and the ways that sub-national actors can support and further international climate agreements, such as the Paris Agreement. In this essay, I hope to demonstrate how cities are critical actors in the fight against climate change.

A just transition requires that we address this dichotomy between who emits carbon and whose rights to property, life, culture, and health are most at risk from climate change. As we create a pathway forward, sub-national actors like New York City can play a role in ensuring that the response to climate change includes a just transition....

In April 2019, right before Earth Day, New York City enacted a package of local laws known collectively as the Climate Mobilization Act. This ambitious plan was New York City's commitment to keep global warming below 1.5°C, as set out in the Paris Agreement. Central to the Climate Mobilization Act, is Local Law 97, the building

Figure 14-7. New York City environmental justice leader Peggy Shepard (left) with book co-author Rebecca Bratspies (right) at the release of the *Environmental Justice For All Report*. New York City, NY, 2024.

retrofit law. Local Law 97 imposed enforceable carbon emissions caps on all buildings larger than 25,000 square feet. The roughly 50,000 buildings covered by Local Law 97 collectively contribute 70 percent of the city's overall carbon footprint. Local Law 97 imposes carbon emissions limits on these buildings, and the limits become increasingly stringent over time. The compliance periods begin in 2024 and extend to 2050. When fully implemented in 2050, Local Law 97's emission caps are projected to reduce carbon emissions from New York City buildings by 80 percent. The law also imposes an interim target of 40 percent emissions reductions by 2030.

How can New York City do this? Because the City knows where the greenhouse gas emissions are coming from. Knowledge is power. New York City has been collecting data regarding large buildings' energy and water use since 2010. This information formed the basis for the reduction targets mandated by Local Law 97. The process began slowly, with 2024 targets that were relatively easy for all but the worst performing 20 percent of businesses to meet. By the January 2024 deadline, 90 percent of covered buildings in New York City were in compliance with their 2024 emissions target. The next deadline, in 2030, has much more challenging emissions reduction targets. Meeting these targets will require significant investment and support. The city has many programs intended to help buildings reach their targets, but the approach is not just carrots. There is also a big stick in the form of high fines for noncompliance—$268 per year for every excess ton of carbon emitted. Remember, each person in New York City has a carbon footprint of eleven tons. So, the fines for failure to decarbonize could be large enough to change behaviors. This law will also have significant environmental justice co-benefits—the changes needed to reduce carbon emissions from buildings will also reduce other pollutants. Thus complying with Local Law 97 will simultaneously improve air quality in most vulnerable communities—the communities that were redlined, that are heat vulnerable, that have been systematically overburdened and under-resourced. The pollution reduction co-benefits from Local Law 97 are expected to prevent up to 130 premature deaths and 150 hospital visits annually.

By the 2030 compliance period, Local Law 97 will reduce New York City's carbon emissions by at least six million tons, which is the equivalent of taking 1.3 million cars off the road, or the equivalent of the entire current emissions of San Francisco. Right after New York City enacted the Climate Mobilization Act, New York State passed the Climate Leadership Community Protection Act (CLCPA) which commits the whole state to making significant carbon reductions. The CLCPA requires that New York derive the majority of the state's electricity from renewable energy by 2030. By 2040, the entire energy supply must be emission free. The CLCPA adopted an environmental justice framework for implementing these climate goals, and contains multiple provisions designed to ensure both that the transition does not occur at the expense of already overburdened communities, and that the benefits of the decarbonization process flows to historically disadvantaged communities.

The Climate Mobilization Act legislation is the first-of-its-kind in the country and in the world. If this building retrofit mandate works in New York City, it will prove that this concept can work in other places as well. I hope we see cities across the country, and around the world, rapidly adopting this kind of plan. But this law was not written on *tabula rasa*. Indeed, two years before the Climate Mobilization Act, New York City had enacted two environmental justice laws that are critical background for understanding how the city will move forward. In signing these laws, former-Mayor Bill de Blasio described them as "recogniz[ing] the historic injustices that have disproportionately fallen on low-income residents and communities of color—the burden of pollution and the effects of climate change—and offer[ing] a different path forward."

These New York City ordinances directed municipal attention to the disparate impacts that polluting infrastructure has on low-income communities and communities of color. The recently released *Environmental Justice For All Report,* which lays the groundwork for the City's environmental justice plan, looked backwards and forwards. Looking backwards, the Report documented the profound structural environmental injustices across the city, and the racialized discrimination that drove existing inequities. Looking forward, the Report highlighted the attendant environmental justice/human rights benefits resultant from New York's energy transition and emphasized that as the city moves forward, it must prioritize climate justice and a just transition.

Notes and Questions

1. **"We're still in?"** International law generally considers the state to be a unitary entity—with the national government as the actor capable of representing the state in international decision-making. If the Trump administration withdraws from the Paris Agreement and cancels renewable energy projects but state and local decision-makers

take actions that achieve the United States' Nationally Determined Contributions (NDCs) anyway, is the United States still part of the Agreement?

G. Climate Litigation

Over the past decade, a wave of lawsuits has sought to force governmental actors to take climate action and/or to hold private companies accountable for their contributions to climate change. This kind of climate litigation could mark a fundamental shift in how legal systems address the climate crisis. These cases center on the principle that governments and corporations have legal obligations to protect citizens from the harmful effects of climate change, with courts increasingly willing to entertain arguments that climate inaction violates fundamental rights to life, health, and a safe environment.

Held v. Montana represents a watershed moment in U.S. climate litigation. In 2020, sixteen young Montanans, aged 5 to 22, sued their state government, arguing that Montana's pro-fossil fuel policies violated their Montana state constitutional right to a "clean and healthful environment." In December 2024, the Montana Supreme Court upheld the lower court's landmark ruling in a 6–1 decision, rejecting the state's argument that Montana's greenhouse gas emissions are insignificant on a global scale. Among other findings, the case established that youth plaintiffs have "a sufficient personal stake" in the right to a "stable climate system." 419 Mont. 403 (2024). A similar case brought by Hawaiian youths, *Navahine v. Hawai'i Dept. of Transportation*, resulted in a groundbreaking settlement. Hawai'i not only acknowledged the constitutional right to a life-sustaining climate under the Hawaiian constitution, but also pledged to implement specific plans to decarbonize the state transportation system. To date, cases brought by other youth plaintiffs under the federal and various state constitutions have been less successful.

On the international stage, the *KlimaSeniorinnen* case achieved a historic victory at the European Court of Human Rights in April 2024. The case involved more than 2,500 older Swiss women who argued that their government's failure to adequately mitigate global warming violated their human rights to health and life and puts them at risk of dying during heatwaves. The court ruled that the Swiss government had violated the human rights of its citizens by failing to do enough to combat climate change, in a decision that will set a precedent for future climate lawsuits. This ruling established binding obligations for all 46 member states of the Council of Europe and demonstrated how climate change intersects with age and gender vulnerabilities.

Recent international law developments underscore the judiciary's increasingly prominent role in clarifying state obligations with respect to climate change and environmental rights. Three international tribunals issued climate Advisory Opinions in rapid succession.

First, on May 21, 2024, in response to a request submitted by the Commission of Small Island States, the International Tribunal for the Law of the Sea issued an Advisory Opinion affirming that the Law of the Sea Convention obligated States to use due diligence to prevent, reduce, and control marine pollution caused by greenhouse gas emissions. This State duty to prevent marine pollution included the obligation to enact appropriate domestic laws and to enforce them with sufficient due diligence to ensure that non-state actors comply.

Second, responding to a request submitted by Chile and Colombia, the Inter-American Court of Human Rights issued an Advisory Opinion on state obligations in response to the climate emergency. In this decision, issued July 3, 2025, the Inter-American Court recognized the right to a healthy climate as a substantive element of the right to a healthy environment. The Court found that states had a *jus cogens* obligation to take urgent action to protect the climate system for present and future generations. To fulfil that obligation, the Court stressed that states must act with the highest ambition and must take all necessary measures to protect vulnerable groups and to reduce the impacts from climate change.

Following rapidly on the heels of this Inter-American Court decision, on July 23, 2025, the International Court of Justice responded to a General Assembly request for an Advisory Opinion on State obligations to the climate system by delivering a sweeping opinion articulating State obligations in the context of multiple environmental treaties, customary international law, and the human rights conventions. Calling the risks to the climate system "urgent" and "universal," the ICJ declared that States have a stringent duty of due diligence to prevent harm to the climate system and a duty to cooperate to mitigate climate damage under both customary law and under the relevant climate treaties. The ICJ characterized a state's failure of climate due diligence, including failure to achieve emissions reductions commitments under the Paris Agreement, as internationally wrongful acts. The Court declared that the human right to a healthy environment included the right to a stable climate system and suggested that the principle of *non refoulment* may extend to those displaced by climate change.

In addition to suits against governments demanding action, there is also an uptick in state court litigation pursuing remedies against corporate actors for their role in climate change. This kind of climate litigation increasingly targets major fossil fuel companies, often referred to as "climate majors," through various legal strategies. These cases typically fall into several categories: lawsuits seeking damages for climate-related harms, cases demanding disclosure of climate risks to investors, and litigation challenging corporate climate misinformation campaigns. Major oil companies like ExxonMobil, Shell, Chevron, and BP face mounting legal pressure worldwide, with plaintiffs arguing these corporations have known about climate risks for decades while actively working to delay climate action. In the United States, many of these cases have been brought by state attorneys general invoking public nuisance law and consumer protection statutes to hold companies accountable for their role in driving climate change.

To date, this litigation has not produced the kinds of legal victories necessary to change behaviors. The following excerpt provides an analysis of the causation challenges that have impeded environmental justice claims in climate litigation.

Maytal Gilboa, Yotam Kaplan & Roee Sarel, *Climate Change as Unjust Enrichment*

112 GEORGETOWN L.J. 1039 (2024)

To establish a tort claim, it is not enough to show that the defendant acted wrongfully and that some harm occurred; it must also be shown that the harm is a but-for result of the defendant's actions, meaning a plaintiff is required to preponderantly prove that its harm would not have occurred absent the defendant's wrongdoing. The nature of climate litigation makes it difficult for plaintiffs to overcome the tort requirements of causation. It is difficult to attribute the future harms of global warming to specific defendants in terms of proving a causal link.

Climate change is not a result of any single polluting activity, but rather a complex result of actions taken over years by multiple entities. Douglas Kysar points out the following difficulties: first, some climate events (such as hurricanes and droughts) do occur irrespective of climate change; second, the "extraordinary numerosity of greenhouse gas emitters" might give rise to a tort defense of "consequentialist alibi" by showing that any polluter's emissions are so small in comparison to total emissions that the effect is negligible.

To illustrate these difficulties, consider a recent case in which the city of Hoboken, New Jersey, filed a lawsuit against a group of oil and gas companies, led by Exxon Mobil Corp., demanding compensation for harms caused by sea level rise. In its decision, the New Jersey district court stated that "[a]lthough it is more than plausible that fossil fuels ... led to the effects of global warming that Hoboken is now facing, this does not amount to but-for causation." This statement shows that not much has changed in the way courts approach the difficulties in establishing the requirement of causation in climate litigation, as there exist "daunting evidentiary problems for anyone who undertakes to prove ... the degree to which the actions of any individual oil company, any individual chemical company, or the collective action of these corporations contribute, through the emission of greenhouse gasses, to global warming." The problem that these statements address is straightforward. Even if all scientists generally agree that GHG emissions cause global warming in the long run, it is very difficult to identify the amount that each specific emitter contributes to, for example, the global processes of melting glaciers and resulting sea level rise. This is especially true given that many of these massive losses are expected to materialize in the far future. Tort doctrine and compensatory damages, with their strong emphasis on harms, cannot overlook these difficulties and therefore fail to provide a remedy when the causal link to a concrete harm cannot be established.

Proposals for more relaxed theories of causation have not been accepted in climate litigation and are largely considered controversial by tort scholars.

Against this backdrop, it is unsurprising that courts have been reluctant to accept climate litigation claims based in tort law, at times even considering climate change as lying outside the scope of adjudication given its complexity. Note that these difficulties are not only applicable for negligence, but also for strict liability, which also requires proof of causation and harm.

Notes and Questions

1. Climate rights? Do you think there is a human right to a stable climate? A constitutional right? What would this mean in practice? How might such a right complement or conflict with other rights?

2. Shared responsibility? Does it make sense to hold fossil fuel companies legally responsible for climate change when consumers and governments also made choices that contributed to the problem? Where should accountability begin and end? How might lawsuits against "climate majors" differ in their justice impacts compared to suits against governments? Which approach is more likely to create meaningful change for affected communities?

3. Litigation tracking. While advocates for climate justice have not recorded many courtroom victories so far, there are a *lot* of climate cases currently pending in courts around the world. For any advocate interested in legal theories and outcomes of these cases, one indispensable resource is the Sabin Center for Climate Change Law, hosted by Columbia Law School. The Sabin Center maintains databases of climate change litigation both globally and domestically within the United States. According to the U.S. database, for example, as of June 2025 there were 202 climate cases grounded in claims under the Clean Air Act, 27 climate cases invoking the 14th Amendment of the U.S. Constitution, 304 climate cases asserting claims under state impact assessment laws, and 43 climate cases asserting common law claims.

4. Climate change attribution. While it remains difficult to attribute any individual hurricane, heat wave, wildfire, or other event specifically to climate change, the science of climate attribution is developing rapidly and may help inform better policymaking and questions of liability in the near future. For a thorough examination of this dynamic area of research and policy, see Michael Burger, Jessica Wentz & Radley Horton, *The Law and Science of Climate Change Attribution*, 45 Columbia J. Envtl. L. (2020).

H. Climate Adaptation

Whatever we might do to reduce carbon emissions in the future, whatever regulatory tools, diplomatic frameworks, or technology developments we might embrace, the fact is that the Earth's climate has changed already due to man-made carbon emissions and will continue to change in succeeding generations. An important question then is how people should adapt to these changes in order to meet basic needs and to achieve thriving communities in the future. A corollary question for purposes of this book is how to ensure that climate adaptation happens fairly and inclusively for all affected people and communities. One can easily imagine a scenario, for example, where rising sea levels around South Florida inspire wealthy homeowners to relocate to higher ground, leaving lower-income people locked into mortgages near sea level to face recurrent threats of flooding. What, if anything, may be done to help all people with the adaptations that our rapidly changing climate will require? The answer to this question is varied and continually expanding with developments in law, policy, and technology. In the next chapter, we will explore concepts of climate adaptation through the concept of **resilience** to the impacts of climate-related disasters. For the concluding section of this chapter, we will endeavor to introduce the concept of climate adaptation and suggest valuable resources for continuing study in this dynamic area of law and public policy.

For a comprehensive examination of climate adaptation from multiple perspectives within the legal academy, *see* Michael B. Gerrard & Katrina Fischer Kuh, The Law of Adaptation to Climate Change: United States and International Aspects (2012).

Under the second Trump administration, the federal government has abandoned climate adaptation as an official strategy and is seeking to claw back millions of dollars granted to communities for climate resilience planning. However, many state and local governments continue to fund climate adaptation plans. A wealth of resources to support this climate adaptation planning by states and local communities is available through the Georgetown Climate Center's Adaptation Clearinghouse, available online at www.georgetownclimate.org/adaptation. Among the resources available on the Adaptation Clearinghouse is the report excerpted below addressing adaptation strategies particularly to support minority and low-income communities.

Georgetown Climate Center, *Opportunities for Equitable Adaptation in Cities*

(2017)

Two of the biggest challenges facing the United States—and the world—are the income inequalities that put the health and well-being of our poorest populations at risk, and climate change, which affects our most vulnerable populations even more than the public as a whole. The effects of climate change—including rising temperatures in urban areas ... and increased extreme storms and stormwater—will disproportionally affect overburdened and low-income people and communities who are already facing significant economic and social challenges. Our success or failure in preparing for the impacts of climate change will be measured by how well we protect the most vulnerable and affected members of our communities, already suffering from a range of challenges including lack of economic opportunity, racism, and pollution.

In April 2016, the Georgetown Climate Center (GCC) and the Urban Sustainability Directors Network (USDN) convened a workshop bringing together nearly 50 thought leaders on equity and climate adaptation. The workshop focused on city-level actions that would support social justice goals and better prepare communities for the effects of climate change. Participants included city officials, representatives of environmental justice and social justice organizations, state and federal partners, and funders who support this work. Workshop participants were challenged to reflect on their own planning processes and identify ways that communities can address unequal risks;

increase diversity, community participation, and leadership in adaptation planning; and ensure that climate change preparation efforts are benefiting and not negatively affecting those most at risk of impacts. Workshop participants discussed adaptation strategies, policies, and projects that could help cities achieve social justice, economic development, and climate adaptation goals.

... Participants identified the following key lessons over the course of the workshop:

- Achieving equitable adaptation outcomes will require an inclusive process that gives community members, especially low-income residents and people of color, the opportunity to envision and set adaptation priorities and influence investments, policies, and programs pursued in their communities.
- In many cities, a long history of mistrust between public agencies and community members will need to be addressed before and throughout the process for collaborative planning to be successful. This will require a long-term commitment to relationship building that is institutionalized and not project-specific.
- Cities can address inequity within their own agencies by hiring more inclusively and identifying ways that city agencies currently reinforce inequities (e.g., holding meetings at inconvenient times for working people or failing to include interpreters or notices in representative languages).
- Public agencies will benefit from partnering with others, including community-based organizations, community institutions, and foundations, to address climate and equity goals.
- Recognizing that climate change will affect some ... groups disproportionately, cities can address equity concerns by directing resources to those areas and groups facing the greatest risks.
- Equitable adaptation asks city leaders and staff to think not only about how and where they direct resources, but also how certain policies might have negative consequences for particular groups or communities. For example, low-income homeowners in floodplains will face increasing economic strain from rising flood insurance rates; this may force some homeowners to drop insurance coverage, which is the last line of defense in the event that flood impacts occur.
- Climate policies can address larger issues such as poverty, housing security, and racial equity. Likewise, policies and activities that are not traditionally seen as "climate adaptation," such as workforce development and arts festivals, can be linked with adaptation initiatives to improve the economic and social resilience of residents.
- Addressing climate change and equity will involve a long process of experimentation and creativity. Some cities and community-based organizations are already pushing boundaries and trying to identify best practices. Participants in the workshop shared ways that they are integrating equity considerations into their adaptation work; these examples are featured throughout this workshop summary.

Notes and Questions

1. **"Adaptation" defined.** The Intergovernmental Panel on Climate Change (IPCC) has defined climate "adaptation" to mean "the process of adjustment to actual or expected climate and its effects. In human systems, adaptation seeks to moderate or avoid harm or exploit beneficial opportunities. In some natural systems, human intervention may facilitate adjustment to expected climate and its effects." IPCC 5TH ASSESSMENT REPORT, SUMMARY FOR POLICYMAKERS (2014). The definition recognizes that adaptation may take place *before* climate impacts are experienced ("anticipatory adaptation") or may follow as a *consequence* of climate impacts ("autonomous adaptation"). What examples of each type of adaptation can you imagine for communities on low-lying Pacific islands affected by rising sea levels?

2. **Migration is the solution?** If all efforts toward climate mitigation fail to achieve substantial reduction of greenhouse gases, can climate migration save us? May the population of the American Gulf Coast avoid repeated hurricane damage by migrating to the American Midwest? May the American Southwest escape prolonged drought by migrating to the Pacific Northwest?

Addressing the proper role for climate adaptation, the IPCC says this: "Without additional mitigation efforts beyond those in place today, and even with adaptation, warming by the end of the 21st century will lead to high to very high risk of severe, widespread and irreversible impacts globally. . . ." Even more bluntly, "Adaptation can reduce the risks of climate change impacts, but there are limits to its effectiveness. . . ." IPCC, *supra*, at 17–19. What "limits" might you see to the effectiveness of northward migration as a remedy for climate change, particularly for low-income communities and people of color?

3. **Adaptation resources.** Adaptation requires resources. And as noted by the Georgetown Climate Center, "equitable adaptation" may require the reallocation of resources toward vulnerable communities. Through such investments, "Climate policies can address larger issues such as poverty, housing security, and racial equity." How might that work? To use two examples from the Georgetown Climate Center, how exactly might investments in "workforce development" and "arts festivals" contribute to climate adaptation as well as social equity? Resources, of course, do not always equate to money and may include such things as training and reference materials, which may be obtained free of charge through such sources as the Georgetown Climate Center's Adaptation Clearinghouse. Among the trove of materials linked through the Adaptation Equity Portal, see the training modules produced by the NAACP: *Our Communities, Our Power: Advancing Resistance and Resilience in Climate Change Adaptation—Action Toolkit.* Here you will find information addressing such diverse topics as community banking, emergency management, and LGBTQIA+ engagement in climate adaptation efforts. Peruse the training modules and see if some ideas here would help your community adapt to anticipated impacts of climate change in your area. In return, what ideas for adapting to climate change might you have to share with others?

Chapter 15

Disaster Justice

Figure 15-1. Aftermath of Hermit's Peak/Calf Canyon Fire, Mora County, New Mexico. Photo: Cliff Villa, 2022.

A. Introduction

Simon Romero, *"Burning Down a Way of Life": Wildfire Rips Through a Hispanic Bastion*

N.Y. Times, May 5, 2022

As rushing flames neared the remote mountains where his family has lived for generations, Miguel Martinez knew he had to move fast and flee with only the clothes on his back.

"I left behind 25 goats, 50 rabbits, 10 chickens and two dogs," said Mr. Martinez, 71, who escaped his home in the village of El Oro this week for an evacuee shelter. "I have no idea if my house is standing or if my animals are alive. I need to prepare for the possibility everything was wiped out."

More than a dozen wildfires are raging this month across the Southwest, as fire season stretches earlier than ever into spring. But the country's largest active blaze, a megafire that has ballooned across more than 165,000 acres in northern New Mexico, has evolved with such ferocity that it threatens a multigenerational culture that has endured for centuries.

Like Mr. Martinez, many who have fled the megafire, known as the Calf Canyon/Hermits Peak fire, are descendants of Hispanic settlers who arrived in New Mexico long before the United States came into existence. They intermarried with Native Americans, honed ways to grow crops in parched lands and preserved an archaically influenced form of Spanish that can still be heard in the aisles of the local Walmart....

Shaped by challenges that range from conquering armies to long economic slumps, these far-flung Hispanic villages withstood one test after another. But the worst drought in at least 1,200 years, marked by intense and unwieldy fire activity, is something new.

"These fires are burning down a way of life that's lasted hundreds of years," said Rob Martinez, New Mexico's state historian and an Albuquerque native whose parents hailed from Mora and Chacon, two outposts in the fire zone....

Paula Garcia fled Mora, with a population of about 800, first for Las Vegas [N.M.] and then Santa Fe. She said she had helped her 82-year-old father pack up his tools before escaping herself as the fire approached their tight-knit community....

Ms. Garcia ... said she attributed her community's persistence to "pure grit."

"We've lived there so long because of our querencia," said Ms. Garcia, a term she defined as "a cultural longing, a pull, that keeps us there."

Such ties to the land have origins in Spain's colonization of New Mexico, which began in 1598, years before the English first settled in the Virginia colony of Jamestown. The colonists and their descendants persisted in relative isolation on the Spanish Empire's northern fringe.

New Mexico remains the nation's most heavily Hispanic state, with nearly 48 percent of the population claiming Hispanic or Latino heritage. The small towns, villages and ranching outposts in the counties hit by the fire, where Hispanics account for about 80 percent of the population, still defy easy classification....

* * *

Like exposure to hazardous waste and toxic air pollutants, and the many other threats to human health and the environment already explored in this book, disasters such as Hermit's Peak/Calf Canyon Fire in 2022 often have disproportionate effects on certain segments of our population, including racial and ethnic minorities, women and children, the elderly, and low-income peoples. While disasters have commonly been viewed as "social equalizers," affecting everyone in a community regardless of status or station, other experts such as Professor Rob Verchick have observed, "In nearly every disaster, it is the poor and other vulnerable groups who suffer most."

Following Hurricane Katrina in August 2005, many observers examined the disparate impacts on the largely poor and Black communities in New Orleans through the lens of environmental justice. *See, e.g.*, Eileen Gauna, *Katrina and Environmental Injustice*, Jurist (Oct. 10, 2005) ("Katrina ... was an exceptionally large echo of a socioeconomic political condition known popularly as environmental injustice"); Center for Progressive Reform, *An Unnatural Disaster: The Aftermath of Hurricane Katrina* 6 (Sept. 2005) ("Race, class, and injustice were key dimensions" of government's failure to protect Katrina victims); National Environmental Justice Advisory Council, *The 2005 Gulf Coast Hurricanes and Vulnerable Populations—Recommendations for Future Disaster Preparedness/Response* 3 (Aug. 2006).

Environmental justice, or *injustice*, can indeed help explain many of the impacts from disasters on certain populations. However, the emerging study of "disaster justice" may add some unique and valuable dimensions to environmental justice as described in earlier chapters of this book. For one thing, the impacts of disasters on certain populations may not always trace to some human action, such as the siting of a new industrial facility or the burning of fossil fuels; the impacts may result from human *inaction*, such as government's failure to provide for evacuation before a storm. For another thing, the impacts from disasters may be much more immediate. While the risks of toxic exposures, for example, are often measured by increased chances of cancer over a lifetime, the fatalities from a wildfire or earthquake may begin instantly and tallied over days and weeks. Finally, the potential remedies for disaster injustice may be different in kind from environmental remedies, requiring planning and mitigation measures by expert agencies on down to individual households.

2017 was a particularly bad year for disasters. In August, Hurricane Harvey dropped 51 inches of rain in one Houston neighborhood, a North American record. Two weeks later, Hurricane Irma would cause catastrophic damage in the Caribbean and Florida Keys before making landfall in Florida as the most intense hurricane to strike the continental U.S. since Katrina in 2005. In another two weeks, Hurricane Maria made a direct hit on Puerto Rico, becoming the deadliest and costliest hurricane to ever strike the island. Hurricane Maria would cause the longest blackout in U.S. history and leave the island suffering in many ways that continue to this day.

At the same time as record storms were devastating the Central and Eastern parts of the United States in 2017, record wildfires were burning in the West. Massive fires from Washington State to Southern California consumed not just timberlands but entire communities at the wildland-urban interface. In California, the Tubbs Fire in October 2017 charred swaths of Napa and Sonoma Counties, almost leveling the Santa Rosa community of Coffey Park. According to state fire investigators, the Tubbs Fire destroyed 5,636 structures, including more than 4,650 residential buildings, and resulted in 22 fatalities. Cal-Fire, *Tubbs Investigation Report*, Case No. 17CALNU010045 3

Figure 15-2. Aftermath of wildfires in Lahaina, Maui. Photo: U.S. EPA, 2023.

(Jan. 20, 2019). At the time, the Tubbs Fire was the most destructive fire in California history. However, the Tubbs Fire was quickly surpassed by the Camp Fire the next year. In November 2018, the Camp Fire incinerated the mountain town of Paradise, California, and surrounding communities, destroying 18,804 structures. Cal-Fire, *Top 20 Most Destructive California Wildfires* (Feb. 19, 2019). The Camp Fire was also the deadliest wildfire in California history, claiming an official count of 86 lives.

The death toll from the Camp Fire in 2018 was surpassed in 2023 by the horrific wildfires on the Hawaiian island of Maui. Exploding from a brush fire on August 8, 2023, the fire storm had particularly devastating impacts on the West Maui town of Lahaina, the former capital of the Hawaiian Kingdom and a community rich in history and cultural value to the Native Hawaiian population. With 102 confirmed deaths, the Maui wildfires in 2023 were the deadliest American wildfire in more than a century. Jacey Fortin & Adeel Hassan, *Death Toll of Maui Wildfire Now at 102*, N.Y. Times, Aug. 9, 2024.

Besides the staggering losses of life and property, the wildfires, hurricanes, and other extreme events of the past decade demonstrated some of the long-expected consequences of climate change. In the first assessment report by the Intergovernmental Panel on Climate Change, the IPCC predicted in 1990 that rising ocean temperatures may affect "the frequency and intensity of coastal storms and hurricanes." *See* IPCC, *Climate Change: The 1990 and 1992 IPCC Assessments* 106 (July 1992). With anticipated increases in heat, drought, and pests, the IPCC also predicted, "Losses from wildfire will be increasingly extensive." *Id.* at 88. With further prescience, the IPCC warned, "The most vulnerable human settlements are those especially exposed to natural hazards; e.g., coastal or river flooding, severe drought, landslides, severe wind storms and tropical cyclones." *Id.* at 89. We are now living in the future that scientists predicted 30 years ago. The principal question for this chapter is how to keep people safe now and into the future.

This chapter is not limited to consideration of "natural" disasters. In fact, many disaster scholars and managers now question whether indeed there is such a thing as a "natural disaster." *See, e.g.*, Greg Bankoff, *No Such Thing as Natural Disasters*, HARVARD INT'L REV. (Aug. 23, 2010); *There Is No Such Thing as a Natural Disaster: Race, Class, and Hurricane Katrina* (Chester Hartman & Gregory D. Squires, eds., 2006). Hurricanes and wildfires occur in nature, of course, but in the age of climate change, the fury and frequency of such events may be quite unnatural. Moreover, there is no "disaster" from hurricanes or wildfire until someone is injured in some way. Conversely, some events that we may consider "disasters" may have no basis in nature at all, such as the September 11 terrorist attacks in 2001 and the BP Deepwater Horizon oil spill into the Gulf of Mexico in 2010.

As Professor Dan Farber has observed, what marks some incidents as "disasters" is not so much a basis in natural phenomena as the kinds of human impacts and risk management choices a disaster may elicit. Daniel Farber, *Symposium Introduction: Navigating the Intersection of Environmental Law and Disaster Law*, 2011 BYU L. REV. 1783, 1788 (2011). Modern definitions of "disaster" reflect this broader conception. For example, the definition of "major disaster" in the federal Stafford Act includes not just "any natural catastrophe," but also "*regardless of any cause*, any fire, flood, or explosion ... which ... causes damage of sufficient severity and magnitude to warrant major disaster assistance ..." Stafford Act § 102(2), 42 U.S.C. § 5122 (emphasis added).

This chapter may therefore consider the justice implications of oil spills and industrial accidents, as well as earthquakes, hurricanes, wildfires, and other "natural" catastrophes. Most importantly, this chapter will also consider measures that both public entities and private actors may take to help keep people safe from disasters.

In this chapter, we will provide theoretical and statutory grounding to help prepare advocates for the pursuit of disaster justice in impacted communities. We will examine the related concepts of **vulnerability** and **resilience** in communities experiencing disasters. We will then survey the emerging field of Disaster Law, drawing foundations from the **disaster cycle** of readiness, response, and recovery, plus statutory authority including the federal **Stafford Act**. Finally, we will conclude the chapter by returning to the communities of northern New Mexico impacted by the Hermit's Peak/Calf Canyon Fire, considering how community members have fared and what we have learned to help keep people safer next time.

B. Vulnerability and Resilience

Many disasters may strike suddenly and with little warning. In ancient times and continuing today in some circles, disasters were often accorded supernatural origins, giving rise to potential exemptions from liability for "Acts of God." *See, e.g.*, Clifford J. Villa, *Is the 'Act of God' Dead?*, 7 WASH. J. ENVTL. L. & POL. 320 (2017). In modern times, we may be less inclined to blame the heavens for fates that befall us. Indeed, people who study disasters, from perspectives of law, geography, sociology, or other disciplines, often attempt to predict the impacts from disasters in terms of **vulnerability** and **resilience**. Vulnerability, in general, describes the susceptibility of certain communities or individuals to some form of adverse impact from an incident, including damages to private property or public infrastructure, losses in economic activity or ecosystem services, as well as bodily injury or death. Resilience, in general, describes the capacity of that community or individual to withstand harmful impacts and recover from the incident. This section will explore these related concepts, beginning with an excerpt from one formative article introducing the concept of "Disaster Justice."

1. Vulnerability

Robert R.M. Verchick, *Disaster Justice: The Geography of Human Capability*

23 DUKE ENVTL. LAW & POLICY FORUM 23 (2012)

We can think of "community hazard" as a combination of a community's "physical vulnerability" and its "social vulnerability." Here, "community" means, as a geographer might put it, "the totality of social system interactions" contained within a "defined geographic space." Depending on one's interest, that could be anything from a neighborhood or a census tract, to a city or a county. Physical vulnerability refers to a community's physical exposure to a place-based risk—for example, a flood, an earthquake, or a wildfire. Physical vulnerability should be read to include "geophysical characteristics" (geology, hydrology, climate, and so on), as well as important aspects of the built infrastructure that, if they failed, would present their own difficulties (such as a dam or a nuclear facility). Social vulnerability refers to the susceptibility of a community's population groups to the impacts of a hazard. This susceptibility, as Susan Cutter defines it, "is not only a function of the demographic characteristics of the population (age, gender, wealth, etc.), but also more complex constructs such as health care provision, social capital, and access to lifelines (e.g., emergency response personnel, goods, services)." The community-hazard framework expands the scope of disaster policy in significant ways. In this view, the factors are not just geophysical; they are also economic, social, and political. They involve a community's natural infrastructure as well as its built infrastructure. The protection of soil-stabilizing forests and storm-slowing coastal marshes becomes an important consideration in disaster policy. So too do bridge maintenance and regular improvements to data and cell-phone networks. This leads us to see the relationship between risk-reduction and the broader concept of "sustainability." The framework's emphasis on the ability to rebound as well as withstand reveals the relationship between risk reduction and the broader concept of "resilience" in all its physical, social, and economic aspects. Within this broader framework—encompassing environmental protection, public works, and more—disaster research has gradually honed in on one social factor of critical concern: inequality. Studies consistently show that in a disaster, poor people and people of color are more likely to suffer property damage, injury, and death. The most significant factor, the literature suggests, is that low-income and minority populations are simply more likely to live in older, denser, disaster-prone neighborhoods, with shoddy housing and inadequate services.

Government assistance programs—often crucial in the wake of a large catastrophe—tend to favor middle-class homeowners over less affluent renters or the homeless. Studies following the 1989 Loma Prieta Earthquake in the San Francisco Bay area have documented the many ways that federal assistance programs failed to meet the needs of the homeless, Latino farm workers, and low-income African-Americans. Louisiana's post-Katrina assistance programs raised similar concerns. Using federal funds, the state developed programs to promote the construction of rental housing and to compensate homeowners for the costs of rebuilding. Because of funding limitations, the rental-repair programs were only able to support the repair of less than one-third of the 82,000 rental units lost to Hurricanes Katrina and Rita. As for homeowners, nearly three-quarters of Road Home applicants had gaps between the received rebuilding resources and the actual costs of repair. The average shortfall for African-Americans was roughly $8,000 more than it was for whites. This discrepancy was caused by the grant formula, which was based on a home's pre-storm value, and African-Americans often lived in housing markets with depressed values.

Poor people and people of color also tend to suffer more psychological effects from disaster than victims who are wealthier or white. According to the literature, "poor, minorities, and single mothers may already feel a lack of control over their lives, and the dislocation and increased uncertainty about the future add to underlying and persistent stress." Elderly African-Americans, in particular, have been found to recover more slowly from "psychosocial" trauma than whites, an effect partially attributable to financial insecurity.

While social scientists emphasize the vulnerabilities of race and class, we should not forget that other demographic characteristics are also important. Age is often a big factor. Because the elderly tend to have more health problems, reduced mobility, and fixed incomes, they are often at higher risk of death or injury during disasters. Following the 2003 European heat wave, which killed an estimated 70,000 people, the World Health Organization reported that "in European cities, the elderly suffered the greatest effects of heat-waves," adding that elderly women bore a higher risk of dying than elderly men. In New Orleans, the elderly made up 60 percent of Katrina's death toll. In its investigation of fatalities from the 2011 Japan tsunami, the Japanese newspaper, Yomiuri Shimbun, estimated that more than 65 percent of those who died were over sixty years old. Children also tend to be more vulnerable in times of disaster and recovery. Physically, their smaller bodies put them at higher risk for allergies, infections, malnutrition, and other health problems. Children recovering from disasters often require emotional support and counseling to help them process confusing or frightening experiences.

Gender can also play a key role. Women, for instance, were hit particularly hard by Hurricane Katrina. Of the 180,000 Louisianans who lost their jobs after the storm, 103,000—or 57 percent—were female. Of the thousands of households that lost public housing services in New Orleans when they were summarily closed after the storm, 88 percent were headed by women. Men's median annual income rose after the storm, in part due to the rise in heavy-labor jobs like demolition and construction. Women, who were more likely to work in the healthcare, education, and hospitality sectors, saw their median income decline. Such widespread destruction, of course, dramatically increased stress within families, predictably leading to soaring reports of domestic violence. Indeed, research shows that evacuations and disasters are often accompanied by increases in violence against women and girls.

Notes and Questions

1. **Physical vulnerability.** After the scenes of devastation in New Orleans following Hurricane Katrina, some people around the country questioned the wisdom of rebuilding a city subject to all the physical hazards of existence between the Mississippi River and the Gulf of Mexico. But how "safe" is your community? Is your community also subject to hurricanes? Floods? Tornadoes? Wildfires? Winter storms? Earthquakes? Between Hurricane Katrina in 2005, Hurricane Sandy in 2012, and the one-two-three assault of Hurricane Harvey, Hurricane Irma, and Hurricane Maria in 2017, we know that the entire Gulf Coast and Atlantic Seaboard are subject to the ravages of hurricanes. We know that the entire West Coast is subject to wildfires. We know that the entire watershed of the Mississippi River is subject to flooding. The Midwest has twisters. The Southwest faces drought. For a more comprehensive review of physical hazards by geographical regions of the United States, *see* Denis Binder, *The Nature of Extreme Natural Risks in the Natural Environment*, 7 Wash. J. Envtl. L. & Pol. 340 (2017).

Every state is also subject to earthquakes, but some regions are more susceptible than others. The San Andreas Fault most infamously threatens Northern California, triggering the Great San Francisco earthquake of 1906 and the Loma Prieta earthquake of 1989. Even graver danger may be posed by the Cascadia Fault in the Pacific Northwest, capable of producing "the worst natural disaster in the history of North America," with odds of one in three for a massive "Cascadia subduction zone" earthquake in the next 50 years. Kathryn Schultz, *The Really Big One*, The New Yorker, July 20, 2015, at 52, 54. Given this physical hazard in the Pacific Northwest, should Seattle be relocated? Where would Seattle go? If we do not relocate Seattle, may we question the wisdom of any other places where people choose to live?

2. **Social vulnerability.** In the excerpt above, Professor Verchick conceptualizes "community hazard" as a combination of both physical vulnerability and social vul-

nerability. FEMA defines "social vulnerability" to mean "the susceptibility of social groups to adverse impacts of natural hazards, including disproportionate death, injury, loss, or disruption of livelihood." FEMA, National Risk Index Technical Documentation at 4-1 (March 2025). While the risk of earthquakes and other "natural" phenomena might be estimated by application of geology and other physical sciences, can we also attempt to estimate risks based upon factors of social vulnerability? In fact, as Professor Verchick has noted, geographers including Susan Cutter have developed a "social vulnerability index" (SVI) to estimate and compare risks in communities across the country. As further explained by Professor Verchick:

> Cutter's team began by collecting socioeconomic data for 1990 for all 3,141 counties in the United States. Starting with more than 250 variables, they winnowed the field (through various statistical means) to ... a subset of the eleven most important variables, which "explained 76.4 percent of the total variance among all counties." They were: (1) personal wealth, (2) age, (3) density of the built environment, (4) single-sector economic dependence, (5) housing stock and tenancy, (6) race—African American, (7) ethnicity—Hispanic, (8) ethnicity—Native American, (9) race—Asian, (10) occupation, and (11) "infrastructure dependence" (as in being employed by a transportation service or public utility).
>
> ... On this basis, Cutter's team found that "[a]s expected, the vast majority of U.S. counties exhibit moderate levels of social vulnerability." But some regions carried higher risk. With a few notable exceptions, the most vulnerable communities were located in the southern half of the country, stretching from southern California to Florida. These regions not only had greater racial and ethnic variation but were also growing quickly, resulting in crowded, flimsy housing stock. The least vulnerable counties were located mainly in New England, along the eastern slopes of the Appalachian Mountains, and in the Great Lakes Region. In all, 12.5 percent of U.S. counties were deemed "most vulnerable." New York County (otherwise known as Manhattan) ranked first in vulnerability due to density as well as its racial, ethnic, and socioeconomic profiles. Other high-risk counties included San Francisco County, Bronx County, and Benton County—home of the Hanford Nuclear Reservation—the economy of which was dominated by a single public utility. The safest bets, like Poquoson, Virginia, or Tolland, Connecticut, were more homogenous and often presented a face that was more "suburban, wealthy, white, and highly educated."

Verchick, *Disaster Justice*, at 47–48.

3. Your community? Building on the work of Susan Cutter and other researchers, the federal Centers for Disease Control and Prevention (CDC) developed an online database and GIS tool for identifying the SVI score in any city, county, or region of the United States. For SVI methodology, see Flanagan et al., *A Social Vulnerability Index for Disaster Management*, 8 J. Homeland Security & Emergency Mgmt 1 (2011). To launch the SVI tool, visit https://www.atsdr.cdc.gov/place-health/php/svi/index.

html or simply type "cdc svi" in any Internet browser. Applying this tool, what is the SVI score for your community? Which of the eleven variables identified above do you believe may most influence the SVI score for your community?

Based upon research from Cutter and others, and drawing upon data from the SVI, FEMA developed its own GIS tool known as the National Risk Index. The National Risk Index integrates data from the SVI with data on physical hazards and "community resilience" across the United States. For FEMA's methodology in developing this tool, see Casey Zurak et al., *The National Risk Index: Establishing a Nationwide Baseline for Natural Hazard Risk in the US*, 114 NATURAL HAZARDS 2331 (2022). As explained by FEMA, "The National Risk Index is designed to serve as a nationwide, comparable measure of community risk for all counties and Census tracts in US states and the District of Columbia, calculated within and across 18 significant hazard types." FEMA, NATIONAL RISK INDEX TECHNICAL DOCUMENTATION (March 2025). The 18 "hazard types" evaluated by the National Risk Index appear in Figure 15-3.

Avalanche	Heat Wave	Strong Wind
Coastal Flooding	Hurricane	Tornado
Cold Wave	Ice Storm	Tsunami
Drought	Landslide	Volcanic Activity
Earthquake	Lightning	Wildfire
Hail	Riverine Flooding	Winter Weather

Figure 15-3. Hazard types evaluated by FEMA National Risk Index. March 2025.

At a glance, which of these 18 hazards do you believe pose a significant threat to your community? Have you experienced any of these threats directly? For FEMA's estimate of risks in your community, launch the National Risk Index tool at the following link: https://hazards.fema.gov/nri/. Do FEMA's results for your community match your own perceptions of risk in your community? If not, how do they differ?

4. Children and older adults. In the article from Professor Verchick, how does a person's age relate to their potential vulnerability in a disaster? In a disaster like Hurricane Katrina, who is more at risk: a six-year-old or sixty-year-old? A six-year-old obviously cannot drive a car, wade through flood waters, or comprehend evacuation orders the way we might expect of an adult. **Children** may also be more vulnerable to toxic exposures in contaminated air, water, food, and land, as explored in previous chapters. In addition, children may be more susceptible to psychological trauma, resulting in a range of behaviors and mental health symptoms including anxiety, depression, bullying, and substance abuse. Tara Powell & Lori K. Holleran-Steiker, *Supporting Children After a Disaster: A Case Study of Psychosocial School-Based Intervention*, 45 CLINICAL

Soc. Work J. 176 (2015) (observing that "Children are one of the most vulnerable groups during and after a natural disaster").

On the other hand, what disproportionate impacts may **older adults** face from a disaster? Consider the following:

> The greatest mortality during and immediately after the 2005 hurricane and subsequent flooding of the Greater New Orleans (GN) area was among the elderly. Those over age 60—some 15% of the New Orleans population before the storm—accounted for approximately 75% of bodies found immediately after; 40% were over 70. These high mortality rates can be attributed to several factors, including lack of evacuation facilities, infirmities that made evacuation difficult if not impossible, and high levels of poverty and isolation....

Vincanne Adams et al., *Aging Disaster: Mortality, Vulnerability, and Long-Term Recovery Among Katrina Survivors*, 30 Med. Anthropology 247, May 30, 2011. Since Hurricane Katrina, every new disaster sadly appears to reconfirm these exceptional risks to older adults. For one horrific example, following the deadly Camp Fire in November 2018, 77 percent of the bodies recovered and identified were reported over the age of 65. Laura Newberry, *Poor, Elderly and Too Frail to Escape: Paradise Fire Killed the Most Vulnerable Residents*, L.A. Times, Feb. 10, 2019.

Even more deadly than wildfire is **extreme heat**. "Extreme heat is now the leading cause of weather-related deaths in the United States," killing more people all other weather-related events combined, including hurricanes and tornadoes. Danielle Arigoni, Climate Resilience for an Aging Nation 44 (2023). Arigoni observes that "[e]xtreme heat is uniquely dangerous for older adults because many lack the ability to readily adjust to extreme heat as a result of weakened cardiovascular circulation or preexisting health conditions such as heart disease and diabetes...." *Id.* For example, the "heat dome" that struck the Pacific Northwest in 2021, pushing temperatures in Portland, Oregon, up to an astronomical 116 degrees F, resulted in some 72 deaths, with victims an average age of 67. *Id.* at 45. For a wealth of materials and resources concerning the dangers of extreme heat and how these dangers may be managed, see www.heat.gov (last visited November 23, 2025).

As Americans continue to age and disasters multiply and expand, how might law or policy help address related risks? As a matter of Equal Protection jurisprudence under the Fourteenth Amendment, the Supreme Court has afforded no special protection or recognition for age as a suspect class. *See Massachusetts Bd. of Retirement v. Murgia*, 427 U.S. 307 (1976). However, legal protections may be found under federal statutory law, including the federal Age Discrimination Act of 1975, 29 U.S.C. § 6101 (2018) (Subject to certain exceptions, "no person in the United States shall, on the basis of age, ... be denied the benefits of, or be subjected to discrimination under any program or activity receiving Federal financial assistance"). Remedies may also be found under state laws to protect children and the elderly. *See, e.g.*, Cal. Welf. & Inst. Code § 15610.07 (California law defining abuse of an elder or a dependent adult to include physical abuse, neglect, abandonment, isolation, or deprivation of care); NMSA 1973,

§ 30-6-1D (prohibiting "knowingly, intentionally, or negligently and without justifiable cause, causing or permitting a child" to be abused). How would you want public and private authorities to assure the protection of your own children or parents or grandparents from the risk of disasters?

5. Disability. Closely associated with the disproportionate risk of disasters to older adults are the risks to people with physical or mental disabilities. Of all the people age 65 and older whose homes were flooded or otherwise damaged by Hurricane Katrina, almost half (48 percent) reported at least one disability, and more than one-quarter (26 percent) reported two or more disabilities. Disabilities included visual and hearing impairments, cognitive difficulties, as well as mobility limitations. Thomas Gabe, Gene Falk & Maggie McCarty, Congressional Research Service, *Hurricane Katrina: Social-Demographic Characteristics of Impacted Areas* at 17 (Nov. 4, 2005). Of course, disabilities are not limited to the elderly, and neither are the associated vulnerabilities to disasters. In the Tubbs Fire of October 2017, for example, one of the deaths in Santa Rosa, California, was a 27-year-old woman in a wheelchair who could not escape the flames that consumed the Journey's End Mobile Home Park. Eloísa Ruano González & Mary Callahan, *Victims Identified in Deadly Sonoma, Napa and Mendocino County Fires*, PRESS DEMOCRAT, Oct. 12, 2017. In the aftermath of Hurricane Maria in 2017, researchers found that the leading factors for hurricane-related mortalities in Puerto Rico included pre-existing heart disease followed by diabetes. Raul Cruz-Cano & Erin L. Mead, *Causes of Excess Deaths in Puerto Rico after Hurricane Maria: A Time-Series Estimation*, 109 AM. J. PUB. HEALTH 1050 (2019).

What can the law do to protect people with disabilities from the risks of disasters? Among other statutory protections, the Americans with Disabilities Act (ADA), 42 U.S.C. § 12131 *et seq*., and state analogues might prove of value in the disaster context. Title II of the ADA provides in relevant part that "[n]o qualified individual with a disability shall, by reason of such disability, be excluded from participation in or be denied the benefits of the services, programs, or activities of a public entity, or be subjected to discrimination by any such entity." 42 U.S.C. § 12132. Courts have found the ADA to require public authorities to include the needs of people with disabilities in their planning for disaster response. *See, e.g., Brooklyn Center for Independence v. Bloomberg*, 980 F. Supp. 2d 588 (S.D.N.Y. 2013) (New York City violated ADA by failure to plan for needs of disabled in emergency evacuation, transportation, and sheltering); *Communities Actively Living Independent & Free v. City of Los Angeles*, 2011 WL 4595993 (C.D. Cal) (Los Angeles violated ADA and California Disabled Persons Act by, among other things, failing to include provisions in the State's emergency preparedness program "to notify people with auditory impairments or cognitive disabilities of an emergency").

For a more thorough consideration of the potentially disproportionate impacts of disasters on disabled persons, and law and policy available to address these concerns, see Lance Gable, *Disasters and Disability*, *in* THE CAMBRIDGE HANDBOOK OF DISASTER LAW AND POLICY, John Travis Marshall et al., eds. 525 (2022).

6. Gender. A growing body of literature examines the differentiated impacts of disasters on men and women. As indicated in the brief excerpt from Professor Verchick above, gender-based marginalization is a contributing factor in populations' overall social vulnerability. This means that women, girls, and trans or nonbinary people are generally more susceptible to the harmful impacts of disasters than their cisgender male counterparts. Elaine Enarson, one early scholar in the field of gender and disaster research, describes how the "human experience" is often universalized in disaster, which overlooks issues specifically affecting women and girls:

> The striking disregard for gender in disaster studies is derived in part from generalizations about "human" behavior arising from decades of gender-blind research studies on preparedness, risk communication, emergency response, economic recovery, emergent organizations, public administration, and vulnerability. The result is a body of knowledge that both fails to specifically investigate gender in men's lives, and generalizes the knowledge gained "through men's eyes" to all persons. This covert grounding of disaster theory in men's lives benefits neither women nor men. Perhaps when critical gender studies are integrated into the canon and gender analysis comes to life in practice, we can speak of human experience in disasters.

ELAINE ENARSON, WOMEN CONFRONTING NATURAL DISASTER: FROM VULNERABILITY TO RESILIENCE 2 (2012).

What sort of issues are overlooked in a male-centric approach to disaster studies, and at what cost? As compared to men, women are overall more likely to, among other things, live below the poverty line; experience partner abuse and sexual assault; live with disabilities or mental illness; or need access to medical services including for reproductive health. Enarson at 3. These disparities are further exacerbated for women of color as compared to their white counterparts. *Id.* More recent literature observes continuing disparities across genders and need for further research in this area:

> There are major gender-based inequities in the realm of climate change and extreme weather events, including: poverty, full enjoyment of human rights and freedom from violence, access to healthcare, education, training, technology dissemination, as well as political engagement and policy formation.... Climate change and extreme weather events have social, economic, and political impacts, but the nexus between gender inequality, climate vulnerability, and the impacts of climate-induced disasters is understudied.
>
> Lack of autonomy can exacerbate the impacts of climate change and extreme weather events, making women even more vulnerable and less able to adapt. The impacts of climate change and extreme weather events can therefore intensify existing vulnerabilities, making women more exposed to violence due to migration, displacement, and other negative impacts, compounding victimization of women. Displacement related to climate change and extreme weather events can also lead to non-economic loss and damage, including loss of culture and heritage. Efforts to increase and strengthen auton-

> omy can reduce vulnerability to the impacts of climate change and extreme weather events and increase resilience and adaptive capacity. Therefore, efforts to reduce poverty, strengthen human rights, improve participation in economic, social, and political life, including through policy formation, technology transfer, and education and training, can all contribute to enhanced resilience to the impacts of climate change and extreme weather events.

Lisa Benjamin & Adelle Thomas, *Gender and Climate Justice—Implications for Policy Formation in the Caribbean Region*, 66 Loyola L. Rev. 329, 331–32 (2020).

Beyond climate-driven events, researchers have identified disproportionate impacts on women and girls following from a range of natural hazards. For example, the Indian Ocean tsunami in 2004, triggered by a massive subsea earthquake, claimed more than 220,000 lives in fourteen countries including India. In the decade that followed, one of the Indian states hit hardest by the tsunami experienced a staggering escalation of domestic partner violence, including a 232 percent rise in sexual violence. Smitha Rao, *A Natural Disaster and Intimate Partner Violence: Evidence Over Time*, 247 Social Sci. & Med. 112804 (2020).

Literature regarding disaster impacts on trans or nonbinary populations remains limited, but indicates another gender-based area of social vulnerability that is often overlooked in dominant disaster paradigms. *See, e.g.*, J.C. Gaillard et al., *Beyond Men and Women: A Critical Perspective on Gender and Disaster*, Disasters 429, 433 (2017). As one more recent commentator observed:

> Transgender communities are rarely included in environmental disaster planning and programming, while they are frequently left out of recovery and response efforts. And transgender women in particular confront roadblocks to essential shelter and relief services due to discriminatory gender stereotypes. This discrimination fuels the transgender community's existing mistrust of healthcare systems, which further contributes to their underuse of social services amid a natural disaster.... In the midst of a disaster, emergency medical providers routinely undervalue hormone medications and treatments for HIV and AIDS.... Disaster shelters can also be dangerous places for transgender people, particularly ones that fail to affirm their gender or protect them from physical harassment. Often, shelters force transgender people into gendered housing that does not match their gender identity. And when transgender individuals use congregate showers, their bodily exposure to other shelter survivors invites verbal and physical attacks if their perceived genitals do not match their gender identity. Unsurprisingly, some transgender individuals simply avoid shelters altogether.

Zacary E. Wilson-Fetrow, *Meaningless Involvement: How Traditional Modes of Involvement Exclude Transgender People from Environmental Justice*, 48 Ecology L.Q. 843, 885–86 (2021).

7. Immigrants. Immigrant communities are another diverse group with heightened vulnerabilities to disasters. The deadliest disaster in U.S. history, the COVID-19 epidemic, resulted in more than one million confirmed deaths in the United States. Within these staggering losses, many immigrant communities suffered the worst. One study by UCLA examined COVID mortalities in California, which has the largest immigrant population in the United States. After the first year of the pandemic, the study revealed that Latinos, many from immigrant families, experienced COVID mortalities almost six times higher than "non-Hispanic whites." David E. Hayes-Bautista, Paul Hsu, & Giselle D. Hernández, *COVID Casts Stark Light on Structural Inequities in California* (2021). As with other forms of environmental injustice, these stark disparities often reflect systemic inequities in society. For example, the UCLA researchers found that Latinos in California on average had lower salaries, less health insurance, greater exposure as "essential workers" to co-workers and customers, and larger households with more workers and children. *Id.*

After Hurricane Katrina, Congress amended the Stafford Act specifically to address vulnerabilities based upon limited English proficiency. *See* Post-Katrina Emergency Management Reform Act of 2006, Pub. L. No. 109-295, 120 Stat. 1355 (2006), amending Stafford Act § 308, codified at 42 U.S.C § 5151(a). With this amendment, states who fail to provide for Limited English Proficiency communities could be subject to enforcement action including loss of federal disaster assistance.

Beyond language barriers, other important differences may make immigrant communities more vulnerable during disasters. In many immigrant communities, there may be ingrained distrust of government, financial institutions, charitable organizations, or legal professionals. With distrust of banks, immigrants may be more likely to maintain savings in cash, which could be lost in a fire or flood. In a disaster, immigrants may worry about the loss of critical immigration documents. Immigrants may also experience heightened levels of prejudice based on national origin. In one notorious incident, for example, then New Orleans mayor Ray Nagin, speaking on camera during a town hall meeting in the wake of Hurricane Katrina, elicited great applause from a crowd by asking, "How do I make sure that New Orleans is not overrun by Mexican workers?" For one harrowing story of discrimination against a Syrian-American family following Hurricane Katrina—and the lawyers who help in the end—*see* Dave Eggers, Zeitoun (2009).

Finally, many individual immigrants and families may have legitimate concerns about seeking emergency aid and disaster assistance based upon their immigration status. Undocumented immigrants are, in fact, entitled to many forms of emergency care, including temporary shelter, food, water, and medical care. Consistently over the years, including the first Trump administration, FEMA maintained, "Your information is confidential [and] FEMA shares that information only with the state and designated agencies that provide disaster assistance, with your permission only." FEMA, *Non-Citizens Can Apply for FEMA Assistance*, Nov. 15, 2016 (encouraging "non-citizen" residents of North Carolina to seek emergency aid and disaster assistance following

Hurricane Matthew). Nevertheless, FEMA (at this writing) remains a part of the U.S. Department of Homeland Security (DHS), which also includes U.S. Immigration and Customs Enforcement (ICE), so the potential concerns of undocumented persons interacting with FEMA are certainly understandable. For a full analysis of the statutory rights and challenges of immigrant communities in receiving disaster assistance in the United States, *see* Ashley Morey, *No Shelter from the Storm: Undocumented Populations and Federal Disaster Aid*, 11 SEATTLE J. SOC. J. 257 (2012).

As a student-lawyer in a law school clinic, or an attorney in a legal aid organization, how might you advise a client who has immigration concerns as well as substantial losses from a declared disaster?

2. Resilience

In contrast to increased vulnerability, increased resilience can help communities and individuals survive the impacts of disasters and recover quickly. There are many ways to define and conceptualize resilience. Here is one description from Professor J.B. Ruhl:

> Although there are numerous variations, a good working definition [of resilience] as used in natural and social sciences is "the capacity of a system to experience shocks while retaining essentially the same function, structure, feedbacks, and therefore identity." One hallmark of system resilience thus is the capacity to maintain a high level of consistency of behavioral structure in the face of a dynamic environment of change.

J.B. Ruhl, *General Design Principles for Resilience and Adaptive Capacity in Legal Systems—With Applications to Climate Change Adaptation*, 89 N.C. L. REV. 1373, 1374–76 (2011).

From this beginning, Professor Ruhl proceeds to distinguish two approaches to resilience, what he terms "engineering resilience" and "ecological resilience." According to Ruhl, "The engineering resilience strategy is to devote all system resources to staying near the equilibrium, the goal being to snap back." By contrast, "ecological resilience relies on adjustments to system processes as the means of managing overall system integrity." *Id.* at 1377. Thus, disaster justice advocates might pursue resilience to coastal storm surge either through engineering measures (e.g., higher, reinforced seawalls) or through ecological measures (e.g., reshaping wildlife habitat or relocating human communities away from flood zones).

Another way of considering resilience is through the dichotomy suggested previously by Professor Verchick's discussion of vulnerability, considering *physical* resilience and *social* resilience. With *physical* resilience, one might imagine building structures designed to withstand maximum wind speeds anticipated in future hurricanes and typhoons. With *social* resilience, one might imagine, for example, a community prepared to help each community member find safe shelter from the storm. For further exploration of the concept of social resilience and its potential value to traditionally vulnerable communities, consider the following excerpt:

Sidney Shapiro, *Preface: An Ounce of Prevention*

CENTER FOR PROGRESSIVE REFORM, FROM SURVIVING TO THRIVING: EQUITY IN DISASTER PLANNING AND RECOVERY (Sept. 2018)

The story is now familiar. An area of the United States is battered by a superstorm, hurricane, or other climate disaster, resulting in a calamity for the people who live and work there. The Federal Emergency Management Agency (FEMA) offers emergency assistance, but since it is not enough to address the harms that occurred, Congress acts to provide hundreds of millions of dollars of additional assistance.

But imagine a counter-narrative, with a significantly better outcome. In that story, we would have paid attention—before disaster ensued—to how environmental protection and planning can prevent and minimize the harm that disasters cause to people, their housing, and the infrastructure of our cities, states, and territories. Steps to inform the public about risks, to adopt protective measures, and to enforce health, safety, and environmental standards could have minimized the human suffering and loss and minimized the economic costs associated with recovery.

One reason for our oversight is that we tend to think about the varied functions of government as distinct. Agencies that protect us from health, safety and environmental risks are separate and operate under different laws than do agencies that address human needs, education, and other forms of our collective welfare. So we tend to overlook the role that these protections play in minimizing the impact of disaster. But viewed through a wider lens, all of these agencies' work ideally serves the same goal: promoting social resilience. People and their neighbors are socially resilient when they have the capacity to survive, adapt, and grow in the face of misfortune and change.

These two types of government activities are mutually supportive. As this report details, investments in health, safety, and environmental protection on the front end can reduce the need for financial or other assistance for human needs after disaster strikes. Environmental protection measures cannot prevent all of the harms that will occur in the wake of weather disasters. Nor can social support services and disaster relief alleviate all the loss and suffering in the wake of disasters. By partnering to promote social resilience, these agencies can use their resources more effectively and better achieve their shared goals....

When we fail to prevent and minimize preventable harms, we ignore Ben Franklin's sage advice, "An ounce of prevention is worth a pound of cure." A recent study by the National Institute of Building Sciences highlights the accuracy of that maxim in the context of disaster response. The study recommends measures that governments and property owners can take to reduce the impact of disaster events that would prevent 600 deaths, 1 million nonfatal injuries, 4,000 cases of post-traumatic stress disorder

(PTSD), and that would save $6 for every $1 spent on these protections funded through select federal agencies.

We also ignore the reality that our most vulnerable citizens are the ones who suffer the most in violent storms and other disasters. Many people share the heartache of losing a house, valuable keepsakes, and other property. But while these harms are shared among many, the most vulnerable residents are often the people least able to manage the temporary and permanent consequences imposed on them by weather disasters.

Social resilience is about the capacity of people and their communities to withstand, recover from, and prosper after disruption. In the case of climate and other weather disasters, measures that promote resilience include natural and human systems that reduce the force of storms or the likelihood of other disasters, preparedness plans that protect people when disaster occurs, and health, safety, and environmental protection measures that focus on anticipating and preparing for weather-related events in ways that prevent (or minimize) harm to people and their property. Resilience is also enhanced by strong social networks, access to information to make sound choices, and policies that recognize and account for the varied needs and capacities of different communities and populations. It is about ensuring people have access to health care, education, and training they need to accommodate the dislocation that occurs when disasters wreak havoc on the communities in which they live.

* * *

Outside of academia, efforts to promote community resilience have been supported broadly by public and private initiatives and at every level of government across the country. *See, e.g.*, Georgetown Climate Center, *Lessons in Regional Resilience: Case Studies on Regional Climate Collaboratives*, Jan. 2017 (discussing resilience initiatives by local governments from Seattle, Washington, to Miami, Florida).

On a national level, the U.S. Department of Homeland Security (DHS), together with other federal departments and agencies, has recognized and emphasized the need for building community resilience. In 2011, President Obama issued a formal directive "aimed at strengthening the security and resilience of the United States through systematic preparation for the threats that pose the greatest risk to the security of the Nation, including acts of terrorism, cyber attacks, pandemics, and catastrophic natural disasters." Presidential Policy Directive/PPD—8: National Preparedness, Mar. 30, 2011. For the purpose of this national goal, the directive defined "resilience" to mean "the ability to adapt to changing conditions and withstand and rapidly recover from disruption due to emergencies."

Consistent with this directive, FEMA has invested in efforts to promote resilience nationwide. In 2024, FEMA released its first National Resilience Guidance, described as offering "a unifying vision of resilience and the principles and steps all communities and organizations in every sector and discipline can take to increase their resilience." FEMA, National Resilience Guidance: A Collaborative Approach to Build-

ING RESILIENCE (August 2024), available online at https://www.fema.gov/sites/default/files/documents/fema_national-resilience-guidance_august2024.pdf.

FEMA also manages significant funding authorized by Congress for grant programs such as the Hazard Mitigation Assistance Grants, available to states, tribal nations, local and territorial governments. For details, see https://www.fema.gov/grants/mitigation.

Together with academic partners, FEMA continues to promote resilience through research, to include efforts to identify factors that contribute the most to community resilience. FEMA defines "community resilience" to mean "the ability of a community to prepare for anticipated natural hazards, adapt to changing conditions, and withstand and recover rapidly from disruptions." NATIONAL RISK INDEX at 4-3. In order to measure community resilience on a local level, FEMA has drawn upon substantial academic investigation led by Susan Cutter and colleagues at the University of South Carolina. The top factors contributing to community resilience have been collected into six broad categories, with examples provided below:

Baseline Resilience Indicators for Communities

University of South Carolina (2020)

Social Resilience:

- % Households with at least one vehicle
- % Population proficient English speakers
- Psychosocial support facilities per capita
- Food security rate

Economic Resilience:

- % Owner-occupied housing units
- % Labor force employed by federal government
- % Employees not in farming, fishing, forestry, tourism, or extractive industry

Community Capital:

- % Current population born in state
- % Immigrant population residing in U.S. > 5 years
- Religious organizations per capita
- Civic organizations per capita

Institutional Resilience:

- Population stability over last 5 years
- Proximity of county seat to state capital
- Local disaster training
- Disaster aid experience over last 10 years

Housing/Infrastructural Resilience:

- % Housing units not mobile homes
- Availability of evacuation routes
- # Public schools per capita
- % Population with access to broadband internet service

Environmental Resilience:

- % Land in wetlands
- % Pervious surfaces
- % Efficient water use
- % Energy efficiency per consumer

For the full list of Baseline Resilience Indicators for Communities (BRIC), see https://www.sc.edu/study/colleges_schools/artsandsciences/centers_and_institutes/hvri/data_and_resources/bric/index.php.

Academia and government researchers are not alone in their promotion of community resilience and recognition of the indicators noted above. For one final perspective on resilience in this section, consider this observation from the NAACP Environmental & Climate Justice Program, focusing on community resilience promoted by "**social cohesion**":

> A key aspect of community resilience is social cohesion. There are many definitions of social (or community) cohesion; we like this definition from The Organisation for Economic Co-operation and Development: "A cohesive society works towards the well-being of all its members, fights exclusion and marginalization, creates a sense of belonging, promotes trust, and offers its members the opportunity of upward social mobility."
>
> Put simply, a spirit of cooperation defines socially cohesive communities. What does this have to do with emergency management? To have a community that works well together in times of crisis, there must be strong relationships, trust, and a spirit of cooperation, unity, and mutuality to mitigate the shocks of a disaster.

NAACP Environmental & Climate Justice Program, *In the Eye of the Storm: A People's Guide to Transforming Crisis & Advancing Equity in the Disaster Continuum* (2018) at 37, https://www.naacp.org/climate-justice-resources/in-the-eye-of-the-storm/.

Notes and Questions

1. **"Engineering resilience" vs. "ecological resilience."** Professor Ruhl's distinction between "engineering resilience" and "ecological resilience" may be readily grasped in the context of natural catastrophes: Can we build a structure strong enough to withstand the next hurricane/flood/fire/winter storm/earthquake (engineering resilience) or can we create a system flexible enough to adjust and adapt to changes without losing

its essential identity and function (ecological resilience)? In his article, as suggested by the title, Professor Ruhl theorizes that legal systems, as well as physical structures, can exhibit either engineering resilience or ecological resilience. For one example of engineering resilience in a legal system, Professor Ruhl points to the U.S. Constitution, which "was designed to be hard to alter in design and has proven so...." Ruhl continues, "By contrast, the American common law system offers an example of ecological resilience: it is a highly dispersed structure of courts throughout the nation, all working to craft doctrine under a loose set of process rules.... The result is a high capacity for swings in behavior in response to changing conditions without altering the system's basic structure and process design." Ruhl at 1380–81.

What are the relative advantages you see of each approach to designing a legal system capable of functioning in a disaster context? Do you want hard and fast rules to provide clarity and structure to potentially chaotic conditions? Or do you want the flexibility to adapt to changing conditions and circumstances that cannot possibly be anticipated in advance? Can you have some of both?

To put these questions in a concrete context, consider the BP Deepwater Horizon oil spill in the Gulf of Mexico in 2010. When the *Deepwater Horizon* (DWH) drill rig caught fire on April 20, 2010, killing eleven crewmembers, and sank two days later, crude oil from the well a mile below the surface spewed uncontrolled for at least eighty-seven days. By some official estimates, more than two hundred million gallons of oil discharged to waters of the Gulf over this time, making it one of the biggest oil spills in world history. As an example of "engineering resilience" in the legal system, the federal Oil Pollution Act, 33 U.S.C. § 2702 (2018), clearly made responsible parties liable for the costs of cleanup and damages, to include recovery for losses in "subsistence use" and "profits and earnings capacity." *Id.* § 2702(b)(2)(C), (E). Consider these categories of liability in the unique circumstances described below:

> Louisiana is home to roughly 25,000 Vietnamese-Americans, most of them living near the Gulf Coast. Their communities, which grew out of the wave of refugees in the 1970s, are almost all economically dependent on fishing and crabbing. Indeed, it is estimated that thirty to fifty percent of all commercial fishers in the Gulf are of Vietnamese descent. In addition to supporting the local economy, fishing also nourished an array of reciprocal bonds among family, friends, and business associates. Vietnamese-American fishers fed their families with their catch. They bartered it for fruits, vegetables, and other goods. A fisher may donate a recent haul to a spring festival or "pound" (that is, reward) the minister with tuna after a stirring sermon. At a wedding, the bride's family might be showered with a hundred pounds of blue crab.

Verchick, *supra*, at 58–59. Can legal systems ever "engineer" for every circumstance that might be encountered after a disaster? How might the concept of "ecological resilience" apply to protect the interests and values of the Vietnamese-American fisher community in this example?

2. Social cohesion. One contributor to social resilience, promoted by the NAACP and other NGOs, as well as academia and government, is known as "social cohesion." How is social cohesion defined in the excerpt above? How is social cohesion built and maintained?

Recent research continues to suggest that social cohesion may play a significant role in promoting community resilience. However, conclusions have been mixed. In one thorough review and analysis of literature examining the role of social cohesion during the COVID-19 pandemic, researchers found indications that social cohesion at the national level may have related positively to health outcomes in the early stages of the pandemic, a "rally around the flag" effect. In later stages of the pandemic, however, as policy responses to the pandemic (e.g., vaccination) worked to fracture national unity, social cohesion at the group level may have contributed to adverse health outcomes. As one potential adverse consequence, the United States and United Kingdom—two of the nations best prepared for managing pandemics—experienced some of the highest rates of illness and death from COVID-19. Paul Ware, *Social Cohesion and COVID-19: Integrative Review*, 13 Interactive J. Med. Research 51214 (Nov. 21, 2024).

3. Mental health. Among the dozens of variables in the BRIC is "Psychosocial support facilities per capita," an indicator of mental health within a given community. The important role of mental health in pre-disaster resiliency and post-disaster recovery has long been acknowledged by researchers. Fran H. Norris & Carrie L. Elrod, *Psychological Consequences of Disaster*, in Methods for Disaster Mental Health Research (2005) (reviewing studies published between 1981 and 2004). Many of the same groups that may be more vulnerable to other impacts of disasters may be most vulnerable to impacts on mental health. Such impacts commonly include depression, anxiety, and Post-Traumatic Stress Disorder (PTSD). These vulnerable groups include children, women, disabled persons, low-income people, and ethnic minorities. Studies have found, for example, that women may be twice as likely as men to develop PTSD following a disaster. *Id.* at 32. People with substance abuse disorders and pre-existing mental disorders may also be at high risk for mental health impacts following disasters. Suresh Bada Math et al., *Disaster Management: Mental Health Perspective*, 37 Indian J. Psych. Med. 261 (Jul–Sept. 2015).

Often overlooked, another group at risk for mental health impacts following disasters are disaster relief workers. "Disaster relief workers encounter considerable stress while providing services to people affected by a disaster and … are at risk for compassion fatigue, burnout and vicarious traumatization." *Id.* As such, "it is essential to monitor the disaster relief workers mental and physical health status during disaster pre-deployment …, deployment …, and post-deployment phase. …" *Id.*

Measures for building and maintaining resilience against adverse mental health impacts following disasters may include "art therapy, … group discussions, drama; … engaging in activities such as yoga, meditation, prayers, relaxation, sports and games; spiritual activities; [and] educating parents and teachers." *Id.* As one example of measures for maintaining good mental health, EPA and other responders supporting cleanup activities following the Maui wildfires participated in a morning and evening *pule* (blessing), led by native hosts, to open and close field work each day. For more on the Maui wildfires and the central role of Native Hawaiian cultural values guiding the response, see the EPA StoryMap at https://storymaps.arcgis.com/stories/543ef95291704045a8943866f4c84b04.

4. Older adults. As previously noted, older adults (often identified as people 65 years or older) may have disproportionate vulnerabilities to disasters. Aging by itself may not always lead to heightened risk; in some ways, it may lead to greater resilience. For example, older adults may prove more resilient than other age groups to anxiety, depression, or other adverse mental health responses to disasters. Norris & Elrod, *supra*, at 32. However, Danielle Arigoni, an expert on aging policies and programs, observes that often "increased age amplifies other vulnerabilities in physical and mental health, cognition, financial well-being, isolation, mobility, and access...." Arigoni at 28. Understanding these vulnerabilities allows policymakers, planners, caregivers, and individuals the opportunity to evaluate and implement a range of strategies to enhance resilience for older adults. Such strategies include the following:

- Invest in redundant and sustainable energy systems, ensuring refrigeration for medications, power for elevators and medical equipment, heating and cooling for homes.
- Identify specific locations within each neighborhood where older adults live and any mobility challenges or other special needs they may have.
- Plan in advance for people with dementia and other cognitive impairments that may challenge self-care and the ability to follow emergency instructions.
- Deploy media forms, including "low-tech modes," that will ensure the ability to communicate with older adults in urgent circumstances.

Arigoni at Table 4-1. Consistent with foundational principles of environmental justice, planning for disaster resilience should encourage the direct engagement of older adults, addressing their unique concerns and benefiting from their accumulated expertise and wisdom. Planning may also benefit from the experiences of community leaders and organizations active in promoting "age-friendly" disaster resilience.

One of these organizations, Together New Orleans, has leveraged public and private funding to construct "Community Lighthouses," solar- and battery-powered resilience hubs that will make heating, cooling, phone-charging, and other community services available in the event of emergencies. As of 2025, ten such hubs have already been constructed at churches and community centers across New Orleans, with more hubs planned to allow walkable access within many neighborhoods. For more information on the work of Together New Orleans, including volunteer outreach to individual community members, find the organization website at the following link: https://www.togethernola.org/.

C. Disaster Law Fundamentals

Observing the devastation in New Orleans and other areas impacted by Hurricane Katrina in 2005, scholars from diverse fields including emergency management and environmental law began to develop a new branch of integrated study and practice that soon came to be known as Disaster Law. The first book dedicated to disaster law appeared in 2006 and a third edition was published in 2015. DANIEL A. FARBER, ROBERT R.M. VERCHICK, JAMES MING CHEN, LISA GROW SUN, DISASTER LAW AND POLICY (3rd ed. 2015). According to Professor Dan Farber, one thing that identifies disaster law as a distinct field is the existence of "a number of distinctive statutes, such as the Stafford Act...." Moreover, and perhaps most importantly, "disaster law as a whole is unified by the concept of risk management," which is the central concern of what Farber calls the "circle of disaster." Daniel Farber, *Symposium Introduction: Navigating the Intersection of Environmental Law and Disaster Law*, 2011 BYU L. REV. 1783, 1790–91 (2011).

For the benefit of students, lawyers, and other advocates who may be called upon at some point to assist diverse individuals or communities impacted by disasters, this section provides a brief introduction to the "Disaster Cycle" followed by key elements of the Stafford Act and other statutes contributing to the body of disaster law.

1. The Disaster Cycle

The field of disaster law is distinguished by its focus on risk management through what many observers describe as a "circle" of disaster stages. Professor Verchick describes the "Circle of Risk Management" as including stages of "Planning, Response, Compensation, and Recovery." Verchick, *supra*. Professor Dan Farber suggests it includes stages of "mitigation, emergency response, insurance/liability compensation, government assistance, [and] rebuilding...." Daniel Farber, *Symposium Introduction: Navigating the Intersection of Environmental Law and Disaster Law*, 2011 BYU L. REV. 1783, 1791 (2011). For purposes of this brief section, we will refer to the "Disaster Cycle" and simplify it to three stages, all conveniently beginning with the letter R, as depicted in Figure 15-4.

Before further consideration of these three R's, we should make a few broad observations from this figure. In general, greater investments in readiness may contribute to a more immediate and effective response when a disaster strikes and faster recovery for the affected communities. Also, as a cycle, there is no beginning nor end. As Los Angeles County recovers from the devastating fires in January 2025, it must also maintain readiness to respond to the next fire that erupts in the county. While the stages may thus overlap and blend at times, the Disaster Cycle nevertheless provides a useful framework for comprehending disaster law and policy, as this brief section may demonstrate.

a. Readiness (or "preparedness") refers generally to "actions taken to plan, organize, equip, train, and exercise to build and sustain the capabilities necessary to prevent, protect against, mitigate the effects of, respond to, and recover from those threats that pose the greatest risks...." U.S. DEPT. OF HOMELAND SECURITY, NATIONAL PREPAREDNESS

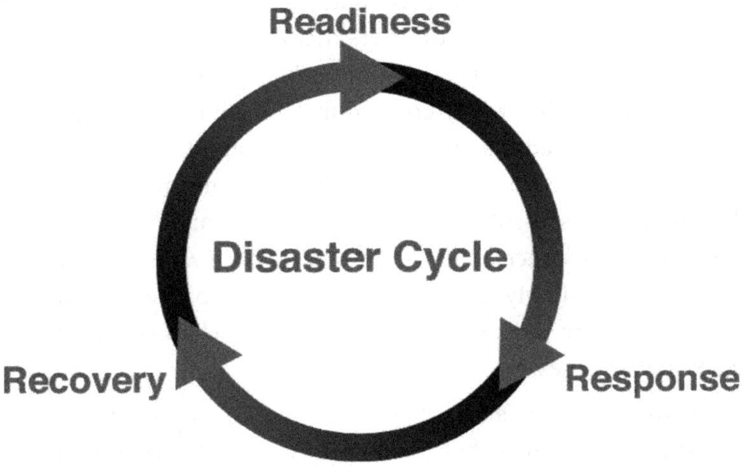

Figure 15-4. Disaster Cycle. Graphic: Tony Anderson, University of New Mexico School of Law.

GOAL (2nd ed. Sept. 2015), at A-2 (defining "National Preparedness"). Importantly, readiness in this sense is not merely a static condition of being "ready" to respond to an incident, but also a state of active and continuous preparation for foreseeable threats.

Elements of readiness such as planning, organizing, equipping, and training engage all levels of government, and many businesses, nonprofit organizations, and private individuals. Of course, the capacity to engage in readiness activities is not equally distributed across all communities and individuals. One obvious limitation is available resources. A single parent working two jobs in order to make ends meet each month cannot be expected to have the same capacity to participate in readiness training or to maintain a recommended level of personal savings in case of emergencies. As one review of related studies concluded:

> The literature suggests that socially vulnerable or disadvantaged households have lower levels of disaster preparedness. For example, [multiple studies] all find that earthquake preparedness (that is, possession of first-aid kits, emergency food supplies, evacuation plans, and fire extinguishers) is less common in low income and minority populations. [One 2003 study] finds that both low income and Black households are less likely to have adequate shuttering to protect homes from hurricane damage. Similarly, [a 1999 study] note[s] that Black households have constrained access to hurricane preparedness supplies. Scholars also observe that minority and lower income homeowners are less likely to hold earthquake [] and flood insurance instruments [].

Sammy Zahran et al., *Social Vulnerability and the Natural and Built Environment: A Model of Flood Casualties in Texas*, DISASTERS, Oct. 24, 2008, at 539–40.

What can advocates do to address this inequality? First, it is certainly an appropriate role of government to plan for the protection of all people in the event of an emergency or disaster situation. Indeed, much of the planning improvements since

Hurricane Katrina have focused on this continuing challenge. On a national level, planning for most emergencies and disasters that require a federal response is led by FEMA through the *National Response Framework*. Recent revisions of the NRF have emphasized protection of the "whole community," which the NRF defines specifically to include "children; older adults, individuals with disabilities and others with access and functional needs; those from religious, racial, and ethnically diverse backgrounds; people with limited English proficiency; and owners of animals, including household pets and service and assistance animals." FEMA, NATIONAL RESPONSE FRAMEWORK (4th ed. 2019) at 5. Accordingly, the unique needs of each of these groups and all other members of a community must be taken into account when governments engage in readiness planning activities.

Consistent with federal law and policy as well as state, local, and tribal policy and legislation, all states and many tribal and local governments have emergency plans in place addressing "all hazards," regardless of whether they represent a "natural" disaster. *See, e.g.*, State of Florida Comprehensive Emergency Management Plan (2024); California State Emergency Plan (2024); State of Texas Emergency Management Basic Plan (Jan. 2025). Planning in each of these documents should address the needs of vulnerable communities and individuals—and be updated regularly to ensure such needs are fully addressed.

In addition to government planning, resources are available to help vulnerable communities and individuals improve their own readiness for emergencies. One good online source of information maintained by FEMA is www.ready.gov, which provides helpful suggestions to family members, including young people, on how to prepare for specific threats such as earthquakes, floods, and winter weather. Recognizing the limited access to and use of online materials by some community members, many planning agencies also offer training in person at convenient locations. In New York City, for example, the *Ready New York* program will send emergency management experts upon request to "your workplace, school, community center, or house of worship" in order to help community members "learn about the hazards you may face in New York City and prepare for all types of emergencies. . . ." https://www1.nyc.gov/site/em/ready/ready-new-york.page.

b. Response. Ready or not, when disaster strikes, some response may be required. FEMA defines "response" in this context to include "actions to save lives, protect property and the environment, stabilize communities, and meet basic human needs following an incident." FEMA, NATIONAL RESPONSE FRAMEWORK (4th ed. 2019), at 1. For most emergencies, such as a car crash or house fire, response may be provided entirely by "first-responders," including local law enforcement and fire authorities. Larger, more complex incidents such as the 2023 train derailment in East Palestine, Ohio, may require involvement from state or federal authorities.

For a major catastrophe such as an earthquake or hurricane in the United States, the public mind often thinks first of FEMA. In 2025, the Trump administration floated the idea of abolishing FEMA, leaving states to manage disasters on their own. This facile idea ignores the fact that many states and territories cannot afford disaster response and assistance on the scale that the federal government can provide. (For fiscal year 2025, FEMA's annual budget exceeded $33 billion, to include disaster relief funds and grants to state, local, and tribal entities.) Leaving disaster response to the states could also leave Indian tribes without any disaster assistance. The idea of abolishing FEMA further ignores the reality that many major disasters require coordination of response across multiple states and jurisdictions. Such coordination may have life-or-death consequences, as agency turf battles at the time of a disaster could be a disaster in itself. To avoid that kind of delay, most federal and state response plans designate lead agencies to serve defined roles during an emergency or disaster. For example, under the *National Response Framework*, Emergency Support Function #1 (ESF #1: Transportation), if an earthquake destroyed part of the federal highway system or required closure of national airspace, the designated lead federal agency would be the U.S. Department of Transportation for purposes of managing those aspects of the disaster response. If the same earthquake breached a levee or impaired a sewage treatment system, the lead federal agency for response to those concerns would be the U.S. Army Corps of Engineers (ESF #3: Public Works). Likewise, if the earthquake caused an oil spill from a ruptured pipeline, the designated lead federal agency for responding to the oil spill would be the U.S. EPA (ESF #10: Oil and Hazardous Materials Response). NATIONAL RESPONSE FRAMEWORK (4th ed. 2019), Table 4: Emergency Support Functions and ESF Coordinators.

Similar designations are often made in advance by state, local, and tribal governments, requiring multiple agencies from various levels of governments to coordinate efficiently and effectively in order to achieve a common mission. To establish and maintain such coordination quickly and throughout a disaster response, federal policy (and federal funding) requires all agencies, on every level, to adopt the **Incident Command System (ICS)**. Under ICS, agencies maintain their individual authorities and jurisdiction, but must operate under certain response doctrines, for example, operating within certain organizational structures such as Unified Command. ICS may appear bewildering to most members of the public, but effective community advocates will decipher the bureaucracy, request copies of organization charts and operating plans, and identify particular moments in time and place where community input may be most influential. For a head-start on comprehending the Incident Command System, *see* Clifford J. Villa, *Law and Lawyers in the Incident Command System*, 36 SEATTLE U. L. REV. 1855 (2013).

c. Recovery. As defined by FEMA, recovery includes "the restoration and strengthening of key systems and resource assets that are critical to the economic stability, vitality, and long-term sustainability of the communities themselves. These include health (including behavioral health) and human services capabilities and networks, public and private disability support and service systems, educational systems, community social networks, natural and cultural resources, affordable and accessible housing, infrastructure systems, and local and regional economic drivers." FEMA, NATIONAL DISASTER RECOVERY FRAMEWORK (2nd ed. 2016) at 1–2. Among the guiding principles most relevant to vulnerable communities, FEMA emphasizes that the recovery stage (as with readiness) focuses on service to the "whole community." By this, FEMA explains—

> Understanding legal obligations and sharing best practices when planning and implementing recovery strategies to avoid excluding groups is critical. Actions, both intentional and unintentional, that exclude groups of people based on race, color, ethnicity, national origin (including limited English proficiency), religion, sex, sexual orientation, gender identity, age, or disability can have long-term negative consequences on entire communities and may violate law.

National Disaster Recovery Framework at 10. By potential violations of law, FEMA cites federal statutes specifically including the Americans with Disabilities Act (ADA), Title VI of the Civil Rights Act of 1964, the Fair Housing Act of 1968, and the Age Discrimination Act of 1975.

If all of this sounds good (or somewhat abstract), when most people think of lawyers and the Disaster Cycle, they think immediately of the recovery stage and questions of compensation. What are the limits of my client's homeowners insurance policy? Can the federal government be liable for the failures of a levee constructed by the Army Corps of Engineers? Should BP have to compensate the Vietnamese-American fishers along the Gulf Coast for injuries to their cultural resources? Should a local government be liable for constructing public housing in a floodplain? Could a local government be liable if it refuses to replace public housing in a floodplain? Could a public utility be liable for power lines that ignite a wildfire during a windstorm? Could a public utility be liable if it preemptively shuts down power lines before a windstorm and interrupts the flow of oxygen to an elderly person on a Continuous Positive Airway Pressure (CPAP) machine? Obviously, questions of compensation after a disaster may keep lawyers employed for a long time and keep justice advocates searching for better solutions.

2. Disaster Law

The major federal law governing disasters in the United States is the Robert T. Stafford Disaster Relief and Emergency Assistance Act, Pub. L. No. 100-707, 102 Stat. 4689 (1988) ("Stafford Act"), which amended the Disaster Relief Act of 1974, Pub. L. No. 93-288, 88 Stat. 243 (1974). As amended, the Stafford Act provides the major authority for federal assistance following a declaration by the president of a national "emergency" or a "major disaster." The Stafford Act also provides federal funding for "predisaster hazard mitigation." While no substitute for complete review of the statute itself, we share from the Stafford Act some key provisions:

Sec. 102. Definitions (42 U.S.C. § 5122)

(1) "Emergency" means any occasion or instance for which, in the determination of the President, Federal assistance is needed to supplement State and local efforts and capabilities to save lives and to protect property and public health and safety, or to lessen or avert the threat of a catastrophe in any part of the United States.

(2) "Major disaster" means any natural catastrophe (including any hurricane, tornado, storm, high water, winddriven water, tidal wave, tsunami, earthquake, volcanic eruption, landslide, mudslide, snowstorm, or drought), or, regardless of cause, any fire, flood, or explosion, in any part of the United States, which in the determination of the President causes damage of sufficient severity and magnitude to warrant major disaster assistance under this Act to supplement the efforts and available resources of States, local governments, and disaster relief organizations....

Sec. 201. Federal and State Disaster Preparedness Programs (42 U.S.C. § 5131)

(a) The President is authorized to establish a program of disaster preparedness that utilizes services of all appropriate agencies and includes—(1) preparation of disaster preparedness plans for mitigation, warning, emergency operations, rehabilitation, and recovery; (2) training and exercises; [and] (3) postdisaster critiques and evaluations....

Sec. 203. Predisaster Hazard Mitigation (42 U.S.C. § 5133)

(b) The President may establish a program to provide technical and financial assistance to State and local governments to assist in the implementation of predisaster hazard mitigation measures that are cost-effective and are designed to reduce injuries, loss of life, and damage and destruction of property....

Sec. 308. Nondiscrimination in Disaster Assistance (42 U.S.C. § 5151)

(a) [Regulations issued by the President] shall include provisions for insuring that the distribution of supplies, the processing of applications, and other relief and assistance activities shall be accomplished in an equitable and impartial manner, without discrimination on the grounds of race, color, religion, nationality, sex, age, disability, English proficiency, or economic status.

Sec. 316. Protection of Environment (42 U.S.C. § 5159)

An action which is taken [pursuant to provisions of this statute], which has the effect of restoring a facility substantially to its condition prior to the disaster or emergency, shall not be deemed a major Federal action significantly affecting the quality of the human environment within the meaning of the National Environmental Policy Act....

Sec. 401. Procedure for Declaration (42 U.S.C. § 5170)

(a) All requests for declaration by the President that a major disaster exists shall be made by the Governor of the affected State. Such a request shall be based on a finding that the disaster is of such severity and magnitude that effective response is beyond the capabilities of the State and the affected local government and that Federal assistance is necessary.... Based on the request of a Governor under this section, the President may declare under this Act that a major disaster or emergency exists.

(b) The Chief Executive of an affected Indian tribal government may submit a request for a declaration by the President that a major disaster exists....

(c) In providing assistance to an Indian tribal government under this subchapter, the President may waive or adjust any payment of a non-Federal contribution....

Sec. 402. General Financial Assistance (42 U.S.C. § 5170a)

In any major disaster, the President may—

(1) direct any Federal agency … to utilize its authorities and the resources granted to it under Federal law … in support of State and local assistance response and recovery efforts …

(2) coordinate all disaster relief assistance (including voluntary assistance) provided by Federal agencies, private organizations, and State and local governments …

(4) assist State and local governments in the distribution of medicine, food, and other consumable supplies, and emergency assistance; and

(5) provide accelerated Federal assistance and Federal support where necessary to save lives, prevent human suffering, or mitigate severe damage, which may be provided in the absence of a specific request. …

Sec. 403. Essential Assistance (42 U.S.C. § 5170b)

(a) Federal agencies may on the direction of the President, provide assistance essential to meeting immediate threats to life and property resulting from a major disaster, as follows:

(1) Utilizing, lending, or donating to State and local governments Federal equipment, supplies, personnel, and other resources …

(3) Performing on public or private lands or waters any work or services essential to saving lives and protecting and preserving property or public health and safety, including—

(A) debris removal;

(B) search and rescue, emergency medical care, emergency mass care, emergency shelter, and provision of food, water, medicine, durable medical equipment, and other essential needs …

(C) clearance of roads and construction of temporary bridges …

(D) demolition of unsafe structures which endanger the public. …

(b) The Federal share of assistance under this section shall be not less than 75 percent of the eligible cost of such assistance.

Sec. 406. Repair, Restoration, and Replacement of Damaged Facilities (42 U.S.C. § 5172)

(a)(1)(A) The President may make contributions—(A) to a State or local government for the repair, restoration, reconstruction, or replacement of a public facility damaged or destroyed by a major disaster …

Sec. 408. Federal Assistance to Individuals and Households (42 U.S.C. § 5174)

(a)(1) [T]he President, in consultation with the Governor of a State, may provide financial assistance and, if necessary, direct services, to individuals and households in the State who, as a direct result of a major disaster, have necessary expenses and serious needs....

(h)(1) No individual or household shall receive financial assistance greater than $25,000 under this section with respect to a single major disaster.

(h)(2) The limit established under [the preceding] paragraph shall be adjusted annually to reflect changes in the Consumer Price Index....

Sec. 415. Legal Services (42 U.S.C. § 5182)

Whenever the President determines that low-income individuals are unable to secure legal services adequate to meet their needs as a consequence of a major disaster... the President shall assure that such programs are conducted with the advice and assistance of appropriate Federal agencies and State and local bar associations.

Sec. 502. Federal Emergency Assistance (42 U.S.C. § 5192)

(a) In any emergency, the President may—(8) provide accelerated Federal assistance and Federal support where necessary to save lives, prevent human suffering, or mitigate severe damage, which may be provided in the absence of a specific request....

Sec. 503. Amount of Assistance (42 U.S.C. § 5193)

(a) The Federal share for assistance provided under this title shall be equal to not less than 75 percent of the eligible costs.

(b)(1) Except as provided in paragraph (2), total assistance provided under this title for a single emergency shall not exceed $5,000,000.

(b)(2) The limitation described in paragraph (1) may be exceeded when the President determines that—(A) continued emergency assistance is immediately required; (b) there is a continuing and immediate risk to lives, property, public health or safety; and (c) necessary assistance will not otherwise be provided on a timely basis.

Notes and Questions

1. Punctuated equilibrium. In contrast to federal environmental legislation, which has remained largely stagnant since 1990, federal disaster legislation has been the subject of continual activity by Congress through numerous amendments to the Stafford Act since 1988. Most of these amendments have followed major catastrophes including Hurricane Katrina in 2005, Hurricane Sandy in 2012, and the devastating hurricane plus wildfire season of 2017. *See, e.g.*, the Post-Katrina Emergency Management Reform Act of 2006, Pub. L. No. 109-295, 120 Stat. 1355 (2006); the Sandy Recovery Improvement Act of 2013, Pub. L. No. 113-2, 127 Stat. 4 (2013); and the Disaster Recovery Reform Act of 2018, Pub. L. No. 115-254, 132 Stat. 3438 (2018).

Legal scholars, adopting theory from evolutionary biologists, have described this pattern as "punctuated equilibrium," characterized by periods of relative stasis followed by moments of disjunction that create opportunities for law to advance. *See, e.g.*, Mark

Niles, *Punctuated Equilibrium: A Model of Administrative Evolution*, 44 J. Marshall L. Rev. 253 (2011). Consistent with this pattern, for example, Congress used post-Sandy legislation to address an original defect in the Stafford Act that allowed a state governor—but not a tribal leader—to request the declaration of a major disaster or emergency. The amended text in Stafford Act § 401 (major disaster declaration) and § 501 (emergency declaration) fixed this defect, supporting federal principles of tribal sovereignty. *See* Heidi Adams, *Sovereignty, Safety, and Sandy: Tribal Governments Gain (Some) Equal Standing Under the Hurricane Sandy Relief Act*, 2 Am. Indian L.J. 376 (2013).

When the next major catastrophe strikes the United States, what amendments to the Stafford Act or other disaster legislation might you seek at that time on behalf of one of the vulnerable groups considered in this chapter?

2. "Emergency" vs. "major disaster." Consider the Stafford Act definitions of "emergency" and "major disaster." Which category of incident is broader? In the following scenarios, consider whether the Stafford Act would support declaration of either an emergency or a major disaster. If authorized by the Stafford Act, consider whether or not such a declaration would be appropriate in these circumstances.

a. State and local officials in Michigan attempt to save money in a financial crisis by switching to a new source for city water. Failure to treat this new water properly causes contamination of city drinking water and widespread health impacts including lead poisoning in children.

b. Federal contractors, attempting to investigate an abandoned mine on a steep mountain slope, accidentally trigger a blow-out that releases three million gallons of contaminated mine water. The bright orange mine water flows into a river eventually crossing three states and multiple towns and tribal lands in the Southwest.

c. A train operated by a major railroad company transports hazardous materials and derails in a small town in rural Ohio. The accident causes a fire and release of toxic chemicals, requiring evacuation of the local community. Three days later, company officials and emergency managers, fearing a catastrophic explosion of chemicals that remain in the tanker cars, approve a "controlled burn" that results in a massive plume of smoke that spreads contamination across a much broader area. Health impacts including headaches and nausea are widely reported and cleanup costs ultimately exceed one billion dollars.

d. A new infectious disease appears in China and spreads quickly around the world. In the United States, the disease causes significant illness and death in all fifty states plus tribal nations and territories. At this time, little is understood about how the disease is transmitted and no vaccines have been developed yet to contain it.

3. Other "emergency" authorities. Beyond the Stafford Act, emergency declarations may be authorized under other legal authorities, including other federal and state statutes. The National Emergencies Act, 50 U.S.C. §§ 1601 *et seq.*, authorizes the President to declare a "national emergency," which may trigger emergency authorities under other statutes. For example, under authority of the National Emergencies Act, President Trump declared a "national energy emergency" on January 20, 2025, encouraging EPA and the U.S. Department of Energy to lower motor vehicle fuel restrictions under the Clean Air Act. *See* "Declaring a National Energy Emergency," White House Fact Sheet (Jan. 20, 2025).

The Public Health Service Act, 42 U.S.C. § 247d, authorizes the Secretary of Health and Human Services (HHS) to declare a "public health emergency." Declaration of a public health emergency authorizes HHS to "take such actions as may be appropriate ... including ... investigations into the cause, treatment, or prevention of a disease or disorder...." Declaration of a public health emergency also authorizes HHS to access a Public Health Emergency Fund "to rapidly respond to [] immediate needs...." 42 U.S.C. § 247d(a)–(b). Both the National Emergencies Act and Public Health Service Act, in addition to the Stafford Act and many other legal authorities, were invoked in 2020 to support the nationwide response to the COVID-19 pandemic.

In response to the Flint Water Crisis, the U.S. EPA declared an "emergency" under authority of the federal Safe Drinking Water Act § 1431, 42 U.S.C. § 300i. The order directed the State of Michigan and City of Flint to take immediate actions to repair the drinking water system. U.S. EPA Office of Enforcement and Compliance Assurance, In the matter of: City of Flint, Michigan, Michigan Dept. of Environmental Quality, and the State of Michigan, Emergency Administrative Order, Jan. 21, 2016.

In addition to the Safe Drinking Water Act, many other environmental statutes allow emergency declarations and response actions. On the federal level, these include the Oil Pollution Act (OPA) to address spills of oil to water and the Comprehensive Environmental Response, Compensation, and Liability Act (CERCLA) to address releases of hazardous substances in the environment. OPA authorities, found in Clean Water Act § 311, authorize designated officials for the U.S. EPA (inland waters) and U.S. Coast Guard (marine waters) to "direct or monitor all Federal, State, and private actions to remove a discharge." 33 U.S.C. § 1321(c)(1)(B)(ii). Similarly, CERCLA provides designated officials with authority to respond immediately to releases of hazardous substances into the environment [§ 104(a)], to issue orders where conditions may present an "imminent and substantial endangerment to the public health or welfare or the environment" [§ 106(a)], and to exceed a presumptive funding cap of $2 million in the event of an "emergency" [§ 104(c)(1)(A)(ii)]. 42 U.S.C. §§ 9604(a), 9604(c), 9606(a).

EPA invoked the emergency authority under CERCLA to exceed the $2 million cap in order to respond to the spill of some three million gallons of contaminated water from the Gold King Mine in southwestern Colorado caused by EPA contractors on August 25, 2015. By the end of the emergency action, EPA had spent over $30 million on the emergency response and may spend hundreds of millions more for long-term cleanup. *See* Clifford J. Villa, *Gold King Mine Spill: Environmental Law and Legal Protections for Environmental Responders*, 2019 Utah L. Rev. 263 (2019).

As in the case of Flint, communities affected by the Gold King Mine spill, including the Navajo Nation, requested a "major disaster" declaration under the Stafford Act. The federal government denied these requests. Do you see why?

4. Invitation only? Can the president, through FEMA and other federal agencies, respond to emergencies and disaster situations if no affected state or tribe requests a declaration? Review the excerpted provisions from Stafford Act § 402 (General Federal Assistance) and § 403 (Essential Assistance). What do you see as differences between these two sections in assistance authorities and triggering mechanisms? Why would an affected state or tribe decline to make such a request in a serious emergency or disaster situation?

After Hurricane Katrina, President Bush and his FEMA Administrator Michael Brown were criticized for delaying the federal response to this catastrophe while awaiting specific requests from state officials. Did the Stafford Act require the president to wait for such requests? For one perspective on this question, *see* Stephen M. Griffin, *Stop Federalism Before It Kills Again: Reflections on Hurricane Katrina*, 21 St. John's J. Legal Comment 527 (2007). One important lesson learned from Hurricane Katrina is that the federal government may sometimes need to act to protect affected communities, even without a specific request from the proper government officials. This notion is now embedded in the response doctrine of "leaning forward," which encourages federal agencies to err on the side of acting if they are uncertain whether or not to act in an emergency situation. FEMA, National Response Framework (4th ed. 2019) at 7 ("A forward-leaning posture is imperative for incidents that may expand rapidly in size, scope, or complexity, as well as incidents that occur without warning").

5. Public Assistance. Often the single largest benefit of a major disaster declaration is the availability of Public Assistance under Stafford Act § 406 to assist state and local government in the "repair, restoration, reconstruction, or replacement" of damaged public facilities or nonprofit facilities. Under this authority, state and local governments regularly receive billions of dollars for repairing or replacing government buildings, public schools, public housing, hospitals, roads, bridges, electrical grids, drinking water and sanitation systems, and other public infrastructure, with a state cost-share of 25 percent. On a case-by-case basis, FEMA may also approve reductions in state cost-share. 44 C.F.R. § 206.47. Following the major disaster declaration for Hurricane Helene, for example, the cost-share for North Carolina was reduced to 10 percent for Public Assistance and reduced to zero for 180 days of debris removal and other emergency measures.

In the year following Hurricane Maria, for example, FEMA obligated $3.3 billion in Public Assistance to Puerto Rico, reportedly restoring to the island 100 percent of hospitals, 99 percent of drinking water, 99 percent of electrical service, and 99 percent of cell service. FEMA funding for public infrastructure was also supplemented and exceeded by funding from the U.S. Department of Housing and Urban Development, with $20 billion awarded to the Government of Puerto Rico through Community Development Block Grants. https://www.fema.gov/hurricane-maria.

6. Individuals and Households Program. Beyond assistance to public entities and nonprofit institutions, the Stafford Act under § 408 authorizes direct assistance to disaster victims under the Individuals and Households Program (IHP). The IHP authorizes funding for a variety of housing needs, including rent for temporary housing and repairs to owner-occupied housing. Note, however, that IHP benefits are subject to a cap under the statute, 42 U.S.C. § 5174(h) (no greater than $25,000 per individual or household with respect to a single major disaster). FEMA has adjusted this cap over time, so that as of 2025, it stood at $43,600 with respect to any single major disaster. FEMA, Notice of Maximum Amount of Assistance Under the Individuals and Households Program, 89 Fed. Reg. 84923 (Oct. 24, 2024). If your home was destroyed in an earthquake, fire, or flood, how far would that go toward rebuilding your home?

Many disaster victims obviously rely on homeowners insurance to rebuild, but that does not always work due to common policy exclusions, particularly for damages from floods and earthquakes. Moreover, many older homeowners who have paid off their house may not have homeowners insurance. Many others simply cannot afford insurance. As such, additional assistance is often needed, and sometimes available through programs such as low-interest loans available to individual homeowners through the U.S. Small Business Administration (SBA). After Hurricane Maria, SBA provided $1.8 billion in low-interest to 52,228 homeowners. At the same time, FEMA provided $1.4 billion to 462,000 households through the IHP program. https://www.fema.gov/hurricane-maria.

7. Legal services. Stafford Act § 415 authorizes the president to provide low-income individuals with legal services "to meet their needs as a consequence of a major disaster." What kind of services might this include? Could it include representation of disaster victims in claims against the federal government for disaster assistance? Would this present a conflict of interest? In practice, FEMA provides funding to independent organizations such as the American Bar Association's Young Lawyers Division to provide "Disaster Legal Services" for declared major disasters. https://www.fema.gov/fact-sheet/disaster-legal-services. If you will be a "young lawyer" in the near future, you could be practicing in this area before you know it.

8. Forward progress? Consider the opportunities that resources from a major disaster declaration could bring to an underserved community. Could you replace or redesign some damaged highways to allow for non-motorized transportation? Could you replace large, old coal-fired power plants and decayed electrical grids with smaller, community-based solar, wind, or tidal energy sources? Could you replace old buildings with energy-efficient and climate resilient constructions?

One common complaint about FEMA assistance has been that it is designed simply to return communities to conditions before a disaster, regardless of whether those pre-disaster conditions ensured any level of safety. If so, then FEMA in Puerto Rico might spend billions of dollars to replace a decrepit electrical grid with another decrepit electrical grid that will fail just as completely as the last one did in Hurricane Maria. FEMA appears, however, to have recognized this illogic and taken steps to address it. Among other things, in 2018, FEMA obtained new authority from Congress to "replace or restore the function of a facility or system to industry standards without regard to the pre-disaster condition of the facility or system" impacted by Hurricane Maria. Bipartisan Budget Act of 2018, Sec. 20601, Pub. L. No. 115-123, 132 Stat. 64 (2018). FEMA has also authorized funding for repair of homes to create a "stronger, more resilient structure ... to withstand future natural events." https://www.fema.gov/hurricane-maria (discussing replacement of wooden house structure with stronger concrete house structure).

How far can such improvements go with FEMA funding under Public Assistance and the Individuals and Households Program? In conjunction with this question, consider the effect of Stafford Act § 316, waiving requirements for environmental assessments under the National Environmental Policy Act (NEPA) where FEMA funding will be used for purposes of "restoring a facility substantially to its condition prior to the disaster or emergency." 42 U.S.C. § 5159. While most environmentalists and environmental justice advocates routinely argue for expanded NEPA analysis to consider potential impacts of a federal action on diverse communities, are there also cases where diverse communities may oppose such analysis?

9. Predisaster mitigation. Consistent with principles of resilience and the Benjamin Franklin adage that "an ounce of prevention is worth a pound of cure," the Predisaster Mitigation (PDM) program established by Stafford Act § 203 provides annual funding to states, U.S. territories, federally recognized tribes, and local communities with the goal "to reduce overall risk to the population and structures from future hazard events." *See* FEMA, *Predisaster Mitigation Grant Program*, https://www.fema.gov/pre-disaster-mitigation-grant-program. As a condition for PDM funding, FEMA requires state, territorial, tribal, and local governments to develop and adopt "hazard mitigation plans." As of January 2025, according to FEMA, all 50 states, 5 territories, 193 tribal governments, 21,579 local governments, and the District of Columbia have approved hazard mitigation plans in place, covering more than 80 percent of the U.S. population. https://www.fema.gov/hazard-mitigation-plan-status. For a compilation of ideas for mitigation projects to address the risks of drought, earthquake, flood, windstorms, winter storms, storm surge, tornados, wildfire, and other common hazards, *see* FEMA, MITIGATION IDEAS (Jan. 2013).

Based on the prior discussion of resilience indicators, how do you see that mitigation efforts might help promote ecological resilience, mental health, or social cohesion?

D. Disaster Justice in Practice: New Mexico's Hermit's Peak/ Calf Canyon Fire

Putting all of this together—vulnerabilities and resilience, disaster law and policy—what does Disaster Justice look like in the "real" world? This final section of the chapter looks back at the communities in New Mexico impacted the Hermit's Peak/ Calf Canyon Fire of 2022. Three years later, what have we learned? What elements of vulnerability exacerbated impacts from the fire? What indicators of resilience helped promote recovery? What have planners and responders learned that will help avoid impacts or respond more effectively next time? What roles are available for lawyers and other community advocates and how can they be more effective in the next disaster?

The Hermit's Peak/Calf Canyon Fire, in the mountains of northern New Mexico, began as two fires started by the U.S. Forest Service. The Hermit's Peak fire began April 6, 2022, when a prescribed burn that day escaped containment four hours later. The Calf Canyon fire resulted from a burn pile in January 2022 that smoldered through the winter and erupted on April 19, 2022. The two fires merged and by May 2, 2022, had grown with ferocity, requiring evacuation of multiple villages and communities in the northern New Mexico counties of Mora and San Miguel. At the request of New Mexico Governor Lujan Grisham, President Biden issued a major disaster declaration on May 4, 2022. Following the onset of summer monsoon rains, the Hermit's Peak/Calf Canyon Fire finally reached 100 percent containment by August 21, 2022. FEMA, HERMIT'S PEAK/CALF CANYON CLAIMS PROGRAM AND POLICY GUIDE 7 (May 23, 2024).

The Hermit's Peak/Calf Canyon Fire proved to be 2022's largest wildfire in the United States and the largest wildfire in the recorded history of New Mexico. The fire burned more than three hundred forty-one thousand acres (an area larger than the City of Los Angeles), with 58 percent on private lands and 41 percent on federal lands. The fire destroyed over 150 homes and 900 other structures including barns and sheds. According to one fire victim, whose family settled in the region in the 1840s, the fire "ruined the lives of thousands of people." Simon Romero, *The Government Set a Colossal Wildfire. What Are Victims Owed?*, N.Y. TIMES, June 22, 2023.

To understand the thousands of people impacted by the 2022 fire, we can start with statistics. Overall, New Mexico is one of the poorest states in the country and the most Hispanic. The communities of northern New Mexico impacted by the fire are even more so: 57 percent "low-income" and 84 percent "people of color" according to EJSCREEN. Statistics such as low-income and high minority population may predict high "social vulnerability" for this area. But such a conclusion deserves a closer look. For example, supplementing the cash economy, many people here live significantly off the land. In the limited growing season above seven thousand feet, they harvest hay and raise sheep and cattle. From surrounding forests, they gather herbs and wood for heating, lumber, and other uses. In the fall, they fill freezers with elk meat to get through the long winters.

Concerning physical hazards, FEMA data characterize this region as low risk for hurricanes or tornados, but high risk for wildfire. Balancing high risk for wildfires plus social vulnerability, community resilience may play an important role in this region. In terms of the resilience indicators noted in this chapter, individual factors may cut in different directions. For example, a high number of mobile homes in this region may indicate less resilience, while "owner-occupied housing" may indicate greater resilience. Population stability may support community resilience. And the factor for "current population born in state" may be unparalleled here, as many current residents were not only "born in state," but represent families who preceded statehood and the founding of the United States.

Stability and sustainability measured in generations or centuries may lend this region "social cohesion." For centuries, community members banded together for survival, facing harsh climates and even invading armies. They developed cooperative systems including *acequias* that provided communal water. They have "grit," as community member Paula Garcia observed. They have *querencia*, a deep love of the land and commitment to land stewardship. That connection extends to each other. Neighbors care for neighbors. They run the Volunteer Fire Department. When the fires came in 2022, volunteers cleared firebreaks, put out spot fires, helped with evacuations, and supported emergency shelters. Most extraordinarily, throughout the largest fire in state history, not one life was lost.

Still, the Hermit's Peak/Calf Canyon Fire resulted in massive losses for the impacted communities, losses that can't ever be measured completely, but certainly total in the billions of dollars. In the wake of the fire, thousands of civil suits have been filed against the United States for igniting the fires. Suits have been filed on behalf of diverse parties including individual fire victims, school districts, utilities, and local government.

While litigation remains pending, an alternative scheme for compensation has been established through federal legislation, the Hermit's Peak/Calf Canyon Fire Assistance Act, signed by President Biden on September 30, 2022. Pub. L. No. 117-180, 136 Stat. 2114 (2022). The federal law made nearly $4 billion available for compensation, supplemented by an additional $1.5 billion approved by Congress in December 2024, for a total compensation fund of now nearly $5.5 billion. Alaina Mencinger, *Congress Approves $1.5 Billion for Hermits Peak/Calf Canyon Victims in Funding Deal*, Santa Fe New Mexican, Dec. 21, 2024.

In addition to providing federal funding for compensation, the Hermit's Peak/Calf Canyon Fire Assistance Act responded substantively to many concerns that have long been raised by advocates for disaster justice. For example, in this largely Hispanic region of northern New Mexico, all forms were made available in both English and Spanish. Reflecting new FEMA policy (2021) addressing "heirs property," FEMA allowed proof of ownership claims to be made in many ways beyond official deeds, to include church records, letters from local officials, and sworn declarations. FEMA, HERMIT'S PEAK/CALF CANYON CLAIMS PROGRAM AND POLICY GUIDE at 23–25. In contrast with policy governing other major disasters under the Stafford Act, the FEMA claims process under the Hermit's Peak/Calf Canyon Act authorized compensation for personal losses including vehicles, farm equipment, livestock, and veterinarian bills. *Id.* at 38–39. Importantly, and consistent with growing concerns for cultural and subsistence values, the FEMA process authorized compensation for loss of natural resources including firewood, herbs, and meat procured through hunting. *Id.* at 38. Each of these categories of potential compensation responded directly to concerns expressed by the communities impacted by the fire.

In terms of procedural justice, the Hermit's Peak/Calf Canyon claims process reflected innovations designed to help claimants navigate the claims process. The FEMA claims office, for example, appointed each claimant with a "Navigator" to provide a variety of assistance. Among other things, "the Navigator may support the claimant in identifying losses that can be eligible" for compensation. The Navigator may also "provide other support as requested, such as informing the claimant of other available federal financial assistance or referring the claimant to other state, local, and/or tribal resources and programs." *Id.* at 11–12.

As of June 2025, FEMA's Hermit's Peak/Calf Canyon claims office has paid out over $2.5 billion in compensation to more than eighteen thousand individuals and businesses. https://www.fema.gov/hermits-peak. The claims process has not been without its critics and many parties continue to litigate rather than rely on the claims process to satisfy all of their concerns. Phaedra Haywood & Alaina Mencinger, *Four Plaintiffs Seek Over $1B from Feds Over Denied Hermits Peak/Calf Canyon Damage Claims*, SANTA FE NEW MEXICAN, Dec. 20, 2024. Importantly, the broader scope of potential compensation only applies to losses from the Hermit's Peak/Calf Canyon Fire, not to losses from every other disaster that may follow. Still, this special legislation may provide a model for future law and policy, especially as the cultural and subsistence values gain more recognition and the needs of individual communities receive closer consideration.

In the meantime, many lessons will be drawn from this tragic event. In June 2022, while the forests were still burning, the U.S. Forest Service issued the first "lessons learned" report. In that report, the Chief of the Forest Service observed:

> Climate change is leading to conditions on the ground we have never encountered. We know these conditions are leading to more frequent and intense wildfires. Drought, extreme weather, wind conditions and unpredictable weather changes are challenging our ability to use prescribed fire as a tool to combat destructive fires.

U.S. FOREST SERVICE, GALLINAS-LAS DISPENSAS PRESCRIBED FIRE DECLARED WILDFIRE REVIEW (June 2022).

Two years later, researchers from Colorado State University published the results of a study focusing on "governance approaches for post-wildfire program implementation." WILLIAM COLE BEUTTNER & COURTNEY A. SCHULTZ, CHALLENGES AND OPPORTUNITIES IN POST-WILDFIRE RESPONSE AND RECOVERY: A CASE STUDY FROM THE HERMIT'S PEAK-CALF CANYON WILDFIRE (2024). Collating and analyzing the results of interviews with organizational leaders from federal, state, and local governments and NGOs, the researchers identified many common concerns that may merit further consideration, to include the following—

- The Stafford Act Individual Assistance program would not offer temporary housing to individuals who did not previously have housing with sewer, water, or electricity connections, impacting low-income residents impacted by the fires.
- The Stafford Act Public Assistance program is based upon reimbursement, creating substantial barriers for poor communities who cannot afford infrastructure repairs up front.
- Stafford Act assistance was initially limited to the direct impacts from the wildfires, excluding impacts from "cascading events" such as flooding that predictably followed the fires.

Flooding often follows fires after vegetation is wiped away, denuded hillsides erode, and creek channels fill with sediment. In the case of the Hermit's Peak/Calf Canyon Fire, flash flooding was particularly devastating as summer monsoon rains hit the burn scars on the mountains, causing three deaths by drowning. Nicholas Gilmore, *Lawsuit Blames Federal Government's Negligence in Hermits Peak/Calf Canyon Fire for Later Flooding Deaths*, SANTA FE NEW MEXICAN, Oct. 23, 2023.

Three years after the Hermit's Peak/Calf Canyon Fire in 2022, impacted community members continue to put their lives back together. As the steep mountainsides and valley floors recover green growth, many community members still rely on bottled water as public water systems remain impaired. Emily Withnall, *The Aftermath of the Hermit's Peak and Calf Canyon Fires*, HIGH COUNTRY NEWS, Dec. 1, 2024. Many community members, even those whose homes survived the flames, still suffer related flooding. People, including older adults, worry about the long-term effects of smoke inhalation. Within a culture defined by grit and *querencia*, community members struggle with trauma and wonder about the future.

By the deadline in March 2025, more than twenty-one thousand fire victims had filed a "notice of loss" with the FEMA claims office, creating a lengthy line for compensation. Alaina Mencinger, *"It's Far From Over": Three Years after New Mexico's Worst Wildfire, Recovery Progresses Slowly*, TAOS NEWS, April 7, 2025. But in the end, all was not lost. Miguel Martinez, who was forced to evacuate ahead of the flames, leaving behind "25 goats, 50 rabbits, 10 chickens and two dogs," told the N.Y. Times in 2022, "I have no idea if my house is standing or if my animals are alive." With the care of neighbors, the animals survived and the house in the village of El Oro remains standing in 2025. While so much has been lost in this community, so much has been saved and remains worth protecting today.

Figure 15-5. The kids are alright. Goats in El Oro, New Mexico. Photo: Cliff Villa, 2025.

Chapter 16

Food Justice

Figure 16-1. Street art in Cali, Colombia. Translation: "At harvest time, we will reap the truth for the peace and reconciliation of our disappeared." The saying refers to the plight of millions of peasants (many Afro-descendent and Indigenous) who were forced off their land during the civil war in Colombia. The resulting food insecurity drove even more people off their lands. Photo: Rebecca Bratspies, 2019.

A. Introduction

From the beginning of the environmental justice movement, advocates recognized that environmental justice included the need for access to safe, nutritious, and appropriate food. *See* Principles of Environmental Justice (1991) #3 ("Environmental justice calls for universal protection from ... poisons ... that threaten the fundamental right to clean air, land, water and *food*") (emphasis added). Thirty years later, the IPCC 6th Assessment Report warned with *high confidence* that "climate change has reduced food security." Between the unmet needs identified in 1991 and the current challenges in a changing world, food justice is a growing and dynamic area of study and practice.

Concerns for "food justice" encompass questions about how food is produced, who has access to that food (and on what terms), the nature and quality of the available food as well as the wastes produced at every step of the food lifecycle. In this concluding chapter of the book, we will take a quick look at a few food justice questions, including food sovereignty and structural inequities in the global food system; problems of local "food deserts"; challenges and opportunities for addressing food loss and waste; the worldwide struggle for food security; and the realities of food oppression. We examine each of these topics through the lens of environmental justice.

Pathfinder on Food Justice

For a solid foundation in food justice *see* ANDREA FREEMAN, RUIN THEIR CROPS ON THE GROUND (2024); JOSHUA SBICCA, FOOD JUSTICE NOW!: DEEPENING THE ROOTS OF SOCIAL STRUGGLE (2018); GARRETT BROAD, MORE THAN JUST FOOD: FOOD JUSTICE AND COMMUNITY CHANGE (2016); and SARU JAYARAMAN, FORKED: A NEW STANDARD FOR AMERICAN DINING (2016).

For a selection of contemporary academic literature demonstrating the diversity of concerns and perspectives on food justice, in addition to the articles noted later in this chapter, *see* Smita Narula, *Beyond Reform: Food Sovereignty and the Future of Global Food Systems,* 31 IND. J. GLOB. LEGAL STUDS. 141 (2024); R. D. Cordova Montes, *Using International Human Rights Law to Address Hunger in the U.S.*, 6 BUS. ENTREPRENEURSHIP & TAX L. REV. 1 (2022); Ursula Ramsey, *Seed Libraries and Food Justice: Cultivating an Effective Legal and Policy Environment,* 25 GEORGETOWN J. POV. L. & POL'Y 193 (2018); Ernesto Hernández-López, *Sustainable Food and the Constitution,* 50 ARIZ. ST. L.J. 549 (2018); Dan DePasquale, Surbhi Sarang, & Natalie Bump Vena, *Forging Food Justice Through Cooperatives in New York City*, 45 FORDHAM URB. L.J. 909 (2018); Rebecca Bratspies, *Owning All the Seeds: Consolidation and Control in Agricultural Biotechnology,* 47 ENVTL. L. 583 (2017); Marc-Tizoc González, *Criminalizing Charity: Can First Amendment Free Exercise of Religion, RFRA, and RLUIPA Protect People Who Share Food in Public?*, 7 U.C. IRVINE L. REV. 291 (2017); Melanie Pugh, *A Recipe for Justice: Support for a Federal Food Justice Interagency Working Group*, 72 FOOD & DRUG L.J. 341 (2017); Stephen Lee, *The Food We Eat and the People Who Feed Us*, 94 WASH. U. L. REV. 1249 (2017); Julia Guarino, *Tribal Food Sovereignty in the American Southwest*, 11 J. FOOD L. & POL'Y 83 (2015); Margot Pollans & Michael Roberts, *Setting the Table for Urban Agriculture*, 46 URB. LAW. 199 (2014); Anastasia Telesetsky, *Community-Based Urban Agriculture as Affirmative Environmental Justice*, 91 U. DET. MERCY L. REV. 259 (2014); Erika George, *Incorporating Rights: Child Labor in African Agriculture and the Challenge of Changing Practices in the Cocoa Industry*, 21 U.C. DAVIS J. INT'L L. & POL'Y 59 (2014).

In popular media, *see* Eric Schlosser, FAST FOOD NATION (2001) and the Richard Linklater documentary film of the same name (2006). Valuable online resources include Farmworker Justice (www.fwjustice.org); JustFood.org (www.justfood.org); and USDA Urban Agriculture (https://www.nal.usda.gov/afsic/urban-agriculture).

B. Food Sovereignty

Food sovereignty is an overarching concept that incorporates a wide range of concerns that fall under the umbrella of food justice. At the first global forum on food sovereignty, held in Mali in 2007, a coalition of civil society groups issued the Declaration of Nyéléni, which defined food sovereignty as "the right of peoples to healthy and culturally appropriate food produced through ecologically sound and sustainable methods." This definition was an outgrowth of decades of advocacy by groups like Via Campesino working to build food systems designed around the needs of those who produce, distribute, and consume food rather than a system designed to respond to the profit demands of markets. Food sovereignty reframes discourse about the right to food to include the array of distributional, environmental, and social justice issues inherent to the current globalized extractive, industrial food system. It includes considerations of social equity, food security, food systems transformation, community participation and agency, and environmental sustainability.

Smita Narula, *Beyond Reform: Food Sovereignty and the Future of Global Food Systems*

31 Ind. J. Glob. Legal Studs. 141 (2024)

The 2006–2008 food crisis "challenged the reigning liberalizing ideology for global food provisioning," exposed the vulnerability of communities subjected to the whim of volatile global markets, and revealed the consequences of a long-term prioritization of "economic growth led by finance capital and export-oriented industrialization at the expense of investments in rural and agricultural production, social safety nets, and basic infrastructure." . . .

Then-World Bank President Robert B. Zoellick announced the Bank's intention to "create a 'Green Revolution' for sub-Saharan Africa by assisting countries to boost productivity throughout the agricultural value chain and help small-holder farmers to break the cycle of poverty." This approach, however, merely extended industrial agricultural practices to small-scale farmers rather than pursuing alternative food systems.... By promoting fertilizers, hybrid seeds, and integration into global supply chains, development agencies essentially tried to fold subsistence producers into the same resource-intensive, export-oriented model that had fueled price volatility and food shortages in the first place. Such top-down interventions lock in unsustainable practices instead of empowering locally adapted agroecological approaches driven by farmers themselves.

Globalization and the financialization of food systems have also enabled large agribusiness actors to exert tremendous control over food production, processing, and retailing, further impoverishing rural communities while causing irreparable environmental harm....

In the face of persistent global hunger and mounting environmental concerns, a paramount question for both policymakers and stakeholders alike is: how do we achieve food security, now and into the future? Social movements around the world that have been formed in response to the ill effects of our corporate-controlled industrial food system are saying that *food sovereignty is the how.* In other words, the way governments can ensure the right to food for present and future generations, reduce the alarming rates of food insecurity, help address climate change, and preserve biodiversity is by ensuring the right of people to define their own food and agricultural systems, and produce food through ecologically sound and sustainable methods, such as agroecology.

Food sovereignty originated as a peasant-led response to the destructive impacts of corporate globalization on local food production, expanding over time into a broader discourse and movement around ecological sustainability, democratic control, and social transformation of food systems. Food sovereignty discourse emerged in 1996 from the international peasant movement La Via Campesina as a counter to neoliberal globalization policies that were seen as undermining local food systems and food security. La Via Campesina first defined food sovereignty as "the right of each nation to maintain and develop its own capacity to produce its basic foods respecting cultural and productive diversity. We have the right to produce our own food in our own territory. Food sovereignty is a precondition to genuine food security." The 1996 definition—which arose partly in response to the impacts of agreements like the North American Free Trade Agreement that enabled dumping of subsidized agricultural products and undermined local farmers—focused on national sovereignty over food production, rejecting WTO policies that eroded countries' ability to be food self-sufficient.

Over time, food sovereignty discourse has expanded to emphasize ecologically sustainable methods, the human right to food, democratic control of food systems, and food as more than just a commodity. The 2007 Nyéléni Declaration broadened the definition of food sovereignty to signify "the right of peoples to healthy and culturally appropriate food produced through ecologically sound and sustainable methods, and their right to define their own food and agricultural systems." The Declaration "emphasize[d] a collective, transnational vision wherein food sovereignty imagines 'new social relations free of oppression and inequality.'" Importantly, food sovereignty is not "a simple one size fits all solution." Rather, it is a commitment to bringing about systemic change, and about ensuring that "human beings hav[e] direct, democratic control over the most important elements of their society."

Seen in this light, the struggle for food sovereignty is "a transformative political project that seeks to decentralize power in the food system, restore ecological balance, and put forward an alternative development paradigm" that addresses socio-economic injustices and is responsive to environmental crises. Although a dominant and globalized industrial food system has emerged over the past sixty to seventy years, a plurality of food systems continues to operate and survive in its shadows. Among these alternative systems are ones that prioritize "small-scale production activities, the involvement of local communities, an alternative perception of quality personal or informal ties, organic practices, welfare, or the application of alternative sales and logistics models....

Food sovereignty offers a much-needed counter-narrative to the dominant ways in which mainstream actors frame the problem of hunger. Specifically, food sovereignty disrupts the idea that food insecurity will be solved by charity or technological innovations, or by increasing food production and the attendant commodification of food-producing resources. Instead, this approach emphasizes the right of communities to shape their own food systems, and the obligations of States under international human rights law to ensure access to safe, nutritious, and culturally appropriate food in a non-discriminatory, participatory, and accountable manner. As explored further below, the food sovereignty approach also points to different solutions and requires a robust, systemic response that addresses the root causes of food insecurity and democratizes food systems governance.

C. Food Deserts

The problem of "food deserts" can be seen in almost any community in the United States where there are high populations of low-income and minority people. Instead of Whole Foods or Trader Joe's, Safeway or Piggly-Wiggly, or other full-service grocery stores, poor communities often have no choice but to obtain food from corner convenience stores emphasizing beer and chips, or from fast-food restaurants such as McDonald's, Burger King, and KFC. Such sources offer the advantage of cheap calories, at the expense of nutrition and community health. Potential solutions to this problem are many and varied, some with potential drawbacks, as explored in the following excerpt.

Deborah N. Archer & Tamara C. Belinfanti, *We Built It and They Did Not Come: Using New Governance Theory in the Fight for Food Justice in Low-Income Communities of Color*

15 SEATTLE JOURNAL FOR SOCIAL JUSTICE 307 (2016)

Meet Anthony. Anthony is eighteen years old and lives with his mother, Mary, in Anacostia, a residential neighborhood in Southeast Washington, D.C. There are no supermarkets in his neighborhood—the closest grocery store is 20 minutes away by bus. One or two corner stores in the neighborhood sell milk, cereal, and other packaged foods. Mary shops for groceries twice a month "when she has the money." On rare occasions she also shops for fruits and vegetables at a farmers market, though she has to travel for over 45 minutes on two buses and a train to reach it. Anthony rarely eats breakfast at home, and when he does it usually consists of dry cereal. His typical breakfast comes from either McDonald's or a hot dog stand he passes on his way to school. If he is home for lunch, he usually has "something like a hot pocket." More often, his lunch comes from his neighborhood McDonald's or a Chipotle near his school. For dinner, he usually eats at McDonald's if he is in his neighborhood or Chipotle if he is at school. On the occasions when Anthony and Mary have dinner together, they eat Chinese take-out; their favorite dishes are orange chicken, chicken nuggets, and fries.

Anthony gets food from McDonald's more than any other establishment because "it is cheap and there is one every three blocks" in his neighborhood. Anthony "does not like or dislike" his food options because, as he says, "I'm used to it, it's all I know."

Anthony lives in a food desert—a neighborhood that is more than a mile away from a supermarket or other large retailer that sells fresh fruits and vegetables. In essence, food deserts are communities, both urban and rural, with severely limited access to healthy and affordable food. In the United States, approximately 23.5 million people live in food deserts. Most of these people are Black or Brown. Blacks, Latinos, and Native Americans tend to travel farther, have fewer choices, and pay more for food than Whites. Compared to Whites, Blacks are half as likely to have access to a chain supermarket, while Latinos are a third less likely to have access to a chain supermarket.

While residents of food deserts have difficulty accessing healthy food, they often have easy access to fast food and convenience stores. Fast food restaurants offer high-calorie, filling meals at bargain prices. But fast food affordability comes at a severe cost to residents' nutrition and health. The average distance between an individual's home to a grocery store as compared to a fast food restaurant is relevant to his or her food choices. "When fast food restaurants are closer than supermarkets to a neighborhood, the neighborhood is more likely to make unhealthy food choices." While food deserts are characterized by a dearth of full-service supermarkets, they often have an abundance of small corner markets. However, "fresh and nutritious produce is rarely available at these small stores, and the type of food generally tends to be of poorer quality and less healthy, high in sugars and saturated fats."

In examining food deserts, many researchers found a link between poverty, access to fresh nutritious foods, and diet-related health problems. This link leads to a paradox of poor health: "Many Americans, particularly low-income people and people of color, are overweight yet malnourished. They face an overwhelming variety of processed foods, but are unable to procure a well-balanced diet from the liquor stores and mini-marts that dominate their neighborhoods." Life in food deserts leads to a lack of food security—these are environments in which "all persons [cannot obtain] at all times a culturally acceptable, nutritionally adequate diet through local non-emergency sources."

Food deserts and food insecurity have received considerable attention from various stakeholders, such as state and local governments, community organizations, and private sector institutions. These stakeholders have sought to overcome food insecurity by turning food deserts into oases by providing "access" to fresh, healthy food. However, many of their solutions—building supermarkets and sponsoring farmers markets—have missed the mark. Residents of food deserts did not flock to grocery stores to purchase fruits and vegetables. As a result, many stakeholders blame the residents of food deserts for their own predicament, lamenting, to paraphrase *Field of Dreams*, "we built it but they did not come."

... Food deserts have largely been framed as problems of proximity. If the problem is proximity to grocery stores, then the solution should be simple: create incentives and opportunities to develop grocery stores in underserved, low-income communities of color. Community organizations worked to bring farmers markets, policy makers and government officials provided financial and tax incentives for the development of full-service supermarkets, and the private sector responded by building supermarkets in many underserved communities. In recent years, the U.S. government distributed more than $500 million, through the Healthy Food Financing Initiative, to encourage grocery stores to open in underserved communities. Many states have also invested substantial resources to spur the development of healthy food options in poor communities plagued by diet-related health problems. However, these investments have not always resulted in healthier communities—supermarkets came to food deserts, but, in many of the communities, the residents neither came to the supermarkets nor bought the newly available healthy food.

In some communities, the development of full-service supermarkets did not alter residents' buying habits. Although community members shopped at the new supermarket, they often bought the same foods they previously bought. Several recent studies have documented this phenomenon around the country. For a National Bureau of Economic Research study, residents agreed to allow researchers to track all of their bar-coded food purchases. The study confirmed that low-income neighborhoods had less physical access to healthy food. However, the study also concluded that individual food preferences, not proximity to full-service supermarkets, dominated the choices people made. Participants who were low-income and had lower levels of education but who lived in wealthier communities with proximity to healthy foods made food choices that were similar to the choices made by low-income people living in low-income neighborhoods with less physical access to healthy food.

Similar results were reached in studies of food desert interventions in Philadelphia and in the United Kingdom. In the Philadelphia study, researchers studied the impact of opening full-service supermarkets in food deserts. After studying purchasing habits over six months, the researchers found that the presence of supermarkets did not lead to increased fruit or vegetable intake of residents or impact body mass index. Ultimately, researchers concluded that "the effectiveness of interventions to improve physical access to food and reduce obesity by encouraging supermarkets to locate in underserved areas therefore remains unclear."

Rather than seeing the results of these studies as a prompt to further investigate the complex reasons people experience difficulty accessing healthy food, many have been content to declare the problem of food deserts solved, or to claim that food deserts were never really the threat to public health that many believed them to be. Yet poor nutrition and food insecurity remain, despite the geographical proximity of supermarkets or other sources of whole foods. Indeed, in the aforementioned study by the National Bureau of Economic Research, researchers found that no more than a tenth of the variation in food bought could be explained by people's proximity to a grocery store. One danger in this finding is that rather than further engaging to unearth and address all of the challenges and opportunity costs people face in accessing food, private industry may stop investing in full-service grocery stores in low-income communities, government entities may move to end tax incentives or other benefits, and non-profits may turn their attention and resources to "more pressing" concerns.

Others have taken the publication of these studies as an opportunity to blame the victims, declaring that access was improved and the remaining issues are about individuals having the desire to change behavior. Some in the food justice movement call residents' behavior a "lifestyle choice" and point to a perceived cultural preference for unhealthy, processed foods. For example, in a survey of community-supported agriculture initiatives ("CSA"), managers were asked, "what do you think are some of the reasons that it is primarily European-American people who seem to participate in CSAs?" Respondents did not question access and affordability or raise issues about structural inequalities. Instead, the CSA managers made remarks such as "Hispanics aren't into fresh, local, and organic products," "I believe that food is affordable to all; it's just a matter of different values . . . ," and "low income people shop elsewhere unless they are given freebies like WIC."

These responses stigmatize the choices of affected communities rather than respond to the systemic and structural barriers that impact access and lead those people to make the choices they do. The result is condemning individuals who may not have the wealth, information, or resources to participate in the food market on the terms set by others. The problem of access to healthy, affordable food is not as simple as reducing the distance a resident must travel to healthy food sources. Advocates, government entities, and members of the private sector must take a step back and examine whether they have truly addressed the access problem by focusing on the meaning of access and the specific barriers for each community.

Notes and Questions

1. **Food desert.** Do *you* live in a food desert? If you do now, or ever have before, what measures would help you or your neighbors better address needs for safe, nutritious food? Can you think of any legal measures that would also help?

2. **Food "mirage."** As Archer & Belinfanti suggest above, the problem of food deserts may not be solved by simply building new supermarkets in underserved communities. Such efforts, in fact, may lead to the problem of the "food mirage," which occurs when "full-service grocery stores appear plentiful but, because food prices are high, healthful foods are economically inaccessible for low-income households." Archer & Belinfanti, *supra*, at 317. What should accessible mean in terms of access to nutritious food?

3. **Farmers markets.** New York City offers a matching program that doubles the value of federal Supplemental Nutrition Assistance Program (SNAP) benefits when those benefits are spent on fruits and vegetables at farmers' markets. This program dovetails with parallel efforts to establish farmers markets in underserved communities of color and/or with high poverty rates. The idea is to simultaneously advance a host of interrelated goals including supporting small-scale agriculture, reducing food miles traveled, and improving access to fresh, healthy food in underserved communities. Is

this responsive to the points that Archer and Belinfanti raise? Could such a program work in your community?

4. "Hispanics aren't into fresh food." *Perdón?* While remarks such as this may surprise (and offend) many Hispanics, cultural differences may play some important part in determining whether or not a business, such as a new supermarket, will be embraced by a local community. In the fall, the air around any successful supermarket in New Mexico should be wrapped in the aroma of roasting chiles. In Seattle, any worthy grocery store must deliver Copper River sockeye salmon in season. In Queens, New York, tamarind, pigeon peas, and plantains are critical foodstuffs. And in Miami, papayas, mangoes, and coconuts are essential for salsas, marinades, and preserves. To what extent should cultural food practices be part of assessing whether or not the needs of a community are being met? Should the interests of procedural justice require that community members be involved when new food stores are proposed? If so, how would this community involvement work?

D. Food Security and Climate Change

Goal 2 of the UN Sustainable Development Goals is to end hunger, achieve food security, and promote sustainable agriculture. Targets for achieving this goal include ending hunger and all forms of malnutrition by 2030. Unfortunately, the world is not on track to accomplish this goal.

The UN Food and Agriculture Organization (FAO) defines food security as a status where "all people, at all times, have physical and economic access to sufficient, safe, and nutritious food that meets their dietary needs and food preferences for an active and healthy life." Rather than advancing toward this goal, the FAO reports that worldwide hunger has been rising. In 2023, nearly 30 percent of the global population (2.33 billion people) were moderately or severely food insecure, meaning they did not have regular access to adequate food. Worse, 864 million people (10.7 percent of global population) suffered severe food insecurity that posed grave risks to their health and well-being. U.N. FAO, The State of Food Security and Nutrition in the World (2024). The global rise in food insecurity tracks the increasing frequency of droughts, natural disasters, and other anticipated impacts of climate change.

The United Nations report below addresses how climate change and land use impact food security. It was written in 2019, when, according to the FAO, 150 million fewer people suffered food insecurity.

Intergovernmental Panel on Climate Change, *Special Report: Climate Change and Land*

An IPCC Special Report on climate change, desertification, land degradation, sustainable land management, food security, and greenhouse gas fluxes in terrestrial ecosystems (Aug. 7, 2019)

Climate change creates additional stresses on land, exacerbating existing risks to livelihoods, biodiversity, human and ecosystem health, infrastructure, and food systems (high confidence). Increasing impacts on land are projected under all future GHG emission scenarios (high confidence). Some regions will face higher risks, while some regions will face risks previously not anticipated (high confidence). Cascading risks with impacts on multiple systems and sectors also vary across regions (high confidence)....

Current levels of global warming are associated with moderate risks from increased dryland water scarcity, soil erosion, vegetation loss, wildfire damage, permafrost thawing, coastal degradation and tropical crop yield decline (high confidence). Risks, including cascading risks, are projected to become increasingly severe with increasing temperatures. At around 1.5°C of global warming the risks from dryland water scarcity, wildfire damage, permafrost degradation and food supply instabilities are projected to be high (medium confidence). At around 2°C of global warming the risk from permafrost degradation and food supply instabilities are projected to be very high (medium confidence). Additionally, at around 3°C of global warming risk from vegetation loss, wildfire damage, and dryland water scarcity are also projected to be very high (medium confidence). Risks from droughts, water stress, heat related events such as heatwaves and habitat degradation simultaneously increase between 1.5°C and 3°C warming (low confidence).

The stability of food supply is projected to decrease as the magnitude and frequency of extreme weather events that disrupt food chains increases (high confidence). Increased atmospheric CO2 levels can also lower the nutritional quality of crops (high confidence).... [G]lobal crop and economic models project a median increase of 7.6% (range of 1 to 23%) in cereal prices in 2050 due to climate change, leading to higher food prices and increased risk of food insecurity and hunger (medium confidence). The most vulnerable people will be more severely affected (high confidence).

In drylands, climate change and desertification are projected to cause reductions in crop and livestock productivity (high confidence), modify the plant species mix and reduce biodiversity (medium confidence).... [T]he dryland population vulnerable to water stress, drought intensity and habitat degradation is projected to reach 178 million people by 2050 at 1.5°C warming, increasing to 220 million people at 2°C warming, and 277 million people at 3°C warming (low confidence).

... The supply of food is defined in this report as encompassing availability and access (including price). Food supply instability refers to variability that influences food security through reducing access. Asia and Africa are projected to have the highest number of people vulnerable to increased desertification. North America, South America, Mediterranean, southern Africa and central Asia may be increasingly affected by wildfire. The tropics and subtropics are projected to be most vulnerable to crop yield decline....

The level of risk posed by climate change depends both on the level of warming and on how population, consumption, production, technological development, and land management patterns evolve (high confidence). Pathways with higher demand for food, feed, and water, more resource-intensive consumption and production, and more limited technological improvements in agriculture yields result in higher risks from water scarcity in drylands, land degradation, and food insecurity (high confidence).

... Urban expansion is projected to lead to conversion of cropland leading to losses in food production (high confidence). This can result in additional risks to the food system. Strategies for reducing these impacts can include urban and peri-urban food production and management of urban expansion, as well as urban green infrastructure that can reduce climate risks in cities (high confidence).

* * *

Law professor Rebecca Bratspies examines legal and ethical concerns for the use of genetically engineered crops to address food security in the following article.

Rebecca M. Bratspies, *Hunger and Equity in an Era of Genetic Engineering*

7 U.C. Irvine Law Review 195 (2017)

The challenge of resolving food insecurity as populations continue to grow is often framed as a binary choice: either farmers will have to glean higher yield from existing farmland under new less favorable conditions, or more land will be converted to agriculture. The latter option has obvious negative environmental ramifications, so policymakers focus on techniques designed to increase production on existing croplands. With this framing, genetically engineered crops are touted as the clear answer. These claims about genetic engineering are built on a series of contested propositions. First, that undernourishment is a production problem susceptible to resolution by increased production. Second, that genetically engineered crops are necessary to increase yield. Third, that only through genetic engineering can we rapidly produce crop varietals able to thrive in the face of climate change. If these propositions were true: *if* undernourishment were a production problem, *and* genetically engineered crops increased yields, *and* these crops were the best way to ensure continued or increased production as growing conditions deteriorate, this would be virtually unanswerable moral claim. However, there is, as yet, no reason to believe that any of these claims are accurate.

Do Genetically Engineered Crops Actually Increase Food Production?

Over the past few decades, genetically engineered crops have been touted as the answer to world hunger, to pesticide overuse, and to negative environmental impacts of agriculture more generally. The assumption is that these crops are necessary to meet the food security needs of a burgeoning human population.... Opponents of the technology were accused of fearmongering, fraud, and worse.

Yet, ... food insecurity flows from inequitable distribution of food rather than from underproduction. Arguments about increased yield alone are therefore not responsive to the actual contours of the food insecurity problem. Indeed, this framing marginalizes the importance of more equitable distribution of existing food, and of minimizing food waste.

Moreover, it is not at all clear that genetically engineered crops increase yield. Reviewing the many dueling studies claiming that crop yields have either increased, held steady, or decreased, the National Research Council concluded that genetically engineered crops "do not have greater potential yield than [non-genetically engineered] counterparts." ... In short, the technology's performance is much more tepid than the extravagant claims made on its behalf.

One thing is clear: two decades of genetically engineered crops has done little to solve the problem of food insecurity. The tantalizing prospect that genetic engineering could help feed the world's hungry has so far "been a somewhat empty promise." Indeed, the pattern has been one in which the benefits claimed for these crops repeatedly fail to materialize....

Of course, the current array of genetically modified crops was not engineered with reducing food insecurity in mind, so measuring them against that yardstick is not entirely fair. But that is, in many ways, the problem. These crops were developed by a few large multinational corporations as a tool for enhancing the scope, scale, and profitability of industrial agriculture. They embody a vision agriculture built around private ownership of patented seeds that are licensed, not sold, to farmers. Because farmers can only purchase the right to use seeds for a single growing season, farmers can no longer save seed. Moreover, because this business model is built on trade secrets and patent rights, the free exchange of germplasm and agronomic information ... is inhibited. That structure at best renders the poorest of the poor invisible to seed developers' decision-making, and at worst, compounds the problems of poverty and food insecurity associated with treating food as global commodities....

What Are the Equity Ramifications of Genetically Engineered Crops?

If we recognize, as we must, that food insecurity and undernutrition are not just functions of food production, we are left with questions of equity and power—why do people starve or suffer food insecurity amidst plenty? How do we change the patterns of distribution and consumption that produce these dismal results? Those are not questions of science or of production. They hint at a problem that is not amenable to a technical solution. Yet, purported technical solutions abound.

The decade-long Golden Rice saga is a good illustration of what happens when decision-makers insist on pursuing purely technical solutions to problems created by poverty and inequity. Golden Rice is rice that has been genetically engineered to contain beta carotene in an attempt to ward off vitamin A deficiencies that lead to blindness and death. In 2000, *Time Magazine* profiled Golden Rice on its cover, proclaiming *This Rice Could Save a Million Kids a Year*. Golden Rice instantly became the poster child for biotechnology, a life-saving negation of the assertion that agricultural biotechnology only generated benefits for multinational corporations. Monsanto and other agricultural biotech companies mounted a slick ad campaign using Golden Rice to stake out moral high ground in debates over genetic engineering. These ads sought to inextricably link "the dream of a tomorrow without hunger" to biotechnology as "the science that promises hope." Critics found themselves accused of perpetuating a "nutritional holocaust," and of condemning poor children to suffer and die. Recently, an open letter from 104 Nobel Laureates demanded, "How many poor people in the world must die before we consider [opposition to Golden Rice] a 'crime against humanity'"?

To say that Golden Rice has failed to live up to this "world changing" hype would be a significant understatement. When it was featured on *Time*'s cover, an at-risk child would have had to eat fifteen pounds of Golden Rice per day to obtain the benefits described in the article. Responding to that disconnect, Michael Pollen called it "the world's first purely rhetorical technology" designed "to win an argument rather than solve a public-health problem." Greenpeace, a staunch opponent of genetic engineering, called Golden Rice an "overpriced public relations exercise." Even the Rockefeller Foundation, which bankrolled the Golden Rice project, acknowledged that the industry advertisements and public relations campaigns built around Golden Rice had "gone too far," and were promising benefits that the technology could not, and might never be able to deliver....

The choice to pursue a technology-based solution to a problem rooted in poverty had consequences. There are alternative, equally valid perspectives about whether vitamin A deficiency, and by implication issues of hunger and diet-related disease more broadly, are problems in need of technical or social solutions. Had the hundreds of millions of dollars spent developing Golden Rice been instead used to support the pre-existing, albeit less glamorous poverty alleviation efforts, or straightforward initiatives to provide vitamin A supplements directly to vulnerable populations, perhaps today's statistics would look very different. As Peter Rosset, director of Food First, emphasized, "People do not have vitamin A deficiency because rice contains too little vitamin A but because their diet has been reduced to rice and almost nothing else." Poverty is the core issue in vitamin A deficiency and in food insecurity more generally. Technology, by itself, cannot solve the problem.

Notes and Questions

1. **The climate change-food security connection.** The Special Report of the IPCC notes, "Risks to food security include availability and access to food, including population at risk of hunger, food price increases and increases in disability adjusted life years ..." In your words, how is food security exacerbated by climate change and land-use impacts?

Figure 16-2. Urban garden with hoophouse on formerly vacant land in Detroit, Michigan. Photo: Cliff Villa, 2022.

2. Food loss and waste. In the United States, more than one-third of the food that reaches our homes and plates is never eaten. **Food waste** is the single most common material in municipal landfills, responsible for 58 percent of landfill methane—a potent greenhouse gas. **Food loss** describes the loss of food from the human food supply chain from the point of production to the retail sector. Together, annual food loss and waste in the United States contribute greenhouse gas emissions equivalent to 60 coal-fired power plants, consuming enough water to supply 50 million homes each year. EPA, USDA, & FDA, National Strategy for Reducing Food Loss and Waste and Recycling Organics (June 2024). For scholarly introduction to related concerns, see Sarah J. Morath, *Regulating Food Waste*, 48 Texas Envtl. L.J. 239 (2018); Alexandra I. Evans & Robin M. Nagele, *A Lot to Digest: Advancing Food Waste Policy in the United States*, 58 Nat. Resources J. 177 (2018).

Reducing food loss and waste can contribute significantly to climate mitigation and waste management while at the same time helping to combat hunger and reduce food insecurity. Communities across the country are finding and implementing innovative means of reducing food loss and waste, with support from all levels of governments. At the federal level, EPA, for example, has built an online resource, the Excess Food Opportunities Map, to help connect potential generators of excess food (e.g., educational institutions, correctional facilities, hospitality industry, restaurants and food services) with potential recipients of excess food (e.g., composting facilities; anaerobic digestion facilities; food banks, food pantries, and soup kitchens). EPA and USDA also provide grant funding for many state, local, and tribal initiatives in this space. The State of Oregon, for example, has established the Bad Apple Campaign to help educate and "inspire households to reduce the amount of food they throw away at home." Montgomery County, Maryland, is one leader in food composting, expanding its composting infrastructure and providing technical assistance to businesses and residents to encourage participation in food scrap recycling programs.

Access to curbside composting, anaerobic digesters, and related services and infrastructure, however, may raise additional concerns for distributive justice, as relatively wealthy urban areas such as Seattle and Austin can afford conveniences that rural or lower income communities cannot. For discussion, see Dharma Khalsa, *Such a Waste: The Environmental Justice Shortcomings of Modern Composting Programs*, 22 VERMONT J. ENVTL. L. 45 (2022).

What services do you have in your community for reducing food waste? Do you consider these services accessible or affordable? What more might you want to see in your community or other communities that may be underserved in this area today?

E. Food Oppression and Poverty

Attorney and geographer Danielle Purifoy explains food justice as an emerging movement that is to be seen as distinct from the sustainable food movement. She provides the example of food served in school cafeterias to illustrate this point. She also observes the proliferation of food policy councils to address community concerns to government officials.

Danielle M. Purifoy, *Food Policy Councils: Integrating Food Justice and Environmental Justice*

24 DUKE ENVTL. LAW & POLICY FORUM 375 (2014)

Like environmental justice, food justice centers its activities on achieving equality for low-income and low-access communities. Rather than aiming for food practices and policies—like do-it-yourself food cultivation and expensive fresh food markets—which require significant disposable income and presume easy access to other necessary resources, food justice aspires to establish healthy food as a fundamental right and to eliminate barriers to its access. The term "food justice" is defined in several ways, likely as a result of its recent emergence as a social movement. Some have attempted to define it in terms of the injustices it is designed to combat, such as advocating against "the maldistribution of food, poor access to a good diet, inequities in the labour process and unfair returns for key suppliers along the food chain." Others, like attendees of the 2012 Food + Justice = Democracy conference, define it as "the right of communities everywhere to produce, process, distribute, access, and eat good food regardless of race, class, gender, ethnicity, citizenship, ability, religion, or community." The conference attendees also defined "good, healthy food and community wellbeing" as "basic human rights." In the 2000 edition of the journal *Race, Poverty, and the Environment*, which was devoted to the food system, the editors observed that the environmental justice definition of the environment as the place "where we live, work, and play," could be extended to "where, what, and how we eat." In all these interpretations, the food justice movement is a direct critique of the global industrial food system and the negative impacts of its policies, laws, and practices on human health, the environment, culture, and equity.

One important example of a food justice challenge is the source and quality of food served in school cafeterias. Although problems are pervasive in school food programs across the United States, they are particularly dire in under-resourced public schools, which often do not have the means to create alternative school food programs or to secure resources for farm-to-school programs. However, the food justice framework views impacted communities as leaders in defining the problems and helping to craft viable solutions. In a case study examined in Gottlieb and Joshi's *Food Justice*, public school students from New Orleans—a city with a rich local food culture—were served cafeteria food that was imported from distant sources, "tasted terrible" and did not support the local economy. The middle school activists in the study, called the Rethinkers, defined the problem in their schools not only as a matter of where their food came from and its quality, but also as a problem of the broader conditions of the cafeterias where they ate, and the amount of time they were given to eat their food. Their advocacy also extended to support the local shrimp industry, which, as they learned, was being displaced because of imports of cheap, chemical-laden shrimp from abroad.

Rather than relying on an authoritative, top-down solution to the problem, the students ensured that they had a say in the outcome, appealing to the school district Superintendent for eliminating "junky eating utensils," using healthy, local food sources, and placing local shrimp on the menus. In this way, Gottlieb and Joshi suggest, the movement for food justice is about advancing "opportunities for moving toward a more just, healthy, democratic, and community-based system."

Advocacy around food justice in the United States has manifested in many forms, from activism around domestic food law and policy (most notably, around the federal Farm Bill, which has historically created farm subsidies for commodity crops (e.g., corn, soybeans, wheat) and public assistance funds for food to low-income individuals and families) or around developing programs and institutions designed to reconfigure local and regional food systems such that they will provide all communities with greater and more equitable access to safe, healthy, and local food. Urban agriculture, community supported agriculture (CSAs), kitchen gardens, co-ops, and local food artisans joined the menu of other food initiatives, most of which targeted hunger at an individual level. Food policy councils, first established in Knoxville, Tennessee, in 1981, have rapidly proliferated in the past decade as forums through which concerned citizens and government officials can collaborate on resolving critical challenges to the local food system.

This concentration on local food systems, with which local residents are most familiar, creates new opportunities not only for bolstering local economies, but also for

Figure 16-3. Cornfield in Walton, Nebraska. Photo: Shirley Trout, 2019.

gradually altering the global food system as localized policies are replicated across the nation.

* * *

Attorney Rebecca Goldberg considers the lessons and goals of the food justice movement as ways to involve the concerns of impoverished communities in policy debates. She draws parallels between the food justice movement and the early days of the environmental justice movement.

Rebecca L. Goldberg, *No Such Thing as a Free Lunch: Paternalism, Poverty, and Food Justice*

24 Stanford L. & Pol'y Rev. 35 (2013)

[T]he food justice movement relies heavily on equality-based rhetoric, but the movement has generally failed to grapple with the disparate needs of the various groups it encompasses, or to articulate a coherent vision of an equitable food system. While a grand unifying theory of equitable food policy might be an unrealistic goal, the environmental justice movement—on which the food justice movement has largely patterned itself—provides an excellent model for how the food justice movement might move beyond feel-good discussions about the need for across-the-board justice and toward a deeper analysis of complex problems such as the ones raised in this article. The current struggles of the food justice movement are in many ways reminiscent of the early days of the environmental justice movement, which began with a fairly diffuse coalition of grassroots activists coalescing around concerns about the distribution of environmental harms and their impact on racial minorities and the poor. When lawyers made a somewhat tardy appearance on the scene, it was not immediately clear how the concerns of the grassroots movement could or should translate into legal or policy actions. Soon, however, the environmental justice movement became, among other things, an influential voice for policy-level change, and it continues to wield that influence today.

The environmental justice movement's involvement in policy debates has often led it to confront the types of difficult issues discussed in this article. For example, the environmental justice movement has often faced situations where an impoverished community expresses a preference for a policy that will harm the community's environment. Paternalistic government actions are sometimes available that would protect the community's environment, albeit against the community's wishes. The conflict between the community's preference and the government's power is particularly stark in situations involving Indian tribes, whose ability to self-govern can in many situations be overridden by the federal government. Such situations pose a conflict for the environmental justice movement, because they create tension between two of the movement's central values: anti-discrimination and environmental protection....

The specific issue of Indian tribes that want to allow storage of spent nuclear fuel and other hazardous waste on their land has generated a particularly large body of scholarship.... "The unique characteristics of Native-American environmental struggles illustrate the epistemological inadequacies of a distributive paradigm of environmental injustice," Sheila Foster asserts, ultimately concluding that these struggles demonstrate that environmental injustice manifests itself not only in unequal distribution of environmental harm, but also in the decision-making process around environmental issues. Alice Kaswan responds to Foster's "community preferences model" by arguing that the specific situation of tribal environmental decision making demonstrates a layering of distributive justice issues on top of sovereignty concerns.

The specific issues of paternalism and equality that the environmental justice movement has focused on are somewhat different from the food policy issues raised in this article. This is because much of the environmental justice literature is about siting disputes that rest on an assumption that some community must bear an environmental burden; the question is how to choose a location. This raises somewhat different questions about equality and justice than are faced by the food justice movement. But the environmental justice movement's scholarship on these topics nonetheless offers a model for how the food justice movement ... might begin to engage with the issues discussed in this article.

To be sure, one should not overstate the extent to which the environmental justice movement has resolved the similar issues that it has faced (and continues to face). A mere proliferation of scholarship does not necessarily represent a move toward coherence or relevance, and the debates discussed above have not resulted in any kind of official determination about the environmental justice movement's vision. However, these debates have been one part of the movement's journey from the nascent, doctrinally underdeveloped movement that Gerald Torres described in 1996 to the prominent movement that today commands real influence over federal government policymaking and has the ability to win meaningful legislative victories. This type of effective role in policymaking is only possible if a group is able to take a position on difficult, real-world problems. While the environmental justice movement certainly does not always speak with one voice, enough of its members are able to coalesce behind specific measures ... such that the movement can be effective.

The food justice movement should follow the lead of the environmental justice movement and use the types of difficult questions discussed here to analyze, refine, and express its core values. If it does not do so, the movement will significantly reduce its ability to contribute in a meaningful way to current debates around food policy, many of which involve paternalistic proposals that either target or disproportionately affect the poor. These include not only other proposed uses of zoning to address obesity and other proposals to modify [the Supplemental Nutrition Assistance Program] (SNAP), but also ongoing efforts to improve the school lunch program and otherwise influence what children eat at school; various proposals to limit or influence portion sizes (which can affect low-income consumers who might take advantage of inexpensive large sizes to share one serving among several people); and the numerous recent proposals to tax unhealthy food, which would have a regressive effect on low-income consumers. Broader food justice topics, such as labor and wage protections for farm workers, also implicate questions about paternalism toward disadvantaged groups.

Furthermore, the food justice movement's failure to articulate a coherent vision of justice hinders the movement's ability to analyze any policy, paternalistic or otherwise, that poses a conflict between substantive goals relating to food consumption and what we might call personhood goals such as autonomy. Put differently, this failure of vision makes it hard for the movement to address the tension that so often exists between the substantive goal of healthy food for the poor and other things the poor might value—anything from autonomy to low prices....

That process will likely need to begin with an intra-movement conversation—whether through scholarship or other media—that addresses head-on the tensions that the food justice movement so far has largely ignored. As the history of the environmental justice movement shows, it takes time and effort for a movement to transition from observing problems to proposing (and successfully fighting for) workable solutions. That leap cannot be made if the movement's own goals are under-developed to the point where it is paralyzed by issues that force it to choose between competing values.

* * *

Law professor Andrea Freeman links the notion of food oppression to social invisibility, decreased social status, and other conditions. Freeman shares the example of milk to illustrate harms posed to vulnerable groups.

Andrea Freeman, *The Unbearable Whiteness of Milk: Food Oppression and the USDA*

3 U.C. Irvine Law Review 1251 (2013)

Food oppression is institutional, systemic, food-related action or policy that physically debilitates a socially subordinated group. Politically and financially weak communities absorb the external costs of food oppression, rendering these costs largely invisible to the mainstream. The effects of the oppression also increase the harmed groups' vulnerability by constraining their political voices, reducing their work capacity, and draining the energy of household and community members who must care for the sick and take on the responsibilities that ill members cannot fulfill. In the long term, food oppression diminishes already vulnerable populations in numbers and in power. Illness arising from food oppression also leads to social invisibility, decreased social status, depression, and despair.

Food oppression is a difficult concept for many to embrace because of the powerful rhetoric regarding personal choice that is endemic in the United States. This rhetoric attributes ill health to individual weakness, regardless of the very real constraints that shape nutritional intake, particularly in low-income, urban communities. The focus on the individual that dominates medical, scientific, and social views of health carries harmful consequences. By ignoring the structural aspects that shape consumption choices, this myopic perspective forecloses effective prevention and treatment of illnesses that disproportionately harm vulnerable communities.

Social position, which reflects the amount of privilege individuals possess along multiple axes, including race, class, gender, sexual orientation, physical ability, and immigration status, dictates how much disposable income and access to nutritious food people have. These factors, in turn, largely determine what we eat. More than taste, preference, willpower, or a commitment to health and fitness, structural forces shape diets. When fast food dominates a person's diet, the reasons are complex and manifold. They include government-corporate partnerships that place fast food in schools, government assistance checks that stretch further in a fast-food restaurant than a produce aisle, public transportation that fails to provide routes between low-income neighborhoods and grocery stores, and government subsidies that artificially lower the price of fast food. Fast food tends to offer more bang for the buck, calories for dollars, making it a sound economic choice for many low-income African American and Latina/o households.

Fast food corporations exploit these harsh realities by devoting millions of dollars to race-targeted marketing annually, including Spanish-language advertising, McDonald's "365 Black" and "Me Encanta" websites, the reconfiguration of restaurants to accommodate large Latina/o families, and the introduction of culture-specific food items. Health problems linked to fast food, including heart disease, strokes, cancer, and diabetes, affect low-income African Americans and Latina/os more frequently and more seriously than whites. In "Fast Food: Oppression Through Poor Nutrition," I introduced the theory of food oppression to explain how government actions and policy that lead to the dominance of fast food in low-income, inner-city African American and Latina/o communities contribute to these health disparities.

Notes and Questions

1. **Paternalism?** Rebecca Goldberg writes about the conflict between community preferences and policy decisions. She writes, "Paternalistic government actions are sometimes available that would protect the community's environment, albeit against the community's wishes." Goldberg provides an example of the conflict between the community's preferences and the government's power in situations involving Indian tribes. What central values are at stake in these conflicts?

2. **Free lunch.** Nine states provide universal free lunch to all students in public school. Does that policy undermine Danielle Purifoy's analysis, or does it make her points even more important? Since 2022, most states also now participate in "Summer EBT," a USDA program that provides low-income families with $120 per child over the three summer months to help cover the time when students are not getting free meals at school. In June 2025, Texas Governor Gregg Abbott vetoed legislation that would have allowed Texas to participate in the Summer EBT program, defying his Republican-controlled state legislature which supported the program and agreed to pay administration costs. Taylor Goldenstein, *Abbott Vetoes Summer Food Aid Program, Forgoing $450M in Federal Funds*, Houston Chronicle, June 23, 2025. If you were the Governor of Texas, what needs would you place above feeding hungry children?

3. **Philanthropy?** During the first Trump administration, Communications and Media Studies Professor Garrett Broad described the competition for resources among food justice advocates. He advised that "community-based food justice organizers and their supporters in law and policy must proactively articulate and demonstrate what makes for successful programs, and then communicate that message to funders, donors, and policymakers at multiple levels of society and government." Garrett M. Broad, *After the White House Garden: Food Justice in the Age of Trump*, 13 J. Food L. & Pol'y 33 (2017). Is food justice philanthropy? In the face of a hostile federal government, food programs often rely on private donors, but the majority of private philanthropic giving goes to food programs that do not directly benefit underserved communities suffering from food injustice. What obstacles do food justice advocates confront in conducting outreach to stakeholders, government agencies, and corporations?

Index